Fodor's 2020

NEW YORK CITY

D0179328

Welcome to New York City

From Wall Street's skyscrapers to the neon of Times Square to Central Park's leafy paths, New York City pulses with an irrepressible energy. History meets hipness in this global center of entertainment, fashion, media, and finance. World-class museums like MoMA and unforgettable icons like the Statue of Liberty beckon, but discovering the subtler strains of New York's vast ambition is equally rewarding: ethnic enclaves and shops, historic streets of dignified brownstones, and trendy bars and eateries all add to the urban buzz.

TOP REASONS TO GO

★ **Landmarks:** With towering edifices and awe-inspiring bridges, the skyline says it all.

★ **Shopping:** Whether you're in the market for top designers or inexpensive souvenirs.

★ **Food:** Dim sum to pizza and everything in between, NYC has what you're craving.

★ **Museums:** Art is it, with museums like the Guggenheim and galleries all over town.

★ **The Dazzle:** From the lights of Broadway to celebrity sightings, NYC is full of stars.

★ **Brooklyn and Elsewhere:** Cool neighborhoods and restaurants are a subway ride away.

Contents

Fodor's Features

MAPS

Gateway to the New World:
Statue of Liberty and Ellis Island.....91
The Metropolitan Museum of Art....336
The American Museum
of Natural History...............366

EXPERIENCE NEW YORK CITY

24 ULTIMATE EXPERIENCES

New York City offers terrific experiences that should be on every traveler's list. Here are Fodor's top picks for a memorable trip.

1 See Art at the Met

NYC has some of the finest art museums in the world and the Metropolitan Museum of Art houses 5,000 years of human creativity—from the ancient Egyptian Temple of Dendur to Warhol's *Mao*. *(Ch. 11)*

2 Listen to an Opera

Lincoln Center is the performing arts hub for jazz, opera, and ballet. It's also worth a visit for architecture buffs. *(Ch. 11)*

3 Ride the Ferry

The Staten Island Ferry offers great views of both Lower Manhattan and the Statue of Liberty—all for free. The trip is especially good at night. *(Ch. 3)*

4 Discover Your Past

Through interactive exhibits, photographs, audio recordings, and artifacts, Ellis Island and the Statue of Liberty remind us that we are a nation of immigrants. *(Ch. 3)*

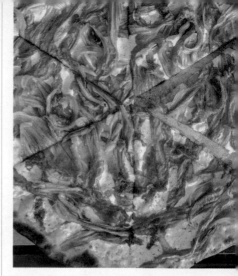

5 Eat Pizza!

You must eat at least one slice while visiting the city. There are good pizzerias in almost every corner of the five boroughs, but Lombardi's in NoLIta is among the most famous. *(Ch. 4)*

6 Walk to Brooklyn

The Brooklyn Bridge is the prettiest bridge in New York, and walking across is an iconic activity, delivering some of the best views of Lower Manhattan. *(Ch. 3)*

7 Grab a Show

New York is synonymous with Broadway— the dozens of theaters in the area around Times Square are home to some of the greatest theater performances on earth. *(Ch. 10)*

8 See Downtown Art

Don't miss the downtown galleries and the acclaimed Whitney Museum of American Art, housed in a beautiful building designed by Renzo Piano. *(Ch. 7)*

9 Pay Your Respects

The reflecting pools at the 9/11 Memorial were built where the World Trade Center once stood and are a beautiful tribute and a somber experience. *(Ch. 3)*

10 Go Museum-Hopping on the Upper East Side

Visit the Dutch Masters at The Frick Collection, Klimt's *Woman in Gold* at the Neue Galerie, or the Frank Lloyd Wright-designed Solomon R. Guggenheim Museum. *(Ch. 11)*

11 Visit Williamsburg

Just over the river, Williamsburg is a concentration of boutiques and vintage stores, casually chic restaurants, and perfectly Instagrammable street art. *(Ch. 14)*

12 Buy a Good Book

New York City has a surprisingly high number of awesome independent bookstores, including the highly esteemed than Three Lives in Greenwich Village. *(Ch. 6)*

13 View the Skyline

There's no better way to understand the scope of New York City than from on high. Check out one of the the three best: the Empire State Building, Top of the Rock, or One World Observatory. *(Ch. 9, 10, 3)*

14 Visit Central Park

Central Park is almost 850 acres of green space—from manicured lawns and beautiful stone structures to ponds and groves of trees—is a much appreciated oasis. *(Ch. 12)*

15 Walk the High Line

Experience world-renowned art, kooky art installations, gourmet food and drinks, views of the skyline, and above all, excellent people-watching. *(Ch. 7)*

16 Hang Out in Washington Square

Washington Square Park is small but lively—you'll find protesters, jugglers, musicians, dog walkers, and hip NYU students lounging on their unofficial "quad." *(Ch. 7)*

17 Eat World Cuisine

Vegan Ethiopian, Yemeni flatbread, or Korean Barbecue, this city of immigrants offers food from all over the world, especially in Queens, the queen of the outer boroughs. *(Ch. 15)*

18 Laugh Along

New York is a breeding ground for comics and there's a chance to see everybody from Judah Friedlander to Samantha Bee. Caroline's is a classic, but Upright Citizens Brigade draws a younger crowd. *(Ch. 10)*

19 Walk the Boardwalk

Visit Coney Island and see a different side of the city. The boardwalk is a quirky and crowded—a fun place to spend an afternoon. *(Ch. 14)*

20 Watch the Crowds

A magnificent transportation hub, Grand Central Terminal's Beaux Arts main hall has a 120-foot-high blue ceiling with a sparkling mural of constellations. *(Ch. 9)*

21 Go Shopping in SoHo

One-of-kind boutiques stand next to uber-popular designer stores, but you may wish to stop for a coffee or cocktail at a fashionable watering hole. *(Ch. 4)*

22 Discover the History and Culture of Harlem

Harlem has stood at the heart of African American culture for most of the 20th century. Now, it's experiencing a cultural and dining revolution while maintaining a sense of neighborhood charm. *(Ch. 13)*

23 Celebrate Pride

The Stonewall Riots in Greenwich Village are celebrated each June in the outrageous, loud, and colorful Pride parade that marches down past the Stonewall Inn from the Flatiron District. *(Ch. 6)*

24 The American Museum of Natural History

The largest natural history museum in the world has more that 30 million artifacts from the sea, land, and outer space, suitable for kids aged 8 to 80. *(Ch. 12)*

WHAT'S WHERE

1 Lower Manhattan. This area includes the Financial District and TriBeCa. Heavy-duty landmarks anchor the southern tip of Manhattan, including Wall Street and Battery Park City. Ferry terminals dispatch boats to Staten Island, Governors Island, Ellis Island, and the Statue of Liberty. The 9/11 Memorial & Museum, One World Trade Center, and the Brooklyn Bridge are also found here.

2 SoHo, NoLIta, Little Italy, and Chinatown. Luxe shops dominate in SoHo these days, while NoLIta, to the east, has lots of boutiques and restaurants. Little Italy is a shrinking zone of rather touristy eateries while, farther south, Chinatown teems with street vendors, Chinese herb shops, and dim sum joints.

3 The East Village and the Lower East Side. Once a gritty neighborhood of artists and punks, the East Village is now a melting pot of NYU students, young professionals, and old-timers. You'll find some of the best people- and pooch-watching from a bench in Tompkins Square Park. The once seedy, now trendy Lower East Side has lots of live-music clubs, indie clothing shops, and wine bars.

4 Greenwich Village and the West Village. Artists with rent-controlled apartments, older gay folks (plus the Stonewall National Monument), and university students still live here among wealthy tech entrepreneurs, celebrities, and socialites, and the bars and restaurants they all frequent.

5 Chelsea and the Meatpacking District. With hundreds of galleries in a seven-block radius, Chelsea is the center of the city's contemporary-art scene. To the south, the Meatpacking District has evolved into a swanky restaurant and club scene by night and—with the High Line, the Whitney Museum of American Art, and high-end boutiques—a prime daytime destination, too.

6 Union Square, the Flatiron District, and Gramercy Park. Bustling Union Square Park hosts the city's best greenmarket. Nearby is private and elegant Gramercy Park. The Flatiron is a mix of office and apartment buildings, along with a giant Eataly Italian market and plenty of other restaurants and bars.

WHAT'S WHERE

7 Midtown East and Murray Hill. Midtown from 5th Avenue to the East River is the refined big sister of Midtown West, with grand hotels, shopping, the Chrysler Building, and Grand Central Terminal. Murray Hill is a mix of quiet tree- and town-house-lined streets and attractions like the Empire State Building and the Morgan Library.

8 Midtown West. Head to 42nd Street to see Times Square in all its neon and mega-screen glory. Towering office buildings line Broadway up to Columbus Circle. At Rockefeller Center are the famous ice rink and Christmas tree (in season).

9 The Upper East Side. The Upper East Side is home to more millionaires than any other part of the city. Along 5th Avenue here is Museum Mile, which includes the Guggenheim and Metropolitan Museum of Art. Madison Avenue's haute boutiques are another notable draw.

10 The Upper West Side. Wide sidewalks and ornate prewar buildings set the tone, and the American Museum of Natural History and Lincoln Center are big draws. Nearby is the pastoral heart of New York: Central Park. Much farther north is the Cloisters, a branch of the Metropolitan Museum of Art devoted to medieval art.

11 Harlem. A hotbed of African American and Hispanic American culture for almost a century, Harlem still sizzles. Many of the brownstone-lined blocks have been refurbished, and there are plenty of boutiques, restaurants, music clubs, and churches.

12 Brooklyn. New York's largest borough would be the country's fourth-largest city. Its distinctive neighborhoods include Brooklyn Heights, Williamsburg, DUMBO, Park Slope, Coney Island, and Brighton Beach, among others.

13 Queens, the Bronx, and Staten Island. Queens is known for its diverse communities and cuisine. The Bronx may be best known for Yankee Stadium, but the New York Botanical Garden and Bronx Zoo also score home runs. Staten Island's best-known feature might be the ferry, but there are reasons to stick around.

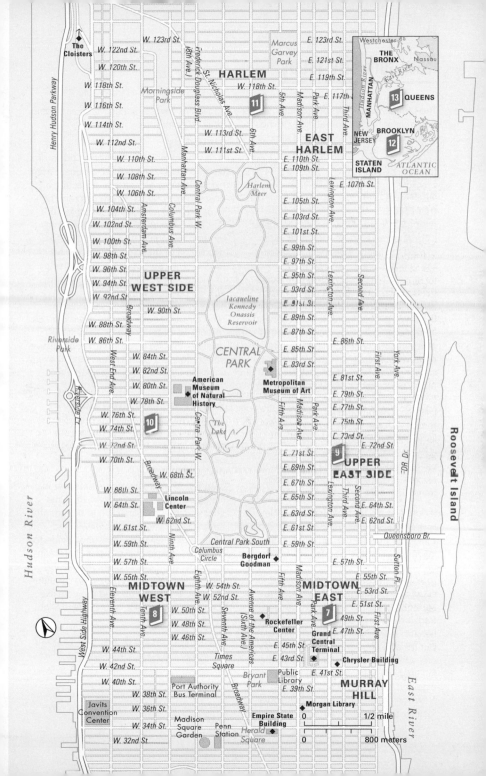

New York City Today

The phrase "in a New York minute" exists for a reason: in this frenetic city, things really do change in a flash, and almost everybody's in a hurry. With the constant ebb and flow, it can be hard to keep up. Here is just some of what New Yorkers are talking about.

POLITICS

As it always has, New York City remains a confluence of political ideals that lean toward the liberal side, while balancing the enormous egos and ambitions of its elected officials. In 2014, Democrat Bill de Blasio took over as mayor from Republican-turned-Independent Michael Bloomberg—the fourth-longest-serving NYC mayor in history, with 12 years in office. From the start, Mayor de Blasio (who was re-elected in 2017) faced challenges to his populist values and plans for economic equality across the five boroughs. He had to pick up where billionaire Bloomberg left off, attempting to rein in some of the seemingly limitless large-scale real estate development and private-public partnerships his predecessor facilitated, while still keeping more favored policies that improved public transit, schools, and parks intact.

It doesn't help that De Blasio and New York State Governor Andrew Cuomo have their own friction, leaving city and state leadership somewhat at odds with each other. It's been especially hard for locals to endure the city's desperate need for subway improvements, but the state's control of the eternally cash-strapped transit authority—leaving plenty of debate, but very few subway upgrades. But it's all a familiar song for New Yorkers, who have endured more than their fair share of political strife in both the long and short terms. On the bright side, New Yorkers possess a strong survival instinct to get along with each other—it

applies to politics just as much as to daily subway commutes.

ECONOMY

A few quick positive economic indicators: New York is experiencing its biggest hotel expansion in a generation, attracting a host of new brands—from high-end boutiques to budget chains—all across the city. The city has 92 hotels in the pipeline to open through 2019 and 2020, with nearly half of these properties slated for the outer boroughs—a key indicator of the recent visitor trend to visit, and stay in, boroughs beyond Manhattan. Tourists keep on coming: 2017 had a record number of visitors—more than 62 million, up from the previous year's 60 million—making it the eighth consecutive year of tourism growth. And there's every indication that the city will continue to set records.

BATTLE OF THE BOROUGHS

While visitors are discovering all things Brooklyn right now, New Yorkers are steadily refocusing their trend-spotting gaze on Queens. And it's no wonder—the borough has long-standing residential communities, cheap ethnic eats, established attractions like MoMA PS1, the second-biggest Chinatown in the country, Long Island City's skyline views, and what is generally an easy subway ride to Midtown. Add less-expensive-than-Manhattan (and Brooklyn) hotel rooms and rents, the current and projected development boom, and proposed projects like the QueensWay (aka "the Queens High Line").

Keep an eye on the Bronx, too: it's home to Yankee Stadium, the magnificent New York Botanical Garden, the Bronx Zoo, and a growing number of breweries and new developments—proof that the dynamic city of New York is always evolving.

THE ARTS

Some of the biggest movers and shakers in the New York art scene have been moving and shaking off dust after recent renovations, perhaps suggesting that the art world will be more focused on exhibition spaces than the exhibitions themselves. In recent years, the Whitney Museum of American Art debuted its state-of-the-art new space in the Meatpacking District, complete with terraces opening onto the High Line and stunning views of the Hudson. Meanwhile, the Metropolitan Museum of Art opened the Met Breuer inside the Whitney's old digs to display its growing collection of contemporary art, as it refines plans to renovate its Modern Wing. The Tenement Museum expanded its scope in late 2017, with an exhibit re-creating the life of immigrants in New York post–World War II. Looking ahead, the American Museum of Natural History is undergoing a six-story addition to improve navigation and add facilities for research and education, and the Lower East Side's Lowline underground park is making slow but steady progress; both are set to be completed about 2020.

WHAT'S NEW?

There's always plenty going on in New York, but keep in mind that project plans and opening dates can change. Check before you travel.

The Pier 57 development at West 15th Street in Hudson River Park originally was a shipping terminal when it opened in 1952. Today, the pier's 12 acres are under construction with a so-called SuperPier that includes plans to introduce new retail, dining, and an elevated park and entertainment space, as well as a home to Google offices; its construction completion is anticipated in late 2019.

The South Street Seaport is wrapping up a $514 million makeover that included replacing the existing complex at Pier 17 with a sleek new dining and office complex, featuring a 60,000-square-foot landscaped rooftop. The reopening rolled out in phases starting in 2018.

Coney Island's New York Aquarium opened its new, $158 million *Ocean Wonders: Sharks!* exhibit in 2018. New features include a roof deck and a walk-through coral tunnel with sharks swimming overhead.

The new Hudson Yards neighborhood opened to the public in March 2019, with new retail, dining, arts venues, a hotel, and even sights. You'll want to check out the shwarama-shape Vessel; the Spanish-themed food court curated by Chef José Andrés is always drawing oohs and satiated ahs; and shoppers are starting to head to the city's first Neiman Marcus department store.

The L Train, which runs from 8th Avenue along 14th Street all the way to Canarsie in southeast Brooklyn, is the primary gateway to the increasingly popular Williamsburg neighborhood. Unfortunately, service will be greatly disrupted nights (after 8 pm) and weekends for the duration of a major (years-long) renovation project.

What to Eat and Drink in New York City

PASTA

When acclaimed chef Missy Robbins opened Lilia in Williamsburg, it was an instant hit and the pace hasn't slowed down since. What we love about Lilia: the minimalist-yet-cozy space, the handmade pasta (especially the agnolotti), the great wine list, and the unpretentious vibe.

PIZZA

New Yorkers take their pizza seriously, and choosing a favorite pizzeria is an extremely subjective matter. That said, a few places stand out from the rest. Roberta's in Bushwick is one of the city's best spots for wood-fired pizza, a casual space with DIY vibes.

BAGELS AND LOX

It doesn't get more classic New York than a bagel piled high with cream cheese, lox, tomatoes, onions, and capers. Though there are plenty of bagel shops around the city, Russ & Daughters has served generations of New Yorkers bagels, smoked salmon, knishes, and rugelach since 1914.

OYSTERS

It's easy to forget that New York City is a beach town, but the fresh seafood here is not to be missed. Almost every upscale restaurant and bar in the city has oysters on the menu, and you'd be missing out not to try some local shellfish.

PASTRAMI SANDWICHES

When Harry Met Sally may have immortalized Katz's Delicatessen on the silver screen, but this place has been a New York institution since 1888. Presidents, celebrities, and visiting heads of state have all lined up at the counter to sample the classic pastrami on rye. Grab a ticket and take your pick of pastrami, hand-carved corned beef, brisket, hot dogs, and matzo ball soup. (Don't forget the pickles.)

FARM-TO-TABLE FARE

The term "farm-to-table" has become overused, but to really understand what it's all about, visit Marlow & Sons by restaurateur Andrew Tarlow, who brought farm-to-table dining to Brooklyn before it was a thing. He sources from farmers and butchers in and around New York, and the menu changes daily, depending on what's fresh and in season.

MEXICAN FOOD

Drawing inspiration from Mexico City, Oaxaca, Baja, and the Yucatán, New York City's Mexican restaurants are a cut above. Standouts for everything from fine dining to street tacos include Cosme (by famed Mexico City chef Enrique

Oysters

Olvera), La Esquina (a subterranean speakeasy taco shop), and Los Tacos No. 1 (inside Chelsea Market).

DIM SUM

The ultimate weekend brunch, dim sum is a Chinatown staple. Bring a group and prepare to feast on dim sum classics, like dumplings, rice rolls,

scallion pancakes, and the original egg rolls stuffed with veggies and chicken. Don't forget the jasmine tea, and save room for almond cookies.

GREEK CUISINE

Astoria, Queens, is known for its Greek restaurants, but Taverna Kyclades rules them all. This is the place to come for fried calamari and

grilled octopus, homemade spanakopita, and kebabs in a place with humble, unassuming decor. Just be prepared to wait: this restaurant doesn't take reservations, and it's perennially packed.

OLD-SCHOOL ITALIAN DESSERTS

The neon sign shining in the night beckons visitors to Veniero's like moths to the flame. Open since 1894, this East Village pasticceria is a proper old-school Italian bakery with marble floors, stained glass, and a pressed-tin ceiling. It's also heaven for anyone with a sweet tooth. The cannoli are a great choice, but the sleeper hit is the utterly addictive pignoli (cookies made with almond paste and dotted with pine nuts).

BURGERS

The burger at the NoMad Bar consistently ranks among the city's best. The beef patty has plenty of suet (the fat from around the cow's kidneys) and bone marrow, and comes topped with white cheddar and a house-made secret sauce. Wash it down with one of the bar's signature cocktails.

New York City's Best Cocktail Bars

RAINES LAW ROOM
Hidden behind a nondescript door in Chelsea and past a heavy velvet curtain, this Victorian-style lounge offers plush sofas arranged around low tables in intimate little nooks, damask wallpaper, a fireplace, antique mirrors, and vintage photographs in gold frames.

UNION POOL
Located in an old pool-supply store under a rather unappealing section of the BQE, this Williamsburg lounge is a hot spot for live music and DJ sets. On weekends, the party lasts into the early morning with several rooms providing different atmospheres, including an open-air courtyard with a taco truck.

WESTLIGHT AT THE WILLIAM VALE
At 23 stories, the Westlight towers over the other buildings in Williamsburg like an alien spaceship. Enjoy craft cocktails and small plates by acclaimed chef Andrew Carmellini. When the weather's nice, grab a seat out on the terrace with the city's best views of Manhattan.

EMPLOYEES ONLY
Look for the neon psychic sign to find this award-winning speakeasy, where the cocktails are treated like works of art. The space channels Art Deco New York, with green glass shelves, vintage artifacts, and white-jacketed bartenders shaking and stirring concoctions with theatrical flair.

THE BACK ROOM
New York is famous for its speakeasies, but this is one of the only remaining spots that actually *was* a speakeasy during Prohibition. To find the bar, look for the toy shop sign, descend a staircase, walk through a dark alley, up another set of steps, and through a door that opens onto an ornate lounge.

BEMELMANS BAR AT THE CARLYLE

For a classic New York night on the town, this swanky Upper East Side haunt inside the Carlyle Hotel can't be beat. White-jacketed waiters whisk martinis and classic cocktails to the sophisticated patrons sitting at round tables positioned around the room adorned with murals by Ludwig Bemelmans.

HOTEL DELMANO

Inspired by the weathered old drinking dens of New Orleans, this unmarked bar on a corner in Williamsburg is beloved by locals for its romantic atmosphere and great cocktails. There's also a raw bar with oysters and other small plates, like local cheeses.

DEATH & COMPANY

This East Village stalwart is known for serving some of the most complex cocktails around. The menu is practically a book and the descriptions are bound to list ingredients you've never heard of, but the expert staff can help guide you to the drink that'll tickle your fancy.

IDES BAR AT THE WYTHE HOTEL

Brooklyn's original boutique hotel has one of the best bars in the borough. Walk through the lobby and take the elevator up to the sixth floor, where the Ides bar awaits with floor-to-ceiling windows and excellent views. There's a great selection of cocktails, beer, wine, and small plates.

DEAR IRVING

This elegant unmarked lounge on Irving Place features a design that goes farther back in time the deeper you go. Start in the 1960s in a room that evokes Mad Men-era New York, continue into the 1920s, then back in time to the 1880s, and finally into the back room that evokes Marie Antoinette.

New York City's Best Art Museums

NEUE GALERIE

The Neue Gallery is a time capsule of Austrian elegance housed in the historic William Starr Miller residence on 5th Avenue, offering an impressive supply of Klimts and Schieles—not to mention a mean sacher torte in its Café Sabarsky.

THE JEWISH MUSEUM

The Jewish Museum is much more than a contemporary art museum. With innovative exhibits like a virtual reality design exhibition or Leonard Cohen retrospective, the museum pushes boundaries. Drop by for one of the morning coffee talks with curators to learn more about the unique programming.

LESLIE-LOHMAN MUSEUM OF GAY AND LESBIAN ART

Tucked inside a classic SoHo warehouse turned residence, this well-curated apartment-size collection of works by LGBTQ+ artists packs a punch—not just through activism for its own community and New York at large, but also via the intersection of pop culture and art.

METROPOLITAN MUSEUM OF ART

A vast, encyclopedic institution, the Met is one of the world's great museums and has one of the most extensive collections of human artifacts. But it's not the dusty, creaky place you might imagine; instead, it delivers thoughtful exhibitions of history, art, design, and objects, not to mention the Met Gala, the city's most glamorous party.

BROOKLYN MUSEUM

While the Met may steal all the glory, those in the know visit the Brooklyn Museum for its comprehensive and exciting collections of Egyptian, American decorative, and African arts. The museum also attracts visitors for its smashing contemporary shows—come for the new and stay for the old.

WHITNEY MUSEUM OF AMERICAN ART

The Whitney offers contemporary and historical perspectives on American art while continually redefining what contemporary and American art is. Its Biennial is a thermometer of artistic production, while the Renzo Piano–designed building on the Hudson is an agile backdrop.

MUSEUM OF MODERN ART

The MoMA is Manhattan's oldest museum dedicated to modern art, where modernist masters are presented alongside contemporary powerhouses. The collection is rich in 20th-century European and American art, including masters such as Picasso, Pollock, and Pipilotti Rist.

GUGGENHEIM MUSEUM

This impressive museum, founded by wealthy New York patron of the arts Solomon Guggenheim, is filled with work by luminaries like Kandinsky and Calder—all displayed inside Frank Lloyd Wright's sculptural spiral building, an icon of New York architecture.

FRICK MUSEUM

Henry Clay Frick's collection and 5th Avenue manse is a treasure trove filled with Europe's most beloved masters, who, sure, may be dead white men but whose brushes transcend subject—just take a look at Thomas Gainsborough's *Grace Dalrymple Elliott* and Jean-Honoré Fragonard's *Progress of Love.*

QUEENS MUSEUM

It makes sense that the most diverse place on earth would have a museum to represent the true meaning of diversity. The Queens Museum's programming ranges from traditional art shows to community-based activism to participative performance across all mediums, demographics, and locations in the borough.

Under-the-Radar Things to Do in NYC

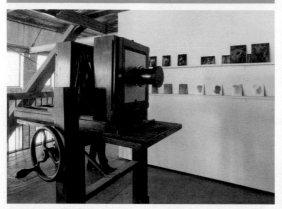

PIONEER WORKS

In Red Hook, Brooklyn, the 19th-century headquarters of the Pioneer Works machine manufacturing company has been converted into a contemporary art center. It hosts artists in residence, who have studio space upstairs, and puts on temporary exhibitions on the ground floor.

GOVERNORS ISLAND

From May to October, Governors Island is accessible by ferry. There are special events like the Jazz Age Lawn Party, as well as more permanent attractions—like oyster bars, public art installations, and glamping tents, so you can even spend a night on the island.

HALLETT NATURE SANCTUARY IN CENTRAL PARK

One of Central Park's best-kept secrets was closed to the public for 79 years. This 4-acre patch of wilderness—one of the park's three woodlands—is home to native flora and fauna and can now be toured with the Central Park Conservancy.

THE MORGAN LIBRARY

Gilded Age banker J. P. Morgan constructed this gorgeous edifice to house his collection of rare books and medieval and Renaissance art, and today it's one of the city's most enchanting museums. Ogle the ornate library with its shelves of leather-bound books and peek inside Morgan's office and vault.

ROOSEVELT ISLAND TRAM

Take the cherry-red Roosevelt Island Tram across the East River and spend some time exploring Roosevelt Island. This 2-mile stretch of land has a dark yet fascinating history as home to a Smallpox Hospital, infamous asylums, and a prison, the vestiges of which you can still see today. It's also home to the FDR Four Freedoms Park, designed by renowned architect Louis Kahn in homage to Franklin Delano Roosevelt.

DONALD JUDD FOUNDATION

Fans of minimalist art should plan a visit to the Judd Foundation at 101 Spring Street in SoHo, where the artist lived and worked before the neighborhood was cool. (Imagine this: he bought the textile factory for just $68,000 in 1968.) It's a fascinating look at Judd's aesthetic philosophy—he designed much of the furniture himself and used the space to display his own work and art by his friends, including Dan Flavin. Be sure to book in advance; reservations are required.

The Morgan Library

THE NEW YORK EARTH ROOM

It may seem crazy that in SoHo, where real estate prices rise through the roof, there's a room containing nothing but a massive pile of dirt, but that's exactly what the New York Earth Room is. Commissioned by the Dia Art Foundation in 1977, land artist Walter De Maria installed 280,000 pounds of dirt in 3,600 square feet of space, and it's been there ever since. The installation is free to visit, but don't try to walk on it.

NEW YORK DISTILLING COMPANY

One of the only craft distilleries within city limits, the New York Distilling Company in Williamsburg produces three types of gin and two kinds of rye, which are stocked in many local bars and liquor shops. Stop by for a tour and tasting on weekend afternoons. At the attached bar, the Shanty, you can sip craft cocktails made using its spirits. Beware: these gins are potent.

STREET ART MURALS IN BUSHWICK

Brooklyn in general is known for its street art, but to find the highest concentration of murals, head to Bushwick, home of the Bushwick Collective, which puts on a huge block party every year. You'll find that the streets around the Jefferson Street L stop—in particular Troutman Street—are lined with full-scale works by established street artists like Beau Stanton, Icy & Sot, Buff Monster, Fumero, and many others.

THE NOGUCHI MUSEUM

This museum in Queens founded by Japanese-American sculptor Isamu Noguchi might be one of the most peaceful places in all of New York. Outside, there's a small sculpture garden. Inside, the galleries are filled with Noguchi's stone sculptures and famous paper lanterns.

New York City's Best Outdoor Adventures

SWIMMING

The city's free outdoor public pools, found in all five boroughs, are generally open throughout the summer. Favorites include the giant Hamilton Fish on the Lower East Side; the magnificent McCarren Park pool on the border between Williamsburg and Greenpoint in Brooklyn; the Astoria Pool in Queens; and Lasker Pool, in the northeast corner of Central Park.

For a more exclusive splash, many of the city's hotels offer day passes (for a price) to their rooftop pools.

BOATING

Several outfitters, including Manhattan by Sail, operate schooners that cater to large groups and have some themed trips. If you like to paddle, Manhattan Kayak offers kayak as well as stand-up paddleboard

lessons and tours. Manhattan's Downtown Boathouse has several locations and offers free kayak instructional trips.

ICE-SKATING

Come fall, outdoor skating rinks open throughout the five boroughs. The Rink at Rockefeller Center tends to be packed, so for more space to practice your double axels, head to Lasker Pool

Swimming

in the northeast part of Central Park or out to the LeFrak Center in Brooklyn's Prospect Park.

BIKING

Bicycling is a favorite outdoor activity around the five boroughs. Citi Bike, the NYC bike-sharing program, makes it easy to bike around in Manhattan, Brooklyn, and Queens, but renting a bike for the day will give you more opportunities to cruise around town and get off the beaten path. There are countless bike paths around the city (the NYC Department of Transportation and NYC Bike Maps are excellent resources) but a perennial favorite waterside ride is the West Side Bike Path, which goes all the way up to the Little Red Lighthouse and the George Washington Bridge. For something a little different, head out to

Bay Ridge, where you can ride south from Owl's Head Park with stunning views of the Verrazzano-Narrows Bridge. If you prefer to cycle out of the way of cars, both Central Park and Prospect Park are car free. (Cars still travel Central Park's transverse drives, but these don't intersect with the scenic loop.)

RUNNING

Running or jogging is the easiest way to enjoy some outdoor activity. All you really need is a pair of running shoes and you're good to go. There are plenty of park and waterside trails throughout the five boroughs and it's easy to find a scenic path. To leave the route planning to someone else, and to do some sightseeing while you get your exercise, why not join a group run? You'll meet some like-minded

people, and there's often the option of going out for food or drinks after. Free Tours by Foot has free group runs in Central Park (tipping at the end is encouraged).

BIRD-WATCHING

When it comes to bird-watching, a lot people think New York City is just about pigeons and seagulls (and those bright green parakeets in Green-Wood Cemetery), so it may come as a surprise that the five boroughs offer some magnificent bird-spotting opportunities. The New York City Audubon Society has an extensive list of places to go birding and the New York City Department of Parks and Recreation has a full roster of bird-watching events.

What to Buy in NYC

BOOKS

Bibliophiles have plenty of great places to shop in New York, but the king of all the city's bookstores is The Strand, offering some 18 miles of books. From rare leather-bound editions to the latest best sellers, you'll find whatever you're looking for.

MODEL WATER TOWER KIT

Forget about model airplanes. For a truly New York souvenir, pick up one of Boundless Brooklyn's model water tower kits, which pay homage to the city's humble yet ubiquitous water towers. Made from 100% recycled materials, each kit comes with step-by-step instructions. They're sold at dozens of stores around the city, including the museum shops at the New Museum and the Museum of the City of New York as well as independent boutiques around the city.

VINTAGE CLOTHING

It should come as no surprise that New Yorkers have style in spades. Shop where the cool kids shop and go vintage at the city's secondhand and vintage stores. Some of the best can be found in Brooklyn. Try Beacon's Closet, which gets swarmed with hipsters on the weekends, or Housing Works, which benefits people living with and affected by HIV/AIDS. Both have multiple locations throughout the city. Screaming Mimi's in the West Village is a long-established store. We also love 10 ft. Single by Stella Dallas, which has a massive selection of vintage clothes from the recent past and a huge selection of midcentury cocktail dresses, coats, and clothes for men.

VINYL RECORDS

For vintage vinyl, locals head to Rough Trade's massive outpost in Williamsburg. This London-based store sells LPs, CDs, and books in a space outfitted with recycled shipping containers. It also hosts concerts, signings, and other events. Check the website for the full schedule.

SPECIALTY TEA

This little jewel box of a shop in Greenpoint is as much a pleasure to visit for its design as for its specialty teas. Bellocq sources matcha and rare teas from the Himalayas, as well as more standard black, green, white, and herbal teas from India, China, and Japan. Packaged in beautiful yellow canisters, the teas make excellent gifts.

LOCAL CRAFTS

For one-of-a-kind creations by local artisans and designers, there's no better place to shop than Artists & Fleas. Launched in Williamsburg, the multi-merchant marketplace now has three New York locations in Williamsburg, Chelsea Market, and SoHo. You can find everything from clutches printed with cheeky phrases to custom clocks made from old hardcover books.

Rough Trade

JEWELRY
Embrace the "Made in Brooklyn" ethos at one of Williamsburg's many jewelry shops. Catbird is especially known for its thin stackable rings, but also makes engagement rings, necklaces, earrings, and bracelets using ethically sourced diamonds, opals, and other gems. In addition to pieces by its in-house studio, it stocks items by other local designers, too.

AFRICAN IMPORTS
At the massive semi-enclosed Malcolm Shabazz Market in Harlem, you can find clothes, jewelry, woven baskets, oils, and decorative objects from Senegal, Nigeria, Kenya, and other African countries all together under one roof. It was inspired by the Malcolm Shabazz Mosque, where Malcolm X preached during the 1950s and '60s.

HOME DECOR
New York is full of quirky and one-of-a-kind design and decor shops. Anybody interested in buying something truly unique for their home should visit the multi-story ABC Carpet & Home. It's a sensory overload of contemporary furniture and rare antiques, with a huge range of prices to match. For fun kitchen supplies, Fishs Eddy is a must-visit for upcycled vintage plates and silverware as well as novelty kitchen items. If you're looking for high design, look no further than the MOMA Design Store, which outlets on 53rd Street or on Spring Street in SoHo.

PERFUME
Though now you can find its perfumes all over the country, the D.S. & Durga brand started in a Bushwick apartment. Made by a husband-and-wife team, each fragrance is meant to evoke a specific time and place, whether it be the cosmic desert town of Marfa or the heat and spice of Bombay. Find their scents at Barneys New York and other retailers around the city. Other places to shop for your signature New York scent include Aedes Perfumery, Bond No. 9, and Le Labo.

Free Things to Do in NYC

CHELSEA GALLERIES
The best way to see a wide range of art at no cost is to explore Chelsea galleries. With most spaces located between 22nd and 27th Streets, west of 10th Avenue, you'll get your share of the cultural experience. And for an extra-special trip, attend one of the Thursday night openings with free wine.

HIGH LINE
Curving along Gansevoort Street in the Meatpacking District to West 34th Street, the High Line takes visitors through the city on the road less traveled. Dating back to 1934, the abandoned freight rails have been transformed into a public park, filled with gardens, art displays, and select special events.

THE CATHEDRAL CHURCH OF ST. JOHN THE DIVINE
This Manhattan marvel is known as the largest cathedral in the world. Stop by the church anytime to look around the facilities, which are filled with plenty of interesting historical tidbits. While official tours cost a small fee, you can roam the 11.3-acre grounds and the building free of charge.

CENTRAL PARK
No trip to New York is complete without a visit to this 843-acre public park, which is worth exploring in every season. Designed by Frederick Law Olmsted and Calvert Vaux, the sprawling beauty makes you forget you're in a crowded city. Keep an eye out for the Alice in Wonderland and Balto statues.

BROOKLYN BREWERY
If you want to look behind the scenes at one of the city's famous breweries, head to the Brooklyn Brewery. Located in Williamsburg, it hosts a wide range of free tours on weekends. Pick up a free ticket at least an hour prior to the tour and make sure to bring your ID.

MUSEUM AT THE FASHION INSTITUTE OF TECHNOLOGY
With a mix of permanent and rotating exhibits, the museum houses work from designers such as Dior, Chanel, and Balenciaga: more than 4,000 pairs of shoes, 50,000 clothing pieces and accessories, and 30,000 textiles.

Brooklyn Bridge

BROOKYLN BRIDGE

The Brooklyn Bridge gives the more than 4,000 pedestrians who cross it each day a stunning view of the city's skyline and waterfront. The walk is about a mile long with views of the Statue of Liberty, the Empire State Building, the Chrysler Building, the World Trade Center, and much more.

STATEN ISLAND FERRY

The 25-minute ride from Manhattan to Staten Island offers views of the Statue of Liberty, Ellis Island, and the city skyline. More than 22 million people travel on the ferry each year, with about 109 trips per day. With five boats on rotating schedules, you can catch the ferry regularly throughout the day.

GRAND CENTRAL TERMINAL

After officially opening its doors in 1913, Grand Central Terminal has become an iconic New York City landmark. More than 750,000 people pass through the terminal every day, but few look up to admire the constellations painted on the ceiling of the main concourse by Paul Helleu.

New York City with Kids

ZOOS

The Bronx Zoo is the country's largest city zoo, home to more than 4,000 animals. Spend a whole day here so you don't have to choose between Congo Gorilla Forest and Tiger Mountain. The Central Park Zoo is small but popular.

CONEY ISLAND

At Coney Island, the whole family can enjoy a walk along Coney Island's famous boardwalk to take in the beach, Luna Park's amusement rides, the landmarked Cyclone wooden roller coaster (54-inch height requirement), minor-league baseball games at the Cyclones' stadium (MCU Park), Nathan's hot dogs, and the New York Aquarium.

BROADWAY SHOWS

The Lion King is still a firm favorite with kids, but it has solid competition with the likes of *Aladdin, Wicked, Frozen,* and Off-Broadway shows like *Stomp,* the *Gazillion Bubble Show,* and *Blue Man Group.* Kids' shows are popular, so it's rare to find tickets at TKTS booths; book ahead if possible. Preteens and teens who are too cool for the Disney musical experience might appreciate Sam Eaton's mind-boggling display of magic and mentalism in *The Quantum Eye,* held Off-Broadway at Theatre 80 in St. Mark's Place. The New Victory Theater is New York City's only theater dedicated to presenting family-friendly works.

MUSEUMS

There's a museum for every age, interest, and attention span in New York City. Some are aimed squarely at the younger set, but you shouldn't limit yourself or your kids to "children's" museums; most—especially the big players like MoMA, the Guggenheim, the Met, and the Whitney—offer programs to engage younger visitors (just ask at the admission desk).

That said, sometimes toddlers want play places designed specifically for them, like the play center and interactive exhibits created for the under-five set at the Children's Museum of Manhattan and the arts-and-crafts rooms and ball pit at the Children's Museum of the Arts.

The American Museum of Natural History is a top choice for kids of all ages and interests, visitors and locals alike: the giant dinosaurs and the huge blue whale alone are worth the trip, as is the live Butterfly Conservatory (October through May). You'll also find an IMAX theater, ancient-culture displays, and fabulous wildlife dioramas. The space shows at the Hayden Planetarium (tickets sold separately) are a big bang with kids.

Nearby, the often overlooked DiMenna Children's History Museum—in the New-York Historical Society—invites kids (ages eight and up) to connect to the lives of real New York children from the past through hands-on activities that include video games, cross-stitching, and interactive maps.

The American Museum of Natural History

The Lower East Side Tenement Museum also offers a glimpse into the lives of early New Yorkers, in this case immigrant families. Guided tours (for ages six and up) visit restored tenement apartments where costumed "residents" bring history to life.

You can also explore the history of public transit in NYC—from horsepower to the subway—at the New York Transit Museum. Housed in an old subway station in downtown Brooklyn, this museum has an old bus to pretend-drive, vintage subway cars, and retro ads and maps.

Also in Brooklyn is the Brooklyn Children's Museum, which, although a trek from the subway, has great hands-on exhibits (best suited for under-eights) like an interactive greenhouse.

The *Intrepid* Sea, Air & Space Museum, an aircraft carrier turned museum, houses the world's fastest jets, a Cold War–era submarine, the first space shuttle, the interactive Exploreum Hall, flight simulators, and more.

When museums try to make learning fun, they often fall flat, but the National Museum of Mathematics makes learning kaleidoscopic—and yes, fun—through interactive puzzles, games, displays, and hands-on tools like square-wheel tricycles.

PARKS AND PLAYGROUNDS

If you're looking for space to let off steam in Manhattan, the 843-acre Central Park is a good start. You can row boats on the lake, ride a carousel, explore the zoo, rent bikes, picnic, or just wander and enjoy the park's musicians, performers, and 21 playgrounds.

Head to DUMBO (short for Down Under the Manhattan Bridge Overpass) for family-friendly Brooklyn Bridge Park, a picnic-perfect waterfront park with several inventive playgrounds. Jane's Carousel, a public swimming pool, and a variety of kid-centric music, arts, and kite-flying festivals.

If it's too hot or too cold, head to Chelsea Piers, between 18th and 23rd Streets along Manhattan's Hudson River. With a climbing wall, batting cages, ice-skating rinks, basketball and volleyball courts, indoor soccer fields, bowling, sailing, golf, gymnastics, and an Explorer Center with a ball pit and slides, it's a five-block energy outlet for kids of all ages.

New York City Sports Teams

No city in the world can claim such a long and storied sports heritage as the Big Apple. Indeed, even the term "Big Apple" is rooted in sports history, as a reference to 1920s horse racing in and around the city. With more than a dozen professional sports teams—many of them playing in major leagues—this town is downright fanatical about competition. It has also hosted some of the all-time greatest players and sporting events: Jackie Robinson and Babe Ruth made baseball history; the 1958 NFL championship, played at Yankee Stadium between the New York Giants and the Baltimore Colts, is considered "the greatest game ever played" (although it's worth noting that the New York team lost). There are big-time sports happening almost every day in the five boroughs. And even if you can't catch an event live, you can almost surely find it playing in a local bar, where you may encounter fans unlike those anywhere else, sports-logo tattoos and all. *For more information about sports, see Sports and the Outdoors in Travel Smart New York City.*

BASEBALL

Few teams are more synonymous with a city than the **Yankees** are with New York. The team has one of baseball's best all-time win records, as well as the best regular-season win percentage (.569 as of 2018). They play at Yankee Stadium in the Bronx, and their famous players have included Yogi Berra, Joe DiMaggio, Lou Gehrig, Reggie Jackson, Derek Jeter, Roger Maris, and Babe Ruth. They currently have a total 27 World Series titles, and 40 American League pennants. Over in Queens, the **New York Mets** play at Citi Field, with a proud fan base and legacy all their own. Famous past players include Dwight Gooden, Keith Hernandez, Willie Mays, and Darryl Strawberry. While they don't boast quite as many

titles as the Yankees (only two World Series championships and five National League pennants), they're considered the city's scrappy underdog, and all of New York cheered when they made it to the World Series in fall 2015 (eventually losing to the Kansas City Royals). Although the two teams are in different leagues, they play each other several times a year in what's known as the Subway Series, making the intracity rivalry as fierce as ever.

BASKETBALL

Part of the fun of witnessing the NBA **New York Knicks** in action at Madison Square Garden from October to June is getting an eyeful of the celebrities often in attendance. Their past few seasons may have been underwhelming, but with two NBA championships, eight conference titles, and greats like Carmelo Anthony, Patrick Ewing, and Walt Frazier on their past roster, it's hard to escape the team's legacy in the basketball world and throughout the city. Since 2012, they've had rivals in the city, with the **Brooklyn Nets** returning to NYC's most populous borough. Games are played at the Barclays Center, with former team owner Jay-Z and other notables often in attendance at the games.

FOOTBALL

Loyalty is a big thing with NYC sports fans, and some **New York Giants** fans are so loyal they even claim to bleed Giants' blue, whereas **New York Jets** fans' rallying cry "J-E-T-S Jets Jets Jets!" is so mighty that if you listen closely on game days, you can almost hear it from across the Hudson River. Both teams play in New Jersey, at MetLife Stadium, from September through February. The Giants have won four Super Bowls (most recently in 2011 against the New England Patriots) and 11 conference titles, led by such players as Eli Manning, Michael Strahan, and Lawrence Taylor. The lower-key Jets, meanwhile, are known as the city's underdog, with only one Super Bowl title (all the way back in 1968) and four division titles. They still have racked up big names like Curtis Martin, Don Maynard, and Joe Namath.

HOCKEY

Back in 1928, the **New York Rangers** were the first American team to win the NHL's championship Stanley Cup, and today's fans are just as eager as back then to get it back, when they play each season at Madison Square Garden. Famous players like Brian Leetch, Henrik Lundqvist, and Mark Messier have helped the team win a total of two Stanley Cups and two conference titles. Meanwhile, the **New York Islanders** relocated from their suburban Long Island stadium to Brooklyn's Barclays Center in 2015. Since they haven't won a Stanley Cup since the early 1980s, maybe Brooklyn will help them get their mojo back. Their pre-1980s glories include four Stanley Cups and five conference titles.

SOCCER

Soccer fans can choose between the city's two Major League Soccer teams during its season, March through October: the **New York Red Bulls** and **New York City Football Club.** Devoted Bulls fans head to the soccer-specific Red Bull Arena in Harrison, New Jersey, near Newark, while the New York City FC play in the hallowed baseball grounds of Yankee Stadium.

OTHER SPORTS

If you can't pick a team, consider a less contentious sport, like tennis—the **U.S. Open** brings the best in tennis to the USTA Billie Jean King National Tennis Center in Queens in late summer. You could also try to catch a matchup in smaller-scale college games, rugby, minor-league baseball, or even **Gotham Girls** roller derby. Or plan an early November trip to witness the fan favorite **NYC Marathon**, the largest marathon in the world, with more than 50,000 runners from around the globe.

Sitting in a TV Audience

Tickets to tapings of TV shows are free but can be hard to get, especially on short notice. Most shows accept advance requests by email or phone, or online—but for the most popular shows, you might have to wait a few months. Same-day standby tickets are often available, but be prepared to wait in line for several hours, sometimes starting at 5 or 6 am, depending on how hot the show is, or the wattage of that day's celebrity guests. Remember that standby tickets do not guarantee a seat in the audience.

THE SHOWS

The Daily Show with Trevor Noah. Jon Stewart may have moved on, but host Trevor Noah is glad to welcome you to free tapings of *The Daily Show* just like his predecessor did. Reservations can be made online only, with tickets released gradually for future shows, so check the website often to RSVP for your preferred date. Only the person whose name is on the reservation can check in, and all attendees must be at least 18. The big caveat is that a reservation doesn't guarantee entry, so get in line early. Check the website for more details. ⊠ *733 11th Ave., at 52nd St., Midtown West* ⊕ *www. showclix.com/event/TheDailyShowWith-TrevorNoah* 🎟 *Free* Ⓜ *A, C, E to 50th St.*

Good Morning America. Robin Roberts, George Stephanopoulos, and Michael Strahan, among others, host this early-morning news and entertainment show. It airs live, weekdays from 7 to 9 am, and ticket requests (free but required if you want a studio tour after the show) can be made online. If you just want to be part of the outdoor audience, you can gather on the corner of West 44th Street and Broadway to participate in outdoor segments. Check the website for more information. ⊠ *7 Times Sq., at 44th St. and Broadway, Midtown West* ⊕ *www.abcnews.go.com/ GMA/part-times-square-audience/story?id=12883468* Ⓜ *1, 2, 3, 7, N, Q, R, S, W to Times Sq.–42nd St.*

Late Night with Seth Meyers. *Saturday Night Live* alum Seth Meyers took the reins as host of *Late Night* on NBC in 2014, when former host Jimmy Fallon departed for the *Tonight Show*. Tickets are available online up to two months in advance. Same-day standby tickets are handed out at 9 am at the NBC Experience Store (49th Street entrance). Monologue-rehearsal tickets are available at the NBC Experience Store at 11:30 am. Guests must be 16 or older to be in the audience. ⊠ *30 Rockefeller Plaza, Midtown West* ☎ *212/664–3056* ⊕ *www.1iota.com/show/461/Late-Night-with-Seth-Meyers* Ⓜ *B, D, F, M to 47th–50th Sts./Rockefeller Center.*

The Late Show with Stephen Colbert. After hosting the *Late Show* for 22 years, David Letterman passed the torch to former *Colbert Report* host Stephen Colbert in 2015. While Colbert's fictional conservative persona did not follow him to his new gig at the Ed Sullivan Theater, his loyal audience did, so expect competition for tickets. The show is usually taped daily at 5:30 pm; check the website and the show's social media for updated details and new ticket releases. You must be 16 or older to sit in the audience. ⊠ *Ed Sullivan Theater, 1697 Broadway, between 53rd and 54th Sts., Midtown West* ☎ *212/975–5853* ⊕ *colbert.1iota. com/show/536/The-Late-Show-with-Stephen-Colbert* Ⓜ *1, C, E to 50th St.; B, D, E to 7th Ave.*

Live! with Kelly and Ryan Sparks fly on this morning program, which books an eclectic roster of guests to chat with hosts Kelly Ripa and Ryan Seacrest. Tickets are available online about six weeks in advance. Standby tickets become available weekdays at 7 am at ABC Studios. Children under 10 are not permitted in the audience. ⊠ *7 Lincoln Sq., at 67th St. and Columbus Ave., Midtown West* ☎ *212/456–3054* ⊕ *www.1iota.com/Show/326/LIVE-with-Kelly–Ryan* Ⓜ *1 to 66th St.–Lincoln Center.*

Saturday Night Live. After four decades of laughs, *SNL* continues to push buttons, nurture comedic talents, and captivate audiences. All "live from New York." Standby tickets (only one per person) are distributed at 7 am on the day of the show at the West 49th Street entrance to 30 Rockefeller Plaza. You may ask for a ticket for either the dress rehearsal (8 pm) or the live show (11:30 pm). Requests for advance tickets (two per applicant) must be submitted by email only, during the month of August, to *snltickets@nbcuni.com*; recipients are determined by lottery. You must be 16 or older to sit in the audience. ⊠ *NBC Studios, 30 Rockefeller Plaza, between W. 49th and W. 50th Sts., Midtown West* ☎ *212/664–3056* ⊕ *www.nbc.com/tickets* Ⓜ *B, D, F, M to 47th–50th Sts./Rockefeller Center.*

Today. The *Today Show* doesn't have a studio audience, but if you get yourself to the corner of Rockefeller Center and West 49th Street well before 7 am, with some posterboard and markers (fun signs always get camera time), comfortable shoes (you'll be on your feet for hours), and a smiley, fun attitude, you might get on camera. America's first morning talk-news show airs weekdays from 7 to 10 am in the glass-enclosed, ground-level NBC studio. ⊠ *Rockefeller Plaza, W. 49th St., Midtown West* ⊕ *www.today.com* Ⓜ *B, D, F, M to 47th–50th Sts./Rockefeller Center.*

The Tonight Show Starring Jimmy Fallon. In 2014, *Saturday Night Live* veteran Jimmy Fallon packed up his impressions and sketches, his roster of star friends, and his house band (The Roots) and moved from *Late Night* to the *Tonight Show*, filling the big comedic shoes of Jay Leno and Johnny Carson before him. He also moved the show back to New York from Los Angeles, where it had originally resided until 1972. Visit the website to reserve free tickets; they're released during the first week of the month prior to the show. ■TIP➔ The show's Twitter feed (@FallonTonight) has up-to-date information. ⊠ *30 Rockefeller Plaza, Studio 6B, Midtown West* ☎ *212/664–3506* ⊕ *www.tonightshow.com/tickets* Ⓜ *B, D, F, M to 47th–50th Sts./Rockefeller Center.*

The Wendy Williams Show. If you're interested in saying "How you doin'?" to the queen of celebrity gossip and news and one of the top-rated talk shows on daytime TV, Wendy tapes live at 10 am, Monday through Thursday, and tapes a second show on Thursday at 2 pm. Check the online calendar to select the show you would like to attend; you'll receive an email response if there are seats available. Guests must be over 18. The dress code is business casual and bright colors are preferred. ⊠ *221 W. 26th St., between 7th and 8th Aves., Chelsea* ⊕ *www.wendyshow.com* Ⓜ *1 to 28th St.*

Seeing a Broadway Show

Costly ticket prices can make attending a Broadway show a less common outing for even the most devout theater-loving New Yorkers, but if there's a short list of quintessential New York experiences you should have at least once in your life, then seeing a live theater performance on Broadway is at or near the top of the list. Whether you see a long-running musical like *Book of Mormon* or *Phantom of the Opera* or a newer play from one of the city's many non-profit companies, put theater on your list of must-dos. New York has upward of 200 "legitimate" theaters (meaning those with theatrical performances, not movies), and many more ad hoc venues—parks, churches, lofts, galleries, rooftops, even parking lots.

BROADWAY AND OFF-BROADWAY—WHAT'S THE DIFFERENCE?

There are 41 officially designated "Broadway" theaters in New York, and although you might expect their shows to be the best ones in town, the designation depends on theater capacity (which must count at least 500 seats), not quality. Nearly all are within a few blocks of Times Square. A show must be performed in a Broadway theater as part of the eligibility requirements for a Tony Award. Off-Broadway theaters, which are scattered throughout the city, have 100 to 499 seats; Off-Off-Broadway venues seat fewer than 100.

WHAT'S ON?

The *New York Times* (⊕ *www.nytimes.com/events*) listings are probably the single best place to find out what's happening in the city. The *New Yorker*'s Goings On About Town listings (⊕ *www.newyorker.com*) are more selective, while *New York* magazine (⊕ *www.nymag.com*) gives a slightly more opinionated spin. The theater sites ⊕ *www.playbill.com*,

⊕ *www.theatermania.com*, and ⊕ *www.offoffonline.com* (for Off-Off-Broadway) provide more detailed information. Sites like ⊕ *www.broadway.org*, run by The Broadway League; ⊕ *www.offbroadway.com*, run by the League of Off-Broadway Theatres and Producers, are each a wealth of information.

BUYING TICKETS AT FULL PRICE

How much do tickets sell for, anyway? The average price paid for a Broadway show runs about $110, but standard prices for most musicals is about $169 up to $249. Nonmusical comedies and dramas cost from $30 to $175. Off-Broadway show can be considerably chepaer.

Unless you want to see the hottest new thing (or *Hamilton*), scoring tickets is fairly easy. The website for the show will tell you what going rates are (and usually if any deals are available) and will provide a link to the official ticket seller. Whenever possible, buy tickets in advance—months ahead for a popular new show. In general, Saturday evenings and weekend matinees are the toughest and priciest tickets to buy. **Telecharge** and **Ticketmaster** handle sales for most shows. Service charges on internet ticket sales are high. Avoid these by buying your tickets in person at the theater box office. Most expensive are typically "premium" tickets with the best views and those offered by resellers, who are legal ticket brokers that often have tickets for the hottest shows; you'll pay a huge premium for the most popular shows. Beware of Craigslist, which is full of ticketing scams.

For smaller Off-Broadway shows, try **Ticket Central,** on Theater Row; service charges are nominal here.

■**TIP→ Although online ticket services provide seating maps to help you choose, the advantage of going to the box office is** twofold: there are no add-on service fees, and a ticket seller can personally advise you about sight lines—and knee room—for the seat location you are considering. Broadway box offices do not usually have direct phone lines; their walk-in hours are generally 10 am until curtain.

BUYING DISCOUNT TICKETS

The cheapest—though chanciest—ticket opportunities are found at participating theater box offices on the day of the performance. So-called "rush" tickets, usually about $25–$40, may be distributed by lottery and are usually for front-row (possibly neck-craning) seats, though it can vary by theater; there are also standing-room-only seats available on occasion (usually for under $30). Check the comprehensive planner on ⊕ www.nytix.com, or go to the show's website to discover whether they make such an offer and how to pursue it. Obstructed-view seats or those in the very rear balcony are sometimes available at deeply discounted rates, for advance purchase.

For advanced discount purchases, the best seating is likely available by using a discount code. Procure these codes, good for an average of 20% to 50% off, online. (You need to register on each website.) The excellent no-subscription-required ⊕ www.broadwaybox.com posts nearly all discount codes currently available for Broadway shows. As with the discount codes provided through online subscriber services—**TheaterMania** and **Playbill**—to avoid service charges, you must bring the printout to the box office, and make your purchase there. You can also download mobile ticketing apps, such as **TodayTix,** which offer discounted last-minute and advance tickets.

For seats at up to 50% off the usual price, get same-day discount tickets by going to one of the **TKTS booths** (⊕ www. tdf.org): there's one in Times Square,

others at Lincoln Center and South Street Seaport. Although they do tack on a $5-per-ticket service charge—and not all shows are predictably available—the broad choices and ease of selection make TKTS the go-to source for the flexible theatergoer. You can browse available shows for that day online or via the TKTS app (⊕ www.tdf.org/tktsapp), or check the electronic listings board near the ticket windows to mull over your options while you're in line. At the Times Square location (under the red glass staircase), there is a separate "Play Express" window (for nonmusicals); and if you buy tickets today, you can come back within the next seven days to make another purchase without having to wait on line. The Times Square and South Street Seaport booths are open daily; Lincoln Center's is closed on Monday. Check the website for the specific hours. All ticket sales are for shows on that same or the next day. Credit cards and cash are accepted at all locations. ■TIP➜ Ticket-booth hours may vary over holiday periods; also note that the longest lines are generally within the first hour of the booths' opening

CONTACTS Playbill. ⊕ www.playbill. com. **Telecharge.** ☎ 212/239–6200, 800/447–7400 ⊕ www.telecharge. com. **TheaterMania.** ☎ 212/352–3101, 866/811–4111 ⊕ www.theatermania.com. **Ticket Central.** ⊠ Playwrights Horizon, 416 W. 42nd St., between 9th and 10th Aves., Midtown West ☎ 212/279–4200 ⊕ www.ticketcentral.com Ⓜ A, C, E to 42nd St.–Port Authority. **Ticketmaster.** ☎ 866/448–7849 for automated service, 800/745–3000 ⊕ www.ticketmaster. com. **TKTS Times Square.** ⊠ Duffy Sq., 47th St. and Broadway, Midtown West ☎ 212/912–9770 ⊕ www.tdf.org/tkts Ⓜ 1, 2, 3, 7, N, Q, R, S to Times Sq.–42nd St. **TodayTix.** ☎ 855/464–9778 ⊕ www. todaytix.com.

NYC's Waterfront Parks

If Central Park makes you think, "Been there, done that," head to one of the city's many waterfront parks. Many New Yorkers are still discovering some of these ever-expanding green getaways, too.

BATTERY PARK CITY

Built on landfill jutting out into the Hudson River, Battery Park City is a high-rise residential neighborhood on the west side of Lower Manhattan, with the Hudson River Park promenade running along the Hudson River. There are a handful of reasonably priced outdoor restaurants with stunning views of the Statue of Liberty. If you have kids, don't miss Battery Park's excellent Teardrop Park, with its long slide, and the delightful SeaGlass carousel.

GETTING HERE

By subway: South Battery Park: 1, R, W to Rector Place; 4, 5 to Bowling Green. North Battery Park: 1, 2, 3, A, C to Chambers Street; E to World Trade Center. By bus: M9, M20, M22.

BROOKLYN BRIDGE PARK

Over in Brooklyn, a former industrial site running along a narrow stretch of Brooklyn waterfront from Vinegar Hill to Brooklyn Heights has been turned into an 85-acre, 1.3-mile-long park featuring grassy lawns, rocky outcrops, bike paths, playgrounds, sports fields, basketball courts, and a carousel. There are picnic areas, seasonal food stands by high-profile restaurants, music and film festivals in summer, water-taxi service to Governors Island, and thousands of visitors and locals taking advantage of it all. Perhaps the best feature of this new hipster destination is one that's been here all along: the picture-postcard views of the Brooklyn and Manhattan Bridges and the Manhattan skyline.

GETTING HERE

By subway: A, C to High Street; F to York Street. Instead of taking the subway, you could take either a water taxi (⊕ *www. nywatertaxi.com*) or the East River Ferry (⊕ *www.nywaterway.com*) to Fulton Ferry Landing, or you could walk across the Brooklyn Bridge.

THE EAST RIVER PARK

This landscaped waterfront park, stretching from Montgomery Street to 12th Street along the Manhattan side of the East River, is one of the Lower East Side's best-kept secrets, with ball fields, bike paths, tennis courts, playgrounds, gardens, and picnic areas—along with impressive views of the Brooklyn skyline and the Williamsburg Bridge. You have to cross a footbridge over the FDR Drive to get to the park.

GETTING HERE

By subway: J, M, Z to Essex Street; F to 2nd Avenue. By bus: M14D, M21, M22.

GOVERNORS ISLAND

A fairly recent addition to the city's parks scene, this little island feels like a small town just 800 yards from the tip of Manhattan. Tourists love the unparalleled views of the New York Harbor and Lower Manhattan, and locals love the out-of-city experience. The 172-acre park, built in part from landfill from subway excavations, was a base for the U.S. Army and Coast Guard for almost two centuries. Until 2003, it was off-limits to the public, which could be why the 19th-century homes here are so well preserved. The island is open to the public daily from May to October, with programs including art showings, concerts, and family events. You can take a bike over on the ferry or rent one on the island. For more information, including updated ferry schedules and a calendar of activities, go to ⊕ *www.govisland.org*.

GETTING HERE

A seven-minute ferry ride ($3; free on weekend mornings) takes passengers to Governors Island from a dock at the restored, cast-iron Battery Maritime Building (10 South Street), near the Staten Island Ferry. Get to the ferry by subway: 1 to South Ferry; 4, 5 to Bowling Green; or R, W to Whitehall Street. By bus: M15, M20, M55.

THE HIGH LINE

Once an elevated railroad track that serviced the long-ago factories along the lower west side, the High Line was converted into a linear park (like a promenade) that integrates landscaping with rail-inspired design and provides a fresh perspective on the city. Vegetation here includes 210 species of plants, trees, and shrubs intended to reflect the wild plants that flourished for decades after the tracks were abandoned in 1980. The park—30 feet above street level—is open between Gansevoort Street (around 12th Street) in the Meatpacking District and 34th Street in Midtown. Swooping views of the Hudson River, an extended sight line of the Meatpacking District, and the Whitney Museum of American Art are the highlights. For information on tours, public programs, and a calendar of events, go to ⊕ *www.thehighline.org* or call ☎ *212/500–6035*. Note that the park is often extremely crowded, especially on afternoons and weekends.

GETTING HERE

The High Line is accessible at Gansevoort and every two blocks between 14th and 30th Streets, with elevator access at 14th, 16th, 23rd, 30th, and 34th Streets; no bikes are allowed. It's two blocks west of the subway station at 14th Street and 8th Avenue, served by the A, C, E, and L. You can also take the C, E to 23rd Street and walk two blocks

west. The 1, 2, 3 stops at 14th Street and 7th Avenue, three blocks away. By bus: M11, M14D, M23, M34.

THE HUDSON RIVER PARK

This 5-mile greenway park hugs the Hudson River from 59th Street to Battery Park. Although the park has a unified design, it's divided into seven distinct sections that reflect the different Manhattan neighborhoods just across the West Side Highway. Along with refurbished piers with grass and trees, there are also attractions like the *Intrepid* Sea, Air & Space Museum at Pier 86 across from 46th Street. A few blocks south, the Circle Line and World Yacht offer boat tours of the Hudson. At Piers 96 and 40, the Downtown Boathouse (⊕ *www.downtownboathouse.org*) offers free kayaking. There's a mammoth sports center, **Chelsea Piers,** between Piers 59 and 61, and a playground, mini-golf course, and beach volleyball court at Pier 25. The park also sponsors free tours and classes, including free fishing. For a calendar of events and activities, go to ⊕ *www.hudsonriverpark.org*. North of Hudson River Park is one of Manhattan's better-known parks, **Riverside Park.**

GETTING HERE

Hudson River Park is on the far west side of the city, adjacent to the West Side Highway. Crosstown buses at 14th, 23rd, and 42nd Streets will get you close, but you'll still have to walk a bit. It's worth it.

New York City Museums, an Overview

From the grand institutions along Fifth Avenue's museum mile to an underground museum in a converted subway station in Brooklyn to the dramatic new Whitney Museum in the Meatpacking District, New York City is home to an almost overwhelming collection of artistic riches, so it's a good idea to plan ahead. This overview includes museums listed elsewhere in the book; check the index for full listings.

MAJOR MUSEUMS

It's hard to create a short list of top museums in New York City, because, well, there are just so many of them. That said, ambitious art lovers will likely focus on the big five. One of the most visited museums in the world, the vast **Metropolitan Museum of Art** (known locally as "the Met," not to be confused with the Metropolitan Opera, also known as "the Met") has a collection that consists of more than 2 million works of art representing 5,000 years of history. Some of the Met's modern art collection is showcased at the Met Breuer, in the former Whitney Museum building. The **Whitney Museum of American Art** itself, which moved from its Upper East Side home to the Meatpacking District in 2015, is one of the city's most memorable museums, famous as much for its High Line and Hudson views as for its expansive indoor and outdoor exhibition spaces. With its world-famous dinosaur exhibits, its halls of fossils, gems, and human evolution, and its planetarium, the **American Museum of Natural History** is one of the most celebrated museums in the world. Both the **Museum of Modern Art (MoMA)** and the **Solomon R. Guggenheim Museum** are known for their incredible spaces—MoMA, a maze of glass walkways, was designed by Yoshio Taniguchi, while the nautilus-like Guggenheim is a masterwork of Frank Lloyd Wright—as well as for their superlative

collections of contemporary art and space-specific shows.

OTHER TOP MUSEUMS

There are many other important museums in the city. The **Frick Collection,** an elegant art museum in the neoclassical mansion of industrialist Henry Clay Frick, is a refined experience for its works, decor, and architecture. The **Morgan Library and Museum** is another mansion-museum founded on the vast and varied collections of a magnate—in this case J. P. Morgan. The **American Folk Art Museum** is dedicated to American folk art and the work of contemporary self-taught artists, while the **New Museum** is the only museum dedicated solely to contemporary art in Manhattan. There are several museums to satisfy design lovers, including the **Museum of Arts and Design,** the **Museum at FIT,** the **Skyscraper Museum,** the **Museum of Illustration** and the **Museum of Comic and Cartoon Art** at the **Society of Illustrators,** and the **Cooper Hewitt, Smithsonian Design Museum,** packed with hands-on activities for grown-ups. Speaking of lovers, the provocative, adults-only **Museum of Sex** explores the history, evolution, and cultural significance of sex, while the **Museum of American Finance** satisfies our curiosity about money and Wall Street.

NEW YORK–SPECIFIC MUSEUMS

It's appropriate that the city's oldest museum, the **New-York Historical Society,** is dedicated to the city itself. Founded in 1805, this neighbor of the American Museum of Natural History offers a unique and comprehensive overview of the city's history, as well as quirky and compelling exhibits. Other New York–centric museums include the **Museum of the City of New York,** the **Lower East Side Tenement Museum,** the **Merchant's House Museum,** the **Fraunces Tavern Museum,** the

Ellis Island Immigration Museum, the **New York City Fire Museum,** the **National 9/11 Memorial & Museum,** and the **New York Transit Museum.**

CULTURALLY SPECIFIC MUSEUMS

New York City is often referred to as a melting pot, which explains the profusion of culture-specific museums dedicated to sharing the broad and specific stories, struggles, and experiences of certain cultural and ethnic groups—often overlooked in mainstream museums. **El Museo del Barrio** focuses on Latin American and Caribbean art and features a popular collection of hand-carved wooden folk-art figures from Puerto Rico. The **National Museum of the American Indian (Smithsonian Institution)** explores the diversity of Native American peoples through cultural artifacts, and regular music and dance performances. The **Jewish Museum,** the **Museum of Jewish Heritage,** and the **Museum at Eldridge Street** explore Jewish culture and art, and the Jewish experience in New York. The **Asia Society and Museum,** the **Museum of Chinese in America (MOCA),** the **Japan Society,** and the **Rubin Museum of Art** are dedicated to the art and experiences of Asian communities. Other notable ethnic- or culture-specific museums include the **Leslie-Lohman Museum of Gay and Lesbian Art,** the **Ukrainian Museum,** and the **Studio Museum in Harlem** (for artists of African descent locally, nationally, and internationally).

OUTER-BOROUGH MUSEUMS

The **Brooklyn Museum** is the second-biggest museum in New York City and home to an impressive collection of European and American paintings and sculptures, an outstanding Egyptian collection, the Elizabeth A. Sackler Center for Feminist Art, and a memorial sculpture garden of salvaged architectural elements from throughout New York City. A visit to

Queens means innovative and experimental art at **MoMA PS1** and the small museum and garden of the **Noguchi Museum,** dedicated to the art of Isamu Noguchi, a prominent Japanese-American sculptor. Other top museums in Queens include the **Museum of the Moving Image** and the **Queens Museum.** The enchanting **Cloisters Museum and Gardens** (an outpost of the Met museum) in Fort Tryon Park in Upper Manhattan is a bit of a trek relative to other city museums, but it's almost guaranteed that you'll find it worth the trip.

CHILDREN'S MUSEUMS

Some kids' museums are fun just for the kids, like the **Children's Museum of the Arts,** the **Children's Museum of Manhattan,** and the **Brooklyn Children's Museum,** but many are fun for the entire family. Kids of all ages will appreciate the fleet of jets, the flight simulator and other hands-on activities, the space shuttle *Enterprise,* and the *Growler* submarine at the Intrepid **Sea, Air & Space Museum.** Other crowd-pleasers include **Madame Tussauds New York** and the **National Museum of Mathematics.** The **DiMenna Children's History Museum** (at the New-York Historical Society) has interactive exhibits geared to help kids connect with children throughout New York's history.

GALLERIES

There are countless art galleries in Manhattan and Brooklyn worth visiting; check neighborhood chapters for specific listings. Your interest in these may vary depending on what shows are on at what times, so we also recommend checking the listings in *New York Magazine* and the *New York Times.*

What to Watch and Read Before You Go to New York City

Books

JUST KIDS BY PATTI SMITH

In her National Book Award–winning memoir, artist, poet, and punk-rock-movement founder Patti Smith creates a beautiful love letter: both to her dear friend, the deceased photographer Robert Mapplethorpe, and to the New York City of their shared youth, where the two lived and learned as artists in the late 1960s and '70s. With a mix of poetry, dream, and sobering reality, Smith is adept at capturing the mood of being young in the city at this particular time, and all those fleeting, poignant moments that exist right on the brink of change, success, and heartbreak.

THE GOLDFINCH BY DONNA TARTT

This Dickensian feat of a novel spans Manhattan from the dark corners of the East Village to the wealthy enclave of the Upper East Side and everywhere in between. Linked to the book's other characters through one major tragedy (and subsequent smaller ones), the novel's antihero is full of moral contradictions and personality flaws, but his journey (from a preteen into adulthood) is fascinating, and it's impossible not to want to follow along.

SOUR HEART BY JENNY ZHANG

Jenny Zhang's heartfelt story collection links together the experiences of first- and second-generation Chinese Americans living throughout Queens and Brooklyn. Her sharp, funny writing describes what it's like to grow up in a country that your parents aren't quite a part of—with the weight of all their expectations and sacrifices on your shoulders—and illustrates a human experience important to the New York (and American) story.

OPEN CITY BY TEJU COLE

Open City's narrator Julius, a Nigerian immigrant and medical fellow at Columbia, likes to walk, and, through his urban meanderings, readers get to explore great expanses of a city that Julius views with respect and wonder, from the sidewalks and skyscrapers to the many versions of life he encounters. Julius observes the crowded yet solitary nature of big-city life and, as an immigrant, displays a keen awareness of the other cultural influences that make up New York.

THE MAMBO KINGS PLAY SONGS OF LOVE BY OSCAR HIJUELOS

This Pulitzer Prize–winning novel traces the lives of two brothers before, during, and after their glory days as performing musicians, moving from Havana to New York City during the height of the mambo trend in the 1950s (at their peak, meeting Desi Arnaz and earning a musical cameo on I Love Lucy). The story is filled with the memories and music of life in the Bronx streets, apartments, hotels, and nightclubs during the pair's heyday.

HERE IS NEW YORK BY E.B. WHITE

E. B. White's 1948 Manhattan might not look much like the city today, but this work encapsulates a certain fervor and mythology associated with a New York writer deeply in awe of his city. The short read is full of nostalgic Manhattan views and White's expert observations, making it a perfect little book to savor en route to the Big City.

LET THE GREAT WORLD SPIN BY COLUM MCCANN

Weaving together the narratives of several loosely related New Yorkers, this novel circles around a cast of characters and events that all occur around the same date in 1974. Central to one particular day is real-life tightrope walker Philippe Petit's harrowing traipse between the Twin Towers of the World Trade Center (curious readers should also watch *Man on Wire*, the 2008 documentary film on Petit). The multiple, overlapping narratives of McCann's National Book Award–winning novel showcase both the diversity and unity of experience the city is capable of producing.

BONFIRE OF THE VANITIES BY TOM WOLFE

Through a central crime told from several points of view of the people involved (a Wall Street trader living on Park Avenue, a bullish assistant district attorney, and an alcoholic tabloid journalist), this satirical novel strives to encapsulate much of the mood of 1980s New York City: less-than-pretty aspects of racism, classism, vapid excess, and bitter greed. While it's funny and full of farce, Wolfe used his skills as a journalist to base much of the novel on real happenings and characters.

EXTREMELY LOUD AND INCREDIBLY CLOSE BY JONATHAN SAFRAN FOER

After his father's tragic death in 9/11, a grieving nine-year-old kid goes on a mission through the five boroughs, making all sorts of human connections throughout the city along the way, and hoping to put together some missing pieces that might help heal his grief. It's a quick read and a beautiful story not just about 9/11 and loss, but about family, history, and human connection. The movie version stars Sandra Bullock and Tom Hanks.

THE WEARY BLUES BY LANGSTON HUGHES

Hughes's poetry here is about Harlem—its life forces, culture, art, and music—during its 1920s renaissance. The young poet borrowed blues and jazz elements to write poetry about black music and life in a way that had seldom been done before, and his work is at once personal, lyrical, and a resounding voice for the African American experience at the time.

MANNAHATTA: A NATURAL HISTORY OF NEW YORK CITY BY ERIC SANDERSON

This book is not just for lovers of natural history: there's a certain magic to be gained from reading it before a visit to New York, and reimagining the streams, hills, and woods that once made up the Manhattan of today, now so crowded with asphalt and chrome. With illustrations, and future insights on combating climate change by returning some of the city to its wildness, *Manhatta* reminds you of the natural world in everything, even in the country's most populated city.

Movies

WHEN HARRY MET SALLY

This Billy Crystal and Meg Ryan classic tops the list because it's great in both its categories, as a romantic comedy *and* a New York movie. Much like the pair's long-running friendship and budding romance in the film, this movie is cute and fun to be around, filled with wanderings throughout the city (and its iconic scene at Katz's Deli), and culminating as many rom-coms do—with a desperate, romantic run through New York City's streets.

HOME ALONE 2: LOST IN NEW YORK

There's something magical about New York City at Christmastime, and New York Christmas movies, when done right (*Miracle on 34th Street, Elf, You've Got*

Mail), give you warm-and-fuzzy feelings about both the holiday season and the city. *Home Alone 2* is an especially fun one because of how much New York you get through Kevin's explorations and antics: Rockefeller Center, Central Park, the Empire State Building, and the Plaza Hotel—even a cameo by a certain former New Yorker—all make their way into this family-friendly screwball film with basically the same plot as the first one.

DO THE RIGHT THING

With his *Chronicles of Brooklyn* series, renowned filmmaker Spike Lee dedicates a whole slew of fantastic movies (*He Got Game, She's Gotta Have It, Red Hook Summer*) to life and black culture in this outer borough, one of the greatest being 1989's *Do The Right Thing*. Starring a young Spike Lee himself, Brooklyn's Bed-Stuy neighborhood on a hot summer day is the setting for a poignant film about community, racial tension, and police brutality.

BIRDMAN

An unbelievable number of Academy Awards went to this artsy dark comedy back in 2015, about a past-his-prime movie star (Michael Keaton) who attempts to produce a Broadway show while his identity (and mental health) slowly start to unravel. The cinematography—especially *Birdman*'s magical-realistic walks through streets of New York, and a particular underwear-clad scene in Times Square—make it a strange but beautiful film.

THE GODFATHER

This quintessential New York mob movie (there have been many, of different form and value, before and after it) remains a respected classic masterpiece in New York, Italian-American, and all popular cinema. Organized-crime stereotypes aside, its depictions of life in Staten Island and Little Italy are a glimpse into the Italian-American experience in 1940s and '50s New York City.

THE CENTRAL PARK FIVE

After a white woman was assaulted while jogging in Central Park, the terrible, highly publicized crime escalated into of one of New York's most infamous wrongful-conviction sagas. In a documentary featuring perspective from the falsely convicted teens, Ken Burns thoroughly investigates all incidents around the case, and also explores the culture of fear and racism in 1980s New York—a factor that played its own important part in this tragedy.

WEST SIDE STORY

The musical drama about love, feuds, and racial clashes in the 1950s takes place on New York's Upper West Side, a demographically different neighborhood then than it is today. The 1961 movie is a classic, and Puerto Rican singer and actor Rita Moreno gives one of the films best performances in her supporting role as Anita.

PARIS IS BURNING

This 1990 documentary showcases "Ball Culture," the underground events and performances in communities of black and Latino gay men, transgender women, and drag queens in 1980s New York City. With colorful ball scenes that have inspired parts of *RuPaul's Drag Race*, this film introduced "vogueing" and other cultural gems to mainstream culture. The more colorful scenes are parsed with interviews, where subjects tackle topics of gender, race, and other social issues.

THE BIG SHORT

Based on the nonfiction book by Michael Lewis (other movies made from his books are *Liar's Poker*, a semiautobiographical account of his time on Wall

Street during the 1980s, and *Moneyball*), this is the story of the greedy banks and bad loans leading up to the 2008 housing-market collapse—and the people who saw it coming. It's a stylized, uniquely depicted drama that would be even funnier if it were less true. Elsewhere in the New York financial-drama category, the original *Wall Street* deserves a nod, as do *Wolf of Wall Street* and *Boiler Room*.

PARIAH
In writer-director Dee Rees first feature film, a young black woman growing up in Fort Greene, Brooklyn (where it was largely filmed), explores identity and belonging through sexuality, family, and the greater community. Adepero Oduye, the young actress playing Alike, gives a touching performance, in a beautiful film about sexual identity and coming of age in Brooklyn.

GANGS OF NEW YORK
A 19th-century Lower Manhattan neighborhood (with a painstakingly detailed set design by Martin Scorsese) is the battleground in this blockbuster. Characters fight for place and survival in 1860s New York City, when Irish immigrants, and anti-immigration sentiment—along with poverty, gangs, and street violence—were prevalent. Heavy hitters like Leonardo DiCaprio, Liam Neeson, and Daniel Day-Lewis make it both a great film and an interesting period piece.

Television Shows

GOSSIP GIRL
Centered around the lives of overprivileged teenagers growing up on Manhattan's Upper East Side, this dramatic series (based on the books by Cecily von Ziegesar) provides a fictionalized glimpse into the lives of the *crème de la crème* of Manhattan society—the limo rides, Hamptons vacations, penthouses, and elite private schools—along with all the secrets, lies, scandals, and plot twists you might expect.

SEX AND THE CITY
This classic HBO show was groundbreaking in its time for featuring a group of cosmopolitan (and cosmopolitan-drinking) women talking about sex and dating in a frank and refreshing way. Besides the infuriatingly large apartments, its depictions of New York and its themes around the turn of the millennium are entertaining and expansive.

BROAD CITY
It's nice to see a female friendship on television that's not about drama or men, and *Broad City*'s stars (and real-life best friends) Abby and Liana have great on-screen chemistry, creating an entertaining comedy about their friendship and lives in New York. In their own New York–artist dream story, the writers and stars of the show began with a YouTube series, picked up by Comedy Central with the help of fan-turned-producer Amy Poehler. Their writing and takes on New York life are fresh, young, and funny.

GIRLS
An update of what *Sex and the City* was to women in the early aughts, *Girls* is also about a group of female friends living in New York City (mostly Williamsburg and other parts of Brooklyn, in this case), but with very millennial problems in a very millennial New York. While not without flaws, Dunham's show deserves credit for the honesty and humor (and smart writing) with which it portrays a certain demographic of overprivileged and overeducated youth trying to "make it" in the New York City of today.

FRIENDS

Irreverent but addictive, this light comedy-drama about twenty- to thirtysomethings living around Greenwich Village (in unrealistically nice apartments) ran for 10 seasons in the '90s and early 2000s. Still probably one of the most popular sitcoms ever, Friends follows the theme of New York shows that are about little else but the intertwining lives of its New Yorker characters and the city itself.

MAD MEN

Named for Madison Avenue and the many ad firms there during the 1960s—a dynamic era for advertising in the United States—there's more to this show than the costumes and astonishing number of cigarettes and martinis consumed. The writing is smart, characters are intriguing (especially, of course, the mysterious Don Draper, played by Jon Hamm), and there are quite a few historical landmarks woven in that make it feel enlightened as a period piece.

NYPD BLUE

Cops in the fictional 15th Precinct (based on the Ninth Precinct in Lower Manhattan) have dark, intense jobs, but often darker, messier private lives. The crime drama ran for 12 seasons beginning in the early 1990s, weaving in issues of alcoholism, corruption, drug overdoses, and terrorism. Rumor has it that a revival show is in the works at ABC.

THE KNICK

This Cinemax show is set in the Knickerbocker, a hospital in an impoverished, unsanitary area of Lower Manhattan during the early 1900s. The gritty lawlessness of downtown Manhattan and the brutalities of early Western medicine make for fascinating viewing, and the show doesn't shy away from portraying opium dens, illegal abortions, and botched experimental surgeries, along with such themes as the racism, classism, and sexism of the time.

EMPIRE

This extremely popular musical drama focuses on a large entertainment company that functions much like a royal dynasty, and not without the same amount of complications and drama. Though much of the actual filming happened in Chicago, everything about Empire, from the scandals and power grabs to the fashion and hip-hop interludes, screams New York.

SEINFELD

The original "show about nothing" features comedian Jerry Seinfeld and his group of friends as they get themselves into sometimes unfortunate, always comical, and usually quintessential New York situations: mishaps at the Puerto Rican Day Parade, Macy's Day Parade, NYC Marathon, and in New York subways and delis, as well as conflicts over parking spaces, cutthroat apartment hunting, bad neighbors and roommates—even 212 versus 646 area codes.

REAL HOUSEWIVES OF NEW YORK

ROHNY is the original edition of the much-loved,-hated, and-loved-to-be-hated franchise about "housewives" in cities across America. Apropos of New York City culture, very few of the women on this edition are actually housewives, but hustling entrepreneurs and businesswomen themselves. The show moves through their failures and successes, friendships and frenemies, Hamptons mortgages, preschool admissions, and charity gala drama. Viewing from the beginning (the first season began in 2008) is a fun move through the trends and changes of the city's wealthy over the decade.

Chapter 2

TRAVEL SMART NEW YORK CITY

2

Updated by
Kelsy Chauvin

★ **CAPITAL:**
Albany

👥 **POPULATION:**
8,550,405

💬 **LANGUAGE:**
English

$ **CURRENCY:**
U.S. Dollar

☎ **AREA CODES:**
212, 332, 347, 646, 718, 917, 929

⚠ **EMERGENCIES:**
911

🚗 **DRIVING:**
On the right

⚡ **ELECTRICITY:**
120–220 v/60 cycles; plugs have two or three rectangular prongs

🕐 **TIME:**
EST

🌐 **WEB RESOURCES:**
www.nycgo.com,
www.mta.info/nyct,
www.broadwaybox.com

11 Things You Need to Know Before You Visit New York City

It can feel vast, loud, and confusing, yet New York City also can be manageable. There are simple and brilliant ways to not only survive each new day in the big city, but to navigate and even enjoy its magnificent chaos. Best of all, the effort is worth it. Because every penny saved or minute spared can be applied to something delightful later.

GET ORIENTED

Manhattan is best navigated by studying the street grid. Forget north and south, and think uptown and downtown, along the avenues. Avenues are mostly one-way, with odd numbers pointing downtown and even numbers heading uptown. Streets run crosstown (roughly east and west), generally linking the East River to the Hudson River. Their directions vary, but mostly odd-numbered streets are westbound. The area below 14th Street is older and doesn't follow the grid so neatly; many streets are on funny diagonals and have names rather than numbers. Broadway is the big boulevard that diagonally connects lower Manhattan to Inwood and the Harlem River. Fifth Avenue separates east from west street addresses (e.g. 25 E. 39th St. stands across Fifth Avenue from 25 W. 39th St.).

THE SUBWAY IS USUALLY YOUR BEST CHOICE

In Manhattan, subways and buses generally run uptown, downtown, or crosstown, just like the streets. Despite its many flaws, the subway is usually the fastest way to get around, especially in Manhattan. But if you can't manage stairs, the bus may be a better alternative; plus all buses have wheelchair ramps. Subways and buses cost $2.75 per ride (plus $1 for the Metrocard). Anyone can buy a one-week unlimited-ride pass for $33.

However, at off-peak times like late weeknights and weekends (especially Sundays), when subways are infrequent or suspended for tunnel maintenance, a yellow taxi or rideshare may be a better and faster alternative, despite the higher cost. The bold may venture onto the blue wheels of CitiBike bikeshare, which is a great option for both time and budget—but only for seasoned urban cyclists.

GETTING TO THE AIRPORT CAN BE TRICKY

JFK Airport is about an hour's taxi ride and a flat rate of $50–$70 to Manhattan; though the AirTrain to the A or E subway is a reasonable option for just $7.75 total, and around 90 minutes to Midtown Manhattan. From Newark (EWR) Airport, wise travelers skip pricey New Jersey taxis and instead take the AirTrain to Newark Airport Station, then transfer to an NJ Transit train into New York Penn Station. For LaGuardia, a taxi is best, since only buses (not trains) provide its measly mass-transit option. Shared rides can be arranged via Lyft, Via, or Uber. Or you can catch an airport shuttle bus like NYC Airporter or Newark Airport Express (around $30 one-way). Just beware that all of NYC's airports are far away, so build in at least an hour more than you think you'll need to catch your flight.

LEARN SIDEWALK ETIQUETTE

While it may seem obvious, NYC sidewalks are busy shared public thoroughfares where pedestrians converge and occasionally collide. Think of them more like foot highways, made for motion, not stopping. We beg you, don't get too caught up in your selfies, and never, ever walk with your eyes glued to your phone. In especially congested areas, pedestrians are wise to "pull over" from the flow before pausing for that quick pic. And know that any place you stop, somebody else probably wants that entrance you're blocking.

IT'S SAFE

In 2018, NYC once again saw crime rates fall. And while New York City is still the safest big city in the U.S., it's still a dynamic metropolis of nearly nine million people, and anything can happen—good or bad. The golden rule remains to stay ever aware of where you are and who's around you. That applies on the street, in a bar, in an art gallery, crossing the Williamsburg Bridge, or picnicking in Central Park: pay attention.

KNOW YOUR NEIGHBORHOODS
Every NYC neighborhood has a character of its own. From Wall Street and Chinatown, to Times Square and Lincoln Center, each one can captivate visitors with its particular atmosphere. Among the most notable are Greenwich Village for its historically Bohemian scene; Tribeca and Soho for their boutiques, galleries, and cobblestones; and Williamsburg for trendy restaurants. Visitors thirsty for nightlife may prefer the East Village or Lower East Side; while theater lovers should take Midtown Manhattan.

THE INS AND OUTS OF DINING OUT
Fine dining is always on the menu in Manhattan, where scoring a table at a hot new eatery can top off a foodie's perfect trip. The most reliable way to snag that dream table is to reserve it well in advance, either directly with the restaurant, or with an app like OpenTable or Resy. For last-minute attempts at a fully booked restaurant, show up in person during non-peak dining hours (i.e. not at 12:30 or 8 pm), be very kind to the almighty host, be flexible, and hope for a cancellation (or see if you can eat at the bar). Also, a few NYC restaurants still accept only cash.

NOT ALL STREET FOOD IS CREATED EQUAL
So you're between meals, peckish, and spy a hotdog/knish/falafel cart. Can you trust its quality? Odds are that it's fine—especially if there's a weekday queue of workers, a telling mark of a well-kept cart serving something delicious. On the other hand, with so many great takeout shops and quality food trucks (especially downtown), you may be wiser instead to spend your $3 snack budget on a great slice of pizza, a taco, or a waffle to go.

PLAN AHEAD
Just like locking in a great restaurant reservation, catching the best NYC entertainment means planning ahead. So if your dream visit hinges on catching a top Broadway show, buy that ticket first, then buy your NYC flights to plan your trip around it. This applies to any show or other major attractions with high demand and timed-ticket reservations (especially in summer), such as the Statue of Liberty's crown, the Top of the Rock observatory, or the 9/11 Memorial & Museum. If you're too late for seats at a great show, last-minute tickets can always be had through TKTS discount booths, and the NYC CityPASS lets you skip the line at several attractions. Or just dig a little deeper and try for something different, like a live jazz or comedy show.

NOT EVERYTHING COSTS AN ARM AND A LEG
High-priced admissions and show tickets can get old fast. Fortunately, some things are still free, starting with NYC's best free cruise past the Statue of Liberty: a ride on the Staten Island Ferry. Similarly grand views can be had for free on the Brooklyn Heights Promenade or crossing one of the East River bridges. Most museums here offer free-entry periods every week (albeit with long lines), and the city's parks and riverfronts offer free recreation, sports, and public art. In summer, free outdoor concerts, festivals, flea and farmers markets, film screenings, open-air theater, and other events turns the whole city into one of the country's most affordable destinations.

DON'T FORGET THE OUTER BOROUGHS
They're less crowded, more affordable, and dotted with landmarks and amazing, authentic eateries: they're the outer boroughs! That is, Brooklyn, Queens, the Bronx, and Staten Island. Set aside at least one day to explore beyond Manhattan. It could take you to a botanical garden, ballpark, beach, national landmark, or renowned museum. No matter where you wind up, it will feel like your own special discovery.

Getting Here

If flying into one of the three major airports that service New York—John F. Kennedy (JFK), LaGuardia (LGA), or New Jersey's Newark Liberty (EWR)—pick your mode of transportation for getting to Manhattan before your plane lands. Tourists typically either take a car service or head to the taxi line, but those aren't necessarily the best choices, especially during rush hour. Public transportation, especially if you're traveling light and without young children, is a swift, inexpensive option.

Once you're in Manhattan, getting around can be a breeze when you get the hang of the subway system. Better yet, if you're not in a rush and the weather's cooperating, just walk—it's the best way to discover the true New York. Not quite sure where you are or how to get where you're headed? Ask a local. You may be surprised at how friendly the city's inhabitants are, debunking their reputation for rudeness. In the same getting-there-is-half-the-fun spirit, there are also boat and bus journeys that let you see the city from a whole new perspective.

✈ Air Travel

Generally, most international flights go in and out of John F. Kennedy or Newark Liberty airport, while domestic flights go in and out of both of these, as well as LaGuardia Airport.

AIRPORTS

The major air gateways to New York City are LaGuardia Airport (LGA) and John F. Kennedy International Airport (JFK) in the borough of Queens, and Newark Liberty International Airport (EWR) in the state of New Jersey.

TRANSFERS—CAR SERVICES

Car services can be a great convenience, because upon request the driver can meet you in the baggage-claim area and helps with your luggage (though more likely, the driver will wait in the car to rendezvous with you in a designated airport-pickup zone). Airport flat rates are often comparable to taxi fares, but some car services charge for parking and wait time at the airport. To eliminate these expenses, other car services require you to telephone their dispatcher (or order a car through an app) when you land so they can send the next available car to pick you up. The New York City Taxi and Limousine Commission rules require all car services to be licensed and pick up riders only by prior arrangement; if possible, call 24 hours in advance for reservations or at least a half day before your flight's departure. Drivers of nonlicensed vehicles ("gypsy cabs") often solicit fares outside the terminal in baggage-claim areas. Don't take them: you run the risk of an unsafe ride in a vehicle that may not be properly insured and will almost certainly pay more than the going rate. Reserving a car with Lyft, Uber, Juno, or other ride-sharing services is another option—just be sure you know which airport terminal you're at before setting the pickup location.

For phone numbers, see Taxi Travel.

TRANSFERS—TAXIS AND SHUTTLES

Outside the baggage-claim area at each of New York's major airports are yellow-cab stands where a uniformed dispatcher connects passengers with taxis (*see Taxi Travel*). Cabs are not permitted to pick up fares anywhere else in the arrivals area, so if you want a taxi, take your place in line. Shuttle services generally pick up passengers from designated spots along the curbs.

GO Airlink NYC, NYC Airporter, and SuperShuttle run vans and some buses from JFK, LaGuardia, and Newark (NYC Airporter does not run to Manhattan from Newark) airports to popular spots like Grand Central Terminal, the Port Authority Bus Terminal, Penn Station, and hotels in Manhattan. Fares on NYC Airporter, for instance, cost about $15–$18 one-way and $28–$34 round-trip per person to or from JFK or LGA. Those rates are significantly cheaper than taking a taxi if you're on your own, but probably not if there are two or more of you traveling together. If you choose to use such services, keep in mind that customers' satisfaction with them is very mixed; online reviews often complain of rude employees and significant waits for vans to both arrive and reach their destinations. In any case, allow extra time for the shuttle's other pickups and drop-offs along the way.

TRANSFERS FROM JFK INTERNATIONAL AIRPORT

The rate for traveling between JFK and Manhattan by yellow cab in either direction is a flat fee of $52.80 plus surcharges and tolls (which average about $6). The trip takes 40–60 minutes. Prices are roughly $25–$55 for trips to most other locations in New York City. You should also tip the driver for safe driving and good service (around 10%–20% of the final fare).

JFK's AirTrain ($5) connects JFK Airport to the New York City subway (A, E, J, and Z trains) and the Long Island Rail Road (LIRR)—both of which take you to Manhattan or Brooklyn. The Air-Train monorail system runs 24 hours, though it's far less frequent overnight.

■ TIP➔ **Not sure which train to take? Check** ⊕ *citymapper.com/nyc,* ⊕ *www.iridenyc. com,* **or** ⊕ *tripplanner.mta.info* **(or their corresponding apps) for the best route to your destination.** Subway travel between

JFK and Manhattan takes about an hour and costs $3.75 in subway fare (including the $1 fee for a refillable MetroCard) plus another $5 for the AirTrain. The LIRR travels between JFK's AirTrain stop (Jamaica Station) and Penn Station in around 30 minutes, for about $17, including the AirTrain fee. When traveling *from* Manhattan to JFK via subway, take the E train to Sutphin Boulevard or take the A train to the Howard Beach station; then, in either case, transfer to the AirTrain. If you are riding the A train, be sure to take an A train marked "Far Rockaway" or "Rockaway Park," *not* an A train bound for "Lefferts Boulevard."

TRANSFERS FROM LAGUARDIA AIRPORT

Taxis cost $30–$50 (plus tip and tolls) to most destinations in New York City, and take at least 20–40 minutes.

For $2.75 (pay with a MetroCard or exact change in coins, no pennies and no dollar bills) you can ride the Q70 bus to the Woodside–61st Street subway station in Queens (with connections to the 7 train, or to the LIRR, with service to Penn Station) or to the Jackson Heights–Roosevelt Avenue subway stop, where you can transfer to the E, F, M, R, and 7 trains and reach many points in Manhattan and Brooklyn. Another option is to take the M60 bus to its end point at 106th Street and Broadway on Manhattan's Upper West Side, with connections en route to several New York City Subway lines (2, 3, 4, 5, 6, A, B, C, D, N, and Q trains). Allow at least 60 minutes for the entire trip to Midtown, and perhaps a bit more during heavy traffic or rain.

TRANSFERS FROM NEWARK AIRPORT

Taxis to Manhattan cost $50–$70 plus tolls and tip and take 20–45 minutes in light traffic; inquire with the airport's taxi dispatcher about shared group rates,

Getting Here

too. If you're heading to the airport from Manhattan, there's a $17.50 surcharge on top of the normal taxi rate, plus tolls and a customary tip.

AirTrain Newark, an elevated light-rail system, can take you from the airline terminal to the Newark Liberty International Airport Station. From here you can take New Jersey Transit (or, for a much higher price, Amtrak) trains heading to New York Penn Station. It's an efficient and low-cost way to get to New York City, particularly if you don't have many in your group and aren't carrying massive amounts of luggage. Total travel time to New York Penn Station via New Jersey Transit is approximately 30 minutes and costs $13. By contrast, a similar, slightly faster trip (about 25 minutes) via Amtrak costs roughly $28. The AirTrain runs every three minutes from 5 am to midnight and every 15 minutes from midnight to 5 am. Note that New Jersey Transit trains first make a stop at the confusingly named Newark Penn Station before they reach New York Penn Station, their final stop. If you're not sure when to get off the train, ask a conductor or fellow passenger.

Coach USA, with Olympia Trails, runs Newark Airport Express buses that leave for Manhattan and stop at Port Authority, Bryant Park (at 42nd Street and 5th Avenue), and Grand Central Terminal about every 15–30 minutes until midnight. The trip takes roughly 45 minutes, and the fare is $16 (plus a $1 administrative fee). Buses headed to Newark Airport depart at the same intervals, from the same Manhattan locations.

TRANSFERS BETWEEN AIRPORTS

There are several transportation options for connecting to and from area airports, including shuttles, AirTrain and mass transit, and car service or taxi. SuperShuttle and NYC Airporter run vans and buses between Newark, JFK, and LaGuardia airports. AirTrain provides information on how to reach your destination from any of New York's airports. Note that if you arrive after midnight at any airport, you may wait a long time for a taxi. There is also no shuttle service on NYC Airporter at that time.

🛥 Boat Travel

The Staten Island Ferry runs across New York Harbor between Whitehall Street (next to Battery Park in Lower Manhattan) and St. George terminal in Staten Island. The free 25-minute ride gives you a view of the Financial District skyscrapers, the Statue of Liberty, and Ellis Island.

New York Water Taxi shuttles passengers to the city's many waterfront attractions between the Hudson River (on Manhattan's west side) and the East River (on its east side), including stops in Lower Manhattan (for access to the 9/11 Memorial Museum) and the South Street Seaport, as well as multiple locations in Brooklyn.

An all-day pass on the water taxi is $37; a similar pass that also allows passengers to visit major attractions like the Empire State Building or 9/11 Memorial Museum as part of their sightseeing package starts at $59.

Also consider NY Waterway, which runs ferry service across the Hudson River between Manhattan and ports in New Jersey and upstate New York. In addition, the NYC Ferry operates along the East River, connecting Manhattan with Brooklyn, Queens, and, seasonally, with Governors Island (the ferries also connect several locations within Brooklyn and in Long Island City, Queens).

NY Waterway ferries offer single-trip ($9–$21.50) and monthly passes ($196–$642.50); the price varies greatly based on the the length of the trip. The NYC Ferry (operated by Hornblower) has one-way tickets for $2.75, or you can buy a 30-day pass for $121.

🚌 Bus Travel

Most city buses in Manhattan follow easy-to-understand routes along the island's street grid. Routes go north and south on the avenues and east and west on the major two-way crosstown streets: 96th, 86th, 79th, 72nd, 66th, 57th, 42nd, 34th, 23rd, and 14th. Bus routes usually operate 24 hours a day, but service is infrequent late at night. Traffic jams can make rides maddeningly slow, especially along 5th Avenue in Midtown and on the Upper East Side. Certain bus routes provide express or "limited-stop service" during weekday rush hours, which saves travel time by stopping only at major cross streets and transfer points. A sign posted at the front of the bus indicates limited service; ask the driver whether the bus stops near where you want to go before boarding.

To find a bus stop, look for a light-blue sign (green for a "limited" bus, which skips more stops) on a green pole; bus numbers and routes are listed, with the stop's name underneath.

Bus fare is the same as subway fare: $2.75. Pay when you board with exact change in coins (no pennies, no dollar bills, and no change is given) or with a MetroCard.

MetroCards (see Public Transportation) allow you one free transfer between buses or from bus to subway; when using coins on the bus, you can ask the driver for a free transfer coupon, good for one change to an intersecting bus route. Legal transfer points are listed on the back of the slip. Transfers generally have time limits of two hours.

Several routes in the city now have so-called Select Bus Service (SBS) rather than limited-stop service. These routes include those along 1st and 2nd Avenues and 34th Street in Manhattan, as well as the M60, which travels between LaGuardia Airport and 125th Street in Harlem. The buses, which are distinguished from normal city buses by signs identifying the bus as SBS on the front, make fewer stops. In addition, riders must pay for their rides upon boarding with either a MetroCard, or before boarding with coins (but not pennies) at a machine mounted on the street. The machine prints out a receipt. This receipt is the only proof of payment, so be sure to hold onto it for your entire SBS trip or risk a fine for fare evasion.

Bus route maps and schedules are posted at many bus stops in Manhattan, major stops throughout the other boroughs, and ⊕ mta.info. Each of the five boroughs of New York has a separate bus map; they're available from some station booths, but rarely on buses. The best places to obtain them are the information kiosks in Grand Central Terminal and Penn Station, and the MTA website.

■ TIP➔ Visit ⊕ bustime.mta.info for real-time bus-arrival updates at any bus stop in the city.

Most buses that travel outside the city depart from the Port Authority Bus Terminal, on 8th Avenue between 40th and 42nd Streets. You must purchase your ticket at a ticket counter, not from the bus driver, so give yourself enough time to wait in line. The terminal is connected to the subway (A, C, E, N, Q, R, S, W, 1, 2, 3, and 7 lines), which offers direct travel on to Penn Station, Grand Central Terminal, and more. Several bus lines

Getting Here

serving northern New Jersey and Rockland County, New York, make daily stops at the George Washington Bridge Bus Station from 5 am to 1 am. The station is connected to the 175th Street station on the A line of the subway, which travels down the west side of Manhattan.

A variety of discount bus services, including BoltBus and Megabus, run direct routes to and from cities such as Philadelphia, Boston, and Washington, D.C., with the majority of destinations along the East Coast. These budget options, priced from as little as $10 one-way (sometimes even less, if you book well in advance), depart from locations throughout the city and can be more convenient than traditional bus services.

🚘 Car Travel

If you plan to drive into Manhattan, try to avoid the morning and evening rush hours and lunch hour. Tune in to traffic reports online or on the radio (e.g., WCBS 880 or 1010 WINS on the AM radio dial) before you set off, and don't be surprised if a bridge is partially closed or entirely blocked with traffic.

Driving within Manhattan can be a nightmare of gridlocked streets, obnoxious drivers, and seemingly suicidal jaywalkers and bicyclists. Narrow and one-way streets are common, particularly downtown, and can make driving even more difficult. The most congested streets of the city generally lie between 14th and 59th Streets and 3rd and 8th Avenues. In addition, sections of Broadway near Times Square (from 42nd to 47th Street) and Herald Square (33rd to 35th) are closed to motorized traffic. This can create gridlock and confusion in nearby streets.

GASOLINE

Gas stations are few and far between in Manhattan. If you can, fill up at stations outside Manhattan, where prices are generally cheaper. In Manhattan, you can refuel at stations along 10th and 11th Avenues south of West 57th Street, and in other locations scattered throughout the island. Some gas stations in New York require you to pump your own gas; others provide attendants (which is always the case in New Jersey).

PARKING

Free parking is difficult to find in Midtown, and on weekday evenings and weekends in other neighborhoods. If you find a spot on the street, check parking signs carefully, and scour the curb for a faded yellow line indicating a no-parking zone, the bane of every driver's existence. Violators may be towed away or ticketed literally within minutes. If you do drive, use your car sparingly in Manhattan. If you can't find public parking, pull into a guarded parking garage; note that hourly rates (which can be $40 or more for just two hours) decrease somewhat if a car is left for a significant amount of time. ■ TIP➔ BestParking (⊕ nyc.bestparking.com) helps you find the cheapest parking-lot options for your visit; search by neighborhood, address, or attraction.

ROAD CONDITIONS

New York City streets are generally in good condition, although there are enough potholes and bad patch jobs to make driving a little rough in some areas, as on sections of 2nd and 3rd Avenues, and along Broadway. Road and bridge repairs seem neverending, so you may encounter the occasional detour or a bottleneck where a three-lane street narrows to one lane. Many drivers don't slow down for yellow lights here—they (foolishly) speed up to make it through the intersection, sometimes unaware of mounted police cameras that capture their license plates. Heavy rains can cause street flooding in some areas, most notoriously on the Franklin D. Roosevelt Drive (known as the FDR Drive and sometimes as East River Drive), where the heavy traffic can grind to a halt when little lakes suddenly appear on the road.

RULES OF THE ROAD
On city streets the speed limit is 25 mph, unless otherwise posted. No right turns during red lights are allowed within city limits, unless otherwise posted. Be alert for one-way streets and "no left turn" intersections.

The law requires that front-seat passengers wear seat belts at all times. Children under 16 must wear seat belts in both the front and back seats. Always strap children under age four into approved child-safety seats. It is illegal to use a handheld cell phone while driving in New York State. Police have the right to seize the car of anyone arrested for DWI (driving while intoxicated) in New York City.

CAR RENTALS
When you reserve a car, ask about cancellation penalties, taxes, drop-off charges (if you're planning to pick up the car in one destination and leave it in another), and surcharges (for being under or over a certain age, additional drivers, or driving across state or country borders or beyond a specific distance from your point of rental). All these things can add substantially to your costs. Request car seats and extras such as GPS when you book.

Rates are sometimes—but not always— better if you book in advance or reserve through a rental agency's website, or if you pick up or drop off at an airport. There are other reasons to book ahead, though: for popular destinations (like NYC), during busy times of the year, or to ensure that you get certain types of cars (vans, SUVs, exotic sports cars).

■TIP➔ Make sure that a confirmed reservation guarantees you a car. Agencies sometimes overbook, particularly for busy weekends and holiday periods.

Rates in New York City average $70–$120 a day and $300–$500 a week (plus tax) for an economy car with air-conditioning, automatic transmission, and unlimited mileage. Rental costs are lower outside New York City, specifically in such places like Hoboken, New Jersey, and Yonkers, New York. If you already have a membership with a short-term car-rental service like Zipcar, it's likely more convenient and cost-effective for your car needs in the city.

CAR-RENTAL INSURANCE
If you own a car and carry comprehensive car insurance for both collision and liability, your personal auto insurance probably covers a rental, but read your policy's fine print to be sure. If you don't have auto insurance, you should probably buy the collision- or loss-damage waiver (CDW or LDW) from the rental company. This eliminates your liability for damage to the car. Some credit cards offer CDW coverage, but it's usually supplemental to your own insurance and may not cover special vehicles (SUVs, minivans, luxury models, and the like). If your coverage is secondary, you may still be liable for loss-of-use costs from the car-rental company (again, read the fine print). If you're planning on using credit-card insurance, use that card for *all* transactions, from reserving to paying the final bill.

You may also be offered supplemental liability coverage. The car-rental company is required to carry a minimal level of liability coverage insuring all renters, but it may not be enough to cover claims in

Getting Here

a really serious accident if you're at fault. Your own auto-insurance policy should also protect you if you own a car; if you don't, you have to decide whether you are willing to take the risk.

U.S. rental companies sell CDWs and LDWs for about $9 a day; supplemental liability is usually more than $10 a day. The car-rental company may offer you all sorts of other policies, but they're rarely worth the cost. Personal accident insurance, which is basic hospitalization coverage, is an especially egregious rip-off if you already have health insurance.

■ TIP➜ You can decline insurance from the rental company and purchase it through a third-party provider such as AIG's Travel Guard (⊕ www.travelguard.com)—$9 per day for $35,000 of coverage.

Ⓜ Metro/Public Transport

When it comes to getting around New York, you have your pick of transportation in almost any neighborhood you're likely to visit. The subway and bus networks are extensive, especially in Manhattan, although getting across town can take some extra maneuvering. If you're not pressed for time, consider taking a public bus (see Bus Travel); they generally are slower than subways, but you can also see the city as you travel. Yellow cabs (see Taxi Travel) are abundant, except during the evening rush hour, when many drivers' shifts change, and in bad weather, when they get snapped up quickly. If it's late at night or you're outside Manhattan, using a ride-sharing service such as Lyft or Uber may be a good idea. Like a taxi ride, the subway is a true New York City experience; it's also often the quickest way to get around. However, New York (especially Manhattan) is really a walking town, and depending on the time

of day, the weather, and your destination, hoofing it could be the easiest and most enjoyable option.

During the height of weekday rush hours (especially from 7:30 to 9:30 am and 5 to 7 pm), avoid Midtown if you can—subways and streets are jammed, and travel time on buses and taxis can easily double.

Subway and bus fares are $2.75 per ride. Reduced fares are available for senior citizens and people with disabilities; there are some restrictions during rush hours on express buses and the Long Island and Metro-North railroads. Kids under 44 inches ride free with a paying adult.

You pay for mass transit with a MetroCard, a plastic card with a magnetic strip. (The MTA is also planning to introduce electronic contactless payment options beginning at select stations around mid-2019). There is a $1 fee for any new MetroCard purchase. (There is a $5.50 minimum card purchase at station booths; this minimum does not apply at vending machines.) A Single Ride Ticket (sold only at MetroCard vending machines) is $3. As you swipe the card through a subway turnstile or insert it in a bus's card reader, the cost of the fare is automatically deducted. With the MetroCard, you can transfer free from bus to subway, subway to bus, or bus to bus, within a two-hour period.

MetroCards are sold at most (but not all) subway stations and some stores—look for an "Authorized Sales Agent" sign. The MTA sells two kinds of MetroCards: unlimited-ride and pay-per-ride. Seven-day unlimited-ride MetroCards ($33) allow bus and subway travel for a week. If you expect to ride more than 11 times in one week, this is the card to get. Unlike in most other cities, there are no single-day unlimited MetroCards.

Unlike unlimited-ride cards, pay-per-ride MetroCards can be shared between riders. (Unlimited-ride MetroCards can be used only once at the same station or bus route in an 18-minute period.)

You can buy or add money to an existing MetroCard at a MetroCard vending machine, available at most subway station entrances (usually near the station booth). The machines accept major credit cards and ATM or debit cards. Many also accept cash, but note that the maximum amount of change they return is $6, which is doled out in dollar coins.

■ TIP→ Open ⊕ subwaytime.mta.info for real-time updates on train arrivals in individual stations (and FYI, subway stations now have cellular access).

SUBWAY

The subway system operates on more than 840 miles of track 24 hours a day and serves nearly all the places you're likely to visit. It's cheaper than a cab, and during the workweek it's often faster than either taxis or buses. The trains are well lighted and air-conditioned. Still, the New York subway is hardly problem-free. Many trains are crowded, the older ones are noisy, the air-conditioning can break, and platforms can be dingy and smelly. Homeless people sometimes take refuge from the elements by riding the trains, and panhandlers and buskers head there for a captive audience. Although trains usually run frequently, especially during rush hours, you never know when some incident somewhere on the line may stall traffic. In addition, subway construction sometimes causes delays or limitation of service, especially on weekends and after 10 pm on weekdays.

You can transfer between subway lines an unlimited number of times at any of the numerous stations where lines intersect. If you use a MetroCard to pay your fare, you can also transfer to intersecting MTA bus routes for free. Such transfers generally have a time limit of two hours.

Most subway entrances are at street corners and marked by lampposts with an illuminated Metropolitan Transportation Authority (MTA) logo or globe-shape green or red lights—green means the station is open 24 hours and red means the station closes at night (though the colors don't always correspond to reality). Subway lines are designated by numbers and letters, such as the 3 line or the A line. Some lines run "express" and skip stops, and others are "local" and make all stops. Each station entrance has a sign indicating the lines that run through the station. Some entrances are also marked "uptown only" or "downtown only." Before entering subway stations, read the signs carefully. One of the most frequent mistakes visitors make is taking the train in the wrong direction. Maps of the full subway system are posted in the middle of every train car and usually on the subway platform. You can usually pick up free paper maps at station booths.

For the most up-to-date information on subway lines, call the MTA's Travel Information line or visit its website. The MTA Weekender, MTA TripPlanner, and Citymapper apps and websites are a good source for figuring out the best line to take to reach your destination, as is Google Maps. Alternatively, ask a station agent.

ACCESSIBILITY ISSUES

Although the city is working to retrofit subway stations to comply with the ADA, many stations, including major ones, are not yet fully accessible, and they are unlikely to be so in the near future. Accessible stations are clearly marked on subway and rail maps. Visitors in wheelchairs have better success with public buses, all of which have wheelchair lifts

Getting Here

and "kneelers" at the front to facilitate getting on and off. Bus drivers provide assistance.

🚗 Ride-Sharing

An increasingly popular option is booking a car through one of the ride-share apps like Lyft, Uber, Juno, or Via, which match passengers with available drivers. After booking a car through one of their respective apps, you can trace its journey to you via GPS, and you get a notification once it has arrived. These services are sometimes cheaper than a taxi, but sometimes more expensive. Most of the services offer a car-pool option that allows passengers to share rides at a discounted fare. However, when "surge pricing" is in effect (when it's raining or at other high-demand times), ride-share rates can skyrocket. The apps do let you get an estimate on rates before you book, but Juno and Via offer fixed "surge-free" or ride-share discounted rates regardless of demand, weather, or traffic. Payment and tipping (if applicable) are also done via the apps. Unlike in some other cities, only licensed livery drivers are allowed to work for the ride-share companies in New York City (hence the sometimes higher rates).

🚕 Taxi Travel

Yellow taxis are almost everywhere in Manhattan, cruising the streets looking for fares. They are usually easy to hail on the street or from a cabstand in front of major hotels, though finding one at rush hour or in the rain can take some time (and assertiveness). Even if you're stuck in a downpour or at the airport, do not accept a ride from a "gypsy cab." If a cab is not yellow and does not have a

numbered aluminum medallion bolted to the hood, you could be putting yourself (or at least your wallet) at risk by getting into the car.

A taxi shows that it's available with its rooftop light. If the numbers are lit, the cab driver is ready to take passengers— by law, he or she is required to take passengers to any location in New York City as well as Newark Airport and two adjoining counties, although only NYC and Newark locations are metered. Once the meter is engaged (off-meter rates are prohibited; even JFK and out-of-town "flat" fares must be recorded by the meter for the passenger's protection), the fare is $2.50 just for entering the vehicle, which includes the first 0.3 mile, and 50¢ for each unit thereafter. A unit is defined as either 0.3 mile when the cab's cruising at 6 mph or faster or as 60 seconds when the cab is either not moving or moving at less than 6 mph. New York State adds 50¢ to each cab ride. There's also a 50¢ night surcharge added between 8 pm and 6 am, and a much-maligned $1 peak-hour surcharge is tacked on between 4 pm and 8 pm as well as a congestion surcharge of $2.50 for rides below 96th Street in Manhattan. Lastly, there is also a 30¢ "improvement surcharge" for all rides. All taxi drivers are required to accept credit cards as payment. On rare occasions, some who prefer cash claim their machines are broken when that isn't actually the case. If a driver waits until the end of the ride to mention a broken machine and you want to pay by credit card, you can ask the driver to *turn off the meter* and drive you to an ATM to see if this extra hassle is worth it.

One taxi can hold a maximum of four passengers (an additional passenger under the age of seven is allowed if the child sits on someone's lap). You must pay any bridge or tunnel tolls incurred during your trip (they are automatically added to the meter). In order to keep things moving quickly, all taxi drivers are required to use an E-ZPass in their cabs to automatically pay tolls, and they must pass the discounted toll rate along to the passenger; the total toll amount is added to the final fare. Taxi drivers expect a 10%–20% tip, which should be awarded for safe driving and good service.

To avoid unhappy taxi experiences, try to know where you want to go and how to get there before you hail a cab. ■ TIP→ Know the cross streets of your destination (for instance, "5th Avenue and 42nd Street") before you enter a cab. Also, speak simply and clearly to make sure the driver has heard you correctly—few are native English speakers, so it never hurts to make sure you've been understood. If headed for a far-flung location in Brooklyn or Queens, it can be helpful to pull up the location using Google Maps or a similar app, especially if the driver doesn't have GPS of his own. When you leave the cab, remember to take your receipt. It includes the cab's medallion number, which can help you track the cabbie down in the event that you've left your possessions in the cab, or if you want to report an unpleasant ride with the city's 311 service (or even to compliment your driver for a great experience). Any charges, such as those for bridges, are itemized on the receipt; you can double-check to make sure you were charged correctly.

Yellow taxis can be difficult to find in parts of Brooklyn, Queens, the Bronx, and Staten Island. To help with this issue, in 2013 the city of New York created a brand-new class of taxi service: apple-green Boro Taxis, which act like yellow taxis: they charge the same metered rates, accept credit cards, and must take

you to any location within the city of New York. The difference is that green taxis are only allowed to pick up fares in non-Manhattan boroughs and in Manhattan locations above 96th Street.

If you're outside Manhattan and can't find a yellow or green taxi, it may be more convenient and less expensive to call a car service. Locals and staff at restaurants and other public places can often recommend a reliable company that's headquartered a particular neighborhood or borough. For example, Arecibo Car Service offers low rates from Brooklyn to any of NYC's airports. Most services offer flat-rate fares, but always confirm the fee when calling for the ride; a 10%–20% tip is customary.

🚊 Train Travel

For information about the subway, see Metro/Public Transport.

Metro-North Railroad trains take passengers from Grand Central Terminal to points north of New York City, both in New York State and Connecticut. Amtrak trains arrive at Penn Station. For trains from New York City to Long Island and New Jersey, take the Long Island Rail Road (LIRR) and New Jersey Transit, respectively; both operate from Penn Station. Although Penn Station does not have a telephone contact or website, each individual train line provides information. The commuter PATH trains to New Jersey offer service to Newark, Jersey City, Harrison, and Hoboken; the main Manhattan PATH stations are located at 33rd Street and the World Trade Center.

Before You Go

🌐 Passport

All visitors to the United States require a valid passport that is valid for six months beyond your expected period of stay.

🪪 Visa

Except for citizens of Canada and Bermuda, most visitors to the United States must have a visa. If you are from one of the 38 designated members of the Visa Waiver Program, then you only require an ESTA (Electronic System for Travel Authorization) as long as you are staying for 90 days or less. However, some changes were made in the Visa Waiver Program in 2015, and nationals of Visa Waiver nations who have traveled to Iran, Iraq, Libya, Somalia, Sudan, Syria, or Yemen no longer qualify for ESTA. Also, if you have been denied a visa to visit the United States, your application for the ESTA program most likely will be denied.

✏️ Immunizations

There are no immunization requirements for visitors traveling to the United States for tourism.

🇺🇸 US Embassy/Consulate

Most foreign countries operate consulates in New York City, some within their missions to the United Nations (though some are separate offices).

📅 When to Go

High Season: Fall—particularly from Labor Day through Christmas—is usually the most expensive time of the year to visit New York City, with the period from Thanksgiving through Christmas Eve the most expensive time of all, when hotel rates can sometimes double. Spring, especially from mid-March through Memorial Day, can also be expensive, but prices depend almost as much on which major conventions and meetings are taking place as anything else. Keep in mind that most Broadway shows, major museum exhibitions, and opera, ballet, and classical music productions open between October through May. A few major events in the fall (particularly the New York City Marathon) also drive up rates for shorter periods.

Low Season: New York City is at its cheapest in the winter, particularly from early January through mid-March (before Spring Break). Airfares may drop, and hotels typically offer their lowest rates during this time; it's not unheard of to find a luxurious hotel offering rooms for half the regular rate during these months. You may face bone-chilling winds and an occasionally traffic-snarling snowstorm, but you're just as likely to experience some mild afternoons sandwiched by frigid nights. If you want to see the city during the festive holiday season, look at the period from Christmas Day to just before New Year's Eve, when there is often a drop in prices for both airfares and hotels.

Shoulder Season: Despite its popularity with tourists, summer can offer a respite from high hotel and airline prices, though certainly not from sweltering temperatures. Some high-end restaurants close in August, when New Yorkers often head for cooler climates, and few new Broadway shows open during this period. Occasional lulls in the late spring can also offer better hotel rates.

Essentials

Activities

BASEBALL

New York City is a baseball town, and many travelers will want to see a game if they come during the season. You can usually get seats for any game except a major draw (a match-up between the Yankees and Mets, for instance), or a major playoff game if you are willing to sit in the cheap seats. The subway gets you directly to the stadiums of both New York–area major-league teams, as well as their minor-league affiliates.

Brooklyn Cyclones

BASEBALL/SOFTBALL | FAMILY | The Mets-affiliated minor-league Brooklyn Cyclones are named for Coney Island's famous wooden roller coaster. They play 38 home games at MCU Park, next to the boardwalk, with views of the Atlantic over the right-field wall and Luna Park amusement park over the left-field wall. Most people make a day of it, with time at the beach and amusement rides before an evening game. Take the D, F, N, or Q subway to the Coney Island–Stillwell Avenue Station, and walk one block to the right of the original Nathan's Famous hot dog stand. ⊠ *MCU Park, 1904 Surf Ave., at 19th St., Coney Island* ☎ *718/372–5596* ⊕ *www.brooklyncyclones.com* Ⓜ *D, F, N, Q to Coney Island–Stillwell Ave.*

New York Mets

BASEBALL/SOFTBALL | FAMILY | The New York Mets play at Citi Field, at the next-to-last stop on the 7 train in Queens. ⊠ *Citi Field, 123-01 Roosevelt Ave., at 126th St. and Roosevelt Ave., Flushing* ☎ *718/507–8499* ⊕ *www.mets.com* Ⓜ *7 to Mets–Willets Point.*

New York Yankees

BASEBALL/SOFTBALL | FAMILY | The Yankees defend their turf at Yankee Stadium in the Bronx, accessible via the B, D, and 4 trains. ⊠ *Yankee Stadium, 1 E. 161st St., at River Ave., Bronx* ☎ *718/293–6000* ⊕ *www.mlb.com/yankees* Ⓜ *4, B, D to 161st St.–Yankee Stadium.*

Staten Island Yankees

BASEBALL/SOFTBALL | FAMILY | For another fun, family-oriented experience, check out the Staten Island Yankees, one of New York's minor-league teams, which warms up many future New York Yankees players. The stadium, a five-minute walk from the Staten Island Ferry terminal, has magnificent views of Lower Manhattan and the Statue of Liberty. ⊠ *Richmond County Bank Ballpark, 75 Richmond Terr., St. George* ☎ *718/720–9265* ⊕ *www.siyanks.com* Ⓜ *Staten Island Ferry.*

BASKETBALL

The men's basketball season runs from late October through April. New York City has two NBA teams, the Brooklyn Nets and the New York Knicks, as well as a WNBA team, the New York Liberty.

Brooklyn Nets

BASKETBALL | FAMILY | The Brooklyn Nets are across the East River, in the swanky Barclays Center. The stadium is easily reachable by 11 different subway lines (nine at the center, but two more are nearby) and the LIRR. ⊠ *Barclays Center, 620 Atlantic Ave., at Flatbush Ave., Prospect Heights* ☎ *917/618–6700 for box office* ⊕ *www.nba.com/nets* Ⓜ *2, 3, 4, 5, B, D, N, Q, R to Atlantic Ave.–Barclays Center.*

New York Knicks

BASKETBALL | The New York Knicks arouse intense hometown passions, which means tickets for home games at Madison Square Garden are hard to come by even when the team is not playing as well as it should. Try StubHub to score tickets. ⊠ *Madison Square Garden, 4 Pennsylvania Plaza, between 31st and 33rd Sts. and between 7th and 8th Aves., Midtown West* ☎ *212/465–5867* ⊕ *www.*

Essentials

nba.com/knicks Ⓜ *1, 2, 3, A, C, E to 34th St.–Penn Station.*

New York Liberty
BASKETBALL | The New York Liberty, a member of the WNBA (Women's National Basketball Association), had its first season in 1997. The season runs from May through September, with home games played a short Metro-North Railroad ride away at the Westchester County Center in White Plains, New York. ✉ *New York* ☎ *212/465–6073 for tickets* ⊕ *liberty. wnba.com.*

BICYCLING

In recent years, bicycling the streets of Manhattan and the outer boroughs has become more mainstream and much less the sole province of bike messengers and zealots. The city government and biking organizations have both helped make it safer, and drivers and pedestrians are more aware that bikes are likely to be on the road, too. Still, traffic volumes are sky-high on weekdays, and drivers can be pushy or downright threatening, so it's best to take to a bike only if you're a seasoned city rider. Check the NYC Department of Transportation's website for a cycling map that shows the best routes and roads with designated bike lanes, as well as local road rules, including for taking a bike on public transit. Google Maps offers a bike-route navigation option for New York, too, using bike lanes as much as possible.

For biking under more controlled conditions, head to New York's major parks. Central Park has a 6-mile circular drive with a couple of climbs. Since April 2018, the park's roadways are permanently closed to car traffic, making cycling here particularly appealing.

Beware of renting a bike from the many illegal vendors that hang out on the streets near Central Park, especially by Columbus Circle. It's usually better to rent from a business with an actual storefront; there are a number of reputable bike shops within a few blocks of the park. Most bike-rental stores have copies of the very handy official NYC Bike Map, which is published annually and shows traffic flow and bike lanes for all of New York City. The map and other bicycling resources can also be found at the Department of Transportation's website, ⊕ *www.nyc.gov/bikes.*

The busy bike lane along the Hudson River Park's esplanade parallels the waterfront from West 59th Street south to the esplanade of Battery Park City. Rentals are available within the linear park. The lane also heads north, connecting with the bike path in Riverside Park and the esplanade between West 72nd and West 100th Streets, continuing all the way to the George Washington Bridge. From Battery Park it's a quick ride up to the Wall Street area, which is relatively deserted on weekends, and over to the bike lane along the East River.

As of 2017, the 3.3-mile circular drive in Brooklyn's Prospect Park is closed to cars year-round. It has a long, gradual hill that tops off near the Grand Army Plaza entrance.

Bike and Roll NYC
BICYCLING | This company offers bike rentals on the Upper West Side, near the American Museum of Natural History. ✉ *451 Columbus Ave., between 81st and 82nd Sts., Upper West Side* ☎ *212/260– 0400* ⊕ *bikeandrollnyc.com* Ⓜ *1 to 79th St.; B, C to 81st St.–Museum of Natural History.*

New York City Department of Transportation
BICYCLING | A PDF version of the annual Bike Map is available from the site, as is lots of other information about cycling in the city. ☎ *311* ⊕ *www.nyc.gov/bikes.*

Toga Bike Shop

BICYCLING | This established bike shop also offers rentals near Lincoln Center. ✉ *110 West End Ave., at 64th St., Upper West Side* ☎ *212/799–9625* ⊕ *www. togabikes.com* Ⓜ *1 to 66th St.–Lincoln Center.*

Unlimited Biking

BICYCLING | This company offers bike rentals as well as organized biking tours. ✉ *Multiple locationsNew York* ☎ *212/749–4444* ⊕ *www.unlimitedbiking.com.*

Waterfront Bicycle Shop

BICYCLING | If you are downtown and want to take advantage of the Hudson River Park bike path, this shop rents bikes in the West Village. ✉ *391 West St., between Christopher and W. 10th Sts., West Village* ☎ *212/414–2453* ⊕ *www. bikeshopny.com* Ⓜ *1 to Christopher St.– Sheridan Sq.*

CITI BIKE BICYCLE SHARE

New York's bike-sharing program debuted in 2013 with hundreds of stations, the majority in Manhattan south of Central Park and northern Brooklyn; hundreds more have rolled out since then, with expansions covering most of Manhattan, deeper into Brooklyn, into Long Island City and Astoria in Queens, and even across the Hudson River to Jersey City. The three-speed, 40-pound, bright-blue bikes, which are either charming or clunky depending on your perspective, are outfitted with automatic lights and bungee cords to secure small bags and other items. There are also a very small number of electric bikes that gently motor on with your pedaling; they are rarely available. They don't come with helmets, though: wearing one is recommended but not mandatory.

After buying a Citi Bike pass, you are able to check out a bike an unlimited number of times over either 24 hours ($12) or three days ($24). What is limited is your time with a particular bike: from the moment you unlock a bike at one station and return it to another must be 30 minutes or less, or you face additional charges added to your credit card (a lost bike is $1,200). As soon as you return one bike, you're free to get another— even one from the same dock.

Before you pull a bike from one of the bays and start the 30-minute clock running, spend a little time planning your route. Citi Bike's website (⊕ *www. citibikenyc.com*) and apps are helpful, because they show the best routes to destinations and which of the computerized outdoor stations have bikes available, and—just as important—which have empty docks available for your returned bike.

Citi Bike

BICYCLING | The Citi Bike website and apps, for Android and iOS, help locate nearby bike stations and the best route to reach destinations. ✉ *New York* ☎ *855/245–3311 for customer service* ⊕ *www.citibikenyc.com*

Group Bike Rides
Bike New York

BICYCLING | Bike New York runs a 40-mile, five-borough bike ride the first Sunday in May. ✉ *New York* ☎ *212/870–2080* ⊕ *www.bike.nyc.*

Five Borough Bicycle Club

BICYCLING | The Five Borough Bicycle Club organizes day and weekend rides. ✉ *New York* ☎ *347/688–2925* ⊕ *www.5bbc.org.*

New York Cycle Club

BICYCLING | The New York Cycle Club sponsors regular rides for every level of ability. ✉ *New York* ⊕ *www.nycc.org.*

Time's Up!

BICYCLING | Time's Up!, a nonprofit advocacy group, leads free recreational rides

Essentials

and workshops for cyclists; the Central Park Moonlight Ride, departing from Columbus Circle at 10 pm the first Friday of the month (though not every month), is a favorite. ⊠ *New York* ☎ *212/802–8222* ⊕ *www.times-up.org.*

BOATING, KAYAKING, AND PADDLEBOARDING

Downtown Boathouse

BOATING | The Downtown Boathouse, at Pier 26 in TriBeCa, offers free kayaks with instruction and all necessary equipment. The season runs from late May to early October, but it's strictly first-come, first-served. ⊠ *Pier 26 Boathouse, near N. Moore St. at the Hudson River, TriBeCa* ⊕ *www.downtownboathouse.org* Ⓜ *1 to Franklin St.; A, C, E to Canal St.*

Loeb Boathouse

BOATING | Central Park has rowboats (plus a Venetian gondola for evening glides) on the 22-acre Central Park Lake. Rent your rowboat, which holds up to four people, at Loeb Boathouse, near East 74th Street, from April through November ($15 an hour). Gondola rides (complete with gondolier) are available during the same period and can be reserved ($45 per half hour); the gondola hold up to six people. ⊠ *East side of Central Park between 74th and 75th Sts., Central Park* ☎ *212/517–2233* ⊕ *www.thecentralparkboathouse.com/boats.php* Ⓜ *6 to 77th St.; Q to 72nd St.*

Manhattan Community Boathouse

BOATING | FAMILY | Operated by Manhattan Community Boathouse is the Pier 96 Boathouse in Midtown West, where you can take a sturdy kayak out for a paddle for free on weekends from late May through early October and on Monday, Tuesday, and Wednesday evenings from June through the end of August. This walk-up kayaking program is offered on a first-come, first-served basis (no reservations are taken in advance) and is suitable for people of all ages and abilities. Kayaks, paddles, life jackets, and basic instructions are provided. All participants must sign a liability waiver and know how to swim. ⊠ *56th St. at the Hudson River, Midtown West* ⊕ *www.manhattancommunityboathouse.org* Ⓜ *1, A, B, C, D to 59th St.–Columbus Circle.*

Manhattan Kayak + SUP

BOATING | Manhattan Kayak + SUP gives kayak and stand-up paddleboard (SUP) lessons for all levels and runs trips on the Hudson River between May and late September, including a fun New York After Dark tour for $65. ⊠ *Pier 84, 555 12th Ave., at 44th St., Midtown West* ☎ *212/924–1788* ⊕ *www.manhattankayak.com* Ⓜ *A, C, E to 42nd St.–Port Authority.*

FOOTBALL

MetLife Stadium

FOOTBALL | Both the New York Jets and New York Giants actually play in New Jersey, at this massive stadium in the New Jersey Meadowlands. On game days, NJ Transit offers direct service to the Meadowlands station from Seacaucus Junction and Hobken (both reachable from Penn Station). There's also bus service from the Port Authority. ⊠ *One MetLife Stadium Dr.* ☎ *201/559–1515, 201/559–1300 for box office* ⊕ *www.metlifestadium.com.*

New York Giants

FOOTBALL | The football season runs from August through December. The enormously popular New York Giants play at MetLife Stadium in East Rutherford, New Jersey. Most seats for Giants games are sold on a season-ticket basis. However, single tickets are occasionally available at ⊕ *giants.com* or on ticket resale sites like the NFL Ticket Exchange (by Ticketmaster) or StubHub. ⊠ *New York* ☎ *201/935–8222 for tickets* ⊕ *www.giants.com.*

New York Jets
FOOTBALL | Like the New York Giants, the New York Jets also play at MetLife Stadium. Jets tickets are likewise hard to come by, with most snapped up by fans before the season opener. ⊠ *New York* ☎ *800/469–5387 for tickets* ⊕ *www. newyorkjets.com.*

HOCKEY
The regular season for hockey runs from October through early April, and the playoffs go through June.

New Jersey Devils
HOCKEY | The New Jersey Devils take the ice at the Prudential Center—aka The Rock—in Newark, New Jersey. ⊠ *Prudential Center, 25 Lafayette St., Newark* ☎ *973/757-6600 box office* ⊕ *www. nhl.com/devils* Ⓜ *NJ Transit or PATH to Newark Penn Station.*

New York Islanders
HOCKEY | The New York Islanders hockey team plays in the Barclays Center in Brooklyn. ⊠ *Barclays Center, 620 Atlantic Ave., at Flatbush Ave., Prospect Heights* ☎ *917/618–6700* ⊕ *islanders.nhl.com* Ⓜ *2, 3, 4, 5, B, D, N, Q, R to Atlantic Ave.–Barclays Center.*

New York Rangers
HOCKEY | The New York Rangers, one of the oldest teams in the National Hockey League, operate out of Madison Square Garden. ⊠ *Madison Square Garden, 4 Pennsylvania Plaza, between 31st and 33rd Sts. and between 7th and 8th Aves. New York* ☎ *212/465–6000* ⊕ *rangers.nhl. com* Ⓜ *1, 2, 3, A, C, E to 34th St.–Penn Station.*

ICE-SKATING
There are many opportunities for ice-skating during the season. Central Park has two rinks, both open from late October through early April, including the beautifully situated Wollman Rink, which has skating until long after dark beneath the lights of the city. Skate rentals are available at all rinks.

Lasker Rink
ICE SKATING | FAMILY | The Lasker Rink, at the north end of Central Park, is usually less crowded than Wollman. ⊠ *Midpark near 106th St., Upper West Side* ⊹ *Park entrance at 110th St. and Lenox Ave.* ☎ *917/492–3856* ⊕ *www.laskerrink.com* Ⓜ *B, C to Cathedral Pkwy.–110th St.; 2, 3 to Central Park North–110th St.*

LeFrak Center at Lakeside Prospect Park
ICE SKATING | FAMILY | In Brooklyn, the beautiful LeFrak Center at Lakeside Prospect Park, which opened in 2013, also offers seasonal skating, though it's a bit of a hike from the nearest subway stations. ⊠ *171 East Dr., southeast corner of Prospect Park, Prospect Park* ☎ ⊕ *lakesidebrooklyn.com* Ⓜ *Q to Parkside Ave.; B, S to Prospect Park.*

The Rink at Rockefeller Center
ICE SKATING | FAMILY | The outdoor rink in Rockefeller Center, open from October through mid-April, is much smaller in real life than it appears on TV and in movies, with only 150 skaters permitted at a time—though it *is* as beautiful, especially when Rock Center's enormous Christmas tree towers above it. Reservations can be booked in advance via the website and are recommended—especially around the holidays. Otherwise, tickets are first-come, first-served, so be prepared to wait (early morning is the best time to get on the ice quickly). Be prepared to pay, too: skating rates are $25–$33 for adults, which doesn't include skate rental ($12.50). ⊠ *5th Ave., between 49th and 50th Sts., lower plaza, Midtown West* ☎ *212/332–7654* ⊕ *www. therinkatrockcenter.com* Ⓜ *B, D, F, M to 47th–50th Sts./Rockefeller Center.*

Essentials

The Rink at Winter Village at Bryant Park

ICE SKATING | The skating rink at the Winter Village at Bryant Park has "free" skating, although this doesn't include skate rental ($15–$19) or the likely fee to either buy a lock for a locker or have bags checked ($10–$15). Winter Village's rink is open from November through early March, daily from 8 am to 10 pm. A FastPass (available online, includes skate rental and bag check) allows you to skip the line; it costs $30. ⊠ *476 5th Ave., between 40th and 42nd Sts. (closer to 6th Ave.), Midtown West* ☎ *917/438–5170* ⊕ *wintervillage.org/skate* Ⓜ *B, D, F, M to 42nd St.–Bryant Park.*

Sky Rink at Chelsea Piers

ICE SKATING | FAMILY | Chelsea Piers' Sky Rink has two year-round indoor rinks overlooking the Hudson. ⊠ *Pier 61, W. 21st St., at the Hudson River, Chelsea* ☎ *212/336–6100* ⊕ *www.chelseapiers. com/sr* Ⓜ *C, E to 23rd St.*

Wollman Skating Rink

ICE SKATING | FAMILY | One of two ice-skating rinks in Central Park, Wollman is more centrally located. Be prepared for daytime crowds, especially on weekends. ⊠ *North of 6th Ave. and Central Park S. entrance, between 62nd and 63rd Sts., Central Park* ☎ *212/439–6900* ⊕ *www. wollmanskatingrink.com* Ⓜ *1, A, B, C, D to 59th St.–Columbus Circle; N, R, W to 5th Ave./59th St.; F to 57th St.*

JOGGING

All kinds of New Yorkers jog, some with dogs or babies in tow, so you always have company on the regular jogging routes. What's not recommended is setting out on a lonely park path at dusk. Go running when and where everybody else does. On Manhattan streets, roughly 20 north–south blocks make a mile.

In Manhattan, Central Park is the busiest spot, specifically along the nearly 1.6-mile path circling the Jacqueline Kennedy Onassis Reservoir. A runners' lane has been designated along park roads; the entire loop road is a hilly 6 miles. A good 1.75-mile route starts at the Tavern on the Green along the West Drive, heads south around the bottom of the park to the East Drive, and circles back west on the 72nd Street park road to your starting point. Riverside Park, along the Hudson River bank in Manhattan, is glorious at sunset. You can cover 3 miles by running from West 72nd to West 100th Streets and back, and the Greenbelt trail extends roughly 4 more miles north to the George Washington Bridge at 181st Street. Other favorite Manhattan circuits are the Battery Park City esplanade (just over a mile), which connects to 4 more miles of jogging paths in Hudson River Park, as well as to sections of the East River Esplanade.

New York Road Runners (*NYRR*)

RUNNING | The New York Road Runners (NYRR) organize the spectacular annual New York City Marathon the first Sunday in November, as well as a variety of other races and running activities throughout the year. ☎ *855/569–6977* ⊕ *www.nyrr. org.*

🍴 Dining

Ready to take a bite out of New York? Hope you've come hungry. In a city where creativity is expressed in innumerable ways, the food scene takes center stage, with literally thousands of chances to taste what Gotham is all about. Whether lining up at street stands, gobbling down legendary deli and diner grub, or chasing a coveted reservation at the latest celebrity-chef venue, New Yorkers are a demanding yet appreciative audience.

Every neighborhood offers temptations high, low, and in between, meaning there's truly something for every taste, whim, and budget. No matter how you approach dining out here, it's hard to go wrong. Planning a day of shopping among the glittering flagship boutiques along 5th and Madison Avenues? Stop into one of the Upper East Side's storied restaurants for a repast among the "ladies who lunch." Clubbing in the Meatpacking District? Tuck into a meal at eateries as trendy as their patrons. Craving authentic ethnic? From food trucks to hidden joints, there are almost more choices than there are appetites. Recent years have also seen entire food categories, from ramen to meatballs to mac 'n' cheese, riffed upon and fetishized, and at many restaurants you find an almost religious reverence for seasonal, locally sourced cuisine.

And don't forget—New York is still home to more celebrity chefs than any other city. Your chances of running into your favorite cookbook author, Food Network celeb, or paparazzi-friendly chef are high, adding even more star wattage to a restaurant scene with an already through-the-roof glamour quotient. Newfound economic realities, however, have revived appreciation for value, meaning you can tap into wallet-friendly choices at every level of the food chain. Rest assured, this city does its part to satisfy your appetite. Ready, set, eat.

CHILDREN

Although it's unusual to see children in the dining rooms of Manhattan's most elite restaurants, dining with youngsters in New York does not have to mean culinary exile. Many of the restaurants reviewed here are excellent choices for families, and are marked as such.

RESERVATIONS

It's always a good idea to plan ahead. Some renowned restaurants like Per Se, Daniel, Brooklyn Fare, and Momofuku Ko are booked weeks or even months in advance. If that's the case, you can get lucky at the last minute if you're flexible—and friendly. Most restaurants keep a few tables open for walk-ins and VIPs. Show up for dinner early (5:30) or late (after 10), and politely inquire about any last-minute vacancies or cancellations.

Occasionally, an eatery may take your credit-card number and ask you to call the day before your scheduled meal to reconfirm: don't forget or you could lose out, or possibly be charged for your oversight.

WHAT TO WEAR

New Yorkers like to dress up, and so should you. Whatever your style, dial it up a notch. Have some fun while you're at it. Pull out the clothes you've been saving for a special occasion and get glamorous. Unfair as it is, the way you look can influence how you're treated—and where you're seated. Generally speaking, jeans and a button-down shirt suffice at most table-service restaurants in the $ to $$ range. Few places require a jacket or jacket and tie, but if you have doubts, call the restaurant and ask.

TIPPING AND TAXES

In most restaurants, tip the server 15%–20%. (To figure out a 20% tip quickly, just move the decimal point one place to the left on your total and double that amount.) Tip at least $1 per drink at the bar, and $1 for each coat checked. Never tip the maître d' unless you're out to impress your guests or expect to pay another visit soon. Your restaurant bill will include a charge for a sales tax of 8.875%.

Essentials

SMOKING
Smoking is prohibited in all enclosed public spaces in New York City, including restaurants and bars.

HOURS
New Yorkers seem ready to eat at any hour. Many restaurants stay open between lunch and dinner, some have late-night seating, and still others serve around the clock. Restaurants that serve breakfast often do so until noon or later. Restaurants in the East Village, Lower East Side, SoHo, TriBeCa, and Greenwich Village are likely to remain open late, whereas Midtown spots and those in the Theater and Financial districts and uptown generally close earlier. Unless otherwise noted, the restaurants listed are open daily for lunch and dinner.

PRICES
Be sure to ask the price of the daily specials recited by the waiter; the charge for specials at some restaurants is noticeably out of line with the other prices on the menu. Beware of the $10 bottle of water; ask for tap water instead, and always review your bill.

If you eat early or late, you may be able to take advantage of a prix-fixe deal not offered at peak hours. Most upscale restaurants have great lunch deals.

Credit cards are widely accepted, but many restaurants (particularly smaller ones downtown) accept only cash. If you plan to use a credit card, it's a good idea to confirm that it is acceptable when making reservations or before sitting down to eat.

WHAT IT COSTS AT DINNER			
$	$$	$$$	$$$$
RESTAURANTS			
under $13	$13–$24	$25–$35	over $35

CHECK BEFORE YOU GO
The nature of the restaurant industry means that places open and close in a New York minute. It's always a good idea to phone ahead and make sure your restaurant is still turning tables.

⊕ Health/Safety
New York City is one of the safest large cities in the country. However, do not let yourself be lulled into a false sense of security. As with visitors in any large city, unsuspecting tourists in New York remain particularly easy marks for pickpockets and hustlers.

After the September 11, 2001, terrorist attacks, security was heightened throughout the city and some NYPD measures have remained. Never leave any bags unattended, and expect to have yourself and your possessions inspected thoroughly in such places as airports, sports stadiums, city buildings, and sometimes subway stations or museums.

Ignore the panhandlers on the streets and subways, along with people who offer to hail you a cab (like outside Penn Station, the Port Authority, and Grand Central), and limousine and gypsy-cab drivers who (illegally) offer you a ride.

Keep jewelry out of sight on the street; better yet, leave valuables at home. Don't carry wallets, passports, smartphones, or other gadgets in your back pockets, and make sure bags and purses stay closed.

Avoid deserted blocks in unfamiliar neighborhoods. A brisk, purposeful pace helps deter trouble wherever you go.

The subway runs around the clock and is generally well trafficked until midnight (and until at least 2 am on Friday and Saturday nights), and overall it is very safe. If you do take the subway late at night, ride in the center car, with the conductor. Watch out for shady characters lurking around the inside or outside of stations and bus shelters.

When waiting for a train, head to the center of the platform, and stand far away from its edge, especially when trains are entering or leaving the station. Once the train pulls into the station, avoid empty cars. While on the train, don't engage in verbal exchanges with aggressive riders. If a fellow passenger makes you nervous while on the train, trust your instincts and change cars. When disembarking, stick with the crowd until you reach the street.

Travelers Aid International helps stranded travelers, airport passengers, and unaccompanied children, and works closely with the police and other social service agencies.

■TIP➔ Distribute your cash, credit cards, IDs, and other valuables between a deep front pocket, an inside jacket or vest pocket, and a hidden money pouch.

🛏 Lodging

There are more hotel rooms than ever in New York City, as exciting new properties continue to open their doors not only in Manhattan but in Brooklyn and the outer boroughs as well. But does that mean that New York is cheap? Well, we wouldn't say *cheap,* but you can still find some deals, especially if you're not set on a specific property or neighborhood, and if you don't mind a few extra minutes of commuting time.

Hotels continue to slash rates based on market sensitivity—especially if you and all of those other Internet-savvy shoppers are willing to wait until the last minute. That said, if you want to stay in a specific place and the rate seems reasonable, book it—it's just as likely to go up, especially during peak seasons (spring and fall).

How to choose? The first thing to consider is location. *(Check out our "Where Should I Stay?" chart.)* Many New York City visitors insist on staying in the hectic Midtown area—and options are improving there—but other neighborhoods are often just as convenient. Less touristy areas, such as Gramercy, the Lower East Side, the Upper West Side—even Brooklyn—provide a more realistic sense of New York life, too.

Also consider timing: the least expensive months to book rooms in the city are January and February. If you're flexible on dates, ask the reservationist if there's a cheaper time to stay during your preferred traveling month—that way you can avoid peak dates, like Fashion Week and the New York City Marathon. Be sure to ask about possible weekend packages that could include a third night free. (The Financial District in particular can be a discount gold mine on weekends.)

Another source of bargains? Chain hotels. Many have moved into the city and charge reasonable room rates. In addition to favorites like the Sheraton, Hilton, and Hyatt brands, there are Best Westerns, Days Inns, and Comfort Inns. These rates aren't as low as you find outside Manhattan, but they're certainly getting closer.

Essentials

NEED A RESERVATION?

Hotel reservations are a necessity when planning your trip to New York. Competition for clients also means properties must undergo frequent improvements, especially during July and August, so when booking, ask about any renovations, lest you get a room within earshot of noisy construction, or temporarily (and inconveniently) without amenities such as room service or spa access.

SERVICES

Unless otherwise noted, all hotels listed have private baths, central heating, air-conditioning, and private phones. Many now have wireless Internet (Wi-Fi) available, though it's not always free. Most large hotels have video or high-speed checkout capability, and many can arrange babysitting. Pools are a rarity, but most properties have gyms or health clubs, and sometimes full-scale spas; hotels without facilities usually have arrangements for guests at nearby gyms, sometimes for a fee.

ACCESSIBILITY

Despite the Americans with Disabilities Act (ADA), the level of accessibility seems to differ from hotel to hotel. Some properties may be accessible by ADA standards for people with mobility disabilities, but not for people with hearing or vision impairments, for example.

If you have a hearing impairment, check whether the hotel has devices to alert you visually to the ring of the telephone, a knock at the door, and a fire/emergency alarm.

If you're bringing a service dog, you're not required to let the hotel staff know ahead of time (they must accommodate your service dog regardless); however, you may wish to notify them in advance as a courtesy.

FAMILY TRAVEL

New York has gone to great lengths to attract family vacationers, and hotels have followed the family-friendly trend. Some properties provide such diversions as in-room video games. Most full-service Manhattan hotels provide babysitting, and stroller rental, but be sure to make these arrangements when booking, not when you arrive. New York City hotel rooms are smaller than average, and some may not accommodate roll-away beds even though many hotels offer them. Most hotel rooms in New York City have a maximum number of legal occupants, so check with the hotel instead of making assumptions.

WHAT ABOUT AN APARTMENT RENTAL?

Many people looking to save money on accommodations look for apartments to rent on a short-term basis. Whether you use AirBnB or some other platform, understand that apartment rentals of non-owner-occupied units for less than 30 days are illegal in New York City (and often prohibited by building regulations). Scams are common, so if you rent an apartment, take special care to rent in a way that you are fully covered if something goes wrong. Always pay with a credit card, and never wire money. Ever. Most listed apartments in New York City are illegal. You can legally rent a room in an occupied apartment or house but generally not the full unit for your own private use.

DOES SIZE MATTER?

If room size is important to you, ask how many square feet a room has, not just if it's big. A hotel room in New York is considered large if it's 500 square feet. Very large rooms are 600 square feet. To stay anywhere larger, book a multiroom suite. Small rooms are a tight 150–200 square feet, sometimes less.

PRICES

There's no denying that New York City hotels are expensive, but rates run the full range. For high-end hotels like the Mandarin Oriental at Central Park, prices start at $795 a night for a standard room in high season, which runs from September through December. At the lower end of the spending spectrum, a bunk at the Jane starts at $99 for a single. But don't be put off by the prices printed here—many hotels slash their rates significantly for promotions and online-only deals.

Prices in the reviews are the lowest cost of a standard double room in high season.

WHAT IT COSTS			
$	$$	$$$	$$$$
FOR TWO PEOPLE			
under $300	$300–$449	$450–$600	over $600

💲 Money

In New York, it's easy to get swept up in a debt-inducing cyclone of $60-per-person dinners, $120 theater tickets, $20 nightclub covers, and $300 hotel rooms. But one of the good things about the city is that you can spend in some areas and save in others. Within Manhattan, a cup of coffee can cost from $1 to $4, a pint of beer from $3 to $12, a slice from $1.50 to $9, and a sandwich from $6 to $20. Generally, prices in the other four boroughs are slightly lower than those in Manhattan.

The most generously bequeathed treasure of the city is the arts. The stated admission fee of $25 at the Metropolitan Museum of Art is a suggestion for New York State residents and is mandatory for outside visitors. Admission is valid for three days and also includes the Met Breuer and the Cloisters. Many other museums in town have special times during which admission is free. The Museum of Modern Art, for instance, is free on Friday from 4 to 8. In summer a handful of free music, theater, and dance performances, as well as films (usually screened outdoors), fill the calendar each day.

Prices in this guide are given for adults. Reduced fees are typically available for children, students, and senior citizens.

🍸 Nightlife

New Yorkers are fond of the "work hard, play hard" maxim, but the truth is, Gothamites don't need much of an excuse to hit the town. Any day of the week could easily be mistaken for a Friday or Saturday; the bottom line is that when the the mood strikes, there are always plenty of choices in this 24-hour city. Whether it's raising a glass in a historic saloon, a dimly lit cocktail den, or a swanky rooftop lounge; checking out the latest band; or laughing it up at a comedy show, it isn't hard for visitors to get a piece of the action.

The nightlife scene still resides largely downtown—in the dives and speakeasies of the East Village and Lower East Side, the classic jazz joints and piano bars of the West Village, and the Meatpacking District's and Chelsea's "see-and-be-seen" clubs. Midtown, especially around Hell's Kitchen, has developed a vibrant scene, too, and plenty of upscale hangouts dot the Upper East and Upper West Sides. Brooklyn and Harlem are go-to destinations for in-the-know locals.

Keep in mind that *when* you go is just as important as *where* you go. A club that

Essentials

is packed at 11 pm might empty out by midnight, and a bar that raged last night may be completely empty tonight. *Time Out New York* magazine has a good list of roving parties (⊕ *www.timeout.com/newyork*), as does *Urban Daddy* (⊕ *www.urbandaddy.com/new-york*). Scour industry-centric websites, too, like *Eater* and *Grub Street,* which catalog the comings and goings of many a nightlife impresario. *New York* magazine and the *New York Times* have listings of cabaret and jazz shows, the latter mainly in its Friday and Sunday arts sections. Bear in mind that a venue's life span is often measured in months, not years. Phone ahead or check online to make sure your target hasn't closed or turned into a polka hall (although, you never know—that could be fun, too).

🎭 Performing Arts

The streets of New York alone are stage-worthy. With so many people faking it 'til they make it, daily life can take on the feeling of performance—to exhausting, and inspiring, effect. No wonder that the city draws a constant influx of actors, singers, dancers, and musicians from around the globe, all striving for their big break and infusing the city with a crackling creative energy. This fiercely competitive scene produces an unrivaled wealth of culture and art that many New Yorkers cite as the reason they're here, and that millions more are determined to travel for.

Although costly ticket prices can make attending a Broadway show a less common outing for even the most devout theater-loving New Yorkers, that's not true of many other kinds of more affordable performances. Whether the audiences are primarily local or not, it's their discernment that helps drive the arts scene, whether they are flocking to a concert hall to hear a world-class soprano deliver a flawless performance, or crowding into a cramped café to support fledgling writers reading from their own work.

New York has upward of 200 "legitimate" theaters (meaning those with theatrical performances, not movies), and many more ad hoc venues—parks, churches, lofts, galleries, rooftops, even parking lots. The city is also a revolving door of special events: summer jazz, one-act-play marathons, film festivals, and music and dance celebrations from the classical to the avant-garde, to name just a few.

🛍 Shopping

The Big Apple is one of the best shopping destinations in the world, rivaled perhaps only by London, Paris, and Tokyo. Its compact size, convenient subway system, and plentiful cabs (or Uber or Lyft rides) make it easy to navigate with plenty of bags in tow. But what it really comes down to is the staggering number and variety of stores. If you can't find it in New York, it probably doesn't exist.

If you like elegant flagships and money is no object, head to Midtown, where you'll find international megabrands like Louis Vuitton, Yves Saint Laurent, and Gucci, as well as famed department stores Bergdorf Goodman and Barneys. Nearby Madison Avenue has couture from Carolina Herrera and Vera Wang, and 5th Avenue is lined with famous jewelry stores such as Tiffany, Van Cleef & Arpels, and Harry Winston. This is also the neighborhood to indulge in bespoke goods, such as handmade shoes from John Lobb. If you like designer pieces but can't afford them, don't despair—there are plenty of upscale consignment shops around the city where you can find last season's Chanel suit or a vintage YSL jacket.

The small, independent shops that once lined SoHo have largely been displaced by the likes of J.Crew and UNIQLO, but if you want to hit the chains, this is a great place to do it, because the neighborhood also provides high-quality people-watching and superb lunches. Poke around on the side streets and in nearby NoLIta for outposts of smaller local and foreign designers and, if you're craving some of old SoHo's artistic spirit, don't discount the street vendors' stalls, which sell handmade jewelry and simple cotton dresses.

The East Village and Lower East Side are hotbeds of creativity and quirky coolness, with little boutiques selling everything from retro furniture to industrial-inspired jewelry. They're tucked among bars and old tenement buildings. The Meatpacking District is another great shopping destination to find chic designer stores like Diane von Furstenberg and rag & bone along with independently owned boutiques. And if you jaunt over to Brooklyn, you'll discover that some of the city's hippest designers are hanging out at boutiques just across the East River.

Tipping

The customary tipping rate for taxi drivers is 10%–20%; bellhops are usually given $2 per bag in luxury hotels, $1 per bag elsewhere. Hotel maids should be tipped $2 per day of your stay. A doorman who hails or helps you into a cab can be tipped $1–$2. You should also tip your hotel concierge for services rendered; the size of the tip depends on the difficulty of your request, as well as the quality of the concierge's work. Tour guides should be tipped 15%–20% if you

enjoyed the tour. Waiters should also be tipped 15%–20%, though at higher-end restaurants, a solid 20% is more the norm. Tip $1 or $2 per drink you order at the bar, or possibly more if you're ordering something especially time-consuming to make.

Taxes

A sales tax of 8.875% applies to almost everything you can buy retail, including restaurant meals. However, prescription drugs and nonprepared food bought in grocery stores are exempt. Clothing and footwear costing less than $110 (per item) also are exempt.

Visitor Information

The Grand Central Partnership staffs a number of information kiosks in and around Grand Central Terminal and also offers free tours of the neighborhood.

NYC & Company is the city's official tourism and visitor information resource. Check out its impressive website (⊕ www.nycgo.com) and official NYC Information Centers (located in Midtown in Times Square and Macy's Herald Square as well as in Lower Manhattan at City Hall Park).

The Downtown Alliance has information on the area encompassing City Hall south to Battery Park, and from the East River to West Street; the Times Square Alliance covers the Times Square area.

Contacts

✈ Air Travel

AIRLINE SECURITY ISSUES Transportation Security Administration (*TSA*). ⊕ *www.tsa.gov.*

AIRPORT INFORMATION JFK International Airport (*JFK*). ☎ *718/244–4444* ⊕ *www.jfkairport.com.* **LaGuardia Airport** (*LGA*). ✉ *Flushing* ☎ *718/533–3400* ⊕ *www.laguardiaairport.com.* **Newark Liberty International Airport** (*EWR*). ☎ *973/961–6000* ⊕ *www.newarkairport.com.*

SHUTTLE SERVICE GO Airlink NYC. ☎ *212/812–9000, 877/599–8200* ⊕ *www.goairlinkshuttle.com.* **NYC Airporter.** ☎ *718/777–5111* ⊕ *www.nycairporter.com.* **SuperShuttle.** ☎ *800/258–3826* ⊕ *www.supershuttle.com.*

JFK TRANSFER INFORMATION AirTrain JFK. ☎ *877/535–2478* ⊕ *www.airtrainjfk.com.* **Long Island Rail Road (LIRR).** ☎ *511* ⊕ *www.mta.info/lirr.*

NEWARK AIRPORT TRANSFER INFORMATION AirTrain Newark. ☎ *888/397–4636* ⊕ *www.airtrainnewark.com.* **Coach USA—Newark Airport Express.** ☎ *908/354–3330, 877/894–9155* ⊕ *newarkairportexpress.com.*

TRANSFER BETWEEN AIRPORTS AirTrain. ☎ *800/247–7433* ⊕ *www.panynj.gov/airtrain.*

⛵ Boat Travel

FERRIES New York Water Taxi (*NYWT*). ☎ *212/742–1969* ⊕ *www.nywatertaxi.com.* **NY Waterway.** ☎ *800/533–3779* ⊕ *www.nywaterway.com.* **NYC Ferry.** ⊕ *www.ferry.nyc.* **Staten Island Ferry.** ☎ *311, 212/639–9675* ⊕ *www.siferry.com.*

🚌 Bus Travel

BUSES IN NEW YORK Metropolitan Transportation Authority (MTA) Travel Information Line. ☎ *511* ⊕ *www.mta.info.*

BUSES TO NEW YORK BoltBus. ☎ *877/265–8287* ⊕ *www.boltbus.com.* **Coach USA.** ☎ *800/877–1888* ⊕ *www.coachusa.com.* **Go Buses (by Academy Bus).** ☎ *855/888–7160* ⊕ *www.gobuses.com.* **Greyhound.** ☎ *800/231–2222* ⊕ *www.greyhound.com.* **Megabus.** ☎ *877/462–6342* ⊕ *us.megabus.com.* **New Jersey Transit.** ☎ *973/275–5555* ⊕ *www.njtransit.com.* **Trailways.** ☎ *800/225–6815* ⊕ *www.trailways.com.*

BUS STATIONS George Washington Bridge Bus Station. ✉ *4211 Broadway, between 178th and 179th Sts., Washington Heights* ☎ *800/221–9903* ⊕ *www.panynj.gov.* **Port Authority Bus Terminal.** ✉ *625 8th Ave., at 42nd St., Midtown West* ☎ *212/564–8484* ⊕ *www.panynj.gov.*

Ⓜ Metro/Public Transport

SCHEDULE AND ROUTE INFORMATION Metropolitan Transportation Authority (MTA) Travel Information Line. ☎ *511* ⊕ *www.mta.info.*

SUBWAY INFORMATION Citymapper. ⊕ *www.citymapper.com.* **MTA The Weekender.** ⊕ *web.mta.info/weekender.* **MTA Trip Planner.** ☎ *511* ⊕ *tripplanner.mta.info.*

🚕 Taxi Travel

CAR-SERVICE COMPANIES Arecibo Car Service. ☎ *718/783–6465* ⊕ *www.arecibocc.com.* **Carey.** ☎ *800/336–4646* ⊕ *www.carey.com.* **London Towncars.** ✉ *Long Island City* ☎ *212/988–9700, 800/221–4009* ⊕ *www.londontowncars.com.*

RIDE-SHARE AND APP-BASED CAR SERVICES

Juno (by Gett). ⊕ *gojuno. com.* **Lyft.** ⊕ *www.lyft. com.* **Uber.** ⊕ *www.uber. com.* **Via.** ⊕ *ridewithvia. com.*

🚆 Train Travel

INFORMATION Amtrak. ✉ *Penn Station, Midtown West* ☎ *800/872-7245* ⊕ *www.amtrak.com.* **Long Island Rail Road.** ✉ *Penn Station, Midtown West* ☎ *511* ⊕ *www.mta.info/ lirr.* **Metro-North Railroad.** ✉ *Grand Central Terminal, Midtown East* ☎ *212/532- 4900, 511* ⊕ *www. mta.info/mnr.* **New Jersey Transit.** ✉ *Penn Station, Midtown West* ☎ *973/275-5555* ⊕ *www. njtransit.com.* **PATH.** ☎ *800/234-7284* ⊕ *www. panynj.gov/path.*

TRAIN STATIONS Grand Central Terminal. ✉ *89 E. 42nd St., at Park Ave., Midtown East* ☎ *511* ⊕ *www.grandcentralter- minal.com.* **Penn Station.** ✉ *From 31st to 33rd St., between 7th and 8th Aves., Midtown West* ☎ *511.*

📍 Visitor Information

LOCAL RESOURCES NYC Mayor's Office for People with Disabilities (*MOPD*). ☎ *311* ⊕ *www.nyc.gov/ mopd.* **Reduced-Fare MetroCard.** ☎ *511* ⊕ *www. mta.info/accessibility/ transit.htm.* **Scootaround.** ☎ *888/441-7575* ⊕ *loca- tions.scootaround.com/ nyc.*

LGBT TRAVEL The Center (*Lesbian, Gay, Bisexual & Transgender Community Center*). ✉ *208 W. 13th St., between 7th and 8th Aves., Greenwich Village* ☎ *212/620-7310* ⊕ *www. gaycenter.org.*

ACTIVITIES NYC Depart- ment of Parks & Recreation. ☎ *311* ⊕ *www.nycgov- parks.org.*

HEALTH/SAFETY Travelers Aid International (JFK). ✉ *JFK International Airport Terminals 1, 4, 5, 7, and 8, Queens* ☎ *718/656-4870* ⊕ *www.travelersaid.org/ jfk.*

CITY INFORMATION Downtown Alliance. ☎ *212/566-6700* ⊕ *www. downtownny.com.* **Grand Central Partner- ship.** ☎ *212/883-2420* ⊕ *www.grandcentral- partnership.nyc.* **NYC & Company.** ⊕ *www. nycgo.com.* **Times Square**

Alliance. ✉ *Midtown West* ☎ *212/768-1560* ⊕ *www. timessquarenyc.org.*

STATEWIDE INFORMA- TION New York State Division of Tourism. ☎ *800/225-5697* ⊕ *www. iloveny.com.*

Great Itineraries

It's challenging but not impossible to take in the big sights of New York City in a bite-size amount of time. Of course, with more major attractions than almost any other city on earth, New York can prove a hard town to know where to start. Here are two compact plans to sample the very best of the Big Apple, whether it's for one day or five days.

New York City in 1 Day

In one day, the best way to soak up Manhattan is to start early and mix together a bit of both downtown and Midtown. So grab New York's breakfast of champions—coffee and a bagel—and prepare yourself for the morning rush hour on the subway on your way to **Battery Park.** From this southernmost tip of the island, you'll see the **Statue of Liberty, Ellis Island,** and the **Staten Island Ferry Terminal.** Head up Broadway past **Bowling Green** and the famous Charging Bull statue on your way to **Wall Street.** Turn right at the 1846 Gothic Revival–style **Trinity Church** to view giant George Washington at **Federal Hall,** across from the **New York Stock Exchange.** Stroll north, then take a left on Liberty Street to the **World Trade Center** site, home to the **National 9/11 Memorial & Museum** and the 104-story **One World Trade Center.** If time and budget allow, make your way to the top of the the the latter for a bird's-eye view of Manhattan (advance ticket reservations are recommended).

Take the subway uptown to spend the afternoon browsing the **Metropolitan Museum of Art** or the **Museum of Modern Art (MoMA).** Take a quick stroll through nearby **Central Park** afterward, and then take a walk downtown to 42nd Street, passing through **Times Square**—best experienced after dark. If you time it right, you may even have time to catch a Broadway show.

New York City in 5 Days

Five days in New York is enough to explore much of the city's culture and sights, along with a few culinary highlights. The first and most important stop is to any subway-station kiosk to buy a seven-day, unlimited-ride MetroCard for $33—it'll help you make your trip much more affordable and easier to get around the city.

DAY 1: LOWER MANHATTAN, SOHO, AND CHELSEA

With its four centuries of history, Lower Manhattan is a prime starting point for your trip. Kick off Day 1 with a visit to **Battery Park, Wall Street, the South Street Seaport,** and **One World Trade Center,** along with a stop at the **National 9/11 Memorial & Museum.** If you get there early enough, you might have time to hop on a ferry and visit either Liberty Island, home to the **Statue of Liberty,** or **Ellis Island,** the entryway for immigrants coming to America from the late 19th century to the mid-20th century. If you're not able to visit, you'll still be able to glimpse them from Manhattan's southernmost tip.

Afterward, drift north toward Canal Street to discover **SoHo** and its unique cast-iron architecture and shops, and continue your walk even farther uptown into Chelsea (a subway ride might be in order here) to walk the **High Line** at sunset. Have dinner and then, if you're big on nightlife, explore the nearby Meatpacking District's many hopping bars and clubs to get your dance on into the wee hours of the morning.

DAY 2: GRAND CENTRAL, 5TH AVENUE, ROCKEFELLER CENTER, AND TIMES SQUARE

Start Day 2 with breakfast at **Grand Central Terminal,** one of NYC's most majestic spaces, where you can gaze up at its ceiling's sparkling constellations and down at the throngs of commuters whizzing through. Head north on **5th Avenue** to check out **Rockefeller Center** (if it's winter, that'll include the ice-skating rink). If you're able to plan ahead, book an NBC studios tour; or just pop into the **NBC Experience Store**. On a clear day, visit the 30 Rock observation deck for a perfect view of the **Empire State Building** and beyond.

Then make a pit stop at the **Museum of Modern Art (MoMA)** to check out one of the world's best modern art museums; must-see exhibits include Andy Warhol's soup cans and *Starry Night* by Vincent van Gogh. After you get your art fill, veer southwest toward **Times Square** to join travelers (and some locals) who converge on the "crossroads of the world" to bask in Broadway's bright lights.

DAY 3: BROOKLYN BRIDGE, CHINATOWN, LOWER EAST SIDE, AND THE EAST VILLAGE

For Day 3, take the subway or water taxi over to Brooklyn and head to **Brooklyn Bridge Park** to view the picturesque lower Manhattan skyline. There you can walk across the **Brooklyn Bridge** back to Manhattan, where you'll end up in **Chinatown,** with its many tasty eateries. Cross Canal Street and walk east past the regal **Manhattan Bridge Arch,** into the **Lower East Side.** The **Tenement Museum** is among the city's most interesting historical experiences, so plan an hour or two there.

Then stroll north through the **East Village** and **Alphabet City,** with a break in **Tompkins Square Park** for eclectic downtown people-watching. Grab a drink at one of the many bars, or treat yourself to cannoli at an old-school Italian bakery.

DAY 4: MUSEUM MILE, CENTRAL PARK, AND THE UPPER WEST SIDE

Infuse some of NYC's best art and history into Day 4 at one of several truly great institutions along the Museum Mile on the Upper East Side. You can invest a couple of hours (or the whole day) exploring the **Metropolitan Museum of Art, Guggenheim, Frick, El Museo del Barrio,** and other history and art institutions. You can also start (or end) your museum-hopping across the park, at the Upper West Side's **American Museum of Natural History.** Regardless of where you start, make sure you spend a few hours exploring **Central Park** and its many picturesque points of interest, like Bethesda Terrace, the carousel, and Belvedere Castle.

As you exit the park on the west side, walk to Broadway for a taste of some of the Upper West Side's authentic delicatessen delights, and top off the evening in Harlem for a show at the historic **Apollo Theater** or smaller jazz clubs.

DAY 5: UNION SQUARE, WASHINGTON SQUARE PARK, WEST VILLAGE

On Day 5, start at **Union Square,** home to a greenmarket (and seasonal holiday crafts market) and surrounded by stores big and small. Don't miss the "18 miles of books" (new and used) for sale at the Strand on Broadway, a local literary institution. Stroll down to **Washington Square Park** to see the famous marble arch and central fountain, hear buskers playing their hearts out, and watch NYU kids hanging out between classes.

Walk toward Bleecker Street, and wander along the winding lanes of the West Village. On Christopher Street, visit the **Stonewall National Monument** and registered city landmark, where the LGBTQ civil-rights movement began; plus other famous watering holes frequented by artistic luminaries throughout the decades.

On the Calendar

Spring

Spring means the start of baseball season with home openers, usually in the first week of April, for both of New York's Major League teams: the Yankees and the Mets.

Sakura Matsuri Cherry Blossom Festival. New Yorkers come out of hibernation en masse at the end of April to witness the extremely popular annual Sakura Matsuri Cherry Blossom Festival at the Brooklyn Botanic Garden. In addition to the blooming cherry trees, there are Taiko drumming performances, Japanese pop bands, samurai swords, martial arts, tea ceremonies, and more. ⊠ *Brooklyn Botanical Garden, 990 Washington Ave., Prospect Heights* ⊕ *www.bbg.org* ⊠ *$15* Ⓜ *2, 3 to Eastern Parkway–Brooklyn Museum; 2, 3, 4, 5 to Franklin Ave.*

Tribeca Film Festival. Founded by Robert De Niro and Jane Rosenthal to contribute to the long-term recovery of Lower Manhattan after 9/11, the Tribeca Film Festival has become one of the world's most prominent film festivals. There are upward of 250 films, more than 1,000 screenings at multiple locations including the Tribeca Film Center (TFC 375 Greenwich St., 2nd fl.), and plenty of buzz. It typically takes place late April to early May. ⊠ *TriBeCa* ⊕ *www.tribecafilm.com.*

Summer

Free outdoor movie festivals are a huge draw in summer: choices include sci-fi movies with a view of Brooklyn Bridge Park (⊕ *www.brooklynbridgepark.org*); indie movies on city rooftops (⊕ *www.rooftopfilms.com*); and classics screened every Monday night in Midtown's Bryant Park (⊕ *www.bryantpark.org*).

Celebrate Brooklyn! Celebrate Brooklyn! is one of the city's most popular free outdoor performing arts festivals, and *the* place to catch excellent live music in the great Brooklyn outdoors. The artists and ensembles reflect the borough's diversity, ranging from internationally acclaimed performers to up-and-coming musicians. The lineup also includes kids' shows, movies with live music, ballet, and more. Performances are rain or shine and free (suggested donation of $5), with the exception of ticketed benefit concerts, which directly support the festival. There are usually about 2,000 chairs, but many people think the best seats are on the lawn, so come early and bring a blanket. Local restaurants set up food and drink stands. ⊠ *Prospect Park Bandshell, 9th St. and Prospect Park W entrance, Park Slope* ⊕ *www.bricartsmedia.org/performing-arts/celebrate-brooklyn* ⊠ *Free* Ⓜ *F, G to 7th Ave.; 2, 3 to Grand Army Plaza.*

Midsummer Night Swing. If you're in town, don't miss the Midsummer Night Swing festival, an outdoor music and dance party in Lincoln Center Plaza that occurs from late June to mid-July. Take lessons with pros or just strut your natural moves on the dance floor. ⊠ *Damrosch Park, 60 Lincoln Center Plaza, Upper West Side* ⊕ *www.midsummernightswing.org* ⊠ *$17–$20 or buy a pass* Ⓜ *1 to 66th St.*

Museum Mile Festival. For one day every June, thousands of locals and visitors celebrate the Museum Mile Festival when museums along 5th Avenue from 82nd Street to 105th Street open their doors for free from 6 pm to 9 pm. There's also dancing and entertainment along the street. ⊠ *Upper East Side* ⊕ *www.museummilefestival.org.*

Summer Streets. Over the first three Saturdays in August, you can join hundreds of thousands of locals to let loose on nearly 7 miles of pedestrianized arterials for Summer Streets. From the Brooklyn Bridge to Central Park, along Park Avenue and connecting streets, New Yorkers hit the car-free streets to run, zipline, dance, experience art, or just ramble along the city's streets in a new way—all for free. ✉ New York ⊕ www.nyc.gov/summerstreets.

Other popular summer festivals and events include Coney Island's **Mermaid Parade,** the **New York International Fringe Festival, SummerStage,** and **Shakespeare in the Park.**

Fall

Brooklyn Book Festival. The Brooklyn Book Festival is a huge, (mostly) free public event with an array of established and emerging authors, readings, panels, discussions, parties, games, and signings—all held in clubs, parks, theaters, and libraries across Brooklyn at the end of September. ✉ New York ⊕ www.brooklynbookfestival.org.

Feast of San Gennaro. Every fall, thousands of locals and visitors flock to Little Italy for the multiday Feast of San Gennaro in mid-September. This festival is a mix of religion, food, colorful parades, and live entertainment. Don't miss the cannoli-eating competition at the beginning of the festival. ✉ Little Italy ⊕ www.sangennaro.nyc.

New York City Marathon. Even if you're not joining the more than 50,000 runners taking a 26.2-mile tour through New York's five boroughs on the first Sunday in November, you'll want to experience the electric atmosphere and the very best of New York with the 2 million spectators who come out to watch and cheer. ✉ New York ⊕ www.tcsnycmarathon.org.

Other top fall events include the **Village Halloween Parade, Macy's Thanksgiving Day Parade,** and the **Rockefeller Center Tree Lighting Ceremony.**

Winter

New York Botanical Holiday Train Show. The New York Botanical Garden's Holiday Train Show is one of the city's top seasonal attractions, especially for families. It runs from the mid-November through mid-January, and you'll find electric trains, more than 150 miniature replicas of city landmarks (made out of twigs and bark), and magical landscapes—all housed in a conservatory, so winter weather can't dampen your spirits. ✉ 2900 Southern Blvd., Belmont ☎ 718/817–8700 ⊕ www.nybg.org ⊠ $20–$25 Ⓜ D, 4 to Bedford Park Blvd.; Metro-North (Harlem local line) to Botanical Garden.

To ring in the **Lunar New Year** in January or February (the date varies), the streets of Chinatown give way to food vendors hawking traditional eats, colorful costumes and decorations, and a major parade of elaborate floats, marching bands, and dragon troupes running from Little Italy through Chinatown and Lower Manhattan. Festivities also take place in Sunset Park in Brooklyn and in the Flushing neighborhood of Queens (⊕ www.betterchinatown.com).

For five days each January, **Winter Jazzfest NYC** (⊕ www.winterjazzfest.com), happens at venues around the city. You can also sign up for a local event like the **Coney Island Polar Bear Plunge** each New Year's Day (and every Sunday at 1 pm, November–April) or the **No Pants Subway Ride** in January (⊕ www.improveverywhere.com).

Best Tours in New York City

In this city dotted with world-famous landmarks, a guided tour is an efficient way to see many sights and learn the neighborhoods. Tours can share insiders' perspectives on where locals eat and play in the city, and reveal fascinating aspects of the city's history, inhabitants, or architecture. Whether you want the classic hop-on, hop-off bus tour to get oriented in the city, or a more personal, interest-specific walk, you'll find it here. ■ TIP→ Some of the bigger tour companies offer discounts if you book in advance online.

🚢 Boat Tours

Circle Line Sightseeing Cruise

TOUR—SIGHT | In good weather, a Circle Line Sightseeing Cruise around Manhattan Island is one of the best ways to get oriented in the city and take the best skyline pictures. Popular options include the Best of NYC ($43), Harbor Lights ($40), and Landmarks ($37) cruises. ⊠ Pier 83, W. 42nd St., Midtown West ☏ 212/563-3200 ⊕ www.circleline42. com ☎ From $18 Ⓜ A, C, E to 42nd St.–Port Authority; 1, 2, 3, 7, N, Q, R, S, W to Times Sq.–42nd St.

★ Classic Harbor Line

BOAT TOURS | FAMILY | Offering more than just sightseeing, this cruise line takes passengers around New York Harbor and along both rivers on its historic luxury yachts and schooners, all with on-board bars. Its unique experiences are fairly priced, and include cruises with live jazz, champagne brunches and sunset tours, wine tastings, and in-depth architecture tours. The company also offers full-day, long-range cruises up the Hudson River to Kingston and Bear Mountain; its fall-foliage cruise is especially lovely. ⊠ Pier 62 at Chelsea Piers, at 22nd St., Chelsea

☏ 212/627-1825 ⊕ www.sail-nyc.com ☎ From $28 Ⓜ C to 23rd St.

Manhattan By Sail

TOUR—SIGHT | Looking for a more historical experience? Manhattan By Sail has several historic boats including an 82-foot schooner dating from the 1920s and the 158-foot-tall Clipper City tall ship. Public sails include themed Sunday brunch sails, a wine-tasting sail, lobster-and-beer-lovers sail, and a jazz sail against stunning moonlit views. The cruises operate mid-April through mid-October. Reservations are advised. ⊠ North Cove Marina at World Financial Center, Financial District ☏ 212/619-0907 ⊕ www. manhattanbysail.com ☎ From $45 Ⓜ A, C to Chambers St.; R, W to Cortlandt St.; 2, 3, 4, 5, A, C, J, Z to Fulton St.

🚌 Bus Tours

Big Bus New York

SCENIC DRIVE | Like its double-decker competitors, Big Bus offers various hop-on, hop-off open-top tours of the city, but its most popular ticket is a two-day pass that includes loops that cover downtown, uptown, and Brooklyn, as well as a night tour or a sightseeing cruise, plus several city attractions. ⊠ Ticket desk, Madame Tussauds, 234 W. 42nd St., Midtown West ☏ 212/685-8687 ⊕ www.bigbustours.com ☎ From $48 Ⓜ A, C, E to 42nd St.–Port Authority; 1, 2, 3, 7, N, Q, R, S, W to Times Sq.–42nd St.

Gray Line New York Sightseeing

TOUR—SIGHT | Gray Line runs various hop-on, hop-off double-decker bus tours, including a downtown Manhattan loop, an upper Manhattan loop, a Brooklyn loop, and evening tours of the city. Packages include 48-hour and 72-hour options plus entrance fees to attractions. ⊠ 777 8th Ave., between 46th and 47th Sts.,

Midtown West ☎ *800/669–0051* ⊕ *www. newyorksightseeing.com* 🚇 *From $49* Ⓜ *A, C, E to 42nd St.–Port Authority; 1, 2, 3, 7, N, Q, R, S, W to Times Sq.–42nd St.*

Free Tours

Big Apple Greeter

TOUR—SIGHT | This free volunteer-led tour service pairs visitors with knowledgeable locals who share insights and tips and cater tours to specific interests. It's like having a friend in town who squires you around and pays for his or her own lunch. Request a greeter at least three weeks before your visit using the online form. ✉ *New York* ☎ *212/669–8159* ⊕ *www. bigapplegreeter.org* 🚇 *Free.*

Central Park Conservancy

TOUR—SIGHT | The Central Park Conservancy offers free guided tours that provide an introduction to the different areas of Central Park—its woodlands, romantic vistas, Conservatory Garden, Seneca Village, and secret corners and off-the-beaten-path walks. Volunteer-led Welcome Tours meet at different points in the park, so check the website for details. Premier tours are ticketed ($15) and provide a more in-depth experience. ✉ *New York* ☎ *212/794–6564* ⊕ *www.centralparknyc. org* 🚇 *Free.*

Free Tours by Foot

TOUR—SIGHT | The walking tours of Manhattan and Brooklyn hosted by Free Tours by Foot are technically free (you pay what you feel the tour was worth at the end). Highlights include sunset walking tours of the High Line, a Brooklyn graffiti and street art tour, and a journey through the storied past of the East Village. Reservations are required for all tours, which run about two hours. ✉ *New York* ☎ *646/450–6831* ⊕ *www.freetoursbyfoot.com* 🚇 *Free (suggested donation).*

Special-Interest Tours

Bike and Roll

TOUR—SIGHT | From Central Park to the Brooklyn Bridge, there's a lot of ground to cover; do yourself a favor and use wheels. Bike and Roll NYC offers guided bike tours with a range of distances and levels of difficulty in Manhattan and across to Brooklyn. There's a popular tour of the waterfront parks and one of Central Park. Rates include bike rentals, helmets, and water. ✉ *New York* ☎ *212/260–0400* ⊕ *www.bikenewyorkci-ty.com* 🚇 *From $40.*

Boroughs of the Dead

TOUR—SIGHT | From tours taking in haunts of various Manhattan neighborhoods to 19th-century true-crime tours to outer-borough ghost walks, the two-hour Boroughs of the Dead tour suggests that the inhabitants of this city truly never sleep—even when they're dead. Don't wait for Halloween to explore the historical crime, gore, and paranormal activities of Manhattan and Brooklyn. No capes, costumes, or gimmicks here: just dark, haunting history. ✉ *New York* ☎ *917/409–8533* ⊕ *boroughsofthedead. com* 🚇 *From $25.*

Local Expeditions

GUIDED TOURS | FAMILY | Local knowledge dives a level deeper with these specialty tours, led by New Yorkers who have crafted themes according to their personal knowledge and expertise. They cover Manhattan, Brooklyn, Queens, and even some New Jersey spots; can be walking, ferry, and/or Citi Bike tours; and span an array of topics—from Chinatown in depth, to Victorian Flatbush in Brooklyn, to the "Yiddish Rialto" days of the East Village. Better still, part of every tour's proceeds go to charity. ✉ *New York* ☎ *917/834–6373* ⊕ *local-expeditions.com* 🚇 *From $20.*

Best Tours in New York City

Shop Gotham

TOUR—SIGHT | If you're on a mission to shop 'til you drop, you won't want to waste time with a map. The fashion-savvy guides at Shop Gotham will save you time and money by guiding you to the best boutiques of SoHo and NoLIta and elsewhere, getting you exclusive shop discounts, VIP access, and also offering styling advice. Private tours are available, too. ⊠ *New York* ☎ *212/209–3370* ⊕ *www.shopgotham.com* ✉ *From $64.*

A Slice of Brooklyn

TOUR—SIGHT | If you're interested in experiencing a more local holiday light tradition far from Rockefeller Center, take A Slice of Brooklyn's bus tour to the festive (and blinding) neighborhood light scene that is Brooklyn's Dyker Heights. The Dyker Lights tour, offered in December, introduces you to some of Brooklyn's less touristed neighborhoods. Other tours include the Original Brooklyn Pizza Tour, a bus tour of iconic Brooklyn pizza joints, and tours of quintessential Brooklyn neighborhoods. ⊠ *New York* ☎ *212/913–9917* ⊕ *www.asliceofbrooklyn.com* ✉ *From $55.*

🚶 Walking Tours

Big Onion Walking Tours

TOUR—SIGHT | The wisecracking PhD candidates of Big Onion Walking Tours lead themed tours—such as Upper East Side: A Clash of Titans, Immigrant New York, and Gangs of New York—as well as renowned multiethnic eating tours and guided walks through neighborhoods from Harlem to the Financial District and Brooklyn. Tours run daily. ⊠ *New York* ☎ *888/606–9255* ⊕ *www.bigonion.com* ✉ *From $25.*

Joyce Gold History Tours of New York

TOUR—SIGHT | The knowledgeable Joyce Gold has been conducting neighborhood walking tours since 1976. Her themed walks—such as Gangs of New York and the Bloody Five Points, and The Flamboyant and the Bohemian—run on weekends, lasting about two hours. ⊠ *New York* ☎ *212/242–5762* ⊕ *www.nyctours.com* ✉ *$25.*

Like A Local Tours

TOUR—SIGHT | Walk like a local, talk like a local, and—best of all—eat like a local with a highly curated tour from Like A Local. Options include the Flatiron Food, History, and Architecture tour, which is a lovely walk from the Flatiron District to Union Square with a lot of tasty stops, photo ops, local history, and private kitchen visits along the way. If you're looking to feel like a hip local in Brooklyn, try the Insider Art Tour of Bushwick, Brooklyn. ⊠ *New York* ⊕ *www.likealocaltours.com* ✉ *From $50.*

The Municipal Art Society of New York

TOUR—SIGHT | The Municipal Art Society conducts a variety of walking tours that emphasize the architecture, history, and changing faces of particular neighborhoods. Options include Edith Wharton's New York, The Bronx's Urban Art, and Storefront: the Disappearing Face of New York. The walking tour of Grand Central explores the 100-year-old terminal's architecture, history, and hidden secrets. ⊠ *Midtown West* ☎ *212/935–3960,* *212/935–3960* ⊕ *www.mas.org/tours* ✉ *From $30.*

New York Food Tours

TOUR—SIGHT | Options from the New York Food walking tours include The Freakiest and Funniest Food ($65), Tastes of Chinatown ($60), Ultimate New York Food & Culture Tour ($60), Everything Chocolate ($60), and an East Village food and culture tour ($75). ⊠ *New York* ☎ *347/559–0111* ⊕ *www.foodtoursofny.com* ✉ *From $60.*

THE STATUE OF LIBERTY AND ELLIS ISLAND: GATEWAY TO THE NEW WORLD

A quintessential part of a visit to New York, the trip to the Statue of Liberty and Ellis Island takes up the better part of a day. It involves a ferry ride, long lines, security checks, and ultimately, the rare opportunity to appreciate some of the most powerful symbols of America right up close. It's worth the effort. It's no overstatement to say that these two sights have played defining roles in American culture.

THE STATUE OF LIBERTY

Impressive from the shore, the Statue of Liberty is even more majestic up close. For millions of immigrants, the first glimpse of America was Lady Liberty, growing from a vaguely defined figure on the horizon into a towering, stately colossus. Visitors approaching Liberty Island on the ferry from Battery Park may experience a similar sense of wonder as they approach. Note that at press time most of Ellis Island is still closed due to damage from Hurricane Sandy. Check www.nps.gov/elis for updates.

What's Here

The 152-foot-tall statue of Liberty, officially named *La Liberté éclairant le monde* ("Liberty Enlightening the World") was a gift from the people of France to the United States. It was designed by French sculptor Frédéric Auguste Bartholdi, built in France, and shipped to America where it was assembled. The statue stands atop an 89-foot-tall pedestal designed by American architect Richard Morris Hunt. The lines of Emma Lazarus's sonnet "The New Colossus" ("Give me your tired, your poor, your huddled masses yearning to breathe free...") are inscribed on a plaque inside the pedestal.

A brand-new informative and entertaining museum opened in May 2019. Highlights include the torch's original glass flame (the current flame is 24-karat gold and lit at night by floodlights), full-scale copper replicas of Lady Liberty's face and one of her giant feet, Bartholdi's alternative designs for the statue, and a model of the interior framework designed by Gustave Eiffel (of Eiffel Tower fame).

The observatory platform at the top of the pedestal is a great place for a photo op; it's 16 stories high, and you'll have all of Lower Manhattan spread out in front of you. The observatory platform is accessible via elevator if you don't want to climb the stairs.

The crown is the statue's highest accessible point. It's reached by stairs (154 of them; about a 20 minute journey) from the observatory platform.

Liberty Island has a pleasant café.

Know Before You Go

Buy your tickets in advance. There are a limited number of same-day standby tickets available at ferry ticket offices, where you catch the ferry but we strongly advise planning early. Once you reach the island, there are no tickets available, and without a ticket there is absolutely no admittance into the pedestal, the crown, or the museum.

You have three choices when buying your ticket to the Statue of Liberty:

A. You can just buy a ferry ticket. This will get you to Liberty Island and Ellis Island but it does not get you into the Statue of Liberty pedestal or the crown (but it does include the new museum). The ferry ticket does include a self-guided audio tour of Liberty Island (there's an adult version and a kids version). Pick up your audio guide when you exit the ferry at Liberty Island.

B. You can buy your ticket with pedestal access; there is no extra charge but you should do this in advance. Pedestal access includes access to the new Statue of Liberty Museum.

C. For crown access, plan *far* in advance, as there are only 320 spots available each day and they sell out months in advance. There is a small extra fee.

Liberty Highlights

■ The surreal chance to stand next to, and be dwarfed by, the original glass torch and the copper cast of Lady Liberty's foot.

■ The vistas of New York from the observatory platform.

Statue Basics

- ☎ 212/363–3200; 877/523–9849 ticket reservations
- ⊕ www.nps.gov/stli
- 🚢 Free; ferry $18.50 round-trip (includes Ellis Island); crown tickets $21.50
- ⊙ Daily 9:30–5; extended hours in summer.

ALTERNATIVE VIEWS

■ The free Staten Island Ferry offers a great view of New York Harbor and of the Statue of Liberty from a distance.

■ Webcams placed around the statue's torch allow you to see what Lady Liberty sees—wide views of the New York City skyline, the Hudson River, and ships in the harbor—from your computer or phone.

■ Liberty Helicopters has sightseeing tours that fly over the crown and torch.

FAST FACT: To move the Statue of Liberty from its initial home on a Paris rooftop to its final home in the New York Harbor, the statue was broken down into 350 individual pieces and packed in 214 crates. It took four months to reassemble it.

FAST FACT: The face of Lady Liberty is actually a likeness of sculptor Frederic-Auguste Bartholdi's mother—quite a tribute.

Foundation of the pedestal to torch: 305'6"

Heel to top head: 111'6"

FAST FACT: Lady Liberty has formidable proportions. Her face is more than 8 feet tall, she has a 35-foot waistline, and she weighs 225 tons (450,000 pounds). Her crown has 7 rays, to represent the 7 continents; each is 9-feet long and weighs about 150 pounds.

ELLIS ISLAND

Chances are you'll be with a crowd of international tourists as you disembark at Ellis Island. Close your eyes and imagine the jostling crowd 100 times larger. Now imagine that your journey has lasted weeks at sea and that your day pack contains all your worldly possessions. You're hungry, tired, jobless, and homeless. This scenario just begins to set the stage for the story of the millions of immigrants who passed through Ellis Island. Between 1892 and 1924, approximately 12 million men, women, and children first set foot on U.S. soil at the Ellis Island federal immigration facility. By the time the facility closed in 1954, it had processed the ancestors of more than 40% of Americans living today.

WHAT'S HERE

The island's main building, now a national monument, reopened in 1990 as the Ellis Island Immigration Museum, with more than 30 galleries of artifacts, photographs, and taped oral histories. The centerpiece of the museum is the Registry Room (also known as the Great Hall). It feels dignified and cavernous today, but photographs show that it took on many configurations over the years, always packed with humanity. While you're here, look out the Registry Room's tall, arched windows and try to imagine what passed through immigrants' minds as they viewed Lower Manhattan's skyline to one side and the Statue of Liberty to the other.

Along with the Registry Room, the museum includes the ground-level Peopling of America Center, which explores immigration to the United States before and after Ellis Island was a portal for immigrants. Graphics and poignant audio stories give firsthand accounts of the immigrants' journeys—from making the trip and arriving in the United States to their struggle and survival here. There is also the American Family Immigration Center, where you can search Ellis Island's records for your own ancestors, and the American Flag of Faces, an interactive display filled with images of immigrants submitted online (submit yours at *FlagofFaces. org*). Outside, the American Immigrant Wall of Honor has inscribed upon it the names of more than 600,000 immigrant Americans.

MAKING THE MOST OF YOUR VISIT

Because there's so much to take in, it's a good idea to make use of the museum's interpretive tools. **Check at the visitor desk for free film tickets, ranger tour times, and special programs.**

Consider starting your visit with a viewing of the free film *Island of Hope, Island of Tears*. A park ranger starts off with a short introduction, then the 25-minute film takes you through an immigrant's journey from the troubled conditions of European life (especially true for ethnic and religious minorities), to their nervous arrival at Ellis Island, and their introduction into American cities. The film is a primer into all the exhibits and will deeply enhance your experience.

The audio tour, which is included in the ticket price, is also worthwhile: it takes you through the exhibits, providing thorough, engaging commentary interspersed with recordings of immigrants recalling their experiences.

ELLIS ISLAND HIGHLIGHTS

• Surveying the Great Hall.

• The moving film *Island of Hope, Island of Tears*.

• Exploring the Peopling of America Center to gain a deeper understanding of the history of immigration in America.

• Reading the names on the American Immigrant Wall of Honor.

• Researching your own family's history.

Ellis Island Basics

☎ 212/363–3200 Ellis Island; 212/561–4588 Wall of Honor information

🌐 www.nps.gov/stli

🎫 Free; ferry from $18.50 round-trip (includes Liberty Island)

🕑 Daily 9:30–5; extended in summer.

IMMIGRANT HISTORY TIMELINE

Starting in the 1880s, troubled conditions throughout Europe persuaded both the poor and the persecuted to leave their family and homes to embark on what were often gruesome journeys to come to the golden shores of America.

1880s 5.7 million immigrants arrive in U.S.

1892 Federal immigration station opens on Ellis Island in January.

1901–1910 8.8 million immigrants arrive in U.S.; 6 million processed at Ellis Island.

1907 Highest number of immigrants (860,000) arrives in one year, including a record 11,747 on April 17.

1910 75% of the residents of New York, Chicago, Detroit, Cleveland, and Boston are now immigrants or children of immigrants.

1920s Federal laws set immigration quotas based on national origin.

1954 Ellis Island immigration station is closed.

New arrivals line up to have their eyes inspected.

FAST FACT: Some immigrants who passed through Ellis Island later became household names. A few include Charles Atlas (1903, Italy); Irving Berlin (1893, Russia); Frank Capra (1903, Italy); Bob Hope (1908, England); Knute Rockne (1893, Norway); and Baron Von Trapp and his family (1938, Germany).

FAST FACT: In 1897, a fire destroyed the original pine immigration structure on Ellis Island, including all immigration records dating back to 1855.

FAST FACT: The first test that immigrants had to pass was known as the "six-second medical exam." As they entered the Great Hall, they were watched by doctors; if anyone seemed disabed, their clothing was marked with chalk and they were sent for a full exam.

Four immigrants and their belongings, on a dock, look out over the water; view from behind.

PLANNING

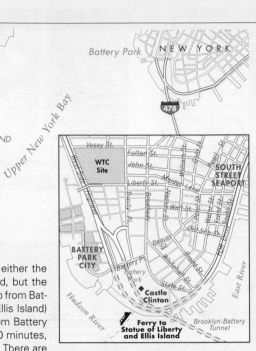

ADMISSION

There is no admission fee for either the Statue of Liberty or Ellis Island, but the ferry ride (which goes round-trip from Battery Park to Liberty Island to Ellis Island) costs $18.50. Ferries leave from Battery Park (see Ch. 3) every 30 to 40 minutes, depending on the time of year. There are often long lines, so arrive early, especially if you have a reserved-time ticket. (Oversize bags and backpacks aren't permitted onboard.) Reserve tickets online—you'll still have to wait in line, both to pick up the tickets (or print your tickets at home) and to board the ferry, but you'll be able to pick up a Monument Pass for access to the pedestal, the museum, and the statue's interior. There is no fee for the Monument Pass, but you cannot enter the Statue of Liberty without it.

WHERE TO CATCH THE FERRY

Broadway and Battery Pl., Lower Manhattan Ⓜ Subway: 4, 5 to Bowling Green.

PLANNING TIPS

Buy tickets in advance. This is the only way to assure that you'll have tickets to actually enter the Statue of Liberty museum and observatory platform.

Be prepared for intense security. At the ferry security check, you will need to remove your coat; at the statue, you will need to remove your coat as well as your belt, watch, and any metal accessories. At this writing, no strollers, large umbrellas, or backpacks are allowed in the statue.

Check ferry schedules in advance. Before you go, check www.statuecruises.com.

Keep in mind that even though the last entry time for the monument is at 4:30 pm, **the last ferry to the Statue of Liberty and Ellis Island is at 3:30 pm.** You need to arrive by at least 3 pm (to allow for security checks and lines) if you want to make the last ferry of the day.

Chapter 3

LOWER MANHATTAN

Updated by
Kelsy Chauvin

👁 Sights
★★★★★

🍴 Restaurants
★★★★☆

🛏 Hotels
★★☆☆☆

💼 Shopping
★★☆☆☆

🍸 Nightlife
★★☆☆☆

NEIGHBORHOOD SNAPSHOT

TOP EXPERIENCES

- Visiting the National 9/11 Memorial & Museum
- Riding the Staten Island Ferry
- Touring Ellis Island and the Statue of Liberty
- Snapping a selfie at Wall Street's *Charging Bull*
- Strolling through the South Street Seaport

PLANNING YOUR TIME

On weekdays, the Financial District sidewalks teem with hurried traders, no-nonsense office workers, speeding messengers, and a steady stream of tourists. On weeknights and weekends, however, the neighborhood turns more residential as parks, restaurants, and shopping areas turn more leisurely and family-friendly.

The district is surrounded by the quintessential sights of New York Harbor, but be prepared for long lines (for both ticketing and security) to visit Ellis Island and the Statue of Liberty, especially on weekends. TriBeCa is one of the more picturesque and quieter neighborhoods in Manhattan, being mostly residential. There are enticing shops, restaurants, and bars, but the neighborhood tends not to be a tourist attraction unless spring's Tribeca Film Festival is on.

GETTING HERE

Many subway lines connect to the Financial District. Fulton Center is serviced by numerous subway lines (2, 3, 4, 5, A, C, J, R, W, Z) and puts you within walking distance of the World Trade Center site, City Hall, and South Street Seaport. To get to the Brooklyn Bridge, take the 4, 5, or 6 to Brooklyn Bridge–City Hall.

For sights around New York Harbor, take the R or W to Whitehall Street, or the 4 or 5 to Bowling Green. (Note that you can also reach the harbor area via the 1 train to South Ferry; it stops in the heart of TriBeCa, at Franklin Street, too.)

QUICK BITES

- **Hudson Eats at Brookfield Place.** The upscale food court and terrace in the Brookfield Place complex has the best of NYC's fast and casual food options ranging from Blue Ribbon Sushi to Black Seed Bagels to Dos Toros Tacos and more. ⊠ *225 Liberty St., at West St., Financial District* ⊕ *bfplny.com* Ⓜ *Subway: E to World Trade Center; N, R, W to Cortlandt St.; A, C to Chambers St.; 2, 3 to Park Pl.; 4, 5 to Fulton St.*

- **La Colombe Torrefaction.** In this airy space just below Canal Street, expect excellent espresso drinks and impressive latte art. Unlike other coffee shops plagued by laptops and customers clad in headphones, none of La Colombe's cafés offer Wi-Fi. ⊠ *319 Church St., at Lispenard St., TriBeCa* ⊕ *www.lacolombe.com* Ⓜ *Subway: A, C, E to Canal St.*

- **Zucker's Bagels & Smoked Fish.** This is one of the few places left in the city that still serves hand-rolled, kettle-boiled New York bagels—plus delicious coffee, smoked fish, and baked goods. ⊠ *146 Chambers St., between Greenwich and Warren Sts., TriBeCa* ⊕ *www.zuckersbagels.com* Ⓜ *Subway: 1, 2, 3 to Chambers St.*

Lower Manhattan, or "all the way downtown" in the parlance of New Yorkers, has long been where the action—and transaction—is.

Originally the Dutch trading post called New Amsterdam (1626–47), this neighborhood is home to historic cobblestone streets next to soaring skyscrapers. This mix of old and new, the whirl of Wall Street, and a concentration of city landmarks make the southern tip of Manhattan essential to any NYC visit. There's no street grid to follow, but Broadway runs straight through the center of the area. To the west are Tribeca and Battery Park City, which have a large proportion of residents in addition to office buildings. At the tip of Manhattan is Battery Park, where you'll find the ferries to the Statue of Liberty and Ellis Island as well as Staten Island. The area east of Broadway is still primarily office buildings, but there are now a fair number of full-time residents.

Financial District

The bustling streets thrum on weekdays with intense traffic and the excitement of big deals, trades, and decisions being made in the vast skyscrapers and financial institutions of Wall Street. Yet beyond this buzz, the Financial District remains among the best neighborhoods to learn about both New York's and America's origins. Colonial-era landmarks include the Federal Hall National Memorial, on the site of the first U.S. capitol and where George Washington was inaugurated as the first president of the United States. Also here are the South Street Seaport's 19th-century brick facades and pedestrian-only Stone Street, one of the city's first thoroughfares. Bounded by the East and Hudson Rivers to the east and west, respectively, and by Chambers Street and Battery Park to the north and south, the Financial District is best appreciated by getting lost in its streets. In recent years, there has been an influx of publishing and media companies, along with a growing residential population and an array of new hotels and developments—all lending to the area's transformation into a well-rounded, day-or-night destination

There's plenty of culture to explore here, and plenty of heritage from distant and more recent history. Be sure to allow ample time to absorb the powerful World Trade Center memorial site, where two 1-acre pools represent the footprints of the fallen Twin Towers.

The southern tip of Manhattan is the key point of departure for Statue of Liberty and Ellis Island tours, which run year-round. This experience should never be dismissed as too touristy. Unlike any other, the excursion is a reminder that New York is a city of immigrants and survivors. The seasonal Governors Island ferry leaves from the Battery Maritime Building (as well as from Pier 6 in Brooklyn).

◉ Sights

Battery Park
NATIONAL/STATE PARK | FAMILY | Jutting out at the southernmost point of Manhattan, tree-filled Battery Park is a respite from the narrow, winding, and buzzing streets of the Financial District. Even if

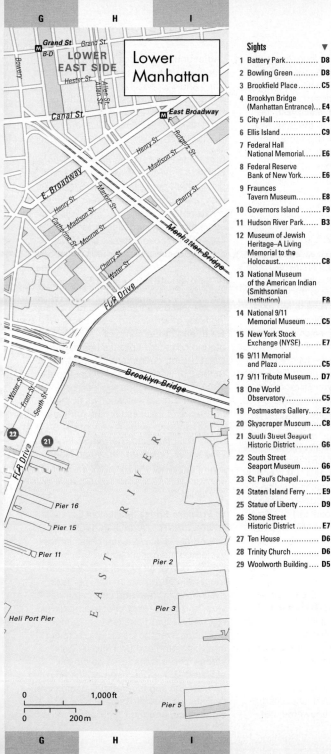

Lower Manhattan

LOWER EAST SIDE

3

Lower Manhattan FINANCIAL DISTRICT

you don't plan to stay for long, carve out a few minutes to enjoy the view, which includes the Statue of Liberty, Ellis Island, and the harbor. The park's main structure is **Castle Clinton National Monument,** the takeoff point for ferries to the Statue of Liberty and Ellis Island. This monument is a former fort erected during the War of 1812 to defend the city. (Its sister fort, Castle Williams, sits across the water on Governors Island.) From 1855 to 1890, it served as America's first official immigration center.

In Battery Park are several memorials, monuments and statues, as well as the lovely SeaGlass Carousel on its east side, where for $5 a spin, you can ride "inside" luminescent fish and enjoy the sensation of floating underwater. Also to the east is the **Staten Island Ferry Terminal,** while to the west is Robert F. Wagner Jr. Park, with its flat, tidy lawn and wide benches from which to view the harbor and summertime performances. ⊠ *Financial District* ⊕ *www.nycgovparks.org/parks/batterypark* Ⓜ *4, 5 to Bowling Green; 1 to South Ferry; R, W to Whitehall.*

Bowling Green

CITY PARK | Perhaps most recognized as the home of Arturo Di Modica's 7,000-pound, bronze *Charging Bull* statue (1989), the small plaza that is Bowling Green, at the foot of Broadway, became New York's first public park in 1733. Legend has it that before that, this was the site upon which Peter Minuit purchased the island of Manhattan from the Native Americans, in 1626, supposedly for what amounted to 24 U.S. dollars. On July 9, 1776, a few hours after citizens learned about the signing of the Declaration of Independence, rioters toppled a statue of British King George III that had occupied the spot for 11 years; much of the statue's lead was melted down into bullets. In 1783, when the occupying British forces fled the city, they defiantly hoisted a Union Jack on a greased, uncleated flagpole so it couldn't be lowered; but

patriot John Van Arsdale drove his own cleats into the pole to replace it with the Stars and Stripes. The copper-top subway entrance across State Street is the original one, built in 1904–05. ⊠ *Broadway and Whitehall St., Financial District* Ⓜ *4, 5 to Bowling Green.*

Brookfield Place (*World Financial Center*)
BUILDING | The four towers of this complex, which range from 34 to 51 stories high, are topped with different geometric ornaments designed by Cesar Pelli and serve as company headquarters for the likes of American Express and Dow Jones. But the glass-domed Winter Garden atrium with its signature palm trees is the main attraction here; it's a pleasant open space that hosts music and dance performances, and also links to a sweeping array of stores and restaurants. At the south end of the complex, an underground concourse passes underneath West Street, connecting the complex to the 9/11 Memorial and Plaza. There's also a pedestrian crosswalk across West Street. The massive windows at the top of the grand staircase on the north side of the atrium provide a view of the 9/11 Memorial Plaza and The Oculus beyond. ⊠ *West St. between Vesey and Liberty Sts., Financial District* 🕾 *212/417–7000* ⊕ *www.brookfieldplaceny.com* Ⓜ *R, W to Cortlandt St.*

★ Brooklyn Bridge (Manhattan Entrance)

BRIDGE/TUNNEL | "A drive-through cathedral" is how the journalist James Wolcott once described the Brooklyn Bridge, one of New York's noblest and most recognized landmarks, perhaps rivaling Walt Whitman's comment that it was "the best, most effective medicine my soul has yet partaken." The bridge stretches over the East River, connecting Manhattan and Brooklyn. A walk across its promenade—a boardwalk elevated above the roadway, shared by pedestrians and (sometimes aggressive) cyclists—is a quintessential New York experience, and the roughly 40-minute stroll delivers exhilarating views. If you start from Lower Manhattan (enter from the east side of City Hall), you'll end up in the heart of Brooklyn Heights, but you can also take the subway to the Brooklyn side and walk back to Manhattan. It's worth noting that from late morning through early evening, especially when the weather is nice, the narrow path gets very congested. Head there early in the morning to find the magical quiet hours. ⊠ East River Dr., Financial District Ⓜ 4, 5, 6 to Brooklyn Bridge–City Hall; J, Z to Chambers St.

City Hall

GOVERNMENT BUILDING | What once marked the northernmost point of Manhattan today houses the office of the mayor, and serves as a gathering place for demonstrators and the news crews who cover their stories. This is one of the oldest City Halls in the country, a striking (but surprisingly small) building dating back to 1803. If the history of local politics and architecture is your thing, free tours are available (sign up in advance online). Inside, highlights include the Rotunda where President Lincoln lay in state in 1865 under a soaring dome supported by 10 Corinthian columns; the Victorian-style **City Council Chamber**; and the **Governor's Room,** an elegantly preserved space with portraits of historic figures, as well as a writing table that George Washington used in 1789 when New York was the U.S. capital. ⊠ City Hall Park, Financial District ☎ 212/788–2656 for tour reservations ⊕ www1.nyc.gov ☜ Free ☉ Tours available some weekdays (reserve online or by phone) Ⓜ 2, 3 to Park Pl.; R, W to City Hall; 4, 5, 6 to Brooklyn Bridge–City Hall; A, C, J, Z to Chambers St.

★ Ellis Island

HISTORIC SITE | **FAMILY** | Between 1892 and 1924 approximately 12 million men, women, and children first set foot on U.S. soil at the Ellis Island federal immigration facility. By the time the facility closed in 1954, it had processed ancestors of more than 40% of Americans living today. The island's main building, now a national monument, is known as the **Ellis Island National Museum of Immigration,** and it tells the story not just of Ellis Island but of immigration from the Colonial era to the present day, through numerous galleries containing artifacts, photographs, and taped oral histories. The museum's centerpiece is the cavernous, white-tile Registry Room (also known as the Great Hall). There's much to take in, so make use of the museum's interpretive tools. Check at the visitor desk for free film tickets, a good audio tour, ranger-led tour times, and special programs.

There is no admission fee for the Statue of Liberty or Ellis Island, but the ferry ride (from Battery Park to Liberty Island to Ellis Island) costs $18.50 round-trip. Ferries leave from Battery Park (and from Liberty State Park in New Jersey) every 30–45 minutes depending on the time of year (buy your tickets online at ⊕ www.statuecruises.com). There are often long lines, so arrive early, especially if you have a timed-entry ticket. There is an indoor-outdoor café on Ellis Island. ⊠ Financial District ☎ 212/561–4588 Ellis Island, 212/561–4500 Wall of Honor information for names of immigrants, 877/523–9849 ⊕ www.ellisisland.org ☜ Free; ferry $18.50 round-trip (includes Liberty Island).

Federal Hall National Memorial

MUSEUM | It's a museum now, but this site has quite a notable claim: George Washington was sworn in here as the first president of the United States, in 1789, when the building was the Federal Hall of the new nation. (You can even view the bible Washington used to swear his oath.) The museum covers 400 years of New York City's history, with a focus on the life and times of what is now the city's Financial District. You can spot the building easily—it was modeled on the Parthenon, and a statue of George

Washington is planted proudly on its (south-facing) stately steps. The National Park Service Visitor Center is on the Pine Street (north side) entrance; meet there for free daily 30-minute ranger-guided tours. ⊠ *26 Wall St., at Nassau St., Financial District* ☎ *212/825–6990* ⊕ *www.nps.gov/feha* ⊠ *Free* ◷ *Closed weekends* Ⓜ *2, 3 to Wall St.; J, Z to Broad St.*

Federal Reserve Bank of New York

BANK | With its imposing mix of sandstone, limestone, and ironwork, the Federal Reserve looks the way a bank ought to: strong and impregnable. The gold ingots in the subterranean vaults here are worth roughly $350 billion—reputedly a third of the world's gold reserves. Hour-long Museum and Gold Vault Tours (conducted twice every weekday and requiring reservations) include a visit to the gold vault, the trading desk, and "FedWorks," a multimedia exhibit center where you can track hypothetical trades. Visitors must show an officially issued photo ID, such as a driver's license or passport, and pass through scanners to enter the building. The Fed advises bringing minimal baggage and arriving 30 minutes before your tour to accommodate security screening; entry is from Maiden Lane. Photography is not permitted. ⊠ *33 Liberty St., between William and Nassau Sts., Financial District* ☎ *212/720–6130* ⊕ *www.newyorkfed.org* ⊠ *Free, including tours* ◷ *Closed weekends* Ⓜ *2, 3, 4, 5, A, C, J, Z to Fulton St.*

Fraunces Tavern Museum

MUSEUM | This former tavern, where General George Washington celebrated the end of the Revolutionary War in 1783, is now a museum covering two floors above the famed restaurant and bar. Here, in his pre-presidential days, Washington bid an emotional farewell to his officers upon the British evacuation of New York. Today, this historic landmark has two fully furnished period rooms—including the Long Room, site of Washington's address—and other modest displays of 18th- and 19th-century American history, as well as temporary exhibits. You'll find more tourists and Wall Street types than revolutionaries in the tavern and restaurant on the ground floor these days, but a cozy Colonial atmosphere and decent hearty meal are available. ⊠ *54 Pearl St., at Broad St., Financial District* ☎ *212/425–1778* ⊕ *www.frauncestavernmuseum.org* ⊠ *$7* Ⓜ *R, W to Whitehall St.; 4, 5 to Bowling Green; 1 to South Ferry; J, Z to Broad St.*

★ Governors Island

NATIONAL/STATE PARK | **FAMILY** | Open seasonally to the public and accessible via a short, free ferry ride, Governors Island is essentially a big, charming park that looks like a small New England town; it's popular with locals for biking by the water, summer festivals, art shows, concerts, and family programs. Wouter van Twiller, a representative for the country of Holland, supposedly purchased the island for his private use, in 1637, from Native Americans for two ax heads, a string of beads, and a handful of nails. The Brits gained firm control of it in the 1670s. In 1784, the island was named for His Majesty's Governors, and it was used almost exclusively by the American military until the 1960s, when the Coast Guard took it over. After their facilities were abandoned in 1995, the island was purchased by the city in 2002 and started welcoming visitors in 2003. The Governors Island ferry departs from the Battery Maritime Building and from Brooklyn's Pier 6. ⊠ *Battery Maritime Building (for Manhattan ferry), 10 South St., Financial District* ⊕ *www.govisland.com* ⊠ *Free (including ferry)* ◷ *Closed Nov.–Apr.* Ⓜ *1 to South Ferry; 4, 5 to Bowling Green; R, W to Whitehall St.*

Museum of Jewish Heritage—A Living Memorial to the Holocaust

MUSEUM | In a granite 85-foot-tall hexagon at the southern end of Battery Park City, this museum aims to educate visitors on the "broad tapestry of Jewish life in the

On a typical weekday, five ferries make roughly 110 trips back and forth between Staten Island and Manhattan, transporting about 70,000 passengers.

20th and 21st centuries—before, during, and after the Holocaust." Architects Kevin Roche and John Dinkeloo designed the six-sided museum to be symbolic of the Star of David, and its three floors of exhibits demonstrate the dynamism of Jewish culture. Visitors enter through a gallery that provides context for the early-20th-century artifacts on the first floor: an elaborate screen hand-painted for the fall harvest festival of Sukkoth, tools used by Jewish tradesmen, and wedding invitations. Other exhibits present the rise of Nazism and anti-Semitism, and the ravages of the Holocaust. Signs of hope are also on display, including a trumpet that Louis Bannet (the "Dutch Louis Armstrong") played for three years in the Auschwitz-Birkenau inmate orchestra. The third floor covers postwar Jewish life. The museum's east wing has a theater, memorial garden, library, galleries, and café. A free audio guide, with narration by Meryl Streep and Itzhak Perlman, is available at the admissions desk. ⌗ *36 Battery Pl., Battery Park City, Financial District* ☎ *646/437–4202*

⊕ *www.mjhnyc.org* ⌗ *$12 (free Wed. and Thurs. 4–8)* ⊘ *Closed Sat. and some Jewish holidays* Ⓜ *4, 5 to Bowling Green; 1, R, W to Rector St.*

National Museum of the American Indian (Smithsonian Institution)

MUSEUM | Massive granite columns rise to a pediment topped by a double row of statues at the impressive Beaux Arts Alexander Hamilton U.S. Custom House (1907), which is home to the New York branch of this Smithsonian museum (the other branch is in Washington, D.C.). Inside, the oval stairwell and rotunda embellished with shipping-theme murals (completed in the 1930s) are worth a long pause. The permanent exhibition, *Infinity of Nations,* is an encyclopedic survey of Native American cultures from across the continent, with the entire museum preserving more than 825,000 art pieces and artifacts dating from ancient to modern times. The venue presents changing exhibitions, videos and films, dance, music, and storytelling programs. ⌗ *1 Bowling Green, between*

State and Whitehall Sts., Financial District ☎ *212/514–3700* ⊕ *www.nmai.si.edu* ✉ *Free* Ⓜ *4, 5 to Bowling Green; 1 to Rector St.; R, W to Whitehall St.; J, Z to Broad St.; 4, 5 to Wall St.*

National 9/11 Memorial Museum

MUSEUM | Beside the reflecting pools on the 9/11 Memorial Plaza is the glass pavilion of the Memorial Museum. The museum descends some seven stories down to the bedrock the Twin Towers were built on, and the vast space displays a poignant, powerful collection of artifacts, memorabilia, photographs, and multimedia exhibits, as well as a gallery that takes visitors through the history of events surrounding both the 1993 and 2001 attacks. You may appreciate the tissue boxes around the museum when experiencing the memorial wall with portraits and personal stories of those who perished. There's also a panoramic media installation about the site's "rebirth," as well as WTC-related art and history temporary exhibits that change throughout the year. Giant pieces of the towers' structural steel and foundations are displayed, along with the partially destroyed Ladder Company 3 fire truck. You can also see the remnants of the Survivors Stairs, which allowed hundreds of people to escape the buildings that fateful September day. ✉ *180 Greenwich St., between Fulton St. and Liberty St. Walkway, Financial District* ☎ *212/266–5211* ⊕ *www.911memorial.org/museum* ✉ *$24 (free Tues. 5–8 pm)* Ⓜ *1, R, W to Cortlandt St.; 2, 3, 4, 5, A, C, J, Z to Fulton Center; E to World Trade Center.*

New York Stock Exchange (NYSE)

BANK | Unfortunately, you can't tour the stock exchange anymore—though the pace on the floor is much less frenetic than it used to be, now that technology has changed how the trading floor works. The building itself, though, at the intersection of Wall and Broad Streets, is still worth ogling. The neoclassical structure, designed by architect George B. Post, opened on April 22, 1903. It has six Corinthian columns supporting a pediment with a sculpture titled *Integrity Protecting the Works of Man,* featuring a tribute to the Gilded Age's sources of American prosperity: Agriculture and Mining to the left of Integrity; Science, Industry, and Invention to the right. As an interesting aside, the Exchange was one of the world's first air-conditioned buildings. ✉ *11 Wall St., between Broadway and Broad St., Financial District* ☎ *212/656–3000* ⊕ *www.nyse.com* Ⓜ *1, R, W to Rector St.; 2, 3, 4, 5 to Wall St.; J, Z to Broad St.*

★ 9/11 Memorial and Plaza

MEMORIAL | Opened to mark the 10th anniversary of 9/11, the somber Memorial occupies a large swath of the 16-acre World Trade Center complex, forming the Memorial Plaza. It comprises two recessed, 30-foot-tall waterfalls that occupy the giant, square footprints where the Twin Towers once stood. Edging the Memorial pools are bronze panels inscribed with the names of the nearly 3,000 people who were killed in the 1993 and 2001 terrorist attacks. Across the plaza are benches, grassy strips, and more than 400 swamp white oak trees harvested from within a 500-mile radius of the site, as well as from Pennsylvania and near Washington, D.C. The 9/11 Memorial is an open-access, free public plaza.

Along Liberty Street on the south side of the site is the elevated Liberty Park, home to Fritz Koenig's *The Sphere,* which for three decades stood on the plaza at the World Trade Center as a symbol of peace. Damaged in the 2001 attack, the sculpture was installed in the park in 2017. On the park's east end stands the yet-unfinished St. Nicholas Greek Orthodox Church and National Shrine, erected to replace the church that was destroyed on 9/11. (At the time of this writing, the church's core structure was built, but exterior and interior finishes remain incomplete.) ✉ *180 Greenwich*

St., between Fulton and Liberty Sts., Financial District ☎ 212/266–5211 ⊕ www.911memorial.org Ⓜ 1, R, W to Cortlandt St.; 2, 3, 4, 5, A, C, J, Z to Fulton St.; E to World Trade Center.

9/11 Tribute Museum

MUSEUM | This project of the September 11th Families' Association opened in 2006 with the intent of putting the events of that day into context—at the time, there was little to see beyond a big construction site. The several galleries include displays about the history and construction of Lower Manhattan; the events of September 11, 2001; the response and recovery efforts after the attacks; and first-person histories. It's a good complement to the broader mission of the separate National 9/11 Memorial & Museum. Guided walking tours by survivors and first responders take in the gallery and the memorial (not the National 9/11 Memorial Museum). ✉ 92 Greenwich St., at Rector St., Financial District ☎ 866/737–1184 ⊕ www.911tributemuseum.org ☞ $15 for galleries; $35 for galleries and guided walking tour Ⓜ 1, R to Rector St.; 2, 3, 4, 5, A, C, J, Z to Fulton St.; E to World Trade Center.

One World Observatory

VIEWPOINT | FAMILY | There are several thrills involved in visiting One World Trade Center, the tallest building in the Western Hemisphere, not the least of which are the spectacular views of Manhattan, Brooklyn, and New Jersey. If you time your visit around dusk, you'll get daytime views as well as sunset and sparkling evening lights. The observatory occupies the 100th, 101st, and 102nd floors of One WTC, and the experience includes an exhilarating trip up in the world's fastest elevators, during which a journey through history is projected on the elevator walls. After you step out at the top, there's also a two-minute video of time-lapse images of Lower Manhattan. The ground floor has exhibits and personal stories about the building of the tower. There are

Brooklyn Bridge Facts 👁

■ Overall length: 6,016 feet

■ Span of twin Gothic-arch towers: 1,595½ feet

■ Distance from top of towers to East River: 272 feet

■ Distance from roadway to the water: 133 feet

■ Number of times the line "If you believe that, I've got a bridge to sell you" is used referring to the Brooklyn Bridge: infinite

several options for dining with a view, including a casual café and a fancier sit-down restaurant (reservations are recommended for the latter). Seasonal events, including Santa, are on the schedule as well. Admission prices rise for "priority" entrance and other combo tickets; the box office, security checkpoint, and observatory entrance are on the West Street side of the tower. You can also purchase advance, timed-entry tickets online. ✉ One World Trade Center, 285 Fulton St., between West and Greenwich Sts., Financial District ☎ 844/696–1776 ⊕ oneworldobservatory.com ☞ $34 Ⓜ 1, R, W to Cortlandt; E to World Trade Center; 2, 3, 4, 5, A, C, J, Z to Fulton St.

Skyscraper Museum

MUSEUM | Why get a crick in your neck—or worse, risk looking like a tourist—while appreciating New York City's famous skyline: instead, at this small museum, you can appreciate highly detailed, hand-carved miniature wood models of Midtown and Lower Manhattan; explore the past, present, and future of the skyscraper—from New York City's Empire State Building to Dubai's Burj Khalifa (taller than the Empire State Building and Chicago's Willis Tower combined); and examine the history of the Twin Towers at the World Trade Center. The museum's exhibits continue to evolve, so expect models of current or future buildings, videos, drawings, floor plans, and talks that reveal the influence of history, real estate, and individuals on shaping city skylines. ⊠ *39 Battery Pl., across from Museum of Jewish Heritage, Financial District* ☎ *212/968–1961* ⊕ *www.skyscraper.org* ⊠ *$5* ⊗ *Closed Mon., Tues.* Ⓜ *4, 5 to Bowling Green.*

South Street Seaport Historic District

HISTORIC SITE | Had this charming cobblestone corner of the city not been declared a historic district in 1977, the city's largest concentration of early-19th-century commercial buildings would have been destroyed. In recent years, the landmarked district has undergone a thorough makeover as a culinary and high-end shopping destination, with seasonal markets, installations, and live entertainment.

At the intersection of Fulton and Water Streets, the gateway to the seaport, is the **Titanic Memorial Lighthouse,** a small white lighthouse that commemorates the sinking of the RMS *Titanic* in 1912. Beyond the lighthouse, Fulton Street turns into a cobblestone pedestrian mall. On the south side of Fulton is the seaport's architectural centerpiece, **Schermerhorn Row,** a redbrick terrace of Georgian- and Federal-style warehouses and countinghouses built from 1810 to 1812. Cross South Street to **Pier 16,** where historic 19th- and 20th-century ships are docked. Pier 16 also is the departure point for various seasonal cruises. (Ship tours are included in the admission to the **South Street Seaport Museum**).

To the north are **Pier 17** and the renovated Tin Building, previously the longtime site of the Fulton Fish Market. Since 2018, the pier is a multilevel dining and office complex with a 60,000-square-foot rooftop that's open to the public and programmed with live shows in summer.

Financial District ☎ *212/732–8257 for event and shopping info* ⊕ *www.south-streetseaport.com* Ⓜ *2, 3, 4, 5, A, C, J, Z to Fulton St.*

South Street Seaport Museum

MUSEUM | FAMILY | Head to this unique Manhattan museum, housed inside Schermerhorn Row's early 19th-century brick buildings, to understand the history of the South Street Seaport—and its importance in making New York the ultimate commercial harbor of early America. The museum's visitor center at 12 Fulton Street leads you to fascinating exhibits within the carefully preserved, landmarked spaces, and ties into displays at the printing house around the corner (211 Water Street) and inside Cannon's Walk (206 Front Street). Many find that the Seaport Museum's main attractions, however, are the the five restored tall ships docked in the harbor at Pier 16. Admission to the museum includes visits (weather permitting) on the 1907 lightship *Ambrose* and the 1885 ship *Wavertree.* There are also public sailings of the 1885 schooner *Pioneer.* The museum organizes walking tours of the area, too. (Creative non-fiction lovers take note: Joseph Mitchell's collection of early New York stories, *Up in the Old Hotel,* brings to life tales from the neighborhood and the hotel that once occupied some of today's South Street Seaport Museum spaces.) ⊠ *12 Fulton St., between Water and South Sts., Financial District* ☎ *212/748–8600* ⊕ *www.southstreetseaportmuseum.org* ⊠ *$12* Ⓜ *2, 3, 4, 5, A, C, J, Z to Fulton St.*

St. Paul's Chapel

RELIGIOUS SITE | For more than a year after the 2001 World Trade Center attacks, the fence of St. Paul's Chapel served as a shrine for visitors seeking solace. People from around the world left tokens of grief and support, or signed one of the large dropcloths that hung from the fence. After serving as a 24-hour refuge where rescue and recovery workers could eat, pray, rest, and receive counseling, the chapel—which amazingly suffered no damage on 9/11—reopened to the public in fall 2002. Open since 1766, St. Paul's is the oldest public building in continuous use in Manhattan and part of the Trinity Church Wall Street parish. Free guided chapel tours are offered Friday at 3 pm. ⊠ *209 Broadway, at Fulton St., Financial District* ☎ *212/602–0800* ⊕ *www.trinity-wallstreet.org/about/stpaulschapel* Ⓜ *2, 3, 4, 5, A, C, J, Z to Fulton St.; E to World Trade Center.*

★ Staten Island Ferry

TRANSPORTATION SITE (AIRPORT/BUS/FERRY/TRAIN) | Some 70,000 people ride the free ferry daily to Staten Island, one of the city's five boroughs, and you too can join them for the city's most scenic commute. Without paying a cent, you get phenomenal views of the Lower Manhattan skyline, the Statue of Liberty, and Ellis Island during the 25-minute cruise across New York Harbor. You also pass tugboats, freighters, and cruise ships—a reminder that this is very much still a working harbor. The ferry sails every 15–30 minutes (24 hours a day, 365 days a year) from the Whitehall Terminal at Whitehall and South Streets, near the east end of Battery Park. You must disembark once you reach the opposite terminal, but you can just get back in line to board again if you don't plan to stay. A small concession stand on each ferry sells a few snacks and beverages (including beer). ⊠ *4 Whitehall St., Financial District* ☎ *212/639–9675* ⊕ *www.siferry.com* ➔ *Free* Ⓜ *1 to South Ferry; R, W to Whitehall St.; 4, 5 to Bowling Green.*

★ Statue of Liberty

MEMORIAL | For millions of immigrants, the first glimpse of America was the Statue of Liberty, and today it remains a powerful symbol of American ideals. *Liberty Enlightening the World,* as the statue is officially named, was presented to the United States in 1886 as a gift from France. The 152-foot-tall figure was

sculpted by Frédéric-Auguste Bartholdi and erected around an iron skeleton engineered by Gustave Eiffel. It stands atop an 89-foot pedestal designed by Richard Morris Hunt, with Emma Lazarus's sonnet "The New Colossus" ("Give me your tired, your poor, your huddled masses...") inscribed on a bronze plaque at the base.

There is no admission fee for either the Statue of Liberty or Ellis Island, but the ferry ride (which goes round-trip from Battery Park to Liberty Island to Ellis Island) costs $18.50 (includes entrance to the statue's pedestal and museum) or $21.50 (also includes access to the statue's crown via a narrow, twisting staircase). Ferries leave from Battery Park (and from Liberty State Park in New Jersey) every 30–45 minutes depending on the time of year (buy your tickets online at ⊕ *www.statuecruises.com*). There are often long lines, so arrive early, especially if you have a timed-entry ticket (strongly recommended; tickets sell out, especially to see the crown). A new museum about the statue's history and legacy, with artifacts including the original torch, is set to open in mid-2019. There is a pleasant indoor-outdoor café on Liberty Island. ⊠ *Liberty Island, Financial District* ☎ *212/363–3200, 877/523–9849 ticket reservations* ⊕ *www.libertyellisfoundation.org* ➔ *Free; ferry $18.50 round-trip (includes Ellis Island), crown tickets additional $3* Ⓜ *4, 5 to Bowling Green; 1 to South Ferry; R, W to Whitehall St.*

Stone Street Historic District

HISTORIC SITE | Amid skyscrapers, the two low-rise blocks of bars and restaurants along historic Stone Street feel more like a village than the center of the financial universe. In the summer, benches and long tables blanket the cobblestone street for a more convivial mood, especially on Thursday and Friday nights. This was Manhattan's first paved street, and today the cluster of buildings along here—with South William and Pearl Streets, and Coenties Alley—make up the Stone Street Historic District. ✉ *Stone, S. William, and Pearl Sts., and Coenties Alley, Financial District* [M] *R, W to Whitehall St.; 1 to South Ferry; 4, 5 to Bowling Green.*

Ten House

MEMORIAL | Just across Liberty Street from the World Trade Center site, the "Ten House" firehouse is officially known as Ladder Company 10 and Engine Company 10. On the morning of September 11, 2001, firefighters on duty here were among the first to respond to New York's terrorist attacks. The companies lost six heroes that day. The "Ten House Bravest Memorial" stands inside the firehouse to commemorate their ultimate sacrifice, and that of other Ten House heroes. Around the corner on Greenwich Street, the 56-foot-long bronze bas-relief FDNY Memorial Wall serves as a tribute to 343 firefighters who perished on 9/11. ✉ *124 Liberty St., at Greenwich St., Financial District* [M] *2, 3, 4, 5, A, C, J, Z to Fulton St.; E to World Trade Center; 1, R, W to Cortlandt St.*

Trinity Church

RELIGIOUS SITE | Occupying a section of land originally granted in 1705 by Queen Anne of England, Trinity Church is considered one of the first and finest examples of Gothic Revival architecture in America. This Episcopal church (the third on this site) was consecrated in 1846 and remained the city's tallest structure until 1890. Among its notable features are its three sets of enormous bronze doors depicting religious and early New York history, and some of the earliest examples of American-made stained glass. The churchyard contains the city's oldest carved gravestone (Richard Churcher, 1681); on its south side, Alexander Hamilton is buried under a white-stone pyramid, not far from a monument commemorating steamboat inventor Robert Fulton (buried in the Livingston family vault with his wife). Trinity's nave is closed for renovation and should reopen by spring 2020; the small Chapel of All Saints remains open to visitors, along with the churchyard. ✉ *74 Trinity Pl., entrance at Broadway and Wall St., Financial District* ☎ *212/602–0800* 🌐 *www.trinitywallstreet.org* [M] *2, 3, 4, 5 to Wall St.; 1, R, W to Rector St.; J, Z to Broad St.*

🍴 Restaurants

The southern tip of the island was once dominated by skyscraper-bound office workers, and starved for recreation and nightlife. But in recent years, FiDi has emerged as a buzzy home to exciting new bars and restaurants, plus parks and waterfront attractions, all intermingled with the neighborhood's venerable steak houses and homey pubs.

Adrienne's Pizza Bar

$$ | **ITALIAN** | **FAMILY** | It's hip to be square at this downtown pizzeria that occupies a long, narrow space with modern decor: father-and-son team Harry and Peter Poulakakos's square (also known as Grandma) pies are worth the trek and are a convenient stop en route to the Statue of Liberty. They also do a mean traditional round pizza, and first-timers should opt for the signature Old Fashioned: thin, crispy crust loaded with tangy tomato sauce, fresh mozzarella, and Parmesan cheese. **Known for:** square, Grandma-style pizza; location way downtown; not-so-friendly service. [$] *Average main: $17* ✉ *54 Stone St., near Hanover Sq., Financial District* ☎ *212/248–3838* 🌐 *www.adriennespizzabarnyc.com* [M] *R, W to Whitehall St.; 4, 5 to Bowling Green.*

Delmonico's

$$$$ | **STEAKHOUSE** | The oldest continually operating restaurant in New York City (since 1837), elegant Delmonico's is steeped in history. It was Manhattan's first fine-dining establishment, with an inventive 19th-century chef de cuisine whose most famous dishes, including eggs Benedict, lobster Newburg, and

The names of those lost on September 11th are commemorated on Memorial Plaza, at the former site of the Twin Towers.

Baked Alaska, are still served. **Known for:** outstanding steak and seafood selection; classic ambience and decor; vast wine selection. $ *Average main: $38* ✉ *56 Beaver St., at William St., Financial District* ☎ *212/509-1114* ⊕ *www.delmonicosny.com* ☯ *Closed Sun. No lunch Sat.* Ⓜ *2, 3 to Wall St.; R to Whitehall St.; 4, 5 to Bowling Green; J, Z to Broad St.*

Financier Patisserie

$ | **CAFÉ** | On the cobblestone pedestrian street that has become the Financial District's restaurant row, this charming pâtisserie serves excellent pastries and delicious savory foods, like mushroom bisque, salads, and hot or cold sandwiches. After lunch, relax with a cappuccino and a *financier* (almond tea cake). **Known for:** exquisite pastries; light lunches; weekday hot spot. $ *Average main: $7* ✉ *62 Stone St., between Mill La. and Hanover Sq., Financial District* ☎ *212/344-5600* ⊕ *www.financierpastries.com* ☯ *No dinner* Ⓜ *2, 3 to Wall St., 4, 5 to Bowling Green; J, Z to Broad St.*

Harry's NYC

$$$ | **STEAKHOUSE** | Its noise-dampening acoustics and maze of underground nooks combine to make Harry's Steak—the fine-dining half of the restaurant (Harry's Café is more casual, but the menu is the same)—one of the city's most intimate steak houses. Settle into a leather booth and start with a shrimp cocktail or other classic appetizer before dining on your favorite cut of beef or one of the fish and pasta options. **Known for:** prime aged porterhouse for two; dark wood-meets-leather interior; weekend brunch. $ *Average main: $35* ✉ *1 Hanover Sq., between Stone and Pearl Sts., Financial District* ☎ *212/785-9200* ⊕ *www.harrysnyc.com* ☯ *Closed Sun.* Ⓜ *4, 5 to Bowling Green; 2, 3 to Wall St.; J, Z to Broad St.*

Manhatta

$$$$ | **AMERICAN** | Enter at street level and rise 60 stories to experience both an exceptional menu and incomparable views at this 2018 addition to the upscale Financial District restaurant scene. The lunch and dinner menus are both short,

World Trade Center Site

On September 11, 2001, terrorist hijackers steered two jets into the World Trade Center's Twin Towers, setting them ablaze and causing their collapse, killing 2,753 people and injuring countless others. The 16 acres of fenced-in rubble and debris that evolved into a construction zone known as "Ground Zero" quickly became a memorial unto itself, a place where visitors and those who lost loved ones could mourn and reflect on what was the single most deadly foreign attack ever to happen on American soil. Exactly a decade later, the 9/11 Memorial Plaza opened, giving thousands of annual visitors a solemn, dedicated place to commemorate the events of that infamous day. After many delays, the accompanying underground National 9/11 Memorial Museum opened in 2014, on the same bedrock once used to support the Twin Towers' foundation. It serves as a fitting, if somber, home to an array of artifacts from 9/11 and its aftermath. The Memorial Plaza's twin reflecting pools are bordered by skyscrapers: the 1,776-foot One World Trade Center, and Towers 3 and 4, each designed by renowned architects and rising 80 and 72 stories, respectively. The site also includes the WTC Transportation Hub, known as the "Oculus," a soaring white-ribbed space designed by Santiago Calatrava.

Known for a time as "Freedom Tower," the 104-story One WTC has a roof that's 1,368 feet tall—a height identical to the original 1 WTC, the "north tower." (The south tower, or original 2 WTC, stood 1,362 feet tall.) An illuminated antenna further increases the skyscraper's height to the symbolic height of 1,776 feet, earning it the rank of tallest building in the Western Hemisphere. Designed by award-winning architect David Childs, One WTC opened to tenants in 2014, while One World Observatory, on its 100th, 101st, and 102nd floors, opened the following year. With its angular, mirrored-glass facade, the Fumihiko Maki–designed 4 WTC anchors the southeastern corner of the complex, and in 2013 was the first tower to open on the site. On its east side, 3 WTC was completed in 2018. At the site's northeast corner, at the corner of Vesey and Church Streets, 2 WTC construction has faced several major delays, and its opening date has yet to be announced.

North of 3 WTC stands the eye-catching Oculus, which serves as the terminal for New Jersey's PATH trains and an underground link to the office and retail center Brookfield Place, as well as 10 subway lines and the Fulton Center transit and retail complex. Inspired by the image of a bird in flight, the building features massive white steel "wings" extending from its riblike substructure. The largely column-free interior and glass-paneled roof allow natural light into the terminal's lower floors. The multilevel hub connects underground to each tower, and offers more than 360,000 square feet of shops and restaurants. As you plan your visit, set aside time to visit other key parts of the 9/11 story, such as St. Paul's Chapel, the 9/11 Tribute Museum, and the "Ten House" firehouse on Liberty Street.

allowing great nuance and care for each dish of seasonal ingredients, prepared with delicate touches of French flair. **Known for:** open kitchen; panoramic high-rise view; no tipping. [$] *Average main: $78* ✉ *28 Liberty St., between Nassau and William Sts., Financial District* ☎ *212/230–5788* 🌐 *www.manhattarestaurant.com* [M] *2, 3, 4, 5 to Wall St.; A, C, J, Z to Fulton St.*

Nobu New York Downtown

$$$$ | **JAPANESE** | At this impressive location in a unique setting of Botticino marble that's part of a century-old building lobby, the sushi stalwart is as bustling and taste bud–tantalizing as ever, serving the innovative Japanese cuisine that namesake master chef Nobu Matsuhisa made famous (though he's rarely in attendance these days). Dishes like fresh yellowtail sashimi with jalapeño, rock shrimp tempura, or miso-marinated Chilean sea bass continue to draw huge crowds. **Known for:** trendy crowd; high-quality sushi; omakase tasting menu. [$] *Average main: $39* ✉ *195 Broadway, at Fulton St., Financial District* ☎ *212/219–0500* 🌐 *www.noburestaurants.com* [M] *2, 3, 4, 5, A, C, J, Z to Fulton St.; E to World Trade Center.*

Ulysses

$ | **AMERICAN** | Squeezed between skyscrapers and the towering New York Stock Exchange, Stone Street is a two-block restaurant oasis that feels more like a village than the center of the financial universe. After the market closes, Wall Streeters head to Ulysses, a big, popular pub with 12 beers on tap and more than 50 bottled beers, plus drink and seasonal specials, and live music. **Known for:** above-average pub grub; lively outdoor atmosphere in summer; beer selection. [$] *Average main: $12* ✉ *95 Pearl St., near Hanover Sq., Financial District* ☎ *212/482–0400* 🌐 *www.ulyssesnyc.com* [M] *R, W to Whitehall St.; J, Z to Broad St.; 2, 3 to Wall St.*

Hotels

Andaz Wall Street

$ | **HOTEL** | **FAMILY** | If space is a priority, head to the southern tip of Manhattan: this sleek chain hotel has generous rooms with large windows, oak floors, and extra-large bathrooms. **Pros:** free Wi-Fi, snacks, and nonalcoholic beverages; excellent, intuitive lighting controls; good value. **Cons:** limited nightlife in the neighborhood; in-house restaurant not open every day; location is a bit far from many major sites. [$] *Rooms from: $299* ✉ *75 Wall St., Financial District* ☎ *212/590–1234* 🌐 *www.hyatt.com* 🛏 *253 rooms* 🍴 *No meals* [M] *2, 3 to Wall St.*

★ The Beekman

$$$$ | **HOTEL** | After sitting abandoned for many years, this historic late-19th-century downtown office building was reborn as a chic hotel that channels old New York, with a popular, clubby lobby bar and restaurants by award-winning chef Tom Colicchio and restaurateur Keith McNally. **Pros:** gorgeous design with notable atrium and lots of character; beautiful, buzzy restaurants and bar; fantastic concierge team. **Cons:** service is inconsistent; lobby bar can be overcrowded; pricey for the location. [$] *Rooms from: $699* ✉ *123 Nassau St., Financial District* ☎ *212/233–2300* 🌐 *www.thebeekman.com* 🛏 *287 rooms* 🍴 *No meals* [M] *2, 3, 4, 5, A, C, J, Z to Fulton St.*

Conrad New York

$ | **HOTEL** | **FAMILY** | A pleasant surprise in a quiet Battery Park City location, this suites-only hotel has many coveted amenities: significant square footage, a breezy rooftop bar, and access to green space in nearby Hudson River Park. **Pros:** spacious rooms with separate living space; very family-friendly; near movie theater and restaurants. **Cons:** decor is understated; removed from Midtown attractions; fee for valet and self-parking. [$] *Rooms from: $291* ✉ *102 North*

End Ave., between Vesey and Murray Sts., Financial District ☎ *212/945–0100* 🌐 *www.conradnewyork.com* 🛏 *463 suites* 🍴 *No meals* [M] *1, 2, 3, A, C to Chambers St.; E to World Trade Center.*

Gild Hall

$ | **HOTEL** | Elegant, cozy, and charming, this boutique sleep from Thompson Hotels offers good value and good design, including beds with padded leather headboards and tartan throw blankets. **Pros:** central Financial District location; chic lobby; stylish room design. **Cons:** small rooms for the price; untraditional location; scant dining options nearby. [$] *Rooms from: $275* ✉ *15 Gold St., at Platt St., Financial District* ☎ *212/232–7700* 🌐 *www.thompsonhotels.com* 🛏 *130 rooms* 🍴 *No meals* [M] *2, 3, 4, 5, A, C, J, Z to Fulton St.*

W New York – Downtown

$ | **HOTEL** | In the heart of the Financial District, this W outpost juxtaposes the neighborhood's historic architecture with sleek surfaces and minimalist style. **Pros:** near popular tourist attractions; restaurant offers some surprisingly affordable fare; modern workout room. **Cons:** no bathtubs in any rooms; not family-friendly; fee for Wi-Fi in rooms. [$] *Rooms from: $250* ✉ *8 Albany St., Financial District* ☎ *646/826–8600* 🌐 *www.wnewyork-downtown.com* 🛏 *217 rooms* 🍴 *No meals* [M] *1, R, W to Rector St.; 4, 5 to Wall St.*

The Wagner at the Battery

$$ | **HOTEL** | **FAMILY** | This elegant hotel, formerly a Ritz-Carlton, provides good-size luxury accommodations—along with some of the best views in the city, including rooms with sweeping vistas of the New York harbor that include the Statue of Liberty and Ellis Island. **Pros:** excellent service; pet- and kid-friendly; unrivaled harbor views. **Cons:** removed from Midtown tourist sights; limited nighttime activities; decor is somewhat nondescript. [$] *Rooms from: $425* ✉ *2 West St., at Battery Park, Financial District* ☎ *212/344–0800* 🌐 *www.thewagnerhotel.com* 🛏 *298 rooms* 🍴 *No meals* [M] *1, R, W to Rector St.; 4, 5 to Bowling Green.*

🍸 Nightlife

The Bar Room

BARS/PUBS | The same year that the Brooklyn Bridge opened (1883), the Temple Court building welcomed its first visitors—though back then it was an office tower, not the lushly restored hotel (The Beekman) it became in 2016. The Bar Room is among the neighborhood's highlights, a splendid ground-floor lounge where libations are priced more for the landmark setting and elegant furnishings than for their quality. Nevertheless, there's no other hotel bar in New York where you can gaze up a nine-story atrium lined with ornate ironwork while sipping a glass of bubbles; just reserve prime seats in advance. ✉ *The Beekman, 5 Beekman St., at Park Row, Financial District* ☎ *212/658–1848* 🌐 *www.thebeekman.com* [M] *R, W to City Hall; 4, 5, 6 to Brooklyn Bridge–City Hall; 2, 3, A, C, J, Z to Fulton St.*

★ The Dead Rabbit

BARS/PUBS | For exquisite cocktails without the dress code or pretentious door policy typical of some New York cocktail dens, venture to the tip of Manhattan for a night of Irish hospitality in a 19th-century-inspired saloon. The ground-floor taproom serves craft beers and whiskeys of the world, while the upstairs parlor shakes and stirs craft cocktails, many utilizing Irish whiskey—accompanied by ragtime music played live on the piano. ✉ *30 Water St., between Broad St. and Coenties Slip, Financial District* ☎ *646/422–7906* 🌐 *www.deadrabbitnyc.com* [M] *1 to South Ferry; R, W to Whitehall St.*

★ Pier A Harbor House

BARS/PUBS | Jutting out from Battery Park, this national landmark served both the harbor police and fire departments, but since 2014 it has been a uniquely restored public complex. Enjoy the nautical details and refurbished original decor across its four areas, each serving seafood and pub food. The Long Bar and the Oyster Bar occupy the main floor and outdoor deck—which gets crowded on summer evenings for the mesmerizing views. The teak-lined, compact, upstairs Commissioner's Bar has a balcony perfect for sipping from the champagne and aperitif menu. The pier's finest cocktails are served in the speakeasy-style Blacktail, pouring Cuban-inspired libations concocted by experts from the Dead Rabbit. ✉ *22 Battery Pl., on west side of Battery Park, Financial District* ☎ *212/785–0153* ⊕ *www.piera.com* Ⓜ *4, 5 to Bowling Green.*

The Wooly Public

BARS/PUBS | Despite the elephant- and woolly mammoth–themed art decorating the walls, the Wooly Public takes its name from the magnificent Woolworth Building in which it's housed. The atmosphere invites both after-work socializing or everyday imbibing of fine cocktails, wine, and beer in the spacious, classically styled bar area. There are weekday happy hour specials (for both drinks and oysters), and DJs and live musicians provide jazz and other mostly mellow tunes on Thursday, Friday, and Saturday evenings. ✉ *9 Barclay St., between Broadway and Church St., Financial District* ☎ *212/571–2930* ⊕ *www.thewoolypublic.com* Ⓜ *R, W to City Hall; 2, 3 to Park Pl.; A, C to Chambers St.; E to World Trade Center.*

 Performing Arts

MUSIC
Winter Garden at Brookfield Place

MUSIC | FAMILY | Brookfield Place, an upscale shopping-and-dining complex across the street from the World Trade Center, provides a showcase for an entirely free program of performing and visual arts, spanning occasional live music and Saturday-morning shows for kids, as well as site-specific installations (with an emphasis on commissioned works), poetry readings, film screenings, and more. Events are presented within Brookfield Place's spectacular 10-story glass-covered Winter Garden atrium, or on its outdoor plaza overlooking the Hudson (weather permitting). In winter that includes an outdoor ice-skating rink. ✉ *230 Vesey St. , at West St., Financial District* ☎ *212/978–1698* ⊕ *www.brookfieldplaceny.com/events* Ⓜ *E to World Trade Center; R, W to Cortlandt St.; A, C to Chambers St.; 2, 3 to Park Pl.; 4, 5 to Fulton St.*

READINGS AND LECTURES
Poets House

READINGS/LECTURES | Situated in a bright and airy building in the residential area of Battery Park City and near the Hudson River, this reading room is an open resource for all ages, with a 70,000-volume library, readings, and other poetry-centric events. ✉ *Battery Park City, 10 River Terr., at Murray St., Financial District* ☎ *212/431–/920* ⊕ *www.poetshouse.org* Ⓜ *1, 2, 3, A, C to Chambers St.*

🛍 Shopping

Known primarily as the home of Wall Street, the Financial District has a few high-end boutiques around Wall Street; better browsing awaits around the South Street Seaport. However, Westfield Place (also known as the Oculus, named after its noteworthy design feature) covers several levels underneath the 9/11 Memorial Plaza. It's a sprawling, upscale mall that has an Apple Store, notable restaurants, and other shops. It connects by a long underground passage to Brookfield Place (previously the Winter Garden), which also has a collection of upscale stores and downtown's best food court.

BARGAIN SHOPPING
★ Century 21

DEPARTMENT STORES | For many New Yorkers this downtown fixture remains the mother lode of discount shopping. Seven floors are crammed with everything from designer shoes to half-price cashmere sweaters to high-end housewares, though you have to sift through racks and fight crowds to find the gems. Devoted shoppers with ample time can uncover some dazzling finds. Don't miss the children's section either, or basement-level luggage bargains. ■ TIP➜ **If you're on the Upper West Side or in Downtown Brooklyn, you can check out more discount shopping at the other two locations, at Broadway and 66th or at City Point, respectively.** ⊠ *22 Cortlandt St., between Broadway and Church St., Financial District* ☎ *212/227–9092* ⊕ *www.c21stores.com* Ⓜ *R, W to Cortlandt St.*

CLOTHING
Kamakura Shirts

CLOTHING | Located amid the high-rise office buildings of the Financial District, the high-end Brookfield Place shopping center seems like an approrpriate home for a U.S. outpost of boutique Japanese shirtmakers Kamakura. Known for impeccable service and timeless style, the designer offers both made-to-measure and ready-to-wear men's dress shirts, as well as custom ties. ⊠ *Brookfield Place, 225 Liberty St., between South End Ave. and West St., Financial District* ☎ *212/619–2484* ⊕ *www.kamakurashirts.com* Ⓜ *R, W to Cortlandt St.; 2, 3, 4, 5, A, C, J, Z to Fulton St.*

GIFTS AND SOUVENIRS
City Store

GIFTS/SOUVENIRS | The official store of NYC sells anything and everything having to do with the city, from books and pamphlets to fun gifts. Pick up NYPD T-shirts, taxicab medallions, garbage truck toys, and dish towels silk-screened with the skyline. The store shuts at 5 pm weekdays and is closed weekends. ⊠ *1 Centre St., at Chambers St., Financial District* ☎ *212/386–0007* ⊕ *a856-citystore.nyc.gov* Ⓜ *4, 5, 6 to Brooklyn Bridge–City Hall.*

MALLS
Brookfield Place Mall

SHOPPING CENTERS/MALLS | Once called the Winter Garden, this space in the World Financial Center is still known for its towering palm trees, expansive views of New York Harbor and the 9/11 Memorial, and luxury stores, including downtown outlets for Gucci, Hermès, and Louis Vuitton, not to mention more down-to-earth shoppping at J. Crew, Bonobos, and Lululemon. There's also a downtown branch of Saks Fifth Avenue Men's Store. More interesting may be the food offerings, including the best food court downtown, Hudson Eats (which has Umami Burger, Black Seed Bagel, and Fuku, a fried chicken shop from from Momofuku restaurateur David Chang), among many other offerings. On the ground floor is Le District, a kind of Eataly for French cuisine. Together, they offer plenty of excellent food options to local office workers and tourists alike. Outside in summer is an outdoor dining area with food stands (and a bar); in winter it becomes an ice-skating rink. And there are events both during the week and on weekends year-round. ⊠ *230 Vesey St., immediately across West St. from the 9/11 Memorial Plaza, Flatiron District* ☎ *212/978–1673* ⊕ *bfplny.com* Ⓜ *Subway: E to World Trade Center; A, C to Chambers St.; 2, 3 to Park Pl.; R, W to Cortlandt St.; 4, 5 to Fulton St.*

The Oculus (*Westfield World Trade Center*)

SHOPPING CENTERS/MALLS | One typically talks about the Oculus as the expansive transportation hub housed under a soaring white riblike structure that looks like nothing less than some prehistoric skeleton. In truth, the interconnecting subway and commuter rail lines lie only at the periphery; what's actually under those ribs is a luxury shopping mall that houses stores from Apple, Breitling, Montblanc, Sephora, Tumi, and many more. Seasonal events and exhibits are hosted in the giant atrium floor. Dining offerings in the Oculus itself include Epicerie Boulud. You'll find the Italian gelateria Grom and the British sandwich chain Pret a Manger in the West Concourse, which leads to the PATH station to New Jersey. The Oculus is connected by an underground passage to the Fulton Center, which has a mezzanine-level food court with one of Lower Manhattan's two Shake Shacks. An expansive Eataly is in yet another connected building. ✉ *185 Greenwich St., between Fulton and Liberty Sts., Financial District* ☏ *212/284–9982* ⊕ *www.westfield.com/westfieldworldtradecenter* Ⓜ *Subway: E to World Trade Center; A, C to Chambers St.; 2, 3 to Park Pl.; R, W to Cortlandt St.; 4, 5 to Fulton St.*

TriBeCa

Tucked on the west side south of Canal Street, residential TriBeCa (the *Triangle Below Canal* Street) has a quieter vibe than most other Manhattan neighborhoods. Walk the photogenic streets, especially the stretch of Federal row houses on Harrison Street, and you'll understand why celebrities and other moneyed New Yorkers own apartments here. The two-block-long Staple Street, with its connecting overhead walkway, is a favorite of urban cinematographers. Although TriBeCa residents' wealth is often hidden behind grand cast-iron facades, you can get a taste of it at posh neighborhood restaurants, cocktail bars, and boutiques, or at the star-studded Tribeca Film Festival every spring.

◉ Sights

★ Hudson River Park
NATIONAL/STATE PARK | FAMILY | The quiet green spaces of New York City are treasured by locals, and one of the best is Hudson River Park, a 5-mile path from Battery Place to 59th Street. This riverside stretch, incorporating the piers that jut out into the Hudson, has been renovated into a landscaped park with walking and cycling paths, a seasonal minigolf course, dog runs, and skate parks. The TriBeCa portion consists of Piers 25 and 26 and has picnic spaces, playgrounds, and a sand volleyball court. The areas adjacent to the West Village (Piers 45 and 46) and near Chelsea (Piers 63 and 64) are equally attractive, with lots of spots for leisure and recreation. To the north, beginning at 72nd Street, is Riverside Park. ✉ *TriBeCa* ☏ *212/627–2020* ⊕ *www.hudsonriverpark.org* Ⓜ *1 to Franklin St. for TriBeCa section of the park.*

Postmasters Gallery
MUSEUM | This gallery, first opened in the East Village in 1984 and open in TriBeCa since 2013, shows new and established conceptual artists of all ages. Postmasters exhibits both young and established artists working in all media, though it seeks out new forms of creative expression that are reflective of the current time. ✉ *54 Franklin St., between Broadway and Lafayette St., TriBeCa* ☏ *212/727–3323* ⊕ *www.postmastersart.com* ✆ *Free* ⊘ *Closed Sun., Mon.* Ⓜ *6, J, N, Q, R, W, Z to Canal St.*

Woolworth Building
BUILDING | Until 40 Wall Street stole the title in 1930, the 792-foot, neo-Gothic Woolworth Building, opened in 1913, was the world's tallest building. For security purposes, the spectacular lobby is no longer open to the public on a daily basis, though special open-house events and architecture tours are available through a few companies, including

WoolworthTours (starting at $20 for a half-hour tour ⊕ *woolworthtours.com*). The lobby is home to a stained-glass skylight and carved wooden sculptures set into the portals to the left and right: one represents namesake F. W. Woolworth counting his nickels and dimes; another depicts the architect, Cass Gilbert, cradling in his arms a model of his creation. ✉ *233 Broadway, between Park Pl. and Barclay St., TriBeCa* ☎ *203/966–9663* ⊕ *woolworthtours.com* ☞ *$20 tour* Ⓜ *2, 3 to Park Pl.; R, W to City Hall; E to World Trade Center.*

🍴 Restaurants

TriBeCa and its restaurants are a playground for the rich and famous. Fortunately, glamorous dining rooms in converted warehouses have been joined by more casual spots.

Bubby's

$$ | **AMERICAN** | **FAMILY** | Neighborhood crowds clamoring for coffee and freshly squeezed juice line up for brunch at this TriBeCa mainstay, but Bubby's is good for lunch and dinner, too, if you're in the mood for comfort food like mac 'n' cheese or fried chicken. The dining room is homey and cozy, with big windows; in summer, patrons sit at tables outside with their dogs. **Known for:** true TriBeCa neighborhood spot; casual atmosphere; plenty of brunch options. Ⓢ *Average main: $18* ✉ *120 Hudson St., at N. Moore St., TriBeCa* ☎ *212/219–0666* ⊕ *www.bubbys.com* Ⓜ *1 to Franklin St.*

Locanda Verde

$$$ | **ITALIAN** | Run by one of Manhattan's top chefs, Andrew Carmellini, this is a consistently fine option for satisfying fare in the neighborhood. The Robert De Niro–backed restaurant inside the Greenwich Hotel is warm and welcoming, with accents of brick and wood and large windows that open to the street, weather permitting, while the menu is full of inspired Italian comfort food that

hits the mark. **Known for:** exquisite pasta dishes; small plates; occasional celebrity sightings. Ⓢ *Average main: $27* ✉ *377 Greenwich St., at N. Moore St., TriBeCa* ☎ *212/925–3797* ⊕ *www.locandaverde-nyc.com* Ⓜ *1 to Franklin St.*

Marc Forgione

$$$ | **AMERICAN** | Restaurant success runs in chef Marc Forgione's blood—his father was one of the New York food scene megastars with his 1980s restaurant, An American Place—but he more than holds his own at this neighborhood restaurant that continues to attract crowds for the ambitious, creative new American cuisine. The menu changes frequently, but whatever you order will be bold, flavorful, and inventive without a hint of preciousness. **Known for:** elevated American fare with worldly influences; superb seafood offerings; romantic atmosphere. Ⓢ *Average main: $31* ✉ *134 Reade St., between Hudson and Greenwich Sts., TriBeCa* ☎ *212/941–9401* ⊕ *www.marcforgione.com* ◷ *No lunch* Ⓜ *1, 2, 3 to Chambers St.*

The Odeon

$$$ | **FRENCH** | **FAMILY** | New Yorkers change hangouts faster than they can speed-dial, but this spot has managed to maintain its quality and flair since 1980: it still feels like *the* spot in TriBeCa to get a late-night bite. The neo–Art Deco room is still packed daily with local office workers and nightly with revelers who appreciate the classic bistro look and fare. **Known for:** perpetually cool late-night downtown hangout; better-than-average bistro fare; good wine list and cocktails. Ⓢ *Average main: $28* ✉ *145 West Broadway, between Duane and Thomas Sts., TriBeCa* ☎ *212/233–0507* ⊕ *www.theodeonrestaurant.com* Ⓜ *1, 2, 3, A, C to Chambers St.*

Tamarind Tribeca

$$$ | **INDIAN** | Many consider Tamarind to be one of Manhattan's best Indian restaurants, and the elegant atmosphere makes it a different experience

from many other NYC Indian eateries. Forsaking the usual brass, beads, sitar, and darkness, the dining room is full of windows and natural light. **Known for:** consistently delicious and sometimes unique Indian fare; multiregional food; elegant setting. [$] *Average main: $28* ✉ *99 Hudson St., at Franklin St., TriBeCa* ☎ *212/775–9000* 🌐 *www.tamarindrestaurantsnyc.com* [M] *1 to Franklin St.; A, C, E to Canal St.*

Hotels

AKA Smyth Tribeca

$$ | HOTEL | Located almost on top of a convenient subway stop, this thoroughly modern hotel with an inviting lobby perfect for lounging makes TriBeCa a welcoming landing spot for visitors. **Pros:** refined service; notable restaurant; excellent subway access. **Cons:** location is far from Midtown attractions; only a frosted-glass partition divides bathroom from sleeping area; bathrooms could have better lighting. [$] *Rooms from: $375* ✉ *85 West Broadway, between Chambers and Warren Sts., TriBeCa* ☎ *212/587–7000* 🌐 *www.stayaka.com/aka smyth tribeca* 🛏 *100 rooms* 🍴 *No meals* [M] *1, 2, 3, A, C to Chambers St.*

Duane Street Hotel

$ | HOTEL | Amid TriBeCa's historic warehouses and trendy art galleries sits this boutique hotel, a fashionable addition to the neighborhood. **Pros:** good value for the area; complimentary bikes provided; stylish rooms with hardwood floors. **Cons:** off-site gym; no 24-hour room service; rooms are on the small side. [$] *Rooms from: $250* ✉ *130 Duane St., at Church St., TriBeCa* ☎ *212/964–4600* 🌐 *www.duanestreethotel.com* 🛏 *43 rooms* 🍴 *No meals* [M] *1, 2, 3, A, C to Chambers St.*

Four Seasons New York Downtown

$$$ | HOTEL | This slick property by the Four Seasons is a luxurious haven near the World Trade Center, with a modern residential-inspired design, a 75-foot indoor pool, an indulgent spa, and CUT restaurant by celebrity chef Wolfgang Puck. **Pros:** sleek design; excellent pool, spa, and gym; convenient (for downtown) location. **Cons:** expensive for the location; limited dining and nightlife options nearby; far from uptown sites and museums. [$] *Rooms from: $559* ✉ *27 Barclay St., TriBeCa* ☎ *646/880–1999* 🌐 *www.fourseasons.com/newyorkdowntown* 🛏 *161 rooms* 🍴 *No meals* [M] *A, C to Chambers St.; 2, 3 to Park Pl.*

The Frederick Hotel

$$ | HOTEL | Located at a busy TriBeCa intersection, the boutique Frederick Hotel is an ideal launching pad for exploring downtown neighborhoods. **Pros:** modern design with NYC touches in historic building; prime downtown location; solid on-site dining and bar. **Cons:** sometimes noisy location; compact rooms; narrow, circuitous hallways. [$] *Rooms from: $329* ✉ *95 West Broadway, at Chambers St., TriBeCa* ☎ *212/566–1900* 🌐 *www.frederickhotelnyc.com* 🛏 *131 rooms* 🍴 *No meals* [M] *1, 2, 3, A, C to Chambers St.*

★ The Greenwich Hotel

$$$$ | HOTEL | Understated and inviting, this boutique hotel manages to fly under the radar even though Robert De Niro is an owner and its rustic Italian restaurant, Locanda Verde, is a local favorite. **Pros:** fabulous restaurant (also available for room service); gorgeous pool; excellent service. **Cons:** some plumbing noise; high prices; the location is far from most subways. [$] *Rooms from: $625* ✉ *377 Greenwich St., between N. Moore and Franklin Sts., TriBeCa* ☎ *212/941–8900* 🌐 *www.thegreenwichhotel.com* 🛏 *88 rooms* 🍴 *No meals* [M] *1 to Franklin St.*

The Roxy Hotel

$$ | HOTEL | Formerly the Tribeca Grand, the Roxy is a stylish downtown property with an emphasis on art, music, and culture that has made it a neighborhood gathering place. **Pros:** great dining and bar scene with live jazz; vinyl record player upon request; complimentary tickets to the on-site Roxy Cinema. **Cons:** rooms get noise from restaurant below; bathrooms have slightly cold design; a bit sceney for some. $ *Rooms from: $395* ✉ *2 6th Ave., between Walker and White Sts., TriBeCa* ☎ *212/519–6000* ⊕ *www. roxyhotelnyc.com* ⚟ *201 rooms* ❝❞ *No meals* Ⓜ *A, C, E to Canal St.*

ⓨ Nightlife

B Flat

BARS/PUBS | The design is red-on-red here, and the Asian-style cocktails are particularly polished at this Japan-meets-1950s-America lounge. Listen to live jazz while nibbling on American and Japanese-inflected treats and sipping inventive libations with international twists. ✉ *277 Church St., between Franklin and White Sts., TriBeCa* ☎ *212/219–2970* ⊕ *www. bflat.info* Ⓜ *1 to Franklin St.; 6, A, C, E, J, N, Q, R, W, Z to Canal St.*

Brandy Library

BARS/PUBS | The most important book in this exquisite wood-paneled "library" is the leather-bound menu listing hundreds of brandies and single-malt scotches. The bottles are on handsome backlighted shelves, though, and you can learn what makes each of them special by chatting with the spirit sommelier—or by buying into one of the lounge's sophisticated tasting classes. ✉ *25 N. Moore St., between Varick and Hudson Sts., TriBeCa* ☎ *212/226–5545* ⊕ *www.brandylibrary. com* Ⓜ *1 to Franklin St.; A, C, E to Canal St.*

M1-5

BARS/PUBS | This lipstick-red, high-ceiling spot is a roomy lounge and playground (as in, billiards, shuffleboard, and darts). There are screens for sports, a long bar, and weekend dance parties—all without a cover charge. Extra points, too, for the bar's name, which cites TriBeCa's warehouse zoning law. ✉ *52 Walker St., between Broadway and Church St.,* *TriBeCa* ☎ *212/965–1701* ⊕ *www.m1-5. com* Ⓜ *6, A, C, E J, N, Q, R, W, Z to Canal St.*

Smith and Mills

BARS/PUBS | Attractive downtown Manhattanites frolic at this tiny gem of a gin mill, where debonair mixologists dispense elixirs (and oysters) from a bar hung with pots and pans. There are cozy table nooks for couples, and while the food is worth a visit, many locals come here late when a craft cocktail craving hits. ✉ *71 N. Moore St., between Hudson and Greenwich Sts., TriBeCa* ☎ *212/226–2515* ⊕ *www.smithandmills. com* Ⓜ *1 to Franklin St.; A, C, E to Canal St.*

Terroir Wine

WINE BARS—NIGHTLIFE | A neighborhood favorite, this fine wine bar is impressive to oenophiles and welcoming to everyone thanks to the extensive wine list, including options by the glass, bottle, or sizable tasting pours. The bar is easy to walk right by on charming Harrison Street, but once inside you will find seats at the bar for wine-centric conversations with the sharp staff or more private nooks for a romantic evening of wine and cheese. ✉ *24 Harrison St., between Greenwich and Hudson Sts., TriBeCa* ☎ *212/625–9463* ⊕ *wineisterroir.com* Ⓜ *1 to Franklin St.*

Tiny's and the Bar Upstairs

BARS/PUBS | In the heart of TriBeCa, this diminutive three-story town house dates all the way back to 1810. The ground floor is home to a restaurant with a wood-burning fireplace in the back, and food is served until late; upstairs, a pressed-copper bar provides an intimate place for cocktails and snacks. This is prime date territory, and Tiny's old-fashioned ambience is perfect for a romantic predinner cocktail. ✉ *135 West Broadway, between Duane and Thomas Sts., TriBeCa* ☎ *212/374–1135* ⊕ *tinysnyc.com* Ⓜ *1, 2, 3 to Chambers St.*

Ward III

BARS/PUBS | You can get a solid Negroni or Manhattan at this exposed-brick watering hole, but where the bar really shines is in its bespoke cocktails. Fight for a seat at the bar if possible to watch the sharply clad barkeeps whip up house specialties, or simply give them a few descriptive words ("spirit-forward," "something with bourbon," "light and refreshing") and let them create a cocktail on the spot to match your thirst. ✉ *111 Reade St., between West Broadway and Church St., TriBeCa* ☎ *212/240–9194* ⊕ *www.ward3. com* Ⓜ *1, 2, 3, A, C to Chambers St.*

✪ Performing Arts

Tribeca Performing Arts Center

ARTS CENTERS | **FAMILY** | The center celebrates theater (with a clever children's series) and dance but is primarily known for jazz. Highlights in Jazz and Lost Jazz Shrines are two of its special series. ✉ *199 Chambers St., between Greenwich and West Sts., TriBeCa* ☎ *212/220–1460 for tickets* ⊕ *www.tribecapac.org* Ⓜ *1, 2, 3, A, C to Chambers St.*

◖ Shopping

Known for its multimillion-dollar lofts and famous residents, TriBeCa is home to some of the most interesting boutiques in the city, though most are geared toward deep pockets, especially the design and clothing stores. Specialty shops still offer deals (usually seasonally), and browsing here may lead to occasional celebrity spotting.

BEAUTY

ONDA Beauty

SPA/BEAUTY | Part spa, part natural beauty boutique, this airy little shop has high standards for sourcing its products. From Ursa Major face wash to Rahua shampoo, only the highest quality—nontoxic, ethical, organic, all-natural—products make it onto the shelves. If you want to try any spa treatments, including facials and Reiki, be sure to book in advance. Side note: actor Naomi Watts is a co-owner. ✉ *117 West Broadway, between Duane and Reade Sts., TriBeCa* ☎ *646/870–9490* ⊕ *ondabeauty.com* Ⓜ *1, 2, 3 to Chambers St.*

CLOTHING

Issey Miyake

CLOTHING | This flagship, designed by Frank Gehry, attracts a nonfashion crowd who come just to gawk at his undulating, 25-foot-high titanium sculpture, *The Tornado.* Miyake's signature style has clothes that are sleek and slim fitting, and made from polyester or ultra-high-tech textiles. This store carries the entire runway collection, as well as Pleats Please and Issey Miyake Fete. ✉ *119 Hudson St., at N. Moore St., TriBeCa* ☎ *212/226–0100* ⊕ *www.tribecaisseymiyake.com* Ⓜ *1 to Franklin St.; A, C, E to Canal St.*

J.Crew Men's Shop at the Liquor Store

CLOTHING | It would be easy to walk right past this place and think it's a bar rather than an outpost of J.Crew for men, both because of the well-preserved watering-hole exterior and because it's filled with manly knickknacks like old hardcovers and vintage photographs. Some of the best finds are the limited-edition suits and cashmere sweaters, as well as non–J.Crew items like Barbour jackets and Ray-Bans. ✉ *235 West Broadway, at White St., TriBeCa* ☎ *212/226–5476* ⊕ *www.jcrew.com* Ⓜ *1 to Franklin St.; A, C, E to Canal St.*

La Garçonne

CLOTHING | The popular online shop has a brick-and-mortar space to display its well-edited collection of clean-lined designer duds in monochromatic hues—unlike the Web store, though, this one only carries women's clothes. Brands like Helmut Lang, Sara Lanzi, and Isabel Marant are perennial favorites. The minimalist, loftlike space also sells some home decor and beauty products. ✉ *465 Greenwich St., between Watts and*

Desbrosses Sts., TriBeCa ☎ 646/553–3303 ⊕ www.lagarconne.com Ⓜ 1 to Canal St.

Nili Lotan

CLOTHING | This Israeli-born designer worked for Ralph Lauren and Nautica before launching her own collection for women. Nili Lotan is known for her knitwear, drapey coats, and love of solid colors. Her whitewashed retail space also sells rare books. ⊠ 188 Duane St., between Greenwich and Hudson Sts., TriBeCa ☎ 212/219–8794 ⊕ www.nililotan.com Ⓜ 1, 2, 3 to Chambers St.

Steven Alan

CLOTHING | The TriBeca flagship of this beloved NYC designer known for his signature casual, cool sportswear is the place to come if your preferred uniform is a cashmere beanie, untucked plaid shirt, and skinny jeans. The rustic space stocks clothing for men and women and sells its own line alongside a curated collection of other designers like Demylee and Rains, as well as beauty products and home accessories. ⊠ 103 Franklin St., between West Broadway and Church St., TriBeCa ☎ 212/343–0692 ⊕ www.stevenalan.com Ⓜ 1 to Franklin St.

HOME DECOR
Korin

HOUSEHOLD ITEMS/FURNITURE | If you're serious about cooking, head to this specialty knife store in TriBeCa. Previously only open to the trade, it is one of the best places to shop for top-quality knives and tableware imported from Japan. ⊠ 57 Warren St., between West Broadway and Church St., TriBeCa ☎ 212/587–7021 ⊕ www.korin.com Ⓜ 1, 2, 3 to Chambers St.

SHOES, HANDBAGS, AND LEATHER GOODS
★ Shinola

SHOES/LUGGAGE/LEATHER GOODS | Proudly based in Detroit, this World War II–era shoe polish brand has been relaunched as a company that builds handcrafted watches, bicycles, leather goods, journals, and pet accessories. Shinola's TriBeCa flagship store also sells American-made products from other brands, such as Filson. ⊠ 177 Franklin St., between Greenwich and Hudson Sts., TriBeCa ☎ 917/728–3000 ⊕ www.shinola.com Ⓜ 1 to Franklin St.; A, C, E to Canal St.

WINE
Verve Wines

WINE/SPIRITS | Run by the former wine director of the outstanding Eleven Madison Park restaurant, this airy neighborhood wine shop brings a hospitality sensibility to its wine vending. From the whimsical neon sign in the window to the regular tasting events featuring local sommeliers, the shop is all about making the best wines in the world fun and accessible. ⊠ 24 Hubert St., between Greenwich and Washington Sts., TriBeCa ☎ 212/810–2899 ⊕ www.vervewine.com Ⓜ A, C, E to Canal St.; 1 to Franklin St.

Chapter 4

SOHO, NOLITA, LITTLE ITALY, AND CHINATOWN

Updated by
Caroline Trefler

◉ Sights	🍴 Restaurants	🛏 Hotels	🛍 Shopping	🍸 Nightlife
★★★☆☆	★★★★★	★★★☆☆	★★★★★	★★★☆☆

NEIGHBORHOOD SNAPSHOT

TOP EXPERIENCES

■ Browsing boutiques and people-watching in SoHo and NoLIta

■ Ogling the out-of-the-ordinary produce and seafood in Chinatown

■ Gallery-hopping in SoHo

■ Eating dim sum in Chinatown

■ Sipping a cocktail in NoLIta

GETTING HERE

SoHo (*South of Ho*uston) is bounded by Houston Street, Canal Street, 6th Avenue, and Lafayette Street. To the east, NoLIta (*No*rth of *Little Ita*ly) is contained by Houston, the Bowery, Kenmare, and Lafayette. Plenty of subways service the area: take the 6, C, or E to Spring Street; the N, R, or W to Prince Street; or the B, D, F, or M to Broadway–Lafayette Street. For Chinatown, farther south, take the 6, J, N, Q, R, W, or Z to Canal Street, or the B or D to Grand Street.

PLANNING YOUR TIME

Most shops SoHo and NoLIta don't open until 10 or 11 am. Most SoHo galleries are closed on Sunday, but it's almost always a madhouse on weekend afternoons because of the stores, though weekdays are somewhat less frenetic. NoLIta is almost always calmer and less crowded.

Little Italy is a small, and most of the restaurants are touristy, with mediocre food. But in mid-September, you won't want to miss the extremely popular Feast of San Gennaro—a huge street fair in honor of the patron saint of Naples. It's not exactly like visiting old Napoli, but it *is* a fun way to take in the sights.

Chinatown bustles with local shoppers all day, but there are more tourists on the weekends, when you may have to duck into a shop or restaurant just for a break from all the sidewalk jostling.

QUICK BITES

■ **The Grey Dog.** Unpretentious and with ample seating, open early till late, and serving breakfast, brunch, lunch, dinner, baked goods, coffee, wine, and beer, the Grey Dog is perfect anytime. ✉ *244 Mulberry St., between Prince and Spring Sts., NoLIta ⊕ www.thegreydog.com Ⓜ Subway: B, D, F, M to Broadway–Lafayette St.; N, R, W to Prince St.*

■ **Saigon Vietnamese Sandwich Deli.** Predating the *banh mi* craze by perhaps a decade, this cash-only storefront serves delicious Vietnamese sandwiches on baguettes that are crusty on the outside and soft on the inside, just as they should be. ✉ *369 Broome St., between Mott and Elizabeth Sts., NoLIta ⊕ www.vietnamese-sandwich.com Ⓜ Subway: J, Z to Bowery; 6 to Spring St.; B, D to Grand St.*

■ **Ladurée New York SoHo.** You can have a sit-down lunch or dinner here. However, the famous macaróns and other baked goods (not to mention the hot chocolate) are definitely worth a quick stop if you are looking for an exquisitely crafted (and exquisitely French) pick-me-up. ✉ *398 West Broadway, between Spring and Broome Sts., SoHo ⊕ www.laduree.us Ⓜ Subway: 6, C, E to Spring St.*

This small swath of downtown is typically jam-packed with locals and visitors, making the neighborhoods perfect for people-watching as you browse, nibble, and wander.

Parts of SoHo and NoLIta are destinations for supertrendy shopping, but both neighborhoods are also chock-full of popular chains and department stores: the boutiques are often overpriced but undeniably glamorous. Little Italy and Chinatown are more about local shopping and Instagram-worthy food shops and stalls. In truth, Little Italy is just a short stretch of Mulberry Street and a few blocks on either side; most of it has been absorbed by Chinatown, which is both sprawling and flourishing.

SoHo

Once the epicenter of the New York art scene, SoHo today is now more synonymous with shopping. A bit of bohemia still exists on the cobblestone side streets, where there are charming restaurants and some art galleries that haven't scattered elsewhere. The main thoroughfares tend to have sidewalks lined with tables of handmade jewelry, hats, purses, and art. If you take the time to look, there's a local vibe here beneath the glitzy boutiques—like the elderly residents speaking Italian on the corners around Sullivan Street and Thompson Street, revealing the neighborhood's Italian past.

◉ Sights

Donald Judd House

HOUSE | A five-story cast-iron building from 1870, 101 Spring Street was the New York home and studio of artist Donald Judd. Although the neighborhood used to be home to many single-use cast-iron buildings, this designated historic building is one of the few that remain. Judd bought it in 1968, and today, guided 90-minute tours (book online, as early as possible, since tours sell out weeks in advance) explore his living and working spaces and include a look at art installations as they were arranged by Judd prior to his death in 1994. Note that climbing stairs is required. ⊠ 101 Spring St., at Mercer St., SoHo 🕾 212/219-2747 ⊕ www.juddfoundation.org 💷 $24 ⊗ Closed Sun., Mon. Ⓜ N, R, W to Prince St.; 6 to Spring St.

Drawing Center

MUSEUM | At this nonprofit organization the focus is on drawings—contemporary and historical. The frequently changing exhibits shown in the three galleries often push the envelope on what's considered drawing; many projects are commissioned by the center. ⊠ 35 Wooster St., between Broome and Grand Sts., SoHo 🕾 212/219-2166 ⊕ www.drawingcenter.org 💷 $5 (free Thurs. 6–8 pm) ⊗ Closed Mon., Tues. Ⓜ 1, 6, A, C, E, J, N, Q, R, W, Z to Canal St.

SoHo, NoLita, Little Italy and Chinatown

Sights ▼

1 Columbus Park.......... **G8**
2 Donald Judd House **E4**
3 Drawing Center **D5**
4 Kimlau Square **I9**
5 Leslie-Lohman Museum of Gay and Lesbian Art **D6**
6 Mahayana Buddhist Temple **I7**
7 Most Precious Blood Church............ **G7**
8 Museum of Chinese in America (MOCA)...... **F6**
9 New York City Fire Museum **A5**
10 New York Earth Room **D3**
11 Ronald Feldman Gallery.......... **E6**
12 St. Patrick's Old Cathedral........... **G3**

Restaurants ▼

1 Balthazar **F4**
2 Balthazar Bakery **F4**
3 Black Seed Bagels **H4**
4 Blue Ribbon Brasserie .. **C4**
5 Blue Ribbon Sushi **C3**
6 Café Altro Paradiso..... **B4**
7 Café Habana **H3**
8 Dominique Ansel Bakery.............. **C4**
9 The Dutch................. **C3**
10 Emporio **G3**
11 Estela..................... **G2**
12 456 Shanghai Cuisine .. **H8**
13 Great NY Noodletown.... **I8**
14 Jing Fong **H8**
15 Joe's Shanghai............ **I9**
16 La Esquina **G5**
17 Le Coucou **F7**
18 Lombardi's Pizza **G4**
19 Lucky Strike **D6**
20 Lure Fishbar **E3**
21 The Mercer Kitchen..... **E3**
22 New Malaysia............. **I8**
23 Osteria Morini Manhattan **F4**
24 Parm...................... **G3**
25 Pasquale Jones......... **G5**
26 Raoul's **C3**
27 Rubirosa **G4**
28 The Smile **G1**
29 Tasty Hand-Pulled Noodles.................... **I9**
30 Uncle Boons............. **H4**
31 Xi'an Famous Foods **I9**

Hotels ▼

1 Arlo SoHo................ **A5**
2 The Broome Hotel **F5**
3 Crosby Street Hotel...... **F4**
4 11 Howard St.............. **F7**
5 Hotel 50 Bowery.......... **I7**
6 Hotel Hugo............... **A4**
7 The James New York–SoHo **C6**
8 The Nolitan Hotel **H5**
9 NOMO SOHO.............. **F6**
10 SIXTY SoHo Hotel........ **C4**
11 Soho Grand Hotel........ **C6**

SoHo and NoLIta Architecture 👁

There are plenty of beautiful people in SoHo and NoLIta, but look up beyond the turn-of-the-20th-century cast-iron "bishop's crook" lampposts, and discover some of New York's most impressive architecture. Look down to see Belgian-brick cobblestones lining some of the streets. Along Broadway and other streets in SoHo, there are "vault lights" in the sidewalk: starting in the 1850s, these glass lenses were set into sidewalks so daylight could reach basements.

The **King of Greene Street**, at 72–76 Greene, between Grand and Canal Streets, is a five-story Renaissance-style 1873 building with a magnificent projecting porch of Corinthian columns and pilasters. These days it's painted in high-gloss ivory. Over at 28–30 Greene Street is the **Queen of Greene Street**, a graceful 1873 cast-iron beauty that exemplifies the Second Empire style with its dormers, columns, window arches, projecting central bays, and roof.

The **Haughwout Building**, at 488–492 Broadway, north of Broome, is best known for what's no longer inside—the world's first commercial passenger elevator, invented by Elisha Graves Otis. The building's exterior is worth a look, though: nicknamed the "Parthenon of Cast Iron," the five-story Venetian palazzo–style structure was built in 1857 to house department-store merchant E. V. Haughwout's china, silver, and glassware store. Each window is framed by Corinthian columns and rounded arches.

Built in 1904, the **Little Singer Building,** at 561 Broadway, is a masterpiece of cast-iron styling, its delicate facade covered with curlicues of wrought iron. The L-shape building's second facade is around the corner on Prince Street.

Over in Little Italy/NoLIta, the magnificent old **Police Headquarters** building at 240 Centre Street, between Broome and Grand, might be familiar from Martin Scorsese's film *Gangs of New York.* The 1909 Edwardian baroque–style structure with its striking copper dome was the headquarters of the New York City Police Department until 1973. It was converted into luxury condos in 1988 but is still known today as the Police Building.

The 1885 Romanesque Revival **Puck Building,** at 295 Lafayette Street, on the southeast corner of Houston, is a former magazine headquarters and now home to REI's New York flagship store on the first and basement levels. There are two gilded statues of Shakespeare's Puck: one just over the door on Lafayette Street and the other on the northeast corner of the building.

Leslie-Lohman Museum of Gay and Lesbian Art

MUSEUM | Founded in 1969 in a basement on Prince Street, the museum has its roots in the collection of its founders, Charles Leslie and Fritz Lohman, two lifelong champions of LGBTQ artists. The well-curated exhibits in the spacious first-floor galleries are usually photographic (and sometimes sexually charged), though the museum's impressive archive leads to new exhibitions in various media as often as eight times a year. ⊠ *26 Wooster St., between Grand and Canal Sts., SoHo* ☎ *212/431–2609* ⊕ *www.leslielohman.org* 🎟 *Free (suggested donation $9)* ⊗ *Closed Mon., Tues.* Ⓜ *1, 6, A, C, E, J, N, Q, R, Z to Canal St.*

Did You Know?

SoHo has one of the greatest concentrations of cast-iron buildings, created in response to the fires that wiped out much of Lower Manhattan in the mid-18th century.

New York City Fire Museum

MUSEUM | In the former headquarters of Engine 30, a handsome Beaux Arts building dating from 1904, retired firefighters volunteer their time in the morning and early afternoon to answer visitors' questions. The collection of firefighting tools from the 18th century to the present includes hand-pulled and horse-drawn engines, speaking trumpets, pumps, and uniforms. A memorial exhibit with photos, paintings, children's artwork, and found objects relating to the September 11, 2001, attacks is also on view—a poignant reminder and tribute to the 343 firefighters who died on 9/11. ✉ *278 Spring St., between Hudson and Varick Sts., SoHo* ☎ *212/691–1303* 🌐 *www.nycfiremuseum.org* 🎫 *$10* [M] *C, E to Spring St.; 1 to Houston St.*

New York Earth Room

MUSEUM | Noted American artist and sculptor Walter De Maria's 1977 avant-garde installation consists, quite simply, of 280,000 pounds of gently sculpted soil (22 inches deep). It fills 3,600 square feet of a second-floor gallery maintained by the Dia Art Foundation since 1980. You can't touch or walk on the dirt, nor can you take photos, but looking at it is quite peaceful. De Maria's equally odd and impressive work *The Broken Kilometer*, an 18.75-ton installation that consists of five columns of a total of 1,000 meter-long brass rods covering the wood floors of an open loft space, is a few blocks away (at 393 West Broadway) and is a good complement. The two installations have the same hours. ✉ *141 Wooster St., 2nd fl., between W. Houston and Prince Sts., SoHo* ☎ *212/989–5566* 🌐 *www.diaart.org* 🎫 *Free* 🕒 *Closed mid-June–mid-Sept.* [M] *N, R, W to Prince St.; B, D, F, M to Broadway–Lafayette St.*

Ronald Feldman Gallery

MUSEUM | Founded in 1971 and located in SoHo since the 1980s, this gallery represents more than 30 international contemporary artists; exhibits include contemporary painting, sculpture, installations, drawings, and prints—some are quite avant-garde. The space also hosts performances and has a large selection of Andy Warhol prints, paintings, and drawings. ✉ *31 Mercer St., between Grand and Canal Sts., SoHo* ☎ *212/226–3232* 🌐 *www.feldmangallery.com* 🎫 *Free* 🕒 *Closed Sun., Mon.* [M] *1, 6, A, C, E, J, N, Q, R, W, Z to Canal St.*

🍴 Restaurants

Eating out in SoHo tends to mean pricey restaurants full of fashionistas and the see-and-be-seen crowd, but the restaurants here are worth the wait—or make a reservation.

Balthazar

$$$ | **FRENCH** | Even with long waits and loud noise levels, most out-of-towners agree that it's worth the effort (make reservations) to experience restaurateur Keith McNally's flagship, a perfectly New York reproduction of a Parisian brasserie. Like the decor, entrées recreate French classics: Gruyère-topped onion soup, steak frites, and icy tiers of crab, oysters, and other pristine shellfish. **Known for:** lively scene; authentically Parisian ambience; outstanding brunch. [$] *Average main: $28* ✉ *80 Spring St., near Crosby St., SoHo* ☎ *212/965–1414* 🌐 *www.balthazarny.com* [M] *6 to Spring St.; N, R, W to Prince St.; B, D, F, M to Broadway–Lafayette St.*

Balthazar Bakery

$ | **BAKERY** | Follow the beguiling scent of fresh-baked bread to Balthazar Bakery, next door to Keith McNally's always-packed Balthazar restaurant, where choices include French breads as well as gourmet sandwiches, soups, and treats to take out (there's no seating). Try the berry noisette tart or coconut cake, or keep it simple with an eggy canelé or a

buttery lemon or chocolate madeleine.
Known for: divine French pastries; fresh
baguettes; even New Yorkers will wait in
line for these baked goods. [$] *Average
main: $11* ⊠ *80 Spring St., near Crosby
St., SoHo* ☎ *212/965–1785* ⊕ *www.
balthazarbakery.com* ⊗ *No dinner* Ⓜ *6 to
Spring St.; N, R, W to Prince St.; B, D, F,
M to Broadway–Lafayette St.*

Blue Ribbon Brasserie

$$$ | **MODERN AMERICAN** | Opened in 1992,
Blue Ribbon still has a reputation not just
as an eclectic, top-notch seafood joint
but also as a serious late-night foodie
hangout, especially for chefs; there are
good meat options, too. Trustafarians,
literary types, chefs, and designers—a
good-looking gang—generally fill this
dark box of a room until 4 am. **Known for:**
matzo-ball soup with seafood; duck club
sandwich; inventive menu. [$] *Average
main: $33* ⊠ *97 Sullivan St., between
Prince and Spring Sts., SoHo* ☎ *212/274–
0404* ⊕ *www.blueribbonrestaurants.com*
⊗ *No lunch* Ⓜ *C, E to Spring St.; N, R, W
to Prince St.*

Blue Ribbon Sushi

$$$ | **JAPANESE** | Sushi, like pizza, attracts
opinionated fanatics, and Blue Ribbon
Sushi gets consistent raves for its sushi
and sashimi; the dark nooks, minimalist
design, and servers with downtown
attitude attract a stylish crowd who
don't mind waiting for a table or chilled
sake. Stick to the excellent raw fish and
specials here if you're a purist, or branch
out and try one of the experimental rolls:
the Blue Ribbon—lobster, *shiso* (Japanese basil), and black caviar—is popular.
Known for: sceney vibe; superfresh sushi;
expensive due to quality and location.
[$] *Average main: $28* ⊠ *119 Sullivan St.,
between Prince and Spring Sts., SoHo*
☎ *212/343–0404* ⊕ *www.blueribbonres-
taurants.com* Ⓜ *C, E to Spring St.; N, R,
W to Prince St.*

Café Altro Paradiso

$$$ | **ITALIAN** | Chef Ignacio Mattos's
sequel to his much-lauded Estela, just
northeast of here, this airy, high-ceilinged
spot is called a café, but it's more of a
paradise of satisfying Italian fare that
includes perfectly prepared pasta dishes.
Hearty meat entrées include caramel-
ized fennel-spiked pork chop. **Known for:**
wine list with unusual Italian and French
bottles; lively atmosphere; linguine with
Maine lobster and chili. [$] *Average main:
$27* ⊠ *234 Spring St., at 6th Ave., SoHo*
☎ *646/952–0828* ⊕ *www.altroparadiso.
com* Ⓜ *C, F to Spring St.*

Dominique Ansel Bakery

$ | **BAKERY** | The cronut, a delectable cross
between a doughnut and a croissant,
was invented by Dominique Ansel in
2013, and the flaky pastries continue to
create a hubbub, with just one inventive
flavor available each month. There are
plenty of other delightful creations as
well, which you can eat in the café or
take with you. **Known for:** sublime hot
chocolate; cookie shot, a chocolate chip
cookie shaped like a cup and filled with
vanilla milk; lines frequently out the door.
[$] *Average main: $8* ⊠ *189 Spring St.,
between Sullivan and Thompson Sts.,
SoHo* ☎ *212/219–2773* ⊕ *www.dominiq
ueanselny.com* Ⓜ *C, E to Spring St.*

The Dutch

$$$ | **AMERICAN** | Perpetually packed with
the see-and-be-seen crowd, chef Andrew
Carmellini's farmhouse-decorated
homage to American cuisine is really an
encapsulation of modern dining trends.
There's an excellent (and pricey) burger at
lunch, greenmarket-driven comfort-food
dishes like fried chicken, and some
serious steak action. **Known for:** top-quality produce and purveyors; well-dressed
crowd; weekend brunch. [$] *Average
main: $30* ⊠ *131 Sullivan St., at Prince
St., SoHo* ☎ *212/677–6200* ⊕ *www.thed-
utchnyc.com* Ⓜ *C, E to Spring St.*

Lucky Strike

$$ | BISTRO | Whether you're lucky enough to nab a table at this sceney SoHo bistro at 1 pm or 1 am, Lucky Strike always seems like the place to be. The French-influenced kitchen offerings are straightforward: croque monsieur, steak frites, and salade niçoise are old standbys, with a turkey burger thrown in to accommodate the *Americain* palate. **Known for:** classic French bistro decor; warm and welcoming vibe; straightforward bistro fare. $ *Average main: $20* ✉ *59 Grand St., between West Broadway and Wooster St., SoHo* ☎ *212/941–0772* ⊕ *www.luckystrikeny.com* Ⓜ *1, A, C, E to Canal St.*

Lure Fishbar

$$$ | SEAFOOD | Decorated like the clubby interior of a sleek luxury liner, Lure serves oceanic fare in multiple culinary styles. From the sushi bar, feast on options like the Lure House Roll—a shrimp tempura roll crowned with spicy tuna and Japanese tartar sauce—or opt for creative dishes from the kitchen, like steamed branzino with oyster mushrooms, scallions, and ponzu sauce, or Manila clams over pancetta-studded linguine. **Known for:** great SoHo location; cool bar scene; lobster roll. $ *Average main: $29* ✉ *142 Mercer St., at Prince St., SoHo* ☎ *212/431–7676* ⊕ *www.lurefishbar.com* Ⓜ *B, D, F, M to Broadway–Lafayette St.; N, R, W to Prince St.*

The Mercer Kitchen

$$$ | ASIAN FUSION | Part of Alsatian superchef Jean-Georges Vongerichten's culinary empire, the celebrity-laden front room of this SoHo spot in the Mercer Hotel is as much about scene as cuisine, which isn't a bad thing. Dishes here look toward Asia (as is the proclivity of Mr. Vongerichten), using simple ingredients and pairings. **Known for:** excellent cocktails; sophisticated service; standout seafood dishes. $ *Average main: $30* ✉ *Mercer Hotel, 99 Prince St., at Mercer St., SoHo* ☎ *212/966–5454* ⊕ *www.* *themercerkitchen.com* 🚫 *No credit cards* Ⓜ *6 to Spring St.; N, R, W to Prince St.; B, D, F, M to Broadway–Lafayette St.*

Osteria Morini

$$$ | ITALIAN | Less formal than chef Michael White's other renowned Italian restaurants (like Marea in Midtown West), Osteria Morini is lively and upbeat, with communal tables at the center and a rock 'n' roll soundtrack. The food nevertheless steals the show: start with a selection of cheeses and cured meats, then move on to hearty pastas and main courses like oven-baked polenta accompanied by either sausage or mushrooms. **Known for:** White Label burger; tasty meatballs; Italian happy hour with snacks. $ *Average main: $27* ✉ *218 Lafayette St., between Spring and Broome Sts., SoHo* ☎ *212/965–8777* ⊕ *www.osteriamorini.com* Ⓜ *6 to Spring St.*

Raoul's

$$$ | FRENCH | One of the first trendy spots in SoHo, this arty French restaurant with closely packed tables and booths has yet to lose its touch, either in the kitchen or atmosphere. Expect a chic bar scene—especially late at night—and bistro-inspired dishes, with oysters and salads to start, and pastas, fish, and meat options for mains. **Known for:** tall, juicy burgers; walls covered with paintings and photos; winding, narrow stairs to the upper room are a bit treacherous in heels. $ *Average main: $30* ✉ *180 Prince St., between Sullivan and Thompson Sts., SoHo* ☎ *212/966–3518* ⊕ *www.raouls. com* ☾ *No lunch weekdays* Ⓜ *C, E to Spring St.*

🛏 Hotels

Arlo SoHo

$ | HOTEL | Affordable rates, a prime location, a popular restaurant and bar, and a funky vibe make up for the tiny rooms at this sleek microhotel. **Pros:** supersleek design; great value for prime

SoHo location; cool events like crafting and mixology classes. **Cons:** small rooms; glass-enclosed bathrooms lack privacy; no in-room minibar. [$] *Rooms from: $199* ✉ *231 Hudson St., near Canal St., SoHo* ☎ *212/806–7000* 🌐 *www.arlohotels.com* 🛏 *325 rooms* 🍴 *No meals* [M] *1 to Canal St.; C, E to Spring St.*

The Broome Hotel

$$ | **HOTEL** | A Federal-style building from 1825 that was an artists' commune in the 1980s has been transformed into a boutique hotel full of local character. **Pros:** excellent location for SoHo shopping and dining; free continental breakfast served on charming patio; good value for the neighborhood. **Cons:** no full-service restaurant on-site; small rooms; inconsistent service. [$] *Rooms from: $359* ✉ *431 Broome St., near Crosby St., SoHo* ☎ *212/431–2929* 🌐 *www.thebroomenyc.com* 🛏 *14 rooms* 🍴 *Free Breakfast* [M] *6 to Spring St.*

★ **Crosby Street Hotel**

$$$$ | **HOTEL** | This whimsical boutique hotel has an eclectic design with colorful furnishings and large, sun-filled rooms with floor-to-ceiling windows. **Pros:** unique, fun design; solicitous service; great bar. **Cons:** small gym; surprisingly expensive; no pool or spa. [$] *Rooms from: $695* ✉ *79 Crosby St., between Prince and Spring Sts., SoHo* ☎ *212/226–6400* 🌐 *www.firmdalehotels.com* 🛏 *86 rooms* 🍴 *No meals* [M] *6 to Spring St.; N, R, W to Prince St.; B, D, F, M to Broadway–Lafayette St.*

11 Howard

$$ | **HOTEL** | A sleek hotel with a design that melds midcentury modern furniture and Scandinavian minimalism, 11 Howard is an excellent downtown base. **Pros:** lots of shopping and dining options nearby; minimalist but comfortable; sleek downtown ambience. **Cons:** vibe feels too cool for some; some guests complain about street noise; Canal Street locale can be a little intense. [$] *Rooms from: $389* ✉ *11 Howard St., near Lafayette St., SoHo* ☎ *212/235–1111* 🌐 *www.11howard.com* 🛏 *213 rooms* 🍴 *No meals* [M] *6, N, Q, R, W to Canal St.*

Hotel Hugo

$ | **HOTEL** | Those who dream of coming home to an NYC loft will be drawn to this stylish property inspired by downtown's industrial-chic residences. **Pros:** great location for walks along the Hudson River; stylish on-site dining and drinking options; rooftop with multiple spaces and fantastic views. **Cons:** space in rooms is tight; not in the prime heart of SoHo, but on the edge of it; fitness center in windowless basement room. [$] *Rooms from: $299* ✉ *525 Greenwich St., between Vandam and Spring Sts., SoHo* ☎ *212/608–4848* 🌐 *www.hotelhugony.com* 🛏 *122 rooms* 🍴 *No meals* [M] *1 to Houston St.*

★ **The James New York – SoHo**

$$ | **HOTEL** | **FAMILY** | This hotel on the edge of SoHo never sacrifices comfort for style, so it's no wonder there's a high percentage of return customers—creative types, businesspeople, fashionistas, and anyone else with deep pockets. **Pros:** stellar service; superb views from tall windows; cool SoHo location. **Cons:** rooftop bar is expensive; bathrooms offer little privacy; noise from the bar can be bothersome. [$] *Rooms from: $429* ✉ *27 Grand St., between Thompson St. and 6th Ave., SoHo* ☎ *212/465–2000* 🌐 *www.jameshotels.com/new-york/soho* 🛏 *114 rooms* 🍴 *No meals* [M] *1, A, C, E to Canal St.*

★ **NOMO SOHO**

$$ | **HOTEL** | Snazzy, fairy-tale-inspired style and a chic SoHo vibe make this hotel a winner for anyone looking for a decadent downtown New York experience. **Pros:** stylish rooms; friendly to electronics addicts; fabulous views from floor-to-ceiling windows. **Cons:** elevators can be slow; standard rooms are on the small side; inconsistent service.

$ Rooms from: $300 ⊠ 9 Crosby St., between Grand and Howard Sts., SoHo ☎ 844/735–3355 ⊕ www.nomosoho.com ⇨ 264 rooms ⦿ No meals Ⓜ 6, J, N, Q, R, W, Z to Canal St.

★ SIXTY SoHo Hotel

$$$ | HOTEL | Formerly SoHo icon 60 Thompson, this stylish hotel has a fabulous rooftop lounge, A60, that remains a warm-weather haven for the well dressed, with sweeping skyline views. **Pros:** central to SoHo nightlife; good dining and drinking options on-site; some rooms have balconies. **Cons:** not family-oriented; expensive minibar; rooftop bar can get crowded. $ Rooms from: $555 ⊠ 60 Thompson St., between Broome and Spring Sts., SoHo ☎ 877/431–0400 ⊕ www.sixtyhotels. com/soho ⇨ 97 rooms ⦿ No meals Ⓜ C, E to Spring St.

SoHo Grand Hotel

$$ | HOTEL | The stalwart SoHo Grand has defined the neighborhood for decades, and as new properties crowd the field, the Grand's low-key sophistication continues to stand out. **Pros:** fashionable, laid-back sophistication; great service; fabulous bar and lounge. **Cons:** closer to Canal Street than to prime SoHo; rooms on small side; not as hip as it used to be. $ Rooms from: $425 ⊠ 310 West Broadway, at Grand St., SoHo ☎ 212/965–3000 ⊕ www.sohogrand.com ⇨ 353 rooms ⦿ No meals Ⓜ 1, 2, 3, A, C, E to Canal St.

☯ Nightlife

BARS

Ear Inn

BARS/PUBS | Since the early 1800s, this watering hole (at one time also a bordello) has been a sturdy New York landmark in a rapidly changing downtown. For those imbibers who prefer a pint of Guinness over the latest cocktail fads, the long wooden bar offers a cozy, unhurried place to raise a glass and rub elbows with New Yorkers. The benches outside are also a perfect spot to relax in the warmer weather, and live music and readings three times a week evoke the bar's artistic heritage. ⊠ 326 Spring St., between Greenwich and Washington Sts., SoHo ☎ 212/226–9060 ⊕ www. earinn.com Ⓜ 1 to Houston St.; C, E to Spring St.

Fanelli's

BARS/PUBS | Linger over lunch or a beer at this well-worn neighborhood bar and restaurant, a down-to-earth SoHo landmark that's been serving drinks (and good burgers, sandwiches, and quiche) since 1847. The old-timey photos on the walls add to the vintage atmosphere, as do the no-nonsense bartenders. ⊠ 94 Prince St., at Mercer St., SoHo ☎ 212/226–9412 Ⓜ N, R, W to Prince St.; B, D, F, M to Broadway–Lafayette St.

Jimmy

BARS/PUBS | On the 18th floor of the trendy James New York – SoHo, Jimmy is an all-season rooftop bar with stellar views and a cozy fireplace. Sit in a corner nook for Empire State Building vistas, or head toward the outdoor pool area (the pool is tiny) to survey the bridges over the East River. Cocktails are a highlight, featuring seasonal ingredients. ⊠ The James New York – SoHo, 15 Thompson St., at Grand St., SoHo ☎ 212/201–9118 ⊕ www.jimmysoho.com Ⓜ C, E to Spring St.; 1, A, C, E to Canal St.

La Compagnie des Vins Surnaturels

WINE BARS—NIGHTLIFE | Cheese, charcuterie, and wine are all temptations at this cozy bar, lined with exposed-brick walls and shelves stocked with wine (the complete list is over 600 bottles). This is the dimly lit sister property of a bar of the same name in Paris; the bottles on the wine list lean heavily toward French options, though by-the-glass options are more varied. ⊠ 249 Centre St., between Broome and Grand Sts., SoHo ☎ 212/343–3660 ⊕ www.compagnienyc. com Ⓜ 6 to Spring St.

Pegu Club

BARS/PUBS | One of the forerunners of New York City's mixologist scene in the early 2000s, the Pegu Club has maintained its charm and dedication to serving excellent cocktails made with top-notch spirits. Modeled on the concept of a 19th-century officers' club in Myanmar, the bar manages to feel expansive and calm even when packed. It's open until the wee hours, making it the perfect spot to cap off a night out. ✉ *77 W. Houston St., 2nd fl., between West Broadway and Wooster St., SoHo* ☎ *212/473–7348* ⊕ *www.peguclub.com* Ⓜ *B, D, F, M to Broadway–Lafayette St., 0 to Bleecker St.*

LIVE MUSIC VENUES
City Winery

MUSIC CLUBS | A combination wine bar and concert space, matched with great food and a calendar packed with great shows, makes this a go-to for a semi-sophisticated night out. Unique events like wine-themed yoga round out the roster. ✉ *155 Varick St., at Vandam St., SoHo* ☎ *212/608–0555* ⊕ *www.citywinery.com* Ⓜ *1 to Houston St.*

🎭 Performing Arts

READINGS AND LECTURES

★ **The Greene Space** (*Jerome L. Greene Performance Space*)

MUSIC | The local public radio stations WNYC and WQXR invite the public into their intimate (125 seats) studio for live shows featuring classical, rock, jazz, and new music; audio theater; conversation; and interviews. It's a great place to get up-close with writers and newsmakers, as well as musicians and actors who might be playing Carnegie Hall, Broadway, or the Met Opera a few days later. ✉ *44 Charlton St., at Varick St., SoHo* ☎ *646/829–4000* ⊕ *www.thegreenespace.org* Ⓜ *C, E to Spring St.; 1 to Houston St.*

★ **The Moth**

READINGS/LECTURES | Dedicated to first-person storytelling, this roving series has spread far beyond New York, where it was founded in 1997 by the writer George Dawes Green. But it's still going strong here: the curated Mainstage shows feature both celebrities and everyday people who worked with The Moth directors to shape their stories. At the much looser, open-mic StorySLAMs, competitors are randomly selected and given just five minutes to tell a story, which must tie in with the night's theme. These tales get told at Housing Works and other venues downtown and throughout the boroughs. ✉ *Housing Works Bookstore Café, 126 Crosby St., between Houston and Prince Sts., SoHo* ☎ *212/742–0551* ⊕ *themoth.org/events* Ⓜ *N, R, W to Prince St.; B, D, F, M to Broadway–Lafayette St.*

THEATER
HERE

THEATER | Celebrating all manner of contemporary, genre-bending productions, the original home of Eve Ensler's *The Vagina Monologues* and Basil Twist's *Symphonie Fantastique* also houses art exhibitions and a lounge to hang out at before or after the show. ✉ *145 6th Ave., between Spring and Dominick Sts., SoHo* ☎ *212/647–0202, 212/352–3101 for tickets* ⊕ *www.here.org* Ⓜ *C, E to Spring St.*

🛍 Shopping

Head to SoHo for both the cheap and the hyperchic. The narrow sidewalks get very busy, especially on weekends, but this is a fun see-and-be-seen neighborhood. There are plenty of familiar high-fashion names like Prada, Chanel, and Louis Vuitton, as well as less expensive chains like Banana Republic and Sephora, which have made land grabs on Broadway. But you can still hit a few clothing and housewares boutiques not found elsewhere in this country. The hottest shopping area runs west from Broadway over to 6th

Avenue, between West Houston and Grand Streets. Don't overlook a couple of streets east of Broadway, too: Crosby and Lafayette have a handful of intriguing shops.

BEAUTY
★ Birchbox
PERFUME/COSMETICS | Cult favorite beauty-subscription service Birchbox has a retail space in SoHo where you can stock up on best-selling products that range from $5 to $200 and include everything from lip balm and stylish mugs to curling irons, headphones, and fragrance. There's a BYOB (Build Your Own Birchbox) section, where users create their own box full of samples. The store also has a separate floor set aside for makeup, hair, and nail services, as well as men's offerings. ⊠ *433 West Broadway, between Prince and Spring Sts., SoHo* ☎ *646/589–8500* ⊕ *www.birchbox.com* Ⓜ *N, R, W to Prince St.*

MiN
PERFUME/COSMETICS | If the selection of grooming products at Duane Reade isn't artisanal or exotic enough for you, head to this sleek boutique where you can shop for unusual scents from Santa Maria Novella and L'Artisan Parfumeur, shaving products from Old Bond Street, quirkier items like mustache wax, and the brand's own signature line of fragrances and candles. ⊠ *117 Crosby St., between Houston and Prince Sts., SoHo* ☎ *212/206–6366* ⊕ *www.min.com* Ⓜ *N, R, W to Prince St.; B, D, F, M to Broadway–Lafayette St.*

BOOKS AND STATIONERY
★ Housing Works Bookstore Cafe
BOOKS/STATIONERY | Operated by a nonprofit that puts all proceeds toward combating AIDS and homelessness, this New York institution has an impressive collection of previously owned books. The café is a popular spot for laptop-toting creatives, and literary and cultural events are held here almost nightly; a full calendar is on the store's website. ⊠ *126 Crosby St., between Houston and Prince Sts., SoHo* ☎ *212/334–3324* ⊕ *www. housingworks.org/locations/bookstore-cafe* Ⓜ *B, D, F, M to Broadway–Lafayette St.; N, R, W to Prince St.*

CHILDREN'S CLOTHING
Les Petits Chapelais
CLOTHING | FAMILY | Designed and made in France, these clothes for kids (from newborn up to age 12) are cute and stylish but also practical. Corduroy outfits have details like embroidered flowers and contrasting cuffs, and soft, fleecy jackets are reversible. T-shirts might have pictures of panda bears or Bob Dylan saying "It's alright, Ma." ⊠ *146 Sullivan St., between Houston and Prince Sts., SoHo* ☎ *212/625–1023* ⊕ *www. lespetitschapelais-nyc.com* Ⓜ *C, E to Spring St.*

CLOTHING
& Other Stories
CLOTHING | The first U.S. outpost of this popular shop owned by Swedish megastore H&M focuses on midrange clothes and bold twists on staples designed in Paris and Stockholm. Chunky sweaters, pointy-toed flats, and printed coats are just the beginning. This is a great place to browse: you're sure to find something delightful and not over-the-top expensive. ⊠ *575 Broadway, between Houston and Prince Sts., SoHo* ☎ *646/767–3063* ⊕ *www.stories.com/us* Ⓜ *N, R, W to Prince St.; B, D, F, M to Broadway–Lafayette St.*

A Bathing Ape
CLOTHING | Known simply as BAPE to devotees, this exclusive label has a cult following in its native Tokyo. At first it may be hard to see what the fuss is about. A small selection of camouflage gear and limited-edition T-shirts for men, women, and children is placed throughout the minimalist space; the real scene stealers are the limited-edition sneakers in funky colors. ⊠ *91 Greene St., between Prince and Spring Sts., SoHo* ☎ *212/925–0222*

⊕ *www.bape.com* Ⓜ *N, R, W to Prince St.; B, D, F, M to Broadway–Lafayette St.*

Agent Provocateur

CLOTHING | If Victoria's Secret is too tame for you, try this British lingerie shop, which has a naughty twist. Show-pieces include corsets, lace sets with contrast-color trim, bottoms tied with satin ribbons, and a few fetish-type leather ensembles. A great selection of stockings is complemented by the garter belts to secure them. ⊠ *133 Mercer St., between Prince and Spring Sts., SoHo* ☎ *212/343–7370* ⊕ *www.agentprovoca-teur.com* Ⓜ *N, R, W to Prince St.; B, D, F, M to Broadway–Lafayette St.*

Alexander Wang

CLOTHING | *Vogue* darling Alexander Wang's flagship boutique is as unfussy and cool as his clothes, with artistic dis-plays amid the racks of perfectly slouchy tank tops, sheath dresses, or edgy ankle boots. ⊠ *103 Grand St., between Greene and Mercer Sts., SoHo* ☎ *212/977–9683* ⊕ *www.alexanderwang.com* Ⓜ *6, J, N, Q, R, W, Z to Canal St.*

American Two Shot

CLOTHING | A carefully edited mix of contemporary and vintage clothes for men and women, as well as fun gift items, are all wittily displayed around this hip boutique. Art installations and pop-up shops (juice bar, anyone?) are sometimes part of the act. ⊠ *135 Grand St., between Crosby and Lafayette Sts., SoHo* ☎ *212/925–3403* ⊕ *www.ameri-cantwoshot.com* Ⓜ *6, J, N, Q, R, W, Z to Canal St.*

Anna Sui

CLOTHING | More like an apartment than a shop, this wonderfully quirky space with its Victorian rock-chick vibe is chock-full of Sui's bohemian and rocker-influenced designs and colorful beauty products. There's a small selection of accessories and purses, too. ⊠ *484 Broome St., between West Broadway and Wooster St., SoHo* ☎ *212/941–8406* ⊕ *www.*

annasui.com Ⓜ *C, E to Spring St.; A, C, E to Canal St.*

The Apartment by The Line

CLOTHING | Imagine stepping into the most understatedly hip SoHo loft and discovering that everything is, in fact, for sale. This online concept store has always focused on craftspeople and the stories behind its highly curated collec-tions, and this brick-and-mortar outpost lets you experience that firsthand. The fashions are mostly for women—think Altuzarra dresses and Pologeorgis coats—but there are also luxe beau-ty products, furnishings and artwork sourced from around the world, and a selection of jewelry. ⊠ *76 Greene St., 3rd fl., between Spring and Broome Sts., SoHo* ☎ *917/460–7196* ⊕ *www.theline. com* Ⓜ *N, R, W to Prince St.*

A.P.C.

CLOTHING | This hip French boutique for men and women sells deceptively simple but elegant clothes in an equally under-stated setting. Choose from sharply cut gabardine and corduroy suits to dark den-im jeans and jackets. For women, best bets include striped sweaters and skinny jeans. ⊠ *131 Mercer St., between Prince and Spring Sts., SoHo* ☎ *212/966–9685* ⊕ *www.apc-us.com* Ⓜ *6 to Spring St.; N, R, W to Prince St.; B, D, F, M to Broad-way–Lafayette St.*

COS

CLOTHING | With COS's monochrome palette, clean lines, and structured styles meant to last, it's hard to believe that this minimalist fashion brand is owned by H&M. Stock up on wardrobe essentials like black dresses, white button-ups, and wool blazers. The leather shoes, handbags, and other accessories are equally elegant. ⊠ *129 Spring St., between Wooster and Greene Sts., SoHo* ☎ *212/389–1247* ⊕ *www.cosstores.com* Ⓜ *N, R, W to Prince St.*

Etro

CLOTHING | This Italian fashion house is known for its trademark paisleys and bold patterns, which cover everything from suits and dresses to lustrous pillows. Etro's downtown location combines the best of Italy with a SoHo loft, with high tin ceilings, brightly colored rugs, and industrial lighting. ⊠ *89 Greene St., at Spring St., SoHo* ☎ *646/329–6929* ⊕ *www.etro.com* Ⓜ *N, R, W to Prince St.; B, D, F, M to Broadway–Lafayette St.*

45R

CLOTHING | Cult-favorite Japanese denim brand 45rpm's New York outpost may be pricey, but fans love the label for its attention to detail, like hand-dyed denim woven on antique looms. The T-shirts are particularly stylish, the non-denim womens wear is ethereal and cozy, and the men's shirts and blazers are elegantly tailored. ⊠ *169 Mercer St., between Houston and Prince Sts., SoHo* ☎ *917/237–0045* ⊕ *www.rby45rpm.com* Ⓜ *N, R, W to Prince St.*

★ Isabel Marant

CLOTHING | If you're after that casually glamorous Parisian vibe, look no further than Isabel Marant. Long a favorite of globe-trotting fashionistas, the tailored jackets, shorts, and flirty dresses are eclectic and sophisticated, with textured, deeply hued fabrics. ⊠ *469 Broome St., at Greene St., SoHo* ☎ *212/219–2284* ⊕ *www.isabelmarant.com* Ⓜ *N, R, W to Prince St.; A, C, E to Canal St.*

Kirna Zabête

CLOTHING | Think of this space as a mini department store for some of the biggest names in fashion, including Alexander Wang, Azzedine Alaïa, Mansur Gavriel, and Ulla Johnson. The store has a fun, pop art–inspired design, with lots of colorful clothes and a wall of neon signs suggesting that shoppers "leave looking lovely" and that "life is short, buy the shoes." ⊠ *477 Broome St., between Greene and Wooster Sts., SoHo* ☎ *212/941–9656* ⊕ *www.kirnazabete. com* Ⓜ *N, R, W to Prince St.; A, C, E to Canal St.*

Maison Kitsuné

CLOTHING | This decades-old French fashion and music label made its stateside debut in this airy, sun-washed boutique for women's and menswear classics with a stylish Japanese-Gallic twist. Fun, colorful prints are the signature. ⊠ *248 Lafayette St., between Prince and Spring Sts., SoHo* ☎ *646/858–2709* ⊕ *www. kitsune.fr* Ⓜ *N, R, W to Prince St.; 6 to Spring St.*

Marc Jacobs

CLOTHING | The designer's only NYC boutique, this sleek, high-ceilinged shop showcases the brand's bright and fun shoes, accessories, and lovingly tailored clothing for men and women in luxurious fabrics: silk, cashmere, wool bouclé, and tweeds ranging from the demure to the flamboyant. The details, though—oversize buttons, circular patch pockets, and military-style grommet belts—add a sartorial wink. ⊠ *113 Prince St., between Wooster and Greene Sts., SoHo* ☎ *212/343–1490* ⊕ *www.marcjacobs.com* Ⓜ *N, R, W to Prince St.; B, D, F, M to Broadway–Lafayette St.*

Marni

CLOTHING | If you're a fan of the boho-chic look, you'll want to check out creative director Francesco Risso's brightly colored clothes at the Italian designer's SoHo outpost. The collection features dresses and jackets in bright colors and quirky prints, and many of the silhouettes are vintage inspired. Accessories are also eye-catching. ⊠ *161 Mercer St., between W. Houston and Prince Sts., SoHo* ☎ *212/343–3912* ⊕ *www.marni. com* Ⓜ *N, R, W to Prince St.; B, D, F, M to Broadway–Lafayette St.*

Miu Miu

CLOTHING | Prada front woman Miuccia Prada established a secondary line (bearing her childhood nickname, Miu Miu) to showcase her more experimental ideas. Look for Prada-esque styles in more daring colors and cuts, such as high-waist skirts with scalloped edges, Peter Pan–collar dresses in bold patterns, and pastel-hued pumps. ✉ *100 Prince St., between Mercer and Greene Sts., SoHo* ☎ *212/334–5156* ⊕ *www.miumiu.com* Ⓜ *N, R, W to Prince St.*

Moncler

CLOTHING | Many New Yorkers swear by this French-Italian brand's coats to keep them warm but stylish throughout the winter or on the ski slopes. The knee length puffer is a firm favorite, but there are all sorts of jackets and accessories spread over the store's three levels, along with pieces created in collaboration with designers like Giambattista Valli and KITH. ✉ *99 Prince St., between Mercer and Greene Sts., SoHo* ☎ *646/350–3620* ⊕ *www.moncler.com* Ⓜ *N, R, W to Prince St.*

★ Opening Ceremony

CLOTHING | It's easy to understand the cultlike status of Opening Ceremony, a concept store filled with eclectic goods. The brand's owners are constantly globe-trotting to soak up the work of foreign designers and bring back the best clothing, products, and vintage items to showcase in their store. Hong Kong, Japan, Brazil, and the United Kingdom have all been represented. The Howard Street address is two connected stores, with stock that includes shoes, kids' clothes, books, and womens and menswear. Both spaces also double as galleries for modern art and installations. ✉ *33–35 Howard St., between Broadway and Crosby St., SoHo* ☎ *212/219–2688* ⊕ *www.openingceremony.us* Ⓜ *6, J, N, Q, R, W, Z to Canal St.*

Paul Smith

CLOTHING | Fans love Paul Smith for his classic-with-a-twist clothes, and this 5,000-square-foot flagship is a temple to his design ethos and inspirations. Victorian mahogany cases complement the dandyish British styles they hold. Embroidered vests; brightly striped socks, scarves, and shirts; and tongue-in-cheek cuff links are all signature Paul Smith looks, along with classic suits and outerwear for men and women. Furniture and a selection of photography books and ephemera are on display as well. ✉ *142 Greene St., between Houston and Prince Sts., SoHo* ☎ *646/613–3060* ⊕ *www.paulsmith.co.uk* Ⓜ *N, R, W to Prince St.; B, D, F, M to Broadway–Lafayette St.*

★ Prada

CLOTHING | This ultramodern, multilevel flagship space, designed by Rem Koolhaas, is both showpiece and showcase. It's worth wandering in to check out the oft-changing artistic display in the central open staircase, even if the luxurious clothes and accessories for men and women are out of your price range. The store stretches from Broadway to Mercer Street, with entrances at both ends. ✉ *575 Broadway, at Prince St., SoHo* ☎ *212/334–8888* ⊕ *www.prada.com* Ⓜ *N, R, W to Prince St.; B, D, F, M to Broadway–Lafayette St.*

Reformation

CLOTHING | Cool girls from Olivia Munn to Taylor Swift love this eco-friendly fashion brand from Los Angeles whose flirty, vintage-inspired dresses and two-piece outfits are made with recycled, leftover, or otherwise sustainable fabrics. There are also locations on Bond Street and on Ludlow Street. ✉ *23 Howard St., between Lafayette and Crosby Sts., SoHo* ☎ *855/756–0560* ⊕ *www.thereformation.com* Ⓜ *6, J, N, Q, R, W, Z to Canal St.*

Reiss

CLOTHING | Think of Reiss as the Banana Republic of Britain—a go-to place for upscale casual-but-tailored clothes. Kate Middleton is a loyal customer. Standouts for women include cowl-neck sweater dresses and A-line skirts. Men's wool combat trousers are complemented by shrunken blazers, military-inspired peacoats, and trim leather jackets. ⊠ *387 West Broadway, between Spring and Broome Sts., SoHo* ☎ *212/925–5707* ⊕ *www.reissonline.com* Ⓜ *N, R, W to Prince St.; C, E to Spring St.*

Saint Laurent Paris

CLOTHING | When Anthony Vaccarello took over the fabled French house, he used Yves Saint Laurent's most classic designs as his palette. And so the same goes for the brand's downtown flagship, its high ceilings, marble walls, and monochromatic aesthetic designed by Vaccarello's predecessor. Browse the designer's elegant womens wear and polished menswear, and don't miss the sleek shoes and structured handbags. ⊠ *80 Greene St., between Spring and Broome Sts., SoHo* ☎ *212/431–3240* ⊕ *www.ysl.com* Ⓜ *N, R, W to Prince St.; 6 to Spring St.*

Saturdays Surf NYC

CLOTHING | Who knew New York had a surfing scene? This cool boutique brings the culture to the heart of SoHo with its boards, men's clothing, surf-focused fine art, and hip accessories. Also here are a coffee counter in the front and a quiet garden in the back. ⊠ *31 Crosby St., between Broome and Grand Sts., SoHo* ☎ *212/966–7875* ⊕ *www.saturdaysnyc. com* Ⓜ *6, J, N, Q, R, W, Z to Canal St.; 6 to Spring St.*

Sean

CLOTHING | This French-pedigreed shop carries classic, understated menswear imported from Europe at reasonable prices. Linen and corduroy painter's coats are best sellers, along with V-neck sweaters and a respectable collection of slim-cut suits. ⊠ *181 Prince St., between Sullivan and Thompson Sts., SoHo* ☎ *212/598–5980* ⊕ *www.seanstore.com* Ⓜ *N, R, W to Prince St.; C, E to Spring St.*

7 for All Mankind

CLOTHING | Whether you're hunting for superskinny, high-waisted, or boot-cut jeans in a dark or distressed finish, this temple to denim has it all. The jeans for men and women are a firm celebrity favorite (Cameron Diaz is a fan), but be warned: although they'll make your derriere look good, they don't come cheap. You'll also find stylish and sexy dresses here, plus sweaters and jackets for men and women. ⊠ *394 West Broadway, between Spring and Broome Sts., SoHo* ☎ *212/226–8615* ⊕ *www.7forallmankind. com* Ⓜ *C, E to Spring St.*

★ Stella McCartney

CLOTHING | Parquet flooring and Art Deco display cases give this multilevel store an understated but chic atmosphere that perfectly matches the clothing aesthetic. The main womens wear collection, done mostly in gauzy, muted colors, is on the top floor, while menswear, sportswear, Adidas by Stella McCartney, and adorable children's clothes are on the lower level. In keeping with McCartney's vegetarianism, fur and leather are verboten. ⊠ *112 Greene St., between Prince and Spring Sts., SoHo* ☎ *212/255–1556* ⊕ *www. stellamccartney.com* Ⓜ *N, R, W to Prince St.; B, D, F, M to Broadway–Lafayette St.*

3X1

CLOTHING | The walls of this large denim shop, which doubles as a factory where you can watch jeans being made, are lined with an assortment of more than 600 varieties of selvage denim. For the ultimate experience, have a bespoke pair made and choose the fabric, buttons, and even the lining material. Everything is hand-cut and sewn by the in-house seamstresses. There are ready-made jeans, too (you can get the hems tailored on the spot). ⊠ *15 Mercer St., between Grand and Howard Sts., SoHo* ☎ *212/391–6969* ⊕ *www.3x1.us* Ⓜ *6, J, N, Q, R, W, Z to Canal St.*

The Webster

CLOTHING | When the French stylist behind this beloved luxury concept store from Miami decided to open an outpost in New York, she renovated a six-floor, landmarked building and injected some of the original store's signature Art Deco sensibilities. The result is a narrow, extremely styled space filled with artful displays of luxury-brand clothes and accessories. Make sure to explore beyond the first floor to find men's and women's clothes and home furnishings. ✉ *29 Greene St., between Grand and Canal Sts., SoHo* ☎ *212/226–1260* ⊕ *www.thewebster.us* Ⓜ *6, J, N, Q, R, W, Z to Canal St.*

★ **What Goes Around Comes Around**

CLOTHING | Professional stylists and celebrities flock here to dig up pristine vintage items like Levi's and Azzedine Alaïa dresses, as well as Hermès scarves and Chanel jewelry. The vintage rock tees (think Black Sabbath, Mötley Crüe) are great finds but can set you back an eye-watering $300–$600. ✉ *351 West Broadway, between Broome and Grand Sts., SoHo* ☎ *212/343–1225* ⊕ *www.whatgoesaroundnyc.com* Ⓜ *6, J, N, Q, R, W, Z to Canal St.*

Woolrich

CLOTHING | In a nod to this brand's almost 200-year history, Woolrich's first retail space is decorated with vintage shearing tools and catalogs from the original Pennsylvania mill. The space is cozy, thanks to throw rugs and industrial-style lighting, and the full Woolrich product line is sold here, from sweaters to blankets and thick winter coats. ✉ *125 Wooster St., between Prince and Spring Sts., SoHo* ☎ *646/371–9968* ⊕ *www.woolrich.com* Ⓜ *N, R, W to Prince St.*

CRAFTS
★ **Purl Soho**

CRAFTS | Anyone with a crafty bent will fall in love with this colorful paradise of top-quality knitting and sewing supplies, gorgeous craft books, and much, much more. Prices aren't cheap, but the salespeople are extra friendly and knowledgeable. It's worth a browse even if you're not planning to buy anything. ✉ *459 Broome St., between Mercer and Green Sts., SoHo* ☎ *212/420–8796* ⊕ *www.purlsoho.com* Ⓜ *6 to Spring St.; 6, A, C, E, J, N, Q, R, W, Z to Canal St.*

FOOD AND TREATS
Harney & Sons

FOOD/CANDY | Fancy a cuppa? Harney & Sons produces more than 250 varieties of tea, which can be sampled at the 24-foot-long tasting bar, surrounded by floor-to-ceiling shelves stocked with tea. Shoppers find classic brews like English breakfast and oolong, along with interesting herbals (ginger and licorice, or mint verbena). There's also a tea salon where you can enjoy a cup with a scone or other light fare. ✉ *433 Broome St., between Broadway and Crosby St., SoHo* ☎ *212/933–4853* ⊕ *www.harney.com* Ⓜ *6 to Spring St.; 6, A, C, E, J, N, Q, R, W, Z to Canal St.*

Jacques Torres Chocolates

FOOD/CANDY | For many, Jacques Torres sets the bar for New York City chocolatiers, and this glass-walled café and shop is the perfect spot to sip richly spiced cocoa and nibble on a chocolate chip cookie or Java Junkie bar. The renowned French chocolatier's chocolate factory is here, too, so you can watch the goodies being made while shopping for bonbons to take home. Chocolate lovers should also check out Torres's 5,000-square-foot chocolate museum, which offers tours Wednesday through Sunday and holds chocolate-making classes. ✉ *350 Hudson St., at King St., SoHo* ☎ *212/414–2450* ⊕ *www.mrchocolate.com* Ⓜ *1 to Houston St.*

MarieBelle

FOOD/CANDY | The handmade chocolates here are nothing less than works of art. Square truffles and bonbons—in flavors like Earl Grey, cappuccino, passion fruit, and saffron—are painted with edible dyes (cocoa butter dyed with natural

4

SoHo, NoLIta, Little Italy, and Chinatown SOHO

coloring) so each resembles a miniature painting. There's a friendly café in back, serving delicious Aztec hot chocolate, made from rich cacao, as well other decadent desserts alongside sandwiches and salads. ✉ *484 Broome St., between West Broadway and Wooster St., SoHo* ☎ *212/226–8901* ⊕ *www.mariebelle.com* Ⓜ *N, R, W to Prince St.; C, E to Spring St.*

HOME DECOR
Canal Street Market

HOUSEHOLD ITEMS/FURNITURE | Some of New York's most interesting designers, artists, and food vendors fill this downtown market hall. Browse minimalist and functional housewares at Leibal's nook, all-natural skin-care products at Smoothie Beauty, and independent magazines at Office Magazine Newsstand. Apart from the anchor vendors, the rest of the stalls rotate, so you never know what gems you'll find. ✉ *265 Canal St., between Broadway and Lafayette St., SoHo* ☎ *646/694–1655* ⊕ *www.canalstreet.market* Ⓜ *6, J, N, Q, R, W, Z to Canal St.*

★ de Vera

HOUSEHOLD ITEMS/FURNITURE | Owner Federico de Vera crisscrosses the globe searching for unique decorative products, so shoppers never know what might turn up here in his fabulous Victorian-era-ish gallery space. Venetian glass vases, Thai Buddhas, and antique rose-cut diamond rings are typical finds. ✉ *1 Crosby St., at Howard St., SoHo* ☎ *212/625–0838* ⊕ *www.deveraobjects.com* Ⓜ *6, J, N, Q, R, W, Z to Canal St.*

Matter

HOUSEHOLD ITEMS/FURNITURE | Beautifully curated, this store appeals to fans of sleek, modern furniture—if money is no object. How about the iconic Tank armchair by Alvar Aalto for a cool $5,900? Or a brass-and-marble pendant lamp by Fort Standard for $5,200? Even if your budget is limited, Matter is worth a visit for inspiration. ✉ *405 Broome St., between Centre and Lafayette Sts., SoHo*

☎ *212/343–2600* ⊕ *www.mattermatters.com* Ⓜ *6 to Spring St.*

★ Michele Varian

HOUSEHOLD ITEMS/FURNITURE | This stylish, multilevel textile designer's shop is a temple to independent designers and artists, featuring a curated collection of everything from furniture to tableware to kids' toys and lots of unique jewelry. Many of the pieces are by local designers, but the boutique also regularly hosts pop-up shops for out-of-town brands. ✉ *27 Howard St., at Crosby St., SoHo* ☎ *212/343–0033* ⊕ *www.michelevarian.com* Ⓜ *6, J, N, Q, R, W, Z to Canal St.*

JEWELRY AND ACCESSORIES
Alexis Bittar

JEWELRY/ACCESSORIES | It's the quintessential New York story—a jewelry designer who got his start selling his first line, made from Depression-era glass, on a corner in SoHo. Now Bittar counts A-list celebs and fashion editors among his fans. He makes clean-line, big-statement jewelry out of vermeil, colored Lucite, pearls, and vintage glass. The store mirrors this aesthetic with a mix of old and new, like antique-white Victorian-era lion's-claw tables and Plexiglas walls. ✉ *465 Broome St., between Mercer and Greene Sts., SoHo* ☎ *212/625–8340* ⊕ *www.alexisbittar.com* Ⓜ *N, R, W to Prince St.; 6, J, N, Q, R, W, Z to Canal St.*

Aurélie Bidermann

JEWELRY/ACCESSORIES | The New York boutique of this French jeweler is all white with pops of color and includes a mural commissioned from a street artist. Bidermann's signature look is bold and inspired by her travels and nature. Look out for lace filigree gold cuffs, large turquoise necklaces, and drop earrings in the shape of gingko leaves. ✉ *265 Lafayette St., between Prince and Spring Sts., SoHo* ☎ *212/335–0604* ⊕ *www.aureliebidermann.com* Ⓜ *N, R, W to Prince St.; 6 to Spring St.*

Broken English

JEWELRY/ACCESSORIES | At the NYC outpost of this L.A. favorite, owner Laura Freedman sells a well-edited selection of jewelry from designers including Anita Ko and Atelier Zobel. Expect delicate and whimsical pieces, from diamond-encrusted ear cuffs to geometric rings. ⊠ *56 Crosby St., between Spring and Broome Sts., SoHo* ☎ *212/219–1264* ⊕ *www.brokenenglishjewelry.com* Ⓜ *6 to Spring St.*

Dinosaur Designs

JEWELRY/ACCESSORIES | The jewelry and housewares designs at this small, Australian-owned brand are inspired by nature and organic shapes. Resin is used to craft jewelry and vases in bold colors like hot pink and orange. The tableware is striking and very covetable. ⊠ *21 Crosby St., between Grand and Howard Sts., SoHo* ☎ *212/680–3523* ⊕ *www. dinosaurdesigns.com* Ⓜ *6, J, N, Q, R, W, Z, to Canal St.*

SHOES, HANDBAGS, AND LEATHER GOODS

Camper

SHOES/LUGGAGE/LEATHER GOODS | Urbanites love this Spanish footwear company for its funky but comfortable shoes. The slip-ons and lace-ups have generously rounded toes and a springy feel. A signature style has pairs of shoes with slightly mismatched designs. ⊠ *110 Prince St., at Greene St., SoHo* ☎ *212/343–4220* ⊕ *www.camper.com* Ⓜ *N, R, W to Prince St.; B, D, F, M to Broadway–Lafayette St.*

The Frye Company

SHOES/LUGGAGE/LEATHER GOODS | There's an old western feel at this 6,000-square-foot mecca to boots, thanks to the exposed brick walls and reclaimed barn doors. Boots can be tattooed—or hot stamped—with your initials while you wait in the lounge. In addition to Frye's famed boots, the store sells flats, oxfords, clogs, and mules. ⊠ *113 Spring St., between Mercer and Greene Sts., SoHo* ☎ *212/226–3793* ⊕ *www. thefryecompany.com* Ⓜ *N, R, W to Prince St.; B, D, F, M to Broadway–Lafayette St.*

Longchamp

SHOES/LUGGAGE/LEATHER GOODS | Its Le Pliage foldable nylon bags may have become a preppy staple, but don't think this label is stuffy—or all about nylon. There's a wide selection of leather handbags as well as wallets, belts, and shoes, and the brand often collaborates with renowned artists. The distinctive store with its eye-catching staircase was designed by celebrity architect Thomas Heatherwick. ⊠ *132 Spring St., between Wooster and Greene Sts., SoHo* ☎ *212/343–7444* ⊕ *www.longchamp.com* Ⓜ *N, R, W to Prince St.*

NoLIta

Many locals would probably say that the spirit of old SoHo is somewhat alive in NoLIta (*No*rth of *Li*ttle *Ita*ly), a charming neighborhood with an artistic spirit, independently run boutiques and restaurants, and a local vibe. The streets here are less frantic and crowded than either SoHo or Chinatown, and each block could provide hours of roaming and ducking into small shops, nursing a cappuccino at a sidewalk café, or lingering over a meal surrounded by stylish New Yorkers. This is downtown, so the prices aren't cheap, but the quality is high and the experience unique.

◉ Sights

St. Patrick's Old Cathedral

RELIGIOUS SITE | If you've seen *The Godfather,* you've had a peek inside New York's first Roman Catholic cathedral—the interior shots of the infamous baptism scene were filmed here. Dedicated in 1815, this church lost its designation as the seat of New York's bishop when the current St. Patrick's opened uptown in 1879. The unadorned exterior of the cathedral gives no hint of the splendors within, which include an 1868 Henry Erben pipe organ. The interior dates from the 1860s, after a large fire gutted most of the original structure. The enormous marble altar surrounded by hand-carved niches (reredos) houses an extraordinary collection of sacred statuary and other Gothic exuberance. Candlelit tours (daily at 11, 1, and 3; fee) of the church and its catacombs, along with Most Precious Blood Church, can be booked through ⊕ www.tommysnewyork.com. ✉ 263 Mulberry St., corner of Mott and Prince Sts., NoLIta ☎ 212/226–8075 ⊕ www. oldcathedral.org Ⓜ N, R, W to Prince St.; 6 to Bleecker St.

 Restaurants

In NoLIta, SoHo's trendy next-door neighborhood, the spirit of old, pre-chain-store SoHo prevails. Diminutive eateries, squeezed between up-and-coming designer boutiques, flank the narrow streets of this atmospheric neighborhood.

Black Seed Bagels

$ | CANADIAN | FAMILY | New York is known for bagels, which tend to be doughy and delicious, but the Montreal-style bagels here have a denser, sweeter dough, with "toppings" (sesame, poppy seed, salt, everything) that are more generous than on the New York bagels. The all-day menu includes sandwich options with cream cheese, smoked salmon, whitefish salad, or baked eggs, with additional lunch choices like a BLT, roast beef with horseradish cream cheese, and a tuna melt, among others. **Known for:** Montreal-style bagels; creative sandwich options; classy decor for a bagel joint. 🏷 Average main: $9 ✉ 170 Elizabeth St., between Spring and Kenmare Sts., NoLIta ☎ 212/730–1950 ⊕ www.blackseedbagels.com Ⓜ 6 to Spring St.

Café Habana

$$ | MEXICAN | FAMILY | The Mexican-style grilled corn, liberally sprinkled with chili powder, lime, and cotija cheese, is undoubtedly worth getting your hands dirty at this crowded, hip luncheonette. Follow up with a classic Cuban sandwich (roast pork, ham, Swiss cheese, pickles, and chipotle mayo), fish tacos, or one of the innovative salads. **Known for:** grilled corn; hearty Mexican fare; take-out shop around the corner. 🏷 Average main: $15 ✉ 17 Prince St., at Elizabeth St., NoLIta ☎ 212/625–2001 ⊕ www.cafehabana. com Ⓜ 6 to Spring St.; N, R, W to Prince St.; J, Z to Bowery.

Emporio

$$ | ITALIAN | The centerpiece of the large, skylighted back room is a wood-fired oven that turns out crisp, thin-crust pizzas topped with quality ingredients like prosciutto and buffalo mozzarella. Try to save some of your carb allowance, though, for house-made pastas like garganelli with pork sausage and house ragù. **Known for:** thin-crust Roman-style pizza; entrées like whole roasted fish; free small bites at the bar during happy hour. 🏷 Average main: $23 ✉ 231 Mott St., between Prince and Spring Sts., NoLIta ☎ 212/966–1234 ⊕ www.emporiony.com Ⓜ B, D, F, M to Broadway–Lafayette St.; N, R, W to Prince St.; 6 to Bleecker St.

★ **Estela**

$$$ | MEDITERRANEAN | Long before Mr. and Mrs. Obama ate dinner here in 2014, this second-floor restaurant with minimalist decor had been on the map for those who appreciate chef Ignacio Mattos's deceptively simple cuisine. The creativity of his creations has a tendency to sneak up on the diner, such as the rye matzo bread under the mashed salt cod, and the sunchoke chips folded into the sumptuous beef tartare. **Known for:** hard-to-get tables; top-notch cocktails; interesting wine list with unique vintages. 🏷 Average main: $27 ✉ 47 E. Houston St.,

between Mott and Mulberry Sts., NoLIta ☎ 212/219–7693 🌐 www.estelanyc.com ⏲ No lunch Mon.–Thurs. [M] 6 to Bleecker St.; B, D, F, M to Broadway–Lafayette St.

La Esquina

$$ | MEXICAN | Anchoring a downtown corner under a bright neon sign, La Esquina looks like a fast-food taqueria, with cheap tacos sold for take-out, but it's actually three superb south-of-the-border spots in one, including a café and brasserie. The real draw is the basement brasserie, like a Mexican speakeasy, accessible (by reservation only) through an unmarked door just inside the ground-floor taqueria. **Known for:** buzzy scene; large portions of Mexican fare; potent margaritas. [$] *Average main: $20* ✉ *114 Kenmare St., between Cleveland Pl. and Lafayette St., NoLIta* ☎ *646/613–7100* 🌐 *www.esquinanyc.com* [M] *6 to Spring St*

★ Le Coucou

$$$$ | FRENCH | If you heard that a Chicago-born chef was taking New York City by storm with classic Parisian fare, you might exclaim "mon Dieu!," but then you realize it's chef Daniel Rose, who earned the approval of critics and diners at his Paris restaurant Spring. Expect updated versions of Gallic classics like sweetbreads with a creamy tarragon sauce, and mains like a duck and foie gras pairing for two, rabbit, or a prime fillet with bone marrow. **Known for:** the talk of the town; prix-fixe lunch; sophisticated space. [$] *Average main: $40* ✉ *138 Lafayette St., at Howard St., NoLIta* ☎ *212/271–4252* 🌐 *www.lecoucou.com* [M] *6, J, N, Q, R, W, Z to Canal St.*

Lombardi's Pizza

$$ | PIZZA | FAMILY | Brick walls, red-and-white-checked tablecloths, and the aroma of delicious thin-crust pies emerging from the coal oven set the mood for dining on some of the best pizza in Manhattan, and Lombardi's has been serving it up since 1905 (though not in the same location). The mozzarella is always fresh, resulting in a nearly greaseless slice, and the toppings, such as meatballs, pancetta, or imported anchovies, are also top quality. **Known for:** traditional New York pizza; always-busy, cash-only spot; clam pizza. [$] *Average main: $24* ✉ *32 Spring St., at Mott St., NoLIta* ☎ *212/941–7994* 🌐 *www.firstpizza.com* 💳 *No credit cards* [M] *6 to Spring St.; J, Z to Bowery; N, R, W to Prince St.*

Parm

$$ | ITALIAN | There's more to this casual NoLIta eatery than the namesake Italian sandwich for which the budding chainlet is named. Founded by chefs Rich Torrisi and Mario Carbone (who are behind other hits like Dirty French, Carbone, and The Grill), Parm has a menu that includes salads, baked clams, and, of course, variations on the eponymous sandwich, including eggplant, meatball, turkey, and chicken, all available as sandwiches or platters. **Known for:** tasty Italian-American staples; plenty of parm options; good-value wine. [$] *Average main: $13* ✉ *248 Mulberry St., between Prince and Spring Sts., NoLIta* ☎ *212/993–7189* 🌐 *www.parmnyc.com* [M] *B, D, F, M to Broadway–Lafayette St., N, R, W to Prince St.*

Pasquale Jones

$$$ | ITALIAN | Just north of of the schlocky restaurants of Little Italy but miles away in terms of quality, Pasquale Jones serves crispy pizza and inventive takes on Italian dishes from the wood oven. A meal in this chic, minimalist restaurant isn't cheap, but remember that service is included in the menu prices, and that makes it better—plus, the food is great. **Known for:** thin-crust pizza; wood-oven-baked chicken alla Romana; good wine list. [$] *Average main: $25* ✉ *187 Mulberry St., at Kenmare St., NoLIta* 🌐 *www.pasqualejones.com* ⏲ *No lunch Mon.* [M] *4, 6 to Spring St.*

Rubirosa

$$ | ITALIAN | Locals have shown an insatiable appetite for this bustling but sophisticated Italian American eatery serving high-quality, classic Italian dishes. You can't really go wrong, so share a half order of pasta alongside a Staten Island–style thin-crust pizza, and maybe a fork-tender veal chop Milanese. **Known for:** vodka-sauce pizza; half orders of some pastas; the wait: put your name on the list early, then have a drink elsewhere. $ *Average main: $22* ⊠ *235 Mulberry St., between Prince and Spring Sts., NoLIta* ☎ *212/965–0500* ⊕ *www. rubirosanyc.com* Ⓜ *6 to Spring St.; N, R, W to Prince St.*

The Smile

$$ | **AMERICAN** | Subterranean and almost hidden, the Smile turns frowns upside down, if you're into lounging among a fashion-conscious clientele in a cozy, brick-walled space. The brunch and lunch menu leans to comfort foods like waffles, egg sandwiches, and avocado toasts, while dinner options, like whole trout, brisket, hanger steak, or roasted chicken, are more ambitious. **Known for:** celeb sightings; straightforward but high-quality food; breakfast served until 4:30 pm. $ *Average main: $16* ⊠ *26 Bond St., between Lafayette St. and the Bowery, NoLIta* ☎ *646/329–5836* ⊕ *www.the-smilenyc.com* Ⓜ *B, D, F, M to Broadway–Lafayette St.; 6 to Bleecker St.*

★ Uncle Boons

$$ | **THAI** | If you're looking for quality Thai in Manhattan, a good choice is Uncle Boons in NoLIta: just be aware that just about everyone else in Manhattan is also trying to get a table at this cute subterranean spot with eclectic art on the walls. Your best bet is to order several items to share, but the *khao soi*, a noodle dish with an ultratender chicken leg swimming in a tangy yellow curry, is so good you'll want it for yourself. **Known for:** high-quality northern Thai fare; great cocktails; Uncle Boons Sister, the more casual spot on Mott St. $ *Average main: $24* ⊠ *7 Spring St., near Elizabeth St., NoLIta* ☎ *646/370–6650* ⊕ *www.*

uncleboons.com ⊘ *No lunch* Ⓜ *J, Z to Bowery; 6 to Spring St.*

 Hotels

The Nolitan Hotel

$$ | **HOTEL** | The cool Nolitan combines a hip, slightly gritty feel with some luxe touches, but don't expect a lot of space to spread out. **Pros:** cool vibe; fun location convenient to lower Manhattan and Brooklyn; fabulous views from some rooms. **Cons:** smallish rooms; gym access five-minute walk away; some street noise. $ *Rooms from: $300* ⊠ *30 Kenmare St., between Elizabeth and Mott Sts., NoLIta* ☎ *212/925–2555* ⊕ *www.nolitanhotel.com* ↩ *57 rooms* ❖ *No meals* Ⓜ *J, Z to Bowery; 6 to Spring St.*

❤ Nightlife

Sweet & Vicious

BARS/PUBS | This unpretentious lounge is high on the sweet factor and luckily low on the vicious attitudes, which helps explain why it's been consistently popular since it opened in 1998. There's a lovely back garden that's more private than the sceney bars you might otherwise hit in SoHo and NoLIta. ⊠ *5 Spring St., between the Bowery and Elizabeth St., NoLIta* ☎ *212/334–7915* ⊕ *www. sweetandvicious.nyc* Ⓜ *6 to Spring St.; J, Z to Bowery.*

🛍 Shopping

NoLIta is a great shopping area, thanks to the abundance of boutiques that range from quirky to elegant. Like SoHo, NoLIta has changed from an understated, locals-only area to a crowded weekend magnet, as much about people-watching as shopping. Still, unlike those of its SoHo neighbor, these stores remain largely independent. Running along the parallel north–south spines of Elizabeth, Mott, and Mulberry Streets, between

Houston and Kenmare Streets, NoLIta's boutiques tend to be small and, as real estate costs dictate, somewhat pricey.

BEAUTY
Le Labo

PERFUME/COSMETICS | If you're bored with the perfume stock at department stores, visit this tiny boutique with a rustic, industrial vibe and resident mixologist who helps create your ideal perfume. After you choose your favorite scents, the perfume is mixed and a personalized label created for your bottle. ⊠ *233 Elizabeth St., between Houston and Prince Sts., NoLIta* ☎ *212/219–2230* ⊕ *www.lelabofragrances.com* Ⓜ *B, D, F, M to Broadway–Lafayette St.*

★ Santa Maria Novella

PERFUME/COSMETICS | A heavy, iron-barred door leads to a hushed, scented inner sanctum of beauty products. At this U.S. outpost of the 600-year-old Florentine company, shoppers can browse intriguingly archaic colognes, creams, and soaps such as rose rice powder, prepared according to both traditional and modern recipes. Everything is packaged in bottles and jars with antique-style apothecary labels. There's also a wide selection of fragrances. ⊠ *285 Lafayette St., between Houston and Prince Sts., NoLIta* ☎ *212/271–0884* ⊕ *buy.smnovella.com* Ⓜ *N, R, W to Prince St.; B, D, F, M to Broadway–Lafayette St.*

BOOKS AND STATIONERY
★ McNally Jackson

BOOKS/STATIONERY | A bibliophile's dream, this cozy independent bookstore in a bright, two-story space has hardwood floors, a café with delicious snacks, and plenty of chairs for lounging and curling up with a book. More than 50,000 books are stocked, including a substantial poetry section downstairs. Upstairs, literature is organized geographically. Author events are held almost nightly. ⊠ *52 Prince St., between Lafayette and Mulberry Sts., NoLIta* ☎ *212/274–1160*

⊕ *www.mcnallyjackson.com* Ⓜ *N, R, W to Prince St.; 6 to Spring St.*

CLOTHING
Creatures of Comfort

CLOTHING | Owner Jade Lai has brought her popular L.A. outpost to New York with this open, airy boutique that racks cool clothes from emerging designers alongside products from around the world. Look for brands like Acne, Band of Outsiders, and the house label, Creatures of Comfort. A small selection of shoes, as well as under-the-radar beauty products, such as Rodin hand cream, rounds out the shelves. ⊠ *205 Mulberry St., between Spring and Kenmare Sts., NoLIta* ☎ *212/925–1005* Ⓜ *6 to Spring St.*

Duncan Quinn

CLOTHING | Described as "Savile Row meets Rock 'n' Roll" by *GQ*, Duncan Quinn provides bespoke services for everything from chalk-stripe suits to collared shirts, as well as ready-to-wear, in a shop not much bigger than its silk pocket squares. Off-the-rack shirts are handmade in Italy, but if you want to splurge, get fitted for one with mother-of-pearl buttons. ⊠ *70 Kenmare St., between Mott and Mulberry Sts., NoLIta* ☎ *212/226–7030* ⊕ *www.duncanquinn.com* Ⓜ *6 to Spring St.; J, Z to Bowery*

★ Everlane

CLOTHING | A cult-favorite online brand has brought its ethically produced (the company discloses fully where and how the products are made), high-quality basics for both men and women to a brick-and-mortar store. With its whitewashed walls, skylights, and electronic checkout, the boutique mimics the website experience, with the bonus that you can try on those colorful cashmere sweaters and silk shirts. The space regularly hosts panels, community events, and photography installations about Everlane's factories. ⊠ *28 Prince St., between Mott and Elizabeth Sts., NoLIta* ⊕ *www.everlane.com*

Ⓜ N, R, W to Prince St.; 6 to Spring St.;
B, D, F, M to Broadway–Lafayette St.

GROUPE

CLOTHING | The longtime SoHo men's
fashion boutique Seize sur Vingt has
evolved to incorporate three different
in-house design brands and an art gallery,
touting itself as an "integrated fashion
collective." You can still splurge on Seize
sur Vingt's exquisitely tailored shirts
and suits, both off the rack or created
bespoke from a mind-boggling array of
fabrics (linen, broadcloth oxford, flannel),
but now there are more moderately
priced options as well, with sweaters,
sneakers, womens wear, and more.
✉ 198 Bowery, between Prince and
Spring Sts., NoLIta ☎ 212/625–1620
⊕ www.groupe.nyc Ⓜ 6 to Spring St.

INA

CLOTHING | The clothing at this couture
consignment store harks back only one
or two seasons, and in some cases, the
items have never been worn. Browse the
racks to spot gems from Lanvin, Chanel,
and Alexander McQueen. There are multiple locations around the city; this outpost
carries offerings for women, while men's
clothes are offered at the location next
door. ✉ 21 Prince St., between Elizabeth
and Mott Sts., NoLIta ☎ 212/334–9048
⊕ www.inanyc.com Ⓜ 6 to Spring St.; B,
D, F, M to Broadway–Lafayette St.

Jay Kos

CLOTHING | There aren't many boutiques
where the owner sometimes whips up
a snack for customers in the boutique's
custom kitchen, but this menswear
designer—famous for dressing Diddy
and Johnny Depp—wanted his boutique
to have a homey feel. The clothes veer
toward the fabulous: suede shoes, linen
suits, and cashmere sweaters, which are
displayed in armoires. ✉ 293 Mott St.,
at Houston St., NoLIta ☎ 212/319–2770
⊕ www.jaykos.com Ⓜ B, D, F, M to
Broadway–Lafayette St.

L'Appartement Sézane

CLOTHING | In a setting inspired by the
high ceilings, floor-to-ceiling windows,
and parquet floors of Parisian apartments
and brasseries, this cult French brand's
store brings its signature French-girl
chic to New York. In addition to the
small permanent collection (called La
Liste), limited-edition seasonal releases
ensure that the in-store stock changes
regularly. Coffee and treats from nearby
Maman are available, and events are held
regularly. ✉ 254 Elizabeth St., between
E. Houston and Prince Sts., NoLIta
☎ 917/261–6190 ⊕ www.sezane.com
Ⓜ B, D, F, M to Broadway–Lafayette St.

Warm

CLOTHING | If you want to feel the love,
come to this little boutique owned by
lifelong surfers Winnie Beattie and her
husband Rob Magnotta. Everything has a
sunny, beachy vibe, from leather sandals,
bikinis, and bleached sweaters to hand-
blown glass vases. There's also a collection of children's books, indie magazines,
housewares, and menswear. ✉ 181 Mott
St., between Kenmare and Broome Sts.,
NoLIta ☎ 212/925–1200 ⊕ www.warmny.
com Ⓜ 6 to Spring St.

GIFTS AND SOUVENIRS

Bulletin Broads

GIFTS/SOUVENIRS | From portraits of
Michelle Obama and "Nevertheless, She
Persisted" mugs to necklaces reading
"Nasty Woman" and greeting cards
with Beyoncé lyrics, this millennial-pink
boutique is a one-stop shop for feminist
products. The women-run business rents
out its shelves to female entrepreneurs
whose wares have previously only been
available on the Internet, and donates
10% of its profits to Planned Parenthood
of NYC. The store regularly hosts events,
many centered around activism. There
are also locations in the Flatiron District
and Williamsburg. ✉ 27 Prince St.,
between Mott and Elizabeth Sts., NoLIta
☎ 646/928–0213 ⊕ www.bulletin.co Ⓜ N,

R, W to Prince St.; 6 to Spring St.; B, D, F, M to Broadway–Lafayette St.

JEWELRY AND ACCESSORIES
Erica Weiner

JEWELRY/ACCESSORIES | The eponymous designer specializes in vintage-inspired jewelry and antiques: delicate Art Deco earrings, vintage lockets, and necklaces fashioned from antique charms. The Erica Weiner collection includes pieces under $200. ✉ *173 Elizabeth St., between Spring and Kenmare Sts., NoLIta* ☎ *212/334–6383* ⊕ *www.ericaweiner. com* Ⓜ *6 to Spring St.; J, Z to Bowery.*

Love Adorned

JEWELRY/ACCESSORIES | Glass cases full of modern and antique jewelry and shelves stocked with perfume and knickknacks beckon you to browse in this airy, romantic shop. Prices are reasonable, plus they do piercings. ✉ *269 Elizabeth St., between Houston and Prince Sts., NoLIta* ☎ *212/431–5683* ⊕ *www.loveadorned. com* Ⓜ *N, R, W to Prince St.; 6 to Spring St.; F to 2nd Ave.*

SHOES, HANDBAGS, AND LEATHER GOODS
Clare V

JEWELRY/ACCESSORIES | L.A. based designer Clare Vivier's New York store displays her signature simple-but-elegant leather fold-over clutches in every size and color, as well as understated totes and duffels. There's a line of men's accessories, plus iPad cases, sunglasses, and other sundries. ✉ *239 Elizabeth St., between Houston and Prince Sts., NoLIta* ☎ *646/484–5757* ⊕ *www.clarev. com* Ⓜ *N, R, W to Prince St.; 6 to Spring St.; F to 2nd Ave.*

Highway

JEWELRY/ACCESSORIES | The Japanese-style, origami-influenced bags here marry form and function. Totes and messenger bags come in durable leather and nylon; popular styles include lots of pockets. ✉ *238 Mott St., between Prince*

and Spring Sts., NoLIta ☎ *212/966–4388* ⊕ *www.highwaybuzz.com* Ⓜ *6 to Spring St.; N, R, W to Prince St.*

John Fluevog Shoes

SHOES/LUGGAGE/LEATHER GOODS | The inventor of the "Angel" sole (protects against water, acid, and "Satan"), Fluevog designs chunky, funky shoes and boots for men and women that are popular with rock stars and those who want to look like them. ✉ *250 Mulberry St., at Prince St., NoLIta* ☎ *212/431–4484* ⊕ *www.fluevog.com* Ⓜ *N, R, W to Prince St.; 6 to Spring St.*

Manhattan Portgage/Token

JEWELRY/ACCESSORIES | Messenger bags are now ubiquitous, but this is the store that started it all. Super durable, the bags come in waxed canvas as well as nylon, and the line has expanded to include totes, duffels, and travel bags, all in unadorned, simple styles. ✉ *258 Elizabeth St., between Houston and Prince Sts., NoLIta* ☎ *212/226–9655* ⊕ *www.manhattanportage.com* Ⓜ *N, R, W to Prince St.; F to 2nd Ave.*

Little Italy

Just east of Broadway, the tangle of pedestrian-friendly blocks surrounding Mulberry Street between NoLIta and bustling Canal Street are still a cheerful salute to all things Italian, although over the decades Little Italy has been whittled down by the sprawl of nearby Chinatown. There are red, green, and white street decorations on permanent display, and specialty grocers and pasta makers still dish up delights, though it's all a bit touristy these days—if it's a great Italian meal you want, you might be wise to look elsewhere. Still, Little Italy is fun to walk around, and several of the classic food stores on Grand Street are worth a stop if you're after an edible souvenir, like a box of classic cannoli. For a bigger and more

The Gangs of Five Points

In the mid-19th century, the Five Points area was perhaps the city's most notorious and dangerous neighborhood. The confluence of five streets—Mulberry, Anthony (now Worth), Cross (now Park), Orange (now Baxter), and Little Water (no longer in existence)—had been built over a drainage pond that was filled in the 1820s. When buildings began to sink into the mosquito-filled muck, middle-class residents abandoned their homes. Buildings were then chopped into tiny apartments that were rented to the poorest of the poor, who at this point included newly emancipated slaves and Irish immigrants fleeing famine. Newspaper accounts at the time tell of daily robberies and other violent crimes. With corrupt political leaders like William Marcy "Boss" Tweed more concerned with lining their pockets than patrolling the streets, keeping order was left to the club-wielding hooligans portrayed in Martin Scorsese's 2002 film *Gangs of New York*. The neighborhood, razed in the 1880s to make way for Columbus Park, has left a lasting legacy: in the music halls where different ethnic groups grudgingly came together, the Irish jig and the African American shuffle combined to form a new type of fancy footwork called tap dancing. Today this is the heart of Chinatown. Residents gather in Columbus Park for tai chi in the morning and sometimes high-spirited board games in the afternoon.

bustling Little Italy, head up to Arthur Avenue in the Bronx, where you'll find several good, affordable restaurants and a cornucopia of authentic Italian goods made for New Yorkers and tourists alike.

Every September, Little Italy's Mulberry Street is home to the giant Feast of San Gennaro, a busy 11-day festival that sizzles with old New York flavors—sausages and onions included.

◉ Sights

Most Precious Blood Church

RELIGIOUS SITE | The National Shrine of San Gennaro, a replica of the grotto at Lourdes, is the high point of Most Precious Blood Church's richly painted interior. The church becomes a focal point during the annual Feast of San Gennaro. Tours of the church and St. Patrick's Old Cathedral can be booked through ⊕ *www.tommysnewyork.com* (daily at 11, 1, and 3; fee). ✉ *109 Mulberry St.,* *between Hester and Canal Sts., Little Italy* ☎ *212/226–6427* Ⓜ *6, J, N, Q, R, W, Z to Canal St.*

Chinatown

Chinatown is a living, breathing, anything-but-quiet enclave with vibrant streets full of food shops selling exotic produce and seafood, Chinese restaurants and bakeries, Buddhist temples, herbalists, discount massage parlors, and barbershops. A quarter of the city's Chinese residents live here, in a neighborhood that started as a seven-block area but now covers some 40-plus blocks above and below Canal Street (encroaching on what was once a thriving Little Italy). Head to **Mott Street,** south of Canal—Chinatown's main thoroughfare—where the first Chinese immigrants (mostly men) settled in tenements in the late 1880s. Walk carefully, as the sidewalks can be slick from the ice underneath the

Some of the storefronts and signage in Chinatown are bilingual—but some are just in Chinese.

eels, blue crabs, snapper, and shrimp that seem to look back at you from seafood displays as you pass by. You can create a movable feast here with delicious soup dumplings, Peking duck, yellow custard cake, and bubble tea—each at a different place in the neighborhood. A city tourist-information kiosk (⊕ www.explorechinatown.com) on a traffic island where Canal, Baxter, and Walker Streets meet can help you with tours, and it also has a map that's useful for unraveling the area's tangled and angled streets.

◉ Sights

Columbus Park
CITY PARK | People-watching is the thing to do in this park. Head toward the Bayard Street section, and if you swing by in the morning, you'll see men and women practicing tai chi; the afternoons bring intense games of cards and mahjongg. In the mid-19th century the park was known as the Five Points—the intersection of Mulberry Street, Anthony (now Worth) Street, Cross (now Park) Street, Orange (now Baxter) Street, and Little Water Street (no longer in existence)—and was ruled by dangerous Irish gangs. In the 1880s a neighborhood-improvement campaign brought about the park's creation. ⊠ *Bounded by Bayard, Mulberry, Worth, and Baxter Sts., Chinatown* ⊕ *www.nycgovparks.org/parks/ M015* Ⓜ *6, J, N, Q, R, W, Z to Canal St.*

Kimlau Square
MEMORIAL | Ten streets converge at this labyrinthine intersection crisscrossed at odd angles by pedestrian walkways. Standing on the concrete island (popular with the pigeons) is the **Kimlau Arch,** named for Ralph Kimlau, a bomber pilot who died in World War II; the arch is dedicated to all Chinese Americans who "lost their Lives in Defense of Freedom and Democracy." A statue on the square's eastern edge pays tribute to a Qing Dynasty official named Lin Zxeu, the Fujianese minister who sparked the First Opium War in 1839 by banning the

drug. ✉ *Chatham Sq., Bowery and E. Broadway, Chinatown* 🌐 *www.nycgovparks.org/parks/kimlausquare* [M] *4, 5, 6 to Brooklyn Bridge–City Hall; J, Z to Chambers St.*

Mahayana Buddhist Temple

RELIGIOUS SITE | This bright and beautiful Buddhist temple is at a very busy corner, at the foot of the Manhattan Bridge Arch on the Bowery, where gilded lions guard the temple's entrance. Inside are a 16-foot-tall Buddha seated on a lotus flower (allegedly the largest Buddha in the city), incense-burning urns, hand-painted prints, and a gift shop full of interesting items on the second floor. ✉ *133 Canal St., at the Bowery, Chinatown* ☎ *212/925–8787* [M] *B, D to Grand St.*

Museum of Chinese in America (MOCA)

MUSEUM | Founded in 1980, this museum is dedicated to preserving and presenting the history of the Chinese people and their descendants in the United States. The current building, near the boundary between Chinatown and Little Italy (many would say it's in Little Italy), was designed by Maya Lin, architect of the Vietnam Veterans Memorial in Washington, D.C. MOCA's core exhibition on Chinese American history, *With a Single Step: Stories in the Making of America,* includes artworks, personal and domestic artifacts, historical documentation, and films. Chinese laundry tools, a traditional general store, and antique business signs are some of the unique objects on display. Rotating exhibitions are on display in another gallery. MOCA sponsors workshops, neighborhood walking tours, lectures, and family events. The museum is free to visit on the first Thursday of the month. ✉ *215 Centre St., between Grand and Howard Sts., Chinatown* ☎ *212/619–4785* 🌐 *www.mocanyc.org* 🎟 *$10* 🕒 *Closed Mon.* [M] *6, J, N, Q, R, W, Z to Canal St.*

🍴 Restaurants

Chinatown beckons adventurous diners with restaurants representing numerous regional cuisines of China, including Cantonese, Sichuan, Hunan, Fujian, Shanghai, and Hong Kong–style cooking. Malaysian and Vietnamese restaurants also have taken root here, and the neighborhood continues to grow rapidly.

456 Shanghai Cuisine

$$ | **CHINESE** | Crowds come to this casual Chinatown eatery for above-average Chinese fare, such as General Tso's chicken, pork buns, and cold sesame noodles, but do yourself a favor and order soup dumplings (*xiao long bao*) as soon as you sit down. You won't regret it: the dumplings, doughy and thin on the outside, encase morsels of crab swimming in a bold, porky broth. **Known for:** superb Shanghai soup dumplings; very affordable; efficient service. [$] *Average main: $14* ✉ *69 Mott St., between Canal and Bayard Sts., Chinatown* ☎ *212/964–0003* [M] *6, J, N, Q, R, W, Z to Canal St.*

Great NY Noodletown

$ | **CHINESE** | **FAMILY** | Although the soups and noodles are unbeatable at this no-frills restaurant, what you should really order are the window decorations—the hanging lacquered ducks and roasted pork, listed on a simple board hung on the wall and superbly served with pungent garlic-and-ginger sauce on the side. Seasonal specialties like duck with flowering chives and salt-baked soft-shell crabs are excellent. **Known for:** Peking duck; affordable and tasty Chinese food; lively atmosphere, with late hours on weekends. [$] *Average main: $12* ✉ *28 Bowery, at Bayard St., Chinatown* ☎ *212/349–0923* 🌐 *www.greatnynoodletown.com* 💳 *No credit cards* [M] *6, J, N, Q, R, W, Z to Canal St.; B, D to Grand St.; F to East Broadway.*

Jing Fong

$$ | CHINESE | FAMILY | On weekend mornings people pack this vast dim sum palace, so be prepared to wait. Once your number is called, take the escalator up to the carnivalesque third-floor dining room, where servers push carts crammed with tasty dim sum goodness, and diners are plied with delights including steamed dumplings, crispy spring rolls, and barbecue pork buns. **Known for:** palatial dining room; dim sum, including adventurous items like chicken feet, tripe, and snails; worthy mango pudding. $ *Average main: $16 ⊠ 20 Elizabeth St., 2nd fl., between Bayard and Canal Sts., Chinatown* ☎ 212/964–5256 ⊕ *www.jingfongny.com* Ⓜ *6, J, N, Q, R, W, Z to Canal St.; B, D to Grand St.*

Joe's Shanghai

$$ | CHINESE | FAMILY | Joe opened his first Shanghai restaurant in Queens in 1995, but buoyed by the accolades showered on his steamed soup dumplings—filled with a rich, fragrant broth and ground pork or a pork-crabmeat mixture—several Manhattan outposts soon followed. The trick is to take a bite of the dumpling and slurp out the soup, then eat the rest. **Known for:** extensive menu, though Shanghai soup dumplings are don't-miss; cash only; fast-moving line. $ *Average main: $17 ⊠ 9 Pell St., between the Bowery and Mott St., Chinatown* ☎ 212/233–8888 ⊕ *www.joeshanghairestaurants. com* ▭ *No credit cards* Ⓜ *6, J, N, Q, R, W, Z to Canal St.; B, D to Grand St.*

New Malaysia

$$ | MALAYSIAN | This Malaysian restaurant, down a nondescript passageway between the Bowery and Elizabeth Street, is worth the wander for Malaysian favorites like roti flatbread with curry and delicious red-bean and coconut-milk drinks. The atmosphere is casual and table service is relaxed, which means you might need to flag down your server. **Known for:** long, varied menu of authentic Malaysian fare; good value; nonalcoholic drinks. $ *Average main: $14 ⊠ 46–48 Bowery, near Canal St., Chinatown* ☎ 212/964–0284 ⊕ *newmalaysiarestaurant.com* Ⓜ *6, J, N, Q, R, W, Z to Canal St.; B, D to Grand St.*

Tasty Hand-Pulled Noodles

$ | CHINESE | The name says it all: the open kitchen at this salt-of-the-earth, cash-only Chinatown restaurant (located on charming, curved Doyers Street) means you can watch the noodle-slinger in action while awaiting your bowl of, yes, tasty hand-pulled noodles. Just choose your ingredients—beef, pork, oxtail, eel, chicken, lamb, or shrimp, among others—and prepare to eat the most delicious bowl of noodles since that last trip to Shanghai. **Known for:** very affordable; good variety of options; small space. $ *Average main: $7 ⊠ 1 Doyers St., at Bowery, Chinatown* ☎ 212/791–1817 ⊕ *www.tastyhandpullednoodles.com* ▭ *No credit cards* Ⓜ *6, J, N, Q, R, W, Z to Canal St.; B, D to Grand St.*

Xi'an Famous Foods

$ | CHINESE | Xi'an's is certainly famous around the five boroughs for its spicy cumin lamb burger, but don't miss out on the chance to explore the generally underrepresented cuisine of western China at this casual cash-only counter-serve spot. Some of the dishes challenge the bounds of boldness in eating (lamb offal soup, anyone?), but it's cheap enough to experiment, so tuck into that bowl of oxtail noodle soup and enjoy. **Known for:** spicy western Chinese fare; lamb burger; good value. $ *Average main: $10 ⊠ 45 Bayard St., between the Bowery and Elizabeth St., Chinatown* ☎ 212/608–4170 ⊕ *www.xianfoods.com* ▭ *No credit cards* Ⓜ *6, J, N, Q, R, W, Z to Canal St.; B, D to Grand St.*

Hotels

Hotel 50 Bowery

$ | **HOTEL** | With a design aesthetic and food offerings inspired by the neighborhood's multifaceted heritage, this thoroughly modern hotel from the Joie de Vivre group takes full advantage of its downtown location. **Pros:** rooms on higher floors have great views; double-paned windows mean no street noise; destination dining and rooftop bar. **Cons:** basement gym with no windows; might feel too cool for some; a subway ride from most uptown tourist sites. [$] *Rooms from: $299* ✉ *50 Bowery, Chinatown* ☎ *212/508–8000* 🌐 *www.jdvhotels.com* 🛏 *229 rooms* 🍴 *No meals* [M] *B, D to Grand St.*

Nightlife

Apotheke

BARS/PUBS | Tucked away down a winding lane deep in Chinatown, this cocktail apothecary is a surprising but happy find in a neighborhood known more for soup dumplings than creative tipples. Influenced by the 19th-century absinthe parlors of Paris, this historically inflected spot is all about drama and presentation, but the the results are a delicious feast for all the senses. ✉ *9 Doyers St., near Pell St., Chinatown* ☎ *212/406–0400* 🌐 *www.apothekenyc.com* [M] *6, J, N, Q, R, W, Z to Canal St.; 4, 5, 6 to Brooklyn Bridge–City Hall.*

Chapter 5

THE EAST VILLAGE AND THE LOWER EAST SIDE

Updated by
Caroline Trefler

◉ Sights	🍴 Restaurants	🛏 Hotels	🛍 Shopping	🍸 Nightlife
★★☆☆☆	★★★★★	★★☆☆☆	★★★★☆	★★★★★

NEIGHBORHOOD SNAPSHOT

TOP EXPERIENCES

- People-watching on St. Marks Place or at Tompkins Square Park
- Getting immersed in the art scene on the Lower East Side
- Shopping at boutiques and vintage clothing stores
- Taking a tour at the Lower East Side Tenement Museum

GETTING HERE

For the East Village, take the R or W subway line to 8th Street–New York University (NYU), the 6 to Astor Place, or the L to 3rd Avenue. To reach Alphabet City, take the L to 1st Avenue or the F to 2nd Avenue. For the Lower East Side, go to the 2nd Avenue stop on the F and then walk southeast, or take the F, M, J, or Z to the Delancey Street–Essex Street stop.

PLANNING YOUR TIME

The East Village lets loose on weekends, when nightlife-seekers descend on the area, filling up the bars and spilling onto the sidewalks. Weekday evenings are less frenetic, with more of a local vibe—although the term "local" around here always means a large number of students from New York University. Daytime is great for shopping in local boutiques, and brunch on weekends generally means lines everywhere, especially for the latest hot spots.

The Lower East Side does not tend to be an early-riser destination any day of the week. Although there's plenty to see during the day, nightfall offers a more exciting vision: blocks that were rows of pulled-down gates during daylight transform into clusters of throbbing bars come evening. On Rivington and Stanton and their cross streets, stores, bars, and cafés buzz all week.

QUICK BITES

- **Il Laboratorio del Gelato.** Ever-changing seasonal varieties make this gelato spot the crème de la crème. About 48 flavors are offered each day, give or take. ⊠ *188 Ludlow St., at E. Houston St., Lower East Side* ⊕ *www.laboratoriodelgelato.com* Ⓜ *Subway: F to 2nd Ave.*

- **Morgenstern's Finest Ice Cream.** Known for unique ice cream flavors like burnt sage and banana curry, the original location still draws long lines, especially in summer. ⊠ *2 Rivington St., between the Bowery and Chrystie St., Lower East Side* ⊕ *www.morgensternsnyc.com* Ⓜ *Subway: F to 2nd Ave.*

- **Mudspot.** The Mudspot hits the spot for excellent take-out coffee and muffins or a casual, quality meal (weekend brunch gets busy, especially on the patio). ⊠ *307 E. 9th St., between 1st and 2nd Aves., East Village* ⊕ *www.mudnyc.com* Ⓜ *Subway: F to 2nd Ave.*

- **Veniero's Pastry.** This Italian bakery has been offering cookies, coffee, and elaborate cakes and tarts since 1894—and the late hours it keeps only sweetens the deal. The fruit-topped minicheesecakes are always a good idea. ⊠ *342 E. 11th St., between 1st and 2nd Aves., East Village* ⊕ *www.venierospastry.com* Ⓜ *Subway: L to 1st Ave.*

Vibrant, bold, and bohemian: the streets of the East Village and the Lower East Side are some of the most electric in New York City. Both neighborhoods have a deep immigrant past, and have evolved into nighttime destinations where you can party until the wee hours any day of the week.

Houston Street runs east–west and neatly divides the East Village (north of Houston) and the Lower East Side (south of Houston). The eastern boundary of the East Village and Lower East Side is the East River; the western boundary is 4th Avenue and the Bowery. So many communities converge in these neighborhoods that each block can seem like a neighborhood unto itself.

This area of downtown is tamer than it used to be (as the arrival of Whole Foods, Starbucks, and several glass-and-chrome condos attests), but a gritty edge lives on in the dive bars, sultry live music venues, and experimental restaurants. Spend time wandering the side streets and you'll be struck by the pastiche of ethnicities whose imprints are visible in the neighborhood's shops, eateries, and, of course, people.

East Village

Many opposites coexist peacefully in the East Village: dive bars and craft-cocktail dens, Ukrainian diners and the latest chef-driven restaurants, stylish boutiques and tattoo parlors. Famous for its nightlife, the East Village has become increasingly more upscale in recent years, with St. Marks Place trading in some of its grit for a hodgepodge of students, well-earning postgrads, and international expats. At its roots, the neighborhood is a community of artists, activists, and social dissenters—and though this is still the essential vibe here, the finish is much more polished these days.

The north–south avenues east of 1st Avenue, from Houston Street to 14th Street, have letters, not numbers, which gives this area its nickname: Alphabet City. Avenues A, B, and C are full of restaurants, cafés, stores, and bars that run from the inexpensive and divey to the pricey and polished, sometimes right next to each other. Parts of Avenues A and B run along Tompkins Square Park. A close-knit Puerto Rican community makes its home around Avenue C, also called "Loisaida" (a Spanglish creation for "Lower East Side"), which is still home to many Latino shops and bodegas but also a growing number of trendy restaurants and bars. Avenue D remains a bit rough around the edges—in part because of the uninterrupted row of housing projects that run along its east side.

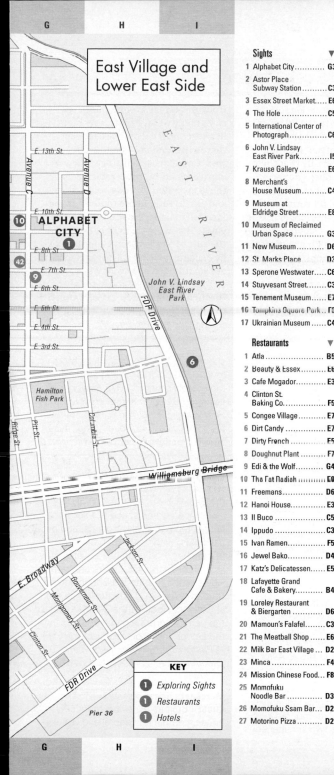

East Village and Lower East Side

Sights ▼

1 Alphabet City **G3**
2 Astor Place
   Subway Station **C3**
3 Essex Street Market..... **E6**
4 The Hole **C5**
5 International Center of
   Photograph **C6**
6 John V. Lindsay
   East River Park **I5**
7 Krause Gallery **E6**
8 Merchant's
   House Museum **C4**
9 Museum at
   Eldridge Street **E8**
10 Museum of Reclaimed
   Urban Space **G3**
11 New Museum **D6**
12 St. Marks Place **D3**
13 Sperone Westwater..... **C6**
14 Stuyvesant Street....... **C3**
15 Tenement Museum..... **E7**
16 Tompkins Square Park .. **F3**
17 Ukrainian Museum **C4**

Restaurants ▼

1 Atla **B5**
2 Beauty & Essex........ **E6**
3 Cafe Mogador........... **E3**
4 Clinton St.
   Baking Co. **F5**
5 Congee Village **E7**
6 Dirt Candy **E7**
7 Dirty French **E5**
8 Doughnut Plant **F7**
9 Edi & the Wolf.......... **G4**
10 The Fat Radish **E6**
11 Freemans **D6**
12 Hanoi House............. **E3**
13 Il Buco **C5**
14 Ippudo **C3**
15 Ivan Ramen.............. **F5**
16 Jewel Bako.............. **D4**
17 Katz's Delicatessen...... **E5**
18 Lafayette Grand
   Cafe & Bakery.......... **B4**
19 Loreley Restaurant
   & Biergarten **D6**
20 Mamoun's Falafel........ **C3**
21 The Meatball Shop **E6**
22 Milk Bar East Village ... **D2**
23 Minca **F4**
24 Mission Chinese Food... **F8**
25 Momofuku
   Noodle Bar **D3**
26 Momofuku Ssam Bar... **D2**
27 Motorino Pizza **D2**
28 Nai Tapas Bar **D4**
29 Oda House............... **F4**
30 Pylos **E4**
31 Russ & Daughters **E5**
32 Saxon & Parole **C5**
33 Shopsin's **E6**
34 Somtum Der............. **E4**
35 Sugar Sweet Sunshine.. **E6**
36 Superiority Burger....... **E3**
37 Supermoon
   Bakehouse **E6**
38 Tim Ho Wan **C3**
39 Vanessa's
   Dumpling House **E7**
40 Veselka.................. **D3**
41 Wildair **E6**
42 Zum Schneider.......... **G3**

Hotels ▼

1 The Bowery Hotel **C5**
2 Hotel Indigo Lower
   East Side, New York..... **E5**
3 Hotel on Rivington **E6**
4 The Ludlow Hotel **E5**
5 PUBLIC **D6**
6 Sister City............... **D6**
7 Sixty LES **E5**
8 The Standard,
   East Village **C4**

Keep Your Eyes Peeled

The East Village's reputation for quirkiness is evinced not only by its residents and sites but also in the many incongruous structures that somehow coexist so easily that they often go unnoticed. Keep your eyes open as you explore the streets. You never know what might turn up.

Look up to see the giant copper statue of Vladimir Lenin that salutes the world from atop a building on Norfolk Street, just south of Houston (it was moved in 2016 from its previous home on the top of 250 Houston Street). Not far away is the shingled Cape Cod–style house perched on the apartment building at the northwest corner of Houston and 1st Avenue, one of the city's many unique rooftop retreats (it's best viewed from the east). Then there's the hidden-in-plain-sight New York Marble Cemetery (⊕ www.marblecemetery.org), established in the 1830s on 2nd Avenue between 2nd and 3rd Streets, where thousands are interred in underground, marble-lined vaults that were thought to prevent the spread of disease in a time marked by cholera epidemics. The gardens are surrounded by 12-foot walls made of Tuckahoe marble, and entered through wrought-iron gates. It's open to the public every fourth Sunday, April through October.

◉ Sights

Astor Place Subway Station
TRANSPORTATION SITE (AIRPORT/BUS/FERRY/TRAIN) | At the beginning of the 20th century, almost all of the city's Interborough Rapid Transit (IRT) subway entrances resembled the one here—an ornate cast-iron replica of a Beaux Arts kiosk marking the subway entrance for the uptown 6 train. This traffic-island entrance, which was—and still is—the stop nearest to the venerable Cooper Union college, is now on the National Register of Historic Places. Inside, plaques of beaver emblems line the tiled station walls (though they're rather grimy these days), a reference to the fur trade that contributed to John Jacob Astor's fortune. Milton Glaser, the Cooper Union graduate who originated the "I [heart] NY" logo, designed the station's murals. ⊠ 8th St. and 4th Ave., traffic island, East Village Ⓜ 6 to Astor Pl.

The Hole
MUSEUM | Run by Kathy Grayson, the former director of the highly influential Deitch Projects, this contemporary-arts gallery generally hosts two simultaneous shows a month. Its artists lean more toward the up-and-coming rather than the establishment. ⊠ 312 Bowery, between Bleecker and E. Houston Sts., East Village ☎ 212/466–1100 ⊕ www.theholenyc.com ⊘ Closed Mon., Tues. Ⓜ 6 to Bleecker St.; B, D, F, M to Broadway–Lafayette St.

John V. Lindsay East River Park
CITY PARK | FAMILY | Running along the East River up to 12th Street, this landscaped green space is a series of connected parks, playgrounds, and baseball fields, with water fountains, plenty of benches, and pedestrian overpasses across the FDR Drive. There are great views of the Manhattan Bridge and Brooklyn. An NYC Ferry dock is located at Corlears Hook, at the southern end of the park, where the park stretches into the Lower East Side near Jackson Street. ⊠ East Village ⊕ www.nycgovparks.org/parks/east-river-park Ⓜ L to 1st Ave.; F to 2nd Ave.

Merchant's House Museum
HOUSE | Built in 1832, this redbrick house, combining Federal and Greek

Revival styles, provides a glimpse into the domestic life of the period 30 years before the Civil War. Retired merchant Seabury Tredwell and his descendants lived here from 1835 until 1933. The home became a museum in 1936, with the original furnishings and architectural features preserved; family memorabilia are on display. The fourth-floor servants' bedroom, where the family's Irish servants slept and did some of their work, offers a look at the lives of Irish domestics in the mid-1800s. Guided tours are at 2 pm; there's an additional tour at 6:30 pm on Thursday, January through September. ⊠ *29 E. 4th St., between the Bowery and Lafayette St., East Village* ☎ *212/777-1089* ⊕ *www.merchantshouse.org* ⊠ *$15* ⊘ *Closed Tues., Wed.* Ⓜ *N, R, W to 8th St.–NYU; 6 to Astor Pl.; B, D, F, M to Broadway–Lafayette St.*

Museum of Reclaimed Urban Space (MoRUS)

MUSEUM | This museum of the East Village's urban activism covers key events from the 1980s to the present, during which period the city's public housing was often woefully mismanaged and hundreds of apartments lay abandoned and crumbling. Photographs and videos fill the small exhibit space inside a tenement's storefront and its basement. Squatters, community gardens, the Tompkins Square riots, and the renaissance of bicycling in the city are all given their due, as is Occupy Wall Street. Tours of community gardens, activist landmarks, and other squats, both legal and otherwise, are also run by the museum. ⊠ *155 Ave. C, between 9th and 10th Sts., East Village* ☎ *973/818–8495* ⊕ *www.morusnyc.org* ⊠ *$5 suggested donation; tours $20* ⊘ *Closed Mon., Wed.* Ⓜ *L to 1st Ave.*

St. Marks Place

NEIGHBORHOOD | The longtime hub of the edgy East Village, St. Marks Place is the name given to idiosyncratic East 8th Street between 3rd Avenue and Avenue A. During the 1950s, beatniks Allen Ginsberg and Jack Kerouac lived in the area; the 1960s brought Bill Graham's Fillmore East (at 105 2nd Avenue), and Andy Warhol's Dom and the Electric Circus nightclub (at Nos. 19–25). The shaved-head punk scene followed, and there's still a chance of seeing some pierced rockers and teenage Goths. Farther down, at No. 33, is where the punk store Manic Panic first foisted its lurid hair dyes on the world. At No. 57 stood the short-lived Club 57, which attracted such 1980s stalwarts as Keith Haring and Ann Magnuson.

These days, there's not much cutting edge left. Some of the grungy facades lead to luxury condos, and the area has become a Little Japan, with several ramen and dumpling shops. The block between 2nd and 3rd Avenues can feel like a shopping arcade, crammed with body-piercing and tattoo salons, and stores selling cheap jewelry and wacky T-shirts. The cafés and bars from here over to Avenue A attract customers late into the night—thanks partly to lower drink prices. ⊠ *8th St. between 3rd Ave. and Ave. A, East Village* Ⓜ *6 to Astor Pl., N, R, W to 8th St.–NYU.*

Stuyvesant Street

NEIGHBORHOOD | Slicing through the block bounded by 2nd and 3rd Avenues and East 9th and 10th Streets, this diagonal street is unique in Manhattan: it's the oldest street laid out precisely along an east–west axis. Among the handsome 19th-century redbrick row houses are the Federal-style **Stuyvesant Fish House** at No. 21, built as a wedding gift for a great-great-granddaughter of the Dutch governor Peter Stuyvesant, and **Renwick Triangle,** an attractive group of Anglo-Italianate brick and brownstone residences that face Stuyvesant and East 10th Streets. ⊠ *Stuyvesant St., East Village* Ⓜ *6 to Astor Pl.; N, R, W to 8th St.–NYU.*

Tompkins Square Park

CITY PARK | FAMILY | This leafy park fills up year-round with locals partaking in picnics and drum circles, and making use of the playground and the dog run. There are movie screenings and music gatherings throughout the summer, a year-round farmers' market by the southwest corner on Sunday, and an annual Halloween dog-costume event. It wasn't always so rosy in the park, though: in 1988, police followed then-mayor David Dinkins's orders to evict the many homeless people who had set up makeshift homes here, and homeless rights and antigentrification activists fought back with sticks and bottles. The park was reclaimed and reopened in 1992 with a midnight curfew, still in effect today. ✉ *From 7th to 10th St., between Aves. A and B, East Village* 🌐 *www.nycgovparks.org/parks/tompkinssquarepark* [M] *6 to Astor Pl., L to 1st Ave.*

Ukrainian Museum

MUSEUM | From the late 19th century through the end of World War II, tens of thousands of Ukrainians made their way to New York City—and particularly to "Little Ukraine," as much of the East Village was known. This museum examines Ukrainian Americans' dual heritage, with a permanent collection made up of folk art, fine art, and documentary materials about immigrant life. Ceramics, jewelry, hundreds of brilliantly colored Easter eggs, and an extensive collection of Ukrainian costumes and textiles are the highlights. **■ TIP→ To continue the experience, have some Ukrainian food at nearby Veselka diner.** ✉ *222 E. 6th St., between 2nd and 3rd Aves., East Village* ☎ *212/228–0110* 🌐 *www.ukrainianmuseum.org* 🎟 *$8* 🕒 *Closed Mon., Tues.* [M] *6 to Astor Pl.; N, R, W to 8th St.–NYU.*

🍴 Restaurants

Once a grungy ghetto for punk rockers and drug addicts, this neighborhood is now a popular foodie destination with great restaurants on every block—from wonderful, inexpensive Asian spots to upscale fine-dining destinations. St. Marks Place is the center of New York's downtown Little Japan, and East 6th Street is its Indian Row.

Atla

$$ | MODERN MEXICAN | A pared-down, more casual version of Mexican superchef Enrique Olvera's hit upscale Flatiron eatery, Cosme, this 90-seat, big-windowed spot does excellent, straightfoward Mexican dishes like chicken enchiladas as well as creative spins like torpedo-shape split-pea *tlacoyo*. The yoga-mat crowd gravitate here in the morning for chia-seed oatmeal and flaxseed chilaquiles. **Known for:** light-filled dining room; good breakfast spot; arctic char–stuffed avocado. [$] *Average main: $17* ✉ *372 Lafayette St., between 2nd and 3rd Sts., East Village* ☎ *646/837–6464* 🌐 *www.atlanyc.com* [M] *B, D, F, M to Broadway–Lafayette St.; 6 to Bleecker St.*

Cafe Mogador

$$ | MOROCCAN | An East Village dining institution, Cafe Mogador has been serving above-average Moroccan cuisine in a date-friendly, candlelit atmosphere since 1983, and it still draws crowds for dinner and brunch. Start with an order of creamy hummus to share, then dig into one of the classic tagine stews, served with couscous, or some tasty meat kebabs. **Known for:** good mezes; popular brunch spot; outdoor tables in summer. [$] *Average main: $17* ✉ *101 St. Marks Pl., near 2nd Ave., East Village* ☎ *212/677–2226* 🌐 *www.cafemogador.com* [M] *L to 1st Ave.*

★ Edi & the Wolf

$$ | **AUSTRIAN** | This rustic-chic Austrian spot is a bit unexpected for the neighborhood, but that hasn't stopped a steady stream of diners from heading to the farther reaches of the East Village since it opened in 2010. The Wiener schnitzel is wonderfully light and grease-free and the delicious highlight of the menu, but if you're in the mood for something else, there's usually a fish option, hearty short ribs, and a vegetarian preparation of spaetzle. **Known for:** fabulous country-style decor; great selection of Central European beers; outstanding schnitzel. [$] *Average main: $23* ✉ *102 Ave. C, at 7th St., East Village* ☎ *212/598–1040* 🌐 *www.ediandthewolf.com* 🕓 *No lunch weekdays* [M] *F to 2nd Ave., L to 1st Ave.*

Hanoi House

$$ | **VIETNAMESE** | Most Vietnamese food in the United States is inspired by the traditions of southern Vietnam because it was largely Vietnamese from the south who left the country after the war ended in 1975. Hanoi House brings a refreshing taste of the north; the pho here, as done in Hanoi, is meatier, darker, and more flavorful, as the broth simmers in cow bones for 12 hours. **Known for:** bun cha with grilled pork and noodles; beef pho with optional additions; delicious options for more daring eaters as well. [$] *Average main: $18* ✉ *119 St. Marks Pl., between 1st Ave. and Ave. A, East Village* ☎ *212/995–5010* 🌐 *www.hanoihousenyc.com* 🕓 *No lunch Mon.–Sat.* [M] *L to 1st Ave.*

Il Buco

$$$ | **MEDITERRANEAN** | The unabashed clutter of vintage kitchen gadgets and tableware harks back to the shopfront's past as an antiques store and adds to the romantic country-house atmosphere. This is a favorite for a cozy, intimate meal of top-notch Mediterranean (mostly Italian and Spanish) food that makes use of meat and produce from local farms. **Known for:** intimate ambience; excellent pasta dishes; casual wine bar around corner. [$] *Average main: $29* ✉ *47 Bond St., between the Bowery and Lafayette St., East Village* ☎ *212/533–1932* 🌐 *www.ilbuco.com* 🕓 *No lunch Sun.* [M] *6 to Bleecker St.; B, D, F, M to Broadway–Lafayette St.*

Ippudo

$$ | **JAPANESE** | Crowds wait hours for the ramen noodles at Ippudo, the first American branch of the famous Japanese chain. Loyal patrons say it's all about the rich pork-based broth (there is a vegetarian version available, though it lacks the depth of flavor), but those in the know order sleeper-hit appetizers like the peppery chicken wings or pork buns. **Known for:** heaping bowls of addictive ramen; worthy appetizers; classy but bustling atmosphere. [$] *Average main: $17* ✉ *65 4th Ave., between 9th and 10th Sts., East Village* ☎ *212/388–0088* 🌐 *www.ippudony.com* [M] *6 to Astor Pl.; N, R, W to 8th St.–NYU.*

Jewel Bako

$$$$ | **JAPANESE** | Arguably the best sushi restaurant in the East Village, this tiny space gleams in a minefield of cheap, often inferior sushi houses. The futuristic bamboo tunnel of a dining room is gorgeous, but try to nab a place at the sushi bar and put yourself in the hands of sushi master Mitsunori Isoda. **Known for:** ultrafresh sushi; fixed-price menus; long sake list. [$] *Average main: $50* ✉ *239 E. 5th St., between 2nd and 3rd Aves., East Village* ☎ *212/979–1012* 🌐 *www.jewelbakosushi.com* 🕓 *Closed Sun. No lunch* [M] *6 to Astor Pl.; N, R, W to 8th St.–NYU.*

Lafayette Grand Cafe & Bakery

$$$ | **FRENCH** | Food-media-darling chef Andrew Carmellini (of Locanda Verde, Bar Primi, and the Dutch) goes Gallic here. There's no culinary trickery, just straightforward and very satisfying bistro fare along the lines of creamy duck-confit-spiked pumpkin risotto, a silky beef tartare, and excellent steak frites. **Known**

for: hearty French fare; homey ambience; breakfast at the café. $ *Average main: $25* ⊠ *380 Lafayette St., at Great Jones St., East Village* ☎ *212/533–3000* ⊕ *www. lafayetteny.com* Ⓜ *6 to Bleecker St.; B, D, F, M to Broadway–Lafayette St.; N, R, W to 8th St.–NYU.*

Mamoun's Falafel

$ | **MIDDLE EASTERN** | **FAMILY** | This cash-only, hole-in-the-wall institution, bustling day and night, is the place to go for speedy, hot, cheap, and delicious Middle Eastern food, particularly the falafel sandwiches topped with tahini. Be warned: the hot sauce is incendiary. **Known for:** cheap and delicious falafel sandwiches; great vegetarian options; late-night noshing. $ *Average main: $7* ⊠ *30 St. Marks Pl., between 2nd and 3rd Aves., East Village* ☎ *212/387–7747* ⊕ *www. mamouns.com* ⊟ *No credit cards* Ⓜ *6 to Astor Pl.; N, R, W to 8th St.–NYU.*

Milk Bar East Village

$ | **CAFÉ** | **FAMILY** | This combination bakery, ice-cream parlor, and sandwich shop with locations around the city boasts quick-serve access to some truly innovative treats from pastry whiz Christina Tosi. Swing by for a kimchi croissant and glass of "cereal" milk, or for treats like the curiously flavored soft-serve ice cream (cereal milk, lemon verbena) or a "candy bar pie" (caramel, peanut-butter nougat, and pretzels atop a chocolate-cookie crust). **Known for:** very sweet sweets; addictive Milk Bar pie cookies and "compost" cookies; several locations around the city. $ *Average main: $7* ⊠ *251 E. 13th St., at 2nd Ave., East Village* ☎ *347/577–9504* ⊕ *www.milkbarstore.com* Ⓜ *L to 3rd Ave.*

Minca

$$ | **JAPANESE** | It may receive less fanfare than some other East Village noodle bars, but the ramen at this tiny spot is among the best in the city; the fact that visiting Japanese students eat here is a good sign. Start with homemade *gyoza* dumplings, then dive your spoon and chopsticks into one of the many types of ramen. **Known for:** spicy pork-broth ramen; expect a wait if you come at prime dining hours; good-value, cash-only option. $ *Average main: $15* ⊠ *536 E. 5th St., between Aves. A and B, East Village* ☎ *212/505–8001* ⊕ *www.newyorkramen.com* ⊟ *No credit cards* Ⓜ *F to 2nd Ave.*

★ Momofuku Noodle Bar

$$ | **ASIAN** | David Chang's first restaurant is still a strong crowd favorite. This riff on the Japanese ramen bar features haute ingredients like Berkshire pork, free-range chicken, and organic produce—and there are plenty of other innovative options on the daily-changing menu, though the mainstay pork buns are pretty much a must-order. **Known for:** creative ramen options from a famous chef; lines out the door at meal times; lively scene. $ *Average main: $17* ⊠ *171 1st Ave., between 10th and 11th Sts., East Village* ☎ *212/777–7773* ⊕ *www.momofuku.com* Ⓜ *L to 1st Ave.*

★ Momofuku Ssäm Bar

$$ | **ASIAN** | This refined David Chang restaurant easily shows its multicultural bent. A selection of country hams is a surprising but delicious way to start a meal, perhaps followed by an Indian-inspired curry and potato appetizer, perfectly glazed barbecue ribs, and a whole-fish preparation. **Known for:** inventive flavor combinations; changing menu; rotisserie duck splurge. $ *Average main: $24* ⊠ *207 2nd Ave., at 13th St., East Village* ☎ *212/254–3500* ⊕ *www.momofuku. com/ssam* Ⓜ *L to 1st Ave.*

Motorino Pizza

$$ | **PIZZA** | The East Village branch of the Williamsburg original serves up authentic Neapolitan pies with slightly charred, delectably chewy crusts. You can't go wrong with any of the signature traditional pizzas, like marinara; margherita with fresh tomatoes, mozzarella, and basil; or a pie with spicy sopressata, sausage, and garlic. **Known for:** Brussels sprouts pizza; interesting seasonal pies; good-value

lunch prix-fixe. $ *Average main: $18* ⌧ *349 E. 12th St., at 1st Ave., East Village* ☎ *212/777–2644* ⊕ *www.motorinopizza. com* Ⓜ *L to 1st Ave.*

Nai Tapas Bar

$$ | TAPAS | At this eclectic tapas joint, chef Ruben Rodriguez puts a modern spin on Galician recipes from his mother and grandmother (his Spanish-born mother has her own tapas restaurant in New Jersey). Traditional tapas like shrimp in garlic sauce, sliced Iberico ham, and *patatas bravas* are on the menu alongside spherified olives, marinated baby back ribs, and Brussels sprouts with diced pork belly. **Known for:** unpretentious spot for a taste of Iberia; flamenco shows on Thursday and Saturday; good selection of Spanish wines. $ *Average main: $20* ⌧ *85 2nd Ave., at 5th St., East Village* ☎ *212/677–1030* ⊕ *www.naitapas. nyc* ⊙ *No lunch weekdays* Ⓜ *L to 3rd Ave.*

Oda House

$$ | EASTERN EUROPEAN | Georgian cuisine isn't as well known as it should be, but try it once and you'll be a believer, especially at this quiet, romantic spot with large windows looking out onto the street. Start with the *khinkali* (meat-and-broth-filled dumplings) and the *adjaruli khachapuri*, a boat-shape bread with melted cheese and an egg in the middle, and then move on to the *chakapuli*, a slow-cooked lamb stew that will warm up any soul on a winter night. **Known for:** Georgian cuisine and wines; adjaruli khachapuri; delicious and varied types of stews. $ *Average main: $20* ⌧ *76 Ave. B, at 5th St., East Village* ☎ *212/353–3838* ⊕ *www.odahouse.com* ⊙ *No lunch Mon.–Thurs.* Ⓜ *L to 1st Ave.*

Pylos

$$$ | GREEK | The perfect setting for a relaxed dinner or an intimate special occasion, this tastefully refined, light-filled East Village restaurant emphasizes rustic cooking from all over Greece. There are delicious versions of hearty comfort-food dishes like pastitsio and moussaka on the menu, but the lighter dishes—especially fish—let the flavors shine through. **Known for:** elevated Greek fare; broad meze selection; clay-baked meat dishes. $ *Average main: $26* ⌧ *128 E. 7th St., near Ave. A, East Village* ☎ *212/473–0220* ⊕ *www.pylosrestaurant. com* ⊙ *No lunch Mon., Tues.* Ⓜ *F to 2nd Ave.; L to 1st Ave.*

Saxon & Parole

$$$ | MODERN AMERICAN | One of the hottest spots on this burgeoning stretch of the Bowery, Saxon & Parole may be named for two 19th-century racehorses, but the food—and the good-looking crowd—at this long-standing, sceney spot is nothing you'd find in a barnyard. The menu is meat-centric, and the burger is one of the best around, but the kitchen also turns out some of the most addictive Brussels sprouts you've ever tasted. **Known for:** trendy but expensive food; house-made whiskey; fun bar scene. $ *Average main: $25* ⌧ *316 Bowery, at Bleecker St., East Village* ☎ *212/254–0350* ⊕ *www.saxonandparole.com* ⊙ *No lunch* Ⓜ *B, D, F, M to Broadway–Lafayette St.; 6 to Bleecker St.; F to 2nd Ave.*

Somtum Der

$$ | THAI | At this bustling restaurant originally based in Bangkok, the namesake *somtum*, a palate-singeing green papaya salad, is the must-order dish before you move on to sharing some of the light, spicy dishes such as, perhaps, the *larb moo*, a mound of minced pork mixed with veggies and chilies. Also worth trying is the fried chicken, which makes you question the Southern United States' monopoly on this crispy bird. **Known for:** authentic Issan cuisine from northeastern Thailand; many spicy dishes, including vegetarian options, good for sharing; small space. $ *Average main: $15* ⌧ *85 Ave. A, between 5th and 6th Sts., East Village* ☎ *212/260–8570* ⊕ *www.somtumder.com* Ⓜ *F to 2nd Ave.; L to 1st Ave.*

Superiority Burger

$ | **VEGETARIAN** | Chef Brooks Headley left a high-profile gig as the head pastry chef at Del Posto to open this walk-in-closet-size veggie burger joint, and even carnivores are glad he did. It's hard to choose the top menu contender: maybe the slider-size, quinoa-and-nut-based burger with Muenster cheese and an umami-loaded tomato sauce, or the veggie version of the Sloppy Joe (called a Sloppy Dave). **Known for:** veggie burgers even carnivores can love; vegetable specials; very limited seating, so take your food to the park or a nearby bar. $ *Average main: $7* ✉ *430 E. 9th St., between 1st Ave. and Ave. A, East Village* ☎ *212/256–1192* ⊕ *www.superiorityburger.com* Ⓜ *L to 1st Ave.*

Tim Ho Wan

$ | **CHINESE** | This dim sum restaurant is best known for the fact of its original Hong Kong location being the most affordable Michelin-starred restaurant on the planet. The Big Apple outlet may or may not win any prestigious culinary awards, but it's certainly proven itself to be one of the best spots for dim sum in the city. **Known for:** affordable dim sum; barbecue pork buns; bright, busy atmosphere. $ *Average main: $9* ✉ *85 4th Ave., at 10th St., East Village* ☎ *212/228–2800* ⊕ *www.timhowanusa.com* Ⓜ *6 to Astor Pl.*

Veselka

$$ | **EASTERN EUROPEAN** | **FAMILY** | Potato pierogi are available 24 hours a day at this East Village stalwart, which opened in 1954; the name means "rainbow" in Ukrainian. The authentic Ukrainian-slash-diner food is the perfect stick-to-your-ribs ending to a night on the town—or beginning to a new day, as the restaurant serves a full array of breakfast staples. **Known for:** welcoming atmosphere; a neighborhood institution; wall paintings. $ *Average main: $13* ✉ *144 2nd Ave., at 9th St., East Village* ☎ *212/228–9682* ⊕ *www.veselka.com*

Ⓜ *6 to Astor Pl.; N, R, W to 8th St.–NYU; L to 1st Ave.*

Zum Schneider

$$ | **GERMAN** | There's always a good time to be had at this garrulous Bavarian spot that serves a variety of German beers and hearty food to complement them. In addition to the usual meaty fare, such as sausages, Wiener schnitzel, and goulash, there are crispy potato pancakes and a few salad options. **Known for:** outside drinking in summer; great beer options; many sausage options. $ *Average main: $16* ✉ *107 Ave. C, at 7th St., East Village* ☎ *212/598–1098* ⊕ *www.zumschneider.com* ☽ *No lunch weekdays* Ⓜ *L to 1st Ave.; F to 2nd Ave.*

🛏 Hotels

★ The Bowery Hotel

$$$ | **HOTEL** | Warmed by rich tapestries and fireplaces, the Bowery Hotel is like an English hunting lodge in Manhattan, and the red-coated doormen, clubby bar, and trendy address makes this a hot property. **Pros:** fun downtown location; happening bar and lobby-lounge area; international crowd. **Cons:** service can be inconsistent; rooms lack luxe touches some might expect; lobby can get too sceney for some. $ *Rooms from: $525* ✉ *335 Bowery, at 3rd St., East Village* ☎ *212/505–9100* ⊕ *www.theboweryhotel.com* ⇥ *135 rooms* ⓞ *No meals* Ⓜ *F to 2nd Ave.; 6 to Bleecker St.*

The Standard, East Village

$$ | **HOTEL** | In the low-rise East Village, this giant, 21-story glass-and-steel building soars above everything around, providing gorgeous views through floor-to-ceiling windows. **Pros:** stylish, sunny rooms with great views; central location for downtown exploring; near hip restaurants and bars. **Cons:** architecture out of character with area; rooms on the small side; no on-site gym or spa. $ *Rooms from: $305* ✉ *25 Cooper Sq., between 5th and 6th Sts., East Village*

☎ 212/475–5700 ⊕ www.standardhotels. com ⚬ 145 rooms ❖ No meals Ⓜ 6 to Astor Pl.; N, R, W to 8th St.–NYU.

ⓨ Nightlife

BARS
Beauty Bar
BARS/PUBS | Grab a seat in a barber chair or under a dryer at this made-over hair salon where, during prime hours, you can get a drink and a manicure for just $10. How's that for multitasking? The DJ spins everything from new wave to soul. It's open until 4 am every night. This is the original of what has now become a mini chain across the United States. ✉ 231 E. 14th St., between 2nd and 3rd Aves., East Village ☎ 212/539–1389 ⊕ www. thebeautybar.com Ⓜ 4, 5, 6, L, N, Q, R, W to 14th St.–Union Sq.

Death & Company
BARS/PUBS | Inventive cocktails, decadent bar bites, and a sultry atmosphere attract a steady stream of New Yorkers with a thirst for finely crafted drinks at prices that are higher than you might expect for the neighborhood. There are staple tipples and a new slate of concoctions unveiled several times a year, all of them mixed by expert bartenders. Seating is first-come, first-served, but the host outside will log your name and text when seats are available; weekends, as you'd expect, can mean a long wait. ✉ 433 E. 6th St., between 1st Ave. and Ave. A, East Village ☎ 212/388–0882 ⊕ www. deathandcompany.com Ⓜ F to 2nd Ave., 6 to Astor Pl.

Holiday Cocktail Bar
BARS/PUBS | If you've been in the city long enough, you'll remember the Holiday as the quintessential New York dive bar, with dim lighting and basic drinks, where everyone felt comfortable despite the slightly uncomfortable bar stools and banquettes. If you've just arrived here, you'll be treated to a similar welcoming ambience, but with new upholstery,

trendier drinks, and interesting bar food. ✉ 75 St. Marks Pl., between 1st and 2nd Aves., East Village ☎ 212/777–9637 ⊕ www.holidaycocktaillounge.nyc Ⓜ F to 2nd Ave.; L to 1st Ave.

Karma
BARS/PUBS | At the top of the hookah-bar heap that has taken this neighborhood by storm, Karma provides a stylish sprawl with Indian decor (dig that wrought-metal statue of Kali) for local scenesters to fill their bowls and suck in the various aromatic tobaccos available. It's also one of the rare NYC venues that still allows cigarette smoking, its permits grandfathered in before the 2003 indoor-smoking ban (heavy-duty ventilation helps clear the air). There's a daily happy hour, as well as live comedy and music shows and DJs nearly every night. ✉ 51 1st Ave., between 2nd and 3rd Sts., East Village ☎ 212/677–3160 ⊕ www.karmanyc. com Ⓜ F to 2nd Ave.; 6 to Bleecker or Spring Sts.

McSorley's Old Ale House
BARS/PUBS | One of New York's oldest saloons (established in 1854) and immortalized by New Yorker writer Joseph Mitchell, McSorley's is a must if you like beer, even if only two kinds of brew are served. McSorley's Light and McSorley's Dark (each served two per order in small glass mugs). It's also essential for history lovers, and though it's usually filled with "bros," the bar is friendlier to women than it was. (The surly motto here once was "Good ale, raw onions, and no ladies.") The food's decent, too. Go early to avoid the down-the-block lines on Friday and Saturday nights. ✉ 15 E. 7th St., between 2nd and 3rd Aves., East Village ☎ 212/473–9148 ⊕ www.mcsorleysoldalehouse.nyc Ⓜ 6 to Astor Pl.

★ Mother of Pearl
BARS/PUBS | This bright and inviting corner bar may catch your eye for its vivid nouveau-tiki style, but once inside, you'll be glad to stay for the innovative

concoctions tucked within the pearlescent menu. Besides the expected rum-forward cocktails—including boozy-fruity punch bowls for groups—co-owner and head bartender Jane Danger employs an array of spirits, along with zingy vegan and vegetarian bar snacks. You're unlikely to find better, friendlier service anywhere in the neighborhood, which merrily reinforces the happy-go-lucky tropical vibe. ⊠ 95 Ave. A, at 6th St., East Village ☎ 212/614–6818 ⊕ www. motherofpearlnyc.com Ⓜ 6 to Astor Pl.; N, R, W to 8th St.–NYU; F to 2nd Ave.

Otto's Shrunken Head Tiki Bar & Lounge
BARS/PUBS | It's a tiki bar that's long been a neighborhood go-to for its easy-breezy attitude, affordable drinks, and hula-crazy eye candy, so drop in to enjoy the bamboo bar, fish lamps, drinks served in shrunken-head mugs, a tattooed punk-rock crowd, and beef jerky for sale. There are live music, comedy, and open mic shows in the back room, and DJs prone to spinning anything from 1950s rock to "Soul Gidget" surf music. ⊠ 538 E. 14th St., between Aves. A and B, East Village ☎ 212/228–2240 ⊕ www.ottosshrunken-head.com Ⓜ L to 1st Ave.

PDT
BARS/PUBS | Those who crave their cocktails with a little cloak-and-dagger might enjoy the mystery of PDT (which stands for "Please Don't Tell"). Make a phone reservation the day of, and then head to Crif Dogs, the unassuming hot dog restaurant. You'll be escorted through the phone booth's false back into the cocktail bar, which is decorated with warm wooden beams and taxidermy. ⊠ 113 St. Marks Pl., between 1st Ave. and Ave. A, East Village ☎ 212/614–0386 ⊕ www. pdtnyc.com Ⓜ 6 to Astor Pl.

★ Pouring Ribbons
BARS/PUBS | This polished, spacious second-floor cocktail bar is named after the way a drink forms iridescent liquid ribbons when it's expertly poured. The menu lists options with a sliding scale that tells you how "spiritous," "refreshing," "comforting," and "adventurous" each one is, and you order accordingly. There are a few food items, too, like cheese and charcuterie, which are a good idea, because you'll be tempted to stay for another round of drinks. ⊠ 225 Ave. B, 2nd fl., between 13th and 14th Sts., East Village ☎ 917/656–6788 ⊕ www.pouringribbons.com Ⓜ L to 1st Ave.

CABARET AND PIANO BARS
Club Cumming
CABARET | When multitalented actor Alan Cumming opened his namesake club in 2017, the East Village saw a welcome return of queer cabaret culture in a former gay-nightclub space. The club hosts nightly musical and spoken-word shows (sometimes multiple per night; usually free) by cutting-edge artists. While they're worth a peek, the compact space is often too popular (i.e., crowded) to view the stage—so if you'd like a little elbow room, aim to catch an early show on a weeknight. ⊠ 505 E. 6th St., at Ave. A, East Village ☎ 917/265–8006 ⊕ club-cummingnyc.com Ⓜ F to 2nd Ave.; 6 to Astor Pl.; L to 1st Ave.

★ Joe's Pub
CABARET | Named for the Public Theater's near-mythic impresario Joseph Papp, and located inside the renovated, historic Public Theater, Joe's is the ultimate cabaret lounge for A-list and longtime-favorite downtown performers who revel in the intimate setting—and for New Yorkers keen to discover marvelous, innovative shows and artists rarely enjoyed elsewhere. The venue serves good food and solid cocktails, and has nary a bad seat, be it at a table, a booth, or the bar—but if you want to occupy one, buy tickets and/or reserve your spot beforehand and make a night of it. ⊠ 425 Lafayette St., between 4th St. and Astor Pl., East Village ☎ 212/539–8778 ⊕ www. publictheater.org/Joes-Pub-at-The-Public Ⓜ 6 to Astor Pl.

🎭 Performing Arts

Danspace Project

DANCE | Founded to foster the work of independent choreographers such as Lucinda Childs and David Gordon, Danspace Project sponsors performances that are as fresh—and idiosyncratic—as the historic church space they occupy. Performance series curated by guest artists are also a regular part of the calendar. ✉ *St. Mark's Church in-the-Bowery, 131 E. 10th St., at 2nd Ave., East Village* ☎ *212/674-8112, 866/811-4111 for tickets* ⊕ *www. danspaceproject.org* Ⓜ *6 to Astor Pl.; N, R, W to 8th St.–NYU; L to 3rd Ave.*

FILM

★ Anthology Film Archives

FILM | Dedicated to preserving and exhibiting independent and avant-garde film, Anthology Film Archives consists of two intimate screening rooms (seating about 200 and 100, respectively) as well as a film repository and a library, all inside a 1919 redbrick courthouse. Cofounded in 1970 by the downtown legend and filmmaker Jonas Mekas, Anthology remains a major destination for adventurous and unusual movies, new as well as old. The Essential Cinema series delves into the works of canonized ground-breaking directors; the frequent festivals are more eclectic. A major expansion set for completion to coincide with the 50th anniversary in 2020 will bring a new library as well as a café and roof terrace. ✉ *32 2nd Ave., at 2nd St., East Village* ☎ *212/505-5181* ⊕ *www.anthologyfilmarchives.org* Ⓜ *F to 2nd Ave.*

MUSIC

SubCulture

CONCERTS | With its exposed brick, structural pillars, theater-style seating, and industrial-chic bar, this intimate subterranean concert hall could just as easily be a cool lounge as a venue for musical theater, Broadway concerts, and occasional classical and jazz performances. Series here have included in-the-round performances of all of Beethoven's string quartets; the piano music of Debussy and Ravel; and concerts from Tony Award–winning composers, featuring guest appearances by various Broadway stars. ✉ *45 Bleecker St., between the Bowery and Lafayette St., East Village* ☎ *212/533-5470* ⊕ *www.subculturenewyork.com* Ⓜ *6 to Bleecker St.; B, D, F, M to Broadway–Lafayette St.*

READINGS AND LECTURES

KGB Bar

READINGS/LECTURES | A nexus of the downtown literary scene, KGB keeps a busy calendar of readings and events, including Sunday Night Fiction and Monday Night Poetry. The name and the Soviet kitsch are a nod to the bar's history as a speakeasy for leftist Ukrainians. The Red Room, a performance space on the third floor, hosts varied nightly events and late-night live jazz. ✉ *85 E. 4th St., between the Bowery and 2nd Ave., East Village* ☎ *212/505-3360* ⊕ *www.kgbbar.com* Ⓜ *F to 2nd Ave.; 6 to Bleecker St.*

★ Nuyorican Poets Cafe

READINGS/LECTURES | The reigning arbiter of poetry slams, the Nuyorican Poets Cafe hosts open-mic events and the influential granddaddy (b. 1989) of the spoken word scene, the Friday Night Poetry Slam. Other performances, including hip-hop open mics, jazz acts, and theatrical performances, round out the schedule. Although tickets for many of the popular shows like the Friday Night Poetry Slam and the Monday-night open mics can be purchased in advance online, it's still a good idea to line up early; the small venue can get packed to the point of standing-room only. ✉ *236 E. 3rd St., between Aves. B and C, East Village* ☎ *212/780-9386* ⊕ *www.nuyorican.org* Ⓜ *F to 2nd Ave.; J, M, Z to Essex St.*

The Poetry Project

READINGS/LECTURES | Launched in 1966, the Poetry Project has been a source of sustenance for poets (and their audiences) ever since. This place has seen performances by Allen Ginsberg, Amiri Baraka, Sam Shepard, Patti Smith, Anne Waldman, and many others. Current readings generally host artists of the same caliber. Prime times are Monday, Wednesday, and Friday. ⊠ *St. Mark's Church in-the-Bowery, 131 E. 10th St., at 2nd Ave., East Village* ☎ *212/674–0910* ⊕ *www.poetryproject.org* Ⓜ *N, R, W to 8th St.–NYU; 6 to Astor Pl.; L to 3rd Ave.*

THEATER
Classic Stage Company
THEATER | At the CSC's cozy 199-seat theater, you can see work by Shakespeare as well as excellent revivals—such as work by Tennessee Williams or Eugene O'Neill—often with a modern spin, reigning theatrical stars, and new scores. ⊠ *136 E. 13th St., between 3rd and 4th Aves., East Village* ☎ *212/677–4210* ⊕ *www.classicstage.org* Ⓜ *4, 5, 6, N, Q, R, W to 14th St.–Union Sq.; L to 3rd Ave.*

La MaMa E.T.C.
THEATER | The late Ellen Stewart founded La MaMa E.T.C. in 1961 in a small Manhattan basement. Since that time, the Experimental Theatre Club has grown continuously, all the while taking risks on unknown works that cross cultures and performance disciplines. (Blue Man Group, for instance, got its start here.) In an effort to keep theater accessible, ticket prices start at $10–$15 across the theater's several venues. ⊠ *66 and 74A E. 4th St., between the Bowery and 2nd Ave., East Village* ☎ *212/352-3101* ⊕ *www.lamama.org* Ⓜ *F to 2nd Ave.; 6 to Bleecker St.*

New York Theatre Workshop
THEATER | Works by new and established playwrights anchor this theater's repertoire. Jonathan Larson's *Rent* got its start here before going to Broadway, and works by Tony Kushner (*Homebody/Kabul*), Caryl Churchill, Amy Herzog, and Paul Rudnick have also been staged here. The CheapTix program makes limited

$25 tickets available. ⊠ *79 E. 4th St., between the Bowery and 2nd Ave., East Village* ☎ *212/460–5475* ⊕ *www.nytw.org* Ⓜ *F to 2nd Ave.; 6 to Astor Pl.*

Performance Space 122 (PS122)
THEATER | Founded in 1980 inside a 19th-century public school building, Performance Space 122 has helped launch the careers of many downtown musicians and artists, both on the fringe and otherwise. After a renovation, it reopened in 2018 with two new theaters and a modernized interior. A new semi-annual themed series, the first of which focused on the changing face of the East Village, presents hybrid and interdisciplinary works that blend performance with installations and readings by different artists with varied visions. ⊠ *150 1st Ave., at 9th St., East Village* ☎ *212/477–5829* ⊕ *www.performancespacenewyork.org* Ⓜ *6 to Astor Pl.; L to 1st Ave.*

★ The Public Theater
THEATER | Fresh, exciting theater keeps people talking about the Public Theater, which was founded in 1954 but has most recently seen such hits as Lin-Manuel Miranda's current Broadway sensation *Hamilton,* and David Byrne and Fatboy Slim's "poperetta" *Here Lies Love,* about Imelda Marcos. Many more noted productions that began here (*Hair, A Chorus Line*) went on to Broadway and beyond. Tickets are available through the website; some discounted tickets are released through the TodayTix app. This is also the company that puts on Shakespeare in the Park in Central Park in summer. ⊠ *425 Lafayette St., south of Astor Pl., East Village* ☎ *212/539–8500, 212/967–7555 for tickets* ⊕ *www.publictheater.org* Ⓜ *6 to Astor Pl.; N, R, W to 8th St.–NYU.*

🛍 Shopping

The East Village is a fabulous hunting ground for indie boutiques and jam-packed vintage stores.

ANTIQUES AND COLLECTIBLES

Lost City Arts

ANTIQUES/COLLECTIBLES | This sprawling shop is one of the best places to shop for 20th-century design furniture, lighting, and accessories. Lost City can also help you relive the Machine Age with their in-house retro-modern line of furniture. ✉ 18 Cooper Sq., at 5th St., East Village ☎ 212/375–0500 ⊕ www.lostcityarts.com Ⓜ 6 to Astor Pl.

BEAUTY

Bond No. 9

PERFUME/COSMETICS | Created by the same fragrance team as Creed, this line of scents is intended to evoke the New York City experience, with a scent for every neighborhood: Central Park, a men's fragrance, is woodsy and "green," and Park Avenue is discreet but not too sweet. This flagship also carries candles and body creams. ✉ 9 Bond St., between Lafayette St. and Broadway, East Village ☎ 212/228-1732 ⊕ www.bondno9.com Ⓜ 6 to Bleecker St.

Kiehl's Since 1851

PERFUME/COSMETICS | At this favored haunt of top models and stylists (and the brand's flagship), white-smocked assistants help you choose between the lotions and potions, all of which are packaged in simple-looking bottles and jars. Some of the products, such as the Ultra Facial Cream, Creme with Silk Groom hairstyling aid, and superrich Creme de Corps, have attained near-cult status among fans. ✉ 109 3rd Ave., at 13th St., East Village ☎ 212/677–3171 ⊕ www.kiehls.com Ⓜ L to 3rd Ave.

CLOTHING

Cloak & Dagger

CLOTHING | The racks of this pint-size shop are lined with trendy pieces from cult-favorite womens wear designers like Samantha Pleet and Sessun, as well as accessories from the likes of A Peace Treaty and Illesteva, all hand-picked by owner and designer Brookelynn Starnes. ✉ 334 E. 9th St., between 1st and 2nd Aves., East Village ☎ 212/673–0500 ⊕ www.cloakanddaggernyc.com Ⓜ 6 to Astor Pl.; L to 1st Ave.

John Varvatos

CLOTHING | This menswear designer has long been inspired by rock 'n' roll. His ad campaigns have starred the likes of Franz Ferdinand and Green Day, so it's fitting that he transformed the former CBGB club into his New York flagship. The space is dotted with vintage pianos, guitars, and vinyl records. And the clothes? The jeans, leather pants, and suede shoes give you rock-star cred, but there are also classic, understated styles for the corporate set. ✉ 315 Bowery, between 1st and 2nd Sts., East Village ☎ 212/358–0315 ⊕ www.johnvarvatos.com Ⓜ 6 to Bleecker St.; F to 2nd Ave.

Resurrection

CLOTHING | If you're serious about vintage—and have deep pockets—Resurrection stocks a treasure trove of pristine pieces from Chanel, Gucci, Halston, Alaïa, and YSL among others. Kate Moss and Chloë Sevigny are fans, and designers like Marc Jacobs and Anna Sui have sought inspiration among the racks. ✉ 45 Great Jones St., between the Bowery and Lafayette St., East Village ☎ 212/625–1374 ⊕ www.resurrectionvintage.com Ⓜ 6 to Bleecker St.

★ Tokio 7

CLOTHING | Even fashion designers like Alexander Wang have been known to pop in to browse at this high-end consignment store. Racks are loaded with goodies from A-list designers such as Gucci, Stella McCartney, Diane von Furstenberg, and Phillip Lim, and the inventory changes all the time. ✉ *83 E. 7th St., between 1st and 2nd Aves., East Village* ☎ *212/353–8443* ⊕ *www.tokio7. net* Ⓜ *6 to Astor Pl.*

Trash and Vaudeville

CLOTHING | This punk mecca is famous for dressing stars like Debbie Harry and the Ramones back in the '70s, and its rock 'n' roll vibe lives on, albeit two blocks from its original location on St. Marks Place. Goths, punks, and pro wrestlers shop here for bondage-inspired pants and skirts, as well as vinyl corsets and mini kilts. ✉ *96 E. 7th St., between 1st Ave. and Ave. A, East Village* ☎ *212/982–3590* ⊕ *www.trashandvaudeville.com* Ⓜ *6 to Astor Pl.; L to 1st Ave.*

HOME DECOR

White Trash

HOUSEHOLD ITEMS/FURNITURE | Looking for a midcentury modern Danish desk? This is your place. Owner Stuart Zamsky crams his store with surprisingly affordable pieces that are mostly from the 1940s through '70s, including tables, lamps, and chairs. Quirkier pieces include paper mobiles from the '70s, old fondue sets, and antique medical-office cabinets. ✉ *304 E. 5th St., between 1st and 2nd Aves., East Village* ☎ *212/598–5956* ⊕ *www.whitetrashnyc.com* Ⓜ *6 to Astor Pl.; F to 2nd Ave.*

JEWELRY AND ACCESSORIES

Verameat

JEWELRY/ACCESSORIES | All the jewelry here is handmade in New York City, and none of it is typical. Design motifs include wrenches, Big Macs, and seahorses. Tilda Swinton is a fan. ✉ *315 E. 9th St., between 1st and 2nd Aves., East Village* ☎ *212/388–9045* ⊕ *www. verameat.com* Ⓜ *6 to Astor Pl.; N, R, W to 8th St.–NYU.*

SHOES, HANDBAGS, AND LEATHER GOODS

Sabah Studio

SHOES/LUGGAGE/LEATHER GOODS | Filled with art, plants, midcentury furnishings, and decorative pieces picked up around the world, this airy boutique sells one thing: handmade leather shoes based on a traditional Turkish style. Updated for modern sensibilities and made by Turkish artisans using centuries-old shoemaking methods, sabahs come in a wide range of colors—from classic black to a whimsical pink suede—but only in one style, for both men and women. The shoes are famously comfortable and known to last years. Colors change seasonally, and children's sizes are available, too. ✉ *49 Bleecker St., between Bowery and Lafayette St., East Village* ☎ *212/228–8754* ⊕ *www.sabah.am* Ⓜ *6 to Bleecker St.; B, D, F, M to Broadway–Lafayette St.*

TOYS

Dinosaur Hill

TOYS | FAMILY | Forget about Elmo and Barbie. This little shop is crammed with quirky gifts for kids like hand puppets and marionettes from Asia, telescopes, and wooden rattles. Don't miss the unusual instruments, such as a cedar *kalimba* (an African thumb piano). ✉ *306 E. 9th St., between 1st and 2nd Aves., East Village* ☎ *212/473–5850* ⊕ *www. dinosaurhill.com* Ⓜ *6 to Astor Pl.; N, R, W to 8th St.–NYU.*

WINE

★ Astor Wines & Spirits

WINE/SPIRITS | Stock up on wine, spirits, and everything else alcohol-related at this beautiful shop; it often has the bottle you can't find anywhere else. Among Astor's other assets are a wine library, a kitchen for cooking classes, and a tasting just about every day of the week. ✉ *399 Lafayette St., at 4th St., East Village* ☎ *212/674–7500* ⊕ *www.astorwines.com* Ⓜ *6 to Astor Pl.; N, R, W to 8th St.–NYU.*

Lower East Side

The Lower East Side (or simply LES) is a center of all things cool: arts and nightlife, restaurants and cafés, boutiques and salons. What was once the "Gateway to America"—and home to waves of Irish, German, Jewish, Hispanic, and Chinese immigrants—is now a quickly gentrifying neighborhood where modern high-rises, the ultracontemporary New Museum, and low-key hangouts all exist in the same corner of Manhattan.

Ludlow Street and Orchard Street in particular are great for exploring the boutiques and galleries wedged between bars and small restaurants. On Friday and Saturday nights, be aware that the neighborhood scene can be as raucous as in a college town, especially on Rivington and Orchard Streets.

The best time to experience the neighborhood's past is by day. The excellent Lower East Side Tenement Museum movingly captures the immigrant legacy of tough times and survival instincts. You might not find many pickles being sold from barrels anymore, but this remains a good place to nosh on delicious Jewish food like matzo-ball soup, corned beef and knishes from Katz's Delicatessen or Russ & Daughters.

◉ Sights

Essex Street Market

MARKET | There are plenty of newfangled food markets around Manhattan and Brooklyn, but the Essex Street Market is an old-school version. Started in 1940 as an attempt by Mayor Fiorello LaGuardia to corral street pushcarts and vendors (and thereby get them off the streets), the Essex Street Market was defined early on by the Jewish and Italian immigrants of the Lower East Side and went through several incarnations. The latest and most exciting is a wholesale move across the street (from 120 Essex Street; scheduled, at this writing, for mid-2019), trading in a windowless and rather cramped space for a light-filled atrium with seating and room for events. All the market's vendors selling meat, fish, cheeses, produce, bread, pastries, fresh juice, coffee, tacos, and more will be moving, along with the eccentric Shopsin's restaurant. There will also be some exciting additions, including the Chinatown Ice Cream Factory. Check the website for updates. ⊠ 88 Essex St., corner of Delancey and Essex Sts., Lower East Side ☎ 212/312–3603 ⊕ www.essexstreetmarket.com Ⓜ F to Delancey St.; J, M, Z to Essex St.

International Center of Photography

MUSEUM | Founded in 1974 by photojournalist Cornell Capa (photographer Robert Capa's brother), this museum continues to put on exhibitions that explore the timely social and political aspects of photojournalism. While the institution has a collection of over 150,000 original prints spanning the history of photography from daguerreotypes to large-scale pigment prints, the public space here, in the first-floor and basement galleries, is devoted to temporary exhibitions. There's a small gift shop and café as well. It's pay-what-you-wish on Thursday night 6–9 pm. ■ TIP→ You can buy a combination ticket ($27 for same-day visit; available Wed.–Sun.) with the New Museum across the street. ⊠ 250 Bowery, between E. Houston and Prince Sts., Lower East Side ☎ 212/857–0000 ⊕ www.icp.org ⊠ $14 ◔ Closed Mon. Ⓜ 6 to Spring St.; F to 2nd Ave.

Krause Gallery

MUSEUM | A handful of interesting small galleries are mixed in among the shops on Orchard and Ludlow Streets, and it's easy to pop in and out to see some fun art. The Krause Gallery is a good one, with frequently changing shows of edgy, contemporary work in a small, two-level space that's been around since 2004. ⊠ 149 Orchard St., between Stanton and Rivington Sts., Lower East Side ☎ 212/777–7799 ⊕ www.krausegallery. com Ⓜ F to 2nd Ave.

Museum at Eldridge Street

MUSEUM | The exterior of this 1887 Orthodox synagogue-turned-museum (and community space), the first synagogue to be built by the many Eastern European Jews who settled in the Lower East Side in the late 19th century, is a striking mix of Romanesque, Gothic, and Moorish motifs. Inside are an exceptional hand-carved ark (used to hold Torah scrolls) of mahogany and walnut, a sculptured wooden balcony, jewel-tone stained-glass windows, vibrantly painted and stenciled walls, and an enormous brass chandelier. Hour-long tours (starting on the hour) are available, and begin downstairs where interactive "touch tables" teach all ages about Eldridge Street and the Lower East Side. The crowning piece of the building's decades-long restoration is a stained-glass window by artist Kiki Smith and architect Deborah Gans, which weighs 6,000 pounds and has more than 1,200 pieces of glass. ✉ 12 Eldridge St., between Canal and Division Sts., Lower East Side ☎ 212/219–0302 ⊕ www. eldridgestreet.org ⛟ $14 ⊘ Closed Sat. Ⓜ F to East Broadway; B, D to Grand St.

New Museum

MUSEUM | This seven-story, 60,000-square-foot structure—a glimmering, metal-mesh-clad assemblage of off-center squares—caused a small neighborhood uproar when it was built in 2007, with some residents slow to accept the nontraditional building. Not surprisingly, given the museum's name and the building, shows are all about contemporary art, often provocative and frequently with a video element. If you're visiting on the weekend, check out the seventh-floor Skyroom and its panoramic views. ■TIP➤ You can buy a combination ticket ($27 for same-day visit; available Wed.–Sun.) with the International Center of Photography across the street. ✉ 235

Bowery, at Prince St., Lower East Side ☎ 212/219–1222 ⊕ www.newmuseum. org ⛟ $18 (pay-what-you-wish Thurs. 7–9 pm) ⊘ Closed Mon. Ⓜ 6 to Spring St., F to 2nd Ave.

Sperone Westwater

MUSEUM | Founded in 1975 in SoHo, Sperone Westwater is now a major part of the "artification" of the Lower East Side. In 2010, the gallery moved into this narrow, nine-story building, which it commissioned for itself—a vote of confidence in both its Bowery surroundings and the continued importance of its artists, who have included Bruce Nauman, William Wegman, Gerhard Richter, and a host of blue-chip minimalists. The changing exhibits, which are frequently politically charged, are always worth a look. ✉ 257 Bowery, between E. Houston and Stanton Sts., Lower East Side ☎ 212/999–7337 ⊕ www.speronewestwater.com ⊘ Closed Sun., Mon. Ⓜ F to 2nd Ave.; 6 to Spring St.; B, D, F, M to Broadway–Lafayette St.

★ Tenement Museum

MUSEUM | Step back in time at the partially restored 19th-century tenement buildings that make up the essence of the Tenement Museum: you can only see the buildings on a guided tour, and they fill up fast, so sign up early. At 97 Orchard Street, themed tours take you through the preserved apartments of several generations of immigrants who lived in the building. The "Hard Times" tour visits the homes of Natalie Gumpertz, a German-Jewish dressmaker (dating from 1878), and Adolph and Rosaria Baldizzi, Catholic immigrants from Sicily (1935). "Sweatshop Workers" visits the Levines' garment shop–apartment and the home of the Rogarshevsky family from Eastern Europe (1918), while "Irish Outsiders" explores the life of the Moores, an Irish-American family living in the building in 1869.

The Tenement Museum offers a fascinating glimpse into the lives of early-20th-century immigrants.

Nearby, at 103 Orchard Street, the *Under One Roof* exhibition explores the lives of immigrant families from Poland, China, and Puerto Rico who lived in the building after World War II. ■**TIP→ A two-hour extended experience tour with a chance for in-depth discussion is hosted daily, as are walking tours of the neighborhood; most tours don't allow kids under five.** ✉ *103 Orchard St., at Delancey St., Lower East Side* ☎ *877/975–3786* ⊕ *www.tenement. org* ✉ *Most tours $25* Ⓜ *B, D to Grand St.; F to Delancey St.; J, M, Z to Essex St.*

🍴 Restaurants

The Lower East Side is a hub of culinary innovation, with everything from molecular gastronomy to hipster Chinese cuisine. You can't walk a block without hitting a place that makes your stomach growl.

Beauty & Essex
$$ | AMERICAN | Enter through the pawnshop (it's real) in front, and you'll find what feels like a grand event, where the clientele are dressed to the nines, the drinks are flowing, and the food—from lemon blackberry pancakes and eggs Benedict at brunch to salmon tartare, pastas, and a thick-cut fillet at dinner—is way better than you'd expect at a party. Dinner is served until at least midnight (Thursday–Saturday until 1 am), a good indication that the party's still happening. **Known for:** fun atmosphere; excellent brunch; extensive menu but standout classics. Ⓢ *Average main: $22* ✉ *146 Essex St., between Stanton and Rivington Sts., Lower East Side* ☎ *212/614–0146* ⊕ *www.beautyandessex.com* ◔ *No lunch weekdays* Ⓜ *F to Delancey St.; J, M, Z to Essex St.*

★ Clinton St. Baking Co.
$$ | AMERICAN | At this down-home casual restaurant, weekend brunch brings a line down the street for what many believe to be the best blueberry pancakes in the city, if not the whole country. Lunch and dinner options include an excellent Black Angus burger, fried chicken, sandwiches,

and salads—and you can get those pancakes at dinner too, without as long a wait. **Known for:** February specialty pancake month; excellent brunch; upscale diner vibe. [$] *Average main: $19* ✉ *4 Clinton St., near Houston St., Lower East Side* ☎ *646/602–6263* 🌐 *www.clintonstreetbaking.com* 🕒 *No dinner Sun.* [M] *F to 2nd Ave.; J, M, Z to Essex St.*

Congee Village
$$ | **CHINESE** | Don't be put off by the name—this boisterous LES icon near Chinatown serves much more than the eponymous rice porridge; indeed, the menu is enormous, covering an encyclopedic range of unusual Cantonese classics. The bamboo-cloaked dining room is great with a group of people, but being wedged in at a communal table with a lively family is part of the experience. **Known for:** big portions; affordable, tasty Cantonese delights; bustling scene. [$] *Average main: $15* ✉ *100 Allen St., near Delancey St., Lower East Side* ☎ *212/941–1818* 🌐 *www.congeevillagerestaurants.com* [M] *F to Delancey St.; J, M, Z to Essex St.; B, D to Grand St.*

★ Dirt Candy
$$ | **VEGETARIAN** | One of the best, most inspired vegetarian restaurants outside California, Dirt Candy shines thanks to chef Amanda Cohen, who knows how to coax every bit of flavor out of vegetables so that they dazzle on the plate and the palate. Some of the standouts include jalapeño hush puppies (with maple butter), cauliflower curry (with a green-pea paneer), and magnificent Brussels sprouts tacos. **Known for:** very creative vegetarian food; refined ambience; make reservations or be prepared for a long wait. [$] *Average main: $17* ✉ *86 Allen St., between Broome and Grand Sts., Lower East Side* ☎ *212/228–7732* 🌐 *www.dirtcandynyc.com* 🕒 *Closed Mon. No dinner Sun., no lunch weekdays* [M] *F to Delancey St.*

Dirty French
$$$ | **FRENCH** | Rich Torrisi and Mario Carbone, the chefs who created a small empire of Italian American restaurants (Parm, Carbone, ZZ's Clam Bar) go Gallic at this cool Lower East Side bistro in the Ludlow Hotel. The name says it all: while the fare is French, the team take many of the dishes on a tour of places like North Africa and Louisiana before the food lands on your table. **Known for:** interesting spices, like Cajun or Moroccan blends; rotisserie meats; all-French wine list. [$] *Average main: $30* ✉ *Ludlow Hotel, 180 Ludlow St., between Houston and Stanton Sts., Lower East Side* ☎ *212/254–3000* 🌐 *www.dirtyfrench.com* [M] *F to 2nd Ave.*

Doughnut Plant
$ | **CAFÉ** | **FAMILY** | The all-American junk-food staple is elevated to high art here, with fresh seasonal ingredients, real fruit, and imported chocolate mixed into the batter. Traditionalists croon over the vanilla-bean doughnut, but there are plenty of exotic flavors to tempt taste buds: the dense, fudgy Blackout is covered in crumb topping; carrot-cake doughnuts have a cream-cheese filling. **Known for:** creative, seasonal flavors in cake and yeast varieties; fudgy Blackout doughnuts; fun decor. [$] *Average main: $5* ✉ *379 Grand St., between Essex and Norfolk Sts., Lower East Side* ☎ *212/505–3700* 🌐 *www.doughnutplant.com* [M] *F to Delancey St.; J, M, Z to Essex St.; B, D to Grand St.*

The Fat Radish
$$ | **BRITISH** | Years ago, the phrase "seasonal British" might have seemed puzzling, but the updated hearty food on the menu at this handsome, hip spot makes it clear that the Brits are totally on trend these days. On the menu are plenty of kale and farro and well-chosen vegetables but also an updated version of a Scotch egg, interesting fish dishes, and a cheeseburger served with duck-fat fries. **Known for:** good British food; fun

scene; craft British brews. $ *Average main: $22* ⊠ *17 Orchard St., near Canal St., Lower East Side* ☎ *212/300–4053* ⊕ *www.thefatradishnyc.com* ⊙ *No lunch Mon.* Ⓜ *F to East Broadway.*

★ **Freemans**

$$$ | AMERICAN | It was Freemans that brought taxidermy, ironic tchotchkes, and lodge-ish dishes like hunters stew, potted pork, and grilled trout to the restaurant scene in 2004 (inspiring many imitators), along with an equally inspired cocktail menu. Down a little-used alleyway on the Lower East Side, this cozy spot continues to draw crowds for its trendy renditions (quinoa linguine, anyone?) of hearty American food and delicious beverages. **Known for:** being perpetually hip; taxidermy decor; excellent cocktails. $ *Average main: $29* ⊠ *End of Freeman Alley, off Rivington St. between the Bowery and Chrystie St., Lower East Side* ☎ *212/420–0012* ⊕ *www.freemansrestaurant.com* Ⓜ *F to 2nd Ave.; J, Z to Bowery.*

★ **Ivan Ramen**

$$ | JAPANESE | Ivan Orkin's improbable but true story is one of the many layers that make New York City's restaurant scene so exciting, authentic, and delicious: the self-described "Jewish kid from Long Island" moved to Tokyo and became a ramen-making master, achieving near legendary status in the Japanese capital. In 2014 he opened this always-packed Lower East Side temple to ramen, where first-timers should try the triple pork, triple garlic *mazemen*, a type of near-brothless ramen. **Known for:** red-chili ramen; rye-based ramen noodles; Japanese fried chicken. $ *Average main: $17* ⊠ *25 Clinton St., between Houston and Stanton Sts., Lower East Side* ☎ *646/678–3859* ⊕ *www.ivanramen.com* Ⓜ *F to 2nd Ave.; J, M, Z to Essex St.*

★ **Katz's Delicatessen**

$$ | DELI | Everything and nothing has changed at Katz's since it first opened in 1888, when the neighborhood was dominated by Jewish immigrants: lines still form on the weekends for giant, succulent hand-carved corned beef and pastrami sandwiches, soul-warming soups, juicy hot dogs, and crisp half-sour pickles. You get a ticket when you walk in and then get it punched at the various stations where you pick up your food; don't lose it or you'll have to pay the lost ticket fee. **Known for:** large pastrami sandwiches; Formica tables and vintage deli decor; weeknights are more laid-back. $ *Average main: $17* ⊠ *205 E. Houston St., at Ludlow St., Lower East Side* ☎ *212/254–2246* ⊕ *www.katzsdelicatessen.com* Ⓜ *F to 2nd Ave.*

Loreley Restaurant & Biergarten

$$ | GERMAN | Start with a good selection of German beer on tap, including seasonal options; add some international options in a can; then up the ante with plates of sausages, schnitzel, and spaetzle; and then top it off with an outdoor beer garden (there's also a brick-walled beer hall with long wooden tables). Did we mention that the beer garden is heated in winter? **Known for:** great daytime happy hour; German craft beers; beer garden is a bit more "concrete" than "garden," but hey, it's Manhattan. $ *Average main: $17* ⊠ *7 Rivington St., near the Bowery, Lower East Side* ☎ *212/253–7077* ⊕ *www.loreleynyc.com* Ⓜ *J, Z to Bowery; B, D to Grand St.; F to 2nd Ave.*

The Meatball Shop

$ | ITALIAN | FAMILY | New York's first full-service meatball restaurant has a pedigreed chef, a professional waitstaff, a wine list, and a hip crowd. And the meatballs, oh, the meatballs: choose beef, pork, chicken, veggie, or "special" ball options that range from chili cheese to Greek lamb and Buffalo chicken; then decide if you want them served in sliders or a hero, as a salad, or as a platter. **Known for:** top-quality ingredients; ice-cream sandwiches for dessert; multiple locations. [$] *Average main: $12* ✉ *84 Stanton St., near Allen St., Lower East Side* ☎ *212/982–8895* 🌐 *www.themeatballshop.com* [M] *F to 2nd Ave.; J, Z to Bowery.*

★ Mission Chinese Food

$$ | **CHINESE** | San Francisco–based chef Danny Bowien is known for his hip restaurant aesthetic and deliciously spicy but not necessarily authentic take on Sichuan cuisine, and this Manhattan outpost keeps to these themes. The Chongquing chicken wings and the kung pao pastrami are standouts for palates that can withstand the fiery Sichuan spices. **Known for:** party scene; creative cuisine and cocktails; make reservations to avoid very long waits. [$] *Average main: $21* ✉ *171 East Broadway, between Rutgers and Jefferson Sts., Lower East Side* ☎ *212/746–2986* 🌐 *www.missionchinesefood.com* 🕓 *No lunch weekdays* [M] *F to East Broadway.*

Russ & Daughters

$$ | **DELI** | For classic smoked fish, caviar, and bagels, you can do no better than this family-owned "appetizing" shop that's been serving customers from the same location since 1914. The lines are long on the weekend and there's no seating, but get a sandwich to go and you'll understand what real smoked salmon tastes like. **Known for:** smoked salmon and all kinds of smoked fish, just for starters; old-school, family-owned business; sit-down restaurant nearby at 127 Orchard Street. [$] *Average main: $13* ✉ *179 E. Houston St., between Allen and Orchard Sts., Lower East Side* ☎ *212/475–4880* 🌐 *www.russanddaughters.com* [M] *F to 2nd Ave.; J, Z to Bowery.*

Shopsin's

$$ | **ECLECTIC** | **FAMILY** | The eclectic menu at this eccentric eatery, which has moved several times since it first opened in Greenwich Village in 1973, runs to literally hundreds of items—from pumpkin pancakes to chilaquiles, and from chili cheeseburgers to lamb-curry soups. Many options, like the mac 'n' cheese pancakes, are whimsical but delicious and have loyal followers (those mac 'n' cheese pancakes are even better with hot sauce). **Known for:** super-eclectic menu; humorously named dishes; many longtime loyal customers. [$] *Average main: $17* ✉ *Essex Market, 88 Essex St., corner of Delancey and Essex Sts., Lower East Side* 🌐 *www.shopsins.com* 🕓 *Closed Mon., Tues. No dinner* [M] *F to Delancey St.; J, M, Z to Essex St.*

Sugar Sweet Sunshine

$ | **CAFÉ** | **FAMILY** | The brainchild of two former Magnolia Bakery employees, Sugar Sweet's cupcakes are believed by many to be far superior; try the chocolate-almond Gooey Gooey, or the cream cheese frosting–topped pumpkin. The flavors are intense but not too-too sweet: the real showstopper is swoon-inducing banana pudding, with crumbled Nilla wafers suspended in vanilla pudding. **Known for:** great cupcakes; banana pudding cupcake; friendly service. [$] *Average main: $6* ✉ *126 Rivington St., between Essex and Norfolk Sts., Lower East Side* ☎ *212/995–1960* 🌐 *www.sugarsweetsunshine.com* [M] *F to Delancey St.; J, M, Z to Essex St.*

Supermoon Bakehouse

$ | **BAKERY** | Supercreative and beautiful baked goods, including the "cruffin"—a cross between a croissant and a muffin, with different fillings—and extravagant croissants (perhaps filled with hazelnut and chocolate ganache and shards of dark chocolate, or a savory version with spinach and cheese) distinguish this colorful bakery. The space and the pastries seem made to be Instagrammed, but the goods are also delicious. **Known for:** inventing the "cruffin"; supercreative flavors of everything; open well into the evening. [$] *Average main: $6* ✉ *120 Rivington St., between Essex and Norfolk*

Sts., Lower East Side ⊕ www.super-
moonbakehouse.com Ⓜ F to Delancey
St.; J, M, Z to Essex St.

Vanessa's Dumpling House

$ | **CHINESE** | One of the best deals in
Chinatown can be found here, with siz-
zling pork-and-chive dumplings (four for
a buck) and plenty of vegetarian options.
This is a casual, order-at-the-counter spot
with a few tables. **Known for:** excellent
dumplings; very budget-friendly; popular
stop before a night of barhopping. Ⓢ Average main: $8 ✉ 118 Eldridge St., near
Broome St., Lower East Side ☎ 212/625–
8008 ⊕ www.vanessasdumplinghouse.
com Ⓜ B, D to Grand St.

Wildair

$$ | **AMERICAN** | Named for a racehorse
that had its stable on the Lower East
Side in pre–Civil War days, this fantastic
wine bar with a streamlined modern
look and brick walls focuses mainly on
natural wines, served with near-revelato-
ry bites of dishes like the 'nduja (spicy,
spreadable pork salume) toast, chunky
yet silky beef tartare, and a fork-tender
Wagyu steak for two. Like the horse
it's named after, this bar will inspire you
to race back for another visit. **Known
for:** attracts foodie types; small menu;
little gem lettuce "salad". Ⓢ Average
main: $19 ✉ 142 Orchard St., between
Rivington and Delancey Sts., Lower East
Side ☎ 646/964–5624 ⊕ www.wildair.
nyc ☉ Closed Sun., Mon. No lunch Ⓜ F to
Delancy St.; J, M, Z to Essex St.

🛏 Hotels

Hotel Indigo Lower East Side, New York

$ | **HOTEL** | Right in the center of a dynam-
ic neighborhood, this hotel is a fantastic
base for good restaurants, nightlife, and
people-watching, and it's hard to beat the
sweeping city views from the restaurant
and bar on the 15th floor. **Pros:** local
flavor, with emphasis on art; steps from
the subway; rooftop bar and restaurant.
Cons: street noise is common in this

all-night neighborhood; small rooms; far
from main tourist attractions. Ⓢ Rooms
from: $250 ✉ 171 Ludlow St., Lower East
Side ☎ 212/237–1776 ⊕ www.hotelin-
digolowereastside.com ➷ 294 rooms
†Ⓞ† No meals Ⓜ F to 2nd Ave.; J, M, Z to
Essex St.

Hotel on Rivington

$$ | **HOTEL** | A pioneer when it opened
back in 2004, this glass-walled hotel
on the Lower East Side is still a great
choice if you want to be in the thick of
the neighborhood's dining and nightlife
scene. **Pros:** cool location and vibe; huge
windows with wonderful New York
views; many rooms have balconies. **Cons:**
feels clubby on weekends; not all rooms
have a view; check-in time is not until
4 pm. Ⓢ Rooms from: $395 ✉ 107 Riv-
ington St., between Ludlow and Essex
Sts., Lower East Side ☎ 212/475–2600
⊕ www.hotelonrivington.com ➷ 108
rooms †Ⓞ† No meals Ⓜ F to Delancey St.;
J, M, Z to Essex St.

The Ludlow Hotel

$ | **HOTEL** | Embodying the effortlessly
cool attitude of the Lower East Side,
this stylish hotel pleases guests with
everything from the cozy lounge with a
limestone fireplace to the romantic trel-
lis-covered garden. **Pros:** hot restaurant
and bar scene; some rooms have terraces and great views; great location for hip
restaurants and shopping. **Cons:** lounge
and courtyard can get crowded; rooms
are small; might be too sceney for some.
Ⓢ Rooms from: $295 ✉ 180 Ludlow
St., Lower East Side ☎ 212/432–1818
⊕ www.ludlowhotel.com ➷ 175 rooms
†Ⓞ† No meals Ⓜ F to 2nd Ave.; J, M, Z to
Essex St.

PUBLIC

$ | **HOTEL** | Ian Schrager's buzzy hotel
brings the Lower East Side the sleek
modern design, state-of-the-art technology, destination dining, and hot bar scene
that define every property he touches.
Pros: minimalist hipster-luxe design; multiple bars and restaurants; hot nightlife

scene. **Cons:** rooms are small, even by NYC standards; noisy heat and air-conditioning; not all rooms have great views. Ⓢ *Rooms from: $250* ✉ *215 Chrystie St., Lower East Side* ☎ *212/735–6000* ⊕ *www.publichotels.com* ⇌ *367 rooms* ⦿ *No meals* Ⓜ *F to 2nd Ave.*

Sister City
$ | **HOTEL** | In a refurbished tenement building, this new minimalist hotel from the owners of the Ace Hotels brand describes itself as an "experiment in essentialism," with a focus on the budget traveler. **Pros:** requisite cool rooftop bar; Floret, the all-day café on the ground floor; great location. **Cons:** design can seem a bit too bare; if you're looking for luxury perks, this isn't for you; far from Midtown tourist sights. Ⓢ *Rooms from: $259* ✉ *225 Bowery, between Rivington and Stanton Sts., Lower East Side* ☎ *646/343–4500* ⊕ *www.sistercitynyc. com* ⇌ *200 rooms* ⦿ *No meals* Ⓜ *F to 2nd Ave.*

Sixty LES
$ | **HOTEL** | This hotel is a great embodiment of the vibe of the neighborhood inhabitants: hip, but friendly when you're acquainted. **Pros:** in the heart of LES nightlife; great views from suites; cool bar scene. **Cons:** occasionally snobby staff; rooms are stylish but dark; some guests complain about noise. Ⓢ *Rooms from: $200* ✉ *190 Allen St., between Houston and Stanton Sts., Lower East Side* ☎ *877/460–8888* ⊕ *www.sixtyhotels.com/lowereastside* ⇌ *141 rooms* ⦿ *No meals* Ⓜ *F to Delancey St.; J, M, Z to Essex St.*

Nightlife

BARS
★ Back Room
BARS/PUBS | The atmospheric Prohibition-era touches here include tin ceilings, chandeliers, velvet wallpaper, mirrored bars, an ample fireplace, and a "hidden" outdoor entrance (which you can find easily enough, through the back alley). Drinks come in old-fashioned teacups or wrapped in paper bags. The clientele are more mature than at some of the other bars in the neighborhood. ✉ *102 Norfolk St., between Rivington and Delancey Sts., Lower East Side* ☎ *212/228–5098* ⊕ *www.backroomnyc.com* Ⓜ *F to Delancey St.; J, M, Z to Essex St.*

Bar Goto
BARS/PUBS | At this stylish *izakaya* from an alum of the Pegu Club, one of the city's foremost cocktail dens, you can expect high-quality, innovative cocktails that make use of the Japanese theme: the Sakura martini is made with sake, gin, maraschino, and cherry blossom, while the Kyoto old-fashioned incorporates rice vodka, gin matcha, and sencha. Small plates to accompany your drinks include a selection of the savory Japanese pancakes called *okonomiyaki* and a few other items. ✉ *245 Eldridge St., between E. Houston and Stanton Sts., Lower East Side* ☎ *212/475–4411* ⊕ *www.bargoto. com* Ⓜ *F, M to 2nd Ave.*

★ Nitecap
BARS/PUBS | Drift down a few stairs into this cozy bar with lots of spots perfect for catching up with friends in its polished nooks, some cushy bar seats, and a few intimate two-seat booths. You'll find friendly service and and a menu listing seasonal cocktails that make use of uncommon infusions and flavor combinations. ✉ *151 Rivington St., between Suffolk and Clinton Sts., Lower East Side* ☎ *212/466–3361* ⊕ *www.nitecapnyc.com* Ⓜ *F to Delancey St.; J, M, Z to Essex St.*

CABARET AND PIANO BARS
The Box
CABARET | A sensation when it opened in 2007, Simon Hammerstein's Roaring Twenties–style cabaret–cum–burlesque show–cum–performance art emporium remains one of the biggest players in any nightlife category. The triumvirate of gorgeousness—design, customers,

and performers—explains why the experience doesn't come cheap. Note the "show fee" of 20% added to your bill, in addition to tip. Check the website to make reservations. ⊠ *189 Chrystie St., between Stanton and Rivington Sts., Lower East Side* ☎ *212/982–9301* ⊕ *www.theboxnyc.com* Ⓜ *F to 2nd Ave.*

LIVE MUSIC VENUES
Arlene's Grocery
MUSIC CLUBS | Crowds of youngsters and longtime New Yorkers pack into this former Puerto Rican bodega that's now a downtown staple for local bands, variety shows, burlesque, the occasional murder-mystery party, and seasonal specialty acts. The drinks are cheap and the vibe is all about the good times. ⊠ *95 Stanton St., between Orchard and Ludlow Sts., Lower East Side* ☎ *212/358–1633* ⊕ *www.arlenesgrocery.net* Ⓜ *F to 2nd Ave.*

★ Bowery Ballroom
MUSIC CLUBS | This legendary theater with Art Deco accents is probably the city's top midsize concert venue. Packing in the crowds here is a rite of passage for musicians (some already big, some on the cusp of stardom), including the Gossip, Yo La Tengo, and the exuberant Go! Team. Grab one of the tables on the balcony (if you can), stand (and get sandwiched) on the main floor, or retreat to the comfortable bar in the basement, which fills up after each show. ⊠ *6 Delancey St., between the Bowery and Chrystie St., Lower East Side* ☎ *212/533–2111* ⊕ *www.boweryballroom.com* Ⓜ *J, Z to Bowery.*

The Delancey
MUSIC CLUBS | From the palm-studded rooftop deck (heated in winter, breezy in summer), to the ground-floor lounge, and down to the basement venue where DJs and rock bands hold court, the multifaceted Delancey, at the foot of the Williamsburg Bridge, is a versatile spot for thirsty lounge lizards. ⊠ *168 Delancey St.,*

between Clinton and Attorney Sts., Lower East Side ☎ *212/254–9920* ⊕ *www.thedelancey.com* Ⓜ *F to Delancey St.; J, M, Z to Essex St.*

Mercury Lounge
MUSIC CLUBS | You have to squeeze past the sardine-packed hipsters in the front bar to reach the stage, but it's worth it. Not only does this top-quality venue specialize in cool bands on the indie scene, but it was also where the late, great Jeff Buckley used to stop by to do spontaneous solo shows. Other big-name musicians follow in his footsteps with occasional pop-up shows of their own. ⊠ *217 E. Houston St., between Ludlow and Essex Sts., Lower East Side* ☎ *212/260-4700* ⊕ *www.mercuryloungenyc.com* Ⓜ *F to 2nd Ave.*

Pianos
MUSIC CLUBS | With two venues for live music and DJs—the Showroom downstairs and the Upstairs Lounge—as well as a full bar that serves food downstairs, there's something for everyone at this Lower East Side staple. It's especially fun late nights and weekends. ⊠ *158 Ludlow St., near Stanton St., Lower East Side* ☎ *212/505-3733* ⊕ *www.pianosnyc.com* Ⓜ *F to Delancey St.; J, M, Z to Essex St.*

Rockwood Music Hall
MUSIC CLUBS | With multiple performers at each of the three intimate venues, there's so much to hear here. Expect music of all types, often from bands or soloists just passing through the city. Performances start as early as 3 pm on the weekends and 6 pm during the week—meaning you can get your live music fix and catch up on sleep, too. Many shows are free, making Rockwood a top spot to catch budding talent. ⊠ *196 Allen St., between Houston and Stanton Sts., Lower East Side* ☎ *212/477–4155* ⊕ *www.rockwoodmusichall.com* Ⓜ *F to 2nd Ave.; J, Z to Bowery.*

🎭 Performing Arts

FILM

Metrograph

FILM | Exclusive premieres, sometimes with celebrity guest speakers, and an ever-changing calendar of both classic and obscure films lure patrons to this boutique movie theater, where six films are usually shown on the two screens each day. Also here are a restaurant and a bar to hang out at before or after the show, a small bookstore for browsing, and a retro candy counter with exotic treats. ⊠ *7 Ludlow St., between Hester and Canal Sts., Lower East Side* ☎ *212/660–0312* ⊕ *www.metrograph. com* Ⓜ *F to East Broadway.*

THEATER

Dixon Place

THEATER | Founded in the 1980s, this small nonprofit theater continues to host worthy, and frequently unconventional and hilarious, performances of theater, music, dance, and more, with a focus on new works. Its popular HOT! Festival of Queer Performance, held in July, is the longest-running LGBTQ festival in the world. Whatever you're seeing—of the some 1,000 shows held here each year—the Lounge, Dixon Place's cheerful bar, is a great place to meet up before the show and connect with artists after. ⊠ *161A Chrystie St., between Rivington and Delancey Sts., Lower East Side* ☎ *212/219–0736* ⊕ *www.dixonplace.org* Ⓜ *J, Z to Bowery; B, D to Grand St.*

🛍 Shopping

Head to the Lower East Side for excellent vintage finds and edgy looks. Once home to multitudes of Eastern European immigrants and crumbling tenement buildings, the neighborhood has transformed from New York's bargain-hunting ground into a hotbed for indie design that includes everything from clothing to furniture. Head here if you want to revamp your look with a trendier style. Ludlow and Orchard Streets are the main drags for boutiques, as well as for galleries, bars, and hip restaurants.

BEAUTY

Aedes Perfumery

PERFUME/COSMETICS | Arguably the best place to buy fragrance in Manhattan, this boutique's super-knowledgeable staff help shoppers find the perfect scent. High-end (and predominantly European) brands like L'Artisan Parfumeur and Astier de Villatte are stocked, along with luxurious skin-care products, pricey candles, and room diffusers. The shop's signature gift wrap is as beautiful as what's inside the box. ⊠ *16A Orchard St., between Hester and Canal Sts., Lower East Side* ☎ *212/206–8674* ⊕ *www.aedes.com* Ⓜ *F to East Broadway.*

CLOTHING

Assembly New York

CLOTHING | Sleekly cut modern and some vintage womens and menswear, as well as an interesting selection of accessories and jewelry, fill this medium-size shop. ⊠ *170 Ludlow St., between E. Houston and Stanton Sts., Lower East Side* ☎ *212/253–5393* ⊕ *www.assemblynewyork.com* Ⓜ *F to 2nd Ave.*

Edith Machinist

CLOTHING | Quintessentially unique vintage accessories, clothes, shoes, and jewelry make this shop, a few steps down from street level, a must-hit for shoppers with a discerning, quirky fashion sense. Recent finds have included a beaded clutch in the shape of the Statue of Liberty, a 1960s Schiaparelli silk scarf, and a pair of floral sequined slippers. ⊠ *104 Rivington St., between Ludlow and Essex Sts., Lower East Side* ☎ *212/979–9992* ⊕ *www.edithmachinist. com* Ⓜ *F to Delancey St.; J, M, Z to Essex St.*

★ Maryam Nassir Zadeh

CLOTHING | A well-chosen collection of clothes, accessories, and objects from some of the most exciting independent

The East Village is predominantly residential and has mostly low-rise buildings.

designers in the world is the draw at this minimalist, industrial-chic boutique. Try on a hot-pink blazer from Eckaus Latta, a colorful patchwork blouse by Sophie Andes Gascon, or a classic silhouette from Paris Georgia. Zadeh's own line is also available, and she sometimes stocks flea market finds from her travels ✉ 123 Norfolk St., between Rivington and Delancey Sts., Lower East Side ☎ 212/673–6405 ⊕ www.mnzstore.com Ⓜ J, M, Z to Essex St.; F to Delancey St.

Oak

CLOTHING | Most of the clothing here comes in black or leather, and the store carries high-end designers in addition to its own line for both men and women. Come here for skinny jeans, oversize sweaters, bomber jackets, and vintage fur and leather finds. ✉ 138 Ludlow St., between Stanton and Rivington Sts., Lower East Side ☎ 646/684–3245 ⊕ www.oaknyc.com Ⓜ F to 2nd Ave.

The Rising States

CLOTHING | An unassuming boutique from a lifelong fashion fan stocks an edited collection of ultrahip pieces for ladies— think quirky dresses, tailored pants, loose tops, and colorful heels and boots—by mostly local designers (like Samantha Pleet and Miranda Bennett) who often drop by the shop. ✉ 168 Ludlow St., between E. Houston and Stanton Sts., Lower East Side ☎ 646/649–2410 ⊕ www.therisingstatesnyc.com Ⓜ F to 2nd Ave.

FOOD AND TREATS

Economy Candy

FOOD/CANDY | FAMILY | Oh, to be a kid in a candy store! Economy Candy has been making life sweeter since 1937, and the floor-to-ceiling shelves and candy-and-nut dispensers here are filled with bulk specialty and brand-name goodies, from every flavor of gummy candy and jelly bean to nuts, halvah, and chocolate-covered everything. There are also everyday chocolates like Baby Ruth, Butterfinger, and M&Ms (available in bulk or in

5-pound bags, by the color). If you've never tried Canadian chocolate bars like Coffee Crisp, Aero, and Crispy Crunch, you're in for a treat. ✉ *108 Rivington St., between Ludlow and Essex Sts., Lower East Side* ☎ *212/254–1531* ⊕ *www.economycandy.com* Ⓜ *J, M, Z to Essex St.; F to Delancey St.*

SHOES, HANDBAGS, AND LEATHER GOODS

Altman Luggage

SHOES/LUGGAGE/LEATHER GOODS | Having trouble fitting all your purchases into your bag? Altman sells top-of-the-line luggage from Rimowa, Samsonite, and Tumi at discount prices. Selections of cosmetic bags and other travel accessories also stock the shelves. ✉ *135 Orchard St., between Rivington and Delancey Sts., Lower East Side* ☎ *212/254–7275* ⊕ *www.altmanluggage.com* Ⓜ *J, M, Z to Essex St.; F to Delancey St.*

Chapter 6

GREENWICH VILLAGE AND THE WEST VILLAGE

Updated by
David Farley

6

👁 Sights ★★☆☆☆ **🍴 Restaurants** ★★★★★ **🛏 Hotels** ★★★☆☆ **👜 Shopping** ★★★★☆ **🍸 Nightlife** ★★★★☆

NEIGHBORHOOD SNAPSHOT

TOP EXPERIENCES

- People-watching in Washington Square Park
- Strolling and window-shopping along the picturesque streets of the West Village
- Relaxing in a café
- Eating your way down Bleecker Street

GETTING HERE

The West 4th Street subway stop—serviced by the A, B, C, D, E, F, and M lines—puts you on the west side of Greenwich Village. Farther west, the 1 train has stops at Houston Street and at Christopher Street–Sheridan Square. The L stops at 8th Avenue, and the A, C, and E trains stop at 14th Street, which is the northern boundary of the West Village.

PLANNING YOUR TIME

A visit to Washington Square Park, in the heart of Greenwich Village, is a must for people-watching and relaxing on a bench (you might also catch some live music performances). There are lots of restaurants and shops in the neighborhood, too.

The West Village—basically from 7th Avenue to the Hudson River—is more residential, and a bit quieter, with carefully tended, tree-lined streets that make the neighborhood a perfect place to roam, camera in hand. Everything from upscale boutiques to cheap pizza joints line Bleecker Street and Greenwich Avenue.

The winding streets of the West Village often seem mazelike, even to many New Yorkers, because most of the streets here are named rather than numbered, and they were established before Manhattan laid out its street-grid system back in 1811. Assume that you're going to get a little bit lost—that's part of the fun—but don't hesitate to ask for directions.

QUICK BITES

- **Caffe Reggio.** Usually packed, this café dates back to the 1920s, making it one of the oldest coffeehouses in the city. Do have a pastry. ✉ 119 MacDougal St., between W. 3rd and Carmine Sts., Greenwich Village ⊕ www.caffereggio.com Ⓜ Subway: A, B, C, D, E, F, M to W. 4th St.

- **Grounded.** Step into this low-key spot for hot or cold brews (tea and coffee)—the specialty lattes are an excellent splurge. ✉ 28 Jane St., between 8th and Greenwich Aves., West Village ⊕ www.groundedcoffee.com Ⓜ Subway: A, C, E to 14th St.; L to 8th Ave.; 1, 2, 3 to 14th St.

- **Joe (West Village).** The coffee is exquisitely prepared at this small corner café, the first of what is now a small chain. ✉ 141 Waverly Pl., at Gay St., Greenwich Village ⊕ www.joenewyork.com Ⓜ Subway: A, B, C, D, E, F, M to W. 4th St.; 1 to Christopher St.–Sheridan Sq.

- **Toby's Estate.** The West Village may be loaded with a legion of coffee spots, but the neighborhood's true java lovers gravitate here for a high-quality perk. It opens at 6:30 am every day. ✉ 44 Charles St., at 7th Ave., West Village ⊕ tobysestate.com Ⓜ Subway: 1 to Christopher St.; 2, 3 to 14th St.

The charming, tree-lined streets of the Village are beloved by New Yorkers (whether they can afford to live there or not) for their cozy restaurants and cafés, chic cocktail bars, and inviting boutiques.

Long the home of writers, artists, bohemians, and bon vivants, "the Village" is made up of Greenwich Village proper (the area surrounding Washington Square Park) and the West Village, from around 7th Avenue to the Hudson River. Greenwich Village, in prime New York University (NYU) territory, has lots of young people, while the West Village is primarily residential, with lots of well-to-do couples and families and a substantial community of older gay men and some lesbians. Both sections have a relaxed, downtown vibe and a distinctly New York style in their stores, corner bars, and trendy restaurants.

Greenwich Village

Many would argue that Washington Square Park is still the beating heart of downtown, a magnet for all kinds of life. People come here to hear live music, stretch out on a picnic blanket, let the pooch loose at the dog run, or bring kids to the playground. The park anchors Greenwich Village, where you can encounter just about every variety of New Yorker, from skateboarders and students to white-collar workers on break to people who look like they've been hanging out in the park for years, playing chess and checkers at the stone tables. This is also a historic part of the neighborhood, with the grand Washington Memorial Arch looking north to two blocks of lovingly preserved Greek

Revival and Federal-style town houses known as "the Row."

"Bountiful" doesn't even begin to describe Greenwich Village's yield of creative genius. In the late 1940s and early 1950s, abstract expressionist painters Jackson Pollock, Lee Krasner, Mark Rothko, and Willem de Kooning congregated here, as did Beat writers Jack Kerouac, Allen Ginsberg, and Lawrence Ferlinghetti. The 1960s brought folk musicians and poets, notably Bob Dylan and Joan Baez. The area's bohemian days may be long gone, but a romantic allure still lingers along the tree-lined streets and at the back of the cafés, behind the frenetic clamor of NYU students and the polished veneer of multimillion-dollar town houses.

👁 Sights

Bleecker Street
NEIGHBORHOOD | Walking the stretch of Bleecker Street between 7th Avenue and Broadway provides a smattering of just about everything synonymous with Greenwich Village these days: NYU buildings, record stores, Italian cafés and food shops, pizza and takeout joints, bars and nightclubs, and funky boutiques. A lazy afternoon here may consist of sampling some of the city's best pizza, grabbing an espresso, and soaking up the downtown fashion scene. Foodies love the blocks between 6th and 7th Avenues for the specialty purveyors like Murray's Cheese (No. 254). At the intersection

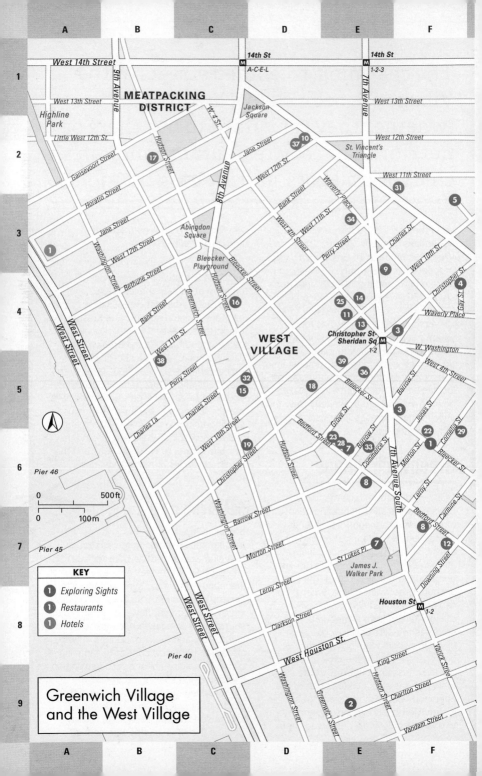

Greenwich Village
and the West Village

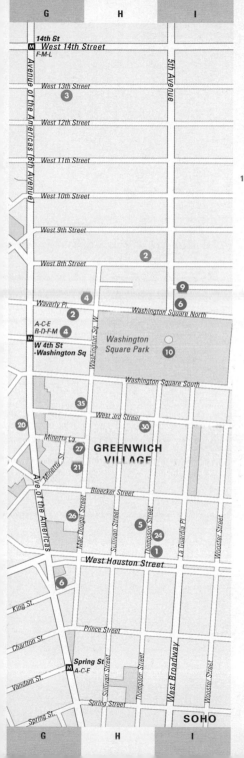

6

Sights ▼

1 Bleecker Street F6
2 Children's
   Museum of the Arts E9
3 Christopher Park E4
4 Gay Street F4
5 Patchin Place F3
6 The Row I4
7 St. Luke's Place E7
8 75 1/2 Bedford St. E6
9 Washington Mews I4
10 Washington
   Square Park I5

Restaurants ▼

1 Arturo's I7
2 Babbo Ristorante G4
3 Bleecker Street Pizza ... F5
4 Blue Hill G4
5 Carbone H7
6 Charlie Bird G8
7 Chumley's E6
8 Do Hwa F7
9 Dominique
   Ansel Kitchen E3
10 Don Angie D2
11 Due West E4
12 Emily F7
13 Empellón Taqueria E4
14 Fedora E4
15 Flip Sigi C5
16 Frankies 570 Spuntino ... C4
17 High Street
   on Hudson B2
18 I Sodi D5
19 Jeju Noodle Bar C6
20 Joe's Pizza G6
21 Kati Roll Company G6
22 Keste Pizza & Vino F6
23 The Little Owl E6
24 Lupa I7
25 Mary's Fish Camp E4
26 Mermaid Oyster Bar G7
27 Minetta Tavern G6
28 Moustache Pitza E6
29 Pearl Oyster Bar F5
30 Pho Bar H6
31 Rahi F2
32 RedFarm C5
33 Sushi Nakazawa E6
34 Taïm E3
35 Tokyo Record Bar H5
36 Via Carota E5
37 Wallflower D2
38 Wallsé B5
39 Westville West E5

Hotels ▼

1 The Jane A3
2 The Marlton H3
3 Walker Hotel G1
4 Washington
   Square Hotel H4

of Bleecker and Carmine Streets is Our Lady of Pompeii Church, where Mother Cabrini, a naturalized Italian immigrant who became the first American citizen to be canonized, often prayed. West of 7th Avenue, the shops get more upscale, with fashion and home-furnishings boutiques featuring antiques, eyeglasses, handbags, shoes, and designer clothing. ⊠ *Greenwich Village* Ⓜ *A, B, C, D, E, F, M to W. 4th St.*

Gay Street

NEIGHBORHOOD | A curved, one-block lane lined with small row houses, Gay Street was probably named after an early landowner and definitely had nothing to do with gay rights. In the 1930s, this tiny thoroughfare and nearby Christopher Street became famous nationwide after Ruth McKenney began to publish somewhat zany autobiographical stories based on what happened when she and her sister moved to No. 14 from Ohio. The stories, first published in the *New Yorker*, birthed many adaptations, including the 1953 Broadway musical *Wonderful Town* and the 1942 and 1955 movies *My Sister Eileen*. ⊠ *Between Christopher St. and Waverly Pl., Greenwich Village* Ⓜ *1 to Christopher St.–Sheridan Sq.; A, B, C, D, E, F, M to W. 4th St.*

Patchin Place

NEIGHBORHOOD | This narrow, gated cul-de-sac off West 10th Street between Greenwich and 6th Avenues has 10 diminutive 1848 row houses. Around the corner on 6th Avenue is a similar dead-end street, **Milligan Place,** with five small houses completed in 1852. The houses in both quiet enclaves were originally built for waiters who worked at 5th Avenue's high-society Brevoort Hotel, long since demolished. Later Patchin Place residents included writers Theodore Dreiser, E. E. Cummings, Jane Bowles, and Djuna Barnes. Milligan Place became popular among playwrights, including Eugene O'Neill. ⊠ *Off W. 10th St., Greenwich Village* Ⓜ *A, B, C, D, E, F, M to W. 4th St.*

The Row

BUILDING | Built from 1833 through 1837, this series of Greek Revival and Federal row houses along Washington Square North, between University Place and MacDougal Street, once belonged to merchants and bankers, then to writers and artists such as John Dos Passos and Edward Hopper. Many are now owned by NYU and used for housing and offices. Although the facades remain beautifully preserved, the interiors have been drastically altered over the years. ⊠ *1–13 and 19–26 Washington Sq. N, between University Pl. and MacDougal St., Greenwich Village* Ⓜ *A, B, C, D, E, F, M to W. 4th St.; N, R, W to 8th St.–NYU; 6 to Astor Pl.*

Washington Mews

NEIGHBORHOOD | A rarity in Manhattan, this pretty, brick-covered street—really a glorified alley—is lined on the north side with the former mews (carriage houses) of the area's homes. Although the street is private, gated, and owned by New York University, which uses many of the buildings for clubs and offices, it's open to pedestrian traffic. ⊠ *From Washington Sq. N to 8th St., between 5th Ave. and University Pl., Greenwich Village* Ⓜ *A, B, C, D, E, F, M to W. 4th St.; N, R, W to 8th St.–NYU; 6 to Astor Pl.*

★ Washington Square Park

CITY PARK | FAMILY | NYU students, street musicians, skateboarders, chess players, and those just watching the grand opera of it all generate a maelstrom of activity in this physical and spiritual heart of Greenwich Village. The 9¾-acre park had inauspicious beginnings as a cemetery, principally for yellow-fever victims—an estimated 10,000–22,000 bodies lie below (a headstone was even unearthed in 2009). In the early 1800s the park was a parade ground and the site of public executions; the notorious Hanging Elm still stands at the northwest corner of the square. Today playgrounds attract parents with tots, dogs go leash-free inside the dog runs, and everyone else seems drawn toward the large central fountain.

Halloween in the Village

All things weird and wonderful, all creatures great and small, all costumes clever and fantastical: New York City has them all—and on All Hallows' Eve they strut through the streets in New York's Village Halloween Parade. White-sheeted ghouls seem dull compared with fishnets and leather, sequins and feathers posing and prancing along 6th Avenue in this vibrant display of vanity and insanity.

In 1974 mask-maker and puppeteer Ralph Lee paraded his puppets from house to house, visiting friends and family along the winding streets of his Greenwich Village neighborhood. His merry march quickly outgrew its original, intimate route and now, decades later, it parades up 6th Avenue, from Spring Street to 16th Street, attracting upward of 60,000 creatively costumed exhibitionists, artists, dancers, and musicians, hundreds of enormous puppets, scores of bands, and more than 2 million spectators. Anyone with a costume can join in, with no advance registration required, although the enthusiastic interaction between participants and spectators makes it just as much fun simply to watch. It's a street event for families and singles alike (though you will be entering very dense crowds), and a joyful night unlike any other.

The parade lines up along 6th Avenue between Canal and Spring Streets from 6:30 to 8:30 pm. The walk actually starts at 7, but it takes about two hours to leave the staging area. It's best to arrive from the south to avoid the crush of participants. Get there a few hours early if possible. Costumes are usually handmade, clever, and outrageous, and revelers are happy to strike a pose. The streets are crowded along the route, with the most congestion below 14th Street. Of course, the best way to truly experience the parade is to march, but if you're not feeling the face paint, it's possible to volunteer to help carry the puppets. For information, visit ⊕ *www.halloween-nyc.com.*

The triumphal European-style **Washington Memorial Arch** at the square's northern flank marks the start of 5th Avenue. The original wood-and-papier-mâché arch, situated a half block north, was erected in 1889 to commemorate the 100th anniversary of George Washington's presidential inauguration. The arch was reproduced in Tuckahoe marble in 1892, and the statues—*Washington as General Accompanied by Fame and Valor* on one side, and *Washington as Statesman Accompanied by Wisdom and Justice* on the other—were added in 1916 and 1918, respectively. ⊠ *5th Ave. between Waverly Pl. and 4th St., Greenwich Village* Ⓜ *A, B, C, D, E, F, M to W. 4th St.*

🍴 Restaurants

Greenwich Village's bohemian days may have faded, but the romantic allure of its tiny bistros, bars, and cafés remains. Around New York University, shabby-chic eateries and take-out joints cater to students, but there is a growing number of more sophisticated dining spots, too.

Arturo's

$$ | PIZZA | FAMILY | Few guidebooks list this classic New York pizzeria, yet the jam-packed room and pleasantly smoky scent foreshadow a satisfying meal. There's a full menu of Italian classics, but pizza is the main event, and the thin-crust beauties are cooked in a coal-fired oven, to emerge sizzling with simple toppings like pepperoni, sausage, and eggplant. **Known for:** classic Big Apple pizza; wacky art on the walls; no reservations on weekends, so long waits. $ *Average main: $22* ⊠ *106 W. Houston St., near Thompson St., Greenwich Village* ☎ *212/535–4480* ◷ *No lunch weeekdays* Ⓜ *1 to Houston St.; B, D, F, M to Broadway–Lafayette St.*

Babbo Ristorante
$$$ | ITALIAN | It shouldn't take more than one bite of tender barbecue squab to understand why it's so hard to get a reservation at this casually elegant restaurant, whose menu strays widely from Italian standards and hits numerous high points in dishes such as rabbit with Brussels sprouts and house-made pancetta. This is the perfect spot for a raucous celebratory dinner with flowing wine and festive banter. **Known for:** palate-pleasing house-made pastas; loud, questionable music; great Italian wine list. $ *Average main: $33* ⊠ *110 Waverly Pl., between MacDougal St. and 6th Ave., Greenwich Village* ☎ *212/777–0303* ⊕ *www.babbonyc.com* ◷ *No lunch Sun., Mon.* Ⓜ *A, B, C, D, E, F, M to W. 4th St.*

Blue Hill
$$$ | MODERN AMERICAN | This tasteful den of a restaurant—formerly a speakeasy—on a quiet side street maintains an impeccable reputation for excellence and consistency under the leadership of chef Dan Barber. Part of the slow-food, sustainable agriculture movement, Blue Hill mostly uses ingredients grown or raised within 200 miles, including the Four Season Farm at Stone Barns Center for Food and Agriculture, Barber's second culinary project in nearby Westchester County. **Known for:** pioneering farm-to-table program; lush, well-executed dishes; sophisticated setting. $ *Average main: $35* ⊠ *75 Washington Pl., between Washington Sq. W and 6th Ave., Greenwich Village* ☎ *212/539–1776* ⊕ *www.*

bluehillfarm.com ◷ *No lunch* Ⓜ *A, B, C, D, E, F, M to W. 4th St.*

Carbone
$$$$ | ITALIAN | It seems like Mario Carbone and Rich Torrisi can do no wrong, and Carbone is a case in point. The achingly popular place not only sticks to the Italian-American formula that has won it (and their earlier restaurant, Torrisi Italian Specialties) acclaim, but goes further: the white-tablecloth restaurant successfully emulates the Big Apple Italian restaurants of the 1950s, with revived dishes like veal marsala, rib eye Diana, and baked clams. **Known for:** well-done red-sauce fare; pricey but huge portions; retro vibe. $ *Average main: $45* ⊠ *181 Thompson St., between Bleecker and Houston Sts., Greenwich Village* ☎ *212/254–3000* ⊕ *www.carbonenewyork.com* ◷ *No lunch Mon.* Ⓜ *A, B, C, D, E, F, M to W. 4th St.*

★ Charlie Bird
$$$ | ITALIAN | Perpetually packed, Italian-leaning Charlie Bird is the brainchild of sommelier Robert Bohr, who was in charge of wine at vino-mad Cru, and chef Ryan Hardy, who made a name for himself at Little Nell in Aspen and has been private chef for Jay-Z and Beyoncé—the restaurant has a hip hop theme. The menu is divided into small and large plates, vegetables, a "raw" section, and pasta. **Known for:** the preferred spot of "cool kids" everywhere; hip-hop on the hi-fi; varied menu. $ *Average main: $33* ⊠ *5 King St., at 6th Ave., Greenwich Village* ☎ *212/235–7133* ⊕ *www. charliebirdnyc.com* Ⓜ *C, E to Spring St.; 1 to Houston St.*

Kati Roll Company
$ | INDIAN | You can think of a kati roll as a South Asian taco: griddled parathas stuffed with savory-spiced grilled meat, shrimp, paneer, chickpea mash, or spiced mashed potato. They're the only things sold at this tiny, popular spot cheerfully festooned with Bollywood posters. **Known for:** tasty kati rolls, mostly to take

Out and On Display: George Segal's sculptures of two gay couples in Christopher Park embody LGBTQ pride in the Village.

out; cheap late-night eats; long lunch lines. $ *Average main: $7* ✉ *99 MacDougal St., near Bleecker St., Greenwich Village* ☎ *212/730–4280* 🌐 *www.thekatirollcompany.com* [M] *A, B, C, D, E, F, M to W. 4th St.*

Lupa

$$$ | **ITALIAN** | Even the most hard-to-please connoisseurs have a soft spot for Lupa, a "downscale" Roman trattoria. Rough-hewn wood and simple preparations with top-quality ingredients define the restaurant, along with the relatively gentle prices for dishes such as ricotta gnocchi with sweet-sausage ragù, house-made salumi, and sardines with golden raisins and pine nuts. **Known for:** lively front room and more private back room; good Italian wines; repeat customers. $ *Average main: $26* ✉ *170 Thompson St., between Bleecker and Houston Sts., Greenwich Village* ☎ *212/982–5089* 🌐 *www.luparestaurant.com* [M] *A, B, C, D, E, F, M to W. 4th St.*

Mermaid Oyster Bar

$$ | **SEAFOOD** | If you're craving a great raw bar, lobster roll, or soft-shell crab sandwich (in season), Mermaid Oyster Bar gives nearby classics Mary's Fish Camp and Pearl Oyster Bar a run for their money. Almost every dish at this clean-lined, neutral-hued spot is a winner, but the lobster bisque, the blackened striped bass, and the spicy seafood bucatini fra diavolo are all standouts. **Known for:** $1.25 oyster happy hour; superior seafood; excellent cocktails. $ *Average main: $24* ✉ *79 MacDougal St., at Houston St., Greenwich Village* ☎ *212/260–0100* 🌐 *www.themermaidnyc.com* ⏲ *No lunch* [M] *1 to Houston St.; A, B, C, D, E, F, M to W. 4th St.*

Minetta Tavern

$$$ | **MODERN AMERICAN** | By converting a moribund 80-year-old Italian restaurant into a cozy hot spot, restaurateur Keith McNally created yet another hit. Try early and often to score reservations, so that you can sample creations like buttery trout meunière, bone marrow on toast,

Bleecker Street's Little Italy

Little Italy can be besieged by slow-moving crowds, touristy shops, and restaurant hosts hollering invitations to dine inside. Bleecker Street between 6th and 7th Avenues, on the other hand, with its crowded cafés, bakeries, pizza parlors, and old-world merchants, offers a more pleasurable, equally vital alternative to the traditional tourist traps.

For an authentic Italian bakery experience, stop by Pasticceria Rocco (No. 243) for wonderful cannoli, cream puffs, and cookies packed up, or order an espresso and linger over the treats.

Step into the past at the old-style (and now high-end) butcher shops, such as Ottomanelli & Sons (No. 285) and Faicco's Pork Store (No. 260), where locals have bought their sausage, prime beef, and custom-cut pork since 1900.

The sweet (or stinky) smell of success is nowhere more evident than at Murray's Cheese (No. 254). The original shop, opened in 1940 by Murray Greenberg (not Italian), was not much larger than the display case that stocked the stuff. Now it's a fromage-lover's emporium, with everything from imported crackers and bamboo cutting boards to a full-service sandwich counter. Samples are frequently served. Educational cheese-tasting classes are held in the upstairs classroom (sign up online in advance). Murray's has expanded to include a Cheese Bar a few doors down (No. 264).

There are also a few popular pizzerias along this strip; Kesté Pizza & Vino (No. 271) serves Neapolitan pies that some would argue rival even Da Michele in Naples. It's also the official location in the United States for the Associazione Pizzaiuoli Napoletani, whose mission is to promote pizzas made in the Neapolitan tradition, using Neapolitan products. Brick-oven favorite John's Pizzeria (No. 278) is a classic New York pizza joint—pies only, no slices!

expertly aged steaks, and the celebrated Black Label burger, a gorgeous assembly of meat with caramelized onions and an added layer of cheese. **Known for:** classic New York dining; original details and mural; tough to get a table. $ *Average main: $30 113 MacDougal St., between Bleecker and 3rd Sts., Greenwich Village 212/475–3850 www.minettatavernny.com No lunch Mon., Tues.* A, B, C, D, E, F, M to W. 4th St.

Pho Bar

$$ | VIETNAMESE | The owners of nearby Saigon Shack couldn't help but notice the insanely long lines at their Vietamese restaurant, so they opened up Pho Bar in late 2018. But this modern space with a wooden floor and tables isn't an annex: Pho Bar kicks it up a notch with excellent takes on the Vietnamese noodle soup, including versions with oxtail, short rib, and soft-shell crab. **Known for:** creative variations on pho; long wait times; airy, comfortable atmosphere. $ *Average main: $15 82 W. 3rd St., between Sullivan and Thompson Sts., Greenwich Village 212/803–3369 phobar.com* A, B, C, D, E, F, M to W. 4th St.

Tokyo Record Bar

$$$ | JAPANESE | An homage to the genre of jewel-box-size restaurant-bars in Tokyo that play vinyl while patrons sip Japanese whiskey and eat feel-good fare, this subterranean, 18-seat spot offers

three seatings per night—6:30, 9:30, and 10:30—for a seven-course Japanese-influenced tasting menu. The offerings change with the season and the chef's whims, but expect dishes and libations such as a shiso-wasabi mojito, nuggets of pork katsu paired with shishito peppers, and a caviar sandwich. **Known for:** changing fixed-price menu; vintage vinyl on the hi-fi; intimate experience. [$] *Average main: $33* ✉ *127 MacDougal St., between 3rd and 4th Sts., Greenwich Village* ☎ *212/420–4777* 🌐 *www.tokyorecordbar.com* 🕒 *No lunch* [M] *A, B, C, D, E, F, M to W. 4th St.*

🛏 Hotels

The Marlton

$$ | HOTEL | Built in 1900 and once home to Jack Kerouac, this stylish boutique property has a residential feel, including a comfortable lobby, with a coffee bar, tufted couches, and shelves lined with books, that attracts guests and locals looking for a quiet place to work. **Pros:** fresh property with luxurious touches; spacious lobby with coffee bar; great Greenwich Village location. **Cons:** very small rooms and bathrooms; no work desks; no room service. [$] *Rooms from: $350* ✉ *5 W. 8th St., between 5th Ave. and MacDougal St., Greenwich Village* ☎ *212/321–0100* 🌐 *marltonhotel.com* 🛏 *107 rooms* 🍴 *Free Breakfast* [M] *A, B, C, D, E, F, M to W. 4th St.*

Walker Hotel

$$ | HOTEL | Among the ghosts of the literary salons and speakeasies of Greenwich Village is the Walker, a boutique property with an Art Deco sensibility, where gas lamps and an inconspicuous facade blend the new hotel with the old character of this tree-lined neighborhood. **Pros:** delivers a true Greenwich Village experience; cozy fireplaces; quiet neighborhood location. **Cons:** small rooms; no connecting rooms; thin walls. [$] *Rooms from: $345* ✉ *52 W. 13th St., between 5th and 6th Aves., Greenwich Village* ☎ *212/375–1300* 🌐 *www.walkerhotel.com* 🛏 *113 rooms* 🍴 *No meals* [M] *1, 2, 3, F, M to 14th St.; L to 6th Ave.*

Washington Square Hotel

$ | HOTEL | Since 1902, this low-key hotel in Greenwich Village has hosted famous people (Ernest Hemingway, the Rolling Stones, and Bob Dylan all stayed here), and today it is popular with visiting New York University parents thanks to its location near Washington Square Park. **Pros:** parkside location; lots of historic character; great hotel bar. **Cons:** NYU students everywhere in the neighborhood; rooms are small; interior rooms don't get much light. [$] *Rooms from: $246* ✉ *103 Waverly Pl., at MacDougal St., Greenwich Village* ☎ *212/777–9515* 🌐 *www.washingtonsquarehotel.com* 🛏 *152 rooms* 🍴 *Free Breakfast* [M] *A, B, C, D, E, F, M to W. 4th St.*

🍸 Nightlife

BARS

★ Existing Conditions

BARS/PUBS | Science and booze merge beautifully at this experimental cocktail bar with exposed brick walls and wooden tables. The cocktail-shaking wizards here are Don Lee and Dave Arnold (from acclaimed spots PDT and Booker & Dax, respectively), who use methods like centrifuging and pressure cooking to concoct very drinkable—and fun—libations, such as a carbonated margarita with clarified strawberries and a waffle-infused bourbon drink spiked with maple syrup. ✉ *35 W. 8th St., between 5th and 6th Aves., Greenwich Village* ☎ *212/203–8935* 🌐 *www.existingconditions.com* [M] *A, B, C, D, E, F, M, to W. 4th St.*

Formerly Crow's

BARS/PUBS | The Bar Formerly Known as the Stoned Crow is anchored in a bibulous subterranean spot where they've been pouring booze since the 1920s. The current incarnation, set on a quiet, stately block near Washington Square Park, is a friendly, dive-y bar with affordable drinks, a lively jukebox, and good pub grub. ⊠ *85 Washington Pl., between 6th Ave. and Washington Sq. W, Greenwich Village* ☎ *212/361–0077* ⊕ *formerlycrows.com* Ⓜ *A, B, C, D, E, F, M to W. 4th St.*

Madame X

BARS/PUBS | This crimson-colored, sexy-dive hangout attracts a steady stream of stylish drinkers, sans attitude. The garden in back is open year-round, thanks to the miracle of outdoor heaters, and Friday and Saturday bring weekly hookah nights. ⊠ *94 W. Houston St., between LaGuardia Pl. and Thompson St., Greenwich Village* ☎ *212/539–0808* ⊕ *www.madamex.com* Ⓜ *C, E to Spring St.; 1 to Houston St.*

124 Rabbit Club

BARS/PUBS | Named for a 19th-century bar at or nearby this address, this tiny, charming, dive-y craft-beer bar is often passed by unnoticed. But ring the bell to enter a hushed, low-lit subterranean bar with funky decor and rabbit images, where the menu dazzles with exotic and seasonal brews on tap and by the bottle (along with a few nice wines). ⊠ *124 MacDougal St., between 3rd and Bleecker Sts., Greenwich Village* ☎ *646/781–0575* ⊕ *rabbitclubnyc.com* Ⓜ *A, B, C, D, E, F, M to W. 4th St.*

Vol de Nuit

BARS/PUBS | Tucked away from the street, the "Belgian Beer Bar" (as everybody calls it) features a European-style, enclosed outdoor courtyard and a cozy interior, all red light and shadows. NYU grad-student types come for the mammoth selection of beers on tap as well as the fries, which are served with Belgian flair in a paper cone, with an array of sauces on the side. ⊠ *148 W. 4th St., at 6th Ave., Greenwich Village* ☎ *212/982–3388* ⊕ *www.voldenuitbar.com* Ⓜ *A, B, C, D, E, F, M to W. 4th St.*

COMEDY CLUBS
Comedy Cellar

COMEDY CLUBS | Every night, laughter fills this subterranean exposed-brick space beneath the writer-friendly Olive Tree Café. The bill features a range of comedians, from hilarious up-and-comers to television and movie personalities like Aziz Ansari and Colin Quinn. ⊠ *117 MacDougal St., between 3rd St. and Minetta La., Greenwich Village* ☎ *212/254–3480* ⊕ *www.comedycellar.com* Ⓜ *A, B, C, D, E, F, M to W. 4th St.*

GAY NIGHTLIFE
★ **Stonewall Inn**

BARS/PUBS | Drink in history—literally. The Stonewall Inn is the bar made famous as the site of the June 1969 Stonewall Riots, when lesbian, gay, bisexual, and transgender patrons fought back against one of the police department's routine raids, ultimately galvanizing America's homosexual civil-rights movement. Today the crowd is a fabulous mix of friendly bargoers who show their pride in this place every day at this legendary (and gay-owned) Village tavern. Drop by to drink anytime from happy hour through late night, to play a round of pool, or to catch a show or dance party upstairs. Just don't miss the plaque out front marking Stonewall as a National Historic Landmark. ⊠ *53 Christopher St., between 7th and Greenwich Aves., Greenwich Village* ☎ *212/488–2705* ⊕ *thestonewallinnnyc.com* Ⓜ *1 to Christopher St.–Sheridan Sq.*

JAZZ VENUES
Bar Next Door

MUSIC CLUBS | It doesn't get more intimate than this dark, inviting music den downstairs from the Italian café La Lanterna. An ever-changing roster of musicians takes the stage here, from emerging artists to featured trios. Come early to grab a seat and tuck into a good thin-crust pizza. In summer, hang out in the lovely garden for a prelude. ⊠ *129 MacDougal St., between 3rd and 4th*

Sts., Greenwich Village ☎ *212/529–5945* ⊕ *www.lalanternacaffe.com* Ⓜ *A, B, C, D, E, F, M to W. 4th St.*

Bitter End

MUSIC CLUBS | On a fabled bohemian block, this Greenwich Village standby has served its share of talent since 1961, with Billy Joel, David Crosby, and Dr. John among the stars who've played here. These days you're more likely to find (much) lesser-known musicians playing blues, rock, funk, and jazz. If you don't like what you hear, there's always the similar **(Le) Poisson Rouge** nearby. ✉ *147 Bleecker St., between Thompson St. and LaGuardia Pl., Greenwich Village* ☎ *212/673–7030* ⊕ *www.bitterend.com* Ⓜ *A, B, C, D, E, F, M to W. 4th St.*

★ Blue Note

MUSIC CLUBS | Considered by many (not least its current owners) to be "the jazz capital of the world," the Blue Note was once the stomping ground for such legends as Dizzy Gillespie, and still hosts a variety of acts, from Chris Botti to jazz to Latin orchestras to Maceo Parker. Expect a steep cover charge except for late shows on weekends, when the music goes from less jazzy to more funky. ✉ *131 W. 3rd St., near 6th Ave., Greenwich Village* ☎ *212/475–8592* ⊕ *www.bluenote.net* Ⓜ *A, B, C, D, E, F, M to W. 4th St.*

The 55 Bar

MUSIC CLUBS | Duck into this slim, Prohibition-era jazz club to catch small ensembles of jazz, blues, and funk players nightly, and channel the Village's groovy legacy while sipping stiff drinks. There are early and late shows (at either 6 or 7 pm and 10 pm), and shows are free or have a nominal cover charge of around $10. ✉ *55 Christopher St., between 7th Ave. S and Waverly Pl., Greenwich Village* ☎ *212/929–9883* ⊕ *www.55bar.com* Ⓜ *1 to Christopher St.–Sheridan Sq.*

Mezzrow

MUSIC CLUBS | Brought to you by the people who run Smalls (just across 7th Avenue from here), Mezzrow is a low-key, subterranean jazz club with a loyal following. Several acts perform nightly, and it's a good idea to make a reservation (see the website) to ensure entry. ✉ *163 W. 10th St. , between 7th Ave. S and Waverly Pl., Greenwich Village* ☎ *646/476–4346* ⊕ *www.mezzrow.com* Ⓜ *1 to Christopher St.–Sheridan Sq.*

LIVE MUSIC VENUES

(Le) Poisson Rouge

MUSIC CLUBS | Head into the street-level or underground entrances to behold this cutting-edge, multipurpose entertainment and dance emporium, whose name means "the Red Fish" (and whose parentheses around "Le" remain a mystery). Blending just the right mix of posh notes (lush decor, fine dining), party nights, reasonable pricing, and brave music programming (retro-pop, jazz, electronic, cabaret, rock, folk—even rollicking drag-queen bingo), the Poisson is an essential NYC fixture. ✉ *158 Bleecker St., at Thompson St., Greenwich Village* ☎ *212/505–3474* ⊕ *www.lepoissonrouge. com* Ⓜ *A, B, C, D, E, F, M to W. 4th St.*

Terra Blues

MUSIC CLUBS | A true charmer, this second-story haven for blues lovers is a cozy Greenwich Village club surprisingly short on NYU students (unlike other places in this neighborhood). Everyone from great national acts like Buddy Guy to local R&B'ers graces the stage year-round. ✉ *149 Bleecker St., between Thompson St. and LaGuardia Pl., Greenwich Village* ☎ *212/777–7776* ⊕ *www.terrablues.com* Ⓜ *A, B, C, D, E, F, M to W. 4th St.; 6 to Bleecker St.*

🎭 Performing Arts

FILM

Angelika Film Center

FILM | Foreign, independent, and specialty films are screened here. Despite its (six) tunnel-like theaters, small screens, and the occasionally audible subway rumble below, it's usually packed with cinephiles. Get a snack at the café while you wait for your movie to be called. ✉ *18 W. Houston St., between Mercer St. and Broadway, Greenwich Village* ☎ *212/995–2570* ⊕ *www.angelikafilmcenter.com/nyc* Ⓜ *B, D, F, M to Broadway–Lafayette St.; 6 to Bleecker St.; N, R, W to Prince St.*

IFC Center

FILM | The IFC Center shows a mix of repertory and first-run independent, art-house, and foreign movies as well as shorts (including cartoons). Despite the modern wire-mesh facade, there are still clues that this was once the much-beloved Waverly Theater. ✉ *323 6th Ave., at 3rd St., Greenwich Village* ☎ *212/924–7771* ⊕ *www.ifccenter.com* Ⓜ *A, B, C, D, E, F, M to W. 4th St.*

PERFORMANCE CENTERS

NYU Skirball

ARTS CENTERS | **FAMILY** | This pristine, wood lined theater on the NYU campus supports emerging artists, with interesting dance, music, and theater events, often in collaboration with international companies. Conferences and a speaker series featuring prominent cultural figures round out the calendar, which also includes many family-friendly events. ✉ *566 LaGuardia Pl., at Washington Sq. S, Greenwich Village* ☎ *212/992–8484, 888/611–8183 for tickets* ⊕ *www.nyuskirball.org* Ⓜ *A, B, C, D, E, F, M to W. 4th St.; N, R, W to 8th St.–NYU.*

READINGS AND LECTURES

Center for Architecture

READINGS/LECTURES | This contemporary glass-faced gallery near Washington Square hosts lively discussions (which may be accompanied by films or other visuals) on topics like modernist architecture in Africa or what to expect when you renovate an apartment. ✉ *536 LaGuardia Pl., between 3rd and Bleecker Sts., Greenwich Village* ☎ *212/683–0023* ⊕ *www.centerforarchitecture.org* Ⓜ *A, B, C, D, E, F, M to W. 4th St.*

New York Studio School

READINGS/LECTURES | The venerable New York Studio School hosts two—always free, almost always on Tuesday and Wednesday—evening lecture series (fall and spring) on contemporary issues in art. Hear from both emerging and established artists and curators, as well as some of the biggest names in art history and criticism. The school building served as the original location of the Whitney Museum. ✉ *8 W. 8th St., between 5th Ave. and MacDougal St., Greenwich Village* ☎ *212/673–6466* ⊕ *www.nyss.org* Ⓜ *A, B, C, D, E, F, M to W. 4th St.*

THEATER

★ Monday Night Magic

THEATER | **FAMILY** | Since 1997, Michael Chaut and three other magician producers have been running these weekly performances in and around Greenwich Village (they've been a permanent fixture at the Players Theatre since 2011). The acts, usually four per night on stage, come from all over the world and often include performers you'd see in much bigger theaters and clubs on other nights. The mind reading and sleight of hand with birds, cards, balls, and handkerchiefs come at a fast pace. Although the acts are tailored to an adult audience, they're also suitable for younger viewers (aged 12 and older), especially on special family nights. ✉ *Players Theatre, 115 MacDougal St., between 3rd and Bleecker Sts., Greenwich Village* ☎ *718/575–1349, 800/838–3006 for tickets* ⊕ *www.mondaynightmagic.com* Ⓜ *A, B, C, D, E, F, M to W. 4th St.*

🍴 Shopping

The Village's poets and artists have long been replaced by New York University buildings and apartments with sky-high rent. Still, if you know where to look, there are charmingly offbeat stores worth exploring here that retain the flavor of the glory days.

BEAUTY

C. O. Bigelow

PERFUME/COSMETICS | Founded in 1838, this is the oldest apothecary-pharmacy in the United States; Mark Twain used to fill prescriptions here. They still fill prescriptions, but the real reason to come is for the hard-to-find brands like Klorane shampoo and Elgydium toothpaste. Bigelow also has its own line of products, including green-tea lip balm and quince hand lotion. ⊠ *414 6th Ave., between 8th and 9th Sts., Greenwich Village* ☎ *212/533–2700* ⊕ *www.bigelowchemists.com* Ⓜ *A, B, C, D, E, F, M to W. 4th St.*

BOOKS AND STATIONERY

★ Goods for the Study

BOOKS/STATIONERY | Lovers of organization, writing, and beautiful things flock to this stationery store from the team behind McNally Jackson bookstore. In addition to a better-than-average selection of normal paper store products—greeting cards from independent artists, notebooks of handmade paper, office supplies from acclaimed designers, hundreds of pens sourced from around the world—the shop also carries art prints from its sister store, Picture Room. ⊠ *50 W. 8th St., between 6th Ave. and MacDougal St., Greenwich Village* ☎ *212/674–4400* ⊕ *www.mcnallyjacksonstore.com* Ⓜ *A, B, C, D, E, F, M to W. 4th St.; N, R, W to 8th St.–NYU.*

CLOTHING

La Petite Coquette

CLOTHING | Everything at this lingerie boutique is unabashedly sexy, and the helpful staff can find the perfect fit. The store's own line of corsets, camisoles, and other underpinnings comes in a range of colors. ⊠ *51 University Pl., between 9th and 10th Sts., Greenwich Village* ☎ *212/473–2478* ⊕ *www.thelittle-flirt.com* Ⓜ *N, R, W to 8th St.–NYU.*

West Village

Small curving streets, peculiar alleys, and historic town houses—it's easy to see why the tree-lined thoroughfares of the West Village (which are primarily residential) are in such high demand. A stroll here reveals charming cafés, the occasional celebrity out and about, and well-dressed children playing in the parks. Visitors come here to get a feel for local life, to daydream about living in New York. Unlike 5th Avenue or SoHo, the pace is slower, allowing shoppers to enjoy the peaceful streets and independent and designer stores. This is the place to come for unusual finds as well as global-brand goods. The West Village section of Bleecker Street is a particularly good place to indulge all sorts of shopping appetites; high-fashion foragers prowl the stretch between West 10th Street and 8th Avenue. Hudson Street and Greenwich Avenue are also prime boutique-browsing territories.

Christopher Street has long been the symbolic heart of New York's gay and lesbian community, though places like Chelsea, Hell's Kitchen, and parts of Brooklyn attract more gay and lesbian residents these days. On Christopher Street, among the cafés and adult shops, is one of the city's most acclaimed Off-Broadway theaters, the Lucille Lortel, where major playwrights like David Mamet, Eugene Ionesco, and Edward Albee have their own sidewalk markers. Nearby, at 51–53 Christopher Street, is the site of the Stonewall Inn and the historic Stonewall riots, one of the most famous, catalyzing events in the LGBTQ civil rights movement. Across the street is a gated triangle named Christopher

Park, where commemorative statues of two life-size gay and lesbian couples have posed for photos since 1992.

Hudson River Park begins in the Financial District and continues along the river all the way to 59th Street. A large, heavily visited area is in the West Village. ⇨ *A listing for the Hudson River Park is in Lower Manhattan.*

👁 Sights

Children's Museum of the Arts
MUSEUM | FAMILY | The CMA encourages children ages 1 to 15 to get creative through a variety of mediums. Along with the requisite children's museum offerings like pencils, chalk, and paint, you'll find a clay bar; a media lab with mounted cameras and a recording studio; a small slide and colorful ball pond that kids can play in; an airy exhibition space with rotating exhibits (and workshops inspired by exhibits); a permanent collection of children's art from more than 50 countries; and classes in ceramics, origami, animation, filmmaking, and more. Check the website for a busy calendar of events. ✉ *103 Charlton St., between Hudson and Greenwich Sts., West Village* ☎ *212/274–0986* ⊕ *www.cmany.org* 🖾 *$13, $30 for family of up to 5 people* 🕙 *Closed Tues., Wed.* Ⓜ *C, E to Spring St.; 1 to Houston St.*

Christopher Park
CITY PARK | You might have to share a bench in this tiny park with George Segal's life-size sculptures of a lesbian couple: titled *Gay Liberation,* the white-painted bronzes were cast in 1980 but not installed until 1992. Standing next to them is a gay male couple, captured mid-chat. ✉ *Bordered by Stonewall Pl. and W. 4th, Grove, and Christopher Sts., West Village* Ⓜ *1 to Christopher St.–Sheridan Sq.; A, B, C, D, E, F, M to W. 4th St.*

75½ Bedford Street
HOUSE | Rising real-estate prices inspired the construction of New York City's narrowest house—just 9½ feet wide and 32 feet deep—in 1873. Built on a lot that was originally a carriage entrance of the Isaacs-Hendricks House next door, this sliver of a building has illustrious past residents including actor John Barrymore and poet Edna St. Vincent Millay. ✉ *75½ Bedford St., between Commerce and Morton Sts., West Village* Ⓜ *A, B, C, D, E, F, M to W. 4th St.*

St. Luke's Place
NEIGHBORHOOD | Steeped in New York City history and shaded by graceful gingko trees, this somewhat-hard-to-find section of Leroy Street has 15 classic Italianate brownstone and brick town houses (1851–54). Novelist Theodore Dreiser wrote *An American Tragedy* at No. 16, and poet Marianne Moore resided at No. 14. (Robert De Niro later lived here for decades—in mid-2012 he sold it for $9.5 million.) The colorful (and corrupt) Mayor Jimmy Walker (first elected in 1926) lived at No. 6; the lampposts in front are "mayor's lamps," which were sometimes placed in front of the residences of New York mayors. This block is often used as a film location: No. 4 was the setting of the Audrey Hepburn thriller *Wait Until Dark.* Before 1890, the James J. Walker Park, on the south side of the street near Hudson, was a graveyard where, according to legend, the dauphin of France—the lost son of Louis XVI and Marie Antoinette—is buried. ✉ *Leroy St., between Bleecker St. and 7th Ave., West Village* Ⓜ *1 to Houston St.*

🍴 Restaurants

The West Village has mastered the art of destination restaurants that feel like neighborhood eateries. Places here are homey, yet remarkable enough to attract diners from all over the city.

Bleecker Street Pizza
$ | PIZZA | FAMILY | Flavor reigns at this bustling corner pizzeria, the perfect place to stop for a stand-up slice at the

counter, or you can plant yourself in the expanded dining room. The thin-crusted Nonna Maria is topped with garlicky marinara, grated and fresh mozzarella, and freshly grated Parmesan, and worth the trek to the West Village. **Known for:** late-night slices; the Nonna Maria; busy spot. $ *Average main: $6* ⊠ *69 7th Ave. S, at Bleecker St., West Village* ☎ *212/924–4466* ⊕ *www.bleeckerstreetpizza.com* Ⓜ *1 to Christopher St.–Sheridan Sq.; A, B, C, D, E, F, M to W. 4th St.*

Chumley's

$$$ | AMERICAN | French writer Simone de Beauvoir visited this hidden Village gem and former famous literary hangout in the 1950s, commenting that the interior was simple yet had "something so rare in America—atmosphere." Today it still has the vibe of a former speakeasy (no sign on the door, for example), but the kitchen takes itself much more seriously these days, churning out top-notch versions of bone-marrow-spiked burgers, foie gras terrine, and harissa-laced cod. The writers might be gone, replaced by patrons with expense accounts, but Chumley's still has that atmosphere. **Known for:** a favorite Village speakeasy; good burgers; photo-lined walls and plenty of history. $ *Average main: $30* ⊠ *86 Bedford St., between Barrow and Grove Sts., West Village* ☎ *212/675–2081* ⊕ *chumleysnewyork.com* ⊗ *Closed Sun. No lunch* Ⓜ *1 to Christopher St.–Sheridan Sq.*

Dominique Ansel Kitchen

$ | BAKERY | Don't come here looking for the cronut, French baker Dominique Ansel's insanely popular Franken-pastry, because you won't find it (for that, head to his other bakery in SoHo). Instead, the cutting-edge baker-wizard conjures up other edible oddities such as garlic-bread croissants, a French toast–like croque monsieur, and beignets sprinkled and filled with matcha powder. **Known for:** shorter lines than the SoHo cronut bakery; inventive baked goods; outdoor tables. $ *Average main: $8* ⊠ *137 7th*

Ave. S, between Charles and 10th Sts., West Village ☎ *212/242–5111* ⊕ *www.dominiqueanselkitchen.com* Ⓜ *1 to Christopher St.–Sheridan Sq.*

★ Don Angie

$$$ | ITALIAN | If you have a hankering for red sauce Italian-American fare, steer clear of Little Italy and book yourself into Don Angie, a restaurant that took a staid cusine, updated it, and made it wholly edible again: quite a task. Sit in the retro front room—featuring checkerboard floors and arched doorways—and chow down on sopressini pasta paired with mussels, pimenton, and sriracha or the excellent (and hugely portioned) lasagna for two, a spiral-shape reimagining of the classic dish. **Known for:** making Italian-American cuisine good; lasagna for two; creative takes on pasta dishes. $ *Average main: $25* ⊠ *103 Greenwich Ave., at 12th St., West Village* ☎ *212/889–8884* ⊕ *www.donangie.com* ⊗ *No lunch* Ⓜ *1, 2, 3 to 14th St.; A, C, E, L to 8th Ave.*

Due West

$$ | AMERICAN | The cocktails at this handsome 65-seat wood-clad gastropub get as much attention and love as the feel-good food created in the kitchen. Grab a seat by the window—in summer they open up, creating a refreshing alfresco ambience—and sip a Negroni or a mezcal-and-beer-laced Old Diablo while grazing on crispy chickpea fritters, pork belly tacos, and gooey hot crab dip. **Known for:** creative cocktails; late-night dining on weekends; good people-watching. $ *Average main: $17* ⊠ *189 W. 10th St., between 4th and Bleecker Sts., West Village* ☎ *646/687–4609* ⊕ *www.duewestnyc.com* ⊗ *No lunch* Ⓜ *1 to Christopher St.–Sheridan Sq.*

Emily

$$ | PIZZA | This beloved Brooklyn pizza and Italian-ish eatery, named for its pie-loving proprietor, has a branch on a charming block in the West Village. The

specialty here is pizza, from Detroit-style grandma pies (think square instead of round, thick instead of thin) to wood-fired pizzas with ingredients like clams, anchovies, and Calabrian chilies. **Known for:** different kinds of pizza; great signature burger; Brooklyn favorite. $ *Average main: $21* ✉ *35 Downing St., at Bedford St., West Village* ☎ *917/935–6434* ⊕ *www.pizzalovesemily.com* Ⓜ *A, B, C, D, E, F, M to W. 4th St.*

Empellón Taqueria

$$$ | MEXICAN | Chef Alex Stupak worked as the pastry chef at the now-closed wd-50, New York's introduction to molecular gastronomy, so when he left to open a taqueria, many diners wondered if they'd be served deconstructed tacos. Instead, they got simple yet well-executed fare using top-notch ingredients, with both straightforward options—fish tempura, lamb, steak—as well as surprising variations, like a taco with sweetbreads and a chorizo gravy. **Known for:** creative takes on tacos; noted chef; different kinds of margaritas. $ *Average main: $25* ✉ *230 W. 4th St., at 10th St., West Village* ☎ *212/367–0999* ⊕ *www.empellon.com* ☾ *No lunch* Ⓜ *1 to Christopher St.–Sheridan Sq.*

Fedora

$$$ | ECLECTIC | Subterranean Fedora was an ancient, little-patronized restaurant until 2011, when the old Italian owner left the building and restaurateur Gabe Stulman took over, revamping the place to attract a younger, hip crowd. The kitchen now churns out French Canadian–accented fare like garlic-cream-topped duck breast and scallops paired with bone marrow. **Known for:** French-Canadian dishes; potent cocktails; narrow space. $ *Average main: $27* ✉ *239 W. 4th St., between Charles and 10th Sts., West Village* ☎ *646/449–9336* ⊕ *www.fedoranyc.com* ☾ *No lunch* Ⓜ *1 to Christopher St.–Sheridan Sq.*

Flip Sigi

$ | PHILIPPINE | If Manila and Mexico City miraculously collided, it would taste a lot like this lively, diminutive Hudson Street spot. Look past the cheeky menu item names—Plan B-Rito, Toss My Salad, Poke Me—and you'll likely enjoy this Filipino-Mex fusion. **Known for:** Filipino-Mexican tacos and burritos; lively atmosphere; poutine with adobo gravy. $ *Average main: $10* ✉ *525 Hudson St., between 10th and Charles Sts., West Village* ☎ *917/639–3262* ⊕ *www.flipsigi.com* Ⓜ *1 to Christopher St.–Sheridan Sq.*

Frankies 570 Spuntino

$$ | ITALIAN | The Frankies—that is, owners and chefs Frank Falcinelli and Frank Castronovo—have a winning formula at their West Village restaurant: serve hearty, not-necessarily-by-the-book Italian-inflected fare using local, organic, and humanely raised ingredients in a laid-back atmosphere. Most menu items change seasonally, but expect good pasta dishes. **Known for:** excellent burrata; chicken liver crostini; friendly neighborhood spot with long menu. $ *Average main: $21* ✉ *570 Hudson St., at 11th St., West Village* ☎ *212/924–0818* ⊕ *www.frankiesspuntino.com* ☾ *No lunch* Ⓜ *A, C, E to 14th St.; L to 8th Ave.*

High Street on Hudson

$$ | AMERICAN | In the morning, High Street churns out deliciously messy egg-and-meat-loaded sandwiches and hearty soups and seasonal salads at lunch; at night, the restaurant reaches a more intimate vibe as the lights go low and bowls of pasta, seafood, and roasted chicken are on offer. Large windows allow for great West Village street viewing. **Known for:** house-made spaghetti; roasted turkey sandwich; "The Bodega" breakfast sandwich. $ *Average main: $18* ✉ *637 Hudson St., at Horatio St., West Village* ☎ *917/388–3944* ⊕ *www.highstreeton-hudson.com* Ⓜ *A, C, E to 14th St.; L to 8th Ave.*

I Sodi

$$$ | ITALIAN | In a city where you can't throw a meatball without hitting an Italian restaurant, this minimalist-designed, Tuscan-focused eatery in the West Village is a real find. Spiky-haired owner Rita Sodi, a Florentine who formerly worked in the fashion industry, ensures the traditional Italian fare coming from the kitchen is satisfying and seasonal. **Known for:** high-quality seasonal Tuscan fare; good pasta dishes; minimalist look. $ *Average main: $28* ⊠ *105 Christopher St., between Bleecker and Hudson Sts., West Village* ☎ *212/414–5774* ⊕ *www. isodinyc.com* ☾ *No lunch* Ⓜ *1 to Christopher St.–Sheridan Sq.*

★ Jeju Noodle Bar

$$$ | KOREAN | Many restaurants have come and gone from this corner location, but it seems the lauded Korean spot, with its tall windows, wood tables, and modern lighting, will be boiling noodles and simmering broths for a while. Specializing in Korean ramen, called *ramyun,* Jeju concocts spicy deliciousness in a bowl, producing cauldrons filled with smooth, rich veal broth bobbing with tender brisket and Wagyu, among other specialties. **Known for:** Korean-style ramen; pork-belly steamed buns; sake and soju lists. $ *Average main: $25* ⊠ *679 Greenwich St., at Christopher St., West Village* ☎ *646/666–0947* ⊕ *jejunoodlebar.com* ☾ *Closed Mon. No lunch* Ⓜ *1 to Christopher St.–Sheridan Sq.*

Joe's Pizza

$ | PIZZA | FAMILY | You might recognize this Village institution from its frequent cameos in TV and film (in *Spider-Man,* Tobey Maguire's Peter Parker was a Joe's delivery boy). But it's the classic gooey New York slice, dripping melted cheese onto paper plates, that *really* makes the place famous. **Known for:** an excellent New York slice; cash only; film cameos. $ *Average main: $6* ⊠ *7 Carmine St., near Bleecker St., West Village* ☎ *212/366–1182* ⊕ *www.joespizzanyc.*

com ⊟ *No credit cards* Ⓜ *A, B, C, D, E, F, M to W. 4th St.*

Kesté Pizza & Vino

$$ | PIZZA | At the back of the long, narrow Keste Pizza & Vino restaurant is a beautiful tiled, wood-fired oven that cooks what might be Manhattan's most authentic Neapolitan pies at 1,000° F. Blistered and chewy around the edges, the margherita pie gives way to a softer center pooled with San Marzano tomato sauce and house-made mozzarella. **Known for:** varieties of authentic Neapolitan pizza; gluten-free option; always busy. $ *Average main: $18* ⊠ *271 Bleecker St., between 6th and 7th Aves., West Village* ☎ *212/243–1500* ⊕ *www.kestepizzeria. com* Ⓜ *1 to Christopher St.–Sheridan Sq.; A, B, C, D, E, F, M to W. 4th St.*

The Little Owl

$$$ | MODERN AMERICAN | This tiny neighborhood joint, with seating for 28 people, is exceptionally eager to please—and this attitude, plus the food, is a winning combination. The menu is just as small, which actually makes it easier to decide what you want; and what you want are the pork-veal-beef-pecorino-cheese meatball "sliders." The unusually juicy pork loin chop, with Parmesan butter beans and dandelion greens, is gigantic and hugely satisfying. **Known for:** perfect West Village neighborhood spot; pork loin chop; raspberry-filled beignets. $ *Average main: $25* ⊠ *90 Bedford St., at Grove St., West Village* ☎ *212/741–4695* ⊕ *www. thelittleowlnyc.com* Ⓜ *1 to Christopher St.–Sheridan Sq.; A, B, C, D, E, F, M to W. 4th St.*

Mary's Fish Camp

$$$ | SEAFOOD | Diners still line up down the street before the restaurant opens for dinner to get a table at this small but bustling seafood shack. The result of a split between Pearl Oyster Bar's partners, Mary's is a more intimate space, but the two have similar menus: excellent fried oysters, chowders, and, of course, the

sweet lobster roll with crisp fries. **Known for:** lobster rolls; hot fudge sundae; friendly staff. $ *Average main: $25* ✉ *64 Charles St., at 4th St., West Village* ☎ *646/486–2185* ⊕ *www.marysfishcamp. com* ⊙ *No dinner Sun.* Ⓜ *1 to Christopher St.–Sheridan Sq.*

Moustache Pitza

$$ | **MIDDLE EASTERN** | There's typically a crowd waiting outside for one of the copper-top tables at this casual Middle Eastern neighborhood restaurant. The focal point is the perfect pita that accompanies tasty salads like lemony chickpea and spinach, hearty lentil and bulgur, or falafel. **Known for:** reliable Middle Eastern fare; good lamb mains; perfect pita. $ *Average main: $14* ✉ *90 Bedford St., between Barrow and Grove Sts., West Village* ☎ *212/229 2220* ⊕ *www. moustachepitza.com* Ⓜ *1 to Christopher St.–Sheridan Sq.; A, B, C, D, E, F, M to W. 4th St.*

Pearl Oyster Bar

$$$ | **SEAFOOD** | There have been many imitators and few real competitors to this West Village seafood institution. Since 1997, Rebecca Charles has been serving arguably the best lobster roll in New York City in a no-frills space down charming, restaurant-lined Cornelia Street—and expanded next door to accommodate the throngs. **Known for:** lobster rolls; sea scallops; maybe too-speedy service. $ *Average main: $26* ✉ *18 Cornelia St., between 4th and Bleecker Sts., West Village* ☎ *212/691–8211* ⊕ *www.pearloysterbar.com* ⊙ *Closed Sun.* Ⓜ *A, B, C, D, E, F, M to W. 4th St.*

Rahi

$$$ | **INDIAN** | Its name means "traveler" in Hindi, and this upscale Indian restaurant with dark wood and white chairs has a menu that travels all over the subcontinent, including regional dishes and modern twists along the way. Think prawn curry in uni butter or *khichdi*, a luscious porridge in this case made with mushrooms and truffles, and doused

with chili oil. **Known for:** lively atmosphere; creative Indian fare; spaghetti squash kofta. $ *Average main: $30* ✉ *60 Greenwich Ave., at Perry St., West Village* ☎ *212/373–8900* ⊕ *www.rahinyc.com* ⊙ *No lunch* Ⓜ *1, 2, 3 to 14th St.*

RedFarm

$$$ | **CHINESE** | Conceived and run by Ed Schoenfeld, an expert on Chinese cuisine, and Joe Ng, known as the dumpling king of New York, this West Village restaurant specializes mostly in—you guessed it—Chinese-style dumplings. The menu at this casual spot with wood beams and wood tables focuses on dim sum—small plates and snacks (often in dumpling form)—as well as Chinese-American dishes like three-chili chicken and chicken in garlic sauce. **Known for:** great dim sum; pastrami egg roll; prices that add up. $ *Average main: $31* ✉ *529 Hudson St., between 10th and Charles Sts., West Village* ☎ *212/792–9700* ⊕ *www.redfarm nyc.com* ⊙ *No lunch* Ⓜ *1 to Christopher St.–Sheridan Sq.*

Sushi Nakazawa

$$$$ | **JAPANESE** | It's all *omakase* at this acclaimed sushi spot from master Daisuke Nakazawa, who practices an old Tokyo style of sushi making—putting all his extremely fresh fish on a thumb-size bundle of rice (sorry, sashimi fans). Reserve at least a month in advance, or try to get a table in the à la carte, no-reservations room adjacent to the restaurant. **Known for:** mind-blowing raw fish (priced to match); hard-to-get tables; Jiro Dreams of Sushi film. $ *Average main: $175* ✉ *23 Commerce St., near Bedford St., West Village* ☎ *212/924–2212* ⊕ *www. sushinakazawa.com* Ⓜ *1 to Christopher St.–Sheridan Sq.; A, B, C, D, E, F, M to W. 4th St.*

Taïm

$ | **MIDDLE EASTERN** | There's a real chef behind this casual, tiny sliver of a restaurant, New York's only gourmet falafel stand. *Taïm* means "tasty" in Hebrew, and Tel Aviv transplant Einat Admony's

MacDougal Street is one of the most popular in Greenwich Village, where you'll find several popular restaurants and bars.

fried chickpea balls are delicious, and available in several beguiling flavors (try them infused with spicy harissa sauce) alongside a tantalizing à la carte salads (the carrot with Moroccan spices is a standout). There's another location in NoLIta, on Spring Street between Mott and Mulberry. **Known for:** eggplant-stuffed sabich sandwich; creative falafel; good smoothies. ⓢ *Average main: $9* ✉ *222 Waverly Pl., near Perry St., West Village* ☎ *212/691–1287* ⊕ *www.taimfalafel.com* Ⓜ *1, 2, 3 to 14th St.; L to 8th Ave.*

Via Carota

$$ | **ITALIAN** | The brainchild of chefs Jody Williams and Rita Sodi, who run Buvette and I Sodi, respectively, just a block or two away from here, Via Carota feels like the perfect West Village Italian eatery. Situated on charming Grove Street, it offers sidewalk tables (or a welcoming long bar to perch at) and consistently serves up unpretentious and above-average Italian fare. **Known for:** great neighborhood ambience; grilled octopus; pastas such as pappardelle with wild boar ragù.

ⓢ *Average main: $21* ✉ *51 Grove St., between 7th Ave. S and Bleecker St., West Village* ☎ *212/255–1962* ⊕ *www. viacarota.com* Ⓜ *1 to Christopher St.– Sheridan Sq.*

Wallflower

$$$ | **FRENCH** | This narrow eatery captures all the trappings of the ideal West Village restaurant: it's down a small tree-lined street, away from the bustle of foot (and automobile) traffic; it's dimly lit and diminutive; it's unassuming and unpretentious. Oh yeah, the seasonal, Gallic-accented food is pretty good, too. **Known for:** French country fare with an international twist; maple bacon–studded burger; seasonal menus. ⓢ *Average main: $33* ✉ *235 W. 12th St., between Greenwich Ave. and 4th St., West Village* ☎ *646/682–9842* ⊕ *www.wallflowernyc.com* ⊙ *No lunch* Ⓜ *1, 2, 3 to 14th St.*

Wallsé

$$$ | **AUSTRIAN** | The modern Austrian menu at Kurt Gutenbrunner's lovely, light-filled neighborhood restaurant has a strong emphasis on Austrian tradition

and urban New York attitude. It's hard to argue with such dishes as Wiener schnitzel with potato-cucumber salad and lingonberries, or venison goulash with spaetzle and Brussels sprouts, and it's often lighter than you'd think Austrian food would be. **Known for:** short-rib goulash; good special-occasion option; great desserts such as Sacher torte. $ *Average main: $35 ✉ 344 W. 11th St., at Washington St., West Village ☎ 212/352–2300 ⊕ www.wallse.com ⟳ Closed Sun. No lunch* Ⓜ *1 to Christopher St.–Sheridan Sq.; A, C, E to 14th St.; L to 8th Ave.*

Westville West

$$ | **AMERICAN** | **FAMILY** | If New York's neighborhoods were small country towns, they'd all have restaurants just like Westville. These adorable spots—now with 7 branches including those in the East and West Village, Chelsea, Wall Street, and DUMBO—serve simple, wholesome fare, at reasonable prices. **Known for:** seasonal veggie sides; good burgers; friendly staff. $ *Average main: $18 ✉ 210 W. 10th St., near Bleecker St., West Village ☎ 212/741–7971 ⊕ www. westvillenyc.com* Ⓜ *1 to Christopher St.– Sheridan Sq.*

Hotels

The Jane

$ | **HOTEL** | To some, the Jane with its appealing public spaces is impossibly chic; to others, the tiny rooms with single beds and a shared unisex bathroom down the hall are reminiscent of Sing Sing. **Pros:** extraordinary value for the neighborhood; hot bar scene; great branch of weekend-brunch favorite Café Gitane. **Cons:** impossibly tiny standard rooms; some rooms have shared bathrooms; noise from the bar. $ *Rooms from: $120 ✉ 113 Jane St., at West St., West Village ☎ 212/924–6700 ⊕ www. thejanenyc.com ⇄ 171 rooms* ❙❖❙ *No meals* Ⓜ *A, C, E to 14th St.; L to 8th Ave.*

▼ Nightlife

BARS

Corner Bistro

BARS/PUBS | Opened in 1961, this lovable neighborhood saloon serves what many think are some of the best (and most affordable) burgers in town. Once you actually get a seat, the space feels nice and cozy, but until then, be prepared to drink a beer amid hungry, sociable patrons. ✉ *331 W. 4th St., at Jane St., West Village ☎ 212/242–9502 ⊕ www. cornerbistrony.com* Ⓜ *1, 2, 3, A, C, E to 14th St.; L to 8th Ave.*

★ Employees Only

BARS/PUBS | The dapper white-coated bartenders at this cocktail bar mix delicious, well-thought-out tipples with debonair aplomb and freshly squeezed mixers. Sip one in the dimly lit bar area and you might feel like you've stepped back in time—if it weren't for the crush of trendy West Village locals and visitors at your back. Look for the green awning that says "EO" and the neon "Psychic" sign out front. Tasty, if pricey, fare is served in the restaurant at the back. ✉ *510 Hudson St., between Christopher and 10th Sts., West Village ☎ 212/242–3021 ⊕ www. employeesonlynyc.com* Ⓜ *1 to Christopher St.–Sheridan Sq.; A, B, C, D, E, F, M to W. 4th St.*

Hudson Bar and Books

BARS/PUBS | Along with its sister branch (Lexington Bar and Books) uptown, the Hudson reflects a literary bent with handsome cigar-bar flair. It's hardly a hushed library; the atmosphere here is more about book decor than serious literature. The seriously clubby look includes wood paneling and leather banquettes, and this is one of the few lounges in NYC where you can still smoke with your classic, seasonal, and signature cocktails. ✉ *636 Hudson St., at Horatio St., West Village ☎ 212/229–2642 ⊕ www.barandbooks. cz/hudson* Ⓜ *A, C, E to 14th St.; L to 8th Ave.*

★ Katana Kitten

BARS/PUBS | This two-floor Japanese cocktail bar hits the mark on all notes. Perch yourself at the bar on the second floor and watch the bartenders shake up sensational Japanese-accented libations, such as a *shiso*-laced G&T or a "Meguroni," with *genever* (a ginlike liquor), aged *umeshu* (a fruit liqueur), and Caffo bitters. There's also a food menu of satisfying *izakaya*-style snacks like *uni*-topped deviled eggs and charred Japanese eggplant. ✉ *531 Hudson St., between 10th and Charles Sts., West Village* ☎ *212/243–3000* ⊕ *www.katanakitten.com* Ⓜ *1 to Christopher St.–Sheridan Sq.; A, C, E to 14th St.; L to 8th Ave.*

★ Little Branch

BARS/PUBS | Top-quality cocktails, dim lighting, and snug booths make this the ideal spot for a conversation with friends (that you can actually hear) or an intimate date. In true speakeasy fashion, despite its sweet location on a busy corner of the West Village, you could wander by never knowing the charm and expert concoctions being stirred up just downstairs. ✉ *22 7th Ave. S, at Leroy St., West Village* ☎ *212/929–4360* Ⓜ *1 to Houston St.*

The Otheroom

BARS/PUBS | Head to the far west Otheroom for a flight of fancy drinking in good company. The menu is reliable and creative, with dozens of microbrews and international wines available by the glass—though choices change weekly, just to keep it interesting. ✉ *143 Perry St., between Greenwich and Washington Sts., West Village* ☎ *212/645–9758* ⊕ *www.theotheroomnyc.com* Ⓜ *1 to Christopher St.–Sheridan Sq.*

White Horse Tavern

BARS/PUBS | According to New York legend, writer Dylan Thomas drank himself to death in this historic West Village tavern founded in 1880. When the weather's nice, try to snag a seat at one of the sidewalk tables for breezy people-watching, and do enjoy the bar's reasonable prices—just don't overdo it like Thomas. ✉ *567 Hudson St., at 11th St., West Village* ☎ *212/989–3956* ⊕ *www.whitehorsetavern1880.com* Ⓜ *1 to Christopher St.–Sheridan Sq.*

Wilfie & Nell

BARS/PUBS | Combine the cozy atmosphere and frothy pints standard at Irish pubs with a well-heeled West Village crowd and you get Wilfie & Nell, a candlelit bar full of communal tables for making new friends. This perpetually crowded neighborhood go-to, with its low ceilings and locally sourced food, is a popular singles spot as well as a good match for night owls: food and brews are served into the wee hours. ✉ *228 W. 4th St., between 10th St. and 7th Ave. S, West Village* ☎ *212/242–2990* ⊕ *www. wilfieandnell.com* Ⓜ *1 to Christopher St.–Sheridan Sq.; A, B, C, D, E, F, M to W. 4th St.*

CABARET AND PIANO BARS

The Duplex

CABARET | No matter who's performing, the big, gay audience hoots and hollers in support of the often kitschy performers at this music-scene staple on busy Sheridan Square, open since 1951. Singers and comedians hold court in the cabaret theater, while those itching to take a shot at open mic head downstairs to the lively piano bar. Warmer seasons bring a most welcome outdoor seating area, offering some of the neighborhood's best people-watching. ✉ *61 Christopher St., at 7th Ave. S, West Village* ☎ *212/255–5438* ⊕ *www.theduplex.com* Ⓜ *1 to Christopher St.–Sheridan Sq.*

Marie's Crisis

PIANO BARS/LOUNGES | Regardless of whatever "Marie's crisis" was or is (each employee seems to have a different story), all the customers here know all the words to show tunes you've never even heard of. Down enough drinks at this ultra-fun West Village joint and you'll be singing along, even if you don't know all the lyrics. ✉ *59 Grove St., at 7th Ave.,*

West Village ☎ *212/243–9323* ⊕ *marie-scrisis.us* Ⓜ *1 to Christopher St.–Sheridan Sq.*

GAY NIGHTLIFE
Henrietta Hudson
BARS/PUBS | The nightly parties at this laid-back West Village HQ for the Sapphic set attract young professional women, out-of-towners, and longtime regulars. Because the DJ and pool table quickly create a crowd, though, lesbians arrive early to stake their claim to a spot, especially on weekends. ⊠ *438 Hudson St., at Morton St., West Village* ☎ *212/924–3347* ⊕ *www.henriettahudson.com* Ⓜ *1 to Christopher St.–Sheridan Sq.*

The Monster
BARS/PUBS | This "Monster" is a friendly one. This local-favorite gay bar has anchored its prime corner spot since 1970 and still serves as a lively piano bar and watering hole at street level, with an energetic disco downstairs programmed with a variety of nightly events, including Sunday tea dances. ⊠ *80 Grove St., between 4th St. and 7th Ave. S, West Village* ☎ *212/924–3558* ⊕ *www.manhattan-monster.com* Ⓜ *1 to Christopher St.–Sheridan Sq.*

JAZZ VENUES
★ Village Vanguard
MUSIC CLUBS | This prototypical jazz club, tucked into a cellar in the Village since the 1940s, has been the haunt of legends like Thelonious Monk and Barbra Streisand. Today you can hear jams from the likes of Bill Charlap and Ravi Coltrane, and on Monday night the sizable resident Vanguard Jazz Orchestra blows its collective heart out. ⊠ *178 7th Ave. S, between 11th and Perry Sts., West Village* ☎ *212/255–4037* ⊕ *www.villagevanguard.com* Ⓜ *1, 2, 3 to 14th St.*

LIVE MUSIC VENUES
SOB's
MUSIC CLUBS | The initials stand for "Sounds of Brazil" (no, not what you— and everybody else—might think), and this is *the* place for reggae, African, and Latin music, with some jazz gigs sprinkled in. Tito Puente Jr. sometimes holds court here, as does calypso's Mighty Sparrow when he's up north. Don't miss the Haitian dance parties, the after-work Latin-groove happy hour, or the bossa-nova brunches. There's usually about a $20 cover charge, and while there is a food menu, it's better to just come for the music. ⊠ *204 Varick St., near Houston St., West Village* ☎ *212/243–4940* ⊕ *www.sobs.com* Ⓜ *1 to Houston St.*

🎟 Performing Arts
FILM
★ Film Forum
FILM | In addition to premiering new international features and documentaries that are otherwise hard to catch on the big screen, this nonprofit with four theaters hosts movies by canonized directors such as Hitchcock, Godard, and Bertolucci; in-depth film series devoted to particular actors or genres; and newly restored prints of classic works. The small concession stand in the lobby serves tasty cakes and freshly popped popcorn. This is no megaplex, but updates in 2018 included new seats with more legroom and a higher slope for better views. ⊠ *209 W. Houston St., between 6th Ave. and Varick St., West Village* ☎ *212/727–8110* ⊕ *www.filmforum.org* Ⓜ *1 to Houston St.; C, E to Spring St.*

🛍 Shopping
The West Village is filled with charming boutiques and restaurants—many of which have retained their vintage charm thanks to exposed brick walls and pressed tin ceilings. Stroll around, get lost on a cobblestone street, and finish a day of shopping with a drink at a cozy bar. Bleecker Street is a particularly good place to indulge all sorts of shopping appetites. Fashion fans forage along the stretch between West 10th

Street and 8th Avenue. Hudson Street and Greenwich Avenue are also prime boutique-browsing territory. Christopher Street, true to its connection with the LGBTQ community, has a handful of shops sporting rainbow flags.

ANTIQUES AND COLLECTIBLES
Kaas Glassworks

ANTIQUES/COLLECTIBLES | From the outside in, this shop is oh-so-charming, with an old-fashioned sign and sandwich board welcoming shoppers and passersby. The specialty here is decoupage that has been turned into quirky trays and paper-weights. Owner Carol Kaas uses antique prints, vintage postcards, historical maps, and ephemera in her work, and custom-izes decoupage trays from wedding invitations, photos, baby announcements, or other paper keepsakes. ⊠ 117 Perry St., between Greenwich and Hudson Sts., West Village ☎ 212/366–0322 ⊕ www.kaas.com Ⓜ 1 to Christopher St.–Sheridan Sq.

BEAUTY
CAP Beauty

SPA/BEAUTY | This is a one-stop shop for natural skin care and wellness products, which means that everything it stocks is 100% free from synthetic ingredients. Brands carried include May Lindstrom, Tata Harper, and Rahua. CAP also does spa treatments, facials, and acupuncture. ⊠ 238 W. 10th St., between Hudson and Bleecker Sts., West Village ☎ 212/227–1088 ⊕ www.capbeauty.com Ⓜ 1 to Christopher St.–Sheridan Sq.

Jo Malone

PERFUME/COSMETICS | Crisp black-and-white decor sets a serene backdrop for sampling tangy scents like lime blossom and mandarin, or Earl Grey and cucumber. Fragrances can be worn alone or layered. The U.S. flagship for the British brand also offers complimentary hand massages (by appointment) and has a sampling bar for creating a bespoke scent. ⊠ 330 Bleecker St., at Christopher St., West Village ☎ 212/242–1454 ⊕ www.jomalone.com Ⓜ 1 to Christopher St.–Sheridan Sq.

BOOKS AND STATIONERY
Idlewild Books

BOOKS/STATIONERY | Named for the pre-1960s JFK Airport, this travel-inspired bookstore is one of the last of its kind in America. It stocks guidebooks, novels, and children's books grouped by destination, and also runs foreign-language classes, ranging from Arabic to German. If those chairs look familiar, it may be because you huddled in one during a layover at the American Airlines terminal. ⊠ 170 7th Ave. S., at Perry St., West Village ☎ 212/414–8888 ⊕ www.idlewildbooks.com Ⓜ 1 to Christopher St.–Sheridan Sq.

★ Three Lives & Company

BOOKS/STATIONERY | One of the city's best book selections is displayed on the tables and counters of this bookshop, which highlights the latest literary fiction and serious nonfiction, classics, quirky gift books, and gorgeously illustrated tomes. The staff members' literary knowledge is formidable, so don't be afraid to ask for their own picks. ⊠ 154 W. 10th St., at Waverly Pl., West Village ☎ 212/741–2069 ⊕ www.threelives.com Ⓜ 1 to Christopher St.–Sheridan Sq.; A, B, C, D, E, F, M to W. 4th St.

CLOTHING
Cynthia Rowley

CLOTHING | The flirty, whimsical dresses at this boutique are perfect for cocktail parties. To complete the look, throw on some of the designer's colorful pumps and sharply tailored coats. ⊠ 394 Bleecker St., between Perry and 11th Sts., West Village ☎ 212/242–3803 ⊕ www.cynthiarowley.com Ⓜ 1 to Christopher St.–Sheridan Sq.

Hotoveli

CLOTHING | This unprepossessing nook stocks some of the most elegant (and expensive) designers in the world, ranging from Lanvin to Yohji Yamamoto. If you have to ask how much an item costs, don't try it on. This location carries clothes for both men and women. ⊠ *271 W. 4th St., between 11th and Perry Sts., West Village* 📞 *212/206–7722* ⊕ *www. hotoveli.com* Ⓜ *1 to Christopher St.– Sheridan Sq.*

Personnel of New York

CLOTHING |"Lifestyle boutique" is an overused term, but it is the best way to describe this indie favorite, which specializes in men's and women's clothing from New York and L.A. designers. The boutique also stocks unusual home goods, such as bottle openers by Japanese designer Tadanori Baba and soap from Juniper Ridge. ⊠ *9 Greenwich Ave., between Christopher and 10th Sts., West Village* 📞 *212/924–0604* ⊕ *www.personelofnewyork.com* Ⓜ *1 to Christopher St.–Sheridan Sq.; A, B, C, D, E, F, M to W. 4th St.*

Screaming Mimi's

CLOTHING | Browse through racks bulging with vintage finds from the 1920s through '90s. Retro wear includes everything from dresses to soccer shirts and prom dresses. Although most of the nondesigner finds are affordable, Screaming Mimi's also carries vintage designer duds from Valentino, Chloé, and Gaultier. ⊠ *240 W. 14th St., between 7th and 8th Ave., West Village* 📞 *212/677–6464* ⊕ *www.screamingmimis.com* Ⓜ *1, 2, 3, A, C, E to 14th St.; L to 8th Ave.*

FOOD AND TREATS
Li-Lac Chocolates

FOOD/CANDY | Feeding the Village's sweet tooth since 1923, Li-Lac indulges shoppers with its almond bark and coconut clusters as well as such specialty items as chocolate-molded Statues of Liberty. The coconut rolls and chocolate-covered graham crackers tempt even the most stubborn dieter. To see how the small-batch chocolates are made, visit Li-Lac's Brooklyn factory. ⊠ *40 8th Ave.,* *at Jane St., West Village* 📞 *212/924–2280* ⊕ *www.li-lacchocolates.com* Ⓜ *A, C, E to 14th St.; L to 8th Ave.*

Sockerbit

FOOD/CANDY | Who knew Scandinavians are obsessed with candy—but there's much more than Swedish fish at this gleaming white candy emporium that stocks hard candies, gummies, licorice, and chocolate. Have fun pronouncing the names of treats like Bumlingar Jordgubb and Zoo Klubba. ⊠ *89 Christopher St., between Bleecker and 4th Sts., West Village* 📞 *212/206–8170* ⊕ *www.sockerbit. com* Ⓜ *1 to Christopher St.–Sheridan Sq.*

JEWELRY AND ACCESSORIES
Ten Thousand Things

JEWELRY/ACCESSORIES | You might find yourself wishing for 10,000 things from the showcases in this elegant boutique, which moved to the West Village from its old TriBeCa haunt. Designs run from delicate gold and silver chains to long Peruvian opal earrings. Many shapes are abstract reflections of natural forms, like twigs or seedpods. Prices start around $180 but quickly rise. ⊠ *237 W. 13th St., between 7th and Greenwich Aves., West Village* 📞 *212/352–1333* ⊕ *www.tenthousandthingsnyc.com* Ⓜ *1, 2, 3, A, C, E to 14th St., L to 8th Ave.*

SHOES, HANDBAGS, AND LEATHER GOODS
Flight 001

SHOES/LUGGAGE/LEATHER GOODS | Frequent flyers can one-stop shop at this travel-themed store that puts a creative spin on everyday accessories. Shop for bright luggage tags, passport holders, satin sleep masks, and innovative storage for everything from shoes to toiletries. ⊠ *96 Greenwich Ave., between 12th and 13th Sts., West Village* 📞 *212/989–0001* ⊕ *www.flight001.com* Ⓜ *1, 2, 3, A, C, E to 14th St.; L to 8th Ave.*

Leffot

SHOES/LUGGAGE/LEATHER GOODS | Simple and understated, this store focuses on one thing: selling top-quality men's shoes. Owner Steven Taffel, who previously worked at Prada, has stocked his shop with selections from John Lobb, Church's, and Edward Green. These shoes are meant to last a lifetime, and many have a price tag to match. Bespoke footwear is also available. ⊠ *10 Christopher St., at Gay St., West Village* ☎ *212/989–4577* ⊕ *www.leffot.com* Ⓜ *1 to Christopher St.–Sheridan Sq.; A, B, C, D, E, F, M to W. 4th St.*

Chapter 7

CHELSEA AND THE MEATPACKING DISTRICT

Updated by
David Farley

7

◉ Sights	🍴 Restaurants	🛏 Hotels	🛍 Shopping	🍸 Nightlife
★★★★☆	★★★★★	★★★☆☆	★★★★★	★★★★★

NEIGHBORHOOD SNAPSHOT

TOP EXPERIENCES

- Gallery-hopping in Chelsea
- Walking along the High Line
- Exploring the Whitney Museum of American Art: the building has light-filled galleries and wonderful views from the terraces
- Eating your way through Chelsea Market
- Shopping the ultrachic boutiques in the Meatpacking District

GETTING HERE

The A, C, E, L, 1, 2, and 3 trains stop at 14th Street for both the Meatpacking District and Chelsea. The latter neighborhood is further served by the C, E, F, M, and 1 lines at 23rd Street and by the 1 train at 18th Street and 28th Street.

PLANNING YOUR TIME

You can plan your visit to the High Line around food: first, work up an appetite by walking downtown along the High Line from 34th Street, and then head to Chelsea Market or any of the nearby restaurants. There are often a few seasonal food vendors on the High Line for impromptu snacking.

The High Line also pairs perfectly with a visit to the Whitney Museum (closed Tuesday).

Chelsea has a dual life: typical gallery hours are Tuesday to Saturday 10–6, but at night the neighborhood changes into a party town, with bars (gay and straight) and high-profile nightclubs that don't rev up until after 11.

To truly appreciate the Meatpacking District, make a 9 pm or later dinner reservation at a hot restaurant, and then hit the bars to see the glitterati.

If shopping is your pleasure, weekdays are great; come after noon, though, or you'll find most spots shuttered.

QUICK BITES

- **Blue Bottle Coffee.** If you're serious about coffee, this outpost of the California-based Blue Bottle is bound to perk you up with its dedication to freshness and flavor. There's a small selection of pastries and snacks as well. ✉ 450 W. 15th St., between 9th and 10th Aves., Chelsea ⊕ www. bluebottlecoffee.com Ⓜ Subway: A, C, E to 14th St.; L to 8th Ave.

- **Donut Pub.** Craving a red-velvet doughnut or an old-fashioned cruller for breakfast, a midafternoon pick-me-up, or something tasty at 3 am? Pull up a stool—this superfriendly spot is open 24/7. ✉ 203 W. 14th St., at 7th Ave., Chelsea ⊕ www.donutpub.com Ⓜ Subway: 1, 2, 3, A, C, E to 14th St.; L to 8th Ave.

- **Stone Street Coffee Company Cafe.** There's no seating in this tiny café, but the coffee, tea, and pastries are top-notch. The hidden bar, Bathtub Gin, has its entrance through the secret door. ✉ 132 9th Ave., between 18th and 19th Sts., Chelsea ⊕ www.stonestreetcoffee. com Ⓜ Subway: A, C, E to 14th St.; L to 8th Ave.

Once the epicenter of New York City's gay dining, nightlife, and shopping scene, Chelsea is still home to plenty of gay New Yorkers, but it's a much more diverse neighborhood than it was in the 1990s, when a dozen gay bars and even more stores and restaurants lined 8th and 9th Avenues. The so-called "scene" is more scattered now, though the area still has a large concentration of excellent restaurants.

It long ago usurped SoHo as the epicenter of New York contemporary art galleries, and there are literally hundreds along the streets here (often several in one building). The area has attracted art enthusiasts for many years, but the 2009 opening of the High Line above 10th Avenue gave new life to this part of the city.

The Highline also catalyzed new development (though Google had established its beachhead long before that) and quickly turned the area into one of the city's most popular destinations for tourists and, increasingly, tech workers. The numbers of tourists surged again with the 2015 arrival of the Whitney Museum of American Art, which firmly established the area as a major art hub and destination.

Chelsea

Most of Chelsea's art galleries are found from about 20th to 27th Streets, primarily between 10th and 11th Avenues. The range of contemporary art on display includes almost every imaginable medium and style; if it's going on in the art world, it'll be in one of the 300 or so galleries here. The galleries described are just a taste of what's available. The best way to explore is to pick a gallery or two and then wander the area.

Hudson River Park runs along the riverfront from lower Manhattan all the way to 59th Street. ⇨ *A listing for the Hudson River Park is in Lower Manhattan.*

◉ Sights

Casey Kaplan
MUSEUM | While many galleries are fleeing Chelsea's high rents for less pricey and more artist-friendly neighborhoods like the Lower East Side or the Upper East Side, Casey Kaplan chose to mark its 20th anniversary in 2015 by moving just a few blocks, into a new 10,000-square-foot, two-story storefront space on West 27th Street. The Kaplan gallery represents contemporary artists from

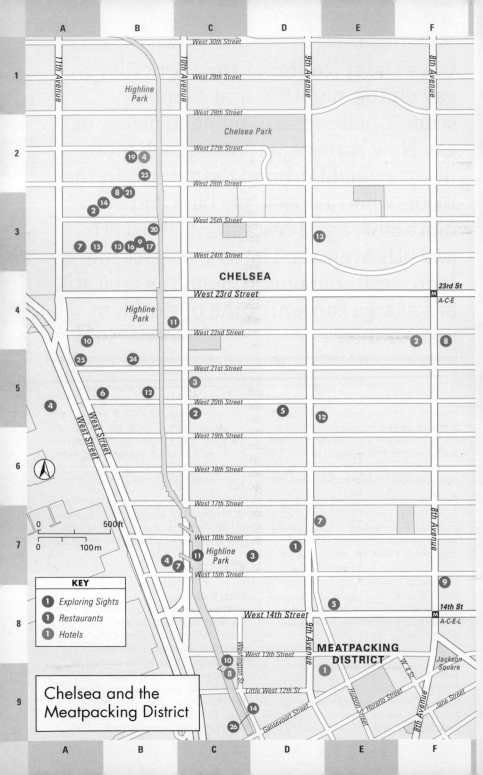

Chelsea and the
Meatpacking District

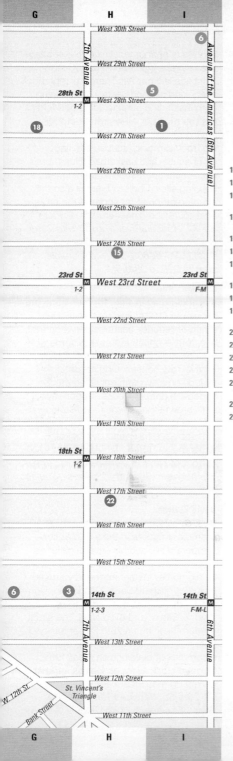

Sights ▼

1 Casey Kaplan.............**I2**
2 Cheim & Reid............**A3**
3 Chelsea Market........**D7**
4 Chelsea Piers **A5**
5 Cushman Row...........**D5**
6 David Zwirner **B5**
7 Gagosian Gallery **A3**
8 Galerie Lelong...........**B2**
9 Gladstone Gallery......**B3**
10 Hauser & Wirth **A4**
11 The High Line............**C7**
12 Jack Shainman
Gallery **B5**
13 Luhring
Augustine Gallery.......**B3**
14 Marlborough Chelsea..**B3**
15 Mary Boone Gallery....**A3**
16 Matthew Marks
Gallery **B3**
17 Metro Pictures..........**B3**
18 Museum at FIT..........**C2**
19 Nancy Hoffman
Gallery **B2**
20 Pace Gallery.............**B3**
21 Paula Cooper Gallery..**B2**
22 Rubin Museum of Art...**H7**
23 Ryan Lee Gallery........**B2**
24 Tanya Bonakdar
Gallery **B5**
25 303 Gallery...............**A5**
26 Whitney Museum
of American Art..........**C9**

Restaurants ▼

1 Buddakan................**D7**
2 Cookshop.................**C5**
3 Coppelia **G8**
4 Del Posto **B7**
5 Gansevoort Market......**E8**
6 La Nacional..............**G8**
7 L'Atelier de
Joël Robuchon..........**B7**
8 Nishi......................**F4**
9 Shorty Tang Noodles....**F8**
10 The Standard Grill **C9**
11 Tia Pol....................**B4**
12 Tipsy Parson.............**D5**
13 Txikito **D3**
14 Untitled
at the Whitney **C9**
15 Zaäu......................**H3**

Hotels ▼

1 Gansevoort
Meatpacking NYC **E9**
2 The GEM
Hotel Chelsea **F4**
3 High Line Hotel...........**C5**
4 Hotel Americano.........**B2**
5 Hotel Hayden **I1**
6 Kimpton Hotel Eventi.....**I1**
7 The Maritime Hotel.....**D7**
8 The Standard,
High Line..................**C9**

7

Chelsea and the Meatpacking District CHELSEA

Europe and the Americas. ⊠ *121 W. 27th St., between 6th and 7th Aves., Chelsea* ☎ *212/645–7335* ⊕ *www.caseykaplangallery.com* ⊜ *Free* ⊙ *Closed Sun., Mon.* Ⓜ *1 to 28th St.*

Cheim & Read

MUSEUM | Louise Bourgeois, William Eggleston, Joan Mitchell, Jenny Holzer, Donald Baechler, and Jack Pierson are among the artists represented at this prestigious gallery. ⊠ *547 W. 25th St., between 10th and 11th Aves., Chelsea* ☎ *212/242–7727* ⊕ *www.cheimread.com* ⊜ *Free* ⊙ *Closed Sun., Mon.* Ⓜ *C, E to 23rd St.*

★ Chelsea Market

MARKET | This former Nabisco plant—where the first Oreos were baked in 1912—now houses more than 50 shops, food vendors, and sit-down restaurants. Probably the biggest draw are the food kiosks (some with counter seating), including favorite taco spot Los Tacos No. 1, Israeli-based sandwich spot Miznon, Amy's Bread, Berlin Currywurst, Ninth Street Espresso, and so much more. Also look for an Anthropologie store, an outpost of Pearl River Mart, a wine bar, upscale groceries, teas, spices, gift baskets, kitchen supplies, and one of New York City's last independent bookstores (Posman Books). The market's funky industrial design—a tangle of glass and metal for an awning, a factory pipe converted into an indoor waterfall—complements the eclectic assortment of shops, but the narrow space can get very crowded. A downstairs level has a few additional food stands as well as bathrooms. ■TIP→ **There is some seating inside, but if the weather's nice, take your goodies to the High Line.** ⊠ *75 9th Ave., between 15th and 16th Sts., Chelsea* ☎ *212/652–2117* ⊕ *www.chelseamarket.com* Ⓜ *A, C, E to 14th St.; L to 8th Ave.*

Chelsea Piers

SPORTS VENUE | **FAMILY** | This sports-and-entertainment complex along the Hudson River between 17th and 23rd Streets, a phenomenal example of adaptive reuse, is the size of four 80-story buildings laid out flat. There's pretty much every kind of sports activity happening both inside and out, including golf (check out the multitier, all-weather outdoor driving range), sailing classes, ice-skating, rock climbing, soccer, bowling, gymnastics, and basketball. Plus there's a spa, elite sport-specific training, and a bowling alley. Chelsea Piers is also the jumping-off point for some of the city's boat tours and dinner cruises. ⊠ *Piers 59–62, Hudson River from 17th to 23rd Sts., entrance at 23rd St., Chelsea* ☎ *212/336–6666* ⊕ *www.chelseapiers. com* Ⓜ *C, E to 23rd St.*

Cushman Row

BUILDING | Built in 1840 for merchant and developer Don Alonzo Cushman, this string of redbrick beauties between 9th and 10th Avenues represents some of the country's best examples of Greek Revival row houses. Original details include small wreath-encircled attic windows, deeply recessed doorways with brownstone frames, and striking iron balustrades and fences. Note the pineapples, a traditional symbol of welcome, on top of the black iron newels in front of No. 416. ⊠ *406–418 W. 20th St., between 9th and 10th Aves., Chelsea* Ⓜ *C, E to 23rd St.*

David Zwirner

MUSEUM | Zwirner is one of the most prominent figures in the world of contemporary art, and his several galleries around the world show multimedia work by big-name, Instagram-friendly artists including Richard Serra, Dan Flavin, Donald Judd, Jeff Koons, Gordon Matta-Clark, Yayoi Kusama, and Alice Neel. The sleek modern building on 20th Street has two floors of exhibition space, and there's a complex of buildings on West 19th Street a block away, as well as another gallery on the Upper East Side. ⊠ *537 W. 20th St., between 10th and 11th Aves., Chelsea* ☎ *212/517–8677* ⊕ *www.*

davidzwirner.com ☒ Free ☉ Closed Sun., Mon. Ⓜ C, E to 23rd St.

Gagosian Gallery

MUSEUM | This internationally renowned modern gallery has two large Chelsea branches (the other is at 522 West 21st Street, between 10th and 11th Avenues) as well as two galleries on the Upper East Side and more than 10 outposts in cities around the world. Perhaps the most powerful dealer in the business, Gagosian Gallery shows works by heavy hitters such as Pablo Picasso, Jean-Michel Basquiat, Urs Fischer, Richard Serra, and pop-art icon Roy Lichtenstein, in addition to less well-known artists. ✉ 555 W. 24th St., at 11th Ave., Chelsea ☏ 212/741–1111 ⊕ www.gagosian.com ☒ Free ☉ Closed Sun. Ⓜ C, E to 23rd St.

Galerie Lelong

MUSEUM | The challenging installations at this large gallery include work by many Latin American artists. Look for art by Yoko Ono, Alfredo Jaar, Andy Goldsworthy, Cildo Meireles, Ana Mendieta, Hélio Oiticica, Nalini Malani, and Petah Coyne. ✉ 528 W. 26th St., between 10th and 11th Aves., Chelsea ☏ 212/315–0470 ⊕ www.galerielelong.com ☒ Free ☉ Closed Sun., Mon. Ⓜ C, E to 23rd St.

Gladstone Gallery

MUSEUM | The international roster of artists at this gallery's two large Chelsea locations includes painter Ahmed Alsoudani, sculptor Anish Kapoor, photographer Sharon Lockhart, and multimedia artists Matthew Barney and Cecilia Edefalk. The other gallery is at 530 West 21st Street, between 10th and 11th Avenues. ✉ 515 W. 24th St., between 10th and 11th Aves., Chelsea ☏ 212/206–9300 ⊕ www.gladstonegallery.com ☒ Free ☉ Closed Sun., Mon. Ⓜ C, E to 23rd St.

Hauser & Wirth

MUSEUM | Currently occupying the former Dia:Chelsea building while its new permanent building is under construction next door, this Hauser & Wirth gallery is the opposite of its narrow town-house location on the Upper East Side. The vast space begs for sprawling exhibits and large-scale works. Emerging and established contemporary artists in the powerful Hauser & Wirth fold include Dieter Roth, Paul McCarthy, Eva Hesse, and Jason Rhoades. ✉ 548 W. 22nd St., between 10th and 11th Aves., Chelsea ☏ 212/790–3900 ⊕ www.hauserwirth.com ☒ Free ☉ Closed Sun., Mon. Ⓜ C, E to 23rd St.

★ The High Line

CITY PARK | FAMILY | Once a railroad track carrying freight trains, this elevated space has been transformed into one of the city's top attractions—a 1½-mile landscaped "walking park," with curving walkways, picnic tables and benches, public art installations, and views of the Hudson River and the Manhattan skyline. Running from Gansevoort Street in the Meatpacking District (at the Whitney Museum of American Art) to West 34th Street, the High Line somehow manages to host about 5 million visitors a year and still feel like a wonderful retreat. That said, the crowds can seem overwhelming when the weather is nice, so visit as early in the morning as possible and avoid the lunchtime and weekend mass of humanity.

One of the main draws of the High Line is the landscaping, which is both wild and cultivated at the same time, and dotted with public art. Chelsea Market Passage, between 15th and 16th Streets, is accented with Spencer Finch's stained-glass art and is home to public art displays, video programs, music performances, and sit-down events. A feature that illustrates the High Line's greatest achievement—the ability to see the city with fresh eyes—is the 10th Avenue Square (between 16th and 17th Streets). This viewing window with stadium seating and large picture windows frames the city below as art, encouraging viewers to linger.

To fully appreciate the High Line, walk a length in one direction (preferably from Gansevoort Street uptown so that you can end with panoramic city and river views) and then make the return journey at street level, taking in the Chelsea neighborhood below. ■TIP➜ **Nearby Chelsea Market and Gansevoort Market are convenient places to pick up fixings for a picnic lunch.** ✉ *10th Ave., from Gansevoort St. to 34th St., Chelsea* ☎ *212/206–9922* ⊕ *www.thehighline.org* Ⓜ *A, C, E, 1, 2, 3 to 14th St.; L to 8th Ave.; 1 to 23rd St. or 28th St.; 7 to Hudson Yards.*

Jack Shainman Gallery

MUSEUM | After being established in 1984 in Washington, D.C., the Jack Shainman Gallery moved to New York's East Village and then SoHo, landing in Chelsea in 1997. The original 20th Street space has been augmented by another at 524 West 24th as well as a vast ex-schoolhouse space in Kinderhook, New York. The galleries all show emerging and established artists such as Nick Cave, El Anatsui, Carrie Mae Weems, Tallur L. N., and Kerry James Marshall. ✉ *513 W. 20th St., between 10th and 11th Aves., Chelsea* ☎ *212/645–1701* ⊕ *www.jackshainman. com* ⊠ *Free* ⊙ *Closed Sun., Mon.* Ⓜ *C, E to 23rd St.*

Luhring Augustine Gallery

MUSEUM | Owners Lawrence Luhring and Roland Augustine have been working with established and emerging artists from Europe, Japan, and America since 1985. Luhring Augustine also has a Brooklyn outpost (at 25 Knickerbocker Avenue in Bushwick) for large-scale installations and long-term projects. Both spaces present fun, innovative shows. ✉ *531 W. 24th St., between 10th and 11th Aves., Chelsea* ☎ *212/206–9100* ⊕ *www.luhringaugustine.com* ⊠ *Free* ⊙ *Closed Sun., Mon. (also Sat. in summer)* Ⓜ *C, E to 23rd St.*

Marlborough Chelsea

MUSEUM | With galleries in London, Barcelona, and Madrid, the Marlborough empire also operates two of the largest and most influential galleries in New York City. The Chelsea location (the other is on 57th Street) shows the latest work of modern artists, with a focus on sculptural forms, such as the boldly colorful paintings of Andrew Kuo. Red Grooms, Richard Estes, and Magdalena Abakanowicz are just a few of the 20th-century luminaries represented. ✉ *545 W. 25th St., between 10th and 11th Aves., Chelsea* ☎ *212/463–8634* ⊕ *www.marlboroughgallery.com* ⊠ *Free* ⊙ *Closed Sun., Mon.* Ⓜ *C, E to 23rd St.*

Mary Boone Gallery

MUSEUM | Based in SoHo in the late 1970s, when the area was a hot showcase for younger artists, the Mary Boone Gallery relocated to Midtown (745 5th Avenue, near 58th Street) in 1996 and then opened this additional branch in a former garage in Chelsea in 2000. The Chelsea space allows for large-scale works and dramatic installations. Over the years, Boone has shown and represented artists including Jean-Michel Basquiat, Jeff Koons, Julian Schnabel, Ross Bleckner, and Ai Weiwei. Boone continues to show established artists such as Barbara Kruger, Pierre Bismuth, and Francesco Clemente, as well as relative newcomers such as Jacob Hashimoto and Hilary Harkness. ✉ *541 W. 24th St., between 10th and 11th Aves., Chelsea* ☎ *212/752–2929* ⊕ *www. maryboonegallery.com* ⊠ *Free* ⊙ *Closed Sun., Mon.* Ⓜ *C, E to 23rd St.*

Matthew Marks Gallery

MUSEUM | With three spaces in the area, there's always something interesting to see at Matthew Marks. Swiss artist Ugo Rondinone made his U.S. debut here, as did Andreas Gursky. Works by Luigi Ghirri, Darren Almond, Jasper Johns, Robert Adams, Nan Goldin, Ellsworth Kelly, and a cast of illustrious others are also shown here. The other two galleries are at 522 and 526 West 22nd Street. ✉ *523 W. 24th St., between 10th and 11th Aves.,*

Chelsea ☎ 212/243–0200 ⊕ www.mat-
thewmarks.com ⊠ Free ⊗ Closed Sun.,
Mon. Ⓜ C, E to 23rd St.

Metro Pictures

MUSEUM | Some of the hottest talents
in contemporary art are shown here,
including Cindy Sherman, Olaf Breuning,
Louise Lawlor, Trevor Paglen, Camille
Henrot, and B. Wurtz. ⊠ 519 W. 24th St.,
between 10th and 11th Aves., Chelsea
☎ 212/206–7100 ⊕ www.metropictures-
gallery.com ⊠ Free ⊗ Closed Sun., Mon.
Ⓜ C, E to 23rd St.

★ Museum at FIT

MUSEUM | What this small three-gallery
museum in the Fashion Institute of Technology (FIT) lacks in size and effects, it
more than makes up for in substance and
style. You may not find interactive manne-
quins, elaborate displays, or overcrowded
galleries at the self-declared "most
fashionable museum in New York City,"
but you will find carefully curated, fun,
and interesting exhibits. The Fashion and
Textile History Gallery, on the main floor,
provides context with a rotating selection
of historically and artistically significant
objects from the museum's permanent
collection of more than 50,000 garments
and accessories (exhibits change every
six months). The real draws, though, are
the special exhibitions in the lower-level
gallery. Gallery FIT, also on the main floor,
is dedicated to student and faculty exhibitions. ⊠ 227 W. 27th St., at 7th Ave.,
Chelsea ☎ 212/217–4558 ⊕ www.fitnyc.
edu/museum ⊠ Free ⊗ Closed Sun.,
Mon. Ⓜ 1, N, R, W to 28th St.

Nancy Hoffman Gallery

MUSEUM | Contemporary painting,
sculpture, drawing, photography, and
video works by an impressive array of
international artists are on display in this
light-filled space with high ceilings and
a seasonal sculpture garden. Among
the artists are Viola Frey, known for her
heroic-scale ceramic male and female
figures, and a strong group of young
artists embarking on their first solo

shows. ⊠ 520 W. 27th St., between 10th
and 11th Aves., Chelsea ☎ 212/966–6676
⊕ www.nancyhoffmangallery.com
⊠ Free ⊗ Closed Sun., Mon. Ⓜ C, E to
23rd St.

Pace Gallery

MUSEUM | The impressive roster of artists
represented by the Pace Gallery includes
a variety of upper-echelon artists, sculp-
tors, and photographers, such as Richard
Avedon, Alexander Calder, Tara Donovan,
Chuck Close, Sol LeWitt, and Robert
Rauschenberg. Pace has two spaces
in Chelsea, including 537 West 24th
Street; a new eight-story flagship gallery
is currently under construction at 540
West 25th Street. There's also a Midtown
location (at 32 East 57th Street). ⊠ 510
W. 25th St., between 10th and 11th
Aves., Chelsea ☎ 212/989–4258 ⊕ www.
thepacegallery.com ⊠ Free ⊗ Closed
Sun., Mon. Ⓜ C, E to 23rd St.

Paula Cooper Gallery

MUSEUM | SoHo pioneer Paula Cooper
moved to Chelsea in 1996 and, after
moving her masterpieces around the
neighborhood, has finally settled into a
stark-white, high-ceilinged space that's
perfect for viewing art. There are now
two galleries (the other is at 521 West
21st Street) that showcase the works of
artists such as Carl Andre, Sam Durant,
Hans Haacke, Donald Judd, and Dan
Flavin. ⊠ 524 W. 26st St., between 10th
and 11th Aves., Chelsea ☎ 212/255–1105
⊕ www.paulacoopergallery.com ⊠ Free
⊗ Closed Sun., Mon. Ⓜ C, E to 23rd St.

Rubin Museum of Art

MUSEUM | This sleek, serene museum
spread over six floors is the largest in
the Western Hemisphere dedicated
to the art of the Himalayas, India, and
neighboring regions. The pieces shown
here include paintings on cloth, metal
sculptures, and textiles dating from
the 2nd century onward. Many of the
works from areas such as Tibet, Nepal,
southwest China, and India relate to
Buddhism, Hinduism, Bon, and other

Chelsea Galleries 101

Good art, bad art, edgy art, downright disturbing art—it's all here waiting to please and provoke in the contemporary art capital of the world. For the uninitiated, the concentration of nearly 300 galleries within a seven-block radius can be overwhelming, and the sometimes cool receptions on entering (and the deafening silence) intimidating. Art galleries are not exactly famous for their customer service, but you don't need a degree in art appreciation to stare at a canvas or installation.

There's no required code of conduct, although most galleries are library-quiet and mobile phones are seriously frowned on. You won't be pressured to buy anything, either; staff will probably be doing their best to ignore you.

Galleries are generally open Tuesday through Saturday from 10 to 6. Gallery hop on a Saturday afternoon—the highest-traffic day—if you want company. You can usually find a binder with the artist's résumé, examples of previous work, and exhibit details (usually including prices) at the front desk; if not, ask. Also ask whether there's information you can take with you.

You can't see everything in one afternoon, so if you have specific interests, plan ahead. Find gallery information and current exhibit details by checking the listings in the New Yorker or the weekend section of the New York Times. Learn more about the galleries and the genres and artists they represent at ⊕ www.artincontext.org.

eastern religions. The fourth-floor Tibetan Buddhist Shrine room presents art and ritual objects as they would be in an elaborate household shrine. Temporary exhibits and a full weekly schedule of music, film, talks, and meditation events are ongoing (check the website). There's a restaurant and bar, and a gift shop on the ground floor. ⊠ 150 W. 17th St., near 7th Ave., Chelsea ☎ 212/620–5000 ⊕ www.rmanyc.org 🖾 $19 (free Fri. 6–10 pm) ⊙ Closed Tues. Ⓜ 1 to 18th St.

Ryan Lee Gallery

MUSEUM | The gallery moved to this third-floor 8,000-square-foot space in 2014 and has since found a whole new audience of millions thanks to RLWindow, which can be viewed from the High Line. RLWindow shows innovative and experimental projects by contemporary artists, including video installations. ⊠ 515 W. 26th St., between 10th and 11th Aves., Chelsea ☎ 212/397–0742 ⊕ www.ryanleegallery.

com 🖾 Free ⊙ Closed Sun., Mon. Ⓜ C, E to 23rd St.

Tanya Bonakdar Gallery

MUSEUM | With two floors of exhibition space, the shows here can spread out. Look for innovative modern work in a variety of media, by the likes of Olafur Eliasson, Uta Barth, Ernesto Neto, Lisa Oppenheim, and Sarah Sze, who represented the United States at the 55th Venice Biennale. ⊠ 521 W. 21st St., between 10th and 11th Aves., Chelsea ☎ 212/414–4144 ⊕ www.tanyabonakdar-gallery.com 🖾 Free ⊙ Closed Sun., Mon. Ⓜ C, E to 23rd St.

303 Gallery

MUSEUM | International cutting-edge artists shown here include photographer Doug Aitken and installation artists Karen Kilimnik and Jane and Louise Wilson. Established in 1984, the gallery has existed in a number of locations but was one of the first to move to Chelsea in the 1990s. It's been in its current space, anchoring the first two floors and mezzanine of a Norman Foster luxury high-rise, since 2016. ✉ *555 W. 21st St., at 11th Ave., Chelsea* ☎ *212/255–1121* 🌐 *www.303gallery.com* 🎫 *Free* 🕒 *Closed Sun., Mon.* [M] *C, E to 23rd St.*

🍴 Restaurants

Several big-name chefs have moved to the western part of this neighborhood in recent years, putting Chelsea on the dining map. For a tasty quick bite or a gift for your favorite foodie, stop by **Chelsea Market.**

Buddakan

$$$ | **ASIAN** | Few—if any—restaurants in Manhattan rival the 16,000-square-foot Buddakan in terms of sheer magnitude and buoyant theatricality. Restaurateur Stephen Starr outdid himself with this New York version of his Philadelphia original: the upstairs bar is a great end-of-day meet-up spot for pert cocktails; the vast downstairs is like a dining hall in a medieval castle, complete with a communal table, and perfect for lush pan-Asian fare. **Known for:** grandiose design; extremely sceney vibe; long menu of Asian dishes. [$] *Average main: $32* ✉ *75 9th Ave., between 15th and 16th Sts., Chelsea* ☎ *212/989–6699* 🌐 *www.buddakannyc.com* 🕒 *No lunch* [M] *A, C, E to 14th St.; L to 8th Ave.*

Cookshop

$$$ | **AMERICAN** | One of far-west Chelsea's first hot restaurants, Cookshop manages a casual elegance while focusing on seasonal, farm-fresh cuisine that continues to wow. Outdoor seating on 10th Avenue is quite peaceful in the evening; during the day you can survey a cross section of gallery-hoppers and shoppers. **Known for:** simple but well-executed, market-driven American cuisine; great cocktails; notable weekend brunch. [$] *Average main: $27* ✉ *156 10th Ave., at 20th St., Chelsea* ☎ *212/924–4440* 🌐 *www.cookshopny.com* [M] *A, C, E to 23rd St.*

Coppelia

$$ | **LATIN AMERICAN** | Named for a legendary ice-cream shop in Havana, Coppelia is neither Cuban nor an ice-cream parlor. Chef Julian Medina has created a 24-hour pan-Latin diner that works on many levels—for a quick breakfast, casual lunch, or late-night bite—with a continent-size menu that emphasizes comfort food. **Known for:** 24-hour dining goodness; good-value pan-Latin fare; excellent pancakes. [$] *Average main: $16* ✉ *207 W. 14th St., between 7th and 8th Aves., Chelsea* ☎ *212/858–5001* 🌐 *www.coppelianyc.com* [M] *1, 2, 3, A, C, E, F, M to 14th St.; L to 8th Ave.*

Gansevoort Market

$ | **INTERNATIONAL** | Once located on Gansevoort Street in the Meatpacking District (hence the name), this 14th Street food hall is one of the best among the rash of gourmet food court openings. Build up a hunger by walking the High Line and then settle in here for a worldly feast that includes Thaimee, with some of the best Thai dishes this side of Queens, and Luzzo's admirable Neapolitan-style pizza. **Known for:** smaller Chelsea Market alternative; food stalls and shared tables; everything from pizza to tacos to ice cream. [$] *Average main: $10* ✉ *353 W. 14th St., between 8th and 9th Aves., Chelsea* ☎ *646/678–3231* 🌐 *www.gansevoortmarketnyc.com* [M] *A, C, E to 14th St.; L to 8th Ave.*

La Nacional

$ | **SPANISH** | Once the kitchen for the 150-year-old Spanish Benevolent Society, La Nacional gives off the vibe of being a hidden private club somewhere in Madrid. The space has been lightened up and modernized a bit with elegant high tables and tall chairs, and this affordable and solid Spanish eatery excels at small plates such as crispy *patatas bravas,* ham croquettes, and garlic shrimp. **Known for:** affordable Spanish fare; large carafes

Did You Know?

If you start by Piers 63 and 64 in Chelsea, you can walk through Hudson River Park all the way to TriBeCa, getting great views of One World Trade Center on the way.

of sangria; Spanish expat clientele. [$] *Average main: $10 ✉ 239 W. 14th St., Chelsea ☎ 917/388–2888 🌐 lanacional.org 🕒 Closed Sun., Mon. No lunch [M] A, C, E to 14th St.; L to 8th Ave.*

L'Atelier de Joël Robuchon

$$$$ | FRENCH | French culinary wizard Joël Robuchon may have gone to that great kitchen in the sky in 2018, but his eponymous restaurant still serves up heavenly haute-Gallic edible gifts for the taste buds. The floor-to-ceiling windows offer Big Apple views with 20 seats at raised tables and 34 at the long bar, and diners can choose between a couple of multicourse or tasting menus (based on seasonal ingredients) or from the long à la carte list. **Known for:** one of the most sophisticated dining experiences in lower Manhattan; more affordable annex, Le Grill; expensive tasting menu. [$] *Average main: $120 ✉ 85 10th Ave., at 15th St., Chelsea ☎ 212/488–8885 🌐 www.joelrobuchonusa.com 🕒 Closed Sun. No lunch [M] A, C, E to 14th St.; L to 8th Ave.*

Nishi

$$$ | ITALIAN | Chef David Chang's attempt at an Asian-Italian mash-up opened in 2016 to mixed reviews until he ditched the Asian aspect, and now this Italian-accented eatery with cozy leather booths and comfortable bar seats has come into its own. Standout starters include fried head-on shrimp and Wagyu crudo, but the real stars of the show here are the pasta dishes, especially thick bucatini noodles smothered in a *ceci e pepe* sauce, a playful take on the classic Roman dish where Chang uses chickpea paste instead of cheese. **Known for:** pasta tasting menu; great daily specials; nicely curated wine list. [$] *Average main: $25 ✉ 232 8th Ave., between 21st and 22nd Sts., Chelsea ☎ 646/518–1919 🌐 nishi.momofuku.com [M] C, E to 23rd St.*

Shorty Tang Noodles

$$ | CHINESE | This sleek Chinese restaurant hails from the family of the Chinese immigrant (Mr. Shorty Tang himself) who introduced New York to Sichuan cuisine in the 1960s. **Known for:** affordable Chinese fare; soup dumplings; friendly service. [$] *Average main: $15 ✉ 98 8th Ave., between 14th and 15th Sts., Chelsea ☎ 646/896–1883 🌐 shortytang.com [M] A, C, E to 14th St.; L to 8th Ave.*

Tía Pol

$$ | SPANISH | It may be sardine-can small, narrow, and dark, but that doesn't stop this popular tapas bar from being packed most nights. This is one of the best tapas spots in town, with a welcoming vibe, a dozen reasonably priced Spanish wines by the glass (and plenty of great bottles), and charm to spare. **Known for:** reasonably priced but high-quality tapas; patatas bravas; good midway stop during a High Line jaunt. [$] *Average main: $15 ✉ 205 10th Ave., between 22nd and 23rd Sts., Chelsea ☎ 212/675–8805 🌐 www.tiapol.com 🕒 No lunch Mon. [M] C, E to 23rd St.*

Tipsy Parson

$$$ | SOUTHERN | If New York's Chelsea neighborhood were magically transported to the American South, the food might taste something like it does at this hip, Southern-accented eatery with a menu of artery-hardening delights. Named for a boozy Southern dessert, the Tipsy Parson and its menu are all about comfort in the belly and soul: fried pickles, homemade peanut butter with crackers, bourbon-laced chicken-liver mousse, and seafood potpie. **Known for:** whiskey and bourbon selection; hot fried chicken; cola-braised short ribs. [$] *Average main: $25 ✉ 156 9th Ave., between 19th and 20th Sts., Chelsea ☎ 212/620–4545 🌐 www.tipsyparson.com 🕒 No lunch Mon. [M] C, E to 23rd St.*

Txikito

$$ | SPANISH | The theme at this diminutive Spanish spot is *cocina vasca,* or the cuisine of the Basque country, one of the most exciting regions in Iberia for eating. Chef Alexandra Raij captures the moment by serving standouts like juicy lamb meatballs in a minty broth, crispy beef tongue, and an addictive crabmeat gratin. **Known for:** bite-size pintxos; olive oil–poached cod; octopus carpaccio. [$] *Average main: $17* ✉ *240 9th Ave., at 25th St., Chelsea* ☎ *212/242–4730* 🌐 *www.txikitonyc.com* ⏲ *No lunch* [M] *C, E to 23rd St.*

Zauo

$$$$ | **JAPANESE** | This Japanese chain's first U.S. location takes the concept of fishing-pole-to-fork quite seriously: diners actually fish for their meal in a plus-size tank right in the dining room. After your fish is caught—there's trout, salmon, fluke, flounder, and others—specify how you want it cooked (tempura, grilled, as sushi), and a short time later that once-swimming fish is on a plate in front of you, ready to be devoured. **Known for:** in-restaurant fishing; ultrafresh fish; large sake selection. [$] *Average main: $40* ✉ *152 W. 24th St., between 6th and 7th Aves., Chelsea* ☎ *646/905–2274* 🌐 *zauo-newyork.com* ⏲ *Closed Sun. No lunch* [M] *1 to 23rd St.*

Hotels

The GEM Hotel Chelsea

$ | **HOTEL** | At this stylish, well-priced boutique hotel, the modern rooms are small but designed to make the most of limited space. **Pros:** great Chelsea location near galleries and restaurants; close to several subway lines; in-room coffeemakers. **Cons:** gym and business center, both on the lower level, feel like a work in progress; rooms may be too small for some; no restaurant or room service. [$] *Rooms from: $270* ✉ *300 W. 22nd St., at 8th Ave., Chelsea* ☎ *212/675–1911* 🌐 *www.thegemhotel.com* 🛏 *81 rooms* 🍴 *No meals* [M] *1, C, E to 23rd St.*

★ High Line Hotel

$$$ | **HOTEL** | A late-19th-century, redbrick, Gothic-style building on the landscaped grounds of a former seminary was transformed into this lovely hotel, full of original architectural details like stained-glass windows and pine floors. **Pros:** historic property with garden and lots of character; quality coffee bar in the lobby; close to the High Line. **Cons:** doesn't have the best subway access; outdoor restaurant only open May–October; no gym on-site. [$] *Rooms from: $495* ✉ *180 10th Ave., at 20th St., Chelsea* ☎ *212/929–3888* 🌐 *www.thehighlinehotel.com* 🛏 *60 rooms* 🍴 *No meals* [M] *C, E to 23rd St.*

Hotel Americano

$$$ | **HOTEL** | Overlooking the High Line, this boutique property captures the artistic and stylish spirit of Chelsea with rooms that are funky yet comfortable, with low platform beds, black vinyl beanbag chairs, and vintage details like touch-tone phones. **Pros:** year-round rooftop pool and bar; views overlooking the High Line; near the thriving gallery scene in Chelsea. **Cons:** low beds; bathrooms lack privacy; some furniture favors form over function. [$] *Rooms from: $480* ✉ *518 W. 27th St., between 10th and 11th Aves., Chelsea* ☎ *212/216–0000* 🌐 *www.hotel-americano.com* 🛏 *56 rooms* 🍴 *No meals* [M] *C, E to 23rd St.*

Hotel Hayden

$ | **HOTEL** | Situated near Penn Station and convenient for Chelsea's attractions, the Hotel Hayden doesn't look like much from outside, but step inside and the stylish ambience unfolds—all the way to your room. **Pros:** good-size rooms for New York; nice view from rooftop restaurant-lounge; in-room Keurig coffee. **Cons:** unattractive, utilitarian-looking facade; street noise can be heard in rooms on lower floors; showers spray water over bathroom floor. [$] *Rooms from: $150* ✉ *127 W. 28th St., between 6th and 7th Aves., Chelsea* ☎ *646/484–4361* 🌐 *www.hotelhaydennyc.com* 🛏 *122 rooms* 🍴 *No meals* [M] *1, N, R, W to 28th St.*

Kimpton Hotel Eventi

$ | **HOTEL** | **FAMILY** | This hotel adds a touch of the Kimpton chain's clever sense of style just below Penn Station in an area desperately in need of new lodging options, with spacious guest rooms, comfortable beds, oversize bathrooms, and floor-to-ceiling windows. **Pros:** complimentary happy hour and morning coffee; relaxing spa; nice gym, plus bikes available to borrow. **Cons:** crowded lobby; few nightlife and dining options nearby; located in a forlorn part of Chelsea. ⓢ *Rooms from: $209* ⊠ *851 6th Ave., at 30th St., Chelsea* ☎ *212/564–4567* ⊕ *www.hoteleventi.com* ⤴ *292 rooms* ⦿ *No meals* Ⓜ *1, N, R, W to 28th St.*

The Maritime Hotel

$$$ | **HOTEL** | The Maritime's white-ceramic tower, the former HQ for the National Maritime Union, was the first luxury hotel to be opened in the Chelsea gallery district, and the property still feels a bit nautical, with small rooms that resemble modern ship cabins. **Pros:** rooms with big porthole windows; great location near Chelsea Market and the Chelsea galleries; fun nautical design elements. **Cons:** street noise; small rooms; no gym or spa. ⓢ *Rooms from: $495* ⊠ *363 W. 16th St., at 9th Ave., Chelsea* ☎ *212/242–4300* ⊕ *www.themaritimehotel.com* ⤴ *126 rooms* ⦿ *Free Breakfast* Ⓜ *A, C, E to 14th St.; L to 8th Ave.*

Nightlife

BARS

★ The 18th Room

BARS/PUBS | Referencing the 18th Amendment of the U.S. Constitution, which banned alcohol, this "secret" cocktail den is a great find. Enter through the fake coffee-supply-company storefront into the Art Deco–bedecked interior to sip high-quality cocktails, many of which are of the bespoke variety: tell the bartender what you like and you'll get an inspired libation. ⊠ *134 9th Ave., between 18th and 19th Sts., Chelsea* ☎ *646/559–1671* ⊕ *the18throom.com* Ⓜ *A, C, E to 14th St.; L to 8th Ave.*

Porchlight

BARS/PUBS | At this southern-inflected bar you can have your cocktails and eat your fried oysters and smoked cheddar biscuits, too. Located in far West Chelsea (a short hike from the subway), this relaxed watering hole from New York restaurateur and hospitality king Danny Meyer is an intimate space to quaff and nibble the night away. ⊠ *271 11th Ave., between 27th and 28th Sts., Chelsea* ☎ *212/981– 6188* ⊕ *porchlightbar.com* Ⓜ *C, E to 23rd St.; 1 to 28th St.*

COMEDY CLUBS

Gotham Comedy Club

COMEDY CLUBS | This 10,000-square-foot club—complete with a chandelier and roomy downstairs lounge—showcases popular headliners such as Roy Wood Jr. and Kate Clinton, and the occasional pop-in by big-name funny folks like Dave Chappelle and Lewis Black. ⊠ *208 W. 23rd St., between 7th and 8th Aves., Chelsea* ☎ *212/367–9000* ⊕ *gothamcomedyclub.com* Ⓜ *1, C, E to 23rd St.*

GAY NIGHTLIFE

Barracuda

BARS/PUBS | The drag shows and free-wheeling, flirty dance nights are what lure a mostly male crowd to this cute, casual neighborhood hangout, far less pretentious (some might say it's adorably divey) than some of its grander Chelsea neighbors. ⊠ *275 W. 22nd St., between 7th and 8th Aves., Chelsea* ☎ *212/645– 8613* Ⓜ *1, C, E to 23rd St.*

Gym Sports Bar

BARS/PUBS | At this gay sports bar, the plentiful flat-screen TVs and cheap Budweisers draw athletic enthusiasts of every stripe, from athlete to armchair. The bar sponsors—and frequently hosts parties for—a number of local gay sports teams. ⊠ *167 8th Ave., at 18th St., Chelsea* ☎ *212/337–2439* ⊕ *www.gymsportsbar.com* Ⓜ *A, C, E to 14th St.; L to 8th Ave.; 1 to 18th St.*

🎟 Performing Arts

DANCE
★ Joyce Theater
DANCE | Set within a former Art Deco movie house in Chelsea, the 472-seat Joyce Theater has superb sight lines and presents a wide range of classical and contemporary dance. Its 48-week season includes a rotating roster of international, national, and New York-based companies. ⊠ *175 8th Ave., at 19th St., Chelsea* ☎ *212/691–9740, 212/242–0800 for tickets* ⊕ *www.joyce.org* Ⓜ *A, C, E to 14th St.; L to 8th Ave.; 1 to 18th St.*

New York Live Arts
DANCE | This Chelsea space serves as the home stage for the innovative Bill T. Jones/Arnie Zane Dance Company. It's also a laboratory for new choreographers and artists in residence, and hosts nonchoreographed events such as panel discussions. ⊠ *219 W. 19th St., between 7th and 8th Aves., Chelsea* ☎ *212/691–6500, 212/924–0077 for tickets* ⊕ *www.newyorklivearts.org* Ⓜ *1 to 18th St.; A, C, E, to 23rd St.*

THEATER
TADA!
THEATER | FAMILY | Vibrant original musicals for family audiences are performed by a cast of talented kids (aged 8–18). Most shows are on weekends, and children's tickets start at reasonable prices. ⊠ *15 W. 28th St., 2nd fl., between Broadway and 5th Ave., Chelsea* ☎ *212/252–1619* ⊕ *www.tadatheater.com* Ⓜ *1, 6, N, R, W to 28th St.*

🛍 Shopping

Chelsea offers one-stop shopping for some of the biggest retail brands, as well as quirky local boutiques.

BOOKS AND STATIONERY
★ Books of Wonder
BOOKS/STATIONERY | FAMILY | Readers young and old delight in Manhattan's oldest and largest independent children's bookstore. The friendly, knowledgeable staff can help select gifts for all reading levels. Don't miss the extensive Oz section, plus the collection of old, rare, and collectible children's books and original children's book art. ⊠ *18 W. 18th St., between 5th and 6th Aves., Chelsea* ☎ *212/989–3270* ⊕ *www.booksofwonder.com* Ⓜ *F, M to 14th St.; L to 6th Ave.*

Posman Books
BOOKS/STATIONERY | Come here for the outstanding selection of contemporary and classic books across genres. Don't miss the cheeky and serious high-quality greeting cards. Look for a second location at 30 Rockefeller Plaza in Midtown West. ⊠ *Chelsea Market, 75 9th Ave., between 15th and 16th Sts., Chelsea* ☎ *212/627–0304* ⊕ *www.posmanbooks. com* Ⓜ *A, C, E to 14th St.; L to 8th Ave.*

CLOTHING
Comme des Garçons
CLOTHING | The designs in this swoopy, gold-adorned space consistently push the fashion envelope with brash patterns, unlikely juxtapositions (tulle and neoprene), and cuts that are meant to be thought-provoking, not flattering. Architecture students come just for the interior design. ⊠ *520 W. 22nd St., between 10th and 11th Aves., Chelsea* ☎ *212/604–9200* ⊕ *www.comme-des-garcons.com* Ⓜ *C, E to 23rd St.*

New York Vintage
CLOTHING | Stylists to the stars, TV costumers, and the deep-pocketed descend upon this boutique to browse racks of prime vintage clothing. Everything is high-end, so don't expect any bargains. Take your pick from Yves Saint Laurent, Madame Grès, and Thierry Mugler items. There's a good selection of handbags and stilettos, too. ⊠ *117 W. 25th St., between 6th and 7th Aves., Chelsea* ☎ *212/647–1107* ⊕ *www.newyorkvintage.com* Ⓜ *F, M to 23rd St.*

HOME DECOR
Room & Board
HOUSEHOLD ITEMS/FURNITURE | Fans of streamlined, midcentury modern furniture ascend to heaven here. This location—set in a landmark 1902 building that was once the warehouse of the Siegel-Cooper Company—is stocked with sleek sofas, beds, and children's furniture as well as accessories like rugs and lamps, 90% of which are made in America. Design aficionados can choose from iconic pieces like seating cubes from Frank Gehry and Eames molded plywood chairs, or items from up-and-coming designers. ⊠ *236 W. 18th St., between 7th and 8th Aves., Chelsea* ☎ *212/204–7384* ⊕ *www.roomandboard. com* Ⓜ *1 to 18th St., 1, 2, 3, A, C, E to 14th St.; L to 8th Ave.*

★ Story
HOUSEHOLD ITEMS/FURNITURE | Launched by former consultant Rachel Shechtman, Story is a concept store with a twist. Every few weeks, it partners with a new sponsor to develop a retail "story," like a magazine spread, which ranges from wearable tech to "home for the holidays." Pop by often to admire the artful displays, and you never know what will be for sale, from chocolates to clothing to books. Story also hosts events such as talks with TED speakers. ⊠ *144 10th Ave., at 19th St., Chelsea* ☎ *212/242–4853* ⊕ *www.thisisstory.com* Ⓜ *A, C, E to 14th St.; L to 8th Ave.*

MUSIC STORES AND MEDIA
Jazz Record Center
MUSIC STORES | If you're seeking rare or out-of-print jazz recordings, this is your one-stop shop. Long-lost Ellingtons and other rare pressings come to light here; the jazz-record specialist also stocks books, collectibles, DVDs, posters, CDs, and LPs. ⊠ *236 W. 26th St., 8th fl., between 7th and 8th Aves., Chelsea* ☎ *212/675–4480* ⊕ *www.jazzrecord-center.com* Ⓜ *1 to 28th St.*

Meatpacking District

Concentrated in a few blocks of what is essentially an extension of the West Village, between the Hudson River and 9th Avenue, from Little West 12th Street to about West 17th Street, the Meatpacking District used to be the center of New York City's wholesale meat industry. There are few meat markets left in this now rather quaint cobblestone area, but it's definitely a figurative meat market at night, when the city's most fashionable denizens frequent the equally trendy restaurants and bars here. The area is also home to some of the city's swankiest retailers, including high-profile fashion designers and labels like Christian Louboutin, Diane von Furstenberg, and Tory Burch. The Whitney Museum of American Art is also here.

◉ Sights

★ Whitney Museum of American Art
MUSEUM | The Renzo Piano–designed museum welcomes visitors with a lively plaza, bold works of contemporary and modern American art, plenty of terraced outdoor spaces, and expansive windows. There are eight floors (not all open to the public), with a restaurant on the ground floor and a café on the eighth floor. The galleries house rotating exhibitions of postwar and contemporary works from the permanent collection that include artists such as Jackson Pollock, Jim Dine, Jasper Johns, Mark Rothko, Chuck Close, Cindy Sherman, and Roy Lichtenstein. Notable pieces often on view include Hopper's *Early Sunday Morning* (1930), Bellows's *Dempsey and Firpo* (1924), Alexander Calder's beloved *Circus,* and several of Georgia O'Keeffe's dazzling flower paintings.

The Whitney experience is as much about the setting as the incredible artwork. The outdoor terraces on floors six, seven, and eight are connected by exterior stairs that provide a welcome reprieve from crowded galleries as well as stunning skyline views. Free tours of the collection and current exhibitions are offered daily. After 7 pm on Friday, the price of admission is pay-what-you-wish. **■TIP→ Skip the long lines and buy tickets in advance, but note that you cannot buy same-day tickets online. They must be purchased the day before.** ✉ *99 Gansevoort St., between Washington St. and 10th Ave., Meatpacking District* ☎ *212/570–3600* 🌐 *www.whitney.org* 🎟 *$25* ⏲ *Closed Tues.* [M] *A, C, E to 14th St.; L to 8th Ave.*

🍴 Restaurants

Europeans, models, actors, and the people who love them stroll the sidewalk like they're on a catwalk, going from one hot restaurant to the next in this cobblestone-laden neighborhood, which has become almost too much of a scene for its own good. There's plenty of great eating here—you just might have to wait awhile (or impersonate a celebrity) to get a table.

Del Posto

$$$$ | ITALIAN | The dining room at Del Posto—with its sweeping staircase, formal decor, and live music from a baby grand—has the feel of an opulent hotel lobby. This is one of the most consistently dazzling special-occasion spots in the city, and the Italian food is stellar. **Known for:** some set menus, including five and eight courses; special-occasion Italian dining; urchin spaghetti. [$] *Average main: $68* ✉ *85 10th Ave., between 15th and 16th Sts., Meatpacking District* ☎ *212/497–8090* 🌐 *www.delposto.com* ⏲ *No lunch weekends* [M] *A, C, E to 14th St.; L to 8th Ave.*

The Standard Grill

$$$ | AMERICAN | Celebs, fashion-industry insiders, and the common folk, too, all cluster at this buzzy restaurant inside The Standard, High Line hotel. The menu is comfort-luxe, with dishes like the over-stuffed lobster roll and hearty Provençal seafood stew. **Known for:** deeply sceney; outdoor seating; seafood-heavy menus. [$] *Average main: $30* ✉ *848 Washington St., between 13th and Little W. 12th Sts., Meatpacking District* ☎ *212/645–4100* 🌐 *www.thestandardgrill.com* [M] *A, C, E to 14th St.; L to 8th Ave.*

Untitled at the Whitney

$$$ | AMERICAN | Located in the handsome Renzo Piano–designed Whitney Museum of American Art at the southern end of the High Line, restaurateur Danny Meyer's Untitled isn't necessarily the masterpiece in his collection of great restaurants, but the minimalist-design eatery is worth a look (and a bite). The deceptively simple dishes explode with flavor: fried chicken thighs paired with zucchini hummus and the chili-roasted scallops are just a couple of the artistically tasty dishes worth trying. **Known for:** artsy surroundings; roasted and fried chicken; seafood cioppino. [$] *Average main: $27* ✉ *Whitney Museum of American Art, 99 Gansevoort St., at West St., Meatpacking District* ☎ *212/570–3670* 🌐 *www.untitledatthewhitney.com* [M] *A, C, E to 14th St.; L to 8th Ave.*

🛏 Hotels

Gansevoort Meatpacking NYC

$$ | HOTEL | Though the nearby Standard, High Line has stolen some of its thunder, there's still plenty to draw guests to this chic Meatpacking District pioneer, starting with the sleek rooms that overlook the city or the Hudson River and the rooftop deck with a 45-foot heated pool. **Pros:** rooftop pool; wonderful art collection; great location for restaurants and shopping. **Cons:** location can seem too trendy, especially at night; service can be slipshod; less attractive building that doesn't match the surroundings. [$] *Rooms from: $425* ✉ *18 9th Ave., at 13th St., Meatpacking District* ☎ *212/206–6700* 🌐 *www.gansevoorthotelgroup.com* 🛏 *186 rooms*

\|◎\| No meals Ⓜ *A, C, E to 14th St.; L to 8th Ave.*

★ The Standard, High Line
$$ | **HOTEL** | This modern architectural statement on the West Side is still one of New York's hottest hotels, with the High Line running underneath it, a lobby full of glamorous types, an authentic beer garden (open year-round; dig the table tennis), and the 18th-floor nightclub that is one of the toughest doors in town. **Pros:** beautiful building with sweeping views; beautiful people; impressive restaurant space. **Cons:** noisy at night; tight rooms; can be too scenev. Ⓢ *Rooms from: $395* ✉ *848 Washington St., between 13th and Little W. 12th Sts., Meatpacking District* ☎ *212/645–4646* ⊕ *www.standardhotels. com* ⌁ *338 rooms* \|◎\| *No meals* Ⓜ *A, C, E to 14th St.; L to 8th Ave.*

Nightlife

BARS
Plunge
BARS/PUBS | The slick rooftop bar of the Gansevoort Meatpacking NYC hotel would be worth visiting even without its sweeping Hudson River and Manhattan views. Sleek and glossy, Plunge has blue Portuguese tiles, an abundance of natural light, cool furnishings, and sexy servers. The music isn't too loud and there is ample space—indoors as well as out. Cocktails are predictably pricey, but there are weekday happy-hour specials from 5 to 7 pm. ✉ *Gansevoort Meatpacking NYC, 18 9th Ave., at 13th St., Meatpacking District* ☎ *212/660–6736* ⊕ *www. plunge.nyc* Ⓜ *A, C, E to 14th St.; L to 8th Ave.*

The Standard Hotel Biergarten
BARS/PUBS | Practically the official bar of the High Line park, the Standard Biergarten is a sprawling, bustling space complete with table tennis, bench tables, and big steins of beer. For food, there's a grill bar and the indoor Living Room lounge. It's unlikely that you'll be able to enter the chic, multivenue hotel rooftop without an advance reservation, so plan accordingly. ✉ *The Standard, High Line, 848 Washington St., at 13th St., Meatpacking District* ☎ *212/645–4646* ⊕ *www. standardhotels.com* Ⓜ *A, C, E to 14th St.; L to 8th Ave.*

The Woodstock
BARS/PUBS | If you've always wanted to sip affordable cocktails and eat pizza in a fashionable wood-paneled rec room done in 1960s style—and who hasn't?— this is the place for you. The Woodstock, first flicking on its lava lamps in 2018, boasts a handful of signature cocktails (try the tequila and blueberry habanero concoction, Light My Fire) and above-average thick-crust pizzas named for '60s-era celebrities. See if you can spot the original Salvador Dalí artworks scattered around the room. ✉ *446 W. 11th St., between 9th and 10th Aves., Meatpacking District* ☎ *212/633–2000* ⊕ *thewoodstocknyc.com* Ⓜ *A, C, E to 14th St.; L to 8th Ave.*

DANCE CLUBS AND DJ VENUES
Cielo
DANCE CLUBS | Avid clubgoers gravitate to this Meatpacking District music-pumping mecca to guzzle cocktails; groove to top flight DJs spinning soulful Latin beats, funk, and techno; boogie on the sunken dance floor; and smoke in the no-frills garden outside. The door can be tight but if you can get in, it's heaven for electronica heads. ✉ *18 Little W. 12th St., between 9th Ave. and Washington St., Meatpacking District* ☎ *212/645–5700* ⊕ *www.cieloclub.com* Ⓜ *A, C, E to 14th St.; L to 8th Ave.*

Shopping

For nearly a century, the industrial western edge of downtown Manhattan was defined by slaughterhouses and meatpacking plants, blood-splattered cobblestone streets, and men lugging carcasses into warehouses before dawn.

But in the late 1990s, the area speedily transformed into another kind of meat market. Many of the old warehouses now house ultrachic shops, nightclubs, and restaurants packed with angular fashionistas. Jeffrey, a pint-size department store, was an early arrival, followed by bigger brands such as Diane von Furstenberg and a few lofty furniture stores. Despite the influx of a few chains—albeit stylish ones like Scoop—eclectic boutiques keep popping up. The one thing that's hard to find here is a bargain.

CLOTHING
Diane von Furstenberg
CLOTHING | At this light-filled New York flagship, try on the iconic DVF wrap dress in myriad patterns. The blouses, shorts, and skirts are equally feminine. ✉ 874 Washington St., at 14th St., Meatpacking District ☎ 646/486–4800 ⊕ www.dvf.com Ⓜ A, C, E to 14th St.; L to 8th Ave.

Jeffrey
CLOTHING | The Meatpacking District really arrived when this Atlanta-based mini Barneys opened its doors. You can find an incredible array of designer shoes—Valentino and red-soled Christian Louboutins are some of the best sellers—plus top labels such as Yves Saint Laurent and Lanvin for both men and women. ✉ 449 W. 14th St., between 9th and 10th Aves., Meatpacking District ☎ 212/206–1272 ⊕ www.jeffreynewyork. com Ⓜ A, C, E to 14th St.; L to 8th Ave.

Rebecca Taylor
CLOTHING | This designer is known for her soft, feminine work, which runs the gamut from sexy to understated, all with a slightly vintage flair. Taylor's downtown location is a serene, spacious environment for browsing racks of silky shirtdresses, embroidered tunics, and ruffled overcoats. Her shoes, handbags, and jewelry are equally romantic. ✉ 34 Gansevoort St., between Greenwich and Hudson Sts., Meatpacking District ☎ 212/243–2600 ⊕ www.rebeccataylor. com Ⓜ A, C, E to 14th St.; L to 8th Ave.

Trina Turk
CLOTHING | Make a beeline to this boutique if you like glowing, happy colors and 1970's-influenced clothing. The shop, designed by Jonathan Adler, showcases Turk's ready-to-wear clothing in a bright, airy setting. Swimwear is a standout, and menswear is also sold here. ✉ 67 Gansevoort St., between Washington and Greenwich Sts., Meatpacking District ☎ 212/206–7383 ⊕ www.trinaturk.com Ⓜ A, C, E to 14th St.; L to 8th Ave.

HOME DECOR
★ RH New York
HOUSEHOLD ITEMS/FURNITURE | You don't have to be in the market for a plush sofa or a chandelier to appreciate a stroll through the massive six-story 90,000-square-foot space of RH (Restoration Hardware), with sections including ones for babies and teens, a soaring central atrium, and a glass elevator to whisk you to the leafy rooftop terrace. There, a restaurant serves elevated comfort food such as truffle-laced pastas, steak sandwiches, and lobster rolls. And who knows? You might just end up leaving with a cool vintage-looking lamp, too. ✉ 9 9th Ave., at 13th St., Meatpacking District ☎ 212/217–2210 ⊕ www.restorationhardware.com Ⓜ A, C, E to 14th St.; L to 8th Ave.

Chapter 8

UNION SQUARE, THE FLATIRON DISTRICT, AND GRAMERCY PARK

8

Updated by
David Farley

◉ Sights	🍴 Restaurants	🛏 Hotels	💼 Shopping	🍸 Nightlife
★★★★★	★★★☆☆	★★★☆☆	★★★★☆	★☆☆☆☆

NEIGHBORHOOD SNAPSHOT

TOP EXPERIENCES

■ Checking out the produce, flowers, and baked goods at the Union Square greenmarket

■ Browsing the miles of books in the Strand bookstore

■ Appreciating the architecture around the perimeter of the historic Gramercy Park

■ Shopping for presents at the outdoor Union Square Holiday Market, which takes place between Thanksgiving and Christmas

■ Having lunch alfresco in Madison Square Park

GETTING HERE

Union Square is a major subway hub, with the 4, 5, 6, L, N, Q, R, and W lines all converging here. For Madison Square Park and the Flatiron District, take the N or R train to 23rd Street (this lets you out on Broadway). The 6 stops at 23rd and 28th Streets (on Park Avenue South).

PLANNING YOUR TIME

Union Square bustles, especially during the summer, with people hanging out on the steps, eating lunch, or watching street performers. Market days—Monday, Wednesday, Friday, and Saturday—are even busier.

This is definitely an area for strolling, shopping, and eating, so plan your visit around a meal—or several. Weekends get very busy, so if you prefer smaller crowds, head to this area on a weekday.

If you're planning to eat at the Shake Shack in Madison Square Park, come before noon to avoid long lines.

There are frequent (and free) art installations in Madison Square Park, and the Madison Square Eats market takes place twice a year.

QUICK BITES

■ **Daily Provisions.** Top-quality sandwiches, delectable pastries, market-fresh salads, and substantial lunch and dinner options are served to eat in or take out at this petite bakery-café that's part of Danny Meyer's empire. ⊠ *103 E. 19th St., between Irving Pl. and Park Ave. S, Union Square* ⊕ *www.dailyprovisionsnyc. com* Ⓜ *Subway: 4, 5, 6, L, N, Q, R, W to 14th St.–Union Sq.*

■ **Irving Farm Coffee Roasters.** Steps from Union Square, this busy little café (known to locals as 71 Irving) roasts its own beans and serves up good people-watching along with espresso drinks, sandwiches, muffins, and snacks. ⊠ *71 Irving Pl., between 18th and 19th Sts., Gramercy* ⊕ *www.irvingfarm.com* Ⓜ *Subway: 4, 5, 6, L, N, Q, R, W to 14th St.–Union Sq.*

■ **Think Coffee.** Maybe you like a little social and environmental awareness with your caffeine, or perhaps the cold-brewed iced coffees, Spanish lattes (made with condensed milk), and cool playlist are sufficient. ⊠ *123 4th Ave., between 12th and 13th Sts., Union Square* ⊕ *www.thinkcoffee.com* Ⓜ *Subway: 4, 5, 6, L, N, Q, R, W to 14th St.–Union Sq.*

Union Square is a hub of activity, and with such a mass of humanity passing through this central subway nexus, there's always good people-watching, whether it's the skateboarders, artists and protesters in the southwest corner, the shoppers at the farmers market, or people just passing through on their way to somewhere else. When that certain brand of New Yorker says they don't like to travel above 14th Street, they're usually thinking about Union Square as the cutoff.

Union Square

The energy of Union Square reaches its peak during greenmarket days (Monday, Wednesday, Friday, and Saturday), when more than 140 regional farmers and food purveyors set up shop on the square's north and west sides to peddle everything from produce to meat and fresh fish to baked goods. The market is a great place to rub elbows with—and get elbowed by—local shoppers and chefs, and a great source for tasty souvenirs (locally produced honeys, jams, pickles, and cheeses) as well as lunch. Find a bench in the park to savor your goodies and take in the scene. Political gatherings sometimes happen here, too.

Even on a nonmarket day, Union Square generally has vendors of all kinds, selling everything from art to jewelry to T-shirts. New York University students, nannies with their charges, and other locals and visitors gather in this open space that can at times feel more like an outdoor version of Grand Central Terminal than a park. Just south of Union Square, on Broadway at 12th Street, is the Strand, a giant institution of a bookstore that attracts book lovers from all over.

◉ Sights

Union Square Park and Greenmarket

CITY PARK | FAMILY | A park, farmers market, meeting place, and the site of rallies and demonstrations, this pocket green space and surrounding public square sits in the center of a bustling residential and commercial neighborhood. The name "Union" originally signified that two main

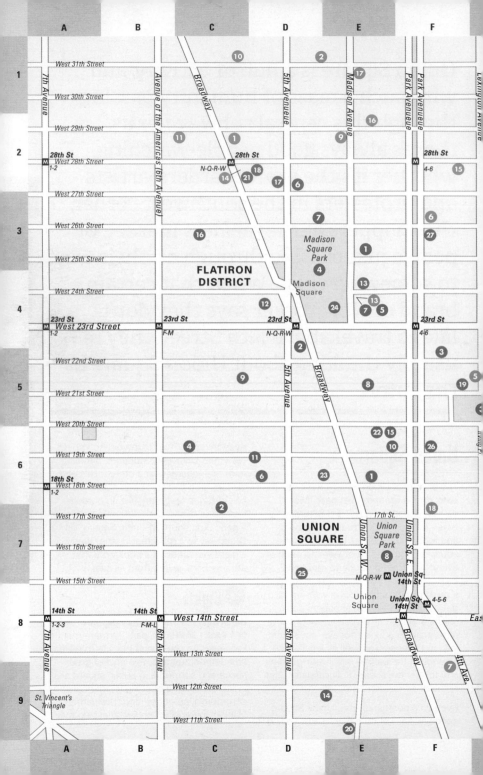

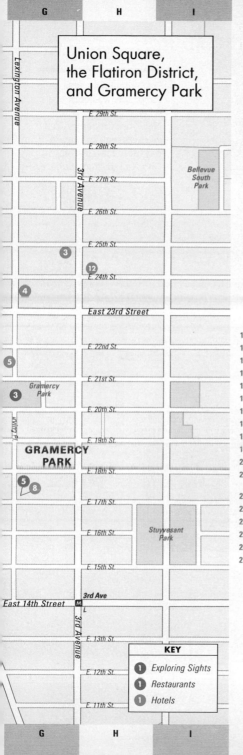

Union Square, the Flatiron District, and Gramercy Park

Sights ▼

1 Appellate Division Courthouse E3
2 Flatiron Building......... D4
3 Gramercy Park.......... G5
4 Madison Square Park.. D3
5 Metropolitan Life Insurance Company Tower E4
6 Museum of Sex D2
7 National Museum of Mathematics D3
8 Union Square Park and Greenmarket.. E7

Restaurants ▼

1 ABC Kitchen.............. E6
2 Aldea...................... C7
3 BLT Prime................. F5
4 Boqueria.................. C6
5 Casa Mono G7
6 The City Bakery D6
7 The Clocktower F4
8 Cosme..................... E5
9 Cote C5
10 Craft...................... E6
11 Dough Doughnuts D6
12 Eataly NYC Flatiron D4
13 Eleven Madison Park.... E4
14 Gotham Bar & Grill E9
15 Gramercy Tavern E6
16 Hill Country C3
17 Ilili....................... D2
18 Made Nice............... D2
19 Maialino F5
20 Nix........................ E9
21 The NoMad Restaurant................ C2
22 Nur E6
23 Rosa Mexicano D6
24 Shake Shack E4
25 Tocqueville D7
26 Union Square Cafe F6
27 Upland F3

Hotels ▼

1 Ace Hotel New York..... C2
2 Arlo NoMad D1
3 Carlton Arms Hotel G3
4 Freehand New York G4
5 Gramercy Park Hotel... G5
6 Hotel Giraffe by Library Hotel Collection.......... F3
7 Hyatt Union Square New York F9
8 The Inn at Irving Place.............. G7
9 The James New York – NoMad...... E2
10 Life Hotel................. C1
11 MADE Hotel C2
12 The Marcel at Gramercy H4
13 The New York EDITION................... E4
14 The NoMad Hotel........ C2
15 Park South Hotel......... F2
16 The Redbury New York E2
17 The Roger................. E1
18 W New York Union Square............. F7

KEY

🔵 Exploring Sights
🔵 Restaurants
🔵 Hotels

roads—Broadway and 4th Avenue—crossed here. It took on a different meaning in the late 19th and early 20th centuries, when the square became a rallying spot for labor protests; many unions, as well as fringe political parties, moved their headquarters nearby.

Union Square is at its best on Monday, Wednesday, Friday, and Saturday (8–6), when the largest of the city's greenmarkets gathers farmers and food purveyors from the tristate area selling fruit and vegetables, plants, fresh-baked pies and breads, cheeses, cider, fish, and meat. Between Thanksgiving and Christmas, artisans sell gift items and food at the large Union Square Holiday Market (⌽ www.urbanspacenyc.com).

New York University dormitories, theaters, and cavernous commercial spaces occupy the restored 19th-century commercial buildings that surround the park, along with some chain stores and restaurants. Statues in the park include those of George Washington, Abraham Lincoln, Mahatma Gandhi (often wreathed in flowers), and the Marquis de Lafayette (sculpted by Frédéric-Auguste Bartholdi, designer of the Statue of Liberty). ⌾ From 14th to 17th St., between Broadway and Park Ave. S, Union Square Ⓜ 4, 5, 6, L, N, Q, R, W to 14th St.–Union Sq.

🍴 Restaurants

There is no shortage of appealing dining options at any price range (including picnic provisions from the wonderful greenmarket, open Monday, Wednesday, Friday, and Saturday) around this central hub.

★ Gotham Bar & Grill

$$$$ | AMERICAN | Every bit as thrilling as when it opened in 1984, this culinary landmark continues to focus on a foundation of simple, clean flavors to create transcendent preparations: no rack of lamb is more tender, no seafood

salad sweeter, and desserts are also memorable. Take a stroll through the Union Square Greenmarket before or after lunch to see the chef's inspirations. **Known for:** invented the concept of "architectural cuisine"; classy space with high ceilings; good-value prix-fixe lunch. Ⓢ Average main: $42 ⌾ 12 E. 12th St., between 5th Ave. and University Pl., Union Square ☎ 212/620–4020 ⌽ www.gothambarandgrill.com ⊘ No lunch weekends Ⓜ 4, 5, 6, L, N, Q, R, W to 14th St.–Union Sq.

Nix

$$ | VEGETARIANVEGETARIAN | Chef John Fraser's "meatless Monday" menu at his Upper West Side eatery, Dovetail, spawned this downtown vegetarian restaurant that offers a sophisticated ambience with its white walls and wood-topped tables. The roasted Brussels sprouts are emboldened with chestnuts and SarVecchio cheese, the pan-roasted gnocchi dance in the bowl with zucchini, mint, and jalapeños, and it's all good enough to make you easily forget about meat. **Known for:** good cocktails; standout gnocchi; intimate setting lit by candles at night. Ⓢ Average main: $19 ⌾ 72 University Pl., between 10th and 11th Sts.,

Union Square ☎ 212/498–9393 ⊕ www.
nixny.com Ⓜ 4, 5, 6, L, N, Q, R, W to 14th
St.–Union Sq.

Rosa Mexicano

$$$ | MODERN MEXICAN | Although the
spacious, colorfully lighted interior might
tip you off that authenticity is best sought
elsewhere, if you're looking for high-qual-
ity Mex-flavored fare, step right up, hom-
bre. Start with an order of guacamole
(made tableside), moving on to the pork
belly and scallop tacos, soul-comforting
chicken tortilla pie, or the crispy pork
shank—all of which taste better with a
margarita. **Known for:** popular happy hour;
potent margaritas; excellent guacamo-
le. Ⓢ Average main: $28 ⊠ 9 E. 18th
St., between 5th Ave. and Broadway,
Union Square ☎ 212/533–3350 ⊕ www.
rosamexicano.com Ⓜ 4, 5, 6, L, N, Q, R,
W to 14th St.–Union Sq.

Tocqueville

$$$ | MODERN AMERICAN | Hidden just
steps from busy Union Square, this
refined, serene dining oasis of excellent
Gallic-American fare is a secret even
to many New Yorkers. Begin with the
signature starter, an unctuous angel-hair
sea-urchin carbonara, before moving on
to dishes like saffron-and-fennel-spiked
grilled octopus, and smoked duck breast
paired with baby bok choy and Asian
pear. **Known for:** underrated haute fare;
good prix-fixe lunch; jacket and tie recommended at dinner. Ⓢ Average main: $33
⊠ 1 E. 15th St., between 5th Ave. and
Union Sq. W, Union Square ☎ 212/647–
1515 ⊕ www.tocquevillerestaurant.com
☺ No lunch Sun., Mon. Ⓜ 4, 5, 6, L, N, Q,
R, W to 14th St.–Union Sq.

Union Square Cafe

$$$ | AMERICAN | This popular New York
culinary institution, in its new location
since 2016, is still firing on all burners,
serving unpretentious yet impressive,
well-executed fare. Since 1985, noted
restaurateur Danny Meyer's American
restaurant has steadily received acclaim,
and the tradition continues in this elegant
two-floor spot a few blocks north of
Union Square. **Known for:** see-and-be-
seen atmosphere; superior burger;
excellent, attentive service. Ⓢ Average
main: $30 ⊠ 101 E. 19 St., at Park Ave. S,
Union Square ☎ 212/243–4020 ⊕ www.
unionsquarecafe.com Ⓜ 4, 5, 6, L, N, Q,
R, W to 14th St.–Union Sq.

🛏 Hotels

★ Hyatt Union Square New York

$$ | HOTEL | Experiencing a bit of "real"
New York (and getting away from
Midtown) is easy at this hip Hyatt with
a prime location just south of Union
Square, near New York University and
at the hub of major subway lines. **Pros:**
convenient and vibrant location; buzzy
dining and drinking outlets in the lobby;
welcoming staff. **Cons:** busy neighborhood means some street noise; some
standard rooms are small; high-traffic
area. Ⓢ Rooms from: $399 ⊠ 134 4th
Ave., between 12th and 13th Sts., Union
Square ☎ 212/253–1234 ⊕ www.hyatt.
com ⇱ 178 rooms ⎮◎⎮ No meals Ⓜ 4, 5, 6,
L, N, Q, R, W to 14th St.–Union Sq.

W New York Union Square

$$ | HOTEL | The W chain's iconic New York
City property continues to attract a mix
of trendsetters and tourists, thanks to its
downtown location and funky reputation.
Pros: landmark building in fashionable
location; great lobby and restaurant;
24-hour room service. **Cons:** room decor
doesn't live up to the hype; some stays
do not include free Wi-Fi; small gym.
Ⓢ Rooms from: $325 ⊠ 201 Park Ave.
S, at 17th St., Union Square ☎ 212/253–
9119 ⊕ www.wnewyorkunionsquare.com
⇱ 270 rooms ⎮◎⎮ No meals Ⓜ 4, 5, 6, L,
N, Q, R, W to 14th St.–Union Sq.

Nightlife

BARS
Rye House

BARS/PUBS | A welcoming bar with slick cocktails and a clever take on comfort food, the Rye House beckons just steps from the chain-store overload of Union Square. Whether you're in the mood for some white-truffle popcorn or want a burger to go with a well-crafted cocktail, this place is a welcome respite from the hustle and bustle. ⊠ *11 W. 17th St., between Broadway and 5th Ave., Union Square* ☎ *212/255–7260* ⊕ *www. ryehousenyc.com* Ⓜ *4, 5, 6, L, N, Q, R, W to 14th St.–Union Sq.*

⬤ Shopping

The several blocks around Union Square and along 5th Avenue between 14th Street and 23 Street have large retail chains like J.Crew, Lululemon, and Anthropologie, as well as some great independent shops. Union Square itself is home to the city's best greenmarket, as well as a holiday market leading up to Christmas.

BEAUTY
Fresh

PERFUME/COSMETICS | Long a beauty favorite, with ingredients that are good enough to eat (think brown sugar, soy, and black tea), this Fresh location has an apothecary-inspired look, with beautifully packaged soaps displayed like pastries in a glass case. Gather around the giant enamel sink to try out soaps and other products. ⊠ *872 Broadway, at 18th St., Union Square* ☎ *212/477–1100* ⊕ *www. fresh.com* Ⓜ *4, 5, 6, L, N, Q, R, W to 14th St.–Union Sq.*

BOOKS AND STATIONERY
★ Strand

BOOKS/STATIONERY | Opened in 1927 and still run by the same family, this monstrous book emporium—home to 2 million volumes, or "18 Miles of Books"—is a symbol of a bygone era, a mecca for serious bibliophiles, and a local institution. The stock includes new and secondhand books, plus thousands of collector's items and merchandise. A separate rare-book room is on the third floor (it closes at 6:15 daily). The basement has discounted, barely touched review copies of new books, organized by author. If you're looking for souvenirs, visit the New York section of the bookstore for New York–centric literature as well as T-shirts and totes. Check the Strand's events calendar for readings. ⊠ *828 Broadway, at 12th St., Union Square* ☎ *212/473–1452* ⊕ *www. strandbooks.com* Ⓜ *4, 5, 6, L, N, Q, R, W to 14th St.–Union Sq.*

CLOTHING
Beacon's Closet

CLOTHING | A simple space, the Manhattan outpost of this long-standing Brooklyn-based icon has a wide selection of gently used modern and vintage clothes. Comb through the racks and you might find pieces from Christian Dior, Marc Jacobs, or AllSaints, as well as stylish items from under-the-radar labels. ⊠ *10 W. 13th St., between 5th and 6th Aves., Union Square* ☎ *917/261–4863* ⊕ *www. beaconscloset.com* Ⓜ *4, 5, 6, L, N, Q, R, W to 14th St.–Union Sq.*

★ Journelle

CLOTHING | This chic New York–based boutique was started by two women who believed that sexy, pretty lingerie should be everyday wear—and comfortable, too. The staff are approachable and helpful. There are now a handful of stores around the city, including in SoHo and on the Upper East Side. ⊠ *14 E. 17th St., between Broadway and 5th Ave., Union Square* ☎ *212/255–7800* ⊕ *www. journelle.com* Ⓜ *4, 5, 6, L, N, Q, R, W to 14th St.–Union Sq.*

FOOD AND WINE
Union Square Wine & Spirits
WINE/SPIRITS | Well-stocked, with attentive sales people and frequent tastings, this wine shop is strategically placed near lots of public transport, though it's not a bargain. ⊠ *140 4th Ave., at 13th St., Union Square* ☎ *212/675–8100* ⊕ *www. unionsquarewines.com* Ⓜ *4, 5, 6, L, N, Q, R, W to 14th St.–Union Sq.*

HOME DECOR
★ ABC Carpet & Home
HOUSEHOLD ITEMS/FURNITURE | If you love eclectic luxury home goods from around the world, this will be your wonderland. Spread over six floors is a superb selection of rugs, antiques, textiles, furniture, and bedding, including sleek sofas and Balinese daybeds. The ground floor is a chic marketplace of antique stemware, ceramic tableware, fine jewelry, and wellness products, while the basement level stocks luxurious items for the bedroom and bathroom. Ascend to higher floors for covetable furniture. There are no less than three in-house restaurants from Jean-Georges Vongerichten, which are destinations in their own right. ⊠ *888 Broadway, at 19th St., Union Square* ☎ *212/473–3000* ⊕ *www.abchome.com* Ⓜ *4, 5, 6, L, N, Q, R, W to 14th St.–Union Sq.*

JEWELRY AND ACCESSORIES
Beads of Paradise
JEWELRY/ACCESSORIES | At what is not your ordinary bead store, the baubles are sourced from around the world. Shoppers can choose silver from Bali and Mexico and ancient glass beads from China, along with semiprecious stones. The store also has a wide range of other trinkets from around the world, including Buddha figurines from Thailand, Madonna candles from Mexico, and Ganesha-printed hangings from India. ⊠ *16 E. 17th St., between 5th Ave. and Broadway, Union Square* ☎ *212/620–0642* ⊕ *www.beadsofparadisenyc.com* Ⓜ *4, 5, 6, L, N, Q, R, W to 14th St.–Union Sq.*

SPORTING GOODS
Paragon Sports
SPORTING GOODS | Three floors stocked with brand-name exercise wear and all kinds of accessories, plus a super-knowledgeable staff working in the shoe department who give advice on what kind of running shoes are right for you, make this a go-to for New Yorkers, whatever their sport. In-store offerings focus on the season, which means lots of swimwear in summer and ski goods in winter, but there's always plenty of running gear. ⊠ *867 Broadway, at 18th St., Union Square* ☎ *212/255–8889* ⊕ *www. paragonsports.com* Ⓜ *4, 5, 6, L, N, Q, R, W to 14th St.–Union Sq.*

TOYS
Kidding Around
TOYS | FAMILY | This independent shop is piled high with old-fashioned wooden toys, sturdy musical instruments, classic kids' books, and plenty of arts-and-crafts materials. ⊠ *60 W. 15th St., between 5th and 6th Aves., Union Square* ☎ *212/645–6337* ⊕ *www.kiddingaroundtoys.com* Ⓜ *F, M to 14th St.; L to 6th Ave.; 4, 5, 6, L, N, Q, R, W to 14th St.–Union Sq.*

Flatiron District

The Flatiron District—anchored by Madison Square Park to the north and Union Square to the south—is one of the city's busiest neighborhoods, particularly along 5th Avenue and Park Avenue South. Once known as Ladies' Mile because of the fashionable row of department stores where women routinely shopped, the area is still a favorite for lady-spotting because of the number of modeling agencies and photography studios here. Lovely Madison Square Park, a pleasant green space hemmed in by some of the neighborhood's most notable architecture—from the triangular Flatiron Building to the dazzling, gold-pyramid-topped New York Life Insurance Building to the

The wedge-shape Flatiron Building got its nickname because of its resemblance to the shape of a clothes iron. Its original name was the Fuller Building.

Metropolitan Life Insurance Tower with its elegant clock face—is the best place to savor the view. Sit and admire the scene with a burger and shake from the park's always-busy Shake Shack, or takeout from the mother (or "mamma mia") of all Italian markets, Eataly, across the street from the west side of the park.

⊙ Sights

Appellate Division Courthouse

GOVERNMENT BUILDING | Figures representing Wisdom and Force flank the main portal of this imposing Beaux Arts courthouse, built in 1899. The structure's purpose coincides with artistic symbolism, and there are statues of great lawmakers, including Moses, Justinian, and Confucius, lining the roof balustrade. In total, sculptures by 16 artists adorn the ornate building, a showcase of themes relating to the law. A branch of the New York State Supreme Court, this court is one of the most important appellate

courts in the country: it hears more than 3,000 appeals and 6,000 motions a year, and also admits approximately 3,000 new attorneys to the bar each year. Inside the courtroom is a stunning stained-glass dome set into a gilt ceiling. The main hall and the courtroom are open to visitors weekdays from 9 to 5. All sessions, which are generally held Tuesday to Thursday at 2 pm, are open to the public (call the main number ahead of time to be sure court is in session, or check the calendar on the website). ✉ *27 Madison Ave., entrance on 25th St., Flatiron District* ☎ *212/340-0422* ⊕ *www. courts.state.ny.us/courts/ad1* ⊗ *Closed weekends* Ⓜ *6, N, R, W to 23rd St.*

Flatiron Building

BUILDING | When completed in 1902, the oddly shaped Fuller Building, as it was originally known, caused a sensation. Architect Daniel Burnham made ingenious use of the triangular wedge of land at 23rd Street, 5th Avenue, and Broadway, employing a revolutionary steel frame that allowed for the building's 22-story, 286-foot height. Covered with a facade of limestone and white terra-cotta in the Italian Renaissance style, the building's shape resembled a clothing iron, hence its nickname. When it became apparent that the building generated strong winds, gawkers would loiter at 23rd Street hoping to catch sight of ladies' billowing skirts. Local traffic cops had to shoo away the male peepers—one purported origin of the phrase "23 skidoo." There is a small display of historic building and area photos in the lobby, but otherwise you have to settle for appreciating this building from the outside. ⊠ *175 5th Ave., bordered by 22nd and 23rd Sts., 5th Ave., and Broadway, Flatiron District* Ⓜ *N, R, W to 23rd St.*

Madison Square Park

CITY PARK | FAMILY | The benches of this elegant tree-filled park afford great views of some of the city's oldest and most charming skyscrapers—the Flatiron Building, the Metropolitan Life Insurance Tower, the gold-crowned New York Life Insurance Building, and even (to the north) the Empire State Building—and serve as a perfect vantage point for people-, pigeon-, and dog-watching. Add free Wi-Fi, Shake Shack, temporary art exhibits, and free summer and fall concerts, and you realize that a bench here is certainly a special place to be.

New York City's first baseball games were played in this 7-acre park in 1845. On the north end of the park, an 1881 statue by Augustus Saint-Gaudens memorializes Civil War naval hero Admiral David Farragut. An 1876 statue of Secretary of State William Henry Seward (the Seward of the term "Seward's Folly," coined when the United States purchased Alaska from the Russian Empire in 1867) sits in the park's southwest corner, though it's rumored that the sculptor placed a reproduction of the statesman's head on a statue of Abraham Lincoln's

body. Madison Square Eats (⊕ *www. madisonsquarepark.org/mad-sq-eats)* is a popular monthlong food market that happens twice a year (spring and fall), across the street. ⊠ *From 23rd to 26th St., between 5th and Madison Aves., Flatiron District* ☎ *212/520–7600* ⊕ *www. madisonsquarepark.org* Ⓜ *N, R, W to 23rd St.*

Metropolitan Life Insurance Company Tower

BUILDING | In 1909, with the addition of the 700-foot tower resembling the campanile of St. Mark's in Venice, this 1893 building became the world's tallest; it was surpassed in height in 1912 (when the Woolworth Building was completed). The building was stripped of much of its classical detail during renovations in the early 1960s but remains a prominent feature of the Midtown skyline. The clock's four faces are each three stories high, and their minute hands weigh half a ton each. If the view from the street doesn't quite cut it, you can reserve a room in the skyline itself: Marriott International and Ian Schrager now operate a luxury hotel, the New York EDITION, in the clock-tower portion of the building. ⊠ *1 Madison Ave., between 23rd and 24th Sts., Flatiron District* Ⓜ *6, N, R, W to 23rd St.*

Museum of Sex

MUSEUM | Ponder the profound history and cultural significance of sex at this 14,000-square-foot museum while staring at vintage pornographic photos, S&M paraphernalia, antimasturbation devices from the 1800s, explicit film clips, vintage condom tins, and a collection of artwork. The Spotlight on the Permanent Collection gallery features revolving artifacts and ephemera, as well as a "Jump for Joy" bounce house (of inflated breasts) that was originally part of an exhibition called *Funland: Pleasures & Perils of the Erotic Fairground.* Other exhibits have probed such topics as desire on the Internet and the sex lives of animals. The subject matter is given serious curatorial treatment, though the gift shop is full of fun sexual kitsch. Only patrons over 18 are admitted. ✉ *233 5th Ave., at 27th St., Flatiron District* ☎ *212/689–6337* 🌐 *www.museumofsex.com* 🎟 *$20.50 ($17.50 before 1 pm weekdays)* [M] *N, R, W to 28th St.*

National Museum of Mathematics (*MoMath*)
MUSEUM | FAMILY | There's no exact formula to get kids excited about math, but the sleek two-floor National Museum of Mathematics (MoMath)—the only cultural institution devoted to math in all of North America—comes close to finding the perfect fun-to-math ratio. Kids can ride square-wheel trikes, create human fractal trees, build virtual 3-D geometric shapes (which can be printed out on a 3-D printer for a fee), use lasers to explore cross sections of objects, solve dozens of puzzles, and generally bend their minds. The popular Robot Swarm exhibition allows kids to explore swarm robotics and interact with two dozen small (Roomba-like) glowing robots, using simple math rules. Exhibits are best suited to kids aged six and up, but preschoolers can still enjoy many interactive exhibits like the Math Square, a light-up floor programmed with math games, simulations, and patterns. **■ TIP→ The museum closes at 2:30 pm the first Wednesday of every month.** ✉ *11 E. 26th St., between 5th and Madison Aves., Flatiron District* ☎ *212/542–0566* 🌐 *www.momath.org* 🎟 *$17* [M] *N, R, W to 28th St.*

🍴 Restaurants

The popular Union Square Greenmarket has done wonders for the dining landscape in the area. Chefs, wanting to be close to the green bounty, have opened up restaurants nearby, particularly in the Flatiron District.

ABC Kitchen
$$$ | AMERICAN | Much more than a shopping break, Jean-Georges Vongerichten's popular restaurant, inside posh housewares emporium ABC Carpet and Home, is like a love letter to greenmarket cuisine. Underneath the exposed concrete beams, a chic crowd devours fresh, flavorful appetizers like the roast carrot and avocado salad or pretzel-dusted calamari, and winning entrées that include pizzas, pastas, and hearty mains. **Known for:** vegetable-forward dishes; healthy power lunches; organic ingredients. [$] *Average main: $31* ✉ *35 E. 18th St., between Broadway and Park Ave. S, Flatiron District* ☎ *212/475–5829* 🌐 *www.abckitchennyc.com* [M] *4, 5, 6, L, N, Q, R, W to 14th St.–Union Sq.*

Aldea
$$$ | PORTUGUESE | Bouley alumnus George Mendes's popular restaurant relies on his Portuguese heritage as inspiration, which he elevates to new heights in this sleek space. Tasting menus allow diners to fully explore the chef's sophisticated cooking techniques and flavors, but it's also possible to order à la carte. Although there are no bad seats, watching Mendes work in his spotless tiled kitchen from one of the seats at the chef's counter in the back is undeniably exciting. **Known for:** chic space and clientele; sea-salted cod; seats at chef's counter. [$] *Average main: $34* ✉ *31 W. 17th St., between 5th and 6th Aves., Flatiron District* ☎ *212/675–7223* 🌐 *www.aldearestaurant.com* 🕒 *Closed Sun. No lunch* [M] *4, 5, 6, L, N, Q, R, W to 14th St.–Union Sq.; F, M to 14th St.*

Boqueria
$$ | **SPANISH** | Perennially packed, this convivial tapas spot has leather banquettes lining the main room and a few seats at the bar, but if you want to make friends, opt for the communal table running down the center of the dining room—if you can get a seat. Fried quail eggs and chorizo on toasted bread are even better than they sound, and the mushroom and ham croquettes are a mainstay. **Known for:** reliable Spanish tapas in a fun atmosphere; communal table; gets very busy (but takes reservations). [$] *Average main: $20* ✉ *53 W. 19th St., between 5th and 6th Aves., Flatiron District* ☎ *212/255–4160* 🌐 *boqueriarestaurant.com* [M] *1 to 18th St.; F, M to 14th St.; L to 6th Ave.; N, R, W to 23rd St.*

The City Bakery
$ | **AMERICAN** | **FAMILY** | This self-service bakery-restaurant is a neighborhood mainstay, with legendary (and giant) cookies, addictive pretzel croissants, and a salad bar that, while pricey, includes impeccably fresh options like baked salmon, roasted vegetables, and soups. There are tables in the somewhat cramped loft space if downstairs is full, as it often is at mealtimes. **Known for:** good breakfast stop; oversize chocolate chip cookies; often lots of strollers and kids. [$] *Average main: $12* ✉ *3 W. 18th St., between 5th and 6th Aves., Flatiron District* ☎ *212/366–1414* 🌐 *thecitybakery.com* 🕑 *No dinner* [M] *4, 5, 6, L, N, Q, R, W to 14th St.–Union Sq.; F, M to 14th St.*

The Clocktower
$$$ | **BRITISH** | On the second floor of the New York EDITION Hotel, this Madison Square Park spot is helmed by British superchef Jason Atherton, who presides over a high-ceilinged, dark-hued dining room. Best described as elevated British tavern fare, the menu offers diners choices like the comforting oxtail-spiked mac 'n' cheese, a hearty pork chop, and butter-roasted Dover sole. **Known for:** clubby ambience; creative cocktails; sophisticated pub food. [$] *Average main: $33* ✉ *Metropolitan Life Insurance Co. Tower, 5 Madison Ave., 2nd fl., between 23rd and 24th Sts., Flatiron District* ☎ *212/413–4300* 🌐 *www.theclocktowernyc.com* [M] *N, R, W to 23rd St.*

★ **Cosme**
$$$ | **MEXICAN** | When Enrique Olvera, chef at Pujol, arguably Mexico's best restaurant, announced he was coming north of the border, New York foodies went loco. Olvera's haute touch to his native cuisine is magic and, coupled with the sleek design (soft lighting, minimalist decor), Cosme makes for a fine dining experience focused on small plates. **Known for:** highly creative Mexican fare; duck carnitas; corn tempura softshell crab. [$] *Average main: $32* ✉ *35 E. 21st St., between Park Ave. S and Broadway, Flatiron District* ☎ *212/913–9659* 🌐 *www.cosmenyc.com* [M] *6, N, R, W to 23rd St.*

Cote
$$$$ | **KOREAN BARBECUE** | This place has blown up the staid New York steak-house formula by infusing Korean twists: that shrimp cocktail may look classic, but just wait till the hot *gochujang* hits your palate. Along with the raw meats to be grilled at your table, kimchi and *banchan* (small plates of Korean treats) arrive, adding layers of taste to your steak dinner. **Known for:** chic but casual atmosphere; excellent bibimbap; Undercote, the downstairs bar. [$] *Average main: $45* ✉ *16 W. 22nd St., between 5th and 6th Aves., Flatiron District* ☎ *212/401–7986* 🌐 *www.cotenyc.com* 🕑 *No lunch* [M] *4, 6 to 23rd St.*

★ **Craft**
$$$$ | **MODERN AMERICAN** | At the flagship of *Top Chef* head judge Tom Colicchio's mini empire of excellent restaurants around the country, the top-notch seasonal fare is exceptionally prepared with little fuss. Expect a menu that hits a variety of high notes, from exuberantly fresh hamachi or braised octopus to

start, stylish salads, hearty but not over-powering pastas, and perfectly cooked mains. **Known for:** dazzling tasting menu; excellent service; sophisticated but welcoming. $ *Average main: $40* ✉ *43 E. 19th St., between Broadway and Park Ave. S, Flatiron District* ☏ *212/780–0880* ⊕ *www.craftrestaurant.com* ◷ *No lunch weekends* Ⓜ *4, 5, 6, L, N, Q, R, W to 14th St.–Union Sq.*

Dough Doughnuts

$ | BAKERY | FAMILY | There's a reason why these doughnuts in multilicious flavors have become a signature at so many cafés throughout Manhattan and Brook-lyn, and at this Manhattan outpost of the Bed-Stuy original, you can get them fresh out of the oven. The ever-popular (though odd sounding) hibiscus version looks gorgeous and has just the right amount of tart fruitiness to balance the sweet-ness of the dough; other favorites include passion fruit, salted chocolate, and cin-namon and sugar. **Known for:** surprising flavors; good coffee, too; this location has long tables to eat in. $ *Average main: $5* ✉ *14 W. 19th St., between 5th and 6th Aves., Flatiron District* ☏ *212/243–6844* ⊕ *www.doughdoughnuts.com* Ⓜ *N, R, W to 23rd St.*

Eataly NYC Flatiron

$$$ | ITALIAN | FAMILY | Both a bustling marketplace and a food hall, Eataly is a veritable temple to all things Italian. You can choose to graze at individual stands, sit down for a meal at one of several restaurants that each specialize in differ-ent aspects of Italian cuisine, or head upstairs to the covered, rooftop *birreria* that is open in all weather and serves hearty Austrian and German food as well as Italian specialties. **Known for:** madden-ing crowds; Italian foods from burrata to gelato; gourmet everything to eat in or take home, at a price. $ *Average main: $25* ✉ *200 5th Ave., at 23rd St., Flatiron District* ☏ *646/398–5100* ⊕ *www.eataly. com* Ⓜ *6, N, R, W to 23rd St.*

★ Eleven Madison Park

$$$$ | MODERN AMERICAN | Luxury, precision, and creativity are the driving forces at this internationally renowned prix-fixe restaurant in a refined high-ceilinged space. Swiss-born chef Daniel Humm oversees the kitchen, concocting unexpected, often whimsical, dishes that change often but have a solid grounding in locavore American tastes. **Known for:** ultimate special-occasion restaurant; shorter tasting menu at the bar; reserve several months ahead. $ *Average main: $225* ✉ *11 Madison Ave., at 24th St., Flatiron District* ☏ *212/889–0905* ⊕ *www. elevenmadisonpark.com* ◷ *No lunch Mon.–Thurs.* Ⓜ *6, N, R, W to 23rd St.*

Hill Country

$$ | BARBECUE | This enormous barbe-cue joint is perfect for big groups and carnivorous appetites. The beef-centric Texas-size menu features meaty ribs and exceptionally succulent slow-smoked brisket; check your diet at the door and go for the moist, fatty option. **Known for:** feel-good Texas-style space; tasty brisket, prime rib, and pulled pork; live music downstairs some nights. $ *Average main: $22* ✉ *30 W. 26th St., between Broadway and 6th Ave., Flatiron District* ☏ *212/255–4544* ⊕ *www.hillcountryny. com* Ⓜ *6, N, R, W to 28th St.; F, M to 23rd St.*

Ilili

$$ | MIDDLE EASTERN | Famed Washington, D.C., restaurateur and chef Philippe Massoud brings his culinary talents to New York City with this bi-level 400-seat eatery that showcases cuisine from his native Lebanon. The menu of innovative Middle Eastern fare includes a dizzying variety of shareable hot and cold meze, as well as mains that run the gamut from to lamb chops with zatar to chicken livers with pomegranate molasses to duck sha-warma with fig jam. **Known for:** creative Lebanese cuisine; small plates; house-baked pita. $ *Average main: $22* ✉ *236*

5th Ave., between 27th and 28th Sts., Flatiron District ☎ *212/683–2929* 🌐 *www.ililinyc.com* [M] *N, R, W to 28th St.*

Made Nice

$$ | **AMERICAN** | For fast, casual dining that delivers way above par, check out this simply decorated spot from the folks behind the stellar Eleven Madison Park. Everything about Made Nice was designed for those who don't have an hour or two to eat but want top-quality food: meals, such as as roasted chicken, curried cauliflower, or tuna niçoise, arrive at diners' tables within 10 minutes of ordering. **Known for:** fast-casual food from noted chef and restaurateur; breakfast sandwiches; milk-and-honey soft serve. [$] *Average main: $13* ✉ *8 W. 28th St., between 5th and 6th Aves., Flatiron District* 🌐 *www.madenicenyc.com* [M] *R, W to 28th St.*

★ The NoMad Restaurant

$$$ | **MODERN AMERICAN** | Named for the hotel, which itself is named for the up-and-coming neighborhood north of Madison Square Park, the NoMad is brought to you by Daniel Humm and Will Guidara, the masterminds behind much-lauded Eleven Madison Park. The atmosphere is a blend of lively and sophisticated (plush velvet chairs and drapes for the hip young crowd), and the food is similarly vibrant yet simple: seared scallops with pumpkin, suckling pig with pear confit and mustard. **Known for:** chic scene; whole roasted chicken for two; classy service. [$] *Average main: $35* ✉ *The NoMad Hotel, 1170 Broadway, at 28th St., Flatiron District* ☎ *347/472–5660* 🌐 *www.thenomadhotel.com* [M] *N, R, W to 28th St.*

★ Shake Shack

$ | **AMERICAN** | Although there are other locations of Danny Meyer's patties 'n' shakes joint around town (including Brooklyn), Madison Square Park is where it all began; there's no indoor seating—just outdoor lines, though you can check the "Shack Cam" from their website to gauge your wait. Fresh Angus beef burgers are ground daily, and for a burger on the go, they're decidedly tasty. **Known for:** top-quality ingredients; vegetarian and non-beef burger and hot dog options; lunchtime lines. [$] *Average main: $8* ✉ *Madison Square Park, near Madison Ave. and 23rd St., Flatiron District* ☎ *212/889–6600* 🌐 *www.shakeshack.com* [M] *6, N, R, W to 23rd St.*

Upland

$$$ | **ITALIAN** | This collaboration between prolific Philly-NYC restaurateur Stephen Starr and Il Buco chef Justin Smillie tastes as if California and Italy miraculously collided. Marrying organic and in-season ingredients with Italian recipes, Upland's standouts include a bucatini alla carbonara that could pass muster with discriminating eaters in the Eternal City or the City of Angels. **Known for:** California-inspired cuisine that New Yorkers can get behind; rustic, airy space; good wine list, with many options by the glass. [$] *Average main: $34* ✉ *345 Park Ave. S, between 25th and 26th Sts., Flatiron District* ☎ *212/686–1006* 🌐 *www.uplandnyc.com* [M] *6 to 28th St.*

Hotels

★ Ace Hotel New York

$$ | **HOTEL** | The Ace is not your ordinary boutique hotel; the lively lobby melds the look of an Ivy League library with the concept of a curiosity cabinet—taxidermy, mosaic tile floors, wooden bookcases, antique sofas—and the vibe is unstuffy and down-to-earth, making it a popular hangout for freelancers and creatives. **Pros:** in-house destination restaurants; supercool but friendly vibe; lobby bar scene. **Cons:** small rooms; caters to a young crowd; may be too sceney for some. [$] *Rooms from: $300* ✉ *20 W. 29th St., at Broadway, Flatiron District* ☎ *212/679–2222* 🌐 *www.acehotel.com/newyork* 🛏 *285 rooms* 🍴 *No meals* [M] *N, R, W to 28th St.*

Arlo NoMad

$ | HOTEL | Aimed at travelers who spend more time out and about than in their rooms, this microhotel opened in 2016 with an emphasis on stylish and functional social spaces, including *Top Chef* alum Dale Talde's restaurant, Massoni, and a rooftop bar with unbeatable views of the Empire State Building. **Pros:** rooms feature smart space-saving design; great restaurant and rooftop bar; fun events. **Cons:** tiny rooms; no in-room minibars; self-check-in isn't for everyone. *$ Rooms from: $220* ✉ *11 E. 31st St., Flatiron District* ☎ *212/806–7000* ⊕ *www.arlohotels.com* ⟿ *250 rooms* ⦿ *No meals* Ⓜ *6 to 33rd St; B, D, F, M, N, Q, R, W to 34th St.–Herald Sq.*

Hotel Giraffe by Library Hotel Collection

$$ | HOTEL | A consistent property with friendly service, large rooms, and lots of repeat customers (particularly business travelers), Hotel Giraffe pleases with nice extras such as a complimentary nightly wine-and-cheese reception. **Pros:** comfortable and friendly lobby to relax in; quiet vibe; nice extras like free breakfast and coffee all day. **Cons:** street noise near lower levels; location a bit off the beaten path; no gym on-site. *$ Rooms from: $449* ✉ *365 Park Ave. S, at 26th St., Flatiron District* ☎ *212/685–7700* ⊕ *www.hotelgiraffe.com* ⟿ *72 rooms* ⦿ *Free Breakfast* Ⓜ *6 to 28th St.*

The James New York – NoMad

$$ | HOTEL | The NoMad outpost of the hip hotel brand that became a phenomenon in SoHo adds another superstylish option to the neighborhood. **Pros:** sleek version of midcentury design; comfy beds; hit Italian restaurant Scarpetta is downstairs. **Cons:** some rooms have views of brick walls; inconsistent service; street noise can be bothersome. *$ Rooms from: $425* ✉ *22 E. 29th St., at Madison Ave., Flatiron District* ☎ *212/532–4100* ⊕ *www.jameshotels.com/new york/nomad* ⟿ *344 rooms* ⦿ *No meals* Ⓜ *6, N, R, W to 28th St.*

Life Hotel

$ | HOTEL | In the former headquarters of *Life* magazine, designed by legendary Beaux Arts architecture firm Carrère & Hastings, this boutique hotel channels the building's past with reclaimed wood paneling, a restaurant named after the magazine's onetime owner (Henry Luce), and a speakeasy-type bar where staffers imbibed during Prohibition. **Pros:** historic building with lots of character; great restaurant and bar; some suites have great Empire State Building views. **Cons:** some rooms are tiny and lack views; no real lobby (street entrance opens onto the restaurant); neighborhood not the most charming. *$ Rooms from: $250* ✉ *19 W. 31st St., between 5th Ave. and Broadway, Flatiron District* ☎ *212/615–9900* ⊕ *www.lifehotel.com* ⟿ *98 rooms* ⦿ *No meals* Ⓜ *B, D, F, M, N, Q, R, W to 34th St.–Herald Sq.*

MADE Hotel

$$ | HOTEL | You'll feel like you made the right choice with a stay at MADE, which takes everything people love about the designer boutique hotel trend (hip design, rooftop bar, buzzy restaurant) and doubles down on the luxury and comfort. **Pros:** cool design; great (seasonal) rooftop bar and restaurant; friendly staff. **Cons:** little storage space; scant in-room amenities (no fridge or iron); some rooms have platform beds that can be hazardous if you get up at night. *$ Rooms from: $395* ✉ *44 W. 29th St., between Broadway and 6th Ave., Flatiron District* ☎ *212/213–4429* ⊕ *www.madehotels.com* ⟿ *108 rooms* ⦿ *No meals* Ⓜ *N, R, W to 28th St.*

★ The New York EDITION

$$ | HOTEL | The landmarked clock tower in the 1909 Metropolitan Life building overlooks Madison Square Park and is also now an übersleek hotel masterminded by renowned hotelier Ian Schrager, with neutral-tone rooms, a luxurious lobby bar, and a highly regarded restaurant by British chef Jason Atheron. **Pros:** on-site

spa; classy atmosphere; upscale restaurant options. **Cons:** decor a bit bland; neighborhood a bit sedate; windowless gym. $ *Rooms from: $400* ⊠ *5 Madison Ave., at 24th St., Flatiron District* ☎ *212/413–4200* ⊕ *www.editionhotels.com/new-york* ⇨ *273 rooms* ❍ *No meals* Ⓜ *N, R, W to 23rd St.*

★ The NoMad Hotel

$$$ | HOTEL | Named for the rapidly emerging "North of Madison" (as in, Madison Square Park) neighborhood in which it's located, this upscale-bohemian property features a gorgeous design by Jacques Garcia, a restaurant by award-winning chef Daniel Humm of Eleven Madison Park fame, and a destination cocktail bar. **Pros:** solicitous service; premier on-site dining and drinking; central location. **Cons:** some rooms have exposed bathtubs that lack privacy; luxury experiences at luxury prices; the bar gets crowded. $ *Rooms from: $550* ⊠ *1170 Broadway, at 28th St., Flatiron District* ☎ *212/796–1500* ⊕ *www.thenomadhotel.com* ⇨ *168 rooms* ❍ *No meals* Ⓜ *N, R, W to 28th St.*

Park South Hotel

$ | HOTEL | In a beautifully transformed 1906 office building, this cozy-chic contemporary hotel is a great vacation base: convenient to getting around but with plenty of on-site appeal. **Pros:** fantastic restaurants and bars; comfortable lobby; good value. **Cons:** some noisy rooms; small rooms and bathrooms; neighborhood may be too quiet for some. $ *Rooms from: $189* ⊠ *124 E. 28th St., between Lexington and Park Aves., Flatiron District* ☎ *212/448–0888* ⊕ *www.parksouthhotel.com* ⇨ *131 rooms* ❍ *No meals* Ⓜ *6 to 28th St.*

The Redbury New York

$$ | HOTEL | Convenient to the action without being smack in the middle of it, the bohemian-chic Redbury is a stylish hotel with three Roman-inspired dining venues by acclaimed restaurateur Danny Meyer, including the pizzeria Marta (reserve

ahead) and wine bar Vini e Fritti. **Pros:** trendy but not over-the-top; excellent dining and drinking venues; good value. **Cons:** sceney restaurant means the lobby can be loud and crowded; lower floors lack views and can feel a bit basement-y; neighborhood rather staid. $ *Rooms from: $325* ⊠ *29 E. 29th St., between Park and Madison Aves., Flatiron District* ☎ *212/689–1900* ⊕ *www.theredbury.com/newyork* ⇨ *257 rooms* ❍ *No meals* Ⓜ *6 to 28th St.*

The Roger

$ | HOTEL | A colorful choice in a rather plain neighborhood, the Roger has a following among repeat visitors who appreciate its local vibe, including photos of NYC. **Pros:** colorful room decor; friendly service; good value. **Cons:** no room service; tiny bathrooms; no free in-room coffee or tea. $ *Rooms from: $191* ⊠ *131 Madison Ave., at 31st St., Flatiron District* ☎ *212/448–7000* ⊕ *www.therogernewyork.com* ⇨ *192 rooms* ❍ *No meals* Ⓜ *6 to 33rd St.*

⊕ Nightlife

BARS

★ The NoMad Bar

BARS/PUBS | A dark, sultry space from the team behind the NoMad Hotel, this bi-level bar impresses with its inviting leather banquettes, extensive golden-lit bar, and tempting list of craft cocktails. There's food, too, which leans toward upscale classics, such as chicken potpie with foie gras and bacon-wrapped hot dogs with black truffle. ⊠ *1170 Broadway, at 28th St., Flatiron District* ☎ *212/796–1500* ⊕ *www.thenomadhotel.com* Ⓜ *6, N, R, W to 28th St.*

Oscar Wilde

BARS/PUBS | If the life-size statue of Oscar Wilde out front doesn't catch your eye, the flamboyant interior surely will. Step inside to behold Manhattan's longest bar (at 118½ feet) and one of the city's most visually striking establishments, where every inch seems occupied by art and objects that blend busy Victorian and baroque styles, colors, and materials—from antique clocks and stained glass to a giant carved-marble fireplace (and Wilde quotes). The building was once home to the 1920s Prohibition Enforcement HQ, but now the bar serves expertly concocted, authentic Prohibition- and Victorian-era tipples. A relatively basic food menu is available, too. ⊠ *45 W. 27th St., between Broadway and 6th Ave., Flatiron District* ☎ *212/213–3066* ⊕ *www.oscarwildenyc.com* Ⓜ *N, R, W to 28th St.*

★ **Raines Law Room**

BARS/PUBS | There's no phone number or big sign for this speakeasy; just ring the bell to enter. Wood-burning fireplaces, deep banquettes, and curtains for privacy all contribute to the intimate vibe—perfect for a date or small group gathering. The little candlelit garden out back is lovely, and put to use: herbs grown here are used in the carefully crafted cocktails. ⊠ *48 W. 17th St., between 5th and 6th Aves., Flatiron District* ⊕ *www.raineslawroom.com* Ⓜ *F, M to 14th St.; 4, 5, 6, L, N, Q, R, W to 14th St.–Union Sq.*

🛍 Shopping

The Flatiron District, north of Union Square, stretches from about 17th Street up to 29th Street, and between 6th Avenue and Lexington. This is one of the buzziest areas in New York, brimming with both large and small stores. Come here if you want to shop the big chains minus the Midtown tourist crowds.

CAMERAS AND ELECTRONICS
Sony Square NYC

CAMERAS/ELECTRONICS | On the ground floor of Sony headquarters, this sprawling space is more a showroom of themed, rotating installations to showcase the latest Sony electronics than it is a store. Take new Playstation games for a spin, experience the latest VR products, preview unreleased products, and even borrow top-of-the-line cameras and lenses to test around the city. The space also hosts events with celebrities and industry experts. ⊠ *25 Madison Ave., at 25th St., Flatiron District* ☎ *212/833–8800* ⊕ *www.sony.com/square-nyc* Ⓜ *6, N, R, W to 23rd St.*

CHILDREN'S CLOTHING
Space Kiddets

CLOTHING | **FAMILY** | The funky (Elvis-print rompers, CBGB onesies) mixes with the old-school (retro cowboy-print pants, brightly colored clogs, Bruce Lee T-shirts) and the high-end (Lili Gaufrette, Kenzo, Boo Foo Woo from Japan) at this casual, trendsetting store for kids. ⊠ *26 E. 22nd St., between Broadway and Park Ave., Flatiron District* ☎ *212/420–9878* ⊕ *www.spacekiddets.com* Ⓜ *6, N, R, W to 23rd St.*

CLOTHING
Anthropologie

CLOTHING | This popular women's clothing and home accessories chain epitomizes bohemian chic. Stock up on flowing dresses, floral-print blouses, and ruffled skirts, and find pastel- and jewel-tone bedspreads and dishware. Don't miss the collection of luxe skin-care and beauty products. ⊠ *85 5th Ave., at 16th St., Flatiron District* ☎ *212/627–5885* ⊕ *www.anthropologie.com* Ⓜ *4, 5, 6, L, N, Q, R, W to 14th St.–Union Sq.*

Madewell

CLOTHING | A J.Crew spinoff, Madewell is ideal for casual women's staples like jeans, T-shirts, and sweaters with a vintage look. The two-story Manhattan flagship has a quirky, homespun design. They have a monogram machine so you can personalize your leather purchases. ⊠ *115 5th Ave., at 19th St., Flatiron District* ☎ *212/228–5172* ⊕ *www.madewell.com* Ⓜ *4, 5, 6, L, N, Q, R, W to 14th St.–Union Sq.*

Holiday Markets

Between Thanksgiving and Christmas, holiday markets—rows of wooden stalls, many with red-and-white-stripe awnings—spring up around town. The gifts and goods vary from year to year, but there are some perennial offerings: colorful handmade knitwear and jewelry; fragrant soaps, candles, and lotions with hand-lettered labels; glittery Christmas ornaments of every stripe; and New York–themed gift items.

While the holiday market in Grand Central Terminal's Vanderbilt Hall is indoors, most vendors set up outside. There's one every year at Columbus Circle, near the southwest entrance to Central Park, and another at Bryant Park, behind the New York City Public Library. The largest and most popular, however, is at the south end of Union Square, where you can go from the greenmarket to the stalls, just like the downtowners who meet in the afternoon or after work to look for unique or last-minute gifts.

HOME DECOR

★ Fishs Eddy

HOUSEHOLD ITEMS/FURNITURE | The dishes, china, and glassware for resale come from all walks of crockery life, including corporate dining rooms and failed restaurants, so you never know what you might find. Fishs Eddy also sells its own lines of dishes and kitchenware, which have both classic and whimsical looks. ■TIP→ The shop is a great place to pick up New York–themed gifts, such as mugs and trays. ✉ 889 Broadway, at 19th St., Flatiron District ☎ 212/420–9020 ⊕ www.fishseddy.com Ⓜ 4, 5, 6, L, N, Q, R, W to 14th St.–Union Sq.

Marimekko

HOUSEHOLD ITEMS/FURNITURE | If you love bright, cheerful patterns, make a beeline to the Marimekko flagship. This 4,000-square-foot store is primarily white, so the colorful merchandise pops. Everything from pot holders and shower curtains to coats and dresses is available here in the Finnish brand's bold signature prints. If you're feeling crafty, pick up a few yards of fabric to create something of your own. ✉ 200 5th Ave., between 23rd and 24th Sts., Flatiron District ☎ 212/843–9121 ⊕ www.marimekko.com Ⓜ 6, N, R, W to 23rd St.

WINE

Bottlerocket Wine & Spirit

WINE/SPIRITS | Fun and approachable, this shop puts a new spin on wine shopping. Vintages are organized by quirky factors like their compatibility with Chinese takeout and whom they'd best suit as gifts (ranging from "Third Date" to "The Boss"). ✉ 5 W. 19th St., between 5th and 6th Aves., Flatiron District ☎ 212/929–2323 ⊕ www.bottlerocket.com Ⓜ 4, 5, 6, L, N, Q, R, W to 14th St.–Union Sq.

Gramercy Park

The haste and hullabaloo of the city calms considerably in the residential neighborhood of Gramercy Park, named for its 1831 gated garden, an early example of the city's best creative urban planning. South of the park, running north to south from 20th Street to 14th Street, is Irving Place, a short street honoring Washington Irving, which also feels calm, green, exclusive; it has a combination of old and new eateries, stores, and architecture.

Sights

Gramercy Park

CITY PARK | You may not be able to enter this private park, but a look through the bars of the wrought-iron fence that enclose it is worth your time, as is a stroll around its perimeter. The beautifully planted 2-acre park, designed by developer Samuel B. Ruggles, dates from 1831, and is flanked by grand examples of early-19th-century architecture and permeated with the character of its many celebrated occupants.

When Ruggles bought the property, it was known as Krom Moerasje (little crooked swamp), named by the Dutch settlers. He drained the swamp and set aside 42 lots for a park to be accessible exclusively to those who bought the surrounding lots in his planned London-style residential square. In 1966 the New York City Landmarks Preservation Commission designated Gramercy Park a historic district. The park is still owned by residents of the buildings surrounding the square (who have keys), although neighbors can now buy visiting privileges. ■TIP→ **Alexander Calder's iconic, monumental outdoor sculpture** *Janey Waney* **(1969) is installed inside the park and can be viewed through the railings.** ⊠ *Lexington Ave. and 21st St., Gramercy* Ⓜ *4, 5, 6, L, N, Q, R, W to 14th St.–Union Sq.; 6 to 23rd St.*

Buildings of 👁 Gramercy Park

Notable Gramercy Park buildings include No. 15, a Gothic Revival brownstone with black granite trim designed by Calvert Vaux that is now home to the National Arts Club, founded in 1898. Next door at No. 16 Gramercy Park South lived the actor Edwin Booth, perhaps most famous for being the brother of Lincoln's assassin. In 1888 he turned his Gothic-trim home into the Players Club, a clubhouse for actors and theatrical types.

🍴 Restaurants

This leafy high-rent neighborhood, which has an old-world, old-money feel, is home to a few gems, tucked away down the long blocks of brownstones. Gramercy is a great place for a stroll before dinner.

BLT Prime

$$$$ | **STEAKHOUSE** | A masculine, lively space is the showcase for bold, appealing Franco-American cuisine. There are poultry, veal, and lamb dishes on the menu—from lemon-rosemary chicken to a lamb T-bone—but the steaks are always the main event, served with a choice of sauce (the béarnaise is perfection). **Known for:** 28-day dry-aged porterhouse; steaks of all kinds; clubby vibe. Ⓢ *Average main: $40* ⊠ *111 E. 22nd St., between Lexington and Park Aves., Gramercy* ☎ *212/995–8500* ⊕ *www.bltprime.com* ☾ *No lunch* Ⓜ *6, N, R, W to 23rd St.*

Casa Mono

$$ | **SPANISH** | Most of the delectable items on the menu at this sceney Iberian small-plates restaurant are made for sharing, but of particular note are all things seared *à la plancha* (grilled on a metal plate), including blistered peppers and garlic-kissed mushrooms. The best seats are at the Casa Mono counter overlooking the chef's open kitchen. **Known for:** high-quality, authentic Spanish tapas; adventurous cuts of meat; Bar Jamón annex around the corner. $ *Average main: $21* ✉ *52 Irving Pl., at 17th St., Gramercy* ☎ *212/253–2773* ⊕ *www.casamononyc.com* Ⓜ *4, 5, 6, L, N, Q, R, W to 14th St.–Union Sq.*

Gramercy Tavern

$$$$ | **AMERICAN** | Danny Meyer's perennially popular restaurant tops many a New Yorker's list of favorite dining spots. In front, the first-come, first-served tavern has a lighter menu along with great craft beers and cocktails, while the more formal dining room has seasonal prix-fixe American options as well. **Known for:** impeccable service; standout seasonal fare; high prices but hospitality is included. $ *Average main: $38* ✉ *42 E. 20th St., between Broadway and Park Ave. S, Gramercy* ☎ *212/477–0777* ⊕ *www.gramercytavern.com* Ⓜ *6, N, R, W to 23rd St.*

Maialino

$$$ | **ROMAN** | Named for its signature dish—suckling pig—the perpetually packed restaurant in the Gramercy Park Hotel is what it might look like if Manhattan and Rome collided: fashionable people eating in an Eternal City ambience, complete with wood-beam ceilings and framed photos on the walls. Try the excellent fried artichokes, spaghetti alla carbonara (made with *guanciale*, or pig cheek, just like in Rome), or any of the hearty roasted main courses. **Known for:** Roman fare in Gramercy; open from breakfast until late night; Bar Maialino, in front, is walk-in only. $ *Average main: $28* ✉ *2 Lexington Ave., at 21st St., Gramercy* ☎ *212/777–2410* ⊕ *www.maialinonyc.com* Ⓜ *6 to 23rd St.*

Nur

$$$ | **MIDDLE EASTERN** | Israeli celeb chef Meir Adoni covers a lot of ground here, serving up whatever is delicious from Morocco to Yemen and everywhere in between, in a tightly packed, low-ceiling space done in netural tones. Standouts include Palestinian tartare (raw beef sprinkled with favas and pine nuts) and main courses like black bass wading in a dashi-chickpea broth or ultratender grilled lamb loin. **Known for:** elevated, creative Middle Eastern dining; chic date atmosphere; Hills of Jerusalem dessert. $ *Average main: $35* ✉ *34 E. 20th St., between Broadway and Park Ave. S, Gramercy* ☎ *212/505–3420* ⊕ *www.nurnyc.com* ◷ *No lunch weekdays* Ⓜ *6 to 23rd St.*

🛏 Hotels

Carlton Arms Hotel

$ | **HOTEL** | Europeans and students know about the chipper, winning attitude of this friendly, no-frills hotel, where the themed rooms are painted by artists on a rotating basis. **Pros:** budget-friendly prices; friendly staff; quieter residential location. **Cons:** no elevator; many rooms have shared baths; no TVs or phones in the rooms. $ *Rooms from: $130* ✉ *160 E. 25th St., at 3rd Ave., Gramercy* ☎ *212/684–8337, 212/679–0680 for reservations* ⊕ *www.carltonarms.com* ⇗ *54 rooms* ◉ *No meals* Ⓜ *6 to 23rd St.*

★ Freehand New York

$ | **HOTEL** | The New York location of this hip hostel-hotel hybrid combines a chic, homey design, four restaurants and bars (including Middle Eastern spot Studio and an outpost of Miami's award-winning Broken Shaker on the roof), and accommodations including everything from rooms with bunk beds to a two-bedroom penthouse suite. **Pros:** destination dining and drinking; great value; fun, social vibe. **Cons:** rooms and suites are on the small side; no bathtubs in any rooms; could be too hip and busy for some. $ *Rooms* from: $132 ⊠ 23 Lexington Ave., between 23rd and 24th Sts., Gramercy ☎ 212/475–1920 ⊕ www.freehandhotels. com ⟿ 395 rooms ❙❍❙ No meals Ⓜ 6 to 23rd St.

★ Gramercy Park Hotel

$$$ | HOTEL | A completely over-the-top, bold design, an impressive art collection, and Danny Meyer's Roman trattoria Maialino make this luxury boutique property—and celebrity magnet—a quintessentially New York experience. **Pros:** trendy bar scene; opulent rooms; parkside location. **Cons:** inconsistent service; expensive bar; might be too sceney for some. Ⓢ Rooms from: $450 ⊠ 2 Lexington Ave., at Gramercy Park, Gramercy ☎ 212/920–3300 ⊕ www. gramercyparkhotel.com ⟿ 190 rooms ❙❍❙ No meals Ⓜ 6 to 23rd St.

★ The Inn at Irving Place

$$ | HOTEL | Fantasies of Old New York— Manhattan straight from the pages of Edith Wharton and Henry James, an era of genteel brick town houses and Tiffany lamps—spring to life at this discreet, romantic inn. **Pros:** romantic and charming; big rooms; excellent breakfast and tea service. **Cons:** rooms show some wear; some street noise; no elevator and lots of stairs. Ⓢ Rooms from: $445 ⊠ 56 Irving Pl., between 17th and 18th Sts., Gramercy ☎ 212/533–4600 ⊕ www. innatirving.com ⟿ 12 rooms ❙❍❙ Free Breakfast Ⓜ 4, 5, 6, L, N, Q, R, W to 14th St.–Union Sq.

The Marcel at Gramercy

$$ | HOTEL | The chic, affordable Marcel gives guests both style and substance in a prime location; for example, the small lobby feels a bit like a swanky nightclub but is still comfortable for lounging. **Pros:** outdoor patio has spectacular views; good value; great Gramercy location. **Cons:** elevators are slow; some rooms are tight on space; decor not to everyone's taste. Ⓢ Rooms from: $309 ⊠ 201 E. 24th St., Gramercy ☎ 212/696–3800

⊕ www.themarcelatgramercy.com ⟿ 136 rooms ❙❍❙ No meals Ⓜ 6 to 23rd St.

▼ Nightlife

BARS

Dear Irving

BARS/PUBS | This cocktail parlor invites guests inside with its name, the beginning of an imaginary love letter to Irving Place, on which the bar resides. Interiors themed for different eras are chic and refined, and just as at sister property Raines Law Room, there are private sections of tables and couches for intimate conversations. Reservations are recommended (make them online), but you can sometimes get a table if you just show up. ⊠ 55 Irving Pl., between 17th and 18th Sts., Gramercy ⊕ www. dearirving.com Ⓜ 4, 5, 6, L, N, Q, R, W to 14th St.–Union Sq.

Old Town Bar

BARS/PUBS | The proudly unpretentious bi-level Old Town is redolent of old New York, which makes sense since it's been around since 1892. The low-key atmosphere and pub-style grub make it a perennially popular spot. ⊠ 45 E. 10th St., between Broadway and Park Ave. S, Gramercy ☎ 212/529–6732 ⊕ www. oldtownbar.com Ⓜ 4, 5, 6, L, N, Q, R, W to 14th St.–Union Sq.

Pete's Tavern

BARS/PUBS | A historic landmark (where O. Henry was a loyal customer), this is one of the bars that claims—with its 1864 date—to be the oldest continuously operating watering hole in the city. Pete's has charm to spare, with its long wooden bar and cozy booths, where locals crowd in for a beer or a fantastic burger. When weather warms up, sidewalk tables with red-and-white-checkered tablecloths on scenic Irving Place are a neighborhood favorite. ⊠ 129 E. 18th St., at Irving Pl., Gramercy ☎ 212/473–7676 ⊕ www. petestavern.com Ⓜ 4, 5, 6, L, N, Q, R, W to 14th St.–Union Sq.

JAZZ VENUES
★ Jazz Standard

MUSIC CLUBS | The Standard's sizable underground room draws top names in the business, and as part of Danny Meyer's southern-food restaurant Blue Smoke, it's one of the few spots where you can get dry-rubbed ribs to go with your bebop. Bring the kids for the Jazz Standard Youth Orchestra concerts every Sunday afternoon. ⊠ *116 E. 27th St., between Park and Lexington Aves., Gramercy* ☎ *212/576–2232* ⊕ *www.jazzstandard.com* Ⓜ *6 to 28th St.*

LIVE MUSIC VENUES
★ Irving Plaza

MUSIC CLUBS | A relatively intimate venue that holds about 1,000 people on two levels, Irving Plaza is known for its packed lineup of both indie and more mainstream acts, though tickets can get a little pricey. The sound system is good and there are several bars. ⊠ *17 Irving Pl., at 15th St., Gramercy* ☎ *212/777–6817* ⊕ *www.irvingplaza.com* Ⓜ *4, 5, 6, L, N, Q, R, W to 14th St.–Union Sq.*

Chapter 9

MIDTOWN EAST AND MURRAY HILL

Updated by
Kelsy Chauvin

⊙ Sights	🍴 Restaurants	🛏 Hotels	🛍 Shopping	🍸 Nightlife
★★★★★	★★★★☆	★★★★★	★★★★★	★★☆☆☆

NEIGHBORHOOD SNAPSHOT

TOP EXPERIENCES

■ Standing in the center of Grand Central Terminal's main concourse and taking in the fiber-optic map of the constellations overhead

■ Strolling down 5th Avenue, where some of the world's top luxury brands have flagship stores—especially around the holidays, when store windows are dressed to impress

■ Enjoying panoramic views of the city at dusk from the top of the Empire State Building

■ Soaking in peace and serenity while ogling the neo-Gothic architecture, stained glass, and sculptures at iconic St. Patrick's Cathedral

GETTING HERE

To get to the east side of Midtown, take the 4, 5, 6, or 7 to Grand Central. The S, or Shuttle, travels back and forth between Grand Central and Times Square.

You can reach the Empire State Building via the B, D, F, M, N, Q, R, and W trains to 34th Street or the 6 to 33rd Street. The 6 also stops at 23rd and 28th Streets.

PLANNING YOUR TIME

The east side of Midtown is somewhat more laid-back than the west side, but there's still lots to keep you busy. Wherever you're headed, try to make sure you at least pass through Grand Central Terminal, one of New York's grandest architectural landmarks—it's a madhouse during rush hours but wonderfully slow on weekends, an ideal time to visit.

If you're planning to visit the Empire State Building when it's less crowded, aim for the morning or after sunset, when the city's evening lights are dazzling. Allow at least two hours for an observation-deck visit.

It's also worth making time for a quick trip out of the United States to visit the "international zone" of the United Nations; take a tour of the buildings and mail a postcard with a unique U.N. stamp.

QUICK BITES

■ **Grand Central Market.** The main level of Grand Central Terminal is home to this gourmet market, a cornucopia of food and beverage options, including Li-Lac Chocolates (Manhattan's oldest chocolatier), delicious Murray's Cheese, and rich coffee by Oren's Daily Roast. ⊠ *Grand Central Terminal east entrance, Lexington Ave. at W. 43 St., Midtown East* ⊕ *www. grandcentralterminal.com/ grand-central-market* Ⓜ *Subway: 4, 5, 6, 7, S to Grand Central–42nd St.*

■ **Little Collins.** This Australian import pays as much attention to what it puts on your plate—try the avocado and feta on toast—as what it pours in your coffee mug—try the flat white (a latte without foam). ⊠ *667 Lexington Ave., near 56th St., Midtown East* ⊕ *www. littlecollinsnyc.com* Ⓜ *Subway: 4, 5, 6 to 59th St.; N, Q, R to Lexington Ave./59th St.; E, M to Lexington Ave./53rd St.*

■ **Lucid Cafe.** A tiny coffee spot in Murray Hill has excellent coffee, espresso, and Belgian hot chocolate, as well as tasty pastries. ⊠ *311 Lexington Ave., at 38th St., Murray Hill* Ⓜ *Subway: 4, 5, 6, 7, S to Grand Central–42nd St.*

Fifth Avenue is Manhattan's dividing line, marking the division of east and west sides, but the avenue itself seems to connote so much of what the island's East Side is all about.

Midtown East is where some of the city's most iconic buildings are found, including the iconic Chrysler Building, Grand Central Terminal, and the mid-century United Nations and Ford Foundation building. It's a bustling business, hotel, and shopping area with residential areas on the periphery (and sometimes in scattered apartment buildings nestled among the office towers), including those in the picturesque Tudor City development, with Gothic-style apartment buildings surrounding a picturesque, treelined park, all overlooking the UN. The other major residential areas include Turtle Bay, in the east 50s between Lexington and 1st avenues, and Sutton Place, in the same area east of 1st Avenue.

Murray Hill is generally thought of as the area east of Fifth Avenue, from 34th Street to 23rd Street, and is predominately residential east of Park Avenue; however, the densely packed blocks between Fifth and Park Avenue South are lined with a mix of hotels, apartment buildings, and office buildings, giving it much the same feel as the rest of Midtown East. The area also has a couple of noteworthy tourist sights: the Empire State Building and the Morgan Library. And two sub-neighborhoods may be of particular interest to tourists who like good food. Lexington Avenue between 24th and 28th streets and the immediately surrounding cross-streets are affectionately known as "Curry Hill" for their large number of Indian restaurants. And Manhattan's Koreatown is centered on a dense stretch of restaurants and stores on 32nd Street between Madison and Broadway.

Midtown East

In terms of architecture, Midtown East has some of the city's most notable gems, including the stately Chrysler Building, considered an Art Deco triumph, and the bustling Beaux Arts masterpiece, Grand Central Terminal. At night the streets are relatively quiet, but the restaurants are filled with expense-account diners and well-heeled locals. Some of the most formal dining rooms and expensive meals in town can be found here. The blocks of 5th Avenue around 57th Street are also a designer label paradise, home to megabrand flagships such as Louis Vuitton and Chanel, and some of the world's most famous jewelry stores, including Tiffany, Van Cleef & Arpels, and Harry Winston. New York's famous department stores like Bloomingdale's and Saks Fifth Avenue have long anchored the upscale shopping scene.

◉ Sights

Chrysler Building
BUILDING | A monument to modernity and the mighty automotive industry, the former Chrysler headquarters wins many New Yorkers' vote for the city's most marvelous and beloved skyscraper

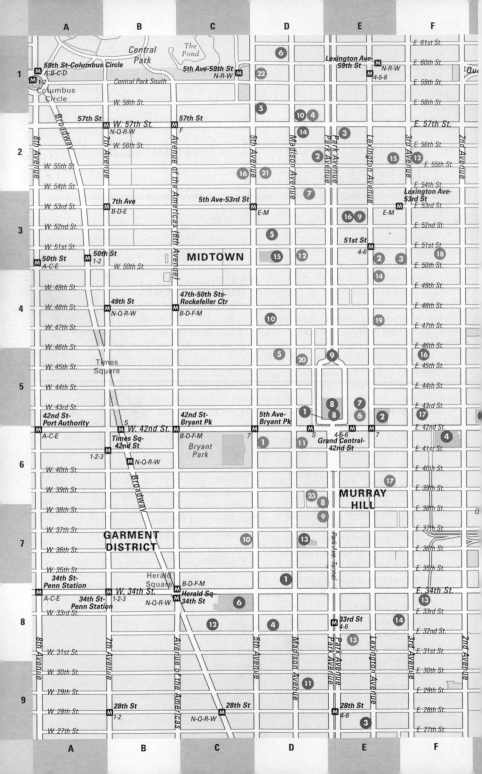

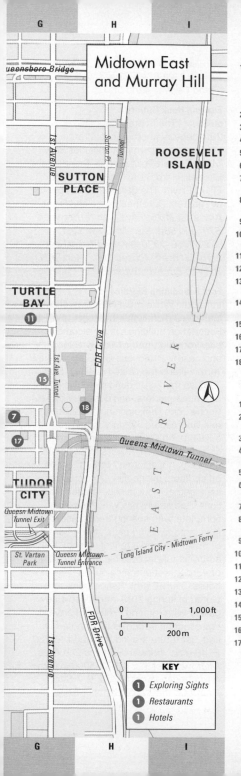

Sights ▼

1 B. Altman Building/New York Public Library—Science, Industry and Business Library (SIBL)..................... **D7**

2 Chrysler Building **E5**

3 Curry Hill **E9**

4 Daily News Building..... **F6**

5 Edwynn Houk Gallery .. **D1**

6 Empire State Building ... **C8**

7 Ford Foundation Building **G5**

8 Grand Central Terminal.................... **E5**

9 Helmsley Building **E5**

10 Hirschl & Adler Galleries **D2**

11 Japan Society........... **G4**

12 Koreatown................ **C8**

13 The Morgan Library & Museum...... **D7**

14 Pace Gallery (Midtown).................. **D2**

15 St. Patrick's Cathedral.. **D3**

16 Seagram Building........ **E3**

17 Tudor City **G6**

18 United Nations Headquarters **H5**

Restaurants ▼

1 Agern..................... **D5**

2 Aquavit and Aquavit Café **D2**

3 BLT Steak................. **E2**

4 Dons Bogam Wine Bar & BBQ........ **D8**

5 Fig & Olive **D3**

6 Fred's Madison Avenue........ **D1**

7 Grand Central Market... **E5**

8 Grand Central Oyster Bar & Restaurant........ **E5**

9 The Grill **E3**

10 Kurumazushi **D4**

11 Marta..................... **D9**

12 P.J. Clarke's.............. **F2**

13 Pio Pio.................... **F8**

14 2nd Ave Deli **E8**

15 Shun Lee Palace......... **E2**

16 Sparks Steak House..... **F5**

17 Sushi Yasuda **F5**

Hotels ▼

1 Andaz 5th Avenue **D6**

2 The Benjamin **E3**

3 Fifty Hotel & Suites by Affinia **F3**

4 Four Seasons Hotel New York **D2**

5 The Gotham Hotel NY .. **D5**

6 Grand Hyatt New York **E5**

7 Hotel Elysée by Library Hotel Collection **D3**

8 Iberostar 70 Park Avenue............. **D7**

9 The Kitano Hotel New York **D7**

10 The Langham, New York, Fifth Avenue........ **C7**

11 Library Hotel by Library Hotel Collection **D6**

12 Lotte New York Palace .. **D3**

13 The Marmara Park Avenue **E8**

14 The Maxwell New York City **E4**

15 Millennium Hilton New York One UN Plaza **G5**

16 The Peninsula New York **C2**

17 Pod 39.................... **E6**

18 Pod 51.................... **F3**

19 Roger Smith Hotel **E4**

20 The Roosevelt Hotel.... **D5**

21 The St. Regis New York **D2**

22 The Sherry-Netherland **D1**

23 The William.............. **D6**

Midtown East and Murray Hill

ROOSEVELT ISLAND

SUTTON PLACE

TURTLE BAY

TUDOR CITY

KEY

Exploring Sights

Restaurants

Hotels

(and the world's tallest for 40 days, until the Empire State Building stole the honor). Architect William Van Alen, who designed this 1930 Art Deco master-piece, incorporated car details into its form: American eagle gargoyles made of chromium nickel sprout from the 61st floor, resembling hood ornaments used on 1920s Chryslers; winged urns festooning the 31st floor reference the car's radiator caps. Most breathtaking is the pinnacle, with tiered crescents and spiked windows that radiate out like a magnificent steel sunburst. View it at sunset to catch the light gleaming off the tip. Even better, observe it at night, when its peak illuminates the sky. The inside is sadly off-limits, apart from the amazing time-capsule lobby replete with chrome "grillwork," intricately patterned wood elevator doors, marble walls and floors, and an enormous ceiling mural saluting transportation and human endeavor. ⊠ *405 Lexington Ave., at 42nd St., Midtown East* Ⓜ *4, 5, 6, 7, S to Grand Central–42nd St.*

Daily News Building (*The News Building*)
BUILDING | The landmark lobby of this Art Deco tower contains an illuminated 12-foot globe that revolves beneath a black glass dome. Around it, spreading across the floor like a giant compass and literally positioning New York at the center of the world, bronze lines indicate mileage to various international desti-nations. Movie fans may recognize the building as the offices of the fictional newspaper *The Daily Planet* in the origi-nal *Superman* movie. On the wall behind the globe you can check out a number of meteorological gauges, which read New York City's weather—especially fun on a windy day when the meters are whipping about. The *Daily News* hasn't called this building home since 1995; only the lobby is open to the public (but that's enough).
■TIP→ **The globe was last updated in 1967, so part of the fun here is seeing how our maps have changed; note Manchuria and East and West Germany.** ⊠ *220 E. 42nd St.,*

between 2nd and 3rd Aves., Midtown East ☎ *212/687–3733* Ⓜ *4, 5, 6, 7, S to Grand Central–42nd St.*

Edwynn Houk Gallery
MUSEUM | The impressive stable of 20th-century photographers repre-sented and shown here includes Sally Mann, Robert Polidori, Nick Brandt, Lalla Essaydi, Herb Ritts, Mona Kuhn, and Elliott Erwitt. The gallery also has prints by masters Dorothea Lange and Diane Arbus. ⊠ *745 5th Ave., 4th fl., between 57th and 58th Sts., Midtown East* ☎ *212/750–7070* ⊕ *www.houkgallery. com* ⊠ *Free* ⊙ *Closed Sun., Mon.* Ⓜ *N, R, W to 5th Ave./59th St.*

Ford Foundation Building
BUILDING | While most Midtown office lob-bies remain off-limits to visitors, the Ford Foundation building's is a welcome res-pite from high-traffic Midtown sidewalks and nearby attractions like Grand Central Terminal and the United Nations. Built in 1967 as the Ford Foundation's New York City headquarters, and designed by Kevin Roche John Dinkeloo and Associates, this landmarked 12-story transparent building of glass, granite, and Corten steel is one of Midtown's most notable buildings, thanks to its open, C-shape office floors overlooking an incredibly lush, secret—but public—garden. This light-filled atrium is a veritable oasis, complete with soaring trees, cascad-ing plants, walking paths, three tiers of plantings, and a reflecting pool. The atrium is fully accessible from the 42nd or 43rd Street entrance during business hours (8 am–6 pm). Renovations com-pleted in spring 2019 introduced a new gallery with rotating exhibits of artwork representing struggles for a more fair and just future around the world. ⊠ *320 E. 43rd St., between 1st and 2nd Aves., Midtown East* ☎ *212/573–5000* ⊕ *www. fordfoundation.org* Ⓜ *4, 5, 6, 7, S to Grand Central–42nd St.*

The restoration and cleaning of Grand Central in the late 1990s uncovered the elaborate astronomical design on the ceiling of the main concourse.

★ Grand Central Terminal

BUILDING | Grand Central is not only the world's largest (48 acres and 44 platforms) and the nation's busiest railway station, but also one of the world's most magnificent public spaces. The **main concourse** stands roughly 12 stories high and is modeled after an ancient Roman public bath. Overhead, a twinkling fiber-optic map of the constellations covers the ceiling. Of course, Grand Central still functions primarily as a railroad station, its majesty preserved in part by Jacqueline Kennedy Onassis's 1975 campaign to save it as a landmark. Underground, trains travel upstate and to Connecticut via the Metro-North commuter rail; the subway connects here as well.

To best admire Grand Central's exquisite Beaux Arts architecture, try to avoid rush hours, and head up one of the staircases at either end, where upscale restaurants occupy the balcony spaces. There you can survey the concourse and feel the terminal's dynamism. Then, if you can find it, head to the southwest corner to reach the **The Campbell** cocktail lounge. Located around and below the main concourse are fantastic shops and eateries—including the eponymous Grand Central Oyster Bar.

The **Municipal Art Society** (☎ 212/935–3960 ⊕ www.mas.org/tours) leads an official daily walking tour for $30 beginning in the main concourse at 12:30 (⊕ www.docentour.com/gct). Alternatively, rent a headset ($9) at GCT Tour windows and take a self-guided audio tour at your own pace (⊕ www.grandcentralterminal.com/tours). ✉ Main entrance, 42nd St. and Park Ave., Midtown East ☎ 212/935–3960 ⊕ www.grandcentral-terminal.com Ⓜ 4, 5, 6, 7, S to Grand Central–42nd St.

Helmsley Building

BUILDING | This Warren & Wetmore–designed 1929 landmark was intended to match neighboring Grand Central Terminal in bearing, and it succeeded, with a gold-and-copper roof topped with an enormous lantern and distinctive dual archways for traffic on Park Avenue.

Stores like Harry Winston go all out for their holiday displays come December.

The building's history gets quirky. When millionaire real-estate investor Harry Helmsley purchased the building in 1977, he changed its name from the New York Central Building to the New York General Building in order to save money by replacing only two letters in the facade (only later did he rename it after himself). In 2010, after a $100 million renovation, the Helmsley Building, no longer under Helmsley ownership (so technically 230 Park, or "the building formerly known as the Helmsley Building and informally still known as the Helmsley Building"), became the first prewar office tower to receive LEED Gold certification for energy efficiency. It remains a defining—and now "green," as opposed to gold—feature of one of the world's most lavish avenues. ⊠ 230 Park Ave., between 45th and 46th Sts., Midtown East ⊕ helmsleybuilding.com Ⓜ 4, 5, 6, 7, S to Grand Central–42nd St.

Hirschl & Adler Galleries
MUSEUM | Although this gallery has a selection of European works, it's best known for American paintings, prints, and decorative arts. The celebrated 19th- and 20th-century artists whose works are featured include Stuart Davis, Childe Hassam, and Suzy Frelinghuysen. Each year, the gallery presents up to a dozen special exhibits exploring historical themes of works culled from its collection. ⊠ 41 E. 57th St., 9th fl., at 5th Ave., Midtown West ☎ 212/535–8810 ⊕ www.hirschlandadler.com ⊠ Free ⏱ Closed Sun. Ⓜ N, Q, R, W to 5th Ave./59th St.

Japan Society
MUSEUM | The stylish, serene lobby of the Japan Society underwent a 2017 renovation by renowned artist Hiroshi Sugimoto and features interior gardens with large bonsai trees and Sugimoto sculptures, all complemented by a second-floor waterfall. The 1971 building itself is a city landmark thanks to its Japanese modernist design by architect Junzo Yoshimura, and its second-floor gallery exhibits works by well-known Japanese artists. Past shows have celebrated the work of contemporary masters including

Takashi Murakami, Yoko Ono, and Daido Moriyama. The society's annual performing arts season (September–June) shares works by established and emerging artists in dance, music, and theater. In July, the museum hosts an annual film festival, Japan Cuts, showcasing contemporary Japanese cinema. ⊠ *333 E. 47th St., between 1st and 2nd Aves., Midtown East* ☎ *212/832–1155* ⊕ *www. japansociety.org* 🎟 *Gallery $12* ⊘ *Gallery closed Mon.* Ⓜ *4, 5, 6, 7, S to Grand Central–42nd St.; E, M to Lexington Ave./53rd St.; 6 to 51st St.*

Pace Gallery (Midtown)

MUSEUM | This leading contemporary art gallery—with two outposts in Chelsea, one in London, and other international locations—focuses on such modern and contemporary artists as Kiki Smith, Julian Schnabel, Mark Rothko, James Turrell, and Tara Donovan. ⊠ *32 E. 57th St., 2nd fl., between Park and Madison Aves., Midtown East* ☎ *212/421–3292* ⊕ *www. thepacegallery.com* 🎟 *Free* ⊘ *Closed Sun., Mon.* Ⓜ *N, Q, R, W to 5th Ave./59th St.*

St. Patrick's Cathedral

RELIGIOUS SITE | This Gothic-style edifice is the largest Catholic cathedral in the United States, seating approximately 2,400 people, and marked by double spires rising 330 feet. "St. Pat's," as locals call it, provides a calm and quiet refuge in the heart of buzzy Midtown, despite the throngs of tourists (the cathedral receives more than 5.5 million visitors annually).

The church dates back to 1858–79, but it was beautifully restored thanks to an extensive $177 million rehabilitation project, completed in 2015. Highlights include the century-old organ in the choir gallery, with its 7,855 pipes; the famous rose window (considered stained-glass-artist Charles Connick's greatest work); and the ornately carved bronze double doors, each weighing 9,200 pounds. In the alcoves around the nave, view

a modern depiction of the first American-born saint, Mother Elizabeth Ann Seton. The church's *Pietà* sculpture is three times larger than the *Pietà* at St. Peter's in Rome.

Daily masses are open and free to the public (check the schedule online) with the exception of Midnight Mass on Christmas Eve, which is a ticketed event. Free guided tours are held at 10 am most days, or you can download the cathedral tour app on its website for a small fee and tour at your leisure. ⊠ *5th Ave., between 50th and 51st Sts., Midtown East* ☎ *212/753–2261 for rectory* ⊕ *www.saintpatrickscathedral.org* Ⓜ *E, M to 5th Ave./53rd St.*

Seagram Building

BUILDING | Ludwig Mies van der Rohe, a pioneer of modernist architecture, built this boxlike bronze-and-glass tower in 1958. The austere facade belies its wit: I-beams, used to hold buildings up, here are merely attached to the surface, representing the *idea* of structural support. The Seagram Building's innovative ground-level plaza, extending out to the sidewalk, has since become a common element in urban skyscraper design, but at the time it was built, it was a radical announcement of a new, modern era of American architecture. Most visitors are distracted by more elaborate figures in the city skyline, but the Seagram is a must-visit for architecture buffs. With its two giant fountains and welcoming steps, it's also a popular lunch spot for Midtown workers. Visit late in the afternoon to avoid crowds. ⊠ *375 Park Ave., between 52nd and 53rd Sts., Midtown East* ⊕ *www.375parkavenue.com* Ⓜ *6 to 51st St.; E, M to Lexington Ave./53rd St.*

Tudor City

BUILDING | In 1925, prominent real-estate developer Fred F. French was among the first Americans ever to buy up a large number of buildings—more than 100, in this case, most of them tenements—and join the properties into a single, massive new complex. He designed a collection of nine apartment buildings and two parks in the "garden city" mode, which placed a building's green space not in an enclosed courtyard, but in the foreground. French also built a 39-by-50-foot "Tudor City" sign atop one of the 22-story buildings, best viewed from the eastern end of 42nd Street. The development's residential towers opened between 1927 and 1930, borrowing a marketable air of sophistication from Tudor-style stonework, stained-glass windows, and lobby-design flourishes. Tudor City has been featured in numerous films, and its landmark gardens—sometimes compared to Gramercy Park, only public—remain a popular lunch spot among office workers. The neighborhood was designated a historic district in 1988. ⊠ *From 40th to 43rd St., between 1st and 2nd Aves., Midtown East* ⊕ *www. tudorcity.com* Ⓜ *4, 5, 6, 7, S to Grand Central–42nd St.*

United Nations Headquarters

GOVERNMENT BUILDING | Officially an "international zone" in the heart of New York City, the U.N. Headquarters sits on an 18-acre tract on the East River, fronted by flags of member states. Built between 1947 and 1961, the complex marked its 70th anniversary in 2015 with the completion of a seven-year $2.1 billion overhaul that retained the 1950s look and feel while upgrading its infrastructure and energy efficiency. The only way to enter the U.N. Headquarters is with the 60-minute weekday guided tour, available in 12 languages; reservations can be made through the website, and you'll need a security pass from the visitors office at 801 1st Avenue. Arrive at least 30 minutes before the start of your tour for security screening, and if you ordered tickets online, be sure to bring your printout. The tour includes the **General Assembly,** major council chambers, and educational details. The tour also includes exhibits on peacekeeping, nuclear

nonproliferation and disarmament, and human rights.

The complex's buildings (the slim, 505-foot-tall green-glass **Secretariat Building**; the much smaller, domed **General Assembly Building**; and the **Dag Hammarskjöld Library**) evoke the influential French modernist architect Le Corbusier, and the surrounding park and plaza remain visionary. The public concourse has a visitor center with a gift shop, a bookstore, and a post office where you can mail postcards with U.N. stamps; bring your passport to add the U.N. stamp. ⊠ *Visitor entrance, 1st Ave. and 46th St., Midtown East* ☎ *212/963–8687* ⊕ *visit.un.org* 🎫 *Tour $22 (plus $2 online surcharge)* ☞ *Children under 5 not admitted* Ⓜ *4, 5, 6, 7, S to Grand Central–42nd St.*

🍴 Restaurants

Midtown East's streets are relatively quiet at night and on weekends, but during the week, the restaurants are filled with expense-account diners celebrating their successes. Indeed, some of the most formal dining rooms and most expensive meals in town can be found here.

Agern

$$$$ | **SCANDINAVIAN** | Set in a vast room in Grand Central that was once hidden to the general public, Agern is the domain of Claus Meyer, most famous for being a cofounder of Copenhagen's highly influential Noma. Here Icelandic chef Gunnar Gislasen mines New York for high-quality ingredients, turning them into palate-pleasing dishes such as apple-glazed pork belly and poached lobster. **Known for:** Noma in New York; prix-fixe menus; superb ingredients. Ⓢ *Average main: $70* ⊠ *Grand Central Terminal, 89 E. 42nd St., between Vanderbilt and Park Aves., Midtown East* ☎ *646/568–4018* ⊕ *www.agernrestaurant.com* 🕑 *Closed Sun. No lunch Sat.* Ⓜ *4, 5, 6, 7, S to Grand Central–42nd St.*

Aquavit and Aquavit Café

$$$$ | **SCANDINAVIAN** | This elegant and refined Scandinavian restaurant in the steady hands of Emma Bengtsson has prix-fixe options that include a ten-course meal, a six-course seasonal affair, and a three-course dinner. Standout dishes are foie gras paired with licorice, sweetbreads with sauerkraut, venison tartare, and for dessert, smoked vanilla crème brûlée. **Known for:** full-flavored, inventive Scandinavian cuisine; house-made aquavit; modern Scandinavian design. [$] *Average main: $105* ✉ *65 E. 55th St., between Madison and Park Aves., Midtown East* ☎ *212/307–7311* 🌐 *www.aquavit.org* 🕒 *Closed Sun. No lunch Sat.* [M] *E, M to 5th Ave./53rd St.*

BLT Steak

$$$$ | **STEAKHOUSE** | Chef Laurent Tourondel may no longer be involved with his namesake steak house, but this classy space, decked out in beige with resin-top black tables, still draws crowds. The no-muss, no-fuss menu with a variety of steaks and other options is nonetheless large, and so are the portions of starters such as crab cakes with celery-infused mayonnaise and ruby tuna tartare with avocado and soy-lime dressing. **Known for:** complimentary Gruyère cheese puffs; thick steaks; grilled lobster. [$] *Average main: $37* ✉ *106 E. 57th St., between Lexington and Park Aves., Midtown East* ☎ *212/752–7470* 🌐 *www.bltsteak.com* 🕒 *No lunch weekends* [M] *4, 5, 6 to 59th St.; N, R, W to Lexington Ave./59th St.*

Fig & Olive

$$$ | **MEDITERRANEAN** | **FAMILY** | Both the cozy tables and the long white marble bar are great options at this bi-level Mediterranean spot with a loyal following. Lunch is an ideal time to partake of shared plates like mix-and-match crostini, cheeses, and meats—not to mention soups, salads, and panini; at night, the place becomes more see-and-be-seen. **Known for:** crostini options; shared plates at lunch; excellent branzino. [$] *Average main: $28* ✉ *10 E. 52nd St., at 5th Ave., Midtown East* ☎ *212/319–2002* 🌐 *www.figandolive.com* 🕒 *No lunch weekends.*

Freds Madison Avenue

$$$ | **AMERICAN** | **FAMILY** | Complementing the luxury department store where it's housed, Freds Madison Avenue at Barneys is a chic day and evening restaurant perched nine floors above the avenue's bustle. Sleek decor and polished servers introduce elegance to a hard day of shopping or navigating Midtown East's weekday crowds; diners savor well-made staples spanning pasta, chopped salads, fresh fish, and vegetarian dishes. **Known for:** weekend brunch; superfresh salads; posh escape from Midtown shopping. [$] *Average main: $30* ✉ *Barneys, 660 Madison Ave., 9th fl., at 61st St., Midtown East* ☎ *212/833–2022* 🌐 *www.barneys.com* [M] *N, R, W to 5th Ave./59th St.; F, Q to Lexington Ave./63rd St.*

Grand Central Oyster Bar & Restaurant

$$$ | **SEAFOOD** | Deep in the belly of Grand Central Terminal, the vast, multiroom Oyster Bar has been a worthy seafood destination since 1913. Sit at the counter for the fried oyster po'boy or to slurp an astounding menu of fresh oysters before a steaming bowl of clam chowder, washed down with an ice-cold beer. **Known for:** all things oyster; straightforward seafood options; gleaming, tiled subterranean space. [$] *Average main: $30* ✉ *Grand Central Terminal, dining concourse, 42nd St. and Vanderbilt Ave., Midtown East* ☎ *212/490–6650* 🌐 *www.oysterbarny.com* 🕒 *Closed Sun.* [M] *4, 5, 6, 7, S to Grand Central–42nd St.*

The Grill

$$$$ | **AMERICAN** | Dining at this sceney, upscale eatery in the sharp, clean Philip Johnson interior of the Seagram Building will transport you to the age of midcentury Mad Men. But the food is even more thrilling—chefs Rich Torrisi and Mario Carbone (Dirty French, Parm, Carbone) took over in 2017 (they also run the adjacent restaurant, The Pool) and have created an

instant classic, one that both updates the American menu and relies on the space's rich history. **Known for:** gorgeous interior for special-occasion dining; steak and anchovy tartare; prime rib trolley service. [$] *Average main: $70* ✉ *99 E. 52nd St., between Park and Lexington Aves., Midtown East* ☎ *212/375–9001* 🌐 *www.thegrillnewyork.com* ⏲ *Closed Sun. No lunch Sat.* 👔 *Jacket required* [M] *E, M to Lexington Ave./53rd St.; 6 to 51st St.*

Kurumazushi

$$$$ | **JAPANESE** | Only a small sign in Japanese indicates the location of this extraordinary restaurant that serves sushi and sashimi exclusively; among the selections are hard-to-find fish imported directly from Japan. Bypass the tables, sit at the sushi bar, and put yourself in the hands of Toshihiro Uezu, the chef and owner. **Known for:** longtime spot for high-quality sushi; attentive staff; impressively expensive. [$] *Average main: $175* ✉ *7 E. 47th St., 2nd fl., between 5th and Madison Aves., Midtown East* ☎ *212/317–2802* 🌐 *www.kurumazushi.com* ⏲ *Closed Sun.* [M] *4, 5, 6, 7, S to Grand Central–42nd St.*

P. J. Clarke's

$$ | **AMERICAN** | This east-side institution has been dispensing great burgers and beer since 1884. Despite renovations and several owners over the years, the original location (there are offshoots in Lincoln Square and Battery Park City) maintains the beveled-glass and scuffed-wood look of an old-time saloon, and the veteran bartenders and loyal patrons are as much a part of the decor as the light fixtures. **Known for:** Cadillac burger (a bacon cheeseburger); old-time saloon; after-work mobs on weekdays. [$] *Average main: $19* ✉ *915 3rd Ave., at 55th St., Midtown East* ☎ *212/317–1616* 🌐 *www.pjclarkes.com* [M] *E, M to 5th Ave./53rd St.; N, R, W to Lexington Ave./59th St.; 4, 5, 6 to 59th St.*

Shun Lee Palace

$$$ | **CHINESE** | If you want inexpensive Cantonese food without pretension, head to Chinatown; if you prefer to be pampered, then this is the place, which has been serving classic Chinese fare in an elegant setting since 1971. Supposedly the dish orange beef was first made here, and indeed, it's worth a sample, but there's so much more. **Known for:** high-price Chinese food; classic orange beef; Beijing duck. [$] *Average main: $29* ✉ *155 E. 55th St., between Lexington and 3rd Aves., Midtown East* ☎ *212/371–8844* 🌐 *www.shunleepalace.net* [M] *N, R, W to Lexington Ave./59th St.; 4, 5, 6 to 59th St.*

Sparks Steak House

$$$$ | **STEAKHOUSE** | Bring a wad of cash to this famed steak house, where magnums of wines that cost more than most people earn in a week festoon the large dining rooms with white tablecloths and plenty of pictures on the walls. Tasty, fresh seafood is given more than fair play on the menu, and the extra-thick lamb and veal chops are also noteworthy—but Sparks is really about dry-aged steak. **Known for:** dry-aged steak; classic sides; the spot where, in 1985, members of the Gambino crime family were gunned down. [$] *Average main: $42* ✉ *210 E. 46th St., between 2nd and 3rd Aves., Midtown East* ☎ *212/687–4855* 🌐 *www.sparkssteakhouse.com* ⏲ *Closed Sun. No lunch Sat.* [M] *4, 5, 6, 7, S to Grand Central–42nd St.*

Sushi Yasuda

$$$ | **JAPANESE** | Devotees mourned the return of namesake chef Naomichi Yasuda to Japan, but things are in able hands with his handpicked successor, Mitsuru Tamura. Whether using fish flown in daily from Japan or the creamiest sea urchin, the chef makes sushi so fresh and delicate it melts in your mouth: the fine selection of sake and beer complements the lovely food. **Known for:** attractive bar; some special appetizers change daily;

stylish, bamboo-lined interior. $ *Average main: $35* ⊠ *204 E. 43rd St., between 2nd and 3rd Aves., Midtown East* ☏ *212/972–1001* ⊕ *www.sushiyasuda. com* ☸ *Closed Sun. No lunch Sat.* Ⓜ *4, 5, 6, 7, S to Grand Central–42nd St.*

🛏 Hotels

Andaz 5th Avenue

$$$ | **HOTEL** | The serene and spacious rooms at this chic, modern property evoke that coveted New York loft feel, with floor-to-ceiling windows that look out over 5th Avenue and the New York Public Library. **Pros:** spacious and stylish rooms; suites have outdoor space; good dining and drinking options. **Cons:** pricey despite some good freebies; busy location might not suit all guests; no closets mean little storage space. $ *Rooms from: $499* ⊠ *485 5th Ave., at 41st St., Midtown East* ☏ *212/601–1234* ⊕ *andaz. hyatt.com* ☛ *184 rooms* ⦿ *No meals* Ⓜ *4, 5, 6, 7, S to Grand Central–42nd St.*

The Benjamin

$$ | **HOTEL** | **FAMILY** | NYC is often called the city that never sleeps, but if a good night's rest is essential for your visit, the Benjamin, with its soothing modern, neutral-hue rooms, may be your choice accommodation—with a menu of 12 pillows to choose from (including buckwheat, water, and Swedish memory varieties), white-noise machines, and 500-thread-count sheets, they've got it covered. **Pros:** sleep-friendly options; kitchenettes in big rooms; gracious staff. **Cons:** decor a bit generic; boring views; dull neighborhood after dark. $ *Rooms from: $349* ⊠ *125 E. 50th St., at Lexington Ave., Midtown East* ☏ *212/715–2500* ⊕ *www.thebenjamin.com* ☛ *209 rooms* ⦿ *No meals* Ⓜ *6 to 51st St.; E, M to Lexington Ave./53rd St.*

Fifty Hotel & Suites by Affinia

$$ | **HOTEL** | **FAMILY** | This popular hotel attracts business travelers, but it's also comfortable for families or leisure travelers—especially the studios and spacious suites, which have full kitchens and a clean, playful design that incorporates oversize chairs and couches. **Pros:** apartment-style living; large rooms; kid- and pet-friendly. **Cons:** pricey Wi-Fi unless you get an online deal; neighborhood activities are limited after dark; traffic noise can get loud. $ *Rooms from: $329* ⊠ *155 E. 50th St., at 3rd Ave., Midtown East* ☏ *212/751–5710, 800/637–8483* ⊕ *www.affinia.com/fifty* ☛ *297 rooms* ⦿ *No meals* Ⓜ *6 to 51st St.; E, M to Lexington Ave./53rd St.*

Four Seasons Hotel New York

$$$$ | **HOTEL** | For better or worse, Four Seasons Hotel New York remains the blueprint for what a Manhattan luxury hotel should be, with stellar service, an imposing lobby done in marble and blond wood, and a well-connected concierge who can get reservations for most of New York's hot tables. **Pros:** spacious and comfortable rooms; perfect concierge and staff service; cocktails in Ty Bar. **Cons:** very pricey; confusing room controls; some furniture could use updating. $ *Rooms from: $995* ⊠ *57 E. 57th St., between Park and Madison Aves., Midtown East* ☏ *212/758–5700* ⊕ *www. fourseasons.com/newyork* ☛ *368 suites* ⦿ *No meals* Ⓜ *4, 5, 6 to 59th St.; N, R, W to Lexington Ave./59th St.*

The Gotham Hotel NY

$$ | **HOTEL** | This sleek hotel has a lot going for it, from good-size rooms to nice amenities, but a clincher is that every room has outdoor space. **Pros:** welcoming staff; central location; every room has a balcony. **Cons:** no on-site gym; some balconies are tiny; valet parking is expensive. $ *Rooms from: $350* ⊠ *16 E. 46 St., between 5th and Madison Aves., Midtown East* ☏ *212/490–8500* ⊕ *www. thegothamhotelny.com* ☛ *66 rooms* ⦿ *No meals* Ⓜ *B, D, F, M to 47th–50th Sts./Rockefeller Center, 4, 5, 6, 7, S to Grand Central–42nd St.*

Grand Hyatt New York

$$ | **HOTEL** | Conveniently located near Grand Central, this large, historic hotel (originally built as the Commodore in 1919) is now a sleek and modern central hub with a fresh-looking lobby that has low-slung leather furniture and two towering Jaume Plensa sculptures. **Pros:** comfy beds; light-filled gym on a high floor; large, well-planned rooms. **Cons:** no in-room minibar; lacking in character; located in a high-traffic area. [$] *Rooms from: $429* ✉ *109 E. 42nd St., between Park and Lexington Aves., Midtown East* ☎ *212/883–1234* 🌐 *newyork.grand.hyatt.com* 🛏 *1,341 rooms* 🍴 *No meals* [M] *4, 5, 6, 7, S to Grand Central–42nd St.*

Hotel Elysée by Library Hotel Collection

$$$ | **HOTEL** | This intimate hotel, a favorite for travelers looking for good value in a desirable Midtown location, offers rooms with a classic European feel, with wooden headboards, rich carpeting underfoot, and—in a few cases—fireplaces, tubs, and balconies. **Pros:** complimentary wine and cheese; individually decorated rooms; cute library. **Cons:** underwhelming lobby; outdated decor; no full-service restaurant. [$] *Rooms from: $475* ✉ *60 E. 54th St., between Madison and Park Aves., Midtown East* ☎ *212/753–1066* 🌐 *www.elyseehotel.com* 🛏 *87 rooms* 🍴 *Free Breakfast* [M] *E, M to 5th Ave./53rd St.*

The Langham, New York, Fifth Avenue

$$$ | **HOTEL** | Setting new standards for luxury, this towering, limestone-clad 5th Avenue hotel is an opulent crash pad for wealthy overseas tourists, captains of industry on long-term stays, and anyone in need of some serious pampering. **Pros:** attentive service; gorgeous spa; quality dining. **Cons:** street noise reported by guests on lower floors; pricey accommodations; high-traffic location. [$] *Rooms from: $595* ✉ *400 5th Ave., Midtown East* ☎ *212/695–4005* 🌐 *www.langhamhotels.com/newyork* 🛏 *234 rooms* 🍴 *No meals* [M] *B, D, F, M, N, Q, R, W to 34th St.–Herald Sq.*

★ **Library Hotel by Library Hotel Collection**

$$ | **HOTEL** | Bookishly handsome, this stately landmark brownstone, built in 1900, is inspired by the nearby New York Public Library: each of its 10 floors is dedicated to one of the 10 categories of the Dewey Decimal System and is stocked with art and books relevant to subtopics such as philosophy, astronomy, or biography—let your interests guide your room choice. **Pros:** fun rooftop bar; access to best-selling e-books via app; complimentary wine and cheese. **Cons:** no full-service restaurant; no gym on-site; no rooms with two double beds. [$] *Rooms from: $399* ✉ *299 Madison Ave., at 41st St., Midtown East* ☎ *212/983–4500* 🌐 *www.libraryhotel.com* 🛏 *60 rooms* 🍴 *Free Breakfast* [M] *4, 5, 6, 7, S to Grand Central–42nd St.*

Lotte New York Palace

$$$ | **HOTEL** | From the moment you enter the gilded gates of these connected mansions, originally built in the 1880s by railroad baron Henry Villard, you know you're somewhere special; there's a reason this hotel is called the Palace. **Pros:** luxury house car service; great service; unmatched views of St. Patrick's Cathedral. **Cons:** high prices; harried staff; expensive Wi-Fi. [$] *Rooms from: $450* ✉ *455 Madison Ave., at 50th St., Midtown East* ☎ *212/888–7000* 🌐 *www.lottenypalace.com* 🛏 *909 rooms* 🍴 *No meals* [M] *6 to 51st St.; E, M to Lexington Ave./53rd St.*

The Maxwell New York City

$ | **HOTEL** | A hopping bar and sunken lounge in the reception area, slick decor, modern art, and clean, comfortable guest rooms make this a hipper hotel than others in the vicinity. **Pros:** central location; sleek rooms; spacious lounges with comfy furniture. **Cons:** thin walls; small rooms; inconsistent service. [$] *Rooms from: $239* ✉ *541 Lexington Ave., between 49th and 50th Sts., Midtown*

East ☎ 212/755–1200 🌐 www.maxwellhotelnyc.com 🛏 696 rooms 🍴 No meals [M] 6 to 51st St.; E, M to Lexington Ave./53rd St.

Millennium Hilton New York One UN Plaza
$ | **HOTEL** | In a sky-high tower near the landmark United Nations building, this Hilton offering starts on the 28th floor and has fabulous views—ask for a room facing west, toward Manhattan's skyline. **Pros:** unbeatable East River and city views; good value; helpful front-door and bell staff. **Cons:** a far walk to the subway; pricey Internet access; corporate vibe. [$] *Rooms from: $299* ✉ *1 United Nations Plaza, 44th St. and 1st Ave., Midtown East* ☎ *212/758–1234* 🌐 *www3.hilton.com* 🛏 *439 rooms* 🍴 *No meals* [M] *4, 5, 6, 7, S to Grand Central–42nd St.*

★ The Peninsula New York
$$$$ | **HOTEL** | Stepping through the Peninsula's Beaux Arts facade onto the grand staircase overhung with a monumental chandelier, you know you're in for a glitzy treat, a treat matched by service that is world-class and personalized. **Pros:** brilliant service; fabulous rooms with convenient controls; unforgettable rooftop bar. **Cons:** extremely expensive; high-traffic area, especially on weekends; limited dining options nearby. [$] *Rooms from: $1,195* ✉ *700 5th Ave., at 55th St., Midtown East* ☎ *212/956–2888* 🌐 *www.peninsula.com/newyork* 🛏 *235 rooms* 🍴 *No meals* [M] *E, M to 5th Ave./53rd St.*

Pod 51
$ | **HOTEL** | If cramped quarters don't bother you, this is one of the best deals in town, with rooms that borrow space-saving ideas from mass transit, including sink consoles like those in an airplane restroom and built-in shelves under the beds. **Pros:** great prices; fun design; buzzy on-site dining and drinking. **Cons:** not for claustrophobes; about half the rooms share baths; no gym. [$] *Rooms from: $179* ✉ *230 E. 51st St., between 2nd and 3rd Aves., Midtown East* ☎ *844/763–7666* 🌐 *www.thepodhotel.com* 🛏 *345 rooms* 🍴 *No meals* [M] *6 to 51st St.; E, M to Lexington Ave./53rd St.*

Roger Smith Hotel
$ | **HOTEL** | This quirky choice is one of the better affordable stays in the city; the art-filled rooms, matched by the murals in the lobby, are homey and comfortable. **Pros:** good location near Grand Central; intimate atmosphere; free yogurt and granola 24/7. **Cons:** street noise; small bathrooms; feels a bit dated. [$] *Rooms from: $297* ✉ *501 Lexington Ave., between 47th and 48th Sts., Midtown East* ☎ *212/755–1400* 🌐 *www.rogersmith.com* 🛏 *130 rooms* 🍴 *No meals* [M] *6 to 51st St.; E, M to Lexington Ave./53rd St.*

The Roosevelt Hotel
$ | **HOTEL** | Named after Teddy, not Franklin, this Midtown icon just steps from Grand Central has an ornate lobby with cushy couches and an old-school bar detailed in heavy wood that makes the place feel like it's from another time, and it is—the property dates from 1924. **Pros:** great public areas; big bathrooms; comfortable rooftop lounge. **Cons:** dated design; limited in-room amenities; no pool or spa. [$] *Rooms from: $199* ✉ *45 E. 45th St., at Madison Ave., Midtown East* ☎ *212/661–9600* 🌐 *www.theroosevelthotel.com* 🛏 *1,015 rooms* 🍴 *No meals* [M] *4, 5, 6, 7, S to Grand Central–42nd St.*

The Sherry-Netherland
$$ | **HOTEL** | With a marble-lined lobby, crystal chandeliers, and wall friezes from the Vanderbilt mansion, the Sherry-Netherland's historic glamour is undeniable, and this tall, luxurious apartment building also has a limited number of hotel rooms, many with decorative fireplaces, antiques, and glorious marble baths. **Pros:** gorgeous lobby; commanding, impeccable location; Cipriani access. **Cons:** small check-in area; rooms vary in taste and decor; interior rooms lack views. [$] *Rooms from: $319* ✉ *781 5th Ave., at 59th St., Midtown East* ☎ *212/355–2800* 🌐 *www.sherrynetherland.com* 🛏 *50*

rooms ¶◎| *No meals* Ⓜ *N, R, W to 5th Ave./59th St.*

★ The St. Regis New York

$$$$ | **HOTEL** | World-class from head to toe, this 5th Avenue Beaux Arts landmark comes as close to flawless as any hotel in New York, with tech-savvy rooms, historic touches, and the iconic King Cole Bar. Butlers have been catering to the whims of each and every guest since the St. Regis first opened its doors in 1904, a touch no other New York hotel can match. **Pros:** classic NYC favorite; rooms combine true luxury with helpful technology; easy-access butler service; superb in-house dining. **Cons:** high price doesn't guarantee a great view; too serious for families seeking fun; standard rooms don't have soaking tubs. Ⓢ *Rooms from: $995* ✉ *2 E. 55th St., at 5th Ave., Midtown East* ☎ *212/753–4500* ⊕ *www. stregisnewyork.com* ⇨ *171 rooms* ¶◎| *No meals* Ⓜ *E, M to 5th Ave./53rd St.*

Nightlife

BARS

The Bar Downstairs

BARS/PUBS | The generic-sounding bar in the basement of the Andaz 5th Avenue hotel may lack a proper moniker, but it certainly has pedigree. Alchemy Consulting, a joint venture from Chicago's Violet Hour and New York's Death & Co., designed the cocktails here; look for spins on the Negroni and Manhattan in the sleek subterranean space. The food menu is similarly upmarket, with Spanish tapas and other small plates. ✉ *Andaz 5th Avenue, 485 5th Ave., at 41st St., Midtown East* ☎ *212/601–1234* ⊕ *newyork5thavenue.andaz.hyatt.com* Ⓜ *B, D, F, M to 42nd St.–Bryant Park; 7 to 5th Ave.; 4, 5, 6, S to Grand Central–42nd St.*

★ The Campbell

BARS/PUBS | Classy tipplers and well-dressed commuters pack into this Grand Central Terminal bar (especially during the evening rush), but you can still have a romantic time in one of Manhattan's more beautiful rooms. The restored space dates to the 1920s, when it was the private office of an executive named John W. Campbell, who entertained friends and colleagues here. Sample the good life as you sip cocktails from club chairs and banquettes. The proprietor also offers the smaller Campbell Palm Court and enclosed, outdoor Campbell Terrace; the latter is just outside in the former taxi driveway. ✉ *Grand Central Terminal, 15 Vanderbilt Ave. entrance, Midtown East* ☎ *212/297–1781* ⊕ *www. thecampbellnyc.com* Ⓜ *4, 5, 6, 7, S to Grand Central–42nd St.*

King Cole Bar

PIANO BARS/LOUNGES | A justly beloved 1906 Maxfield Parrish mural of "Old King Cole" himself, as well as his artful court (made famous by the 18th-century nursery rhyme), adds to the already considerable elegance at this romantic and essential Midtown lounge. Try the Bloody Mary—since this is where the drink was introduced to Americans as a "Red Snapper" back in 1934—and be ready to pay for the privilege of drinking in this legendary establishment. ✉ *St. Regis New York, 2 E. 55th St., between 5th and Madison Aves., Midtown East* ☎ *212/339–6857* ⊕ *www.kingcolebar. com* Ⓜ *E, M to 5th Ave./53rd St.*

GAY NIGHTLIFE

Evolve Bar and Lounge

BARS/PUBS | Filling out a space that's long been the site of a gay establishment, Evolve is a go-to for mostly men to mingle after work and on weekends. The long bar is a watering hole for many regulars, and the smoke-friendly back patio is an added incentive to unwind in a bar unlike others in the neighborhood. Check the bar's social-media pages to see what go-go shows and open-mic lineups are planned. ✉ *221 E. 58th St., between 2nd and 3rd Aves., Midtown East* ☎ *212/355–3395* Ⓜ *4, 5, 6 to 59th St.; N, R, W to Lexington Ave./59th St.*

Townhouse Bar
PIANO BARS/LOUNGES | It's the elegant yin to the casual yang of **Evolve,** which is just across the block at East 58th Street. Distinguished mature men from the Upper East Side meet younger would-be versions of themselves at this "gentlemen's club" and piano bar. The attire is "uptown casual" if not fancier (though jackets are not required), and there are daily happy hours plus weekly special events. ⌧ *236 E. 58th St., between 2nd and 3rd Aves., Midtown East* ☎ *212/754–4649* ⊕ *www. townhouseny.com* Ⓜ *4, 5, 6 to 59th St.; N, R, W to Lexington Ave./59th St.*

🛍 Shopping

If money is no object, put on your best shopping shoes and most glamorous sunglasses and head to Midtown East. Some of the world's most luxurious brands—from Bulgari to Dior—have their flagship stores along 5th Avenue. All the stores *on* 5th Avenue are included in Midtown East, although some might be on the west side of the street and have West in their address.

ANTIQUES AND COLLECTIBLES
A La Vieille Russie
ANTIQUES/COLLECTIBLES | Antiques dealers since 1851, this shop specializes in European and Russian decorative arts, jewelry, and paintings. Behold bibelots by Fabergé and others, enameled or encrusted with jewels. If money is no object, there are also antique diamond necklaces and pieces of china once owned by Russian nobility. The shop is closed on weekends. ⌧ *745 5th Ave., 4th fl., between 57th and 58th Sts., Midtown East* ☎ *212/752–1727* ⊕ *www.alvr.com* Ⓜ *N, R, W to 5th Ave./59th St.*

The Chinese Porcelain Company
ANTIQUES/COLLECTIBLES | Though the name of this prestigious shop indicates one of its specialties, its stock covers more ground, ranging from lacquerware to Khmer sculpture, as well as work by

contemporary Chinese artists. ⌧ *232 E. 59th St., 5th fl., between 2nd and 3rd Aves., Midtown East* ☎ *212/838–7744* ⊕ *www.cpco.co* Ⓜ *4, 5, 6 to 59th St.; N, R, W to Lexington Ave./59th St.*

BOOKS AND STATIONERY
Argosy Bookstore
BOOKS/STATIONERY | Family-owned since 1925, Argosy is a charmingly old-fashioned place to browse for both bargain and priceless books. The shop keeps a scholarly stock of rare books and autographs. It's also a great place to find low-price maps and prints for gifts. ⌧ *116 E. 59th St., between Park and Lexington Aves., Midtown East* ☎ *212/753–4455* ⊕ *www.argosybooks.com* Ⓜ *4, 5, 6 to 59th St.; N, R, W to Lexington Ave./59th St.*

CAMERAS AND ELECTRONICS
Apple Store
CAMERAS/ELECTRONICS | New York's flagship Apple Store features a 32-foot-high glass cube that appears to float over its subterranean entrance—or, at least, it normally does, though the store is under renovation until 2020 (and is being supplemented by an adjacent temporary flagship until then). The Apple-obsessed will be happy to know this location (and the future, renovated store) is open 24/7, holidays included. Make an appointment (well in advance) at the Genius Bar if you need tech help. There's also an Apple Store location in SoHo, in a converted historic post office building, as well as a few other branches around the city. ⌧ *767 5th Ave., at 59th St., Midtown East* ☎ *212/336–1440* ⊕ *www.apple.com* Ⓜ *N, R, W to 5th Ave./59th St.*

CLOTHING
Abercrombie & Fitch
CLOTHING | This brand is known for its casual, preppy clothes for men, women, and kids—but brace yourself for the thumping club music and dim lighting. ⌧ *720 5th Ave., at 56th St., Midtown East* ☎ *212/306–0936* ⊕ *www.*

abercrombie.com Ⓜ *F to 57th St.; N, R, W to 5th Ave./59th St.*

Banana Republic

CLOTHING | Although there are around a dozen Banana Republic stores around the city, come to the flagship for the biggest selection of the brand's classic clothing. Don't miss the Heritage collection or the big clearance racks. ✉ *Rockefeller Center, 626 5th Ave., at 51st St., Midtown East* ☎ *212/974-2350* ⊕ *www.bananarepublic. com* Ⓜ *B, D, F, M to 47th–50th Sts./Rockefeller Center; E, M to 5th Ave./53rd St.*

BCBGMAXAZRIA

CLOTHING | The brand's first four letters are short for "bon chic, bon genre," which means stylish sportswear and embellished, embroidered evening dresses here. The collection ranges from leather pants to maxi dresses. ✉ *461 5th Ave., at 40th St., Midtown East* ☎ *212/991-9777* ⊕ *www.bcbg.com* Ⓜ *B, D, F, M to 42nd St.–Bryant Park.*

★ Brooks Brothers

CLOTHING | The clothes at this classic American haberdasher are, as ever, traditional, comfortable, and fairly priced. Summer seersucker, navy-blue blazers, and the peerless oxford shirts have been staples for generations; the women's and boys' selections have variations thereon. At this flagship store, which Brooks Brothers has occupied since 1915, tailors are on hand for fittings; an appointment is recommended. ✉ *346 Madison Ave., at 44th St., Midtown East* ☎ *212/682-8800* ⊕ *www.brooksbrothers.com* Ⓜ *4, 5, 6, 7, S to Grand Central–42nd. St.*

Burberry

CLOTHING | This six-story glass-and-stone flagship is a temple to all things plaid and British. The iconic trench coat can be made to measure here, and the signature plaid can be found on bikinis, scarves, and wallets. For children, there are mini versions of quilted jackets and cozy sweaters. ✉ *9 E. 57th St., between 5th and Madison Aves., Midtown East* ☎ *212/407-7100* ⊕ *us.burberry.com* Ⓜ *N, R, W to 5th Ave./59th St.*

Chanel

CLOTHING | This Midtown flagship at 15 East 57th Street has often been compared to a Chanel suit—elegant, timeless, and flawlessly crafted. The boutique reopened in late 2018 after an impressive renovation, becoming Chanel's largest store in North America. Come here for the iconic suits and quilted handbags, along with other pillars of Chanel style: chic little black dresses, evening gowns, and yards of pearls. There's also a cosmetics area where you can stock up on the famed scents and nail polish. ✉ *15 E. 57th St., between 5th and Madison Aves., Midtown East* ☎ *212/355-5050* ⊕ *www.chanel.com* Ⓜ *N, R, W to 5th Ave./59th St.; F to 57th St.*

Dior

CLOTHING | Very white and very glossy, this space sets a serene background to showcase the luxe ready-to-wear collection along with handbags, fragrances, and accessories. If you're not in the market for an investment gown or fine jewelry, peruse the latest status bag. Dior Homme menswear boutique is next door at No. 17. ✉ *21 E. 57th St., between 5th and Madison Aves., Midtown East* ☎ *212/931-2950* ⊕ *www.dior.com* Ⓜ *N, R, W to 5th Ave./59th St.; F to 57th St.*

Dolce & Gabbana

CLOTHING | It's easy to feel like an Italian movie star amid these exuberant (in every sense) clothes. Corseted dresses are a favorite; the fabric could be sheer, furred, or leopard print. Men's suits are slim and sharp. In addition to this location, there are also boutiques dedicated exclusively to the women's and children's collections farther up Madison Avenue around East 69th St. ✉ *717 5th Ave., between 55th and 56th Sts., Midtown East* ☎ *212/897-9653* ⊕ *www.dolcegabbana.com* Ⓜ *F to 57th St.; E, M to 5th Ave./53rd St.*

Gucci

CLOTHING | This 46,000-square-foot flagship with floor-to-ceiling glass windows is the largest Gucci store in the world. Here, shoppers find a special "heritage" department, plus goods exclusive to the store. The clothing is edgy and sexy. Skintight pants might be paired with a luxe leather jacket; silk tops leave a little more to the imagination. Many of the accessories, like blingy shades or snakeskin shoes, have Gucci's signature horse-bit detailing. ✉ 725 5th Ave., at 56th St., Midtown East ☎ 212/826–2600 ⊕ www. gucci.com Ⓜ N, R, W to 5th Ave./59th St.; F to 57th St.

H&M

CLOTHING | Of-the-moment trends are packaged for the mass market at this affordable Swedish clothing chain. The 57,000-square-foot flagship is the brand's largest store in the world, though there are numerous others around the city. H&M has collaborated with many designers, including Karl Lagerfeld and Isabel Marant. ✉ 589 5th Ave., between 47th and 48th Sts., Midtown East ☎ 855/466–7467 ⊕ www.hm.com Ⓜ B, D, F, M to 47–50th Sts./Rockefeller Center.

Massimo Dutti

CLOTHING | Owned by Zara, this brand is that more ubiquitous one's older, more sophisticated sibling. The three-story space specializes in sleek basics that are perfect for work or weekends, such as blazers, trench coats, and silky sweaters. ✉ 689 5th Ave., between 54th and 55th Sts., Midtown East ☎ 212/371–2555 ⊕ www.massimodutti.com Ⓜ E, M to 5th Ave./53rd St.

Tommy Hilfiger

CLOTHING | The global flagship prizes classic Americana, with its dark-wood paneling, bookshelf displays, and assorted antiques—and of course the red, white, and blue details. It's filled with tailored suits for men, smart sweater sets and pencil skirts for women, both evening and sportswear, plus a whole floor devoted to denim. ✉ 681 5th Ave., between 53rd and 54th Sts., Midtown East ☎ 212/223–1824 ⊕ usa.tommy.com Ⓜ E, M to 5th Ave./53rd St.

UNIQLO

CLOTHING | At 89,000 square feet, this flagship is the biggest retail space on 5th Avenue, and the biggest UNIQLO in the world (in New York, there are also branches in SoHo and near Herald Square and Brooklyn's Barclays Center). Shoppers can scoop up fashion staples such as sweaters, skinny jeans, and button-down shirts in a rainbow of colors. Don't miss the limited-edition collaborations with big-name designers and stylists. The Heattech clothing range is always a big hit. Weekday mornings are the best time to avoid long lines for the dressing rooms. ✉ 666 5th Ave., at 53rd St., Midtown East ☎ 877/486–4756 ⊕ www. uniqlo.com Ⓜ E, M to 5th Ave./53rd St.

Versace

CLOTHING | The architecture here, with its marble floor and glittering chandeliers, provides the perfect backdrop for the outrageous designs and colors of Versace clothes. The brand's housewares and bedding collection are also available here. ✉ 647 5th Ave., between 51st and 52nd Sts., Midtown East ☎ 212/317–0224 ⊕ www.versace.com Ⓜ E, M to 5th Ave./53rd St.

Zara

CLOTHING | This massive store is one of Zara's biggest in the United States and the place to come for affordable, stylish fashion for men, women, and children. New merchandise arrives twice a week and ranges from classics like blazers to edgier skinny trousers. It's an enticing, airy flagship, plus there are two lounge areas, in case you need a shopping break. ✉ 666 5th Ave., between 52nd and 53rd Sts., Midtown East ☎ 212/765–0477 ⊕ www.zara.com Ⓜ E, M to 5th Ave./53rd St.

DEPARTMENT STORES
Bergdorf Goodman

DEPARTMENT STORES | The ultimate shopping destination, this luxury department store offers ladies (and gentlemen) who lunch designer clothes, a stellar shoe department, and top-notch service. The range of products in the beauty department is unparalleled, and shoppers can complete their look with highlights at the in-house John Barrett salon. The fifth floor is home to more contemporary lines. If you need to refuel, grab a bite at the seventh-floor BG Restaurant, with Central Park views, or a quick bite at the beauty-level Good Dish. ⊠ *754 5th Ave., between 57th and 58th Sts., Midtown East ☎ 212/753–7300 ⊕ www. bergdorfgoodman.com Ⓜ N, R, W to 5th Ave./59th. St.*

★ Bloomingdale's

DEPARTMENT STORES | Only a few stores in New York occupy an entire city block; the uptown branch of this classic New York retail institution is one of them. The main floor is a buzzy, glittery maze of mirrored cosmetic counters and perfume-spraying salespeople. Navigate past this dizzying scene to find good buys on designer clothes, shoes, bedding, housewares, and more. In true upscale Bloomie's style, in-store personal shoppers will help you score styles for yourself (or gifts for others) like a VIP. ⊠ *1000 3rd Ave., main entrance at 59th St. and Lexington Ave., Midtown East ☎ 212/705–2000 ⊕ bloomingdales.com Ⓜ 4, 5, 6 to 59th St.; N, R, W to Lexington Ave./59th St.*

Saks Fifth Avenue

DEPARTMENT STORES | This iconic store remains a high-fashion force and continually revamps its modish offerings with contemporary designer lines, such as Proenza Schouler and Victoria Beckham. The department store now has a designer sneaker shop, as well as an enormous Christian Louboutin shop-within-a-shop. The ground-floor beauty department stocks an incredible array, from classics to edgy. ⊠ *611 5th Ave., between 49th and 50th Sts., Midtown East ☎ 212/753–4000 ⊕ www.saksfifthavenue.com Ⓜ E, M to 5th Ave./53rd St.; B, D, F, M to 47–50th Sts./Rockefeller Center.*

GIFTS AND SOUVENIRS
★ New York City Transit Museum Gallery Annex & Store

GIFTS/SOUVENIRS | Located in the symbolic heart of New York City's transit system, this museum store and gallery features an eclectic array of merchandise all linked to the MTA (Metropolitan Transportation Authority), from straphanger ties to earrings made from old subway tokens. ⊠ *Grand Central Terminal, Vanderbilt Pl. and 42nd St., Shuttle Passage, Midtown East ☎ 212/878–0106 ⊕ www.nytransitmuseumstore.com Ⓜ 4, 5, 6, 7, S to Grand Central–42nd St.*

HOME DECOR
Armani/Casa

HOUSEHOLD ITEMS/FURNITURE | In keeping with the Armani aesthetic, the minimalist furniture and housewares here have a subdued color scheme (gold, gray, cream, and black). Big-ticket items include luxuriously upholstered sofas and sleek coffee tables. The desk accessories and throw pillows are equally understated. ⊠ *Decoration & Design Building, 979 3rd Ave., Suite 1424, between 58th and 59th Sts., Midtown East ☎ 212/334–1271 ⊕ www.armanicasa.com Ⓜ 4, 5, 6 to 59th St.; N, R, W to Lexington Ave./59th St.*

JEWELRY AND ACCESSORIES
Bulgari

JEWELRY/ACCESSORIES | With a marble-lined, jewel-encrusted flagship on 5th Avenue (one of several global Bulgari "temples"), this Italian company is certainly not meek with its branding, which encircles gems, watch faces, and an ever-growing accessories line. There are ornate, weighty rings and other pieces mixing gold with stainless steel, porcelain, and the brand's signature cabochon multicolored sapphires. Wedding and engagement rings are slightly more subdued. ⊠ *730 5th Ave., at 57th St., Midtown East* ☎ *212/315–9000* ⊕ *www. bulgari.com* Ⓜ *N, R, W to 5th Ave./59th St.; F to 57th St.*

Cartier

JEWELRY/ACCESSORIES | Established in 1914, this legendary French jeweler and firm favorite among royals and celebrities is the place to come for exquisite engagement rings, luxury watches, or cuff links. Cartier's iconic designs include the panther motif, the Trinity ring, and Tank watches—all available in its famous 5th Avenue boutique just outside Central Park. (The Cartier Mansion boutique, with additional vintage accessories, is about six blocks south, at East 52nd Street.) ⊠ *767 5th Ave., between 58th and 59th Sts., Midtown East* ☎ *212/457–3202* ⊕ *www.cartier.com* Ⓜ *N, R, W to 5th Ave./59th St.*

H. Stern

JEWELRY/ACCESSORIES | Sleek designs pose in an equally modern setting; smooth cabochon-cut stones, most from South America, glow in pale wooden display cases. The designers make notable use of semiprecious stones such as citrine, tourmaline, and topaz. ⊠ *645 5th Ave., between 51st and 52nd Sts., Midtown East* ☎ *212/688–0300* ⊕ *www. hstern.net* Ⓜ *E, M to 5th Ave./53rd St.*

Harry Winston

JEWELRY/ACCESSORIES | These jewels regularly adorn celebs at the Oscars, and you need an A-list bank account to shop here. The ice-clear diamonds are of impeccable quality and set in everything from emerald-cut solitaire rings to wreath necklaces resembling strings of flowers. No wonder the jeweler was immortalized in the song "Diamonds Are a Girl's Best Friend." Note that the jeweler's flagship is due to reopen after renovations by 2020; you can find the temporary store at 701 5th Avenue, at 55th Street. ⊠ *718 5th Ave.,* at 56th St., Midtown East* ☎ *212/399–1000* ⊕ *www.harrywinston.com* Ⓜ *F to 57th St.; N, R, W to 5th Ave./59th St.; E, M to 5th Ave./53rd St.*

Mikimoto

JEWELRY/ACCESSORIES | The Japanese originator of the cultured pearl, Mikimoto presents a glowing display of high-luster pearls. Besides the creamy strands from their own pearl farms, check out diamond-and-pearl earrings, bracelets, and rings. ⊠ *730 5th Ave., between 56th and 57th Sts., Midtown East* ☎ *212/457–4600* ⊕ *www.mikimotoamerica.com* Ⓜ *F to 57th St.; N, R, W to 5th Ave./59th St.*

Tiffany & Co.

JEWELRY/ACCESSORIES | It's hard to think of a more iconic New York jewelry store than Tiffany, along with its unmistakable blue box. Daydream among the displays of platinum-and-diamond bracelets and massive engagement rings, but head to the sterling-silver floor for more affordable baubles. This flagship is among the world's most famous stores, thanks in part to Truman Capote's 1958 novella *Breakfast at Tiffany's* and the 1961 classic film starring Audrey Hepburn as Holly Golightly. ⊠ *727 5th Ave., at 57th St., Midtown East* ☎ *212/755–8000* ⊕ *www. tiffany.com* Ⓜ *N, R, W to 5th Ave./59th St.; F to 57th St.*

Van Cleef & Arpels

JEWELRY/ACCESSORIES | This French jewelry company is considerably more low-key than many of its blingy neighbors, in both design and marketing ethos (you won't see them opening a store in your average mall). Their best-known design is the cloverleaf Alhambra, which can be found on rings, necklaces, and earrings. ⊠ *744 5th Ave., at 57th St., Midtown East* ☎ *212/896–9284* ⊕ *www.vancleefarpels. com* Ⓜ *N, R, W to 5th Ave./59th St.; F to 57th St.*

SHOES, HANDBAGS, AND LEATHER GOODS

Cole Haan

SHOES/LUGGAGE/LEATHER GOODS | This brand is known for its comfortable but stylish footwear—many shoes have Nike Air cushioning in the heel. All kinds of shoes from sandals to boots and pumps are available. ⊠ *Rockefeller Center, 620 5th Ave., between 49th and 50th Sts., Midtown East* ☎ *212/765–9747* ⊕ *www. colehaan.com* Ⓜ *B, D, F, M to 47–50th Sts./Rockefeller Center.*

Fendi

SHOES/LUGGAGE/LEATHER GOODS | Once known primarily for its furs, Fendi is now synonymous with decadent handbags, and its Madison Avenue flagship is a temple to them. The purses are beaded, embroidered, and fantastically embellished. Leather goods, women's wear, menswear, shoes, watches, and other accessories are also available. ⊠ *598 Madison Ave., between 57th and 58th Sts., Midtown East* ☎ *212/897–2244* ⊕ *www.fendi.com* Ⓜ *N, R, W to 5th Ave./59th St.*

Fratelli Rossetti

SHOES/LUGGAGE/LEATHER GOODS | Don't come here expecting sexy, skyscraper stilettos or any overly trendy looks: this Italian leather-goods company excels at classic shoes. Riding boots are among the most popular items, but there are also pumps, loafers, and slouchy ankle boots. Men can choose from oxfords and boots. There's also a line of leather handbags. ⊠ *625 Madison Ave., between 58th and 59th Sts., Midtown East* ☎ *212/888–5107* ⊕ *www.fratellirossetti. com* Ⓜ *N, R, W to 5th Ave./59th St.; 4, 5, 6 to 59th St.*

Louis Vuitton

SHOES/LUGGAGE/LEATHER GOODS | In the mammoth 57th Street flagship, shoppers get their fill of LV-emblazoned handbags and accessories, as well as the more subtle Damier check pattern and colorful striated leathers. The clothes and shoes here are devastatingly chic, and the merchandising displays alone make the store work a peek. ⊠ *1 E. 57th St., at 5th Ave., Midtown East* ☎ *212/758–8877* ⊕ *www.louisvuitton.com* Ⓜ *N, R, W to 5th Ave./59th St.*

Salvatore Ferragamo

SHOES/LUGGAGE/LEATHER GOODS | Elegance and restraint typify these designs, from handbags and footwear to fragrances and leather goods—all well represented at this multilevel flagship. The company has reworked some of its women's styles from previous decades, like the girlish Audrey (as in Hepburn, for whom the style was designed) ballet flat, released seasonally for limited runs. ⊠ *655 5th Ave., at 52nd St., Midtown East* ☎ *212/759–3822* ⊕ *www.ferragamo.com* Ⓜ *E, M to 5th Ave./53rd St.*

Stuart Weitzman

SHOES/LUGGAGE/LEATHER GOODS | The broad range of (mostly women's) shoe styles, from pumps to tall boots to strappy sandals, is enhanced by an even wider range of sizes and widths. Bridal shoes are hugely popular, if pricey. The label also produces a line of chic handbags. ⊠ *625 Madison Ave., between 58th and 59th Sts., Midtown East* ☎ *212/750–2555* ⊕ *www.stuartweitzman.com* Ⓜ *N, R, W to 5th Ave./59th St.; 4, 5, 6 to 59th St.*

Murray Hill

Murray Hill stretches roughly from 30th to 40th Street between 5th Avenue and the East River, and is a mix of high-rises, restaurants, and bars filled mostly with an affluent, postcollege crowd. The small but solid enclave of Little India (also known as "Curry Hill"), primarily around Lexington and 28th Street, is a good area for sampling authentic cuisine and shopping for traditional clothing and other goods in a handful of boutiques. Farther north, a few side streets are lined with shady trees and town houses, with some

The lights on the top of the Empire State Building often change color to support different holidays and causes.

high-profile haunts, including the Morgan Library and Museum with its striking architecture and rare manuscripts. But no matter why you're here or where you're headed, New York's biggest icon, the Empire State Building, is always inviting your skyward gaze.

⊙ Sights

B. Altman Building/New York Public Library–Science, Industry and Business Library (SIBL)

LIBRARY | FAMILY | What is now a part of the New York Public Library (NYPL) began as a famous retail outpost. In 1906, Benjamin Altman gambled that his fashionable patrons would follow his popular department store in the "Ladies' Mile" shopping district downtown up to this 5th Avenue location. His new emporium, one of the first of the grand department stores on 5th Avenue, blended in with the stately mansions nearby—note its Renaissance Revival style, limestone facade, Ionic columns, and other classical details. The store shuttered in 1989 and

stood vacant until 1996, when the NYPL moved in and formed the high-tech Science, Industry and Business Library. A 33-foot-high atrium unites the building's two floors: the lending library off the lobby and the research collections below. Downstairs, a wall of electronic ticker tapes and TVs tuned to business-news stations beams information and instructions to patrons. ⊠ 188 Madison Ave., between 34th and 35th Sts., Murray Hill ☏ 917/275–6975 ⊕ www.nypl.org ⊘ Closed Sun. Ⓜ B, D, F, M, N, Q, R, W to 34th St.–Herald Sq.; 6 to 33rd St.

Curry Hill

NEIGHBORHOOD | An affectionate play on the name of the neighborhood, Curry Hill is an aromatic three-block cluster of Indian restaurants and one of the city's more exciting dining destinations. There are around two dozen Indian restaurants peppered (or is it spiced?) around Lexington Avenue between 26th and 28th Streets, and while the neighborhood is popular with in-the-know New Yorkers, it is off the beaten tourist track. You'll find

The Lights of the Empire State Building ◉

At night the Empire State Building lights up the Manhattan skyline with a colorful view as awe-inspiring from a distance as the view from the top. The colors at the top of the building are changed regularly to reflect seasons, events, and holidays, so New Yorkers and visitors from around the world always have a reason to look at this icon in a new light.

The building's first light show was in November 1932, when a simple searchlight was used to spread the news that New York–born Franklin Delano Roosevelt had been elected president of the United States. Douglas Leigh, sign designer and mastermind of Times Square's kinetic billboard ads, tried to brighten up prospects at the "Empty State Building" after the Depression by negotiating with the Coca-Cola Company to occupy the top floors. He proposed that Coca-Cola could change the lights of the building to serve as a weather forecast and then publish a small guide on its bottles to decipher the colors. Coca-Cola loved this idea, but the deal fell through after the bombing at Pearl Harbor, when the U.S. government needed office space in the building.

In 1956 the revolving "freedom lights" were installed to welcome people to America; then in 1964 the top 30 floors of the building were illuminated to mark the New York World's Fair.

Douglas Leigh revisited the lights in 1976, when he was made chairman of City Decor to welcome the Democratic Convention. He introduced the idea of color lighting, and so the building's tower was ablaze in red, white, and blue to welcome the convention and mark the celebration of the American Bicentennial. The color lights were a huge success, and they remained red, white, and blue for the rest of the year.

Leigh's next suggestion of tying the lights to different holidays, a variation on his weather theme for Coca-Cola, is the basic scheme still used today. In 1977 the lighting system was updated to comply with energy-conservation programs and allow for a wider range of colors. Leigh further improved this new system in 1984 by designing an automated color-changing system so vertical fluorescents in the mast could be changed.

The Empire State Building's computer-driven LED light system was installed in 2012. It can produce intensely saturated full-color light and dimmable cool white light, allowing for an astonishing range of dramatic or subtle lighting effects. The system is capable of displaying 16 million different colors that can change instantaneously.

For the lighting schedule, visit ⊕ www.esbnyc.com.

---

culinary offerings from regional cuisines, be it a filling biryani or a quick *chaat* (savory snack). Highlights include a *saag paneer* (spinach dish with cheese) or a flavorful tandoori at one of the neighborhood's founding restaurants, Curry in a Hurry (119 Lexington Avenue); creamy *rogan josh* (lamb curry with saffron) or lentil fritters at Sahib (104 Lexington Avenue); and *kati* rolls (meat or veggie filling wrapped in flatbread) and other urban Indian street snacks at Desi Galli (101 Lexington Avenue). Don't leave the neighborhood without sampling a *dosa,* a fermented crêpe often filled with spiced potato and served with dipping sauces, and shopping the spice markets. ⊠ *Lexington Ave., between 26th and 28th Sts., Murray Hill* Ⓜ *6 to 28th St.; N, R, W to 23rd St.*

★ Empire State Building

BUILDING | **FAMILY** | With an iconic silhouette recognizable virtually worldwide, the Empire State Building is an Art Deco monument to progress, a symbol for New York City, and a star in some great romantic scenes, on- and off-screen. Built in 1931 at the peak of the skyscraper craze, this 103-story limestone giant opened after 13 months of construction. The framework rose at a rate of 4½ stories per week, making the Empire State Building the fastest-rising skyscraper ever built.

There are three lines to get to the top: a line for tickets, a line for security, and a line for the elevators. Save time by purchasing tickets online in advance. You can skip to the front of the ticket line and the line for elevators by purchasing an Express ticket to the 86th floor ($65).
■ **TIP➜ If you don't want to pony up for express service, skip that last elevator line at the 80th floor by taking the stairs.**

The 86th-floor observatory (1,050 feet high) has both a climate-controlled glass-enclosed area and an outdoor deck spanning the building's circumference. Don't be shy about going outside into the wind or you'll miss half the experience. The free high-powered binoculars help you see up to 80 miles on clear days. The views from the 102nd-floor observatory are even more awesome—yet fewer visitors make it this far. Even if you skip the journey to the top, step into the building lobby and take in the extraordinary Art Deco decor and especially the ceiling. ⊠ *350 5th Ave., at 34th St., Murray Hill* ☎ *212/736–3100, 877/692–8439* ⊕ *www. esbnyc.com* ⬛ *$38; $58 for 86th-fl. and 102nd-fl. decks; $65 for express to 86th fl.* Ⓜ *B, D, F, M, N, Q, R, W to 34th St.– Herald Sq.; 6 to 33rd St.*

Koreatown

NEIGHBORHOOD | Despite sitting in the shade of the Empire State Building, and within steps of Herald Square, Koreatown (or "K-Town," as it's locally known) is not a tourist destination. In fact, it feels decidedly off the radar and insulated, as though locals wryly planted their own place to eat, drink, be merry, and get a massage—right under the noses of millions of tourists. Technically, Koreatown runs from 31st to 36th Street between 5th and 6th Avenues, though the main drag is 32nd Street between 5th and Broadway. Labeled Korea Way, this strip is home to 24/7 Korean barbecue joints, karaoke bars, and spas, all stacked on top of each other. Fill up on kimchi (spicy pickled cabbage), *kimbap* (seaweed rice), and red-bean doughnuts (delicious), try some karaoke, and then top off your Koreatown experience by stepping into a jade-igloo sauna (at Juvenex Spa, 25 West 32nd Street). Expect a big bang for your buck; you'll rub elbows with locals and get bragging rights over visitors who followed the crowds to Chinatown. ⊠ *From 31st to 36th St., between 5th and 6th Aves., Murray Hill* Ⓜ *B, D, F, M, N, Q, R, W to 34th St.–Herald Sq.; 6 to 33rd St.*

★ The Morgan Library & Museum

MUSEUM | The treasures inside this museum and research center, gathered by John Pierpont Morgan (1837–1913), one of New York's wealthiest financiers, are exceptional: medieval and Renaissance illuminated manuscripts, old-master drawings and prints, rare books, and autographed literary and musical manuscripts. Some crowning achievements on paper include letters penned by John Keats and Thomas Jefferson; a summary of the theory of relativity in Einstein's own elegant handwriting; three Gutenberg Bibles; drawings by Dürer, Leonardo da Vinci, Rubens, Blake, and Rembrandt; the only known manuscript fragment of Milton's *Paradise Lost;* Thoreau's journals; and original manuscripts and letters by

Charlotte Brontë, Jane Austen, Thomas Pynchon, and many others. The Morgan is known for exquisite changing exhibitions that feature its holdings and related objects and art from other collections.

The library shop is housed within an 1852 Italianate brownstone, once the home of Morgan's son, J. P. Morgan Jr. Outside on East 36th Street, the sphinx in the right-hand sculpted panel of the original library's facade is rumored to wear the face of architect Charles McKim. ⊠ *225 Madison Ave., at 36th St., Murray Hill* ☎ *212/685–0008* ⊕ *www.themorgan.org* ▦ *$20 (free Fri. 7–9)* ⊘ *Closed Mon.* Ⓜ *B, D, F, M, N, Q, R, W to 34th St.–Herald Sq.; 6 to 33rd St.*

⑪ Restaurants

This area has a residential feel with plenty of bistros perfect for a casual meal. Lexington Avenue's "Curry Hill" section between 26th and 28th Streets is home to Indian spice shops, cafés, and restaurants.

Dons Bogam Wine Bar & BBQ

$$$$ | **KOREAN BARBECUE** | Meat lovers in particular will enjoy Korean barbecue, and Dons Bogam is a venerable, quality option with a wide variety of choices of meat and seafoods, which are cooked for you on a grill embedded in your table and are served with a wide array of condiments, sauces, embellishments. Don't ignore the appetizers; the dumplings and Korean pancakes are excellent, as are the noodle dishes and bulgogis if you aren't into barbecue. **Known for:** grilled-at-the-table Korean barbecue meat and seafood; spicy Korean stews and noodle dishes (both cold and hot); reservations necessary, even on weeknights. Ⓢ *Average main: $40* ⊠ *17 E. 32nd St., between 5th and Madison Aves., Murray Hill* ☎ *212/683–2200* ⊕ *www.donsbogam. com* Ⓜ *6 to 33rd St.; B, D, F, M, N, Q, R, W to 34th St.–Herald Sq.*

★ Marta

$$ | **ITALIAN** | The excellent cracker-thin crust of the Roman-style pizzas at Marta are a refreshing break from the thicker crust of the Neapolitan pizzas that have overtaken Manhattan in recent years, and we have beloved restaurateur Danny Meyer and chef Lena Ciardullo to thank for it. The high-ceiling dining room belies the casual fare, but the menu is a love letter to salt-of-the-earth Roman food. **Known for:** one of the few places in New York serving Roman-style pizza; buzzy room; Roman dishes. Ⓢ *Average main: $20* ⊠ *Redbury Hotel, 29 E. 29th St., at Madison Ave., Murray Hill* ☎ *212/651–3800* ⊕ *www. martamanhattan.com* Ⓜ *6 to 28th St.*

Pio Pio

$$$ | **PERUVIAN** | **FAMILY** | The long, slender dining room isn't fancy, but you've come for the Peruvian rotisserie chicken, and you'll likely remember Pio Pio's addictive, secret-recipe green sauce most. The weekday lunch special (11–4), which includes a quarter chicken, salad, a side, and a soda, is enough for two meals. **Known for:** juicy rotisserie chicken; lunch special; multiple locations. Ⓢ *Average main: $25* ⊠ *210 E. 34th St., between 2nd and 3rd Aves., Murray Hill* ☎ *212/481–0034* ⊕ *www.piopio.com* Ⓜ *6 to 33rd St.*

2nd Ave Deli

$$ | **DELI** | It may no longer be on 2nd Avenue, but the most recent incarnation of this East Village institution—about a mile uptown, in Midtown—still delivers on its longtime traditional matzo ball soup, overstuffed triple-decker sandwiches filled with house-cured pastrami, and other old-world specialties. Hot open-face sandwiches, like juicy beef brisket, are served with gravy and French fries. **Known for:** long menu of classic deli fare; gefilte fish and lox; brisket and pastrami. Ⓢ *Average main: $23* ⊠ *162 E. 33rd St., between Lexington and 3rd Aves., Murray Hill* ☎ *212/689–9000* ⊕ *www.2ndave-deli.com* Ⓜ *6 to 33rd St.*

Hotels

Iberostar 70 Park Avenue

$ | HOTEL | At this Midtown business-traveler favorite in a quiet neighborhood a couple of blocks from Grand Central, the lobby and rooms of this chain hotel are infused with a soft color palette and modern furniture. **Pros:** some rooms have Empire State Building views; polite service; simple rooms and hotel layout. **Cons:** small rooms and bathrooms; design and art might not suit all tastes; no in-hotel dining. $ Rooms from: $180 ⊠ 70 Park Ave., at 38th St., Murray Hill ☎ 212/973–2400, 800/707–2752 ⊕ www.iberostar.com ⟿ 205 rooms ⦿ No meals Ⓜ 4, 5, 6, 7, S to Grand Central–42nd St.

The Kitano Hotel New York

$$ | HOTEL | Importing much of its sensibility from Japan, the Kitano has touches that include a bilingual concierge and a high-concept Japanese restaurant—it also makes for a notably service-oriented stay. **Pros:** extra soundproofing in guest rooms; cute mezzanine bar area; excellent live jazz. **Cons:** lower-floor views are limited; expensive restaurant; charge for Wi-Fi. $ Rooms from: $359 ⊠ 66 Park Ave., at 38th St., Murray Hill ☎ 212/885–7000, 800/548–2666 ⊕ www.kitano.com ⟿ 150 rooms ⦿ No meals Ⓜ 4, 5, 6, 7, S to Grand Central–42nd St.

The Marmara Park Avenue

$$$ | HOTEL | A popular pick for extended-stay travelers, this sleek property impresses with large rooms complete with the conveniences of home, like wet bars or fully equipped kitchens. **Pros:** lots of amenities in rooms; serene lap pool, sauna, and steam room; many suites have private terraces. **Cons:** neighborhood isn't the most exciting; limited subway access nearby; expensive even for Murray Hill/Midtown. $ Rooms from: $500 ⊠ 114 E. 32nd St., Murray Hill ☎ 212/603–9000 ⊕ park.marmaranyc.com ⟿ 128 rooms ⦿ No meals Ⓜ 6 to 33rd St.

Pod 39

$ | HOTEL | The cheap and cheerful sibling of Pod 51 (on 51st Street) has tight quarters and trendy amenities, including a rooftop bar and ground-floor restaurant by famed chef Alex Stupak. **Pros:** quality taco and cocktail spot; big rooftop with gorgeous views; lobby lounge with Ping-Pong table. **Cons:** tight quarters; buzzy lobby and restaurant might not suit all guests; no gym or pool. $ Rooms from: $229 ⊠ 145 E. 39th St., between Lexington and 3rd Aves., Murray Hill ☎ 844/763–7666 ⊕ www.thepodhotel.com ⟿ 366 rooms ⦿ No meals Ⓜ 4, 5, 6, 7, S to Grand Central–42nd St.

The William

$$ | HOTEL | What was once two connected brownstones home to a social club for Williams College is now a modern, extended-stay hotel with an outpost of the fabulous speakeasy-style cocktail bar Raines Law Room. **Pros:** convenient fully equipped kitchens; central location near Grand Central; good eating and drinking options. **Cons:** color and design may be too bright and modern for some guests; no gym or spa on-site, limited restaurants and nightlife in the neighborhood. $ Rooms from: $350 ⊠ 24 E. 39th St., between Park and Madison Aves., Murray Hill ☎ 646/922–8600 ⊕ www.thewilliamnyc.com ⟿ 33 rooms ⦿ No meals Ⓜ 4, 5, 6, 7, S to Grand Central–42nd St.

ⓨ Nightlife

BARS

5th&Mad

BARS/PUBS | Even in a neighborhood dotted with Irish pubs, the two-story 5th&Mad is a fine drinking establishment with a hearty menu. Head here to relax at its big circular bar and to mingle with a spirited after-work crowd who love the weekday happy hours. DJs lend a clubby vibe Wednesday through Saturday, as do late-night bar hours (until 4 am on weekends). ⊠ 7 E. 36th St., between 5th and

Madison Aves., Murray Hill ☎ *212/725–2353* ⊕ *5thandmad.com* Ⓜ *6 to 33rd St.*

Middle Branch

BARS/PUBS | This enticing, two-story speakeasy-style bar in Murray Hill is located inside a former antiques store—and, like its West Village sibling, Little Branch, there's no sign outside to announce its presence. Cocktail lovers find the brick town house anyway, and inside, linger over small plates, live jazz, and a long list of sophisticated drinks. ✉ *154 E. 33rd St., between 3rd and Lexington Aves., Murray Hill* ☎ *212/213–1350* ⊕ *www.middlebranchnyc.com* Ⓜ *6 to 33rd St.*

👜 Shopping

BOOKS AND STATIONERY
Compleat Strategist

SPECIALTY STORES | A mecca for those who love role-playing games, this shop stocks board games and classic soldier sets, as well as fantasy games. ✉ *11 E. 33rd St., between 5th and Madison Aves., Murray Hill* ☎ *212/685–3880* ⊕ *www.thecompleatstrategist.com* Ⓜ *6 to 33rd St.*

CLOTHING
Dover Street Market

CLOTHING | The New York location is the only U.S. outpost of Rei Kawakubo's Dover Street Market (the others are in London, Tokyo, Singapore, and Beijing). It's basically a multilevel fashion emporium: each floor has mini boutiques from brands including Prada, Alaïa, and Alexander Wang, alongside lesser-known designers. The seven-story building is worth a look just for the people-watching. The in-house Rose Bakery is the perfect spot to refuel with an espresso or berry tart. ✉ *160 Lexington Ave., at 30th St., Murray Hill* ☎ *646/837–7750* ⊕ *newyork.doverstreetmarket.com* Ⓜ *6 to 28th St.*

Chapter 10

MIDTOWN WEST

Updated by
Kelsy Chauvin

⊙ Sights	🍴 Restaurants	🛏 Hotels	🛍 Shopping	🍸 Nightlife
★★★★★	★★★★★	★★★★★	★★★★★	★★★☆☆

NEIGHBORHOOD SNAPSHOT

TOP EXPERIENCES

■ Watching summer film screenings at dusk in Bryant Park

■ Ice-skating at Rockefeller Center

■ Checking out the views from the Top of the Rock; opinions vary on whether the better views are from here or from the Empire State Building. Either way, if you go at night, the city spreads out below in a mesmerizing blanket of lights

■ Soaking in the art and serenity of MoMA's sculpture garden

GETTING HERE

You can get to Midtown via almost all the subways; many trains make numerous stops throughout the area. For Midtown West, the 1, 2, 3, 7, A, C, E, N, Q, R, and W serve Times Square and West 42nd Street. The S, or Shuttle, travels back and forth between Times Square and Grand Central Terminal. The B, D, F, and M trains serve Rockefeller Center.

PLANNING YOUR TIME

Most people think of Times Square when they think of Midtown, but there's so much more going on than just animated billboards and Broadway shows. The Museum of Modern Art (MoMA) is one of the neighborhood's top attractions and certainly worth a visit, as is Bryant Park, a cool oasis for Midtown's workers and locals. If you have enough time, head westward to 12th Avenue to visit the space shuttle *Enterprise* at the *Intrepid* Sea, Air & Space Museum.

Times Square is almost always a frenetic mass of people staring up at the lights or at the costumed street performers. If you're in a hurry to get somewhere, try to avoid walking or cabbing through here. Hotels abound in Midtown, and travelers staying here can take advantage of the prime location, rise early, and be first in line at landmarks, museums, or the TKTS booth for discount day-of theater tickets.

QUICK BITES

■ **Blue Bottle Coffee.** Known for meticulous brewing, freshly roasted organic beans (prepared in a Brooklyn roastery), and delicious treats and pastries, the Rock Center outpost of this California coffee favorite is the perfect, if pricey, refueling spot in frantic Midtown. ⊠ *1 Rockefeller Plaza, Concourse Level* ⊕ *www.bluebottlecoffee.com* Ⓜ *Subway: B, D, F, M to 47–50th Sts./ Rockefeller Center; E, M to 5th Ave./53rd St.*

■ **Café Grumpy.** Stop by this Garment District outlet of the New York minichain and turn any sign of grumpiness into a smile with coffee roasted at the Greenpoint, Brooklyn, location. All pastries are baked at the Lower East Side branch: the black-pepper-and-cardamom banana bread is a standout. ⊠ *200 W. 39th St., between 7th and 8th Aves.* ⊕ *www. cafegrumpy.com* Ⓜ *Subway: 1, 2, 3, 7, N, Q, R, S, W to Times Sq.–42nd St.*

■ **Zibetto Espresso Bar.** You won't find any seats here, but you will find arguably the best espresso in New York. ⊠ *1385 6th Ave, at 56th St.* ⊕ *www.zibettoespresso.com* Ⓜ *Subway: F to 57th St.*

Big is the buzz in Times Square, where giant TV screens, towering skyscrapers, and Broadway theaters play starring roles alongside megastores and over-the-top street performers. Love it or hate it, Times Square is the flashy and flashing heart of Midtown, and a visit to New York demands a photo op there. Just don't forget that there's plenty more to see and experience beyond this famous crossroads of 7th Avenue and Broadway.

Luckily, you needn't go far to get away from the crowds. Drift west to 9th Avenue—also known as Hell's Kitchen (where the restaurant scene is heavenly)—and calmer side streets, home to a mixed bag of locals, many of whom work in the theater industry. There are lots of eclectic restaurants, pretheater dining options, and cute boutiques for shopping. Head over to the Avenue of the Americas (6th Avenue) and discover Bryant Park's Zen green space, stretched out like a yoga mat at the back door of the New York Public Library (another refuge from Midtown madness).

You can score good seats to some of the hottest Broadway and Off-Broadway shows for half the going rate at the TKTS booth in Duffy Square at 47th Street and Broadway. Although people think of Broadway as the heart of the theater scene, few theaters actually line the thoroughfare. For some of the grande dames, head west on 45th Street. There are several Broadway beauties here, including the **Booth,** the **Schoenfeld,** the

Jacobs, the **Music Box,** and the **Imperial.** On the southern side of 45th Street there's the pedestrians-only **Shubert Alley,** distinguished by colorful posters advertising the latest hit plays and musicals, and the **Shubert Theatre,** one of Broadway's most lustrous gems. Head west along 44th Street to see the **Helen Hayes,** the **Broadhurst,** the **Majestic,** and the **St. James.**

You might be surprised to learn that Chelsea is not the only gallery hub in the city; 57th Street between 5th and 6th Avenues is home to some of the city's most prestigious galleries, including Marian Goodman and the Marlborough Gallery.

◉ Sights

★ Bryant Park
CITY PARK | FAMILY | This lovely green space spread out among landmarks and skyscrapers is one of Manhattan's most popular parks. Tall London plane trees line the perimeter of the sunny central lawn,

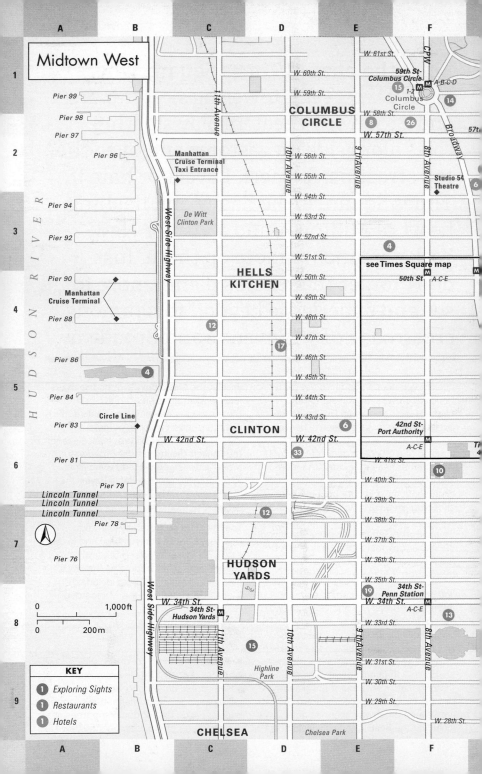

Midtown West

COLUMBUS CIRCLE

HELLS KITCHEN

CLINTON

HUDSON YARDS

CHELSEA

Pier 99
Pier 98
Pier 97
Pier 96
Pier 94
Pier 92
Pier 90
Pier 88
Pier 86
Pier 84
Pier 83
Pier 81
Pier 79
Pier 78
Pier 76

HUDSON RIVER

West Side Highway

Manhattan Cruise Terminal Taxi Entrance

De Witt Clinton Park

Manhattan Cruise Terminal

Circle Line

Lincoln Tunnel
Lincoln Tunnel
Lincoln Tunnel

11th Avenue
10th Avenue
9th Avenue
8th Avenue
Broadway
CPW

W. 61st St.
W. 60th St.
W. 59th St.
W. 58th St.
W. 57th St.
W. 56th St.
W. 55th St.
W. 54th St.
W. 53rd St.
W. 52nd St.
W. 51st St.
W. 50th St.
W. 49th St.
W. 48th St.
W. 47th St.
W. 46th St.
W. 45th St.
W. 44th St.
W. 43rd St.
W. 42nd St.
W. 42nd St.
W. 41st St.
W. 40th St.
W. 39th St.
W. 38th St.
W. 37th St.
W. 36th St.
W. 35th St.
W. 34th St.
W. 34th St.
W. 33rd St.
W. 31st St.
W. 30th St.
W. 29th St.
W. 28th St.

59th St-Columbus Circle
Columbus Circle
1-2
A-B-C-D

Studio 54 Theatre

see Times Square map
50th St
A-C-E

42nd St-Port Authority
A-C-E

34th St-Penn Station
A-C-E

34th St-Hudson Yards
7

Highline Park

Chelsea Park

57th

14
8
26
4
6
12
17
4
6
33
12
15
19
13
10
15

0   1,000ft
0   200m

KEY

1 Exploring Sights
1 Restaurants
1 Hotels

Sights ▼

1 Bryant Park.............. **H6**
2 Christie's **H4**
3 Findlay Galleries **I2**
4 Intrepid Sea, Air & Space Museum **B5**
5 Marian Goodman Gallery **H2**
6 Marlborough Gallery (Midtown)................ **H2**
7 The Museum of Modern Art (MoMA) ... **H3**
8 NBC Studios............. **H4**
9 New York Public Library Main Branch **I6**
10 The New York Times Building **F6**
11 The Paley Center for Media **H3**
12 The Rink at Rockefeller Center....... **I4**
13 Rockefeller Center...... **H4**
14 Top of the Rock.......... **H4**
15 Vessel **C8**

Restaurants ▼

1 Benoit **H2**
2 Brasserie Ruhlmann......**I4**
3 burger joint **G2**
4 Danji...................... **E3**
5 db Bistro Moderne **H5**
6 Esca **E5**
7 Gabriel Kreuther **H6**
8 Indian Accent **G2**
9 La Bonne Soupe **H2**
10 L'Adresse **H6**
11 Le Bernardin **G3**
12 Legacy Records.......... **D7**
13 Lugo Cucina Italiana **F8**
14 Marea..................... **F1**
15 Plaza Food Hall by Todd English **H1**
16 Quality Meats **H1**
17 Tulcingo del Valle **D4**
18 '21' Club **H3**
19 Uncle Jack's Steakhouse............... **E8**

Hotels ▼

1 The Algonquin Hotel Times Square, Autograph Collection **H5**
2 Archer Hotel New York **H7**
3 Baccarat Hotel & Residences **H3**
4 Bryant Park Hotel....... **H6**
5 City Club Hotel **H5**
6 Dream Midtown **G2**
7 Hotel Metro NYC........ **H7**
8 Hudson New York....... **E2**
9 Hyatt Herald Square New York **H9**
10 Iroquois New York...... **H5**
11 JW Marriott Essex House New York **G1**
12 Kimpton Ink48 Hotel **C4**
13 The London NYC **G3**
14 LUMA Hotel Times Square........... **G6**
15 Mandarin Oriental, New York **F1**
16 The Mansfield Hotel **I5**
17 Moxy NYC Times Square........... **G7**
18 1 Hotel Central Park **H2**
19 Park Hyatt New York ... **G2**
20 The Plaza **H1**
21 The Quin Central Park.... **H2**
22 Refinery Hotel........... **H7**
23 The Ritz-Carlton New York, Central Park **H1**
24 Royalton New York **H5**
25 Shoreham Hotel......... **H2**
26 6 Columbus **F2**
27 Sofitel New York **H5**
28 Viceroy Central Park New York **G2**
29 Warwick New York..... **H2**
30 Wellington Hotel **G2**
31 WestHouse Hotel New York **G2**
32 Whitby Hotel **H2**
33 Yotel New York **D6**

Bryant Park is one of the best places to bring your lunch and people-watch in the city.

overlooking stone terraces, flower beds, and snack kiosks. The garden tables scattered about fill with lunching office workers and folks enjoying the park's free Wi-Fi. In summer you can check out free readings, live jazz, and "Broadway in Bryant Park" musical theater performances. Most popular of all is the summer film festival: locals leave work early to snag a spot on the lawn for the outdoor screenings each Monday at dusk.

At the east side of the park, near a squatting bronze cast of Gertrude Stein, is the stylish Bryant Park Grill, which has a rooftop garden, and the adjacent open-air Bryant Park Café, open seasonally. On the south side of the park is an old-fashioned **carousel** ($3) where kids can also attend storytellings and magic shows. Come late October the park rolls out the artificial frozen **"pond"** (*Oct.–Mar., daily 8 am–10 pm; skate rental $20*) for free ice-skating (bring your own padlock for the lockers). Surrounding the ice rink are the Christmas-market stalls of the **holiday shops,** selling handcrafted goods

and local foods. ⊠ *6th Ave., between 40th and 42nd Sts., Midtown West* ☎ *212/768–4242* ⊕ *www.bryantpark.org* Ⓜ *B, D, F, M to 42nd St.–Bryant Park; 7 to 5th Ave.*

Christie's

STORE/MALL | You could easily spend an hour or more wandering the free, museumlike galleries at the New York outpost of this famous auction house, viewing impressive works of art, estate jewelry, furniture, and other rarely displayed objects of interest that are usually housed in (and most likely, soon to be returned to) private collections. One of the first items to be auctioned here, when it opened in 2000, was the "Happy Birthday" dress worn by Marilyn Monroe when she sang to President Kennedy (it sold for more than $1.2 million). Yes, the auction house has come a long way since James Christie launched his business in England by selling two chamber pots, among other household goods, in 1766. The lobby's abstract Sol LeWitt mural alone makes it worth visiting the

310,000-square-foot space. Hours vary by sale, so call ahead to confirm. ✉ *20 Rockefeller Plaza, 49th St. between 5th and 6th Aves., Midtown West* 🕾 *212/636–2000* ⊕ *www.christies.com* 📧 *Free* Ⓜ *B, D, F, M to 47th–50th Sts./Rockefeller Center; E, M to 5th Ave./53rd St.*

Findlay Galleries

MUSEUM | A 2016 merger between the well-established David Findlay Jr. Gallery and Wally Findlay Gallery led to this combined Midtown space with the same concentration of the former's contemporary and 20th-century American artists—from Frank Stella to Barbara Grad, Byron Browne, and Leonard Nelson—and the latter's presentation of impressionist and postimpressionist works. ✉ *724 5th Ave., 7th fl., between 56th and 57th Sts., Midtown West* 🕾 *212/421–5390* ⊕ *www. findlaygalleries.com* 📧 *Free* ⊘ *Closed Sun., also Mon. fall–spring* Ⓜ *N, Q, R, W to 5th Ave./59th St.*

Gulliver's Gate

MUSEUM | FAMILY | At this attraction in Times Square, "the crossroads of the world," behold miniature, detailed, sometimes animated versions of the world's major cities and sights, starting with a 1,000 square foot scale model of the Big Apple itself (see if you can find the tiny Spider-Man). From there, follow a path through the sprawling exhibit and witness 50 nations and 300 small-scale scenes—from the Eiffel Tower and Big Ben to the Taj Mahal and Machu Picchu—each built by artists and model makers native to the region represented. There are more than 100,000 tiny people throughout, plus more than 3,200 feet of railroad track; thousands of trucks, trains, boats, planes, and cars; and a fully operational mini airport where you can watch planes taking off precisely as they do in real life. Along the way, use a digital key to bring scenes to life, and watch model makers in action in the gallery. ✉ *216 W. 44th St., between Broadway and 8th Ave., Midtown West* 🕾 *212/235–2016*

⊕ *gulliversgate.com* 📧 *$36 (discounts available online)* Ⓜ *1, 2, 3, 7, N, Q, R, S, W to Times Sq.–42nd St.; A, C, E to 42nd St.–Port Authority.*

Intrepid Sea, Air & Space Museum

MUSEUM | FAMILY | Manhattan's only floating museum is a historic, nonprofit, and educational institution like no other. The centerpiece is the *Intrepid*, a 900-foot-long aircraft carrier that was launched in 1943 and decommissioned in 1974. The carrier's most trying moment of service, the day it was attacked in World War II by kamikaze pilots, is recounted in a stirring multimedia presentation. On the ship's various indoor and outdoor decks is a collection of 28 aircraft. The space shuttle *Enterprise*—NASA's original prototype orbiter that paved the way for the space-shuttle program—is housed in a climate-controlled pavilion on the *Intrepid's* flight deck. Surrounding exhibits share the shuttle's history and that of NASA's decades-long space-shuttle program.

Docked alongside the *Intrepid* is the submarine *Growler,* the only American guided missile submarine open to the public. *Growler* offers visitors a first-hand look at life aboard a submarine and a close-up inspection of the once top secret missile command center. Also among the museum's collection is a retired British Airways Concorde, the world's fastest passenger jet. This record-breaking plane—the Concorde Alpha Delta G-BOAD—holds the record for the fastest Atlantic crossing by any Concorde. The museum provides specialized programs and resources to support those with disabilities and their families. ✉ *Pier 86, 12th Ave. at 46th St., Midtown West* 🕾 *212/245–0072, 877/957–7447* ⊕ *www.intrepidmuseum.org* 📧 *$33 (free for U.S. military/veterans)* Ⓜ *A, C, E to 42nd St.–Port Authority.*

Madame Tussauds New York

MUSEUM | FAMILY | Croon with Michael Jackson, Tina Turner, and Taylor Swift,

Ice-skating under the sculpture of Prometheus, at Rockefeller Center, is a winter ritual for many local and visiting families.

pucker up to your favorite heartthrob (be it Justin Bieber or Justin Timberlake), strike a fierce pose with fashionista Heidi Klum, or enjoy a royal chat with the Duke and Duchess of Cambridge, William and Kate. Much of the fun here comes from photo opportunities—you're encouraged to pose with and touch the more than 200 realistic replicas of the famous, infamous, and downright super.

The Marvel 4D Experience includes wax likenesses of heroes like the Hulk, Captain America, Iron Man, and Thor, as well as a short animated movie shown on a 360-degree screen that surrounds the viewer. Other interactive options at the museum include a karaoke café, a celebrity walk down the red carpet, and a Sports Zone where you can see how you measure up to sporting legends like Serena Williams and Eli Manning. Note that closing hours vary during peak seasons, but the last tickets sold are always one hour prior. ⊠ *234 W. 42nd St., between 7th and 8th Aves., Midtown West* ☎ *866/841–3505* ⊕ *www.* madame-tussauds.com ⊠ *$37 (discounts available online)* Ⓜ *1, 2, 3, 7, N, Q, R, S, W to Times Sq.–42nd St.; A, C, E to 42nd St.–Port Authority.*

Marian Goodman Gallery

MUSEUM | Perhaps the most respected contemporary art dealer in town, the Marian Goodman Gallery has been introducing top European artists to American audiences since 1977. The stable of excellent contemporary artists in the Goodman fold includes Gerhard Richter, Jeff Wall, John Baldessari, William Kentridge, Chantal Akerman, and Steve McQueen. ⊠ *24 W. 57th St., between 5th and 6th Aves., Midtown West* ☎ *212/977–7160* ⊕ *www.mariangoodman.com* ⊠ *Free* ⊘ *Closed Sun.* Ⓜ *F to 57th St.*

Marlborough Gallery (Midtown)

MUSEUM | The gallery has an international reputation, representing modern artists such as Magdalena Abakanowicz, Beverly Pepper, and Red Grooms, architect Santiago Calatrava, and photo-realist Richard Estes. Look for sculptures by Tom Otterness, whose whimsical

Art in Rockefeller Center

The mosaics, murals, and sculptures that grace Rockefeller Center—many of them Art Deco masterpieces—were part of John D. Rockefeller Jr.'s plans. In 1932, he put together a team of advisers to find artists who could make the project "as beautiful as possible." Some artists scoffed at the idea of decorating an office building: Picasso declined to meet with Rockefeller, and Matisse replied that busy businessmen wouldn't be in the "quiet and reflective state of mind" needed to appreciate his art. Those who agreed to contribute, including muralists Diego Rivera (from Mexico) and José María Sert (from Spain), were relatively unknown, though a group of American artists protested Rockefeller's decision to hire "alien" artists. More than 50 artists contributed 200 works.

As Rockefeller Center neared completion in 1932, Rockefeller still needed a mural for the lobby of the main buildings, and he wanted the subject to be grandiose: "human intelligence in control of the forces of nature." He hired Rivera. Man at the Crossroads, with its depiction of massive machinery moving mankind forward, seemed exactly what Rockefeller wanted—until it was realized that a portrait of Soviet Premier Vladimir Lenin surrounded by red-kerchiefed workers occupied a space in the center. Rockefeller, who was building what was essentially a monument to capitalism, was less than thrilled. When Rivera was accused of propagandizing, he famously replied, "All art is propaganda."

Rivera refused to remove the offending portrait and, in early 1934, as Rivera was working, representatives for Rockefeller informed him that his services were no longer required. Within a half hour, tar paper had been hung over the mural. Despite negotiations to move the artwork to the Museum of Modern Art, Rockefeller was determined to get rid of the mural once and for all. Not content to have it painted over, he ordered ax-wielding workers to chip away the entire wall. He commissioned a less offensive one (by Sert) instead.

Rivera had the last word, though: he re-created the mural in the Palacio de Bellas Artes in Mexico City, adding a portrait of Rockefeller among the Champagne-swilling swells ignoring the plight of the workers.

The largest of the original artworks that remains is Lee Lawrie's 2-ton sculpture, Atlas. Its building also stirred up controversy, as it was said to resemble Italy's fascist dictator, Benito Mussolini. The sculpture, depicting a muscle-bound man holding up the world, drew protests in 1936. Some even derided Paul Manship's golden Prometheus, which soars over the ice-skating rink, when it was unveiled the same year. Both are now considered to be among the best public artworks of the 20th century.

Lawrie's sculpture Wisdom, over the main entrance of 20 Rockefeller Plaza, is another gem. Also look for Isamu Noguchi's stainless-steel plaque News over the entrance of 50 Rockefeller Plaza and Attilio Piccirilli's 2-ton glass-block panel Youth Leading Industry over the entrance of the International Building at 636 5th Avenue.

bronzes are found in several subway stations. A Chelsea branch specializes in contemporary art. ✉ *40 W. 57th St., between 5th and 6th Aves., Midtown West* ☎ *212/541–4900* ⊕ *www.marlboroughgallery.com* ✉ *Free* ⊙ *Closed Sun.* Ⓜ *F to 57th St.*

★ The Museum of Modern Art (MoMA)

MUSEUM | Housing one of the world's finest collections of modern art, the MoMA is renowned for its permanent exhibits, which include masterpieces by Picasso, Van Gogh, Monet, and Dalí, as well as its first-rate—and highly buzzed-about—multimedia exhibitions. Located north of Rockefeller Center on West 53rd Street, the MoMA's current building design features a maze of glass walkways to permit art viewing from many angles; a high-end restaurant and bar, The Modern; and a cinema that offers curated international film selections and talks.

The museum spans six levels, and it's best to explore from top to bottom, ending on Level 1 at the Abby Aldrich Rockefeller Sculpture Garden. Designed by Philip Johnson, it features Barnett Newman's *Broken Obelisk* (1962–69) and a reflecting pool and trees. Plans for an expansion into the space next door (the former American Folk Art Museum, which has relocated near Lincoln Center) include additional gallery space, an expanded lobby, and the opening of its entire first floor, including the sculpture garden, as a free public space. Construction completion is expected in late 2019. ■**TIP**→ **Entry is free on Friday 4–8 pm, but expect long lines.** ✉ *11 W. 53rd St., between 5th and 6th Aves., Midtown West* ☎ *212/708–9400* ⊕ *www.moma. org* ✉ *$25* Ⓜ *E, M to 5th Ave./53rd St.; F to 57th St.; B, D, E to 7th Ave.*

NBC Studios

FILM STUDIO | You can join the gawking crowds watching news tapings outside the NBC studios (which are in the Art Deco GE Building on Rockefeller Plaza), or you can get even closer to the action (without having to elbow anyone) by taking a slick behind-the-scenes tour of the legendary studios. Tours depart every 20 minutes daily, delving into the history of television and the actual recording studios of some of the network's top shows, like *Saturday Night Live, The Tonight Show Starring Jimmy Fallon,* and *NBC Nightly News.* Tours start at the Shop at NBC Studios (49th Street between 5th and 6th Avenues); advance tickets are sold online (recommended), and children must be at least six years old. ✉ *30 Rockefeller Plaza, 49th St. between 5th and 6th Aves., Midtown West* ☎ *212/664–3700* ⊕ *www.thetouratnbcstudios.com* ✉ *$33* Ⓜ *B, D, F, M to 47th–50th Sts./ Rockefeller Center.*

New York Public Library Main Branch

LIBRARY | The "Library with the Lions" marked its centennial in 2011 as a masterpiece of Beaux Arts design and as one of the great research institutions in the world, a repository for millions of items including books, manuscripts, photographs, maps, periodicals, and more. For the building's current, comprehensive modernization, expect changes to the building that will adapt it to the 21st century. Renovation continues through 2021 and includes the creation of more public space, a new 40th Street entrance, improved infrastructure, and expanded exhibition spaces.

The library's bronze front doors open into **Astor Hall,** which leads to special exhibit galleries and, to the left, a stunning periodicals room with wall paintings of New York publishing houses. Ascend the sweeping double staircase to a second-floor balconied corridor overlooking the hall, with panels highlighting the library's development. Continue up to behold the magisterial **Rose Main Reading Room**, where natural light pours through the massive windows. Third-floor galleries show rotating exhibits on print and photography. On the ground floor, visit the Children's Center to see a display of

Winnie-the-Pooh and friends, the actual dolls owned by Christopher Robin that inspired A. A. Milne's beloved tales. Free hour-long tours leave Monday–Saturday at 11 and 2, and Sunday at 2 from Astor Hall. ⊠ *476 5th Ave., between 40th and 42nd Sts., Midtown West* ☎ *212/930–0800 for exhibit info* ⊕ *www.nypl.org* Ⓜ *B, D, F, M to 42nd St.–Bryant Park; 7 to 5th Ave.*

The New York Times Building

BUILDING | Completed in 2007, this 52-story building with its distinctive, ladderlike ceramic rods is a testament to clean-lined modernism. The architect, Renzo Piano, extended the ceramic rods beyond the top of the building so that it would give the impression of dissolving into the sky. One of the skyscraper's best features—and the one that's open to the public—is the building's lobby atrium, which includes an open-air moss garden with 50-foot paper-birch trees and a wooden footbridge; a 560-screen media art installation titled *Moveable Type*, streaming a mix of the newspaper's near-real-time and archival content; and the New York flagship store of minimalist home-goods designer MUJI. You never know which famous journalists you'll spy on the coffee line in Dean & DeLuca. Unfortunately, tours are not offered. ⊠ *620 8th Ave., between 40th and 41st Sts., Midtown West* ☎ *212/984–8128* ⊕ *www.newyorktimesbuilding.com* Ⓜ *A, C, E to 42nd St.–Port Authority; 1, 2, 3, 7, N, Q, R, S, W to Times Sq.–42nd St.*

The Paley Center for Media

MUSEUM | With an ever-changing exhibition gallery, small cinema, screening room, and a computerized catalog of more than 160,000 television and radio programs, the Paley Center for Media's New York outpost examines the constantly evolving state of media. Temporary exhibits on the first floor may showcase anything from game shows to sporting events through photographs, recordings, and artifacts. The center also hosts public seminars, lectures, and screenings that explore the history of broadcasting. The fourth-floor library is a top draw here: if you want to see an archived awards show, news program, sitcom, or historic event, simply check into a semiprivate computer terminal, enter your search terms, and enjoy. Possibly the most entertaining part of these TV shows from yesteryear is the fact that the original commercials are still embedded in many of the programs. If ads are your thing, you can watch compilations of classic commercials. ⊠ *25 W. 52nd St., between 5th and 6th Aves., Midtown West* ☎ *212/621–6800* ⊕ *www.paleycenter.org* ⤶ *$10 (suggested admission)* ⊙ *Closed Mon., Tues.* Ⓜ *E, M to 5th Ave./53rd St.; B, D, F, M to 47th–50th Sts./Rockefeller Center.*

The Rink at Rockefeller Center

SPORTS VENUE | **FAMILY** | Set (in season) in the shadow of the giant Rockefeller Center Christmas tree, the city's most iconic ice-skating rink is a quintessential experience for visitors and a longstanding tradition for many locals. General-admission skating is on a first-come, first-served basis, so it is best to come early, and on weekdays, to avoid crowds. First Skate tickets ($40–$65, reserved online) allow 7 am access to the rink, followed by a complimentary hot chocolate or coffee and pastry or breakfast. VIP Skate packages ($60–$150) allow guests to skate past the long lines and include skate rental, 90 minutes of ice time, and hot chocolate and cookies. Other packages include Christmas Show and VIP Skate (from $121), which covers orchestra seating for the Radio City Christmas Spectacular as well as admission to the rink, skate rental, and refreshments. The rink is a café in summer. ⊠ *30 Rockefeller Plaza, between 49th and 50th Sts., Midtown West* ⊕ *www.therinkatrockcenter. com* ⤶ *$25–$33; $12.50 skate rental* ⊙ *Closed mid-Apr.–Sept.* Ⓜ *B, D, F, M to 47th–50th Sts./Rockefeller Center; E, M to 5th Ave./53rd St.*

Rockefeller Center

BUILDING | Comprising more than 100 shops and 50 eateries, the Rockefeller Center complex runs from 47th to 52nd Street between 5th and 6th Avenues. Special events dominate the central plazas in spring and summer. In December an enormous twinkling tree towers above the ice-skating rink, causing huge crowds of visitors from across the country and the globe to shuffle through with necks craned and cameras flashing.

The world's most famous ice-skating rink (see The Rink at Rockefeller Center) occupies Rockefeller Center's sunken lower plaza from October through mid-April and converts to a café in summer. The gold-leaf statue of the Greek hero **Prometheus** hovers above, forming the backdrop to zillions of photos. The lower plaza also provides access to the marble-lined concourse underneath Rockefeller Center, which houses restaurants, a post office, and clean public restrooms.

Rising from the Lower Plaza's west side is the 70-story Art Deco **GE Building.** Here Rockefeller commissioned and then destroyed a mural by Diego Rivera. He replaced it with the monumental American Progress by José María Sert, still on view in the lobby, flanked by additional murals by Sert and English artist Frank Brangwyn. Up on the 65th floor is the landmark **Rainbow Room,** a glittering big-band ballroom dating to 1934. Higher up, **Top of the Rock** has what many consider the finest panoramic views of the city. ⊠ From 47th to 52nd St. between 5th and 6th Aves., Midtown West ⊕ www.rockefellercenter.com Ⓜ B, D, F, M to 47th–50th Sts./Rockefeller Center; E, M to 5th Ave./53rd St.

Times Square

NEIGHBORHOOD | Hands down, this is the most energetic part of New York City, a cacophony of flashing lights and shoulder-to-shoulder crowds that many New Yorkers studiously avoid. Originally named after the New York Times (whose headquarters have since relocated to 8th Avenue), the area has seen many changes since the first subway line, which included a 42nd Street station, opened in 1904. While the area was once a bastion of the city's unseemly side, today it's a vibrant, family-friendly destination with pedestrian stretches that have lined Broadway Plaza with tables, chairs, and granite benches. There's no longer a visitor center, but you can drop by the official NYC Information Center, a movable kiosk (usually located at West 44th Street) with maps, brochures, coupons, and a bilingual staff.

The focus of the entertainment may have shifted over the years, but showtime is still the heart of Midtown's theater scene, and there are 40 Broadway theaters nearby. Learn about Broadway's history and architecture with a one-hour walking tour ($50) by Manhattan Walking Tours (⊕ www.manhattanwalkingtour.com); or join the two-hour guided Inside Broadway tour ($35; daily at 4 pm ⊕ www.insidebroadwaytours.com) that leaves from the George M. Cohan statue at West 46th Street and Broadway. ⊠ Broadway between 42nd and 48th Sts., Midtown West ☎ 212/768–1560 for Times Square Alliance ⊕ www.timessquarenyc.org Ⓜ 1, 2, 3, 7, N, Q, R, S, W to Times Sq.–42 St.

★ Top of the Rock

VIEWPOINT | Rockefeller Center's multi-floor observation deck, the Top of the Rock, provides views that rival those from the Empire State Building. Arriving pre-sunset affords a view of the city that morphs into a dazzling wash of colors, with a bird's-eye view of the Empire State Building and the Chrysler Building, and sweeping views northward to Central Park and south to the Statue of Liberty. Timed-entry ticketing eliminates long lines. Indoor exhibits include films of Rockefeller Center's history and a model of the building.

Some of the world's most famous paintings hang in the MoMA, including Monet's *Water Lilies*.

Rapid elevators lift you to the 67th-floor interior viewing area, and then an escalator leads to the outdoor deck on the 69th floor for sightseeing through nonreflective glass safety panels. Then, take another elevator or stairs to the 70th floor for a 360-degree outdoor panorama of New York City on a deck that is only 20 foot wide and nearly 200 feet long. Especially interesting is a Plexiglas screen on the floor with footage showing Rock Center construction workers dangling on beams high above the streets. A Sun & Stars ticket ($54) allows you to visit twice and see the city as it rises and sets in the same day. ⊠ *30 Rockefeller Plaza, 50th St. entrance, between 5th and 6th Aves., Midtown West* ☎ *212/698–2000* ⊕ *www. topoftherocknyc.com* ✉ *$36* Ⓜ *B, D, F, M to 47th–50th Sts./Rockefeller Center; E, M to 5th Ave./53rd St.*

★ Vessel

PUBLIC ART | The centerpiece of the new Hudson Yards development, a temporarily named interlocking staircase (which is called "art") is at this writing the hottest tourist ticket in New York City and will likely be a strong competitor to the ever popular High Line. You may think you're in an M. C. Escher lithograph come to life, but it's a selfie paradise up on those stairs. For the foreseeable future, you'll have to book a timed-entry ticket two weeks before your expected visit, or you can try to reserve a same-day pass—either online in the morning or in person through a ticket kiosk at the site—to snag one of the limited same-day passes. Evening times book up the quickest (especially in summer, when it's stlil light out), so those are the most unlikely times you'll find for the same day. It doesn't open until 10 and closes at 9, so you won't be able to do some stair-climbing and picture-taking after imbibing or dining at one of the area's expensive restaurants. On the positive side, it's completely free. ⊠ *20 Hudson Yards, Midtown West* ☎ *646/954–3100* ⊕ *www.hudsonyardsnewyork.com* ✉ *Free (timed-entry ticket is required)* Ⓜ *7 to 34th St.–Hudson Yards.*

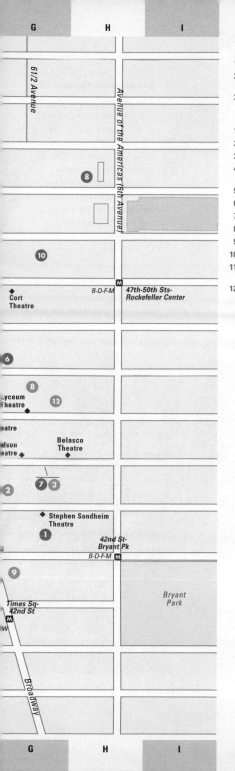

Sights ▼

1 Gulliver's Gate............ **EG**
2 Madame Tussauds
    New York **E8**
3 Times Square............ **F5**

Restaurants ▼

1 Aureole **G7**
2 Becco.................... **B5**
3 Carmine's................ **F6**
4 Ellen's
    Stardust Diner........... **F2**
5 5 Napkin Burger **B5**
6 Havana Central **G5**
7 The Lambs Club........ **G6**
8 Le Pain Quotidien....... **H2**
9 Marseille................. **B6**
10 Ocean.................... **G3**
11 Plataforma
    Churrascaria **C3**
12 Toloache................ **D2**

Hotels ▼

1 Belvedere Hotel.......... **C3**
2 Casablanca Hotel by
    Library Hotel
    Collection................ **G6**
3 The Chatwal
    New York **G6**
4 CitizenM New
    York Times
    Square **E3**
5 DoubleTree Suites
    by Hilton Hotel
    New York City
    –Times Square **F4**
6 Hilton Times Square..... **E7**
7 InterContinental
    New York
    Times Square............. **C6**
8 Kimpton Muse Hotel.... **G5**
9 The Knickerbocker **G7**
10 The Michelangelo
    New York- Starhotels
    Collezione................ **F2**
11 Renaissance New York
    Times Square Hotel...... **F4**
12 Room Mate Grace **G6**
13 The Time New York...... **E3**
14 W New York
    –Times Square **E4**
15 Westin New York
    at Times Square......... **D7**

Did You Know?

The phrase "Great White Way" refers to the stretch of Broadway along the Theater District. Stories vary, but some attribute this nickname to the showy display of lamps that lighted the theater marquees in the early days of incandescent lighting.

🍴 Restaurants

It's true that tourist traps abound on Broadway, but fortunately you needn't head far from Times Square to score a stellar meal. Just move away from the bright lights and the unrelenting foot traffic that clogs the area. On calmer side streets and in adjoining Hell's Kitchen there are excellent dining options for budget travelers and expense-account diners alike. Some of the best steak houses and Italian restaurants are here, and many eateries offer budget pretheater dinners and prix-fixe lunch menus to draw in new business.

Aureole

$$$$ | MODERN AMERICAN | An island of fine modern American dining just a stone's throw from bustling Times Square, Aureole is the second act of a New York classic from Charlie Palmer and his executive chef, Gabriele Carpentiere. The dining room (prix-fixe menus only), with its abundance of flowers, is the place to hobnob with expense-account diners and pretheater revelers. **Known for:** refined dining; prix-fixe menu; barroom with à la carte choices. $ Average main: $96 ⊠ 135 W. 42nd St., between Broadway and 6th Ave., Midtown West 🕾 212/319-1660 ⊕ www.charliepalmer. com ⊘ Closed Sun. No lunch Sat. Ⓜ B, D, F, M to 42nd St.–Bryant Park; 1, 2, 3, 7, N, Q, R, S, W to Times Sq.–42nd St.

Becco

$$$ | ITALIAN | An ingenious concept makes bustling Becco a prime Restaurant Row choice for time-constrained theatergoers. There are two pricing scenarios at this Italian spot: one includes an all-you-can-eat selection of antipasti and three pastas served hot out of pans that waiters circulate around the dining room; the other adds a generous entrée to the mix. **Known for:** one of the better Restaurant Row pretheater options; changing pasta selection; mains including veal shank and rack of lamb. $ Average main:

$26 ⊠ 355 W. 46th St., between 8th and 9th Aves., Midtown West 🕾 212/397-7597 ⊕ www.becco-nyc.com Ⓜ A, C, E to 42nd St.–Port Authority.

Benoit

$$$ | FRENCH | Who needs to go to Paris when the world's most famous French chef, Alain Ducasse, can come to you? The interior of Ducasse's imported Right Bank bistro—cozy red-velour banquettes and wall lamps illuminating each table—is plucked straight from the City of Light, and so is the menu, which doesn't reinvent anything as much as it replicates. **Known for:** classic Parisian bistro fare; wine bar; roasted veal loin. $ Average main: $35 ⊠ 60 W. 55th St., between 5th and 6th Aves., Midtown West 🕾 646/943-7373 ⊕ www.benoitny. com Ⓜ N, R, W to 5th Ave./59th St.; F to 57th St.

Brasserie Ruhlmann

$$$ | BISTRO | Sublime French bistro cookery is on display in a plush 120-seat dining room with just enough Art Deco touches to harmonize with its Rockefeller Center setting. The room has a refined air, but the staff are so friendly that the place could never be stuffy. **Known for:** bistro fare and raw bar; outdoor terrace; French flair. $ Average main: $30 ⊠ 45 Rockefeller Plaza, 50th St. between 5th and 6th Aves., Midtown West 🕾 212/974-2020 ⊕ www.brasserieruhl-mann.com ⊘ No dinner Sun. Ⓜ B, D, F, M to 47th–50th Sts./Rockefeller Center; E, M to 5th Ave./53rd St.

burger joint New York

$ | BURGER | What's a college burger bar, clad in wood paneling and rec-room design straight out of *Happy Days,* doing inside a five-star Midtown hotel? This one-of-a-kind spot with great burgers, hidden behind a heavy red-velvet curtain in the Parker New York hotel, does such boisterous business that lines often snake through the lobby (beat the line by coming at off hours, before noon or midafternoon). **Known for:** not-so-secret

About Hudson Yards

It's rare for a brand-new neighborhood to be built in New York City from scratch. Hudson Yards was constructed on a platform directly above the sprawling train tracks that head west from New York Penn Station, and much of it opened in March 2019. Regardless of how you think about the architecture, there's plenty to draw tourists here who want to eat, shop, or gawk. You will also be able to stay at a new Equinox Hotel, slated to open in June 2019.

Attractions

In addition to the expansive public plazas, Hudson Yards has several other attractions that are meant to draw tourists and locals at all hours of the day and night. The biggest draw is the **Vessel** (temporarily named), an series of interlocking staircases that looks like an M. C. Escher etching come to life. But **The Shed** may be a more substantial addition to the New York arts scene, an interdisciplinary venue that will adapt to whatever happens to be on the bill. Less (or perhaps even more) interesting is **Snark Park,** where you can pay $28 to take selfies with the immersive art installations. Think of it as the Vessel on a decidedly less grand scale and at many times the cost. Still under development at this writing (and with undisclosed pricing) is **The Edge**, an open-air glass-enclosed observation deck on the 100th floor of 30 Hudson Yards that promises some of Manhattan's most spectacular views for those with the stomach to stand outside at that height.

Dining

If you're hungry, there are almost three dozen places to get anything from an wildly expensive celebrity-chef meal to coffee to a fancy cocktail to a black-and-white cookie to some of New York's best ice cream. Many of the restaurants are open now, though some open later in 2019. They include Little Spain, a Spanish food hall by José Andrés; Fuku, a fried chicken stand from David Chang; Kawi, a Korean restaurant by Chef Eunjo Park; a modern British restaurant, Queensyard; a branch of Estiatorio Milos; and a branch of Bouchon Bakery from Thomas Keller, as well as Tak Room, a fine-dining restaurant. But there are other fast-casual places, coffee shops, ice cream stores, candy shops, a bakery, and wine and cocktail bars as well.

Shopping

A giant luxury shopping mall offers everything from mass-market stores like Banana Republic, H&M, Lululemon, Pandora, and Athleta; to luxury retailers Cartier, Coach, Dior, Fendi, Rolex, Tiffany, and Louis Vuitton; to New York City's first Neiman Marcus department store

spot for good-value burgers; retro fast-food joint inside a luxury hotel; crisp fries. [$] *Average main: $9* ✉ *Parker New York, 119 W. 56th St., between 6th and 7th Aves., Midtown West* ☎ *212/708–7414* 🌐 *www.burgerjointny.com* [M] *N, Q, R, W to 57th St.–7th Ave.; F to 57th St.*

Carmine's

$$$ | **ITALIAN** | **FAMILY** | Savvy New Yorkers line up early for the affordable family-style Italian meals at this large, busy Midtown eatery where family photos line the walls, and there's a convivial feeling amid all the Times Square hubbub. Families carbo-loading for a day of sightseeing or a night of theater on Broadway are rewarded with mountains of such classic, toothsome viands as fried calamari, linguine with white clam sauce, chicken parmigiana, and veal saltimbocca. **Known for:** good-value Italian fare; family-style portions; swift service. [$] *Average main: $25* ✉ *200 W. 44th St., between Broadway and 8th Ave., Midtown West* ☎ *212/221–3800* 🌐 *www.carminesnyc.com* [M] *A, C, E to 42nd St.–Port Authority; 1, 2, 3, 7, N, Q, R, S, W to Times Sq.–42nd St.*

Danji

$$ | KOREAN | Helmed by talented chef Hooni Kim, this diminutive white-walled Hell's Kitchen Korean spot stands out among the rows of restaurants that attract theatergoing tourists to the neighborhood, thanks to Kim's inventive and inspired take on Korean cuisine. The menu is split between small, medium, and large plates, each category a combination of traditional Korean fare and more experimental dishes. **Known for:** Korean fire chicken wings; bulgogi beef sliders; great lunch option. [$] *Average main: $21* ✉ *346 W. 52nd St., between 8th and 9th Aves., Midtown West* ☎ *212/586–2880* 🌐 *www.danjinyc.com* [M] *C, E to 50th St.*

db Bistro Moderne

$$$ | FRENCH | Daniel Boulud's "casual bistro" (it's neither, actually) consists of two elegantly appointed dining rooms. The menu features classic dishes like Atlantic salmon and hanger steak exquisitely prepared—as well as the trendsetting (and pricey) "db" hamburger stuffed with braised short ribs, foie gras, and black truffles, credited with kick-starting the gourmet burger trend. **Known for:** db burger; steak frites; worth the price. [$] *Average main: $33* ✉ *55 W. 44th St., between 5th and 6th Aves., Midtown West* ☎ *212/391–2400* 🌐 *www.dbbistro.com* [M] *B, D, F, M to 42nd St.–Bryant Park; 7 to 5th Ave.*

Ellen's Stardust Diner

$$ | AMERICAN | FAMILY | If you haven't had enough Broadway singing and dancing, you'll get a kick out of Ellen's, a retro, 1950s-style diner, complete with a singing waitstaff. The menu focuses on all-American classics like meat loaf and chicken potpie, and the waiters and waitresses serenading you on roller skates possess fittingly Broadway-caliber talent. **Known for:** midcentury food; star-spangled fun; good for families. [$] *Average main: $20* ✉ *1650 Broadway, at 51st St., Midtown West* ☎ *212/956–5151* 🌐 *www.ellensstardustdiner.com* [M] *1 to 50th St.; B, D, E to 7th Ave.*

Esca

$$$ | SEAFOOD | The name is Italian for "bait," and this restaurant lures diners in with delectable crudo preparations—such as tilefish with orange and Sardinian oil or pink snapper with a sprinkle of crunchy red clay salt. It then hooks them with entrées like whole salt-crusted branzino, sea bass for two, or bucatini pasta with spicy baby octopus. **Known for:** elevated, fresh seaside Italian fare; daily-changing menu; exciting wine list. [$] *Average main: $35* ✉ *402 W. 43rd St., at 9th Ave., Midtown West* ☎ *212/564–7272* 🌐 *www.esca-nyc.com* 🕑 *No lunch Sun.* [M] *A, C, E to 42nd St.–Port Authority.*

5 Napkin Burger

$$ | BURGER | This perennially packed Hell's Kitchen burger place and brasserie has been a magnet for burger lovers since day one. Though there are many menu distractions—including matzo ball soup, shrimp tempura, and salad bowls—the main attractions are the juicy burgers, like the original 10-ounce chuck with a tangle of onions, Gruyère cheese, and rosemary aioli. **Known for:** messy, delicious burgers of all kinds; deep-fried delights; wildly indulgent desserts. [$] *Average main: $17* ✉ *630 9th Ave., at 45th St., Midtown West* ☎ *212/757–2277* 🌐 *www.5napkinburger.com* [M] *A, C, E to 42nd St.–Port Authority.*

Gabriel Kreuther

$$$$ | FRENCH | Chef Gabriel Kreuther rose to NYC culinary prominence when he made The Modern (the eatery inside MoMA) one of *the* places for fine dining in the city. After leaving, in 2006 he fired up the burners at this eponymous place across from Bryant Park that, refreshingly, still sends out of the kitchen extremely haute prix-fixe fare, influenced by Kreuther's native Alsace. **Known for:** sturgeon and sauerkraut tart; Euro-chic ambience; haute dining at haute prix-fixe price, but lunch is cheaper. $ *Average main: $155* ⊠ *41 W. 42nd St., between 5th and 6th Aves., Midtown West* ☎ *212/257–5826* ⊕ *www.gknyc.com* ⊗ *Closed Sun.* Ⓜ *B, D, F, M to 42nd St.–Bryant Park.*

Havana Central

$$ | CUBAN | A little slice of Havana in the center of the Big Apple, Havana Central is a great place for reasonably priced group dining and sampling Cuban-Latino standards. Dig into dishes like garlicky chicken, hearty oxtail stew, authentic *mofongo* (smashed, fried plantains), pine-apple-spiked chicken, and well-seasoned skirt steak with a cucumber-and-mango salad. **Known for:** lively, musical atmosphere; rum-driven cocktail menu; Cuban brunch. $ *Average main: $20* ⊠ *151 W. 46th St., between 6th and 7th Aves., Midtown West* ☎ *212/398–7440* ⊕ *www. havanacentral.com* Ⓜ *N, R, W to 49th St.; B, D, F, M to 47th–50th Sts./Rockefeller Center.*

★ Indian Accent

$$$$ | MODERN INDIAN | It didn't take long after chef Manish Mehrotra opened Indian Accent in New Delhi in 2009 that buzz about it being the best resaurant in India began. In 2016, he opened an outlet in a New York; it also didn't take long for buzz to circulate that this was the Big Apple's best Indian eatery, as chef Mehrotra extracts as much flavor out of his ingredients as possible. **Known for:** outstanding prix-fixe Indian dining; stuffed breads;

ghee roast lamb. $ *Average main: $75* ⊠ *123 W. 56th St., between 6th and 7th Aves., Midtown West* ☎ *212/842–8070* ⊕ *www.indianaccent.com* ⊗ *No lunch Sun.* Ⓜ *F to 57th St.*

La Bonne Soupe

$$ | FRENCH | Midtown office workers and in-the-know out-of-towners keep this French restaurant bustling for the ever-popular La Bonne Soupe special—a bowl of excellent soup with bread, salad, a beverage (house wine, beer, soda, or coffee), and dessert. À la carte options include bistro classics like crepes, omelets, salads, quiche, sandwiches, and croques madame and monsieur. Although it's not the hippest place in town, it's plenty satisfying. **Known for:** reliable, good-value French fare; soup special; Midtown lunch hot spot. $ *Average main: $19* ⊠ *48 W. 55th St., between 5th and 6th Aves., Midtown West* ☎ *212/586–7650* ⊕ *www.labonnesoupe. com* Ⓜ *B, D, F, M to 47th–50th Sts./Rockefeller Center.*

L'Adresse

$$$ | AMERICAN | This Russian import has evolved from a coffee-fueled spot to a full-fledged restaurant, calling itself L'Adresse: American Bistro and serving taste bud–tingling international fare. The spacious restaurant, located across from Bryant Park, serves masterful contemporary American dishes from seafood to its famous truffle burger, in addition to a few Russian favorites. **Known for:** truffle burger; halvah latte; polished Midtown dining. $ *Average main: $30* ⊠ *1065 6th Ave., at 40th St., Midtown West* ☎ *212/221–2510* ⊕ *www.ladressenyc.com* ⊗ *No dinner Sun.* Ⓜ *B, D, F, M to 42nd St.–Bryant Park.*

The Lambs Club

$$$$ | MODERN AMERICAN | Restaurateur Geoffrey Zakarian's opulent supper club on the ground floor of the Chatwal Hotel has superb Art Deco detailing, blood-red leather banquettes, and a roaring fireplace. The food is typical Zakarian,

meaning new American cuisine with luxe touches in dishes that span shellfish, seasonal-veggie salads, and classic steak, pork, and duck dishes. **Known for:** famous former private-club patrons like Charlie Chaplin and John Wayne; great breakfasts; clubby vibe. [$] *Average main: $36* ✉ *132 W. 44th St., between 6th Ave. and Broadway, Midtown West* ☎ *212/997–5262* 🌐 *www.thelambsclub.com* [M] *1, 2, 3, 7, N, Q, R, S, W to Times Sq.–42nd St.; B, D, F, M to 47th–50th Sts./Rockefeller Center.*

★ Le Bernardin

$$$$ | SEAFOOD | Head into the serene, teak-panel dining room at this trendsetting French seafood restaurant, and let chef Eric Ripert work his magic with anything that swims—at times preferring not to cook it at all. Deceptively simple dishes such as poached lobster in rich coconut-ginger soup or crispy spiced black bass in a Peking duck bouillon are typical of his style. **Known for:** one of the best seafood spots in the country; prix-fixe only; stellar wine list. [$] *Average main: $155* ✉ *155 W. 51st St., between 6th and 7th Aves., Midtown West* ☎ *212/554–1515* 🌐 *www.le-bernardin.com* 🕒 *Closed Sun. No lunch Sat.* 👔 *Jacket required* [M] *1 to 50th St.; N, R, W to 49th St.; B, D, E to 7th Ave.*

Le Pain Quotidien

$$ | BAKERY | This casual international Belgian chain brings its homeland ingredients with it, treating New Yorkers to crusty organic breads, jams, chocolate, and other specialty products. You can grab a snack to go or stay and eat breakfast, lunch, or dinner at wooden communal or private tables with waiter service. **Known for:** fresh baked goods; open-face sandwiches; cozy atmosphere. [$] *Average main: $14* ✉ *1271 6th Ave., at 50th St., Midtown West* ☎ *646/462–4165* 🌐 *www.lepainquotidien.com* [M] *B, D, F, M to 47th–50th Sts./Rockefeller Center; N, R, W to 49th St.; 1 to 50th St.*

★ Legacy Records

$$$ | ITALIAN | Named for the space's erstwhile occupant, Legacy Recording Studios (where everyone from Jimi Hendrix to Jay-Z recorded), this Italian eatery inside Henry Hall, part of the new Hudson Yards megaproject, is made up of a culinary dream team: chef Ryan Hardy (Charlie Bird, Pasquale Jones); Arvid Rosengren, voted in 2016 as "best sommelier in the world" (by the Association de la Sommellerie); and Jeff Bell, lauded mixologist from PDT, behind the cocktail list. Hardy focuses on the cuisine of northern Italy, specifically the coastal regions. **Known for:** changing risotto options; creative cocktails; hip scene. [$] *Average main: $30* ✉ *517 W. 38th St., between 10th and 11th Aves., Midtown West* 🌐 *www.legacyrecordsnyc.com* [M] *7 to 34th St.–Hudson Yards.*

Lugo Cucina Italiana

$$$ | ITALIAN | The area around Madison Square Garden is a restaurant wasteland with the rare, sparkling exception of this spacious Italian "brasserie," serving comfort food with a dolce vita twist. Stop by for an espresso and pastry in the morning; later, a single menu presents lunch, *aperitivo*, and dinner options, which include grazing portions of salumi, cheeses, and vegetable dishes like eggplant caponata, Tuscan white-bean salad, and grilled zucchini with pine nuts. **Known for:** Italian comfort food and house-made pastas; gnocchi with crab; solid dining in MSG area. [$] *Average main: $25* ✉ *1 Penn Plaza, 33rd St. and 8th Ave., Midtown West* ☎ *212/760–2700* 🌐 *www.lugocucina.com* 🕒 *Closed weekends* [M] *1, 2, 3, A, C, E to 34th St.–Penn Station.*

★ Marea

$$$ | SEAFOOD | Large picture windows in the dining room look out to expansive views of Central Park South at this upscale, seafood-centric Italian eatery. No expense is spared in importing the very best of the ocean's bounty, beginning with crudo dishes—think scallops with orange, wild fennel, and arugula—that are becoming the restaurant's signature. **Known for:** grilled octopus; memorable seafood pastas; baked branzino for two. [$] *Average main: $28* ✉ *240 Central Park S, between 7th Ave. and Broadway, Midtown West* ☎ *212/582–5100* 🌐 *www.marea-nyc.com* [M] *1, A, B, C, D to 59th St.–Columbus Circle.*

Marseille

$$$ | **MEDITERRANEAN** | With great food and a convenient location near several Broadway theaters, Marseille is perpetually packed. The Mediterranean creations are continually impressive, including the bouillabaisse, the signature dish of the region for which the restaurant is named—a mélange of mussels, shrimp, and whitefish in a fragrant broth, topped with a garlicky crouton and served with rouille on the side. **Known for:** three-course dinner; bouillabaisse and steak frites; delicious desserts. [$] *Average main: $25* ✉ *630 9th Ave., at 44th St., Midtown West* ☎ *212/333–2323* 🌐 *www.marseillenyc.com* [M] *A, C, E to 42nd St.–Port Authority.*

Oceana

$$$ | **SEAFOOD** | Entering this restaurant is like walking into the dressy stateroom of a modern luxury ocean liner, a perfect setting for some of the most vivid and delicious seafood in town. Floor-to-ceiling windows look out north and west, and the arrestingly designed raw bar backed with Mediterranean-hue ceramics serves stunningly fresh choices including gorgeous oysters. **Known for:** grilled whole fish; good vegetarian options; ocean liner vibes. [$] *Average main: $35* ✉ *120 W. 49th St., at 6th Ave., Midtown West* ☎ *212/759–5941* 🌐 *www.oceanarestaurant.com* 🕓 *Closed Sun. No breakfast or lunch Sat.* [M] *B, D, F, M to 47th–50th Sts./Rockefeller Center.*

Plataforma Churrascaria

$$$ | **BRAZILIAN** | This sprawling, boisterous Brazilian shrine to meat, with its all-you-can-eat prix-fixe menu, is best experienced with a group of ravenous friends. Start with a trip to the fabulous salad bar, piled with vegetables, meats, and cheeses—but remember, there's about to be a parade of all manner of grilled meats and poultry, from pork ribs to chicken hearts, delivered to the table on long skewers. **Known for:** all-you-can-eat meat; salad bar; good for group meals. [$] *Average main: $35* ✉ *316 W. 49th St., between 8th and 9th Aves., Midtown West* ☎ *212/245–0505* 🌐 *www.plataformaonline.com* [M] *C, E to 50th St.*

Plaza Food Hall by Todd English

$$ | **ECLECTIC** | At this food hall in the basement of the Plaza Hotel, celeb-chef Todd English oversees a series of mini restaurants, each with its own counter and seating ideal for a quick snack or a full-fledged meal. Though the place is made up of individual food concepts, you are seated by a hostess at any available counter and then, once settled, you can get up and survey your choices before sitting down and ordering from your waiter. **Known for:** favorite celebrity-chef dishes; affordable for this upscale neighborhood; everything from seafood to burgers to pizzas. [$] *Average main: $18* ✉ *Plaza Hotel, 1 W. 59th St., at 5th Ave., Midtown West* ☎ *212/986–9260* 🌐 *www.theplazany.com/dining/foodhall* [M] *N, R, W to 5th Ave./59th St.*

Quality Meats

$$$$ | **STEAKHOUSE** | The handsome design at this steak house is inspired by classic New York City butcher shops in its use of warm wood, stainless steel, and white marble. Sit at the bar to peruse the extensive menu of wines and single-malt scotches, or sip a classic martini; then retire to the dining room for memorable fare like foie gras terrine, roasted fish, and sophisticated riffs on steak-house classics from veal chops to short ribs. **Known for:** all manner of prime cuts; inventive variations on classic dishes; signature smoked cocktails. [$] *Average main: $37* ✉ *57 W. 58th St., near 6th*

Ave., Midtown West ☎ *212/371–7777* 🌐 *www.qualitymeatsnyc.com* 🕑 *No lunch weekends* [M] *F to 57th St.; N, R, W to 5th Ave./59th St.*

Toloache

$$ | MEXICAN | The bi-level eatery at this bustling Mexican cantina just off Broadway has a festive vibe, with several seating options: bar, balcony, main dining room, and ceviche bar. Foodies flock here for three types of guacamole (traditional, fruited, and spicy), well-executed ceviches, Mexico City–style tacos with Negra Modelo–braised brisket, and quesadillas with black truffle and *huitlacoche* (a corn tungus known as the "Mexican truffle"). **Known for:** quesadilla with huitlacoche; good Latin flavors; broad tequila selection. [$] *Average main: $21* ✉ *251 W. 50th St., near 8th Ave., Midtown West* ☎ *212/581–1818* 🌐 *www.toloachenyc.com* [M] *1, C, E to 50th St.; N, R, W to 49th St.*

Tulcingo del Valle

$$ | MEXICAN | FAMILY | This authentic Mexican grocery and restaurant serves tacos, tortas, and Pueblan specialties seven days a week from breakfast until dinner. The real stars here are the massive meat platters served with rice, beans, guacamole, salsa picante, and tortillas. **Known for:** authentic Mexican; chicken mole poblano; flavorful juices and drinks. [$] *Average main: $13* ✉ *665 10th Ave., near W. 47th St., Midtown West* ☎ *212/262–5510* 🌐 *www.tulcingorestaurant.com* [M] *C, E to 50th St.*

'21' Club

$$$$ | AMERICAN | Tradition's the thing at this town-house landmark, a former speakeasy that opened in 1929. Chef Sylvain Delpique tries to satisfy everyone with standards like the famous '21' burger and Dover sole with brown butter, as well as more modern dishes, such as sautéed pork belly, but the food is almost secondary to the restaurant's storied past. **Known for:** classic dishes; no jeans or sneakers allowed; old-school Manhattan exclusivity. [$] *Average main: $42* ✉ *21 W. 52nd St., between 5th and 6th Aves., Midtown West* ☎ *212/582–7200* 🌐 *www.21club.com* 🕑 *Closed Sun. No lunch Sat.* 👔 *Jacket required* [M] *E, M to 5th Ave./53rd St.; B, D, F, M to 47th–50th Sts./Rockefeller Center.*

Uncle Jack's Steakhouse

$$$$ | STEAKHOUSE | Surpassing even its celebrated flagship restaurant in Bayside, Queens, Uncle Jack's soars directly into the pantheon of the best steak houses in Manhattan, serving USDA prime steaks dry-aged for 21 days. Despite its corny 3-D sign out front, the interior is vast and traditionally appointed, and service is swift and focused. **Known for:** serious NYC meats; "Yabba Dabba Doo for Two" rib chop; vintage steak house style. [$] *Average main: $69* ✉ *440 9th Ave., between 34th and 35th Sts., Midtown West* ☎ *212/244–0005* 🌐 *www.unclejacks.com* 🕑 *No brunch weekends* [M] *A, C, E to 34th St.–Penn Station.*

🛏 Hotels

The Algonquin Hotel Times Square, Autograph Collection

$ | HOTEL | One of Manhattan's most historic properties, the Algonquin is a landmark of literary history—think oak paneling and pillars in the lobby—but with modernized rooms and contemporary comforts. **Pros:** historic character in spades; knowledgeable staff; hotel cat keeps guests company. **Cons:** some small rooms; might feel a bit old-fashioned; decor could use updates. [$] *Rooms from: $289* ✉ *59 W. 44th St., between 5th and 6th Aves., Midtown West* ☎ *212/840–6800* 🌐 *www.algonquinhotel.com* 🛏 *181 rooms* 🍴 *No meals* [M] *7 to 5th Ave.; B, D, F, M to 42nd St.–Bryant Park.*

Archer Hotel New York

$$ | HOTEL | Rooftop bar Skyglass, with its killer view of the Empire State Building, is the star of this quirky new-build property just south of Bryant Park with a subtly industrial-inspired look that nods to the neighborhood's past. **Pros:** rooftop bar; whimsical design and ambience; reasonably priced for Manhattan. **Cons:** small rooms; lack of amenities including gym or spa; convenient but unglamorous location. $ *Rooms from: $449* ⊠ *45 W. 38th St., between 5th and 6th Aves., Midtown West* ☎ *855/437–9100* ⊕ *www.archerhotel.com* ⮑ *180 rooms* ⦿ *No meals* Ⓜ *B, D, F, M, 7 to 42nd St.–Bryant Park.*

Baccarat Hotel & Residences

$$$$ | **HOTEL** | This polished property provides pure luxury at every corner, from the emphasis on quality service to the glamorous, flower-filled salon and bar where all the drinks are served in Baccarat glassware. **Pros:** glamorous dining and drinking options; all rooms are stocked with Baccarat glassware; serene swimming pool and La Mer spa. **Cons:** very expensive; no coffee machine in standard rooms; inconsistent service. $ *Rooms from: $1,000* ⊠ *28 W. 53rd St., between 5th and 6th Aves., Midtown West* ☎ *212/790–8800* ⊕ *www.baccarathotels.com* ⮑ *114 rooms* ⦿ *No meals* Ⓜ *E, M to 5th Ave./53rd St.*

Belvedere Hotel

$$ | **HOTEL** | **FAMILY** | The main draw of the Belvedere, which was built during the 1920s, is its Times Square/Theater District location; the rooms tend to be dark with a dull design, although they are spacious and have kitchenettes with a microwave, mini-refrigerator, and coffeemaker. **Pros:** helpful staff; rooms are good value; convenient location. **Cons:** can be loud with street noise; slow elevators; Wi-Fi free in only some room categories. $ *Rooms from: $329* ⊠ *319 W. 48th St., between 8th and 9th Aves., Midtown West* ☎ *212/245–7000* ⊕ *www.belvederehotelnyc.com* ⮑ *352 rooms* ⦿ *No meals* Ⓜ *C, E to 50th St.*

Bryant Park Hotel

$$ | **HOTEL** | A city landmark that towers over the New York Public Library and Bryant Park, this sleek hotel is still a Midtown hot spot. **Pros:** gorgeous building; fashionable crowd and setting; across from pretty Bryant Park. **Cons:** views not great from lower floors; not kid-friendly; limited dining and nightlife in the area. $ *Rooms from: $395* ⊠ *40 W. 40th St., between 5th and 6th Aves., Midtown West* ☎ *212/869–0100* ⊕ *www.bryantparkhotel.com* ⮑ *128 rooms* ⦿ *No meals* Ⓜ *B, D, F, M to 42nd St.–Bryant Park; 7 to 5th Ave.*

Casablanca Hotel by Library Hotel Collection

$$ | **HOTEL** | A favorite for the comfortable rooms and great location, the Casablanca evokes the sultry Mediterranean with its colors and decor, including a lobby outfitted with mirrors and mosaics, wooden blinds, and bistro tables—it's all rather theatrical, but then again, so is the neighborhood. **Pros:** great access to the Theater District; free continental breakfast and evening wine-and-cheese reception; access to best-selling e-books via app. **Cons:** exercise facilities at nearby New York Sports Club, not on premises; heavy tourist foot traffic; no full-service restaurant. $ *Rooms from: $369* ⊠ *147 W. 43rd St., between 6th and 7th Aves., Midtown West* ☎ *212/869–1212* ⊕ *www.casablancahotel.com* ⮑ *45 rooms* ⦿ *Free Breakfast* Ⓜ *1, 2, 3, 7, N, Q, R, S, W to Times Sq.–42nd St.*

★ The Chatwal New York

$$$ | **HOTEL** | A lavishly refurbished reincarnation of a classic Manhattan theater club, the Chatwal delivers a stylish, luxury experience with a matching price tag. **Pros:** gorgeous lobby; state-of-the-art room controls and amenities; quality dining, bar, and spa. **Cons:** some find the price too high even for Times Square; tiny pool barely big enough to swim laps in; rooms are not large. $ *Rooms from: $545* ⊠ *130 W. 44th St., between Broadway and 6th Ave., Midtown West* ☎ *212/764–6200* ⊕ *www.thechatwalny.com* ⮑ *76 rooms* ⦿ *No meals* Ⓜ *B, D, F,*

M to 42nd St.–Bryant Park; 1, 2, 3, 7, N, Q, R, S, W to Times Sq.–42nd St.

★ CitizenM New York Times Square

$ | HOTEL | Part of a stylish chain with a refreshing attitude, this hotel is all about giving you everything you need and nothing you don't really require. **Pros:** all-season rooftop bar; cozy lobby full of books and magazines; 20th-floor gym with great views. **Cons:** rooms are tight on space; high-traffic area; streamlined service (no bellboys, self check-in) isn't for everyone. $ Rooms from: $225 ✉ 218 W. 50th St., between Broadway and 8th Ave., Midtown West ☎ 212/461–3638 ⊕ www.citizenm.com ↘ 230 rooms ⦿⃝ No meals Ⓜ 1, C, E to 50th St.; N, R, W to 49th St.

City Club Hotel

$$ | HOTEL | Ocean liner–inspired rooms at the City Club are brisk, bright, and masculine: they're also about the same size as a room on a cruise ship, which means tight quarters, matey, no matter how much you enjoy sharing space with Jonathan Adler ceramics. **Pros:** convenient Midtown location; great restaurant; personal service. **Cons:** no gym; tiny lobby; small rooms. $ Rooms from. $375 ✉ 55 W. 44th St., between 5th and 6th Aves., Midtown West ☎ 212/921–5500 ⊕ www.cityclubhotel.com ↘ 65 rooms ⦿⃝ No meals Ⓜ B, D, F, M to 42nd St.–Bryant Park; 7 to 5th Ave.

DoubleTree Suites by Hilton Hotel New York City–Times Square

$$ | HOTEL | FAMILY | Space is the draw at this 45-story Times Square top dog; every room is a suite, with a separate bedroom and living room (each with a big flat-screen TV), occupying about 400 square feet overlooking Times Square and Broadway—an especially desirable location during the New Year's Eve ball drop. **Pros:** extremely helpful, informed concierge; convenient to the Theater District; quiet, considering the location. **Cons:** fee for Wi-Fi in guest rooms; pricey for a DoubleTree; generic design. $ Rooms

from: $399 ✉ 1568 Broadway, at 47th St., Midtown West ☎ 212/719–1600 ⊕ doubletree3.hilton.com ↘ 468 rooms ⦿⃝ No meals Ⓜ B, D, F, M to 47th–50th Sts./Rockefeller Center; 1 to 50th St.; N, R, W to 49th St.

Dream Midtown

$$ | HOTEL | Part hotel, part Kafkaesque dream, this Midtown spot specializes in style over comfort but is still quite livable, despite some over-the-top design features—and noise from the scenesters headed to the rooftop bar. **Pros:** PHD Terrace penthouse bar; large spa; up-to-the-minute electronics. **Cons:** small rooms; spotty service; might be too sceney for some. $ Rooms from: $429 ✉ 210 W. 55th St., at Broadway, Midtown West ☎ 212/247–2000 ⊕ www.dreamhotels. com/midtown ↘ 219 rooms ⦿⃝ No meals Ⓜ N, Q, R, W to 57th St.–7th Ave.

Hilton Times Square

$ | HOTEL | A glass-and-steel skyscraper atop a 335,000-square-foot retail complex that includes a movie theater and Madame Tussauds Wax Museum, the Hilton Times Square soars 44 stories above Manhattan and overlooks New York City's famous skyline and the Hudson River. **Pros:** great location for Times Square entertainment; convenient to public transportation; big rooms. **Cons:** impersonal feel; nickel-and-dime charges and overpriced food and drink; extremely high-traffic area with expensive parking. $ Rooms from: $299 ✉ 234 W. 42nd St., between 7th and 8th Aves., Midtown West ☎ 212/840–8222, 800/445–8667 ⊕ www.hilton.com ↘ 460 rooms ⦿⃝ No meals Ⓜ 1, 2, 3, 7, N, Q, R, S, W to Times Sq.–42nd St.; A, C, E to 42nd St.–Port Authority.

Hotel Metro NYC

$ | HOTEL | In the heart of Herald Square (and with a rooftop view of Macy's), Hotel Metro has the convenience of location matched with the comfort of a family-run establishment. **Pros:** complimentary coffee and tea 24/7; renovated exercise room has flat-screen TVs; rooftop has views of the Empire State Building. **Cons:** noise seeps in from outside; rooms are tasteful but spartan; high-traffic area. 🛇 *Rooms from: $294* ✉ *45 W. 35th St., between 5th and 6th Aves., Midtown West* ☎ *212/947–2500* ⊕ *www.hotelmetronyc.com* ⇌ *183 rooms* ⦿ *No meals* Ⓜ *B, D, F, M, N, Q, R, W to 34th St.–Herald Sq.*

Hudson New York

$ | HOTEL | Fashionistas and other modish folks who mind their budgets are drawn to this stylish, affordable hotel with its fabulous lobby (resembling a set from *A Midsummer Night's Dream*), multiple bars and lounges perfect for people-watching, and contemporary art that's an escape from the usual hotel design. **Pros:** fabulous, elegant bar; gorgeous Francesco Clemente fresco in lobby; breathtaking Sky Terrace. **Cons:** staff can be cold; tiny rooms; overpriced cocktails. 🛇 *Rooms from: $250* ✉ *356 W. 58th St., between 8th and 9th Aves., Midtown West* ☎ *212/554–6000* ⊕ *www. hudsonhotel.com* ⇌ *878 rooms* ⦿ *No meals* Ⓜ *1, A, B, C, D to 59th St.–Columbus Circle.*

Hyatt Herald Square New York

$$ | HOTEL | Business travelers, tourists, and families alike appreciate this boutique property a stone's throw from Penn Station, with a scenic rooftop bar featuring Empire State Building views. **Pros:** stylish rooms with coffeemakers; friendly and efficient service; location in the thick of it. **Cons:** small workout room; location can be noisy; rooftop bar is seasonal. 🛇 *Rooms from: $349* ✉ *30 W. 31st St., between 5th Ave. and Broadway, Midtown West* ☎ *212/330–1234* ⊕ *newyorkheraldsquare.hyatt.com* ⇌ *122 rooms* ⦿ *No meals* Ⓜ *B, D, F, M, N, Q, R, W to 34th St.–Herald Sq.*

InterContinental New York Times Square

$$$ | HOTEL | A central location mere blocks from the heart of Broadway, Times Square, and restaurant-rich Hell's Kitchen makes the InterContinental a conveniently located draw. **Pros:** central for transportation and entertainment; in-house restaurant menu by celebrity chef; attentive staff. **Cons:** expensive for the neighborhood; corporate vibe; high-traffic area. 🛇 *Rooms from: $515* ✉ *300 W. 44th St., between 8th and 9th Aves., Midtown West* ☎ *212/803–4500* ⊕ *www.interconny.com* ⇌ *607 rooms* ⦿ *No meals* Ⓜ *A, C, E to 42nd St.–Port Authority.*

Iroquois New York

$$$ | HOTEL | Once the home of James Dean (he lived here for two years in the 1950s), the Iroquois is a historic hotel dating back to 1899, with a semisecret cocktail bar that's one of the best in Manhattan. **Pros:** excellent craft-cocktail bar; 24-hour fitness center with Finnish sauna; complimentary coffee and tea in lobby. **Cons:** room decor is dated; most rooms are poorly lit; no roll-away beds available. 🛇 *Rooms from: $550* ✉ *49 W. 44th St., between 5th and 6th Aves., Midtown West* ☎ *212/840–3080* ⊕ *www. iroquoisny.com* ⇌ *117 rooms* ⦿ *No meals* Ⓜ *B, D, F, M to 42nd St.–Bryant Park; 7 to 5th Ave.*

JW Marriott Essex House New York

$$ | HOTEL | With Central Park views and an Art Deco masterpiece of a lobby, the JW Marriott Essex House is a comfortable Midtown hotel full of character. **Pros:** great service; amazing views and easy access to Central Park; gorgeous, timeless architecture and decor. **Cons:** overly complex room gadgetry; expensive bar; traffic clogs up the area during peak hours. 🛇 *Rooms from: $406* ✉ *160 Central Park S, between 6th and 7th Aves., Midtown West* ☎ *212/247–0300* ⊕ *www. marriott.com* ⇌ *426 rooms* ⦿ *No meals* Ⓜ *N, Q, R, W to 57th St.–7th Ave.; F to 57th St.*

Kimpton Ink48 Hotel

$$ | HOTEL | FAMILY | If you want to be near Midtown but a bit removed from the hustle and bustle, this hotel is a great

option, with spacious, reasonably priced rooms, expansive views, a sceney rooftop bar and pool, and great service that make up for a long walk from the nearest subway. **Pros:** friendly staff; beautiful rooftop with great skyline views; large rooms. **Cons:** out-of-the-way location; lobby can feel overly quiet; street noise in lower-floor rooms. [$] *Rooms from: $399* ✉ *653 11th Ave., at 48th St., Midtown West* ☎ *212/757–0088* 🌐 *www.ink48.com* 🛏 *222 rooms* 🍴 *No meals* [M] *C, E to 50th St.*

Kimpton Muse Hotel
$$ | **HOTEL** | Surrealist prints and busts of Thalia, the muse of comedy, adorn the lobby of this polished property, a good pick for guests looking for a Midtown boutique-hotel experience. **Pros:** contemporary interiors; bike rentals and in-room yoga mats available; complimentary morning coffee and tea and evening wine reception. **Cons:** street noise; small gym; many room views are underwhelming. [$] *Rooms from: $399* ✉ *130 W. 46th St., between 6th and 7th Aves., Midtown West* ☎ *212/485–2400* 🌐 *www.themusehotel.com* 🛏 *200 rooms* 🍴 *No meals* [M] *B, D, F, M to 47th–50th Sts./Rockefeller Center.*

The Knickerbocker
$$$ | **HOTEL** | An oasis of elegant, urban sophistication in the heart of Times Square, the Knickerbocker is a soothing counterpoint to the mass of people, lights, and excitement that converge nearby at the crossroads of Broadway and 42nd Street. **Pros:** in Times Square but aesthetically apart from it; spacious gym; fabulous rooftop bar. **Cons:** nearby dining isn't that exciting; small lobby; fee for Wi-Fi. [$] *Rooms from: $500* ✉ *6 Times Sq., entrance on 42nd St., east of Broadway, Midtown West* ☎ *212/204–4980* 🌐 *www.theknickerbocker.com* 🛏 *330 rooms* 🍴 *No meals* [M] *1, 2, 3, 7, N, Q, R, S, W to Times Sq.–42nd St.*

★ The London NYC
$$$$ | **HOTEL** | Stylish and sophisticated, the London NYC merges the flair of both its namesake cities in spacious, tech-savvy suites that are some of the largest in New York, starting at 500 square feet. **Pros:** sophisticated atmosphere; great fitness club; good concierge service. **Cons:** no bathtubs in most rooms; expensive dining options; no spa. [$] *Rooms from: $699* ✉ *151 W. 54th St., between 6th and 7th Aves., Midtown West* ☎ *212/307–5000* 🌐 *www.thelondonnyc.com* 🛏 *562 suites* 🍴 *No meals* [M] *B, D, E to 7th Ave.; N, Q, R, W to 57th St.–7th Ave.*

LUMA Hotel Times Square
$$ | **HOTEL** | Housed in a new glass building, the LUMA offers streamlined contemporary design, a restaurant by James Beard Award–winning chef Jose Garces, and an intimate experience in the heart of busy Midtown Manhattan. **Pros:** great restaurant by an award-winning chef; tech-friendly amenities include plentiful USB ports and a robot butler; simple, functional design. **Cons:** extremely high-traffic area; no gym on-site; small lobby offers little space for lounging. [$] *Rooms from: $399* ✉ *120 W. 41st St., between 6th Ave. and Broadway, Midtown West* ☎ *888/559–5862* 🌐 *www.lumahotels.com* 🛏 *130 rooms* 🍴 *No meals* [M] *1, 2, 3, 7, N, Q, R, S, W to Times Sq.–42nd St.*

★ Mandarin Oriental, New York
$$$$ | **HOTEL** | The Mandarin's commitment to excess is evident in the lobby, on the 35th floor of the Time Warner Center, where dramatic floor-to-ceiling windows look out over Columbus Circle and Central Park. **Pros:** vibrant location near transit and thoroughfares; destination-worthy cocktails and dining; expansive suites. **Cons:** limited Central Park views; occasional service issues; mall-like surroundings. [$] *Rooms from: $795* ✉ *80 Columbus Circle, at 60th St., Midtown West* ☎ *212/805–8800* 🌐 *www.mandarinoriental.com/newyork* 🛏 *198*

rooms †⊙I No meals Ⓜ 1, A, B, C, D to 59th St.–Columbus Circle.

The Mansfield Hotel

$$ | HOTEL | Built in 1904 as lodging for distinguished bachelors, this small, club-by property has an Edwardian sensibility that shows in details like the working fireplace in the lounge, the lobby's coffered ceiling, and a marble-and-cast-iron staircase. **Pros:** handsome decor; business center; 24-hour gym. **Cons:** tiny rooms and bathrooms; air-conditioners are window units; poor lighting in rooms. Ⓢ Rooms from: $319 ⊠ 12 W. 44th St., between 5th and 6th Aves., Midtown West ☎ 212/277–8700 ⊕ www. mansfieldhotel.com ⇨ 126 rooms †⊙I No meals Ⓜ B, D, F, M to 42nd St.–Bryant Park; 7 to 5th Ave.

The Michelangelo New York - Starhotels Collezione

$$ | HOTEL | Italophiles feel like they've been transported to the good life in the Mediterranean at this deluxe hotel, where the long, wide lobby lounge is clad with multihue marble and Veronese-style oil paintings. **Pros:** convenient location for shopping and sights; spacious rooms; Clefs d'Or concierge. **Cons:** noisy air-conditioning units; in-room fixtures need some updating; small closets. Ⓢ Rooms from: $399 ⊠ 152 W. 51st St., at 7th Ave., Midtown West ☎ 212/765–1900 ⊕ www.michelangelohotel.com ⇨ 179 rooms †⊙I No meals Ⓜ B, D, E to 7th Ave.; 1 to 50th St.

Moxy NYC Times Square

$ | HOTEL | Among Midtown's trendy new lodging choices is this good-value hotel (part of a stylish chain) designed with plenty of "moxy," including modern boutique swagger and a vibrant dining and drinking scene. **Pros:** affordable rates; central location near public transit; vibrant on-site restaurants and bars. **Cons:** small rooms and minimal in-room storage; street noise and bright lights flashing outside; sink is in main room instead

of bathroom. Ⓢ Rooms from: $209 ⊠ 485 7th Ave., at 36th St., Midtown West ☎ 212/967–6699 ⊕ moxy-hotels.marriott. com ⇨ 612 rooms †⊙I No meals Ⓜ 1, 2, 3, A, C, E to 34th St.–Penn Station.

1 Hotel Central Park

$$$ | HOTEL | A commitment to next-level eco-friendly policies is evident in the smallest details at this hotel, from in-room chalkboards (instead of note-pads) to triple-filtered water straight from the taps that eliminates the need for bottled water. **Pros:** committed to green policies; room are surprisingly quiet; cozy window seats with great city views. **Cons:** some service inconsistencies; rooms are on the small side; no spa. Ⓢ Rooms from: $450 ⊠ 1414 Avenue of the Americas, at 58th St., Midtown West ☎ 212/703–2001 ⊕ 1hotels.com/central-park ⇨ 229 rooms †⊙I No meals Ⓜ F to 57th St; N, R, W to 5th Ave./59th St.

★ Park Hyatt New York

$$$$ | HOTEL | Occupying the first 25 floors of a towering Midtown skyscraper, this luxury property is the flagship of the global Park Hyatt brand and features one of the best spas in the city. **Pros:** large guest rooms; luxurious furnishings; city views from the fitness center and spa. **Cons:** disappointing views from guest rooms; pricey even for the neighborhood; street noise audible from lower floors. Ⓢ Rooms from: $795 ⊠ 153 W. 57th St., between 6th and 7th Aves., Midtown West ☎ 646/774–1234 ⊕ www.hyatt.com ⇨ 210 rooms †⊙I No meals Ⓜ N, Q, R, W to 57th St.–7th Ave.

★ The Plaza

$$$$ | HOTEL | Eloise's adopted home on the corner of Central Park, this landmark property is one of New York's most storied hotels, hosting all manner of dignitaries, moneymakers, and royalty. **Pros:** historic property with modern amenities; lavish rooms, especially the renovated suites in the Legacy Collection; luxurious Guerlain spa. **Cons:** rooms aren't that big for the money; old-school design not to everyone's taste; fee for Wi-Fi. $ *Rooms from: $895* ☒ *768 5th Ave., at Central Park, Midtown West* ☎ *212/759–3000* ⊕ *www.theplazany.com* ↘ *282 rooms* ❍| *No meals* Ⓜ *N, R, W to 5th Ave./59th St.*

The Quin Central Park

$$$ | HOTEL | This luxury hotel just south of Central Park once housed artists like Marc Chagall and Georgia O'Keeffe, and it still has an emphasis on contemporary art. **Pros:** bright fitness center; spacious rooms; close to neighborhood destinations like Carnegie Hall. **Cons:** 57th Street location might be too busy for some; nightly charge for dogs; no pool or spa. $ *Rooms from: $489* ☒ *101 W. 57th St., at 6th Ave., Midtown West* ☎ *877/234–7033* ⊕ *www.thequinhotel.com* ↘ *208 rooms* ❍| *No meals* Ⓜ *N, R, W to 5th Ave./59th St.; F to 57th St.*

★ Refinery Hotel

$ | HOTEL | Set in a former hat factory, this hotel has a gorgeous year-round rooftop with Empire State Building views, impressively spacious rooms, and several buzzing bars and restaurants. **Pros:** lots of character and lovely, detailed design; rooftop lounge with great views; excellent bars and restaurant. **Cons:** limited dining and nightlife options nearby; the lobby gets crowded with people heading to the rooftop; service can be a bit inconsistent. $ *Rooms from: $299* ☒ *63 W. 38th St., between 5th and 6th Aves., Midtown West* ☎ *646/664–0310* ⊕ *www.refineryhotelnewyork.com* ↘ *197 rooms* ❍| *No meals* Ⓜ *B, D, F, M to 42nd St.–Bryant Park; 7 to 5th Ave.*

Renaissance New York Times Square Hotel

$$$ | HOTEL | This Renaissance adds some chic urban style to a prime Times Square location: the lobby feels like it's been designed for urban court jesters, with oversize furniture; curved, abstract art; and dangling, filament-like sculpture. **Pros:** contemporary design; latest in-room

technology; comfortable beds. **Cons:** rooms can be a bit noisy; high-traffic area; Wi-Fi isn't free. $ *Rooms from: $499* ☒ *714 7th Ave., between 47th and 48th Sts., Midtown West* ☎ *212/765–7676* ⊕ *www.renaissancehotels.com* ↘ *305 rooms* ❍| *No meals* Ⓜ *N, R, W to 49th St.; 1 to 50th St.; B, D, F, M to 47th–50th Sts./Rockefeller Center.*

★ The Ritz-Carlton New York, Central Park

$$$$ | HOTEL | FAMILY | It's all about the park views here, though the above-and-beyond service, accommodating to a fault, makes this renowned property popular with celebs and other guests who can afford premier luxury travel. **Pros:** personalized service; gorgeous furnishings recently renovated; stellar location with Central Park views. **Cons:** guests can be pretentious; limited common areas; overly expensive dining and bar menus. $ *Rooms from: $995* ☒ *50 Central Park S, at 6th Ave., Midtown West* ☎ *212/308–9100* ⊕ *www.ritzcarlton.com/centralpark* ↘ *259 rooms* ❍| *No meals* Ⓜ *F to 57th St.; N, R, W to 5th Ave./59th St.*

Room Mate Grace

$ | HOTEL | FAMILY | A favorite of European visitors and business travelers who work in fashion and entertainment, Grace delivers high-design lodgings on a budget. **Pros:** cool swimming pool lounge; friendly, helpful staff; nice design on a budget. **Cons:** small rooms; little in-room privacy (no door separating shower from main room); high-traffic area. $ *Rooms from: $229* ☒ *125 W. 45th St., between 6th and 7th Aves., Midtown West* ☎ *212/354–2323* ⊕ *www.room-matehotels.com* ↘ *139 rooms* ❍| *No meals* Ⓜ *B, D, F, M to 47th–50th Sts./Rockefeller Center.*

Royalton New York

$$ | HOTEL | The Royalton's lobby bar is one of the prime Midtown meeting spots for local A-listers, along with a new generation of movers and shakers—so be prepared to run the gauntlet of the buzzing

lounge before reaching your room. **Pros:** hip lobby scene; luxurious beds and bathrooms; helpful service. **Cons:** dark hallways; lighting verges on eye-strainingly dim; immediate area is overrun with office workers. $ *Rooms from: $399* ✉ *44 W. 44th St., between 5th and 6th Aves., Midtown West* ☎ *212/869–4400* ⊕ *www.royaltonhotel.com* ⤳ *175 rooms* ¶⊙¶ *No meals* Ⓜ *B, D, F, M to 42nd St.– Bryant Park; 7 to 5th Ave.*

Shoreham Hotel

$ | **HOTEL** | In a neighborhood packed with generic hotels, the Shoreham sports a welcome dose of style, along with proximity to Midtown's attractions. **Pros:** tech-friendly rooms; pet-friendly attitude; stylish decor. **Cons:** not designed for families; limited space; fee for Wi-Fi. $ *Rooms from: $179* ✉ *33 W. 55th St., between 5th and 6th Aves., Midtown West* ☎ *212/247–6700* ⊕ *www. shorehamhotel.com* ⤳ *177 rooms* ¶⊙¶ *No meals* Ⓜ *E, M to 5th Ave./53rd St.; F to 57th St.*

6 Columbus

$$ | **HOTEL** | **FAMILY** | This boutique-style hotel in the shadow of the towering Time Warner Center has the vibe and amenities of downtown lodging with a convenient Midtown location. **Pros:** convenient location; fun in-hotel restaurant; reasonably priced for neighborhood. **Cons:** rooms on lower floors facing 58th Street can be noisy; no gym on-site; some tiny rooms lack desks. $ *Rooms from: $325* ✉ *308 W. 58th St., between 8th and 9th Aves., Midtown West* ☎ *212/204–3000* ⊕ *www.sixtyhotels.com/6columbus* ⤳ *88 rooms* ¶⊙¶ *No meals* Ⓜ *1, A, B, C, D to 59th St.–Columbus Circle.*

Sofitel New York

$ | **HOTEL** | With bilingual signage throughout the hotel, plenty of velvet in the lobby, and European modern design in the rooms—think blond wood and fresh flowers—the Sofitel brings a Gallic flair to Midtown West. **Pros:** central location; touches of French elegance; some suites

with terraces and views. **Cons:** room views vary; no spa or pool; high-traffic area. $ *Rooms from: $299* ✉ *45 W. 44th St., between 5th and 6th Aves., Midtown West* ☎ *212/354–8844* ⊕ *www.sofitel-new-york.com* ⤳ *398 rooms* ¶⊙¶ *No meals* Ⓜ *B, D, F, M to 42nd St.–Bryant Park; 7 to 5th Ave.*

The Time New York

$$$ | **HOTEL** | One of the neighborhood's first boutique hotels, this spot near the din of Times Square is a contemporary retreat with a futuristic glass elevator that transports guests to the second-floor lobby and beyond. **Pros:** popular Serafina restaurant downstairs; surprisingly quiet for Times Square location; good turndown service. **Cons:** service is inconsistent; location isn't for everyone; a bit pricey for the area. $ *Rooms from: $459* ✉ *224 W. 49th St., between Broadway and 8th Ave., Midtown West* ☎ *212/246–5252, 877/846–3692* ⊕ *www.thetimeny.com* ⤳ *167 rooms* ¶⊙¶ *No meals* Ⓜ *1, C, E to 50th St.; N, R, W to 49th St.*

Viceroy Central Park New York

$$ | **HOTEL** | Handsome and finely tailored, this hotel has functional, tech-focused rooms and lots of amenities, including a well-equipped fitness center and plunge pool, a rooftop bar with park views, and a welcoming ground-floor restaurant, Kingside. **Pros:** comfortable, quiet library with "cartender" mixing drinks in late afternoon; generous rooftop space with views of Central Park; appealing restaurant. **Cons:** small, crowded lobby; busy 57th Street location might not suit all guests; Wi-Fi is only complimentary for direct bookings. $ *Rooms from: $399* ✉ *120 W. 57th St., Midtown West* ☎ *212/830–8000* ⊕ *www.viceroyhotelsandresorts.com/ newyork* ⤳ *237 rooms* ¶⊙¶ *No meals* Ⓜ *N, Q, R, W to 57th St.–7th Ave.; F to 57th St.*

W New York - Times Square

$ | **HOTEL** | The W Times Square still stands out in the craziness of Midtown, thanks to its iconic 57-story exterior—so if you want to be in the thick of the action, this is the place to stay. **Pros:** bustling nightlife and happy-hour scene; sleek rooms; 24-hour room service. **Cons:** if you want quiet, head elsewhere; no bathtubs in the smaller rooms; extra fees for Wi-Fi, pets, and parking. $ *Rooms from: $230* ✉ *1567 Broadway, at 47th St., Midtown West* ☎ *855/516–1093* ⊕ *www.wnewyorktimessquare.com* ⤴ *509 rooms* ⦿ *No meals* Ⓜ *1, 2, 3, 7, N, Q, R, S, W to Times Sq.–42nd St.*

Warwick New York
$$ | **HOTEL** | Built by William Randolph Hearst in 1926 for his mistress, Hollywood actress Marion Davies, this grande dame has hosted many from Tinseltown since then, including Cary Grant in the Presidential Suite for 12 years. **Pros:** excellent restaurant and bar; historic property with character; spacious suites. **Cons:** loads of commuter traffic outside; no a/c in the hallways; some rooms have views of an air shaft. $ *Rooms from: $399* ✉ *65 W. 54th St., at 6th Ave., Midtown West* ☎ *212/247–2700, 800/223–4099* ⊕ *www.warwickhotels. com/new-york* ⤴ *426 rooms* ⦿ *No meals* Ⓜ *F to 5/th St.; B, D, E to 7th Ave.*

Wellington Hotel
$ | **HOTEL** | **FAMILY** | A few blocks south of Central Park and Columbus Circle, the Wellington is a good base for visitors who want to see the sights in Midtown and the Upper West Side. **Pros:** central location; chipper, helpful staff; good for big families. **Cons:** dark, often small bathrooms; limited breakfast options; unlimited Wi-Fi is free only when reservation is made directly with hotel. $ *Rooms from: $275* ✉ *871 7th Ave., at 55th St., Midtown West* ☎ *212/247–3900* ⊕ *www. wellingtonhotel.com* ⤴ *700 rooms* ⦿ *No meals* Ⓜ *N, Q, R, W to 57th St.–7th Ave.*

WestHouse Hotel New York
$$ | **HOTEL** | This Art Deco–style hotel is designed to feel like a glamorous private residence: included in the built-in nightly "resident fee" are morning breakfast,

afternoon tea, and hourlong evening canapés with alcoholic and nonalcoholic beverages (all served on the 23rd-floor terrace), as well as in-room snacks and Wi-Fi. **Pros:** many extras included; fresh, luxurious rooms; nice views from the terrace where breakfast and snacks are served. **Cons:** mandatory daily resident fee is included; busy Midtown location lacks nearby quality restaurant and nightlife options; $150 fee for pets. $ *Rooms from: $345* ✉ *201 W. 55th St., between 7th Ave. and Broadway, Midtown West* ☎ *212/707–4888* ⊕ *www.westhousehotelnewyork.com* ⤴ *172 rooms* ⦿ *Free Breakfast* Ⓜ *B, D, F to 7th Ave.; N, Q, R, W to 57th St.–7th Ave.*

Westin New York at Times Square
$$ | **HOTEL** | This giant Midtown hotel has all the amenities and service you expect from a reliable brand, at fairly reasonable prices, including comfortable rooms with coffeemakers, iPhone docks, 24-hour room service, and a spacious work desk. **Pros:** central for Midtown attractions; big rooms; great gym. **Cons:** congested area near the Port Authority; not the best location for prime dining and nightlife; rooms are a bit nondescript. $ *Rooms from: $329* ✉ *270 W. 43rd St., at 8th Ave., Midtown West* ☎ *212/201–2700* ⊕ *www. westinny.com* ⤴ *873 rooms* ⦿ *No meals* Ⓜ *A, C, E to 42nd St.–Port Authority.*

Whitby Hotel
$$$$ | **HOTEL** | Like all Firmdale Hotels, this relatively new (from 2017) boutique property showcases owner–acclaimed designer Kit Kemp's eclectic sensibility—rooms feature exotic fabrics, and an eye-catching installation made of baskets crowns the bar. **Pros:** sophisticated design; excellent afternoon tea; state-of-the-art screening room. **Cons:** mighty expensive; no pool or spa; rooms lack coffeemakers. $ *Rooms from: $795* ✉ *18 W. 56th St., between 5th and 6th Aves., Midtown West* ☎ *212/586–5656* ⊕ *www. firmdalehotels.com* ⤴ *86 rooms* ⦿ *No meals* Ⓜ *F to 57th St.*

Yotel New York

$ | **HOTEL** | Look beyond the gimmicks (a luggage-storing robot, the futuristic white design scheme) and discover one of New York's best-run, most functional lodgings—and at a great price, too. **Pros:** great value; large common outdoor space; access to West Side piers and Javits Center. **Cons:** rooms may be too small for some; limited luggage storage and hanging space; 10th Avenue is a bit remote. [$] *Rooms from: $119* ✉ *570 10th Ave., at 42nd St., Midtown West* ☎ *646/449–7700* 🌐 *www.yotelnewyork.com* 🛏 *713 rooms* 🍴 *No meals* [M] *A, C, E to 42nd St.–Port Authority.*

🍸 Nightlife

BARS

Célon Lounge

BARS/PUBS | Underneath the Bryant Park Hotel—and dramatic arched ceilings—is one of the more unexpected and spectacular spaces in Midtown, thanks to its Moroccan decor and Mediterranean-inspired cocktail and light-fare menus. Expect to sip herbally aromatic craft drinks while international pop music plays, and fashionistas and media types unwind in style. ✉ *Bryant Park Hotel, 40 W. 40th St., between 5th and 6th Aves., Midtown West* ☎ *212/642–2257* 🌐 *www.celonlounge.com* [M] *B, D, F, M to 42nd St.–Bryant Park; 7 to 5th Ave.*

Connolly's Pub & Restaurant

BARS/PUBS | This family-owned, tri-level Irish pub often hosts terrific live music including Irish bands, both traditional and with a modern edge. Top off your night with a shepherd's pie; one bite and you may think you're in Dublin instead of Times Square. ✉ *121 W. 45th St., between Broadway and 6th Ave., Midtown West* ☎ *212/597–5126* 🌐 *www.connollyspubandrestaurant.com* [M] *B, D, F, M, to 47th–50th Sts./Rockefeller Center; N, R, W to 49th St.*

Forty Four

BARS/PUBS | The dimly lit, wood-clad Forty Four is the comfortable lobby bar of the boutique Royalton Hotel. Kick back in a leather sofa to enjoy the chic decor, craft cocktails, and large fireplace—a sexy spot to gear up or wind down after a Broadway show. ✉ *Royalton Hotel, 44 W. 44th St., between 5th and 6th Aves., Midtown West* ☎ *212/944–8844* 🌐 *www.royaltonhotel.com* [M] *B, D, F, M to 42nd St.–Bryant Park; 7 to 5th Ave.*

Joe Allen

BARS/PUBS | Everybody's en route either to or from a show at this "old reliable" on boisterous Restaurant Row, celebrated in the musical version of *All About Eve*. You may even spot a Broadway star at the classic bar—with its robust scotch and whiskey menus—or in the dining room. Still, our favorite thing about Joe's is not the show crowd but the hilarious "flop wall," adorned with posters from musicals that bombed, sometimes spectacularly. (Check out the ones for *Paradox Lust, Got Tu Go Disco,* and *Dude*, the unfortunate sequel to *Hair*.) ✉ *326 W. 46th St., between 8th and 9th Aves., Midtown West* ☎ *212/581–6464* 🌐 *www.joeallenrestaurant.com* [M] *A, C, E to 42nd St.–Port Authority; N, R, W to 49th St.*

Keens Steakhouse

BARS/PUBS | Single-malt scotch aficionados have a delicious dilemma trying to select from 200-plus varieties on the menu at Keens. Given its location just around the corner from Madison Square Garden, this institution founded way back in 1885 sees its share of sports and music fans—but whatever your taste, take a gander at the ceilings, which are lined with thousands of clay pipes that once belonged to patrons. ✉ *72 W. 36th St., between 5th and 6th Aves., Midtown West* ☎ *212/947–3636* 🌐 *www.keens.com* [M] *B, D, F, M, N, Q, R, W to 34th St.–Herald Sq.*

Lantern's Keep

BARS/PUBS | The elegance of cocktail culture from another era is alive and well at Lantern's Keep, an intimate lounge tucked behind the lobby of the Iroquois Hotel. Reservations are recommended for this romantic lounge, where plush seats are huddled around a fireplace. There is no standing room here, resulting in a luxurious, leisurely vibe. Cocktails are works of art and bartenders are helpful at concocting your perfect poison. ✉ Iroquois Hotel, 49 W. 44th St., between 5th and 6th Aves., Midtown West ☎ 212/453–4287 ⊕ www.iroquoisny.com/lanternskeep Ⓜ B, D, F, M to 42nd St.–Bryant Park.

★ Lillie's Victorian Establishment

BARS/PUBS | Delight awaits at this uncommonly large (for Times Square) and flamboyantly decorated bar, with nearly every square inch covered in old English art and sculpture. Don't be thrown off—the cocktails here are inventive and expertly made, as is the tasty, filling pub fare. Consider a table reservation if you're dining around pretheater hours. Lillie's also shares its friendly brand of Victorian charm in its Union Square location. ✉ 249 W. 49th St., between Broadway and 8th Ave., Midtown West ☎ 212/957–4530 ⊕ www.lilliesnyc.com Ⓜ C, E to 50th St.; N, R, W to 49th St.

Morrell Wine Bar and Cafe

WINE BARS—NIGHTLIFE | The vibrant Morrell takes its grape products very seriously, with one of the city's best selections of wine by the glass and an epic array of bottles. In summer you can sip at outdoor tables in the heart of Rockefeller Center. ✉ 1 Rockefeller Plaza, at W. 49th St., Midtown West ☎ 212/262–7700 ⊕ www.morrellwinebar.com Ⓜ B, D, F, M to 47th–50th Sts./Rockefeller Center.

★ The Rum House

BARS/PUBS | Among the glittering lights of Broadway theaters, the Rum House is a destination bar thanks to its attention to the craft of mixing cocktails. The sister lounge to downtown favorite Ward III, this bar has nightly live piano music and creative libations in addition to all the classic cocktails. See if you can figure out where Michael Keaton sat during scenes from the 2015 film Birdman. ✉ 228 W. 47th St., between 7th and 8th Aves., Midtown West ☎ 646/490–6924 ⊕ therumhousenyc.com Ⓜ N, R, W to 49th St.; A, C, E to 42nd St.–Port Authority.

Russian Vodka Room

BARS/PUBS | Forget Russian Samovar across the block—here's where the serious vodka drinking goes down. The Vodka Room features a glowing, sophisticated front room with nightly piano player, a more sumptuous back room, a generous attitude-adjustment hour (that's Russki for happy hour), and an impressive variety of infused vodkas from horseradish to ginger to pepper. For those who crave variety, a vodka tasting menu is available, as are culinary standards like caviar and borscht. ✉ 265 W. 52nd St., between Broadway and 8th Ave., Midtown West ☎ 212/307–5835 Ⓜ 1, C, E to 50th St.

★ Salon de Ning

BARS/PUBS | Take a break from 5th Avenue shopping at this glass-lined penthouse bar on the 23rd floor of the ritzy Peninsula Hotel, where the sumptuous decor is inspired by the historic tale of Shanghai socialite Madame Ning. Drinks are pricey, of course, but what isn't in this neighborhood? The views are worth it, especially from the rooftop terraces. ✉ Peninsula Hotel, 700 5th Ave., at 55th St., Midtown West ☎ 212/903–3097 ⊕ newyork.peninsula.com Ⓜ E, M to 5th Ave./53rd St.

Sardi's

BARS/PUBS | Head to this Broadway institution to drink in vintage Midtown Manhattan at the compact bar, surrounded by caricatures of theater, film, music, and TV stars past and present. ✉ 234 W. 44th St., between Broadway and 8th Ave., Midtown West ☎ 212/221–8440

⊕ www.sardis.com Ⓜ A, C, E to 42nd St.–Port Authority.

CABARET AND PIANO BARS
Don't Tell Mama

CABARET | Composer-lyricist hopefuls and established talents show their stuff until 3 am nightly at this convivial Theater District cabaret. Extroverts will be tempted by the piano bar's open-mic policy as well as by the other showroom's singers, comedians, and drag acts. Those needing a break from the above can find it in the quieter exposed-brick lounge. ✉ 343 W. 46th St., between 8th and 9th Aves., Midtown West ☎ 212/757–0788 ⊕ www.donttellmamanyc.com Ⓜ A, C, E to 42nd St.–Port Authority; C, E to 50th St.

COMEDY CLUBS
Caroline's on Broadway

COMEDY CLUBS | This high-gloss club presents established names as well as comedians on the edge of stardom. Janeane Garofalo, David Alan Grier, Colin Quinn, and Gilbert Gottfried have all headlined, and sometimes their sets are recorded for TV and streaming shows. ✉ 1626 Broadway, between 49th and 50th Sts., Midtown West ☎ 212/757–4100 ⊕ www.carolines.com Ⓜ N, R, W to 49th St.; 1 to 50th St.

Upright Citizens Brigade

COMEDY CLUBS | Raucous sketch comedy, audience-initiated improv, and classic stand-up take turns onstage here at the city's absolute capital for alternative comedy. There are classes available, too. UCB offers ADA accessibility. The troupe also has an outpost in the East Village. ✉ 555 W. 42nd St., near 11th Ave., Midtown West ☎ 212/366–9176 ⊕ hellskitchen.ucbtheatre.com Ⓜ A, C, E to 42nd St.–Port Authority; 1, 2, 3, 7, N, Q, R, S, W to Times Sq.–42nd St.

GAY NIGHTLIFE
Posh

BARS/PUBS | Among Hell's Kitchen's gay lounges, Posh offers an array of special party nights and drag shows, ample room for flirting and dancing, plenty of neon decor (plus artwork by local artists), and long hours to suit any schedule, from 2 pm to 4 am. Daily happy "hour" from 2 to 9 pm draws a steady clientele. ✉ 405 W. 51st St., at 9th Ave., Midtown West ☎ 212/957–2222 ⊕ www.poshbarnyc.com Ⓜ C, E to 50th St.

Therapy

BARS/PUBS | With slate floors, wood-paneled walls, and a small stone-filled pond, the design at this spacious lounge in Hell's Kitchen is as upscale as its mostly male clientele, which includes older uptown professionals and the twentysomething hipsters who love them (and vice versa). Hungry? There's a solid menu of small dishes. ✉ 348 W. 52nd St., between 8th and 9th Aves., Midtown West ☎ 212/397–1700 ⊕ www.therapy-nyc.com Ⓜ C, E to 50th St.

JAZZ VENUES
Birdland

MUSIC CLUBS | This place gets its name from saxophone great Charlie "Yardbird" (or just "Bird") Parker, so expect serious musicians such as John Pizzarelli, the Dave Holland Sextet, and Arturo O'Farrill's Afro-Cuban Jazz Orchestra (on Sunday night). The dining room serves moderately priced American fare with a Cajun accent. ✉ 315 W. 44th St., between 8th and 9th Aves., Midtown West ☎ 212/581–3080 ⊕ www.birdlandjazz.com Ⓜ A, C, E to 42nd St.–Port Authority.

★ Dizzy's Club Coca-Cola

MUSIC CLUBS | For a night of jazz with big names and talent but without the pretension, turn to Dizzy's, an intimate club with Manhattan-skyline and Central Park views and southern-inflected cuisine (gumbo, blackened fish dishes) and cocktails. Late-night sessions are ideal for an after-dinner nightcap; some of the drinks, such as the Dizzy Gillespie, are named after jazz legends. ✉ Jazz at Lincoln Center, 10 Columbus Circle, inside the Time Warner Center, 5th fl., Midtown

West ☎ 212/258–9595 ⊕ www.jazz.org/
dizzys Ⓜ 1, A, B, C, D to 59th St.–Columbus Circle.

Iridium
MUSIC CLUBS | This cozy, elite jazz venue
is a sure bet for big-name talent like the
David Murray Black Saint Quartet and
pianist Michael Wolff. The sight lines
are good, and the sound system was
designed with the help of Les Paul,
inventor of the solid-body electric guitar
(Paul used to play here every Monday
night). The rest of the week sees a mix
of artists like Chuck Mangione and the
Eddie Daniels Band. ✉ 1650 Broadway, at
51st St., Midtown West☎ 212/582–2121
⊕ www.theiridium.com Ⓜ 1 to 50th St.;
N, R, W to 49th St.

🎭 Performing Arts

FILM
★ Museum of Modern Art (MoMA) films
FILM | You'll find some of the most engag-
ing international film repertory around
at Roy and Niuta Titus Theaters 1 and 2,
in the MoMA's lower level, and at the
Celeste Bartos Theater, in the lower level
of the Cullman Education and Research
Building on the museum campus.
Sometimes the films tie in with current
art exhibitions. The Contenders series,
which starts each fall, is a chance to
catch up on the past year's releases that
are likely to win awards, or at least stand
the test of time. Movie tickets are available at the museum for same-day screenings (a limited number are released up
to one week in advance). They're free if
you have purchased museum admission
($25); otherwise they cost $12. ✉ 11 W.
53rd St., between 5th and 6th Aves.,
Midtown West ☎ 212/708–9400 ⊕ www.
moma.org/calendar/film Ⓜ E, M to 5th
Ave./53rd St.; B, D, F, M to 47th–50th
Sts./Rockefeller Center.

The Paris Theatre
FILM | Across from the Plaza Hotel stands
the Paris Theatre—a rare, stately remnant

of the single-screen era. Opened in
1948, it retains its wide screen (and
balcony) and is a fine showcase for new
movies, some of them foreign and with
a limited release. The venue is now part
of City Cinemas, and tickets can be
purchased online in advance to ensure
a seat for high-demand screenings. ✉ 4
W. 58th St., between 5th and 6th Aves.,
Midtown West ☎ 212/823–8945 ⊕ www.
citycinemas.com/paris Ⓜ N, R, W to 5th
Ave./59th St.; F to 57th St.

MUSIC
★ Carnegie Hall
MUSIC | FAMILY | Internationally renowned
Carnegie Hall has incomparable acoustics
that make it one of the best venues in
the world to hear classical music, but it's
also strong in jazz, pop, cabaret, and folk
music. Since the opening-night concert
on May 5, 1891, which Tchaikovsky conducted, virtually every important musi-
cian the world has known has performed
in this Italian Renaissance–style building.
The world's top orchestras perform in the
grand and fabulously steep 2,804-seat
Isaac Stern Auditorium; the 268-seat **Weill
Recital Hall** often features young talents
making their New York debuts; and the
subterranean 599-seat **Judy and Arthur
Zankel Hall** attracts big-name artists
such as the Kronos Quartet and Milton
Nascimento to its stylish modern space.
A noted roster of family concerts is also
part of Carnegie's programming.

The Carnegie box office releases $10
rush tickets for some shows on the
day of performance, or you may buy
partial-view seating in advance at 50%
off the full ticket price. Head to the second-floor Rose Museum to learn more
about the famous hall's history through
its archival treasures; admission is free,
and it's open seven days a week, 11 am
to 4:30 pm. ✉ 881 7th Ave., at 57th St.,
Midtown West ☎ 212/247–7800 ⊕ www.
carnegiehall.org Ⓜ N, Q, R, W to 57th
St.–7th Ave.; B, D, E to 7th Ave.; F to
57th St.

New York's Film Festivals

New York's extreme diversity is what makes it a cinephile's heaven: you'll find dozens of festivals. While new releases and premieres dominate the festival scene, the city has its share of retrospective events, especially in summer.

The city's preeminent film event is the annual **New York Film Festival** (⊕ www.filmlinc.com), presented by the Film Society of Lincoln Center, from late September into October. The lineup is announced about a month in advance, and screenings often sell out quickly (though standby tickets are available for most events). Film venues include Lincoln Center's Alice Tully Hall, Walter Reade Theater, and Elinor Bunin Munroe Film Center. In January, the Film Society join forces with the Jewish Museum to produce the **New York Jewish Film Festival** (⊕ www.nyjff.org); in March it joins the MoMA to present **New Directors/New Films** (⊕ www.newdirectors.org), and June brings the society's collaboration on the **Human Rights Watch Film Festival** (⊕ ff.hrw.org), among other festivals and repertory programming throughout the year.

The **Tribeca Film Festival** (⊕ www. tribecafilm.com/festival) takes place in mostly downtown venues for about two weeks starting mid- or late April and shows mainstream premieres along with indie flicks, television debuts, a conversation series, and more.

Fans also flock to other noteworthy annuals like the **New York Asian Film Festival** (⊕ www.asiancin-evision.org) from late July to early August; and the **Margaret Mead Film Festival** (⊕ www.amnh.org/explore/margaret-mead-film-festival) in October or November and **DOC NYC** (⊕ www.docnyc.net) in November, two fall festivals that focus on documentaries from all over.

For kids, the year-round programs of the **New York International Children's Film Festival** (NYICFF ⊕ www.gkids.com) peak in March with an extravaganza of about 100 new films for aged 3–18.

Summer in New York sees a bonanza of alfresco film; screenings are usually free (but arrive early to secure a space; screenings begin at dusk). The **HBO Bryant Park Summer Film Festival** (⊕ www.bryantpark.org) shows classic films at sundown on Monday, June through August. The **Hudson RiverFlicks** (⊕ www.riverflicks.org) series in July and August has movies for grown-ups on Wednesday evening on Pier 63, as well as Family Friday for kids at Pier 46. The Upper West Side has **Summer on the Hudson** (⊕ www. nycgovparks.org) with Wednesday-night screenings on Pier 1, near West 70th Street. **Rooftop Films'** (⊕ www. rooftopfilms.com) Underground Movies Outdoors is more eclectic than most other film series, with shows outdoors in summer on rooftops in all five boroughs. Check the schedule for off-season screenings as well. On Thursday evenings in July and August, check out **Movies with a View in Brooklyn Bridge Park** (⊕ www. brooklynbridgepark.org).

Socrates Sculpture Park (⊕ www. socratessculpturepark.org) in Queens has an internationally inspired Outdoor Cinema festival on Wednesdays, July through August; the NYC skyline serves as a backdrop.

PERFORMANCE CENTERS
Baryshnikov Arts Center
ARTS CENTERS | Famed dancer and actor Mikhail Baryshnikov's longtime vision came to fruition in this modern performing arts venue for contemporary dance, theater, music, and film. The center, set within the Hudson Yards neighborhood, hosts a range of resident artists, including dancers and musical groups, as well as productions by boundary-breaking international choreographers, playwrights, filmmakers, and musicians. The vibrant programming is presented in the center's 238-seat Jerome Robbins Theater and the 136-seat Howard Gilman Performance Space. ⊠ *450 W. 37 St., between 9th and 10th Aves., Midtown West* ☎ *646/731–3200* ⊕ *www.bacnyc.org* Ⓜ *A, C, E to 34th St.–Penn Station, 7 to 34th St.–Hudson Yards.*

★ The New Victory Theater
ARTS CENTERS | FAMILY | In a magnificently restored space from 1900, The New Victory Theater presents an international roster of supremely kid-pleasing plays, music, dance, opera, puppetry, and circus performances. Through the organization's workshops and arts activities, children and their parents can also learn more about other parts of theater (writing, for instance) and kinds of performance, such as break dancing. Count on reasonable ticket prices, high-energy and high-class productions, and the opportunity for kids to chat with the artists after many performances. ⊠ *209 W. 42nd St., between 7th and 8th Aves., Midtown West* ☎ *646/223–3010* ⊕ *www.newvictory.org* Ⓜ *1, 2, 3, 7, N, Q, R, S, W to Times Sq.–42nd St.; A, C, E to 42nd St.–Port Authority.*

★ New York City Center
ARTS CENTERS | Pause as you enter this neo-Moorish building, built in 1923 for the Shriners (cousins of the Freemasons), and admire the ornate decorative details in the lobby and theater. City Center's 2,200-seat main stage is perfectly suited for dance and special theatrical events. Among its varied performances and showcases, the Tony Award–honored Encores! series, generally held in spring, revisits musicals of the past in a concert format—an event that has led to shows returning to Broadway, with the long-running *Chicago* among them. During summer, Encores! Off-Center features concert versions of Off-Broadway musicals. Tickets for City Center's annual Fall for Dance festival sell out quickly. ⊠ *131 W. 55th St., between 6th and 7th Aves., Midtown West* ☎ *212/581–1212 for tickets* ⊕ *www.nycitycenter.org* Ⓜ *N, Q, R, W to 57th St.–7th Ave.; F to 57th St.*

★ Radio City Music Hall
ARTS CENTERS | This landmark was built shortly after the stock market crash of 1929; John D. Rockefeller wanted to create a symbol of hope in what was a sad, broke city. When Radio City Music Hall opened, some said there was no need for performances, because people would get more than their money's worth simply by sitting there and enjoying the grand space. Despite being the largest indoor theater in the world with its city-block-long marquee, it feels warm and intimate. Seventy-five-minute Stage Door walking tours ($30) run year-round. Day-of tour tickets are sold at the Radio City Sweets & Gifts, or at the 51st Street tour entrance during Christmas Spectacular season; advance tickets are available by phone, at the box office, or through the website.

Although there are concerts and events year-round, the biggest draw is the Radio City Christmas Spectacular: more than a million visitors every year come to see the iconic Rockettes dance. Make reservations early, especially if you want to attend near Christmas or on a weekend. You can usually find tickets for all shows until mid-October. Tickets start at $49 per person ($41 for matinees) for the 90-minute show, although there are often promotions and deals. ⊠ *1260 6th Ave.,* between 50th and 51st Sts., Midtown West ☎ 212/465–6000, 866/858–0007 for tickets ⊕ www.radiocity.com Ⓜ B, D, F, M to 47th–50th Sts./Rockefeller Center; N, R, W to 49th St.

The Town Hall
ARTS CENTERS | Founded by suffragists and built in 1921 by famed architectural firm McKim, Mead & White, the Town Hall has been part of NYC's cultural fabric for almost 100 years. Notable Town Hall claims include Strauss's, Stravinsky's, and Isaac Stern's U.S. debuts; Marian Anderson's first NYC recital; Dizzy Gillespie and Charlie Parker's introduction of bebop to the world; and Bob Dylan's first major concert. More recently, the stage has welcomed musicians like Gilberto Gil, Joan Baez, Patti Smith, and David Byrne; comedians like Stephen Colbert and Larry David; the only East Coast staging of Hunter S. Thompson's "The Kentucky Derby Is Decadent and Depraved"; TED Talks Live; and more. ✉ 123 W. 43rd St., between 6th Ave. and Broadway, Midtown West ☎ 212/997–6661, 800/982–2787 for tickets ⊕ www. thetownhall.org Ⓜ 1, 2, 3, 7, N, Q, R, S, W to Times Sq.–42nd St.; B, D, F, M to 42nd St.–Bryant Park.

READINGS AND LECTURES
LIVE from the NYPL
READINGS/LECTURES | The New York Public Library's discussion series includes a rich program of lectures and reading events from the biggest names in books and culture in general. Most programs are held at the famous main library. ✉ Stephen A. Schwarzman Bldg., 5th Ave. at 42nd St., Midtown West ☎ 917/275–6975, 888/718–4253 for tickets ⊕ www.nypl. org/live Ⓜ B, D, F, M to 42nd St.–Bryant Park; 7 to 5th Ave.

THEATER
New Amsterdam Theatre
THEATER | FAMILY | In 1997 Disney refurbished the elaborate 1903 Art Nouveau New Amsterdam Theatre, where Bob Hope, Jack Benny, Fred Astaire, and the Ziegfeld Follies once drew crowds. The Lion King ruled here for the first nine years of its run, followed by Mary Poppins and then Aladdin, which opened in 2014. Frozen debuted here in 2018. ✉ 214 W. 42nd St., between 7th and 8th Aves., Midtown West ☎ 866/870–2717 for tickets ⊕ www.disneyonbroadway. com Ⓜ 1, 2, 3, 7, N, Q, R, S, W to Times Sq.–42nd St.; A, C, E to 42nd St.–Port Authority.

Playwrights Horizons
THEATER | Known for its support of new work by American playwrights, this Off-Broadway theater was the first home for eventual Broadway hits such as Grey Gardens and Wendy Wasserstein's Heidi Chronicles. ✉ 416 W. 42nd St., between 9th and 10th Aves., Midtown West ☎ 212/564–1235, 212/279–4200 for tickets ⊕ www.phnyc.org Ⓜ A, C, E to 42nd St.–Port Authority.

Roundabout Theatre Company
THEATER | This nonprofit theatrical company is known for its revivals of classic musicals and plays. Its main stage, the American Airlines Theatre, is the former Selwyn—the venerable home to the works of Noël Coward, George S. Kaufman, and Cole Porter in their heyday. The Roundabout's other Broadway venues are Studio 54 and the Stephen Sondheim Theatre. The two Off-Broadway stages at the Harold and Miriam Steinberg Center for Theatre on West 46th Street show a mix of classics and works from up-and-coming playwrights. ✉ American Airlines Theatre, 227 W. 42nd St., between 7th and 8th Aves., Midtown West ☎ 212/719–1300 ⊕ www.roundabouttheatre.org Ⓜ 1, 2, 3, 7, N, Q, R, S, W to Times Sq.–42nd St.; A, C, E to 42nd St.–Port Authority.

Signature Theatre Company
THEATER | Designed by the architect Frank Gehry, the company's Pershing Square Signature Center houses three theater

Best Tips for Broadway

Whether forking over hundreds of dollars for a top seat or shoestringing it with a standing-room ticket, you'll have better Broadway experiences to brag about if you take our advice.

Do your homework. Remember—your friend's must-see may not be yours. Subscribe to online newsletters ahead of your trip for access to show reviews, special ticket offers, and more. If it's a classic play or opera, you may enjoy it more if you've read a synopsis before you go.

Reserve and plan ahead. TKTS booth is a great resource if you're up for what the fates make available, but for must-sees, book early. While you're at it, ask whether the regular cast is expected. (An in-person stop at the box office is the most reliable way to score this information, but don't hold them to it unless it's the day of the performance. If there is a change then—and the replacement cast is not acceptable to you—you may get a refund.) For musicals, live music often adds a special zing; confirm when ticketing to avoid surprises on the rare occasion when recorded music is used.

Check theater seating charts. Front mezzanine is a great option; with seats that overhang the orchestra section, they can be better (though not always less expensive) than many orchestra seats. Book with a seating chart at hand (available online and at the box office). Check accessibility, especially at older theaters with multiple flights of stairs and few elevators.

Know when to go. Typically, Broadway shows give eight performances a week. There are nightly performances from Tuesday through Saturday night, and matinees at 2 pm on Wednesday and Saturday and at 3 pm on Sunday (on Monday most theaters are closed, or "dark"). Weekend shows, especially Saturday night, are the most difficult tickets to get. Tuesday is especially promising, and an earlier curtain—sometimes as early as 7 instead of the usual 8 pm—helps ensure a good night's sleep for your next day of touring.

Dress right. You can throw on jeans to go to the theater these days, but personally we feel shorts and sneakers have no place on Broadway (at least in the audience). Bring binoculars if your seats are up high, check bulky coats if a coat check is available, and drop bags and packages off at your hotel room in advance—theater seats tend to be narrow, with little leg room.

Travel smart. Trying to get to the show on time? Unless you don't mind watching the meter run up while you're stuck in traffic, avoid cabs into or out of Times Square. Walk, especially if you're within 10 blocks of the theater. Otherwise, take the subway; many train lines converge in the area. And you don't need to arrive 30 or 40 minutes ahead (15 will do).

Dine off Broadway. Dining well on a budget and doing Broadway right are not mutually exclusive. The key is to avoid eating in Times Square itself—even the national chains are overpriced. Consider eating earlier instead, in whatever neighborhood you're visiting that day. If you're already in Midtown, head west to 9th or 10th Avenue, where prix-fixe deals and good eateries are plentiful and many actors and theater folk live.

spaces. The Tony Award–winning theater company provides a platform for both New York and world premieres, as well as revivals. Tickets tend to be affordable here, starting around $30. A central space with a café and bookstore connects the theaters, so come early, or stay late; the café is open noon to midnight Tuesday through Sunday. ⊠ *Pershing Square Signature Center, 480 W. 42nd St., between 9th and 10th Aves., Midtown West* ☎ *212/967–1913, 212/244–7529 for tickets* ⊕ *www.signaturetheatre.org* Ⓜ *A, C, E to 42nd St.–Port Authority.*

🛍 Shopping

Stretching west from ritzy 5th Avenue, Midtown West covers everything from Herald Square to Times Square, and there's plenty of shopping temptation in between. Whether you're only window-shopping or have money to burn, you'll no doubt find something to strike your fancy, from high-end designers to independent boutiques to major retail brands.

CAMERAS AND ELECTRONICS
★ B&H Photo & Video

CAMERAS/ELECTRONICS | Competitive prices, vast inventory, and a fair return policy make this bustling emporium a favorite with pros and amateurs alike looking for audio and video equipment, new cameras, computers, or tech accessories. Be sure to leave a few extra minutes for the checkout procedure; also, bear in mind that the store is closed Saturday. B&H is also known for its ceiling-height conveyor-belt system to move packages. ⊠ *420 9th Ave., between 33rd and 34th Sts., Midtown West* ☎ *212/444–6615* ⊕ *www.bhphotovideo.com* Ⓜ *1, 2, 3, A, C, E to 34th St.–Penn Station.*

CLOTHING
Forever 21

CLOTHING | The pounding music, plethora of jeggings, and graffiti-covered NYC taxicabs parked inside appeal to tween shoppers. But even if you are older than 21, there's still reason to shop here. This location, clocking in at a whopping 90,000 square feet and perched right on Times Square, is crammed with super-trendy clothes that won't break the bank, such as slouchy sweaters, shirtdresses, and poofy skirts. Menswear and children's clothes are also sold here, and the jewelry is surprisingly well-done. There are several other locations in Manhattan, including Union Square and Herald Square. ⊠ *1540 Broadway, between 45th and 46th Sts., Midtown West* ☎ *212/302–0594* ⊕ *www.forever21.com* Ⓜ *N, R, W to 49th St.; 1, 2, 3, 7, N, Q, R, S, W to Times Sq.–42nd St.*

Gap

CLOTHING | Gap may be as ubiquitous as Starbucks, but it is still a go-to place for classic denim, khakis, and sweaters in a rainbow of colors, as well as on-trend capsule collections from top designers. This Times Square flagship also carries GapBody, GapMaternity, GapKids, and babyGap, and shares its prime corner spot with Old Navy. You'll also find a Gap at Herald Square and several other locations across Manhattan. ⊠ *1514 Broadway, at W. 44th St., Midtown West* ☎ *646/866–5935* ⊕ *www.gap.com* Ⓜ *1, 2, 3, 7, N, Q, R, S, W to Times Sq.–42nd St.; A, C, E to 42nd St.–Port Authority.*

Norma Kamali

CLOTHING | A fashion fixture from the 1980s, Norma Kamali has a thoroughly modern, though still '80s-influenced, line. Her luminously white store carries graphic bathing suits, Grecian-style draped dresses, and her signature poofy "sleeping-bag coats." The in-house Wellness Café sells olive oil–based beauty products. ⊠ *11 W. 56th St., between 5th and 6th Aves., Midtown West* ☎ *212/957–9797* ⊕ *www.normakamali.com* Ⓜ *N, R, W to 5th Ave./59th St.; F to 57th St.*

DEPARTMENT STORES
Macy's
DEPARTMENT STORES | The store's massive, iconic flagship emerged in 2016 from a multiyear renovation that includes a glossier, grander style with acres of marble and video screens. On both the cosmetics and clothing floors, the focus has been shifted to prestige brands like Gucci and Kate Spade. With over 1 million square feet of retail space to explore, it's easy to spend an entire day shopping here. ⊠ *Herald Square, 151 W. 34th St., between Broadway and 7th Ave., Midtown West* ☎ *212/695-4400* ⊕ *www.macys.com* Ⓜ *B, D, F, M, N, Q, R, W to 34th St.–Herald Sq.*

FOOD AND TREATS
Kee's Chocolates
FOOD/CANDY | Owner Kee Ling Tong whips up delicious truffles and macarons with unusual, Asian-inspired flavors. Try the ginger peach and rosewater lychee macarons, or truffles flavored with lemongrass mint and Thai chili. ⊠ *315 W. 39th St., between 8th and 9th Aves., Midtown West* ☎ *212/967-8088* ⊕ *www.keeschocolates.com* Ⓜ *A, C, E to 42nd St.–Port Authority; 1, 2, 3, 7, N, Q, R, S, W to Times Sq.–42nd St.*

HOME DECOR
Muji
HOUSEHOLD ITEMS/FURNITURE | If you're into simple, chic, and cheap style, Muji has you covered. The name of this Japanese import translates to "no brand," and indeed, you don't find logos plastered on the housewares or clothes. Instead, the hallmark is a streamlined, minimalist design. The whole range of goods, from milky porcelain teapots to wooden toys, is invariably user-friendly. ⊠ *620 8th Ave., at 40th St., Midtown West* ☎ *212/382-2300* ⊕ *www.muji.us* Ⓜ *A, C, E to 42nd St.–Port Authority; 1, 2, 3, 7, N, Q, R, S, W to Times Sq.–42nd St.*

MUSEUM STORES
Museum of Arts and Design Store
GIFTS/SOUVENIRS | This well-edited museum gift shop stocks high-quality crafts like beautiful handmade tableware, unusual jewelry, and rugs, often tied into ongoing exhibits. It's a great place to stock up on gifts. ⊠ *2 Columbus Circle, at 8th Ave., Midtown West* ☎ *212/299-7700* ⊕ *thestore.madmuseum.org* Ⓜ *1, A, B, C, D to 59th St.–Columbus Circle.*

★ Museum of Modern Art Design and Book Store
GIFTS/SOUVENIRS | The MoMA's in-house shop stocks a huge selection of art reproductions and impressive coffee-table books about painting, sculpture, film, and photography. Across the street is the **MoMA Design Store,** where you can find Charles and Ray Eames furniture reproductions, vases designed by Alvar Aalto, and lots of clever toys. ⊠ *11 W. 53rd St., between 5th and 6th Aves., Midtown West* ☎ *212/708-9700* ⊕ *store.moma.org* Ⓜ *E, M to 5th Ave./53rd St.*

PERFORMING ARTS MEMORABILIA
One Shubert Alley
GIFTS/SOUVENIRS | This was the first store to sell Broadway merchandise outside of a theater. Today, souvenir posters, tees, and other knickknacks memorializing past and present Broadway hits still reign at this Theater District shop next to the Booth Theatre. ⊠ *222 W. 45th St., between 7th and 8th Aves., Midtown West* ☎ *212/944-4133* ⊕ *www.oneshubertalley.com* Ⓜ *1, 2, 3, 7, N, Q, R, S, W to Times Sq.–42nd St.*

Triton Gallery
GIFTS/SOUVENIRS | Theatrical posters both large and small are available, and the selection is democratic, with everything from Marlene Dietrich's *Blue Angel* to recent Broadway shows like *Hamilton* represented. ⊠ *The Film Center, 690 8th Ave., 6th fl., between 43rd and 44th Sts.,*

*Midtown West ☎ 212/765–2472 ⊕ www.
tritongallery.com Ⓜ A, C, E to 42nd St.–
Port Authority.*

SHOES, HANDBAGS, AND LEATHER GOODS

Manolo Blahnik

SHOES/LUGGAGE/LEATHER GOODS | These
sexy status shoes are some of the most
expensive on the market. The signature
look is a pointy toe with a high, delicate
heel, but there are also ballet flats,
loafers and oxfords, and over-the-knee
dominatrix boots that cost upward of
$1,000. Pray for a sale. ⊠ *31 W. 54th St.,
between 5th and 6th Aves., Midtown
West ☎ 212/582–3007 ⊕ www.manolo-
blahnik.com Ⓜ E, M to 5th Ave./53rd St.*

TOYS

American Girl Place

TOYS | **FAMILY** | Grade-school kids are
crazy for American Girl dolls, whose lines
range from historically accurate characters to contemporary girls with all the
accompanying clothes and accessories.
Bring your doll to this New York flagship
in Rockefeller Plaza for a doll hairdressing
salon and spa, doll hospital, café, Dress
Like Your Doll shop, design-your-own-
doll station, and more. ⊠ *75 Rockefeller Plaza, between 51st and 52nd
Sts., Midtown West ☎ 877/247–5223
⊕ www.americangirl.com Ⓜ B, D, F, M to
47th–50th Sts./Rockefeller Center.*

Chapter 11

THE UPPER
EAST SIDE

Updated by
Joshua Rogol

● **Sights**
★★★★☆

🍴 **Restaurants**
★★☆☆☆

🛏 **Hotels**
★★☆☆☆

🛍 **Shopping**
★★★★☆

🍸 **Nightlife**
★★☆☆☆

NEIGHBORHOOD SNAPSHOT

TOP EXPERIENCES

■ Exploring any of the world-class museums here, followed by a relaxing, restorative lunch

■ Gallery-hopping the UES's so-unhip-it's-now-hip art scene (plus they're free)

■ Window-shopping on Madison Avenue

■ Appreciating the views from the cable car on the ride to Four Freedoms Park on Roosevelt Island

GETTING HERE

Take the Lexington Avenue 4 or 5 express train to 59th or 86th Street. The 6 local train also stops at 59th, 68th, 77th, 86th, and 96th Streets. The 2nd Avenue subway line opened in 2017 with Q train stops at 72nd, 86th, and 96th streets. From Midtown, the F and Q trains let you out at Lexington Avenue and 63rd Street, where you can transfer to the 4, 5, or 6 after a short walk (and free transfer). From the Upper West Side, take one of the cross-town buses, the M66, M72, M79, M86, or M96. You can also take the N, R, or W train to 59th Street and Lexington Avenue.

PLANNING YOUR TIME

The Upper East Side lends itself to a surprising variety of simple but distinct itineraries: exploring the landmarks on Museum Mile; languorous gallery grazing; window-shopping on Madison Avenue; or, for younger crowds of twenty- or thirtysomethings, barhopping on 2nd Avenue. If it's the museums you're after, make sure to plan at least a few hours per museum—with some snack or coffee breaks. There's a lot to see, so try not to plan on visiting more than one museum a day. The Upper East Side's town houses, boutiques, consignment stores, and hidden gardens are easy to miss unless you take some time to wander.

QUICK BITES

■ **Joe (Upper East Side)**
One of the city's best coffee chains, Joe has the kind of quality caffeine and sweets to fuel you up and down Museum Mile (and maybe even around the park). ✉ *1045 Lexington Ave., between 74th and 75th Sts.* ⊕ *www.joenewyork.com* Ⓜ *Subway: 6 to 77th St.*

■ **Lady M Cake Boutique.**
The signature here is the Mille Crepes cake: 20 crepes stacked together with a delicious cream filling. (Thank us later.) There are some salads and basic sandwiches offered as well. ✉ *41 E. 78 St., at Madison Ave.* ⊕ *www.ladym.com* Ⓜ *Subway: 6 to 77th St.*

■ **Two Little Red Hens.**
With first-rate coffee and delicious cupcakes, cheesecake, and cookies to match, this little bakery is a legend with locals. ✉ *1652 2nd Ave., at 86th St.* ⊕ *www.twolittleredhens.com* Ⓜ *Subway: 4, 5, 6, Q to 86th St.*

To many New Yorkers, the Upper East Side connotes old money and high society. Alongside Central Park, between 5th and Lexington Avenues, up to East 96th Street, the trappings of wealth are everywhere apparent: posh buildings, Madison Avenue's flagship boutiques, and doormen in braided livery. It's also a key destination for visitors, because some of the most fantastic museums in the country are here.

There's a reason this stretch of Manhattan is called "Museum Mile": this is where you'll find the **Metropolitan Museum of Art,** the **Solomon R. Guggenheim Museum,** and the **Cooper Hewitt, Smithsonian Design Museum,** as well as a number of art galleries. For a local taste of the luxe life, catwalk down Madison Avenue for its lavish boutiques; strolling the platinum-card corridor between 60th and 82nd Streets is like stepping into the pages of a glossy magazine. Many fashion houses have their flagships here and showcase their lush threads in exquisite settings.

Venture east of Lexington Avenue and encounter a less wealthy—and more diverse—Upper East Side, inhabited by couples seeking some of the last (relatively) affordable places to raise a family south of 100th Street, as well as recent college grads getting a foothold in the city (on weekend nights 2nd Avenue resembles a miles-long fraternity and sorority reunion). One neighborhood particularly worth exploring is northeast-lying Yorkville, especially between 78th and

86th Streets east of 2nd Avenue. Once a remote hamlet with a large German population, Yorkville has several remaining ethnic food shops, 19th-century row houses, and—one of the city's best-kept secrets—**Carl Schurz Park,** which make for a good half-day's exploration, as does catching a glimpse of the most striking residence there, **Gracie Mansion.**

If art galleries appeal, there are some elegant ones on the Upper East Side. In keeping with the tony surroundings, the emphasis here is on works by established masters.

⊙ Sights

Acquavella Galleries
MUSEUM | The 19th- and 20th-century museum-quality art inside this five-story, marble-floored French neoclassical mansion tends to be big-name stuff, from impressionists through pop artists, including Picasso, Lucian Freud, Jean-Michel Basquiat, James Rosenquist, and Wayne Thiebaud. ⊠ *18 E. 79th St.,*

Upper East Side

11

The Upper East Side

between 5th and Madison Aves., Upper East Side ☎ *212/734–6300* ⊕ *www.acquavellagalleries.com* 🎫 *Free* ⊘ *Closed weekends (open Sat. during select exhibitions or by appointment)* Ⓜ *6 to 77th St.*

Asia Society and Museum

MUSEUM | The Asian art collection of Mr. and Mrs. John D. Rockefeller III forms the core of this museum's holdings, which span territory from Pakistan to Java and date back to the 11th century BC, and include Hindu stone sculpture, Tibetan Buddhist paintings, Vietnamese ceramics, Han Dynasty bronzes, and Japanese woodblock prints. Founded in 1956, the society has a regular program of lectures, films, and performances, in addition to changing exhibitions of traditional and contemporary art. Trees grow in the glass-enclosed, skylighted Garden Court Café, which serves an eclectic Asian lunch menu and weekend brunch. Admission is free Friday 6–9 pm (September to June). A free audio tour is included with admission, or you can take a free guided tour at 2 daily and 6:30 on Friday. ✉ *725 Park Ave., at 70th St., Upper East Side* ☎ *212/288–6400* ⊕ *www.asiasociety.org/ny* 🎫 *$12* ⊘ *Closed Mon.* Ⓜ *6 to 68th St.–Hunter College.*

Blum & Poe New York

MUSEUM | This contemporary art gallery may be a relative newbie on the Upper East Side art scene (it opened in 2014), but as one of L.A.'s top art galleries, Blum & Poe was quick to settle into its renovated town house on East 66th Street and establish itself in the New York art world. Past exhibits have featured artists including Hugh Scott-Douglas, Kishio Suga, Yun Hyong-Keun, and Zhu Jinshi. ✉ *19 E. 66th St., between 5th and Madison Aves., Upper East Side* ☎ *212/249–2249* ⊕ *www.blumandpoe.com* ⊘ *Closed Sun., Mon.* Ⓜ *6 to 68th St.–Hunter College; F, Q to Lexington Ave.–63rd St.*

Carl Schurz Park

CITY PARK | FAMILY | Facing the East River, this park, named for a German immigrant who was a prominent newspaper editor in the 19th century, is so tranquil you'd never guess you're directly above the FDR Drive. Walk along the promenade and take in views of the river and the Roosevelt Island Lighthouse across the way. To the north are Randalls and Wards Islands and the RFK Bridge (aka the Triborough Bridge)—as well as the more immediate sight of locals pushing strollers, riding bikes, or walking their dogs. If you use the 86th Street entrance, you'll find yourself near the grounds of a Federal-style wood-frame house that belies the grandeur of its name: Gracie Mansion. ✉ *From 84th to 90th St., between East End Ave. and the East River, Upper East Side* ☎ *212/459–4455* ⊕ *www.carlschurzparknyc.org* Ⓜ *4, 5, 6, Q to 86th St.*

Castelli Gallery

MUSEUM | One of the most influential dealers of the 20th century, Leo Castelli helped foster the careers of many important artists, including one of his first discoveries, Jasper Johns. Castelli died in 1999, but the gallery continues to show works by Roy Lichtenstein, Andy Warhol, Ed Ruscha, Frank Stella, Robert Morris, and other heavy hitters. ✉ *18 E. 77th St., between 5th and Madison Aves., Upper East Side* ☎ *212/249–4470* ⊕ *www.castelligallery.com* 🎫 *Free* ⊘ *Closed Sun., Mon.* Ⓜ *6 to 77th St.*

Cooper Hewitt, Smithsonian Design Museum

MUSEUM | FAMILY | The Cooper Hewitt is a slick 21st-century museum that has taken an ornate, century-old mansion (once the residence of industrialist Andrew Carnegie) and outfitted it with the latest technologies and amenities to create a highly interactive experience. You don't just *look* at design; you engage it and then take it home. Visitors receive a digital pen that acts as a key to the museum's entire collection of more than 200,000 objects, everything from antique cutlery and Japanese sword fittings to robotics and animation. Museum highlights include giant touch-screen tables where visitors can summon random-yet-relevant items from the museum's collection by drawing a squiggle or a shape; the Immersion Room, where visitors can view and save their favorite wallpapers from the museum's incredible collection or create their own designs; and the Process Lab, where visitors get hands-on to solve design dilemmas.

The focus on design and discovery extends to "SHOP," where limited-edition objects are for sale. There is a café, and an outdoor garden is free and open to the public. Guided tours run daily at 11:30, at 1:30 on weekdays, and at 1 and 3 on weekends. Admission is pay-what-you-wish Saturday evening from 6 to 9. ✉ *2 E. 91st St., at 5th Ave., Upper East Side* 📞 *212/849–8400* ⊕ *www.cooperhewitt. org* 💲 *$18 ($16 online)* Ⓜ *4, 5, 6 to 86th St.*

El Museo del Barrio

MUSEUM | *El barrio,* Spanish for "the neighborhood," is the nickname for East Harlem, a largely Spanish-speaking Puerto Rican and Dominican community; El Museo del Barrio, on the edge of this neighborhood, focuses on Latin American and Caribbean art, with some 10% of its collection concentrated on works by self-taught artists from New York, Puerto Rico, the Caribbean, and Latin America. The more than 6,500-object permanent collection includes over 400 pre-Columbian artifacts, sculpture, photography, film and video, and traditional art from all over Latin America. The collection of 360 *santos,* carved wooden folk-art figures from Puerto Rico, is popular. El Museo hosts performances, lectures, films, and cultural events, including a monthlong Día de los Muertos celebration. ■TIP→ **Admission to El Museo del Barrio gains you free entrance to the neighboring Museum**

of the City of New York. ✉ *1230 5th Ave., between 104th and 105th Sts., Upper East Side* 📞 *212/831–7272* ⊕ *www. elmuseo.org* 💲 *$9 suggested donation* ⊗ *Closed Mon., Tues.* Ⓜ *6 to 103rd St.*

★ Frick Collection

MUSEUM | Henry Clay Frick (1849–1919) made his fortune amid the soot and smoke of Pittsburgh, where he was a coke (a coal fuel derivative) and steel baron, but this lovely art museum, once Frick's private New York residence, is decidedly removed from soot. With an exceptional collection of works from the Renaissance through the late 19th century that includes Édouard Manet's *The Bullfight* (1864), a Chinard portrait bust (1809), three Vermeers, three Rembrandts, works by El Greco, Goya, Van Dyck, Hogarth, Degas, and Turner, as well as sculpture, decorative arts, and 18th-century French furniture, everything here is a highlight.

The Portico Gallery, an enclosed portico along the building's 5th Avenue garden, houses the museum's growing collection of sculpture, and the tranquil indoor garden court is a magical spot for a rest. An audio guide, available in six languages, is included with admission, as are the year-round temporary exhibits. Children under 10 are not admitted ✉ *1 E. 70th St., at 5th Ave., Upper East Side* 📞 *212/288–0700* ⊕ *www.frick.org* 💲 *$22; pay-what-you-wish Wed. 2–6; free first Fri. of the month (except Sept., Jan.)* ⊗ *Closed Mon.* Ⓜ *6 to 68th St.–Hunter College.*

Gagosian Madison Avenue

MUSEUM | If you are looking for ambitious works by the world's most acclaimed artists in a gallery that easily competes with the city's top museums, you have to visit Gagosian. Perhaps the most powerful art dealer in the world, Larry Gagosian has galleries in London, Paris, Rome, Athens, and Hong Kong, among other cities, as well as five galleries in New York. The 980 Madison Avenue location, the contemporary art empire's head-quarters, is a multifloor gallery that has shown works by big names like Warhol, Pollock, Miró, Calder, Twombly, and Hirst. Gagosian also has spaces at nearby 976 Madison Avenue, as well as a store-front space on Park Avenue and 75th Street. ⊠ *980 Madison Ave., near 76th St., Upper East Side* ☎ *212/744–2313* ⊕ *www.gagosian.com* ◻ *Free* ⊙ *Closed Sun.* Ⓜ *6 to 77th St.*

Gracie Mansion

GOVERNMENT BUILDING | The official may-or's residence, Gracie Mansion was built in 1799 by shipping merchant Archibald Gracie, and enlarged in 1966. Ten mayors have lived here since it became the official residence in 1942, though Michael Bloomberg stayed in his own 79th Street town house during his three terms as mayor. He poured millions into renova-tions at Gracie Mansion, rejuvenating both the interior and exterior and turning the second floor into a house museum.

In 2014, the mansion became home to Mayor Bill de Blasio and his family. Visitors to the "People's House"—with all its history and colorful rooms furnished over centuries and packed with American objets d'art—can see that the resident first family of New York City has added its personal touch to the mansion, swap-ping out much of the artwork to better reflect the city's diversity. The collection now includes a bill of sale for a slave, a portrait of Frederick Douglass, and Native American artifacts. Tours are offered on Monday, and reservations must be made online; plan at least two weeks in advance, if possible. ⊠ *Carl Schurz Park, East End Ave., at 88th St., Upper East Side* ☎ *212/676–3060* ⊕ *www1.nyc.gov/gracie* ◻ *Free* ⊙ *Closed Tues.–Sun.* Ⓜ *4, 5, 6, Q to 86th St.*

Jane Kahan Gallery

MUSEUM | This welcoming gallery rep-resents some lofty artists. In addition to tapestries by modern masters like

Pablo Picasso, Joan Miró, and Alexander Calder—one of this gallery's specialties—works by late-19th- and early-20th-centu-ry modern artists like Fernand Léger and Marc Chagall are showcased. There's also an exhibition space (open by appointment only) in the neighborhood at 330 East 59th Street. ⊠ *922 Madison Ave., 2nd fl., between 73rd and 74th Sts., Upper East Side* ☎ *212/744–1490* ⊕ *www.janekahan. com* ◻ *Free* ⊙ *Closed Sun., Mon.; also Sat. July–Aug.* Ⓜ *6 to 77th St.*

The Jewish Museum

MUSEUM | In a Gothic-style 1908 man-sion, the Jewish Museum draws on a large collection of art and ceremonial objects to explore Jewish identity and culture spanning more than 4,000 years. The wide-ranging collection includes a 3rd-century Roman burial plaque, 20th-century sculpture by Elie Nadel-man, and modern art from artists such as Marc Chagall and Man Ray. *Scenes from the Collection,* occupying the entire third floor, contains roughly 600 pieces from ancient to contemporary, many of which are on display for the first time. The space is divided into seven thematic sections complemented by interactive media; displays will rotate at least annual-ly. The museum's changing exhibitions are well curated and lively. Don't leave without checking out the museum's café, Russ & Daughters, an outpost of the longtime Jewish appetizing shop and Lower East Side institution. ⊠ *1109 5th Ave., at 92nd St., Upper East Side* ☎ *212/423–3200* ⊕ *www.thejewishmu-seum.org* ◻ *$18 (free Sat., pay-what-you-wish Thurs. 5–8)* ⊙ *Closed Wed.* Ⓜ *6 to 96th St.*

The Met Breuer

MUSEUM | A great addition to the Metro-politan Museum of Art's already stunning collection, the Met Breuer offers art lovers four floors of rotating exhibits focusing on modern and contemporary art from the 20th and 21st centuries. The former site of the Whitney Museum (now in the Meatpacking District), the Brutalist-style building was designed by Marcel Breuer (pronounced "BROY-er") and also offers performances, art commissions, and educational programs. A ticket to the Met Breuer also includes admission to the Met, a few blocks away on 5th Avenue, and the Cloisters, farther uptown. ✉ 945 Madison Ave., at 75th St., Upper East Side ☎ 212/731–1675 ⊕ www.metmuseum.org/visit/met-breuer 💰 $25 for 3-day ticket (includes the Metropolitan Museum and Met Cloisters); $25 suggested donation for New York State residents (full donation includes 3-day ticket to Metropolitan Museum and Met Cloisters) ۞ Closed Mon. Ⓜ 6 to 77th St.

★ The Metropolitan Museum of Art

MUSEUM | If Manhattan held no other museum than the colossal Metropolitan Museum of Art, you could still occupy yourself for days roaming its labyrinthine corridors. The Metropolitan Museum has more than 2 million works of art representing 5,000 years of history, so it's a good idea to plan ahead; looking at everything here could take a week. The famous **Egyptian collection** (including the Temple of Dendur) is reason enough to visit. Other don't-miss sections include the magnificent **Islamic Galleries,** the collections of impressionist paintings, the **American Wing,** and the **Anna Wintour Costume Center.** Keep in mind that the **British Galleries** are closed for renovations (reopening winter 2020), and the **European Paintings Galleries** will be partially closed in two phases as gallery skylights are replaced between 2018 and 2022. In fall 2018, the Met announced the complete overhaul of the Africa, Oceania, and Americas collections, with work scheduled to begin in 2020. Check the website for updates. Admission includes three-day entry to the museum's modern-art outpost, the Met Breuer (Madison Avenue and 75th Street), as well as the Cloisters Museum and Gardens in northern Manhattan. ✉ 1000 5th Ave., at 82nd St., Upper East Side ☎ 212/535–7710 ⊕ www.metmuseum.org 💰 $25 for 3-day ticket (includes Met Breuer and Met Cloisters); $25 suggested donation for New York State residents (full donation includes 3-day ticket to Met Breuer and Met Cloisters); $7 for audio guide Ⓜ 4, 5, 6 to 86th St.

Mount Vernon Hotel Museum and Garden

HISTORIC SITE | FAMILY | Built in 1799, this former carriage house became a day hotel (a sort of country club) in 1826. Now restored and owned by the Colonial Dames of America, it provides a glimpse of the days when the city ended at 14th Street and this area was a country escape for New Yorkers. A 45-minute tour (the only way to see the museum and garden) passes through the eight rooms that display furniture and artifacts of the Federal and Empire periods. Many rooms have real artifacts such as clothes, hats, and fans that children can handle. The lovely adjoining garden is designed in an 18th-century style. Tours are on demand and can be geared to specific interests; arrive at least a half hour before closing time to allow for tour. ■TIP➔ Entrance is free for children under 12. ✉ 421 E. 61st St., between York and 1st Aves., Upper East Side ☎ 212/838–6878 ⊕ www.mvhm.org 💰 $0 ۞ Closed Mon. Ⓜ 4, 5, 6 to 59th St.; N, R, W to Lexington Ave./59th St.; F, Q to Lexington Ave./63rd St.

Museum of American Illustration

MUSEUM | Founded in 1901, the museum of the Society of Illustrators presents its annual "Oscars," a juried international competition, from January to March. The best in children's book illustration is showcased October through December. In between are eclectic exhibitions on science fiction, fashion, politics, and history illustrations. The Society of Illustrators has also incorporated the holdings of the Museum of Comic and Cartoon Art (MoCCA) into its collections. MoCCA's

Continued on page 343

THE METROPOLITAN MUSEUM OF ART

If the city held no other museum than the colossal Metropolitan Museum of Art, you could still occupy yourself for days roaming its labyrinthine corridors. Because the Metropolitan Museum has more than 2 million works of art representing 5,000 years of history, you're going to have to make tough choices. Looking at everything here could take a week.

Mesmerizing carvings in the ancient Egyptian Temple of Dendur.

Before you begin exploring the museum, check the museum's floor plan, available at all entrances, for location of the major wings and collections. Google Maps will help you find your way through the museum. The service tracks your location with a blue dot and guides you through exhibits, across floors, and to bathrooms and exits. It can even help you avoid the gift shop if you're visiting with kids!

The posted adult admission, is now required for all but permanent residents of New York state. It is still suggested for state residents. Admission includes all special exhibits and same-day entrance to the Met Cloisters (see Chapter 13) and Met Breuer. The Met's audio guide costs an additional $7, and if you intend to stay more than an hour or so, it's worth it. The generally perceptive commentary covers museum highlights and directors' picks, with separate commentary tracks directed at kids.

If you want to avoid the crowds, visit weekday mornings or take on Empty Met Tour (from $165). Also good are Friday and Saturday evenings, when live classical music plays from the Great Hall balcony. If the Great Hall (the main entrance) is mobbed, avoid the chaos by heading to the street-level entrance to the left of the main stairs, near 81st Street. Ticket lines and coat checks are much less ferocious here.

What to see? Check out the museum highlights on the following pages.

Don't forget the Met Breuer. In 2016, the Met moved part of its modern art collection into the former home of the Whitney Museum on Madison Avenue, a few blocks south of the Met's main building on Fifth Avenue. Unlike the main museum and the Met Cloisters, the Met Breuer is closed on Mondays. There are also special exhibits. In 2019, there was discussion of housing park of the Frick Museum's collection in this building with the Frick itself was closed for a major expansion and renovation, but those plans are still forthcoming.

MUSEUM HIGHLIGHTS

Egyptian Art

A major star is the **Temple of Dendur** (circa 15 BC), in a huge atrium to itself and with a moatlike pool of water to represent its original location near the Nile. The temple was commissioned by the Roman emperor Augustus to honor the goddess Isis and the sons of a Nubian chieftain. Look for the scratched-in graffiti from 19th-century Western explorers on the inside. Egypt gave the temple as a gift to the U.S. in 1965; it would have been submerged after the construction of the Aswan High Dam.

Temple of Dendur

The Egyptian collection as a whole covers 4,000 years of history, with papyrus pages from the Egyptian Book of the Dead, stone sarcophagi inscribed with hieroglyphics, and tombs. The galleries should be walked through counterclockwise from the Ancient Kingdom (2650–2150 BC), to the period under Roman rule (30 BC–AD 400). In the latter, keep an eye out for the enormous, bulbous **Sarcophagus of Horkhebil**, sculpted from basalt.

Greek and Roman Art

Today's tabloids have nothing on ancient Greece and Rome. They had it all—sex, cults, drugs, unrelenting violence, and, of course, stunning art. The recently redone Greek and Roman galleries encompass 6,000 works of art that reveal aspects of everyday life in these influential cultures.

The urnlike terracotta kraters were used by the Greeks for mixing wine and water at parties and other events. Given that, it's not surprising that most depict slightly racy scenes. Some of the most impressive can be found in the gallery covering 5th century BC.

On the mezzanine of the Roman galleries, the Etruscan bronze chariot from 650 BC depicts scenes from the life of Achilles. Notice how the simplistic Etruscan style in combination with the Greek influence evolved into the naturalistic Roman statues below.

The frescoes from a bedroom in the Villa of P. Fannius Synistor preserved by the explosion of Mt. Vesuvius in AD 79 give us a glimpse into the stylistic achievement of perspective in Roman painting.

ART TO TAKE HOME

You don't have to pay admission to get to the mammoth gift shop on the first floor. One of the better souvenirs here is also one of the more reasonable: the Met's own **illustrated guide** to 869 of the best items in its collection.

Engelhard Court

An artifact from ancient Greece.

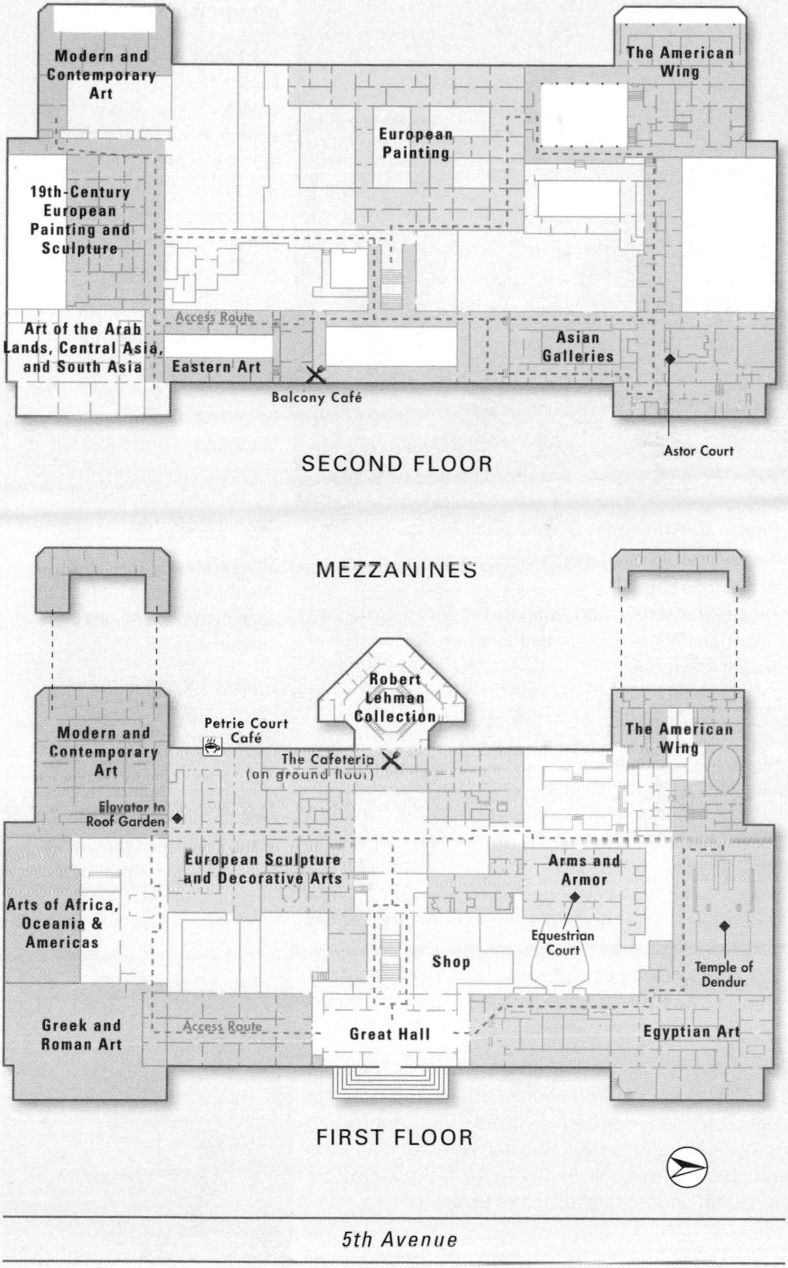

Modern and Contemporary Art

The American Wing

European Painting

19th-Century European Painting and Sculpture

Art of the Arab Lands, Central Asia, and South Asia

Access Route

Eastern Art

Balcony Café

Asian Galleries

Astor Court

SECOND FLOOR

MEZZANINES

Robert Lehman Collection

Petrie Court Café

The Cafeteria (on ground floor)

Modern and Contemporary Art

The American Wing

Elevator to Roof Garden

European Sculpture and Decorative Arts

Arms and Armor

Arts of Africa, Oceania & Americas

Equestrian Court

Shop

Temple of Dendur

Greek and Roman Art

Access Route

Great Hall

Egyptian Art

FIRST FLOOR

5th Avenue

The American Wing of the Metropolitan Museum of Art.

American Wing

After years of extensive renovations, the Met's revitalized **New American Wing Galleries for Paintings, Sculpture, and Decorative Arts** reopened in 2012 with 30,000 square feet of skylit space to showcase one of the best and largest collections of American art in the country.

There's much to see, from Colonial furniture to the works of the great masters, including John Singleton Copley, Gilbert Stuart, Thomas Cole, Frederic Edwin Church, Winslow Homer, and Thomas Eakins, among others. The highlight of the new installation is Emanuel Gottlieb Leutze's magnificent 1851 painting, *Washington Crossing the Delaware*. Hung in an immense gilded frame (recreated from an 1864 photograph of the painting), Leutze's iconic work is displayed just as it was at a fundraiser for Union soldiers in 1864—flanked by Frederic Church's *Heart of the Andes* and Albert Bierstadt's *Rocky Mountains*.

Also not to be missed are John Singer Sargent's *Madame X*, a once-scandalous portrait of a Parisian socialite; the recreation of the entrance hall of the 18th Century Van Rensselaer Manor House in Albany, New York; and the collection of portrait miniatures—detailed watercolors to be carried or gifted as tokens of love.

TIME TO EAT? INSIDE THE MUSEUM

The **Petrie Court Café**, at the back of the 1st-floor European Sculpture Court, has waiter service. Prices range from $12 for a sandwich to $21 for organic chicken salad. Afternoon tea is served from 2:30 pm to 4:30 pm during the week. Dinner is served on weekends.

The **Great Hall Balcony Bar** is located on the second floor belcony overlooking the Great Hall. On Fridays and Saturdays, 4 pm to 8:30 pm waiters serve appetizers and cocktails accompanied by live classical music.

The **cafeteria** on the ground floor has stations for pasta, main courses, antipasti, and sandwiches.

Looking for one of the best views in town? The **Roof Garden** (open May–Oct.) exhibits contemporary sculpture, but most people take the elevator here to have a drink or snack while checking out **Central Park** and the skyline.

Tiffany

Arms and Armor

The **Equestrian Court**, where the knights are mounted on armored models of horses, is one of the most dramatic rooms in the museum. For a bird's-eye view, check it out again from the balconies in the Musical Instruments collection on the second floor.

European Sculpture and Decorative Arts

Among the many sculptures in the sun-filled Petrie Court, **Ugolino and His Sons** still stands out for the despairing poses of its subjects. Ugolino, a nobleman whose family's tragic story is told in Dante's *Inferno*, was punished for treason by being left to starve to death with his grandsons and sons in a locked tower. (It's not clear if putting such a sculpture so near the Petrie Court's café is some curator's idea of a joke or not.) By the way, the redbrick and granite wall on the court's north side is the museum's original entrance.

The newly renovated Wrightsman Galleries for French Decorative Arts on the first floor displays the opulence that caused Louis the XVI to lose his head. The blindingly golden Boiserie from the Hotel de Cabris, a remnant of French 18th century Neo-classical interiors, represents the finest collection of French decorative arts in the country.

Anna Wintour Costume Center

In May 2014, after a two-year renovation, the Met's Costume Institute reopened with a newly designed 4,200-square-foot main gallery, an updated costume conservation laboratory, expanded study and storage facilities, and a new name—the Anna Wintour Costume Center. Named for the legendary Vogue editor-in-chief and Met Trustee (responsible for the annual Met Gala), and housing one of the most comprehensive costume collections in the world, the new Costume Center (northeast end of the museum on the ground floor) is sure to be a huge draw for fashion lovers.

European Paintings

On the second floor, the 13th- to 18th-century paintings are grouped at the top of the Great Hall's stairs.

Recently, the Met spent about $45 million to buy Duccio di Buoninsegna's *Madonna and Child,* painted circa 1300. The last remaining Duccio in private hands, this painting, the size of a piece of typewriter paper, is unimpressive at first glance. The work, though rigid, represents a revolution in Byzantine art. The humanity reflected in the baby Jesus grabbing his mother's veil changed European painting.

TIME TO EAT?
OUTSIDE THE MUSEUM

Because museum admission is good all day, you can always leave for lunch and come back later. A block from the museum, **Caffe Grazie** *(26 E. 84th St., between Madison and Fifth Aves., 212/717–4407)* offers casual Italian dining in a lovely townhouse. Options include omelets, pizzas, sandwiches, and salads, but they're best known for the Italian Bento-Box with its tastings of savory and sweets.

At the fairly inexpensive sit-down eatery **Le Pain Quotidien** *(1131 Madison Ave., at 84th St., 212/327–4900),* the hungry dine at long communal tables on high-quality sandwiches (around $9), salads, and pastries.

Equestrian Court (1930)

Rembrandt's masterful *Aristotle with a Bust of Homer* (1653) shows a philosopher contemplating worldly gains versus values through its play of light and use of symbols. Around Aristotle is a gold medal of Alexander the Great, one of the philosopher's students.

In the room dedicated to **Monet** you can get to all his greatest hits—poplar trees, haystacks, water lilies, and the Rouen Cathedral. The muted tones of Pissaro are followed by a room full of bright and garish colors announcing works by Gauguin, Matisse, and Van Gogh.

Vincent van Gogh,
Wheatfield with Cypresses

Islamic Galleries

In late 2011, after an eight-year renovation, the Met reopened its Islamic galleries, a suite of 15 galleries housing one of the world's premier collections of Islamic art. Now known as the "Art of the Arab Lands, Turkey, Iran, Central Asia, and Later South Asia," the collection comprises more than 12,000 works of art and traces the course of Islamic Civilization over a span of 13 centuries. Highlights include an 11-foot-high 14th century mihrab, or prayer niche, decorated with glazed ceramic tiles; the recently restored Emperor's Carpet—a 16th century Persian carpet that was presented to the Hapsburg Emperor Leopold I by Peter the Great of Russia; the Damascus Room—a Syrian Ottoman reception room decorated with poetic verses; and glass, ceramics, and metalwork from Egypt, Syria, Iraq, and Iran.

Asian Galleries

The serene **Astor Court**, which has its own skylight and pond of real-life koi (goldfish), is a model of a scholar's court garden in Soochow, China.

The Han dynasty (206 BC–AD 220) introduced the practice of sending the dead on to the afterlife with small objects to help them there. Keep an eye out for these **small clay figures**, which include farm animals (enclosed in barnyards) and dancing entertainers.

On display in a glass case in the center of an early-Chinese gallery is a complete set of 14 **bronze altar vessels.** Dating 1100 BC–AD 800, these green and slightly crusty pieces were used for worshipping ancestors. The Met displays some of its finest **Asian stoneware and porcelain** along the balcony overlooking the Great Hall.

The teak dome and minature balconies from a **Jain meeting hall** in western India were carved in the 16th century. Just about the entire surface is covered with musicians, animals, gods, and servants.

WHAT'S NEW

Under construction for two years, the front steps of the Met—one of Manhattan's most iconic meeting places—have reopened as a European-style plaza with additional public seating, a modernized fountain, landscaping, and improved museum access.

Standing eight-armed
Avalokiteshvara

collection is in its own gallery on the second floor, and there are workshops, programs, and a comic festival (MoCCA Fest). ■TIP→ **Admission is free on Tuesday 5–8.** ⊠ *128 E. 63rd St., between Lexington and Park Aves., Upper East Side* ☎ *212/838–2560* ⊕ *www.societyillustrators.org* ⊠ *$15* ⊙ *Closed Sun., Mon.* Ⓜ *F, Q to Lexington Ave./63rd St.; 4, 5, 6 to 59th St.; N, R, W to Lexington Ave./59th St.*

Museum of the City of New York

MUSEUM | The city's present, past, and future are explored through quirky, engaging exhibits on subjects such as architecture, fashion, history, and politics in a Colonial Revival building designed for the museum in the 1930s. The ongoing exhibition *New York at Its Core* explores the sweep and diverse facets of the city's 400-year history through artifacts, photography, archival film, and interactive digital experiences. Don't miss *Timescapes,* a 25-minute media projection that innovatively illustrates New York's physical expansion and population changes, or *Activist New York,* an ongoing exploration of the city's history of social activism. You can also find New York–centric lectures, films, and walking tours here. There's a café, too. After touring the museum, cross the street and stroll through the Vanderbilt Gates to enter the Conservatory Garden, one of Central Park's hidden gems. ⊠ *1220 5th Ave., at 103rd St., Upper East Side* ☎ *212/534–1672* ⊕ *www.mcny.org* ⊠ *$18 suggested donation* Ⓜ *6 to 103rd St.*

Neue Galerie New York

MUSEUM | Early-20th-century German and Austrian art and design are the focus here, with works by artists Gustav Klimt, Wassily Kandinsky, Paul Klee, and Egon Schiele, as well as Josef Hoffmann and other designers from the Wiener Werkstätte, taking center stage. The Neue Galerie was founded by the late art dealer Serge Sabarsky and cosmetics heir and art collector Ronald S. Lauder. It's in a 1914 wood- and marble-floored mansion designed by Carrère and Hastings, which was once home to Mrs. Cornelius Vanderbilt III. An audio guide is included with admission. Children under 12 are not admitted, and teens 12–16 must be accompanied by an adult. **Café Sabarsky,** in an elegant, high-ceiling space on the first floor, is a destination in its own right for Viennese coffee, cakes, strudels, and Sacher tortes. ■TIP→ **Admission is free 6–9 pm on the first Friday of the month.** ⊠ *1048 5th Ave., at 86th St., Upper East Side* ☎ *212/628–6200* ⊕ *www.neuegalerie.org* ⊠ *$22* ⊙ *Closed Tues., Wed.* Ⓜ *4, 5, 6 to 86th St.*

Roosevelt Island

NATIONAL/STATE PARK | FAMILY | The 2-milelong East River slice of land that parallels Manhattan from 48th to 85th Streets is now a quasi-suburb of more than 14,000 people, and the vestiges of its infamous asylums, hospitals, and prisons make this an offbeat historical trip. At its southern tip are the ruins of a **Smallpox Hospital,** built in 1854 in a Gothic Revival style by James Renwick Jr. Neighboring the hospital ruins is **Four Freedoms Park,** a memorial to Franklin Delano Roosevelt designed by architect Louis I. Kahn. The monument has a giant bust of FDR and a wall inscribed with the wartime "Four Freedoms" speech. Visitors can stroll the walkways and enjoy unique views of the United Nations and East River. Group guided walking tours ($15 per person) of FDR Four Freedoms Park are available; email or call in advance to reserve. At the island's north tip is a small park with a lighthouse built in 1872 by island convicts. The first phase of Cornell University's sustainable Tech campus opened in 2017.

You can get here by subway—but it's fun to take the five-minute ride on the **Roosevelt Island Tramway,** which lifts you 250 feet for impressive views of Queens and Manhattan. A visitor center stands to your left as you exit the tram. Free red buses service the island. ✉ *Tramway entrance, 2nd Ave., between 59th and 60th Sts., Upper East Side* ☎ *212/688–4836 for visitor center, 212/204–8831 Four Freedoms Park tours* ⊕ *www.fdrfourfreedomspark.org* ✉ *$2.75 (one-way subway or tram fare)* ⊘ *Four Freedoms Park and Visitors Center Kiosk closed Tues.* ⛴ *Tram leaves approximately every 15 mins* Ⓜ *F to Roosevelt Island.*

★ **Solomon R. Guggenheim Museum**

MUSEUM | Frank Lloyd Wright's landmark curving, nautiluslike museum building is renowned as much for its famous architecture as for its superlative collection of art and well-curated shows. Opened in 1959, shortly after Wright's death, the Guggenheim is acclaimed as one of the greatest buildings of the 20th century. Inside, under a 96-foot-high glass dome, a ramp spirals down, past the artworks of the current exhibits (the ramp is just over a quarter-mile long). The museum has strong holdings of Wassily Kandinsky (150 works), Paul Klee, Marc Chagall, Pablo Picasso, and Robert Mapplethorpe.

Wright's design was criticized by some who believed that the distinctive building detracted from the art, but the design allows artworks to be viewed from different angles and distances. On permanent display, the museum's Thannhauser Collection is made up primarily of works by French impressionists and postimpressionists Van Gogh, Toulouse-Lautrec, Cézanne, Renoir, and Manet. The museum is pay-what-you-wish on Saturday evening from 5 to 8. Lines can be long, so arrive early. The last tickets are handed out at 7:15. The museum also has a (pricey) modern American restaurant, the Wright (at 88th Street), with a stunning design by Andre Kikoski. ■**TIP→ Escape the crowded lobby by taking the elevator to the top and working your way down the spiral.** ✉ *1071 5th Ave., between 88th and 89th Sts., Upper East Side* ☎ *212/423–3500* ⊕ *www.guggenheim.org* ✉ *$25* Ⓜ *4, 5, 6 to 86th St.*

Van Doren Waxter

MUSEUM | This gallery in a historic town house on a tree-lined street merged with its former Lower East Side location in 2019, resulting in an expanded gallery space on the Upper East Side. Van Doren Waxter continues to feature contemporary artists with a focus on the historical connection of their art to works by established artists. ✉ *23 E. 73rd St., between Madison and 5th Aves., Upper East Side* ☎ *212/445–0444* ⊕ *www.vandorenwaxter.com* ✉ *Free* ⊘ *Closed Sun., Mon.* Ⓜ *6 to 77th St.*

🍴 Restaurants

Long viewed as an enclave of the privileged, the Upper East Side has plenty of elegant, pricey eateries that serve the society "ladies who lunch" and bankers (male and female) looking forward to a steak and single-malt scotch at the end of the day. However, visitors to Museum Mile and 5th Avenue shopping areas need not be put off. Whether you're looking to celebrate a special occasion or just want to grab a quick bite, there is something here for almost any budget.

Café Boulud

$$$$ | **FRENCH** | Manhattan's "who's who" in business, politics, and the art world come to hobnob at Daniel Boulud's café-in-name-only, where the food and service are top-notch. The menu is divided into four parts: for example, under La Tradition are classic French dishes such as roasted duck breast Montmorency with cherry chutney; Le Potager tempts with creations inspired by local farmers' markets. **Known for:** elegant UES dining; chic bar scene; both French and international cuisine. ⓢ *Average main: $44* ✉ *Surrey Hotel, 20 E. 76th St., between 5th and Madison Aves., Upper East Side* ☎ *212/772–2600* ⊕ *www.cafeboulud.com/nyc* Ⓜ *6 to 77th St.*

★ Café Sabarsky

$$ | AUSTRIAN | In the Neue Galerie, this stately coffeehouse is meant to duplicate the Viennese café experience and does a good job of it, with Art Deco furnishings, a selection of daily newspapers, and cases filled with cakes, strudels, and Sacher tortes. Museumgoers and locals love to linger here over coffee—so much so that it's sometimes a challenge to find a seat (there's a less aesthetically pleasing outpost of the café in the basement). **Known for:** a slice of Vienna (and Sacher torte) on the UES; hearty Austrian food at night from famous chef; excellent coffee and pastries. $ *Average main: $20* ✉ *Neue Galerie, 1048 5th Ave., near 86th St., Upper East Side* ☎ *212/288-0665* ⊕ *www.kurtgutenbrunner.com* ⊙ *Closed Tues. No dinner Mon., Wed.* Ⓜ *4, 5, 6 to 86th St.*

Calexico (Upper East Side)

$$ | MEXICAN | Named for a border town between Mexico and California, this casual, easygoing Cal-Mex restaurant originated as a food truck in Lower Manhattan before opening four storefronts, three of which are in Brooklyn. At the Upper East Side outpost, you'll find Calexico's usual staples of burritos, quesadillas, tacos, and enchiladas; things to try include frozen margaritas, chipotle-marinated pork tacos, and carne fries smothered in carne asada, cheese sauce, pico de gallo, and sour cream. **Known for:** anything with chipotle pork; chips with house-made guacamole; lively bar scene. $ *Average main: $15* ✉ *1491 2nd Ave., at 78th St., Upper East Side* ☎ *347/967-5955* ⊕ *www.calexico.com* Ⓜ *Q to 72nd St., 6 to 77th St.*

Candle 79

$$ | VEGETARIAN | This vegan eatery, in an elegant bi-level space done in warm, autumnal tones, is far from a health-food stereotype. Entrées like spaghetti and wheat balls and the wild mushroom crepe with tempeh are well executed; the signature seitan piccata is so expertly made that you won't miss the meat. **Known for:** vegan fare delicious for all eaters; organic wines; seitan piccata. $ *Average main: $22* ✉ *154 E. 79th St., at Lexington Ave., Upper East Side* ☎ *212/537-7179* ⊕ *www.candle79.com* Ⓜ *6 to 77th St.*

★ Daniel

$$$$ | FRENCH | Celebrity-chef Daniel Boulud has created one of the most elegant dining experiences in Manhattan in an equally elegant formal (jacket required) dining room with some serious artwork. The prix-fixe menu (there are à la carte selections in the lounge and bar) is predominantly French, with such modern classics as turbot on Himalayan salt, and a duo of dry-aged Black Angus beef featuring red wine–braised short ribs and seared rib eye with mushrooms and Gorgonzola cream. **Known for:** incredible service; special-occasion haute fare; superb cheeses and desserts. $ *Average main: $200* ✉ *60 E. 65th St., between Madison and Park Aves., Upper East Side* ☎ *212/288-0033* ⊕ *www.danielnyc.com* ⊙ *Closed Sun. (except Dec.). No lunch* ⓘ *Jacket required* Ⓜ *6 to 68th St.–Hunter College.*

Flip Sigi (Upper East Side)

$ | PHILIPPINE | If the Philippines and Mexico collided over Manhattan, it might look and taste a lot like this lively, 13-seat Filipino taqueria. Chef Jordan Andino had fun creating (and naming) his menu items, including an egg-and-sausage Plan B-Rito; first-timers should try the F.U.C. **Known for:** unique culinary mash-ups, cleverly named; Filipino cocktails and beer; credit cards only. $ *Average main: $10* ✉ *1752 2nd Ave., between 91st and 92nd Sts., Upper East Side* ☎ *833/354-7744* ⊕ *www.flipsigi.com* Ⓜ *Q to 96th St.*

Heidi's House by the Side of the Road

$$ | AMERICAN | Roughly the size of a studio apartment, this homey bar and restaurant is the epitome of a neighborhood spot. The short menu of comfort foods (hamburgers, a pasta, macaroni

and cheese) changes frequently, but the lobster macaroni and cheese never fails to impress. **Known for:** skillet mac and cheese; wait for a table at Ed's Elbow Room bar next door; nice selection of beer, wine, and cider. $ *Average main: $18* ⊠ *308 E. 78th St., between 1st and 2nd Aves., Upper East Side* ☎ *212/249–0069* ⊕ *www.heidishouse.net* ☾ *No lunch* Ⓜ *Q to 72nd St., 6 to 77th St.*

Lexington Candy Shop

$$ | **DINER** | **FAMILY** | Established in 1925, this corner luncheonette still sports 1940s-era milk-shake mixers, coffee urns, and a soda fountain. Enjoy the epic collection of Coca-Cola memorabilia along with fresh-made sodas, burgers, classic sandwiches, and breakfast all day. **Known for:** good diner fare; Coca-Cola items; neighborhood institution. $ *Average main: $15* ⊠ *1226 Lexington Ave., at 83rd St., Upper East Side* ☎ *212/288–0057* ⊕ *www.lexingtoncandyshop.net* Ⓜ *4, 5, 6 to 86th St.*

The Loeb Central Park Boathouse

$$$ | **AMERICAN** | There are plenty of pushcarts dispensing hot dogs and sodas, but if you're looking to soak up Central Park's magical ambience in an elegant setting, head for the Central Park Boathouse, which overlooks the gondola lake. There you can relax on the outdoor deck with a glass of wine and a cheese plate, or go for a more formal meal inside the restaurant. **Known for:** one of the city's most placid dining experiences; drinks on the outdoor deck; crowded in summer. $ *Average main: $30* ⊠ *E. 72nd St., at Park Dr. N, Upper East Side* ☎ *212/517–2233* ⊕ *www.thecentralparkboathouse.com* ☾ *No dinner Dec.–Mar.* Ⓜ *6 to 77th St.*

Patsy's Pizzeria

$$ | **ITALIAN** | One bite of the nearly perfect coal-oven pizza at the original Patsy's Pizzeria and it's immediately clear why this iconic pizzeria baked Frank Sinatra's favorite slices. Don't try and get too fancy here; just order a "plain pie" and a chicken parmigiana entrée and you'll

know why the trek up to to 118th Street was worth it. **Known for:** coal-oven pies and red-sauce dishes; old-school Italian vibe; cash-only spot. $ *Average main: $15* ⊠ *2287 1st Ave., at 118th St., Upper East Side* ☎ *212/534⊡9783* ⊕ *www.thepatsyspizza.com* ▤ *No credit cards* Ⓜ *6 to 116th St.*

Rotisserie Georgette

$$$$ | **FRENCH** | Georgette Farkas, who spent 17 years as chef Daniel Boulud's marketing and PR person, branched out on her own to become the queen of rotisserie chicken. This elegant spot (now run by executive chef Thomas Castellon) with an altarlike rotisserie in the back of the room might spin the best fowl in the city. **Known for:** foie gras–stuffed chicken; rotisserie duck; plenty of options if you don't want chicken. $ *Average main: $40* ⊠ *14 E. 60th St., between 5th and Madison Aves., Upper East Side* ☎ *212/390–8060* ⊕ *www.rotisserieg.com* ☾ *No lunch Sat.* Ⓜ *4, 5, 6 to 59th St.; N, R, W to 5th Ave./59th St.*

Sfoglia

$$$ | **ITALIAN** | Veiled from the street by linen curtains, this tiny Manhattan offshoot of its Nantucket namesake does a fine impression of a shabby-chic Tuscan farmhouse with its big wooden communal tables and Murano glass chandeliers. But it's the exquisite Italian food, from perfect pastas to fish and meat mains, with its air of photo-styled casual perfection, that has made Sfoglia one of the town's toughest reservations. **Known for:** seasonal Italian fare; fresh, crusty bread with sea salt; reservations needed well in advance. $ *Average main: $33* ⊠ *1402 Lexington Ave., at 92nd St., Upper East Side* ☎ *212/831–1402* ⊕ *www.sfogliarestaurant.com* ☾ *No lunch* Ⓜ *4, 5, 6 to 86th St.*

Sushi of Gari

$$$ | **JAPANESE** | The many options at this popular, casual sushi restaurant range from the ordinary (California roll) to the more unusual, such as miso-marinated

cod or Japanese yellowtail with jalapeño. Japanese noodles (udon or soba) and meat dishes such as teriyaki and *negima-ki* (scallions rolled in thinly sliced beef) are well prepared. Some of the inventive nonsushi items on the menu are worth a try, especially the fried cream-cheese dumplings. **Known for:** sushi with creative sauces and combos; fried cream-cheese dumplings; omakase option. $ *Average main: $35 ⊠ 402 E. 78th St., at 1st Ave., Upper East Side* ☎ *212/517–5340* ⊕ *www.sushiofgari.com* ⊙ *Closed Mon. No lunch weekends* Ⓜ *6 to 77th St.; Q to 72nd St.*

Hotels

★ The Carlyle, A Rosewood Hotel

$$$$ | HOTEL | On the well-heeled corner of Madison Avenue and 76th Street, the Carlyle fuses venerable elegance and Manhattan swank, and calls for the aplomb of entering a Chanel boutique: walk in chin high, wallet out, and ready to impress (and be impressed). **Pros:** perhaps NYC's best Central Park views; chic shopping in neighborhood; delightful dining and bar options. **Cons:** removed from tourist sights of Manhattan; stuffy vibe may not work for families; every room is different, limiting consistency. $ *Rooms from: $725 ⊠ 35 E. 76th St., between Madison and Park Aves., Upper East Side* ☎ *212/744–1600* ⊕ *www.the-carlyle.com* ⤳ *190 rooms* ⦿l *No meals* Ⓜ *6 to 77th St.*

Hôtel Plaza Athénée

$$$$ | HOTEL | Positioned unobtrusively by Central Park on the Upper East Side, the Plaza Athénée (now related in name only to its Parisian cousin) makes stellar service a priority, with a personal sit-down check-in off to the side of the lobby, and extravagant in-room dining service with white tablecloths, candles, and flowers. **Pros:** discerning service; fabulous hotel bar; old-world vibe. **Cons:** lobby can feel dark; may feel stuffy to some; rooms not the most exciting design. $ *Rooms from: $799 ⊠ 37 E. 64th St., at Madison Ave., Upper East Side* ☎ *212/734–9100* ⊕ *www.plaza-athenee.com* ⤳ *143 rooms* ⦿l *No meals* Ⓜ *6 to 68th St.–Hunter College; F, Q to Lexington Ave./63rd St.*

Hotel Wales

$$ | HOTEL | FAMILY | A favorite for in-the-know travelers, this pleasant if unassuming hotel in a sedate neighborhood has small standard guest rooms, but they do have fine oak woodwork, interesting photographs and art, and Gilchrist & Soames bath products. **Pros:** on-site fitness facilities; great neighborhood feel; roof garden. **Cons:** standard rooms are tight on space; if seeking nightlife, go elsewhere; uninspired design. $ *Rooms from: $395 ⊠ 1295 Madison Ave., between 92nd and 93rd Sts., Upper East Side* ☎ *212/876–6000* ⊕ *www.hotelwalesnyc.com* ⤳ *89 rooms* ⦿l *No meals* Ⓜ *6 to 96th St.*

Loews Regency New York Hotel

$$$ | HOTEL | Snazzy and spacious, this Park Avenue hotel has state-of-the-art technology, a 10,000-square-foot spa, and bright, tastefully appointed rooms with notably comfortable beds. **Pros:** friendly and helpful staff; appealing, buzzy bar and restaurant; huge spa and fitness center. **Cons:** design feels a bit generic; limited dining and nightlife options nearby; may seem expensive for what you're getting. $ *Rooms from: $599 ⊠ 540 Park Ave., at 61st St., Upper East Side* ☎ *212/759–4100* ⊕ *www.loewshotels.com/regency-hotel* ⤳ *379 rooms* ⦿l *No meals* Ⓜ *4, 5, 6, N, R, W to Lexington Ave./59th St.*

The Lowell Hotel

$$$$ | HOTEL | Steps from Madison Avenue shopping and the Museum Mile, this old-money refuge on a leafy residential block was built as an upscale apartment hotel in the 1920s and still delivers genteel sophistication and pampering service in an unbeatable location. **Pros:** great location; service with a personal touch; charming decor. **Cons:** cramped lobby; may be too small a hotel for some;

no spa (services can be arranged in your suite). [$] *Rooms from: $855* ✉ *28 E. 63rd St., between Madison and Park Aves., Upper East Side* ☎ *212/838–1400* 🌐 *www.lowellhotel.com* 🛏 *74 rooms* 🍴 *No meals* [M] *F, Q to Lexington Ave./63rd St.*

★ The Mark Hotel
$$$$ | **HOTEL** | The perfect combo of uptown panache and downtown chic, the Mark has striped marble floors, opulently appointed rooms, and a restaurant by renowned chef Jean-Georges Vongerichten. **Pros:** hip design; great service; scene-making restaurant and bar. **Cons:** design may not be to everyone's taste; have to walk slightly further for dining and nightlife options; rooms on lower floors don't have good views. [$] *Rooms from: $725* ✉ *25 E. 77th St., at Madison Ave., Upper East Side* ☎ *212/744–4300* 🌐 *www.themarkhotel.com* 🛏 *105 rooms* 🍴 *No meals* [M] *6 to 77th St.*

The Pierre, a Taj Hotel
$$$$ | **HOTEL** | This iconic grande dame across from Central Park has played host to aristocrats and Hollywood actors, but it prides itself on treating all its guests like royalty. **Pros:** oozes historic charm; great dining and drinking options; excellent location across from Central Park. **Cons:** no full-service spa; staffed elevators can be slow; standard rooms are on the small side. [$] *Rooms from: $675* ✉ *2 E. 61st St., Upper East Side* ☎ *212/838–8000* 🌐 *www.thepierreny.com* 🛏 *189 rooms* 🍴 *No meals* [M] *N, R, W to 5th Ave./59th St.*

Nightlife

BARS

The Auction House
BARS/PUBS | This Victorian-style lounge brings a touch of downtown chic to the sometimes suburban-feeling UES with candlelit tables, high tin ceilings, and velvet couches. Rap and hip-hop fans should look elsewhere (and no baseball caps are allowed), as the only tunes coming out of this joint are usually alternative and rock. If you find yourself downtown on the Lower East Side, check out its sister bar, a speakeasy called The Back Room, once frequented by gangsters like Lucky Luciano and Meyer Lansky. ✉ *300 E. 89th St., between 1st and 2nd Aves., Upper East Side* ☎ *212/427–4458* 🌐 *theauctionhousenyc.com* [M] *4, 5, 6, Q to 86th St.*

Bar Pleiades
BARS/PUBS | The cocktail bar companion to Café Boulud, also in the Surrey hotel, Bar Pleiades is a livelier alternative to the more staid atmosphere at the Carlyle's Bemelmans Bar. The design is classic to a fault, employing a black-and-white theme that's positively Audrey Hepburn–esque. Drinks rotate seasonally, and there are tasty nibbles from the café kitchen. Though it doesn't have the same drink menu, the rooftop bar is a cozy aerie good for people- and skyscraper-watching. ✉ *The Surrey, 20 E. 76th St., between 5th and Madison Aves., Upper East Side* ☎ *212/772–2600* 🌐 *www.barpleiades.com* [M] *6 to 77th St.*

★ The Penrose
BARS/PUBS | Clad with varnished wood and exposed brick that reinforce the cozy vibe, the Penrose fancies itself "the Upper East Local" and has something for everyone. In addition to a well-focused cocktail program that spills over into brunch (think cold-brew negroni), the bar offers a colossal fried chicken sandwich, a late-night menu served daily until 2 am, and even live jazz, blues, and folk music on Sunday nights. ✉ *1590 2nd Ave., between 82nd and 83rd Sts., Upper East Side* ☎ *212/203–2751* 🌐 *www.penrose-bar.com* [M] *Q to 86th St.*

★ The Pony Bar
BARS/PUBS | "Drink craft beer" is the manifesto here, so grab a stool and saddle up to the bar or around one of the barrels fashioned into a table, and take your time poring over the video board displaying

various artisanal lagers and ales. There's usually a heavy focus on NYC and New York State brews. Take advantage of the daily happy hour at 4:20, when beer, wine, and well drinks are all $6. The kitchen stays open late, serving bar fare to soak up some of the suds. ⊠ *1444 1st Ave., at 75th St., Upper East Side* ☎ *212/288–0090* ⊕ *theponybar.com* Ⓜ *Q to 72nd St.*

Session 73

BARS/PUBS | Young-ish patrons and live music (ranging from jazz to blues to funk) set this sizable restaurant and bar apart from others in the neighborhood. If the youth and tunes aren't sufficient, then the eclectic assortment of tequilas and beers on tap probably will be. ⊠ *1359 1st Ave., at E. 73rd St., Upper East Side* ☎ *212/517–4445* ⊕ *www.session73.com* Ⓜ *6 to 77th St.; Q to 72nd.*

Subway Inn

BARS/PUBS | Okay, so it's not *exactly* the original Subway Inn, which stood as an all-time favorite Manhattan dive bar for more than 70 years, until rising rents forced it out of business in 2014. But wander just two avenues east to behold the same iconic neon sign and a few other interior keepsakes at the new location, now a friendly local haunt run by the family of a bartender who spent years slinging drinks at the old watering hole. ⊠ *1140 2nd Ave., at 60th St., Upper East Side* ☎ *212/758–0900* Ⓜ *4, 5, 6 to 59th St.; N, R, W to Lexington Ave./59th St.*

CABARET AND PIANO BARS
★ **The Carlyle**

PIANO BARS/LOUNGES | The hotel's discreetly sophisticated **Café Carlyle** hosts such top cabaret and jazz performers as Christine Ebersole, Judy Collins, John Pizzarelli, Steve Tyrell, and Woody Allen, who swings on the clarinet with the Eddy Davis New Orleans Jazz Band. The less fancy-schmancy (though still pricey) **Bemelmans Bar,** with a mural by the author of the *Madeline* books, features a rotating cast of pianist-singers. ⊠ *35*

E. 76th St., between Madison and Park Aves., Upper East Side ☎ *212/744–1600* ⊕ *www.thecarlyle.com* Ⓜ *6 to 77th St.*

COMEDY CLUBS
Comic Strip Live

COMEDY CLUBS | The atmosphere here is strictly "corner bar," belying its storied history: Eddie Murphy is said to have discovered Chris Rock here, for example. The famous stage also helped launch the careers of funnymen Paul Reiser and Jerry Seinfeld, though these days you're more likely to see fresh faces still trying to find their humorous groove. ⊠ *1568 2nd Ave., between 81st and 82nd Sts., Upper East Side* ☎ *212/861–9386* ⊕ *www.comicstriplive.com* Ⓜ *4, 5, 6, Q to 86th St.*

GAY NIGHTLIFE
★ **Brandy's Piano Bar**

PIANO BARS/LOUNGES | The singing waitstaff warm up the mixed crowd at this delightful and intimate uptown saloon and piano bar, getting everyone in the mood to belt out their favorite tunes. In fact, the Brandy's scene is so cheerful that some patrons call it musical Prozac, keeping depression at bay. ⊠ *235 E. 84th St., between 2nd and 3rd Aves., Upper East Side* ☎ *212/744–4949* ⊕ *www.brandyspianobar.com* Ⓜ *4, 5, 6, Q to 86th St.*

🎭 Performing Arts

PERFORMANCE CENTERS
92nd Street Y

ARTS CENTERS | **FAMILY** | Well-known soloists, jazz musicians, show-tune stylists, and chamber music groups perform in 92Y's 905-seat **Kaufmann Concert Hall.** But the programming is hardly limited to music—its online calendar bristles with popular lectures and readings series featuring big-name film and TV stars, authors, poets, playwrights, political pundits, and media bigwigs (many events are live streamed or archived online). Also worth the Upper East Side trek are the Harkness Dance Festival, film programs, and many family-friendly events. ⊠ *1395 Lexington Ave., at 92nd St., Upper East Side* ☎ *212/415–5500 for tickets* ⊕ *www.92y.org* Ⓜ *6 to 96th St.; 4, 5, 6 to 86th St.*

★ Park Avenue Armory

ARTS CENTERS | Completed in 1881 and occupying an entire city block, this Gothic-style brick building now serves as a splendid arts center but was originally the headquarters, drill hall, and social club for the Seventh Regiment, a National Guard unit called the "Silk Stocking" regiment because its members were mainly drawn from wealthy Gilded Age families. The reception rooms on the first floor and Company Rooms on the second floor were designed by Louis Comfort Tiffany, Stanford White, and other fashionable designers of the time. Eventually the armory was put into the service of art, even as building renovations continue. The huge installations, plays, and immersive concerts here take advantage of the space its 55,000-square-foot drill hall provides. Intimate artist conversations, recitals, and experimental performances are held in the smaller first- and second-floor spaces. ⊠ *643 Park Ave., between 66th and 67th Sts., Upper East Side* ☎ *212/616–3930, 212/933–5812 for tickets* ⊕ *www.armoryonpark.org* Ⓜ *6 to 68th St.–Hunter College, F, Q to Lexington Ave./63rd St.*

READINGS AND LECTURES
Works & Process

READINGS/LECTURES | Insight into the creative process is what the Works & Process program at the Guggenheim is all about. Often drawing on dance and theater works in progress, the live performances are complemented by illuminating discussions with their choreographers, playwrights, and directors. There are very popular holiday concerts, too. ⊠ *Guggenheim Museum, 1071 5th Ave., between 88th and 89th Sts., Upper East Side* ☎ *212/423–3575* ⊕ *www.worksandprocess.org* Ⓜ *4, 5, 6 to 86th St.*

🛍 Shopping

This well-heeled neighborhood is known for its antiques shops and high-end designers, such as Carolina Herrera, Oscar de la Renta, and Tom Ford. Shops are primarily sprinkled along Madison Avenue.

ANTIQUES AND COLLECTIBLES
Keno Auctions

ANTIQUES/COLLECTIBLES | Leigh Keno of *Antiques Roadshow* fame presides over this auction house, which specializes in Americana. As expected, he has a good eye and an interesting inventory; he's sold silver sauceboats from Paul Revere, masterpiece paintings, and Chippendale furniture. Visits are by appointment only. ⊠ *127 E. 69th St., between Park and Lexington Aves., Upper East Side* ☎ *212/734–2381* ⊕ *www.kenoauctions. com* Ⓜ *6 to 68th St.–Hunter College.*

Newel

ANTIQUES/COLLECTIBLES | The huge collection here spans the Renaissance through the 20th century and includes nonfurniture finds, from figureheads to bell jars, that make for prime conversation pieces. Newel is a major supplier of antiques for Broadway shows and luxury department store windows. It's closed on weekends. ⊠ *306 E. 61st St., 3rd fl., between 2nd Ave. and Ed Koch Queensboro Bridge Exit, Upper East Side* ☎ *212/758–1970* ⊕ *www.newel.com* Ⓜ *4, 5, 6 to 59th St.; N, R, W to Lexington Ave./59th St.*

BEAUTY
NARS

PERFUME/COSMETICS | Women adore NARS for its iconic products such as Jungle Red lipstick and multiuse makeup sticks. The NARS flagship has glossy white walls and a red counter, and stocks the full NARS makeup range as well as a collection of "François' Favorite Things," which includes books, films, and photographs that have served as inspiration. ⊠ *971 Madison Ave., between 75th and 76th Sts., Upper East Side* ☎ *212/861–2945*

⊕ www.narscosmetics.com Ⓜ 6 to 77th St.

CHILDREN'S CLOTHING
★ Bonpoint
CLOTHING | FAMILY | Celebrities and mere mortals love this French children's boutique for the beautiful designs and impeccable workmanship—think pony-hair baby booties, hand-embroidered jumpers, and cashmere onesies. The flagship has a loftlike design with whimsical touches, such as a large indoor tree and a cloud sculpture. ✉ 805 Madison Ave., between 67th and 68th Sts., Upper East Side ☎ 212/879–0900 ⊕ www.bonpoint.com Ⓜ 6 to 68th St.–Hunter College.

Infinity
CLOTHING | FAMILY | Prep-school girls and their mothers giggle and gossip over the tween clothes (with more than a few moms picking up T-shirts and jeans for themselves) with Les Tout Petits dresses, Juicy Couture jeans, and tees emblazoned with Justin Bieber. Check out their Instagram at @infinityonmad. ✉ 1116 Madison Ave., at 83rd St., Upper East Side ☎ 212/734–0077 Ⓜ 4, 5, 6 to 86th St.

CLOTHING
Alexander McQueen
CLOTHING | The New York flagship of this iconic fashion house is full of rich details, like intricately patterned floors, and tiny architectural nuances meant to draw the eye, such as feathers in the molding. Now under the helm of Sarah Burton, the designer sells both menswear and women's wear, in styles that lean towards edgy gothic. ✉ 747 Madison Ave., between 64th and 65th Sts., Upper East Side ☎ 212/645–1797 ⊕ www.alexandermcqueen.com Ⓜ 6 to 68th St.–Hunter College; F, Q to Lexington Ave./63rd St.

Balenciaga
CLOTHING | This sleek new flagship on Madison Avenue is a manifestation of creative director Demna Gvasalia's fresh vision for the iconic French fashion house. Minimalist and warehouse-inspired, the boutique lets Gvasalia's clever, colorful designs—asymmetrical jackets, oversize shirts, those infamous Ikea-inspired bags—take center stage and forgoes the typical stuffiness of most Upper East Side high-fashion shops. ✉ 840 Madison Ave., between 69th and 70th Sts., Upper East Side ☎ 212/328–1671 ⊕ www.balenciaga.com Ⓜ 6 to 68th St.–Hunter College.

Barbour
CLOTHING | The signature look here is the British company's waxed-cotton and quilted jackets, available for men and women. The quilted jackets, tweeds, moleskin pants, lamb's-wool sweaters, and tattersall shirts invariably call up images of country rambles. ✉ 1047 Madison Ave., at 80th St., Upper East Side ☎ 212/570–2600 ⊕ www.barbour.com Ⓜ 6 to 77th St.

Calvin Klein 205W39NYC
CLOTHING | Though the namesake designer has bowed out, the label keeps channeling his particular style. The new line reimagines the designer's luxury ready-to-wear line and showcases it in the brand's flagship store alongside art installations. Inspired by classic Americana, clothing for both men and women tends to be soft around the edges, with dashes of both whimsy and timelessness. There are also shoes, accessories, and fragrances. ✉ 654 Madison Ave., at 60th St., Upper East Side ☎ 212/292–9000 ⊕ www.calvinklein.com Ⓜ 4, 5, 6 to 59th St.; N, R, W to Lexington Ave./59th St.

Carolina Herrera
CLOTHING | A favorite of the high-society set (and A-list celebs), Herrera's designs are ladylike and elegant. Her suits, gowns, and cocktail dresses in luxurious fabrics make for timeless silhouettes. The New York flagship also carries her bridal collection. ✉ 954 Madison Ave., at 75th St., Upper East Side ☎ 212/249–6552

⊕ www.carolinaherrera.com Ⓜ 6 to 77th St.

Christopher Fischer

CLOTHING | Featherweight cashmere sweaters, wraps, and throws in every hue, from Easter-egg pastels to rich jewel tones, have made Fischer the darling of the men and women of the preppy set. His shop also carries leather accessories, housewares, and baby clothes. ⊠ 1225 Madison Ave., between 88th and 89th Sts., Upper East Side ☎ 212/831–8880 ⊕ www.christopherfischer.com Ⓜ 4, 5, 6 to 86th St.

Kate Spade

SHOES/LUGGAGE/LEATHER GOODS | The Kate Spade flagship is in a pretty uptown town house, so it feels like shopping in a well-appointed home—albeit one with oversize chandeliers and glamorous custom rugs. The nearly 8,000-square-foot space contains every Kate Spade product, from clothing to shoes and beauty. ⊠ 789 Madison Ave., between 66th and 67th Sts., Upper East Side ☎ 212/988–0259 ⊕ www.katespade.com Ⓜ 6 to 68th St.–Hunter College.

La Perla

CLOTHING | If money is no object, shop here for some of the sexiest underthings around. The collection includes lace sets, corsets, and exquisite bridal lingerie. ⊠ 803 Madison Ave., between 67th and 68th Sts., Upper East Side ☎ 212/570–0050 ⊕ www.laperla.com Ⓜ 6 to 68th St.–Hunter College.

Lanvin

CLOTHING | This French label has been around since 1889 and is the oldest French fashion house still in existence. Lanvin's signature look is understatedly elegant; think tailored dresses, wide-leg pants, and ruffled blouses. ⊠ 849 Madison Ave., between 70th and 71st Sts., Upper East Side ☎ 646/439–0380 ⊕ www.lanvin.com Ⓜ 6 to 68th St.–Hunter College.

★ Ludivine

CLOTHING | Make a beeline for this store if you love French designers. Owner Ludivine Grégoire showcases of-the-moment Gallic (and a few Italian) designers like Vanessa Bruno, Jerome Dreyfuss, and Carvin. ⊠ 1216 Lexington Ave., between 82nd and 83rd Sts., Upper East Side ☎ 212/249–4053 ⊕ www.boutiqueludivine.com Ⓜ 4, 5, 6 to 86th St.

Marina Rinaldi

CLOTHING | If you are a curvy gal and want to celebrate your figure rather than hide it, shop here. A branch of Milanese fashion house Max Mara (which has a store next door at 813 Madison Avenue), Marina Rinaldi sells form-flattering knit dresses, wool trousers, and coats that are tasteful and luxurious. ⊠ 815 Madison Ave., at 69th St., Upper East Side ☎ 212/734–4333 ⊕ www.marinarinaldi.com Ⓜ 6 to 68th St.–Hunter College.

Max Mara

CLOTHING | Think subtle colors and classics in plush fabrics—pencil skirts in heathered wool, tuxedo-style evening jackets, and wool and cashmere overcoats. The suits are exquisitely tailored. ⊠ 813 Madison Ave., at 68th St., Upper East Side ☎ 212/879–6100 ⊕ www.maxmara.com Ⓜ 6 to 68th St.–Hunter College.

Milly

CLOTHING | These bright, cheerfully patterned clothes look as at home on the Upper East Side as they would in Palm Beach or Marrakech. At designer Michelle Smith's U.S. flagship, find flirty cocktail dresses, beach-ready maxis, and boldly patterned bathing suits. ⊠ 900 Madison Ave., at 73rd St., Upper East Side ☎ 212/395–9100 ⊕ www.milly.com Ⓜ 6 to 77th St.

Morgane Le Fay

CLOTHING | The clothes here have a dreamy, ethereal quality that is decidedly feminine. Silk gowns are fluid and soft, while blazers and coats are more tailored.

Her wedding dresses are also popular with brides who want a dreamy but understated look. ✉ *980 Madison Ave., between 76th and 77th Sts., Upper East Side* ☎ *212/879–9700* ⊕ *www.morganelefay.com* Ⓜ *6 to 77th St.*

Oscar de la Renta

CLOTHING | Come here for the ladylike but bold runway designs of this upper-crust favorite. Skirts swing, ruffles billow, embroidery brightens up tweed, and even a tennis dress looks like something you could go dancing in. ✉ *772 Madison Ave., at 66th St., Upper East Side* ☎ *212/288–5810* ⊕ *www.oscardelarenta.com* Ⓜ *6 to 68th St.–Hunter College.*

Otte

CLOTHING | This stylish mini chain has outposts around the city, but the Upper East Side location has the biggest selection of clothing from on-trend designers such as Rachel Comey and Band of Outsiders, as well as its own line. If you want that nonchalant-chic look, like an oversize velvet jacket thrown over skinny jeans, this is your place. ✉ *1281 Madison Ave., between 91st and 92nd Sts., Upper East Side* ☎ *212/289 2644* ⊕ *otteny.com* Ⓜ *6 to 96th St.*

Ralph Lauren

CLOTHING | Even if you can't afford the clothes here, come just to soak up the luxe lifestyle. The designer's women's flagship is housed in a 22,000-square-foot building inspired by the avenue's historic Beaux Arts mansions, complete with its own curving marble staircase and stone floors. In addition to the complete women's collection, the brand's lingerie, housewares, and fine-jewelry and watch salon are here. You can find the men's flagship directly across the street. ✉ *888 Madison Ave., at 72nd St., Upper East Side* ☎ *212/434–8000* ⊕ *www.ralphlauren.com* Ⓜ *6 to 68th St.–Hunter College.*

Roberto Cavalli

CLOTHING | Rock-star style (at rock-star prices) means clothing decked out with fur, feathers, and lots of sparkle. Animal prints are big in this temple to the over-the-top. ✉ *711 Madison Ave., at 63rd St., Upper East Side* ☎ *212/755–7722* ⊕ *www.robertocavalli.com* Ⓜ *N, R, W to 5th Ave./59th St.; F, Q to Lexington Ave.–63rd St.*

Sachin & Babi

CLOTHING | Sachin and Babi Ahluwalia used to source textiles for luxury designers like Oscar de la Renta. Now, they use that same design sensibility to produce a gorgeous line of globally inspired women's formal wear and accessories. The embroidery is exquisite, the colors vibrant. ✉ *1200 Madison Ave., between 87th and 88th Sts., Upper East Side* ☎ *212/996–5200* ⊕ *www.sachinandbabi.com* Ⓜ *4, 5, 6 to 86th St.*

Tom Ford

CLOTHING | Famous for revamping Gucci, Ford does not disappoint with either his eponymous line or his Madison Avenue flagship, a sleek, grandiose temple to glamorous fashion. Women's stilettos and clutches are unabashedly sexy, while men's selections veer toward the traditional and are impeccably tailored. Shirts come in more than 300 hues, and off-the-rack suits start around $3,000. His Black Orchid unisex fragrance is a cult favorite. ✉ *672 Madison Ave., at 61st St., Upper East Side* ☎ *212/359–0300* ⊕ *www.tomford.com* Ⓜ *F, Q to Lexington Ave./63rd St.; N, R, W to Lexington Ave./59th St.*

Tomas Maier

CLOTHING | In 2018, shortly before parting ways with Bottega Veneta as creative director, Tomas Maier designed the luxury Italian company's enormous new flagship on Madison Avenue. The German-born designer also has a self-named store just eight blocks to the north. This elegant, wood-floored space showcases Tomas Maier's understated clothing for men and women as well as jewelry and home goods, such as candles. Best bets include classic black dresses and structured handbags. ✉ *956 Madison Ave.,*

between 75th and 76th Sts., Upper East Side ☎ 212/988–8686 ⊕ www.tomasmaier.com Ⓜ 6 to 77th St.

Tory Burch

CLOTHING | The global flagship of this preppy boho label is housed in an elegantly restored town house. The five-story space features Tory Burch's signature orange-lacquer walls, purple curtains, and gold hardware. If you already own her iconic ballet flats, browse through the ready-to-wear collection, handbags, shoes, and jewelry. Her new Tory Sport line is sometimes available as well. ✉ 797 Madison Ave., between 67th and 68th Sts., Upper East Side ☎ 212/510–8371 ⊕ www.toryburch.com Ⓜ 6 to 68th St.–Hunter College.

Valentino

CLOTHING | No one does a better red than Valentino, and the mix here at this four-story town house is at once audacious and beautifully cut; the fur or feather trimmings, low necklines, and opulent fabrics are about as close as you can get to celluloid glamour. Big spenders can request the VIP suite. ✉ 821 Madison Ave., between 68th and 69th Sts., Upper East Side ☎ 212/772–6969 ⊕ www.valentino.com Ⓜ 6 to 68th St.–Hunter College.

Vera Wang

CLOTHING | This celebrity wedding-dress designer churns out dreamy dresses that are sophisticated without being over-the-top. Choose from A-line and princess styles, as well as slinky sheaths. If money is no object, bespoke wedding dresses are available. An appointment is essential. ✉ 991 Madison Ave., at 77th St., Upper East Side ☎ 212/628–3400 ⊕ www.verawang.com Ⓜ 6 to 77th St.

Vilebrequin

CLOTHING | Allow St-Tropez to influence your summer style. This iconic French swimwear designer began by making classic striped, floral, and solid-color trunks in sunny hues for both men and boys. Nowadays, it's expanded to include a women's line, resort wear, and summery accessories. ✉ 1007 Madison Ave., between 77th and 78th Sts., Upper East Side ☎ 212/650–0353 ⊕ us.vilebrequin.com Ⓜ 6 to 77th St.

DEPARTMENT STORES

Barneys New York

DEPARTMENT STORES | This luxury boutique-style department store continues to provide fashion-conscious and big-budget shoppers with irresistible, must-have items at its uptown flagship store. The extensive menswear selection has a handful of edgier designers, though made-to-measure is always an option. The women's department showcases posh designers of all stripes, from the subdued lines of Armani and rag & bone to the irrepressible Alaïa and Isabel Marant. The shoe selection trots out Prada boots and Loeffler Randall mules; the cosmetics department keeps you in Kiehl's, La Mer, and Chantecaille; jewelry runs from the whimsical (Jennifer Meyer) to the classic (Ileana Makri). The store also has a blow dry bar, a brow bar, several restaurants, and more. ✉ 660 Madison Ave., between 60th and 61st Sts., Upper East Side ☎ 212/826–8900 ⊕ www.barneys.com Ⓜ 4, 5, 6 to 59th St.; N, R, W to Lexington Ave./59th St.

★ Fivestory

DEPARTMENT STORES | Located inside an Upper East Side town house, this luxurious mini department store carries clothing, accessories, shoes, and home decor for men, women, and children in an elegant setting (think marble floors and lots of velvet and silk). It specializes in independent designers but also showcases designs from heavy hitters such as Proenza Schouler and Dior. ✉ 18 E. 69th St., at Madison Ave., Upper East Side ☎ 212/288–1338 ⊕ www.fivestoryny.com Ⓜ 6 to 68th St.–Hunter College.

FOOD AND TREATS

★ La Maison du Chocolat

FOOD/CANDY | Stop in at this artisanal chocolatier's small tea salon to dive into a cup of thick, heavenly hot chocolate. The Paris-based outfit sells handmade truffles, chocolates, and pastries that could lull you into a chocolate stupor. ⊠ *1018 Madison Ave., between 78th and 79th Sts., Upper East Side* ☎ *212/744–7117* ⊕ *www.lamaisonduchocolat.us* Ⓜ *6 to 77th St.*

JEWELRY AND ACCESSORIES

Asprey

JEWELRY/ACCESSORIES | This luxury retailer's claim to fame is jewelry; its own eponymous diamond cut has A-shape facets, but the British brand caters to all tastes. Everything from leather goods and rare books to polo equipment and scarves is available. ⊠ *853 Madison Ave., between 70th and 71st Sts., Upper East Side* ☎ *212/688–1811* ⊕ *www.asprey. com* Ⓜ *6 to 68th St.–Hunter College.*

Fred Leighton

JEWELRY/ACCESSORIES | If you're in the market for vintage diamonds, this is the place, whether your taste is for tiaras, Art Deco settings, or sparklers once worn by a Vanderbilt. The skinny, stackable diamond eternity bands are hugely popular. ⊠ *773 Madison Ave., at 66th St., Upper East Side* ☎ *212/288–1872* ⊕ *www. fredleighton.com* Ⓜ *6 to 68th St.–Hunter College.*

MUSEUM STORES

Metropolitan Museum of Art Store

GIFTS/SOUVENIRS | Highlights of the museum's sprawling shop are a phenomenal book selection, as well as posters, Japanese print note cards, and decorative pillows covered in William Morris prints. Reproductions of statuettes and other objets d'art fill the gleaming cases. Don't miss the jewelry selection, with its Byzantine- and Egyptian-inspired baubles. ⊠ *1000 5th Ave., at 82nd St., Upper East Side* ☎ *212/570–3894* ⊕ *store.metmuseum.org* Ⓜ *4, 5, 6 to 86th St.*

Museum of the City of New York

GIFTS/SOUVENIRS | Satisfy your curiosity about New York City's past, present, or future with the terrific selection of books, cards, toys, and photography posters. ⊠ *1220 5th Ave., at 103rd St., Upper East Side* ☎ *917/492–3330* ⊕ *shop.mcny.org* Ⓜ *6 to 103rd St.*

Neue Galerie

GIFTS/SOUVENIRS | Like the museum, the in-house bookshop and design store focus on German, Austrian, and Central European art. Everything from children's toys to accessories and home decor is available here. ⊠ *1048 5th Ave., at 86th St., Upper East Side* ☎ *212/994–9496* ⊕ *shop.neuegalerie.org* Ⓜ *4, 5, 6 to 86th St.*

★ Shop Cooper Hewitt, Smithsonian Design Museum

GIFTS/SOUVENIRS | Prowl the shelves at this well-stocked museum shop for intriguing urban oddments and ornaments, like sculptural tableware, Alexander Girard dolls, housewares by Alessi, and Japanese notebooks by Postalco. ⊠ *Cooper Hewitt, Smithsonian Design Museum, 2 E. 91st St., at 5th Ave., Upper East Side* ☎ *212/849–8355* ⊕ *shop.cooperhewitt.org* Ⓜ *4, 5, 6 to 86th St.*

SHOES, HANDBAGS, AND LEATHER GOODS

Anya Hindmarch

SHOES/LUGGAGE/LEATHER GOODS | Although arguably most famous for her "I'm Not a Plastic Bag" tote, Hindmarch's real standouts are buttery leather shoulder bags and satchels, which are decidedly understated. Her designs run the gamut from cheeky to ladylike. Leather goods can be embossed with monograms, entire sentences, or a sketch. ⊠ *795 Madison Ave., between 67th and 68th Sts., Upper East Side* ☎ *646/852–6233* ⊕ *www.anyahindmarch.com* Ⓜ *6 to 68th St.–Hunter College.*

Bally

SHOES/LUGGAGE/LEATHER GOODS | If you want to channel your inner princess, you can't go wrong with the ladylike pumps and high-heeled boots here. The mostly leather accessories and clothing are equally tasteful. ⊠ *689 Madison Ave., at 62nd St., Upper East Side* ☎ *212/751–9082* ⊕ *www.bally.com* Ⓜ *F, Q to Lexington Ave./63rd St.*

Bottega Veneta

SHOES/LUGGAGE/LEATHER GOODS | The signature crosshatch weave graces leather handbags, slouchy satchels, and shoes; the especially satisfying brown shades extend from fawn to deep chocolate. The stylish men's and women's ready-to-wear collection is also sold here. ⊠ *740 Madison Ave., between 64th and 65th Sts., Upper East Side* ☎ *212/371–5511* ⊕ *www.bottegaveneta.com* Ⓜ *F, Q to Lexington Ave./63rd St.*

Christian Louboutin

SHOES/LUGGAGE/LEATHER GOODS | Lipstick-red soles are the signature of Louboutin's delicately sexy couture slippers and stilettos, and his pointy-toe creations come trimmed with beads, buttons, or "tattoos." ⊠ *967 Madison Ave., between 75th and 76th Sts., Upper East Side* ☎ *212/396–1884* ⊕ *www.christianlouboutin.com* Ⓜ *6 to 77th St.*

Devi Kroell

SHOES/LUGGAGE/LEATHER GOODS | You may have spotted her snakeskin hobo on celebs such as Halle Berry and Ashley Olsen. This serene space is a perfect backdrop for the designer's luxury handbags and shoes, which are crafted from premium leather. Roomy shoulder bags come in python and calf leather, and evening bags have a touch of sparkle. There's also a selection of jewelry and scarves. ⊠ *717 Madison Ave., between 63rd and 64th Sts., Upper East Side* ☎ *212/888–7755* ⊕ *www.devikroell.com* Ⓜ *F, Q to Lexington Ave./63rd St.*

Hermès

SHOES/LUGGAGE/LEATHER GOODS | The legendary French retailer is best known for its iconic handbags, the Kelly and the Birkin (named for Grace Kelly and Jane Birkin) as well as its silk scarves and neckties. True to its roots, Hermès still stocks saddles and other equestrian items in addition to a line of beautifully simple separates. A men's store is located across the street. ⊠ *691 Madison Ave., at 62nd St., Upper East Side* ☎ *212/751–3181* ⊕ *www.hermes.com* Ⓜ *N, R, W to 5th Ave./59th St.; F, Q to Lexington Ave./63rd St.*

Jack Rogers

SHOES/LUGGAGE/LEATHER GOODS | Beloved by prepsters everywhere, this brand is most famous for its Navajo sandal, worn by Jackie Onassis. You can still buy the Navajo at the Jack Rogers flagship store, as well as other footwear like loafers, boots, and wedges. ⊠ *1198 Madison Ave., between 87th and 88th Sts., Upper East Side* ☎ *212/259–0588* ⊕ *www.jackrogersusa.com* Ⓜ *4, 5, 6 to 86th St.*

Jimmy Choo

SHOES/LUGGAGE/LEATHER GOODS | Pointy toes, low vamps, narrow heels, ankle-wrapping straps—these British-made shoes are sometimes more comfortable than they look. ⊠ *699 Madison Ave., between 62nd and 63rd Sts., Upper East Side* ☎ *212/759–7078* ⊕ *www.jimmychoo.com* Ⓜ *F, Q to Lexington Ave./63rd St.*

John Lobb

SHOES/LUGGAGE/LEATHER GOODS | If you truly want to be well-heeled, pick up a pair of these luxury shoes, whose prices start at around $1,200. Owned by Hermès, John Lobb offers classic styles for men, such as oxfords, loafers, boots, and slippers. They've recently expanded to offer similar cuts in women's styles. Bespoke shoes are also an option. ⊠ *800 Madison Ave., between 67th and 68th Sts., Upper East Side* ☎ *212/888–9797* ⊕ *www.johnlobb.com* Ⓜ *6 to 68th St.–Hunter College.*

Robert Clergerie

SHOES/LUGGAGE/LEATHER GOODS | Although best known for its chunky, comfy wedges, this French brand is not without its sense of fun. The sandal selection includes beaded starfish shapes, and for winter, the ankle boots have killer heels with padded soles. In honor of the opening of this new flagship boutique in 2018, Clergerie launched its new 901 collection, featuring sneakers. ✉ *901 Madison Ave., between 72nd and 73rd Sts., Upper East Side* ☎ *212/207–8600* ⊕ *www.robertclergerie.com* Ⓜ *6 to 68th St.–Hunter College, Q to 72nd St.*

★ Smythson of Bond Street

BOOKS/STATIONERY | Although Smythson still sells stationery fit for a queen— check out the royal warrant from England's HRH—it is also a place to scoop up on-trend handbags, iPad cases, and wallets. The hues range from sedate brown and black to eye-popping tangerine. The softbound leather diaries, address books, and travel accessories make ideal gifts. ✉ *667 Madison Ave., between 60th and 61st Sts., Upper East Side* ☎ *212/265–4573* ⊕ *www.smythson. com* Ⓜ *N, R, W to 5th Ave./59th St.; F, Q to Lexington Ave./63rd St.*

Chapter 12

THE UPPER WEST SIDE

Updated by
Joshua Rogol

⊙ Sights	🍴 Restaurants	🛏 Hotels	🛍 Shopping	🍸 Nightlife
★★★☆☆	★★☆☆☆	★☆☆☆☆	★★★☆☆	★★☆☆☆

NEIGHBORHOOD SNAPSHOT

TOP EXPERIENCES

- Exploring Central Park
- Strolling through Riverside Park past the boat basin
- Standing below the gigantic blue whale at the American Museum of Natural History
- Taking in the views, gardens, and medieval masterpieces at the Met Cloisters

GETTING HERE

The A, B, C, D, and 1 subway lines take you to Columbus Circle. From there, the B and C lines make local stops along Central Park. Along Broadway, the 1 train runs local, while the express 2 and 3 trains stop at 72nd and 96th Streets.

PLANNING YOUR TIME

Broadway is one of the most walkable and interesting thoroughfares on the Upper West Side because of its broad sidewalks and lively mix of retail stores, restaurants, and apartment buildings. If you head north from the Lincoln Center area (around 65th Street) to about 81st Street (about 1 mile), you'll get a feel for the neighborhood's local color, particularly above 72nd Street. Up here you'll encounter residents of every conceivable age and ethnicity either shambling or sprinting along; street vendors hawking used and newish books; and such beloved landmarks as the 72nd Street subway station, the Beacon Theatre, and Zabar's (a market and eatery that will woo all five senses—and may drain your wallet). The Upper West Side's other two main avenues—Columbus and Amsterdam—are more residential but also have myriad restaurants and shops.

If you're intrigued by the city's only Ivy League school, hop the 1 train to 116th Street and emerge smack-dab in front of illustrious Columbia University, founded in Lower Manhattan in 1754 as King's College. Pass through its gates and up the walk to view its open central campus, surrounded by a cluster of buildings so elegant you'll understand why it has long been an iconic NYC destination.

QUICK BITES

- **Hungarian Bakery.** Linger over a danish and bottomless cups of coffee with the Columbia kids and professors at this old-world (cash only) café and bakery. ✉ *1030 Amsterdam Ave., at 111th St.* Ⓜ *Subway: 1 to Cathedral Pkwy.–110th St.*

- **Indie Food and Wine.** In the Elinon Bunin Munroe Film Center, this small, bustling spot keeps busy early until late, with Irving Farm coffee, sandwiches, and salads from the counter. After 5 pm, there's table service. ✉ *144 W. 65th St., between Broadway and Amsterdam Ave.* ⊕ *www.indiefoodandwine.com* Ⓜ *Subway: 1 to 66th St.–Lincoln Center.*

- **Zabar's Cafe.** Fast-track the Zabar's experience with a gourmet coffee and sandwich, pickled lox, or slice of cheesecake. ✉ *2245 Broadway, at 80th St.* ⊕ *www.zabars.com* Ⓜ *Subway: 1 to 79th St.*

The Upper West Side is one of Manhattan's quieter, more residential neighborhoods, with wide sidewalks and a (relatively) slower pace. The Met Cloisters, in Inwood, houses part of the Metropolitan Museum's medieval collection.

The tree-lined side streets of the Upper West Side are lovely, with high stoops leading up to stately brownstones. Central Park, of course, is one of the main attractions here, no matter the season or time of day; though locals know that Riverside Park, along the Hudson River, can be even more appealing thanks to smaller crowds.

The Upper West Side also has its share of cultural institutions, from the 16-acre **Lincoln Center** complex, to the impressive and quirky collection at the **New-York Historical Society,** to Columbus Circle's **Museum of Arts and Design** and the much-loved, soon-to-be-expanded **American Museum of Natural History.**

The Upper West Side

The Upper West side begins at Columbus Circle (59th Street), above which 8th Avenue turns into Central Park West, 9th Avenue becomes Columbus Avenue, 10th Avenue becomes Amsterdam Avenue, and 11th Avenue becomes West End Avenue. It's bordered on the west by the Hudson River, and on the east by Central Park. It technically ends at 110th Street, at Central Park North. It's predominately a residental neighborhood with tree-lined blocks containing a mix of brownstones and apartment buildings. The Avenues are more commerical (except for Central Park West, which is almost entirely residential above 61st Street). The expansive Lincoln Center complex and Fordham University take up almost the entirety of the blocks from 60th to 67th Street, between Amsterdam and Columbus Avenues.

Most people think the area north of 110th Street and south of 125th Street on the west side is just an extension of the Upper West Side. Technically it's Morningside Heights, largely dominated by Columbia University along with a cluster of academic, religious, and medical institutions, including Barnard College and the **Cathedral Church of St. John the Divine.**

◉ Sights

American Folk Art Museum

MUSEUM | FAMILY | The focus of this museum near Lincoln Center is its incredible collection of work by contemporary self-taught artists of the 20th and 21st centuries, including the single largest collection of reclusive Chicago artist Henry Darger, known for his painstakingly detailed collage paintings of fantasy worlds. The gift shop has an impressive collection of handcrafted items. ⌧ *2 Lincoln Sq., Columbus Ave. at 66th*

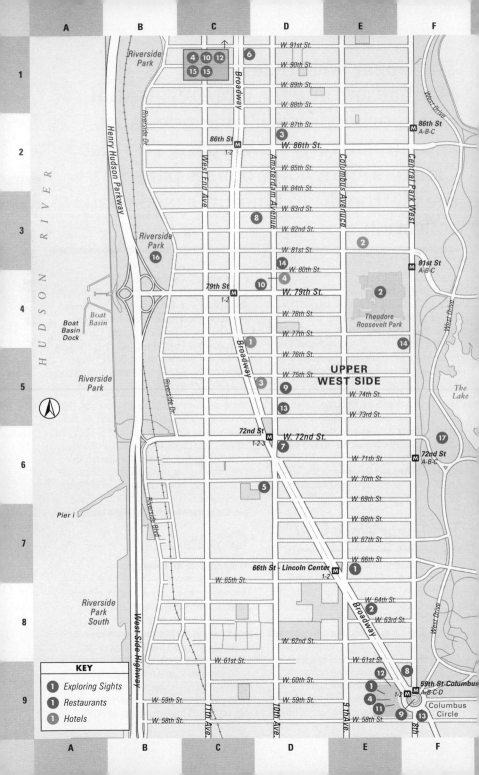

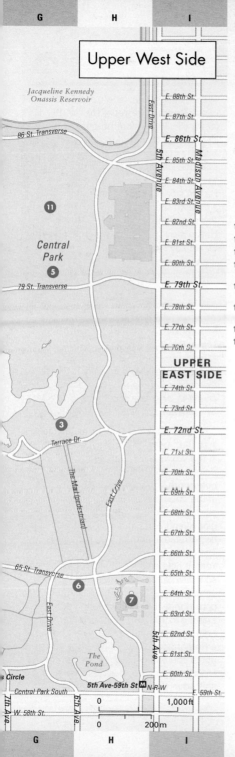

Upper West Side

Sights ▼

1 American Folk
  Art Museum **E7**
2 American Museum of
  Natural History........... **E4**
3 Bethesda Fountain **G6**
4 Cathedral Church of
  St. John the Divine **C1**
5 Central Park **G4**
6 Central Park
  Conservancy: Dairy
  Visitor Center............ **H8**
7 Central Park Zoo........ **H8**
8 Children's Museum
  Of Manhattan **D3**
9 Columbus Circle **F9**
10 Grant's Tomb **C1**
11 Great Lawn **G3**
12 The Met Cloisters........ **C1**
13 Museum of Arts
  and Design **F9**
14 New-York
  Historical Society........ **F4**
15 Nicholas
  Roerich Museum **C1**
16 Riverside Park........... **B3**
17 Strawberry Fields........ **F6**

Restaurants ▼

1 Asiate **E9**
2 Bar Boulud **E8**
3 Barney Greengrass..... **D2**
4 Bouchon
  Bakery & Café........... **E9**
5 Cafe Luxembourg....... **D6**
6 Carmine's Upper
  West Side................. **C1**
7 Gray's Papaya........... **D6**
8 Jean-Georges........... **F9**
9 Levain Bakery.......... **D5**
10 Nice Matin.............. **D4**
11 Per Se **E9**
12 Porter House
  Bar and Grill............. **E9**
13 Salumeria Rosi......... **D5**
14 Sarabeth's **D3**
15 Thai Market **C1**

Hotels ▼

1 Arthouse Hotel
  New York City **C4**
2 The Excelsior Hotel...... **E3**
3 Hotel Beacon............ **D5**
4 The Lucerne **D4**

12

The Upper West Side

AMNH on Film

Does the inside of AMNH look familiar? It should. The museum is a popular location for movies filming in New York. In *Spider-Man 2* (2004), Peter Parker (Tobey Maguire) has yet another bad day wrestling with his secret identity while in the Rose Center. Larry (Ben Stiller) is chased through the halls by a T. rex and outsmarts a monkey in the Hall of African Mammals while working as a night security guard in *Night at the Museum* (2006). AMNH plays a role in *Night at the Museum: Battle of the Smithsonian* (2009) and *Night at the Museum: Secret of the Tomb* (2014), too. In the coming-of-age film *The Squid & the Whale* (2005), Walt Berkman (Jesse Eisenberg) comes to a revelation that he is the squid and his father is the whale in front of the Hall of Ocean Life's famous diorama. And then there's *The Devil Wears Prada* (2006), where Andrea (Anne Hathaway) wins over Miranda (Meryl Streep) by remembering the names of high-society guests while attending a benefit here.

St., Upper West Side ☎ 212/595–9533 ⊕ www.folkartmuseum.org ✉ Free Ⓜ 1 to 66th St.–Lincoln Center; A, B, C, D to 59th St.–Columbus Circle.

★ **American Museum of Natural History**
MUSEUM | FAMILY | With 45 exhibition halls and more than 34 million artifacts and specimens, the world's largest and most important museum of natural history can easily occupy you for a day. The dioramas might seem dated, but are fun. The dinosaur fossils and exhibits, including a massive T. rex, are probably the highlight for many people. Another museum icon—the 94-foot model of a blue whale—is suspended from the ceiling in the **Milstein Hall of Ocean Life.** The AMNH also has plans for an expansion, to open by 2021. Attached to the museum is the **Rose Center for Earth and Space,** with various exhibits and housing the **Hayden Planetarium** and an **IMAX Theater.** The actual entry fee is a donation; you must pay something, but it can be as little as you wish. Just be aware that many of the wonderful features (not to mention special exhibits) cost extra and must be paid for in full, and check the website for special programs, including sleepovers for kids. ✉ Central Park W, at 79th St., Upper West Side ☎ 212/769–5100 ⊕ www.amnh.org ✉ $23 suggested donation, includes admission to Rose Center for Earth and Space; $28 includes an IMAX or space show Ⓜ B, C to 81st St.–Museum of Natural History.

Cathedral Church of St. John the Divine
RELIGIOUS SITE | The largest cathedral in the world, even with its towers and transepts still unfinished, this divine behemoth comfortably asserts its bulk in the country's most vertical city. As such, the cathedral has long been a global landmark, and in 2017 it was at last designated a landmark by New York City. The seat of the Episcopal diocese in New York, it acts as a sanctuary for all, giving special interfaith services that include a celebration of New York's gay and lesbian community. Built in two long spurts starting in 1892, the cathedral remains only two-thirds complete. What began as a Romanesque Byzantine–style structure under the original architects, George Heins and Christopher Grant Lafarge, shifted in 1911 to French Gothic.

Above the 3-ton central bronze doors is the intricately carved **Portal of Paradise,** which depicts St. John witnessing the Transfiguration of Jesus. Step inside to the cavernous nave: more than 600 feet long, it holds some 5,000 worshippers, and the 162-foot-tall dome crossing could comfortably contain the Statue of Liberty (minus its pedestal). The **Great Rose Window** is the largest stained-glass window in the United States. Sunday services are at 8, 9, 11, and 4. Tours including a Highlights Tour and a Vertical Tour are offered throughout the week; check the website for prices and to reserve. ⊠ *1047 Amsterdam Ave., at 112th St., Upper West Side* ☎ *212/316-7540, 866/011-4111 for tour reservations* ⊕ *www.stjohndivine. org* 🖼 *$10, includes self-guided tour; guided tours $12–$20* Ⓜ *1 to Cathedral Pkwy.–110th St.*

Children's Museum of Manhattan

MUSEUM | FAMILY | In this five-story exploratorium, children aged 1–7 are invited to paint their own masterpieces, float boats down a "stream" (weather permitting), rescue animals with Dora and Diego (in an exhibition created in collaboration with Nickelodeon), and walk through giant interactive human organs to explore the connections between food, sleep, and play. Special exhibits are thoughtfully put together and fun. Art workshops, science programs, and storytelling sessions are held daily. ⊠ *212 W. 83rd St., between Broadway and Amsterdam Ave., Upper West Side* ☎ *212/721–1223* ⊕ *www. cmom.org* 🖼 *$14* 🕙 *Closed Mon.* Ⓜ *1 to 79th St.*

Columbus Circle

STORE/MALL | This busy traffic circle at Central Park's southwest corner anchors the Upper West Side and makes a good starting place for exploring the neighborhood if you're coming from south of 59th Street. The central 700-ton granite monument (capped by a marble statue of Christopher Columbus) serves as a popular meeting place. To some people,

Columbus Circle is synonymous with the **Time Warner Center** building (☎ *212/823–6300* ⊕ *www.theshopsatcolumbuscircle. com*) and its several floors of shops and restaurants, including the underground food hall Turnstyle (on the subway-station mezzanine)—a good spot to pick up fixings for a Central Park picnic. It's also home to the Rose Hall performing arts complex, part of Jazz at Lincoln Center. ⊠ *Broadway between 58th and 60th Sts., Upper West Side* Ⓜ *1, A, B, C, D to 59th St.–Columbus Circle.*

Grant's Tomb (*General Grant National Memorial*)

MEMORIAL | Walk through upper Riverside Park and you're sure to notice this towering granite mausoleum (1897), the final resting place of Civil War general and two-term president Ulysses S. Grant and his wife, Julia Dent Grant. As the old joke goes, who's buried here? Nobody—they're *entombed* in a crypt beneath a domed rotunda, surrounded by photographs and Grant memorabilia. Once a more popular sight than the Statue of Liberty, this pillared Classical Revival edifice remains regal and timeless. The words engraved on the tomb, "Let Us Have Peace," recall Grant's speech to the Republican convention upon his presidential nomination. Surrounding the memorial are the so-called rolling benches, covered with colorful mosaic tiles. Made in the 1970s as a public art project, they are now as beloved as they are incongruous with the grand memorial they surround. ■TIP→ **Stop by the visitor center (across the street from the tomb) for a 20-minute film about Grant. Note that the memorial itself is open every other hour due to staffing limitations.** ⊠ *Riverside Dr. and 122nd St., Upper West Side* ☎ *212/666–1640* ⊕ *www.nps.gov/gegr* 🖼 *Free* 🕙 *Closed Mon., Tues.* Ⓜ *1 to 116th St.*

Museum of Arts and Design (*MAD*)

MUSEUM | Housed in a glass and glazed terra-cotta building on the rim of Columbus Circle, the Museum of Arts and

Continued on page 374

AMERICAN MUSEUM OF NATURAL HISTORY

Theodore Roosevelt Memorial Hall

The largest natural history museum in the world is also one of the most impressive sights in New York. Four city blocks make up its 45 exhibition halls, which hold more than 30 million artifacts and wonders from the land, the sea, and outer space. With all those wonders, you won't be able to see everything on a single visit, but you can easily hit the highlights in half a day.

Before you begin, plan a route before setting out. Be sure to pick up a map when you pay your admission. The museum's four floors (and lower level) are mazelike.

Visitors can use the free AMNH Explorer app to navigate the museum. It tracks your location, has turn-by-turn directions, profiles of iconic museum objects, and tours, and guides you to bathrooms and exits. There are free companion apps to support special exhibits; check the website. The museum has devices you can borrow if you don't have an app-friendly phone.

Enter the museum at the below-street-level entrance connected to the 81st Street subway station for the shortest lines (look for the subway entrance to the left of the museum's steps). The entrance on Central Park West, where the vast steps lead up into the impressive, barrel-ceilinged Theodore Roosevelt Rotunda, is central and a good starting place for exploring.

The Rose Center for Earth and Space is attached to the museum. Enter from West 81st Street, where a path slopes down to the entrance, after which elevators and stairs descend to the ticket line on the lower level.

What to see? Check out the museum highlights on the following pages.

✉ Central Park West at W. 79th St., Upper West Side

Ⓜ Subway: B, C to 81st St.

☎ 212/769–5100

🌐 www.amnh.org

💳 $23 suggested donation, includes admission to Rose Center for Earth and Space but not special exhibitions or the Space Show.

🕐 Daily 10–5:45.

Left, Spectrum of Life Wall

MUSEUM HIGHLIGHTS

Left, Woolly Mammoth
Above, Tyrannosaurus rex

Dinosaurs and Mammals

An amazing assembly of dinosaur and mammal fossils covers the entire fourth floor. The organization can be hard to grasp at first, so head to the **Wallace Orientation Center,** where a short film explains how each of the Fossil Halls lead into each other. You'll want to spend at least an hour here—the highlights include a *T. Rex,* an *Apatosaurus* (formerly called a Brontosaurus), and the *Buettneria,* which resembles a modern-day crocodile.

The specimens are not in chronological order; they're put together based on their shared characteristics. Key branching-off points—a watertight egg, a grasping hand—are highlighted in the center of rooms and surrounded by related fossil groups. Check out the touch screens here; they make a complex topic more comprehensible.

Reptiles and Amphibians

Head for the Reptiles and Amphibians Hall on the third floor to check out the Komodo Dragon lizards and a 23-foot-long python skeleton. The weirdest display is the enlarged model of the Suriname toad *Pipa pipa,* whose young hatch from the female's back. The Primates Hall carries brief but interesting comparisons between apes, monkeys, and humans. Also on the third floor is the upper gallery of the famed Akeley Hall of African Mammals.

SPECIAL SHOWS AND NEW EXHIBITS

Special exhibits, the IMAX theater, and the Space Show cost extra. The timed tickets are available in advance at the museum's Web site and are sold same day at the door. Between October and May, don't miss the warm, plant-filled Butterfly Conservatory, where blue morphos, monarchs, and other butterflies flit and feed. Ten minutes is probably enough time to enjoy it.

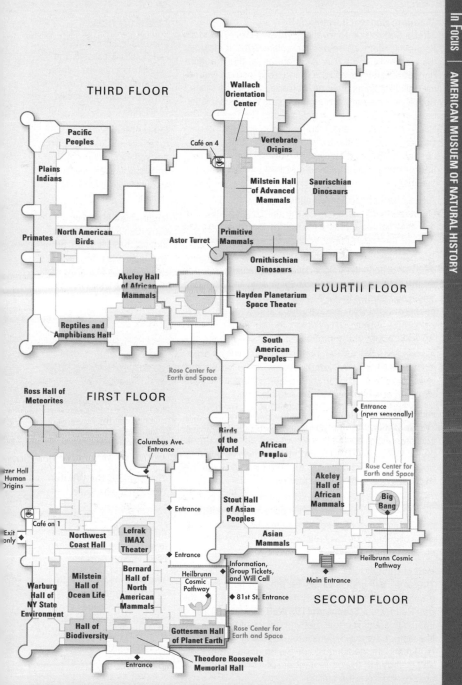

THIRD FLOOR

Pacific Peoples

Plains Indians

Primates

North American Birds

Wallach Orientation Center

Café on 4

Vertebrate Origins

Milstein Hall of Advanced Mammals

Saurischian Dinosaurs

Astor Turret

Primitive Mammals

Akeley Hall of African Mammals

Hayden Planetarium Space Theater

Ornithischian Dinosaurs

FOURTH FLOOR

Reptiles and Amphibians Hall

Rose Center for Earth and Space

South American Peoples

Ross Hall of Meteorites

FIRST FLOOR

Columbus Ave. Entrance

Birds of the World

African Peoples

Entrance (open seasonally)

…zer Hall Human Origins

Café on 1

Entrance

Stout Hall of Asian Peoples

Akeley Hall of African Mammals

Rose Center for Earth and Space

Big Bang

Exit only

Northwest Coast Hall

Lefrak IMAX Theater

Entrance

Asian Mammals

Heilbrunn Cosmic Pathway

Warburg Hall of NY State Environment

Milstein Hall of Ocean Life

Bernard Hall of North American Mammals

Heilbrunn Cosmic Pathway

Information, Group Tickets, and Will Call

Main Entrance

SECOND FLOOR

81st St. Entrance

Hall of Biodiversity

Gottesman Hall of Planet Earth

Rose Center for Earth and Space

Theodore Roosevelt Memorial Hall

Entrance

Theodore Roosevelt Memorial

After a $40 million renovation, the two-story Theodore Roosevelt Memorial re-opened in late 2012. It includes the restored Central Park West entrance, the Theodore Roosevelt Rotunda, and the Theodore Roosevelt Memorial Hall. Highlights are a new bronze statue of a seated Roosevelt, celebratory murals honoring the Conservation President, touch-screen timelines, and film footage. The Hall of North American Mammals was also restored as part of the memorial to Roosevelt; the hall originally opened in 1942 and many of its displays feature scenes from National Parks that were signed into being by the president.

Akeley Hall of African Mammals

Opened in 1936, this hall on the third floor, its 28 dramatically lighted dioramas is one of the most beloved parts of the museum.

The hall was the life's work of the explorer Carl Akeley, who came up with the idea for the hall, raised the funds for the expeditions, gathered specimens, and sketched landscape studies for what would become the stunning backgrounds. (The backgrounds themselves were painted by James Perry Wilson, whose works can be found throughout the museum.)

Akeley died a decade before the hall opened on an expedition in what's now Rwanda. His gravesite is near the landscape portrayed in the gorilla diorama, completed after his death as a memorial to him and his work.

Hall of Human Origins

The Spitzer Hall of Human Origins on the first floor is a comprehensive exhibit that allows visitors to draw their own conclusions about human evolution by presenting both the scientific methods and the material evidence that goes into evolutionary theory.

The exhibit then traces the evolution of our species over six million years of fossil record and spells out our ancestors' physical and intellectual advancements. Highlights include casts of our famous hairy relative "Lucy," who walked the plains of Africa over 1.8 million years ago.

Hall of Biodiversity

The small **Hall of Biodiversity** on the first floor includes a shady replica of a Central African Republic rain forest. Nearby, the **Spectrum of Life Wall** showcases 1,500 specimens and models, helping show just how weird life can get. The wall opens into the gaping Milstein Hall of Ocean Life, designed to give it an underwater glow and to show off the 94-foot model of a **blue whale** that's suspended from the ceiling.

AMNH ON FILM

Does the inside of AMNH look familiar? It should. The museum is a popular location for movies filming in New York. Here are a few of its recent close ups:

Spider-Man 2:
Peter Parker (Tobey Maguire) has yet another bad day wrestling with his secret identity while in the Rose Center.

Night at the Museum:
Larry (Ben Stiller) is chased through the halls by a T. Rex and outsmarts a monkey in the Hall of African Mammals while working as a night security guard.

Blue Whale

The Squid & the Whale:
Walt Berkman (Jesse Eisenberg) comes to a revelation that he is the squid and his father is the whale in front of the Hall of Ocean Life's famous diorama.

The Devil Wears Prada:
Andrea (Anne Hathaway) wins over Miranda (Meryl Streep) by remembering the names of high society guests while attending a benefit here.

ROSE CENTER
FOR EARTH AND SPACE

The vast expanses of space and time involved in the creation of the universe can be hard to grasp even with the guiding hand of a museum, so you may want to visit the center when you're at your sharpest. The stunning glass building's centerpiece is the aluminum-clad Hayden Sphere, 87 feet in diameter. Enclosed within are the planetarium, called the Space Theater, and an audiovisual Big Bang presentation consisting of four minutes of narration by Maya Angelou, indistinct washes of color, and frightening bursts of sound. The rock-filled **Hall of Planet Earth** is particularly timely given the earthquakes and other natural disasters of recent years: one section uses a working earthquake monitor to help explain just what causes such seismic violence.

The Space Theater

At the Space Theater, the stage is the dome above you and the actors, heavenly projections. One of the world's largest virtual reality simulators, the theater uses surround sound and slight vibrations in the seats, to immerse you in scenes of planets, star clusters, and galaxies. *Dark Universe* puts Hollywood effects to shame as it explores the cosmos and just how little we know about it.

Tip: The Museum's Cosmic Discoveries app allows you to take the universe, and all its galaxies and planets, with you when you leave. The app offers images, findings, and bulletins all culled from the museum's archives and curated by the museum's astrophysicists. ⊕ *www.amnh.org/apps*

TIME TO EAT?

Inside the museum:
The **main food court** on the lower level serves sandwiches, pizza, hamburgers and global street food. The animal- and planet-shaped cookies are draws for kids; adults should check out the barbecue station.

The small **Café on 4**, in a turret next to the fossil halls, offers garden views and sells premade sandwiches and salads, soup, yogurt, and desserts.

The über-white **Café on 1**, tucked away beside the Hall of Human Origins, sells warm sandwiches, soup, salads, beer and wine at New York prices.

TIME TO PLAY

Nights at the museum aren't just for kids! Bust out your moonwalk and enjoy a few cosmicpolitans at the Rose Center's monthly One Step Beyond series, featuring live bands, DJs, VJs, cocktails, and dynamic visuals. Get tickets at amnh.org/plan-your-visit/one-step-beyond

TIME TO WATCH

Each October, the AMNH hosts the Margaret Mead Film & Video Festival, the longest-running premiere showcase for international documentaries in the United States. Tickets are made available one month prior to the festival, and online at www.amnh.org/mead

AMNH TALKS TO FODOR'S

Interview with Ellen V. Futter, President of the American Museum of Natural History, conducted by Michelle Delio.

If You Only Have an Hour: The American Museum of Natural History has the world's finest collection of dinosaur fossils, so a visit to the fourth-floor's Fossil Halls, where more than 600 specimens are on display, is a must. An extraordinarily high percentage of the specimens on view—85%—are real fossilized bones as opposed to casts. At most museums those percentages are reversed, so here visitors have the chance to see the real thing including T. rex, velociraptor, and triceratops.

What to Hit Next? The museum also is renowned for its habitat dioramas, which are considered among the finest examples in the world. Visits to the Akeley Hall of African Mammals, the Hall of North American Mammals, and the Sanford Hall of North American Birds provide an overview of the diorama arts—pioneered and advanced at the museum—while allowing visitors to come face-to-face with some glorious and beautiful animals depicted in their natural habitats—habitats which in many cases no longer exist in such pristine conditions.

If You're Looking to Be Starstruck: Even if you don't have time to take in a space show in the Hayden Planetarium, the Rose Center for Earth and Space has lots of fascinating exhibits describing the vast range of sizes in the cosmos; the 13-billion-year history of the universe; the nature of galaxies, stars, and planets; and the dynamic features of our own unique planet Earth—all enclosed in a facility with spectacular award-winning architecture.

Hidden gems

The museum consists of 45 exhibition halls in 25 interconnected buildings so there are gems around every corner. Some lesser-known treasures include:

Star of India: The 563-carat Star of India, the largest and most famous star sapphire in the world, is displayed in the Morgan Memorial Hall of Gems.

Rose Center for Earth and Space

ID PLEASE!

Once a year (usually in May or June—check website for details), the museum invites visitors to share rocks, teeth, shells, insects, feathers, and other curiosities with their scientists and anthropologists. Previous Identification Days have yielded rocks from the Jurassic Period, a fossilized walrus skull, and a 5,000-year-old stone spear point from Morocco. Lines can be long, but it's so interesting.

Black Smokers: These sulfide chimneys—collected during groundbreaking museum expeditions to the Pacific Ocean—are the only such specimens exhibited anywhere. Black smokers form around hot springs on the deep ocean floor and support a microbial community that does not live off sunlight but instead on the chemical energy of the Earth. Some of these microbes are considered the most ancient forms of life on Earth and may offer clues to the development of life here and the possibility of life elsewhere. See them in the Gottesman Hall of Planet Earth.

Spectrum of Life: The Hall of Biodiversity aims to showcase the glorious diversity of life on Earth resulting from 3.5 billion years of evolution. The impressive "Spectrum of Life" display is a 100-foot-long installation of more than 1,500 specimens and models—microorganisms and mammals, bacteria and beetles, fungi and fish. Use the computer workstations to learn more about the species depicted in each area.

Dodo: One of the museum's rarest treasures is the skeleton of a dodo bird, displayed along with other endangered or extinct species in the "Endangered Case" in the Hall of Biodiversity.

Small Dioramas: Tucked along the sides of the Hall of North American Mammals are two easy-to-miss corridors displaying a number of exquisitely rendered dioramas. In these jewel-box-like displays, some a mere 3 foot deep, you will see the smaller animals such as wolves galloping through a snowy night, a Canada lynx stalking a snowshoe hare, and a spotted skunk standing on its hands, preparing to spray a cacomistle, to name just a few of the evocative scenes.

Dinosaur Eggs: In 1993 museum scientists working in the Gobi Desert of Mongolia were the first to unearth fossilized embryos in dinosaur eggs, as well as the fossil of an adult oviraptor in a brooding posture over its nest. This discovery provided invaluable information about dinosaur gestation and revolutionized thinking about dinosaur behavior. Look for the display in the museum's Fossil Halls on the fourth floor.

Ross Terrace: In warmer months the Ross Terrace, with its fountains and cosmic theme, offers a wonderful outdoor spot for resting and reflecting, while providing a spectacular view of the Rose Center for Earth and Space.

Star of India

A diorama featuring a Komodo Dragon, the largest and most powerful lizard in the world.

MOST INTERESTING OBJECT?

What's most interesting about the American Museum of Natural History is not any single object on exhibit, but the sheer range and scope of what you can experience here. Think of it is a field guide to the natural world, the universe, and the cultures of humanity—all under one roof. The experience of visiting the museum is ultimately about awakening a sense of discovery, wonder, awe, and stewardship of this Earth we call home.

Design celebrates joyful quirkiness and personal, sometimes even obsessive, artistic visions. The art is human-scale here, much of it neatly housed in display cases rather than hanging on walls, with a strong focus on contemporary jewelry, glass, ceramic, fiber, wood, and mixed-media works. Exit through the gift shop with its incredible housewares, jewelry, and other artful pieces unseen anywhere else. Thursday evening from 6 to 9 is pay-what-you-wish at the museum. Free docent-led tours are offered daily at 11:30 and 3. ⊠ *2 Columbus Circle, 59th St. at 8th Ave., Upper West Side* ☎ *212/299–7777* ⊕ *www.madmuseum. org* 🖃 *$16* ⊙ *Closed Mon.* Ⓜ *1, A, B, C, D to 59th St.–Columbus Circle.*

★ **New-York Historical Society**

MUSEUM | Manhattan's oldest (and perhaps most under-the-radar) museum, founded in 1804, boasts one of the city's finest research libraries in addition to sleek interactive technology, a children's museum, and inventive exhibitions that showcase the museum's eclectic collections and unique voice. While the permanent collection of more than 6 million pieces of art, literature, and memorabilia sheds light on America's history, art, and architecture, the special exhibitions showcase the museum's fresh insight on all things New York. The Henry Luce III Center for the Study of American Culture includes 100 dazzling Tiffany lamps on display; historic treasures that tell the American story in a novel way; and the Center for the Study of Women's History, with exhibitions that examine the untold stories of women who have impacted and continue to shape the American experience. The **DiMenna Children's History Museum** on the lower level invites children to become "history detectives" and explore New York's past through interactive displays, hands-on activities, and the stories of iconic New York children through the centuries.

Storico, the light-filled restaurant on the first floor (with a separate entrance), serves upscale Italian food at lunch and dinner; Parliament Coffee & Espresso Bar sells beverages, pastries, and light lunch fare. ⊠ *170 Central Park W, at 77th St., Upper West Side* ☎ *212/873–3400* ⊕ *www.nyhistory.org* 🖃 *$21 (pay-what-you-wish Fri. 6–8 pm)* ⊙ *Closed Mon.* Ⓜ *B, C to 81st St.–Museum of Natural History.*

Nicholas Roerich Museum

MUSEUM | An 1898 Upper West Side town house contains this small, eccentric museum dedicated to the work of Russian artist Nicholas Roerich, who immigrated to New York in the 1920s and quickly developed an ardent following. Some 150 of his paintings hang here—notably some vast canvases of the Himalayas. Free chamber music concerts are held many Sunday evenings at 5, except from June through September. ⊠ *319 W. 107th St., between Broadway and Riverside Dr., Upper West Side* ☎ *212/864–7752* ⊕ *www.roerich.org* 🖃 *Free; donations welcome* ⊙ *Closed Mon.* Ⓜ *1 to Cathedral Pkwy.–110th St.*

Riverside Park

CITY PARK | **FAMILY** | Surrounded by the culture and concrete of the Upper West Side, you might not realize that there is an expansive green space running along the Hudson River just blocks away. Riverside Park dishes out a dose of tranquility from 72nd to 158th Street, as does the park's south extension, from about 59th to 72nd Street, still a work in progress. The original sections of Riverside Park, designed by Frederick Law Olmsted and Calvert Vaux of Central Park fame and laid out between 1873 and 1888, have a waterfront bike and walking path.

There are several access points to the park, including one at West 72nd Street and Riverside Drive (look for the statue of Eleanor Roosevelt), where you reach the waterfront path by an underpass. You can then head north along the Hudson River, past the 79th Street Boat Basin. Above it, a ramp leads to the Rotunda, home in warmer months to the seasonal Boat Basin Café, a dog-friendly open-air café that serves lunch and dinner. The 91st Street Garden is a level up from the water: leave the riverside path near 92nd Street by taking another underpass and then heading up the path on the right. ✉ *From 59th to 158th St., between Riverside Dr. and the Hudson River, Upper West Side* 🌐 *www.nycgovparks.org/parks/riversidepark* [M] *1, 2, 3 to 72nd St.*

🍴 Restaurants

The area around Lincoln Center is a fine-dining hub; as you head north you'll find a mix of casual and sophisticated neighborhood spots.

Asiate

$$$$ | **ASIAN** | The unparalleled view of Central Park is reason enough to visit Asiate's pristine dining room, on the 35th floor of the Time Warner Center in the Mandarin Oriental Hotel. The kitchen turns out contemporary dishes with an Asian influence, pairing unlikely ingredients: think foie gras and hazelnut brittle, or branzino and truffles. **Known for:** park view; noted wine list; prix-fixe menus only. [$] *Average main: $100* ✉ *Mandarin Oriental Hotel, 80 Columbus Circle, 35th fl., at 60th St., Upper West Side* ☎ *212/805–8881* 🌐 *www.mandarinoriental.com* [M] *1, A, B, C, D to 59th St.–Columbus Circle.*

★ Bar Boulud

$$$ | **FRENCH** | Acclaimed French chef Daniel Boulud, known for upscale New York City eateries Daniel and Café Boulud, shows diners his more casual side with this lively contemporary bistro and wine bar. The menu emphasizes charcuterie, including terrines and pâtés designed by Parisian charcutier Gilles Verot, as well as traditional French bistro dishes like steak frites and coq au vin. **Known for:** charcuterie and bistro classics; good value from noted chef; three-course pretheater menu. [$] *Average main: $34* ✉ *1900 Broadway, between 63rd and 64th Sts., Upper West Side* ☎ *212/595–0303* 🌐 *www.barboulud.com* [M] *1 to 66th St.–Lincoln Center; 1, A, B, C, D to 59th St.–Columbus Circle.*

★ Barney Greengrass

$$ | **AMERICAN** | At this Upper West Side landmark, brusque waiters send out stellar smoked salmon, sturgeon, and whitefish to a happy crowd packed to the gills at small Formica tables. Split a fish platter with bagels, cream cheese, and other fixings, or get your velvety nova scrambled with eggs and buttery caramelized onions. **Known for:** smoked fish and chopped liver; cash only; less crowded on weekdays. [$] *Average main: $19* ✉ *541 Amsterdam Ave., between 86th and 87th Sts., Upper West Side* ☎ *212/724–4707* 🌐 *www.barneygreengrass.com* ⏲ *Closed Mon. No dinner* 💳 *No credit cards* [M] *1, B, C to 86th St.*

Bouchon Bakery & Café

$$ | **CAFÉ** | Never mind that you're in the middle of a shopping mall—soups and sandwiches don't get much more luxurious than at acclaimed chef Thomas Keller's low-key lunch spot (one floor down from his extravagant flagship, Per Se); it draws long lines for good reason. Fork-and-knife open-face tartines, like the tuna niçoise, are delicious. **Known for:** chicken soup; croque madame; desserts from bakery window. [$] *Average main: $20* ✉ *Time Warner Center, 10 Columbus Circle, 3rd fl., between 58th and 60th Sts., Upper West Side* ☎ *212/823–9366* 🌐 *www.bouchonbakery.com* ⏲ *No dinner* [M] *1, A, B, C, D to 59th St.–Columbus Circle.*

Cafe Luxembourg

$$$ | **FRENCH** | The old soul of the Lincoln Center neighborhood seems to inhabit the tiled and mirrored walls of this lively, cramped French bistro, where West End

Avenue regulars are greeted with kisses, and musicians and audience members pack the room after a concert. The bar's always hopping, and the menu includes classics like steak tartare, *moules frites,* and lobster roll. **Known for:** quintessential UWS bistro; after-concert scene; good service. $ *Average main: $33* ✉ *200 W. 70th St., between Amsterdam and West End Aves., Upper West Side* ☎ *212/873–7411* ⊕ *www.cafeluxembourg.com* Ⓜ *1, 2, 3, B, C to 72nd St.*

Carmine's Upper West Side

$$$ | **ITALIAN** | **FAMILY** | Set on a nondescript block of Broadway, this branch of the Italian mainstay is a favorite for families celebrating special occasions, pre-prom groups of teens, and plain-old folks. They come for the tried-and-true items like fried calamari, linguine with white clam sauce, chicken parmigiana, and veal saltimbocca, all served in mountainous portions. **Known for:** best red-sauce joint on UWS; cheerful scene; antipasti table. $ *Average main: $30* ✉ *2450 Broadway, between 90th and 91st Sts., Upper West Side* ☎ *212/362–2200* ⊕ *www. carminesnyc.com* Ⓜ *1, 2, 3 to 96th St.*

Gray's Papaya

$ | **FAST FOOD** | It's a stand-up, take-out, 24-hour dive: but yes, limos do sometimes stop here for these legendary hot dogs—they are delicious, and quite the economical meal. The recession special is two grilled hot dogs and a drink, and there are cheap breakfast offerings, too, like the quintessential egg and cheese on a roll. **Known for:** fast, affordable Big Apple bites; $10 minimum for credit cards; sugary papaya drinks. $ *Average main: $5* ✉ *2090 Broadway, at 72nd St., Upper West Side* ☎ *212/799–0243* ⊕ *grayspapaya.nyc* Ⓜ *1, 2, 3 to 72nd St.*

Jean-Georges

$$$$ | **FRENCH** | This culinary temple in the Trump International Hotel and Towers focuses wholly on chef célèbre Jean-Georges Vongerichten's spectacular creations. The chef may now have restaurants sprinkled around the globe, but this is where you want to be, as some dishes on the prix-fixe-only menu approach the limits of the taste universe, like foie-gras brûlée with spiced fig jam and ice-wine reduction. **Known for:** masterful haute cuisine; yellowfin tuna ribbons; sesame crab toast. $ *Average main: $178* ✉ *1 Central Park W, at 60th St., Upper West Side* ☎ *212/299–3900* ⊕ *www.jean-georges. com* 🍴 *Jacket required* Ⓜ *1, A, B, C, D to 59th St.–Columbus Circle.*

Levain Bakery

$ | **BAKERY** | **FAMILY** | Completely unpretentious and utterly delicious, Levain Bakery's cookies are rich and hefty (they clock in at 6 ounces each). Choose from the chocolate-chip walnut, dark-chocolate chocolate chip, dark-chocolate peanut-butter chip, or oatmeal raisin: batches are baked fresh daily and taste best when they're warm and melty right out of the oven. **Known for:** huge cookies; flavored breads; muffins and scones. $ *Average main: $9* ✉ *167 W. 74th St., near Amsterdam Ave., Upper West Side* ☎ *212/874–6080* ⊕ *www.levainbakery. com* ☾ *No dinner* Ⓜ *1, 2, 3 to 72nd St.*

Nice Matin

$$$ | **BISTRO** | **FAMILY** | If the Upper West Side and the French Riviera collided, it might look a little bit like Nice Matin. This is a longtime neighborhood favorite, particularly in warm-weather months, when regulars plant themselves at sidewalk tables and gawk at passersby while munching on Gallic fare like pan-roasted monkfish, garlicky mussels, and, of course, steak frites. **Known for:** weekend brunch; Nice burger; lengthy wine list. $ *Average main: $28* ✉ *201 W. 79th St., at Amsterdam Ave., Upper West Side* ☎ *212/873–6423* ⊕ *www.nicematinnyc. com* Ⓜ *1 to 79th St.*

★ Per Se

$$$$ | **AMERICAN** | The New York interpretation of what many consider one of America's finest restaurants (the Napa Valley's French Laundry), Per Se is chef Thomas Keller's Broadway stage—set in a large, understated dining room with great views of Central Park. Keller embraces seasonality and a witty playfulness, and some dishes are world-renowned, such as the tiny cones of tuna tartare topped with crème fraîche, and the "oysters and pearls"—tiny mollusks in a creamy custard with tapioca. **Known for:** reservations needed several months ahead; prix-fixe menus (service included in price); duck foie gras. [$] *Average main: $340* ✉ *Time Warner Center, 10 Columbus Circle, 4th fl., at 60th St., Upper West Side* ☎ *212/823–9335* 🌐 *www.perseny.com* 🕓 *No lunch Mon.–Thurs.* 👔 *Jacket required* [M] *1, A, B, C, D to 59th St.–Columbus Circle.*

Porter House Bar and Grill

$$$$ | **STEAKHOUSE** | With clubby interiors by Jeffrey Beers and an adjoining lounge area, Porter House is helmed by veteran chef Michael Lomonaco. Filling the meat-and-potatoes slot in the Time Warner Center's upscale "Restaurant Collection," this masculine throwback highlights American wines and pedigreed supersize meat; the expertly seasoned fare comes with the usual battery of à la carte sides—creamed spinach, roasted mushrooms, and truffle mashed potatoes. **Known for:** filet mignon tartare; roasted bone marrow; côte de boeuf. [$] *Average main: $55* ✉ *Time Warner Center, 10 Columbus Circle, 4th fl., at 60th St., Upper West Side* ☎ *212/823–9500* 🌐 *www.porterhousenewyork.com* [M] *1, A, B, C, D to 59th St.–Columbus Circle.*

Salumeria Rosi

$$ | **ITALIAN** | Chef Cesare Casella may no longer be associated with this cured meat mecca but he has left the place in a still-delicious state, showcasing dozens of varieties of prosciutto, coppa, mortadella, and more. You can have it carved from a professional slicer for consumption on the spot or purchase it as indulgent takeout. **Known for:** unctuous Italian cured meats; panini menu; Italian fare including lasagna. [$] *Average main: $17* ✉ *283 Amsterdam Ave., between 73rd and 74th Sts., Upper West Side* ☎ *212/877–4800* 🌐 *www.salumeriarosinyc.com* [M] *1, 2, 3 to 72nd St.*

Sarabeth's

$$ | **AMERICAN** | Lining up for brunch here is as much an Upper West Side tradition as taking a sunny Sunday afternoon stroll in nearby Riverside Park. Locals love the bric-a-brac-filled restaurant for sweet morning-time dishes like lemon ricotta pancakes and comforting dinners including chicken potpie and steak frites with truffle herb fries. **Known for:** the UWS place to brunch; afternoon tea with great baked goods; multiple locations. [$] *Average main: $19* ✉ *423 Amsterdam Ave., at 80th St., Upper West Side* ☎ *212/496–6280* 🌐 *www.sarabeth.com* [M] *1 to 79th St.*

Thai Market

$$ | **THAI** | This cozy neighborhood Thai joint, just four blocks from the Cathedral Church of St. John the Divine, is decorated with photos of Thai street markets, along with two substantial red umbrellas that float above the bar. Specialties on the long, enticing menu range from crispy rice crepes with minced shrimp to *gai rad prik* (fried chicken in a sauce of chili, garlic, and tamarind) to marinated skirt steak. **Known for:** authentic Thai option; well-priced lunch specials; the menu's "specialty" dishes. [$] *Average main: $16* ✉ *960 Amsterdam Ave., between 107th and 108th Sts., Upper West Side* ☎ *212/280–4575* 🌐 *thaimarketny.net* [M] *1 to Cathedral Pkwy.–110th St.*

Hotels

Arthouse Hotel New York City

$$ | HOTEL | Bringing modern style to the sometimes stodgy Upper West Side, this hotel (formerly the NYLO) nods to the jazz era—think raucous bar, decadent living room with a fireplace, and tempting restaurants. **Pros:** short walk from Central Park; excellent dining and drinking options; some rooms with terraces and dynamite views. **Cons:** lobby might be too hectic for some; Upper West Side location removed from some attractions; fee for pets. ⓢ *Rooms from: $389* ⊠ *2178 Broadway, at 77th St., Upper West Side* ☎ *212/362–1100* ⊕ *www.arthousehotel-nyc.com* ⋑ *291 rooms* ⦿ *No meals* Ⓜ *1 to 79th St.*

The Excelsior Hotel

$ | HOTEL | Directly across the street from the American Museum of Natural History, this well-kept old-school spot is comfortable, with rooms that have warm lighting, comfortable beds, and work desks with ergonomic chairs. **Pros:** excellent neighborhood-y Upper West Side location near Central Park; near foodie mecca Zabar's and popular burger joint Shake Shack; tranquil environment. **Cons:** spotty front-desk and other staff; rooms are inconsistent; Wi-Fi is not free. ⓢ *Rooms from: $189* ⊠ *45 W. 81st St., between Central Park W and Columbus Ave., Upper West Side* ☎ *212/362–9200* ⊕ *www.excelsiorhotelny.com* ⋑ *198 rooms* ⦿ *No meals* Ⓜ *B, C to 81st St.– Museum of Natural History.*

Hotel Beacon

$$$ | HOTEL | FAMILY | A neighborhood favorite for a reason, this Upper West Side hotel is well situated—three blocks from Central Park, 10 blocks from Lincoln Center, and steps from great gourmet grocery stores (Zabar's, Fairway, and Citarella). **Pros:** kitchenettes in all rooms; great UWS location; excellent service. **Cons:** though comfortable and spacious (at a cost), rooms won't win any design

awards; limited nightlife in the area; no room service. ⓢ *Rooms from: $559* ⊠ *2130 Broadway, at 75th St., Upper West Side* ☎ *212/787–1100* ⊕ *www.bea-conhotel.com* ⋑ *278 rooms* ⦿ *No meals* Ⓜ *1, 2, 3 to 72nd St.*

The Lucerne

$$ | HOTEL | FAMILY | Service is the strong suit at this landmark-facade hotel, whose exterior has more pizzazz than the predictable guest rooms decorated with dark-wood reproduction traditional furniture and chintz bedspreads. **Pros:** close to Central Park and American Museum of Natural History; near good shopping and dining; friendly staff. **Cons:** inconsistent room size; decor a bit outdated; few nightlife options in neighborhood. ⓢ *Rooms from: $309* ⊠ *201 W. 79th St., at Amsterdam Ave., Upper West Side* ☎ *212/875–1000, 800/492–8122* ⊕ *www.thelucernehotel.com* ⋑ *202 rooms* ⦿ *No meals* Ⓜ *1 to 79th St.*

ⓨ Nightlife

BARS

Broadway Dive

BARS/PUBS | It may be called a dive, but this dimly lit, wood-clad bar, covered with various animal busts, is more like a craft beer emporium. A rotating selection of local brews is always on draft, and a to-go fridge stocks bottles and cans for off-site consumption. You'll also find wine on tap, bar shelves with a superb variety of spirits and Scotch whiskies, and a few light bites. ⊠ *2662 Broadway, between 101st and 102nd Sts., Upper West Side* ☎ *212/865–2662* ⊕ *divebarnyc.com/broadway-dive* Ⓜ *1, 2, 3 to 96th St.; 1 to 103rd St.*

The Empire Hotel Rooftop Bar

BARS/PUBS | The only thing better than hanging out in Lincoln Center on a lovely night is hanging out a dozen stories above Lincoln Center and taking in city views. Thanks to the Empire Hotel's sprawling rooftop bar—most of it outdoors, covered by a retractable roof, and heated in winter—you can enjoy that pleasure even on nights that are less than lovely. ⊠ *The Empire Hotel, 44 W. 63rd St., between Broadway and Columbus Ave., Upper West Side* ☎ *212/265–2600* ⊕ *www.empirehotelnyc.com* Ⓜ *1 to 66th St.–Lincoln Center.*

Hi-Life NYC
BARS/PUBS | The fantastic neon signs, padded black walls, large round mirrors, and L-shape bar here make you think you've wandered onto a 1930s movie set. Settle into a booth or banquette and watch the neighborhood bons vivants (and bon-vivant wannabes) leap into action nightly, be it early for the daily happy hour or late weekend nights. ⊠ *477 Amsterdam Ave., at 83rd St., Upper West Side* ☎ *212/787–7199* ⊕ *www.hi-life.com* Ⓜ *1 to 86th St.*

★ Maison Pickle
BARS/PUBS | From the same father-son team who made Jacob's Pickle a neighborhood fave, this pleasant restaurant is deservedly famous for its French-dip sandwich and other filling dishes. But its "old-school but progressive" cocktails, wine, and beer menus keep both of its separate bars busy. This is the sort of place where one visit will make you a regular. ⊠ *2315 Broadway, near 84th St., Upper West Side* ☎ *212/496–9100* ⊕ *www.maisonpickle.com* Ⓜ *1 to 86th St.*

Manhattan Cricket Club
BARS/PUBS | Paying homage to the gentlemen's clubs of yore, this intimate UWS speakeasy (located above Australian restaurant Burke & Wills) welcomes everyone, provided you're in appropriate attire (no sneakers or baseball caps) and possess an appreciation for sophisticated cocktails elegantly served. Delicate bar snacks complement boutique bottled beverages and, more importantly, the club's fine spirits made into classic or creative concoctions. See the host at Burke & Wills for entry through the green

leather door ⊠ *226 W. 79th St., between Broadway and Amsterdam Ave., Upper West Side* ☎ *646/823–9252* ⊕ *www.mccnewyork.com* Ⓜ *1 to 79th St.*

COMEDY CLUBS
Stand Up NY
COMEDY CLUBS | Head to this low-key club that lends a stage to both aspiring comedians and veteran comics who pop in to polish their material. Catch a pre-show drink in the front bar, then join the laughter in the back room for the price of a ticket plus a drink minimum. FYI to parents: the comedy showroom is open to guests 16 and up, as long as those under 18 are with a guardian. ⊠ *236 W. 78th St., between Broadway and Amsterdam Ave., Upper West Side* ☎ *212/595–0850* ⊕ *standupny.com* Ⓜ *1 to 79th St.*

JAZZ VENUES
Smoke Jazz & Supper Club
MUSIC CLUBS | If you can't wait to get your riffs on, head uptown to this lounge near Columbia University, where the music starts at 7 pm and continues with two more shows nightly at 9 and 10:30. Performers include some of the top names in the business, including turban-wearing organist Dr. Lonnie Smith and the drummer Jimmy Cobb (who kept time on Miles Davis's seminal album *Kind of Blue*). ⊠ *2751 Broadway, between 105th and 106th Sts., Upper West Side* ☎ *212/864–6662* ⊕ *www.smokejazz.com* Ⓜ *1 to 103rd St.*

ⓘ Performing Arts

MUSIC
Great Music in a Great Space
MUSIC | This aptly named series of public concerts is inspired by a wide range of musical traditions and performed in St. John the Divine's massive, atmospheric, Gothic-style space. The program showcases composers and performers of choral and instrumental music, often to sold-out crowds. ⊠ *Cathedral Church of St. John the Divine, 1047 Amsterdam*

Ave., at 112th St., Upper West Side
☎ 212/316–7540 ⊕ www.stjohndivine.
org/music/great-music Ⓜ 1, B, C to
Cathedral Pkwy.–110th St.

Jazz at Lincoln Center

MUSIC | FAMILY | A few blocks south of
Lincoln Center itself, this Columbus Circle venue is almost completely devoted
to jazz, with a sprinkling of other genres
mixed in. Stages in Rafael Viñoly's crisply
modern **Frederick P. Rose Hall** include the
1,200-seat **Rose Theater,** where a worthy
Jazz for Young People series joins buoy-
ant adult programming a few times each
year. Also here is **The Appel Room,** an elegant theater with a glass wall overlooking
Columbus Circle. In the smaller **Dizzy's
Club Coca-Cola,** there are often multiple
sets nightly, plus late-night sessions
Tuesday through Saturday, all accompanied by a full bar and restaurant with a
New Orleans–inspired menu. ✉ Time
Warner Center, 10 Columbus Circle, 5th
fl., Broadway at 60th St., Upper West
Side ☎ 212/258–9800, 212/721–6500 for
tickets ⊕ www.jazz.org Ⓜ 1, A, B, C, D to
59th St.–Columbus Circle.

Merkin Concert Hall at Kaufman Music Center

MUSIC | A destination for both old-school
and cutting-edge musical performances,
this concert hall around the corner from
Lincoln Center is a lovely, acoustically
advanced 450-seater that presents
chamber pieces. It's also known for jazz,
world, new music, and especially its
Ecstatic Music Festival (January through
March), when an eclectic group of indie
classical artists more than live up to
their billing. ✉ 129 W. 67th St., between
Broadway and Amsterdam Ave., Upper
West Side ☎ 212/501–3330 ⊕ www.kau-
fmanmusiccenter.org/mch Ⓜ 1 to 66th
St.–Lincoln Center.

Miller Theatre

MUSIC | Adventurous programming of
jazz, classical, early and modern music,
and dance makes up the calendar at this
Columbia University theater, founded in
1988. A well-designed 688-seater, this
is a hall that rewards serious listeners.
✉ Columbia University, 2960 Broadway, at 116th St., Upper West Side
☎ 212/854–1633, 212/854–7799 for
tickets ⊕ www.millertheatre.com Ⓜ 1 to
116th St.–Columbia University.

PERFORMANCE CENTERS
★ **Lincoln Center**

ARTS CENTERS | An internationally
renowned cultural destination, attracting
more than 6.5 million visitors annually, this massive, white-travertine-clad
complex contains Avery Fisher Hall, the
Juilliard School, the New York City Ballet,
and the Film Center of Lincoln Center,
making it one of the most concentrated
places for the performing arts in the
nation. Its 16-acre campus, containing
30 venues in all, was designed by prolific
New York architect Wallace Harrison,
and was built over the course of several
years, as part of an urban renewal effort,
from 1962 to 1969.

Renovations that were done to celebrate its recent 50th-anniversary season
included the remodeled centerpiece of
the plaza, the Revson Fountain, as well
as the completely transformed Alice Tully
Hall. The largest hall, the Metropolitan
Opera House, is notable for its dramatic
arched entrance as well as its lobby's
immense chandeliers and Marc Chagall
paintings, both of which can be seen
from outside. Even the fountain in the
central plaza puts on a show here, with
performances (in season) that include
spouts of water 40 feet high. Tours of
Lincoln Center, including the Met, take
place daily and leave from the atrium;
reservations are recommended and can
be made from the website (⊕ atrium.
lincolncenter.org) or in person. ✉ From
62nd to 66th St., between Broadway/
Columbus and Amsterdam Aves., Upper
West Side ☎ 212/875–5000 for main
switchboard, 212/721-6500 for tickets

⊕ *www.lincolncenter.org* Ⓜ *1 to 66th St.–Lincoln Center.*

Symphony Space

ARTS CENTERS | FAMILY | Although Symphony Space runs an energetic roster of classical, jazz, international, and other kinds of music, it also excels with other kinds of arts programming. On the literary front, its two halls—the **Peter Jay Sharp Theatre** and the **Leonard Nimoy Thalia**—host a celebrated roster of literary events, including Bloomsday on Broadway, the Thalia Book Club, and the famed Selected Shorts series (stories read by prominent actors and produced as a podcast and radio show on National Public Radio). There's also a popular comedy series, Uptown Showdown, as well as Performance in HD screenings from the National Theatre Live, Royal Shakespeare Company, and Royal Opera House, and Secret Science Club North science talks. Plays, films, and "Thalia Docs" (usually true-to-their-roots art-house screenings) round out the adult programming. For the family, turn to the popular **Just Kidding** lineup for a nonstop parade of zany plays, sing-alongs, puppetry, and dance midday Saturday (and sometimes Sunday). ⊠ *2537 Broadway, at 95th St., Upper West Side* ☎ *212/864–5400* ⊕ *www.symphonyspace.org* Ⓜ *1, 2, 3 to 96th St.*

THEATER

★ **Shakespeare in the Park**

THEATER | Some of the best things in New York are, indeed, free—including this summer festival presented by the Public Theater and performed at an open-air stage in Central Park. Many notable performers have appeared here, from Meryl Streep to Morgan Freeman. Tickets are given out (limit two per person) starting at noon on the day of each show, and always run out. What you save in money, you make up for in time and tedium—lines are usually *long*. Line up by midmorning or earlier if there have been good reviews. (A limited number of same-day tickets are also distributed via an in-person lottery at The Public Theater, 425 Lafayette Street, at Astor Place.) The easiest way to score these scarce tickets is to register via a mobile lottery using the TodayTix app between midnight and noon on the day you'd like to attend; an email response after noon confirms (or denies) success. Making a tax-deductible donation to the Public Theater is one way to avoid lines and be sure you get a ticket. ⊠ *Delacorte Theater, Central Park, Midpark, use 81st St. entrance at Central Park W, Upper West Side* ☎ *212/967–7555* ⊕ *www.publictheater.org* Ⓜ *B, C to 81st St.–Museum of Natural History.*

🛍 Shopping

Although largely a residential neighborhood, the Upper West Side has some excellent food stores (including Zabar's) as well as smaller boutiques.

BOOKS AND STATIONERY

Westsider Books & Westsider Records

BOOKS/STATIONERY | This wonderfully crammed space is a lifesaver on the Upper West Side. Squeeze in among the stacks of art books and fiction, or pop outside for the $1 bargains. Don't miss the rare-book collection. Nearby, at 233 West 72nd Street, the record shop has an equally impressive collection of vinyl and CDs. ⊠ *2246 Broadway, between 80th and 81st Sts., Upper West Side* ☎ *212/362–0706* ⊕ *www.westsiderbooks.com* Ⓜ *1 to 79th St.*

CLOTHING

★ **bocnyc**

CLOTHING | Who needs to go downtown for cutting-edge designers? This store stocks sleek designs from the likes of Ulla Johnson, Loeffler Randall, and A.L.C. The selection of bags, shoes, and jewelry is just as stylish. ⊠ *410 Columbus Ave., between 79th and 80th Sts., Upper West Side* ☎ *212/799–1567* ⊕ *www.bocnyc.com* Ⓜ *1 to 79th St.; B, C, to 81st St.–Museum of Natural History.*

Intermix

CLOTHING | Whether you're looking for the perfect daytime dress, a pair of J Brand jeans, or a puffer coat that doesn't make you look like the Michelin man, Intermix sells a well-curated assortment of emerging and established designers. Expect to see designs from DVF, rag & bone, and Missoni. There are a number of locations in the city. ⊠ *210 Columbus Ave., between 69th and 70th Sts., Upper West Side* ☎ *212/769–9116* ⊕ *www.intermixonline.com* Ⓜ *1, 2, 3, B, C to 72nd St.*

Pachute

CLOTHING | This cozy boutique, which means "simple" in Hebrew, specializes in stylish casual wear for women. If your weekend uniform consists of button-down shirts, understated jewelry, and espadrilles, then make a beeline here. There are also locations on the Upper East Side and on Atlantic Avenue in Brooklyn. ⊠ *57 W. 84th St., between Columbus Ave. and Central Park W, Upper West Side* ☎ *212/501–9400* ⊕ *www.pachute.com* Ⓜ *B, C to 86th St.*

FOOD AND TREATS

★ Zabar's

FOOD/CANDY | When it comes to authentic New York food, it's hard to beat rugelach, black-and-white cookies, or lox from this iconic, local-favorite specialty food emporium. Zabar's is massive, so either bring your shopping list or make a beeline straight for the appetizing counter or café, where you can score a cup of gourmet coffee and a slice of New York cheesecake, or the epic combination of nova (smoked salmon) with a cream cheese schmear on a proper bagel. ⊠ *2245 Broadway, at 80th St., Upper West Side* ☎ *212/787–2000* ⊕ *www.zabars.com* Ⓜ *1 to 79th St.*

SHOES, HANDBAGS, AND LEATHER GOODS

Tani

SHOES/LUGGAGE/LEATHER GOODS | Fashionable Upper West Side ladies love this shoe store for its huge selection and patient staff. Tani's selection is mostly classic-with-a-twist, and shoppers find brands that are more cool than sexy, such as Dolce Vita and Camper. ⊠ *131 W. 72nd St., between Columbus and Amsterdam Aves., Upper West Side* ☎ *917/265–8835* ⊕ *www.taninyc.com* Ⓜ *1, 2, 3, B, C to 72nd St.*

Central Park

More than 40 million people visit Central Park each year; on an average summer weekend day, a quarter of a million children and adults flood these precincts, frolicking in the 21 playgrounds and 26 ball fields, and resting on more than 9,000 benches that would span 7 miles if you lined them up. There are more than 55 monuments and sculptures in the park, and countless ways to have fun.

◉ Sights

★ Bethesda Fountain

FOUNTAIN | **FAMILY** | Few New York views are more romantic than the one from the top of the magnificent stone staircase that leads down to the ornate three-tiered Bethesda Fountain. The fountain, dedicated in 1873, was built to celebrate the opening of the Croton Aqueduct, which brought clean drinking water to New York City. The name Bethesda was taken from the biblical pool in Jerusalem that was supposedly given healing powers by an angel, which explains the statue *The Angel of the Waters* rising from the center. The four figures around the fountain's base symbolize Temperance, Purity, Health, and Peace. Beyond the terrace stretches the lake, filled with swans, gondolas, and amateur rowboat captains. At its eastern end is the Boathouse, home of an outdoor café for on-the-go snacks, and a pricier restaurant for more leisurely meals. ⊠ *Midpark at 72nd St. transverse, Central*

Did You Know?

The statue on top of Bethesda Fountain was designed by Emma Stebbins, the first woman to be commissioned for a major work of art in New York City, in 1868.

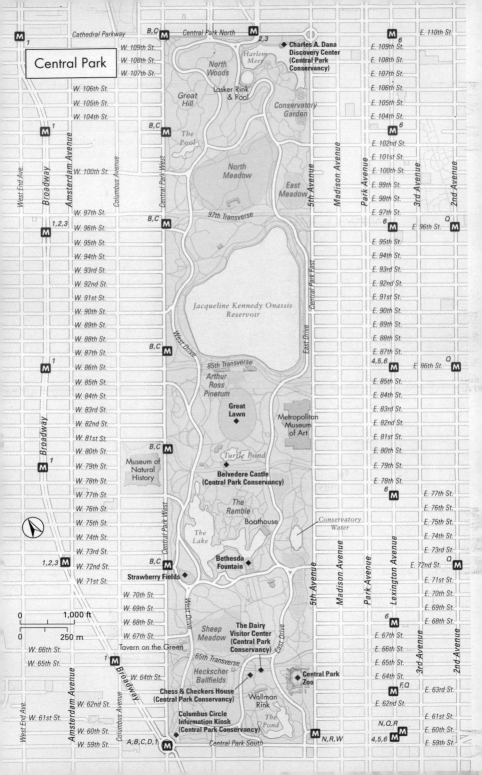

Park ⊕ www.centralparknyc.org Ⓜ B, C to 72nd St.

★ Central Park

CITY PARK | FAMILY | Central Park's creators had a simple goal: to design a place where city dwellers could go to forget the city. Even though New York eventually grew far taller than the trees planted to hide it, this goal has never faltered. A combination escape hatch and exercise yard, Central Park is an urbanized Eden that gives residents and visitors alike a bite of the apple. Indeed, without the Central Park's 843 acres of meandering paths, tranquil lakes, ponds, and open meadows, New Yorkers (especially Manhattanites) might be a lot less sane.

The busy southern section of Central Park, from 59th to 72nd Street, is where most visitors get their first impression. But no matter how many people congregate around here, you can always find a spot to picnic, ponder, or just take in the foliage, especially on a sunny day. Playgrounds, lawns, jogging and biking paths, and striking buildings populate the midsection of the park, from 72nd Street to the reservoir. You can soak up the sun, take in the public art, take pictures at Bethesda Fountain, visit the penguins at the Central Park Zoo, or join the runners huffing counterclockwise on the dirt track that surrounds the reservoir. North of the reservoir and up to 110th Street, Central Park is less crowded and feels more rugged. Not many people know about Lasker Rink & Pool in the northeast corner of the park, a swimming pool that becomes a skating rink in winter—and it's much less crowded than Wollman Rink in the southern part of the park. To find out about park events and a variety of year-round walking tours, visit the website of the Central Park Conservancy.

If you're taking the subway to the park's southernmost parts, then the stops at either Columbus Circle (southwest corner) or 5th Avenue/59th Street (southeast corner) are handy. If headed for points north, the A, B, C, and D subway lines travel along Central Park West (beware of local versus express stops), while the 4, 5, and 6 lines travel along Lexington Avenue, three blocks east of 5th Avenue and the park.

There are many paved pedestrian entrances into the park, from 5th Avenue, Central Park North (110th Street), Central Park West, and Central Park South (59th Street). Four roads, or transverses, cut through the park from east to west—66th, 79th, 86th, and 96th Streets. The East and West drives are both along the north-south axis; Center Drive enters the south edge of the park at 6th Avenue and connects with East Drive around 66th Street. Along the main loop, lampposts are marked with location codes that include a letter—always "E" (for east) or "W" (for west)—followed by numbers, the first two of which tell you the nearest cross street. For example, E7803 means you're near 78th Street; above 99, the initial "1" is omitted, so W0401 is near West 104th Street. Download the Central Park Conservancy's free app for a GPS-enabled map to help you navigate the park. The app also includes an audio guide, self-guided tours, and current events in the park. Central Park has one of the lowest crime rates in the city. Still, use common sense and stay within sight of other park visitors, and in general, avoid the park after dark.

If you haven't packed a picnic and you want a snack, you can usually find one of those rather tired-looking food carts selling pretzels and ice-cream sandwiches. But these days, there are often specialty food carts around, too, mostly in the southern half of the park—your taste buds will thank you. Other reliable options include the café next to the Boathouse Restaurant (midpark at 74th Street), or the park's branch of Le Pain Quotidien (midpark at 69th Street). Both serve sandwiches, soup, pastries, and other satisfying on-the-go grub (and Le Pain also has free Wi-Fi). If you're looking for something a little more iconic, you can stop for brunch, lunch, or dinner at the Tavern on the Green.

As part of a parkwide restoration project named Plan for Play, all 21 playgrounds have undergone or will get an update through the 2010s. Most will see renovations to play structures, plus other improvements that will ensure each one's structural stability and ongoing maintenance for decades to come. ⊠ *Central Park* ☎ *212/794–6564 for Dairy Visitor Center, 212/360–2726 for custom walking tours, 212/310–6600 for Central Park Conservancy* ⊕ *www. centralparknyc.org* Ⓜ *1, A, B, C, D to 59th St.–Columbus Circle; N, R, W to 5th Ave./59th St.*

Central Park Conservancy

CITY PARK | FAMILY | Five visitor centers—the Dairy (midpark at 65th Street), Belvedere Castle (mid-park at 79th Street), the Chess & Checkers House (midpark at 64th Street), the Charles A. Dana Discovery Center (at the top northeast corner of the park at 110th Street, on the shore of Harlem Meer), and the Columbus Circle Information Kiosk (southwest corner of the park at West 59th Street)—have directions, park maps, event calendars, and volunteers who can give you guidance. ⊠ *Dairy Visitor Center, midpark at 65th St., Central Park* ☎ *212/310–6600* ⊕ *www.centralparknyc.org.*

Central Park Zoo

ZOO | FAMILY | Even a leisurely visit to this small but delightful menagerie takes only about an hour, unless, of course, you fall under the spell of the zoo's adorable animals, be they the ever-friendly penguins, the spry snow leopard, or other furry or feathered residents. There are more than 130 species here, but no space for animals like zebras and giraffes to roam; the biggest specimens here are Betty

and Veronica—two lovable grizzly bears. Buying tickets online will save you 10%.

Don't miss the sea lion feedings, possibly the zoo's most popular attraction, daily at 11:30, 1:30, and 3:30. Clustered around the central Sea Lion Pool are separate exhibits for each of the Earth's major environments: penguins and polar bears live at Polar Circle; the highlights of the open-air Temperate Territory are the chattering monkeys; and the Tropic Zone contains the flora and fauna of rain forests. The Tisch Children's Zoo (no additional ticket required) gives kids the opportunity to feed sheep, goats, cows, and pigs. The 4-D theater ($7) shows 15-minute-long family-friendly films that feature sensory effects like wind, mist, bubbles, and scents. Children under 12 are not admitted to the zoo without an adult. ⊠ *Entrance at 5th Ave. and 64th St., Central Park* ☎ *212/439–6500* ⊕ *www.centralparkzoo.org* 🎟 *$14; $20 Total Experience (includes 4-D show)* Ⓜ *6 to 68th St.–Hunter College; N, R, W to 5th Ave./59th St.; F, Q to Lexington Ave./63rd St.*

Great Lawn

CITY PARK | FAMILY | This truly great 14-acre oval has endured billions of footsteps, thousands of ball games, hundreds of downpours, scores of concerts, and even the crush of people attending one papal Mass. Yet it's the stuff of a suburbanite's dream—perfectly tended turf (a mix of rye and Kentucky bluegrass), state-of-the-art drainage systems, automatic sprinklers, and careful horticultural monitoring. The area hums with action on weekends and most summer evenings, when its softball fields and picnicking grounds provide a much-needed outlet for city folk (and city dogs) of all ages. ⊠ *Midpark between 81st and 85th Sts., Central Park* ⊕ *www.centralparknyc.org* Ⓜ *B, C to 81st St.–Museum of Natural History.*

Many Beatles fans come to Strawberry Fields to pay their respects to John Lennon, who was murdered across the street at the Dakota apartments.

Strawberry Fields

MEMORIAL | This memorial to John Lennon, who penned the classic 1967 song "Strawberry Fields Forever," is sometimes called the "international garden of peace." The curving paths, shrubs, trees, and flower beds create a deliberately informal landscape reminiscent of English parks. Every year on December 8, Beatles fans mark the anniversary of Lennon's death by gathering around the star-shape black-and-white "Imagine" mosaic set into the pavement. Lennon's 1980 murder took place across the street at the Dakota apartment building, which was home to Lennon and Yoko Ono and has been the residence of other celebrities from Boris Karloff to Leonard Bernstein. The building's elaborate exterior is best admired from Central Park West, as visitors are not welcome in the lobby and there are no tours. ⊠ *Just off W. 72nd St., Central Park* ⊕ *www.centralparknyc. org* Ⓜ *B, C to 72nd St.*

Inwood

Well north of Harlem, at the very northern tip of Manhattan, Inwood is still essentially the *Upper* Upper West Side, with Fort Tryon Park lying just to its south.

👁 Sights

The Met Cloisters

MUSEUM | Perched on a wooded hill in Fort Tryon Park, near Manhattan's northwestern tip, the Cloisters museum and gardens houses part of the medieval collection of the Metropolitan Museum of Art and is a scenic destination in its own right. Colonnaded walks connect authentic French and Spanish monastic cloisters, a French Romanesque chapel, a 12th-century chapter house, and a Romanesque apse. One room is devoted to the 15th- and 16th-century *Unicorn Tapestries,* which date to 1500—a

388

must-see masterpiece of medieval mythology. The tomb effigies are another highlight. Two of the three enclosed gardens shelter more than 250 species of plants similar to those grown during the Middle Ages, including flowers, herbs, and medicinals; the third is an ornamental garden.

Concerts of medieval music are held regularly, and there are holiday concerts in December (concert tickets include same-day admission to the museum). The outdoor Trie Café is open 11 to 4:15 daily, from April to October, and serves sandwiches, coffee, and snacks. ✉ *99 Margaret Corbin Dr., Fort Tryon Park, Upper West Side ☎ 212/923-3700 ⊕ www.metmuseum.org ✉ $25 for 3-day ticket (includes Metropolitan Museum and Met Breuer); $25 suggested donation for New York State residents (full donation includes 3-day ticket to Metropolitan Museum and Met Breuer)* Ⓜ *A to 190th St.*

Chapter 13

HARLEM

Updated by
Tracy Hopkins

👁 Sights   🍴 Restaurants   🛏 Hotels   🛍 Shopping   🍸 Nightlife

★★☆☆☆   ★★★☆☆   ★☆☆☆☆   ★★☆☆☆   ★★★★☆

NEIGHBORHOOD SNAPSHOT

TOP EXPERIENCES

- Spending an evening at the iconic Apollo Theater
- Visiting the Schomburg Center for Research in Black Culture
- Shopping at Malcolm Shabazz Harlem Market
- Donning your Sunday best for jazz brunch at places like the Red Rooster

GETTING HERE

The 2 and 3 subway lines stop on Lenox Avenue; the 1 goes along Broadway, to the west; and the A, B, C, and D trains travel along St. Nicholas and 8th Avenues (note: the B train does not run on weekends). And yes, as the song goes, the A train is still usually "the quickest way to Harlem."

The city's north–south avenues take on different names in Harlem: 6th Avenue is called both Malcolm X Boulevard *and* Lenox Avenue; 7th Avenue is Adam Clayton Powell Jr. Boulevard (named for the influential minister and congressman); and 8th Avenue is Frederick Douglass Boulevard. West 125th Street, the major east–west street and Harlem's commercial center, is also known as Dr. Martin Luther King Jr. Boulevard.

PLANNING YOUR TIME

Harlem's simplest pleasures are free. Take time to walk the areas around Strivers' Row, Hamilton Heights, Sugar Hill, and 116th Street to see some impressive—and often fanciful—architecture. Hear the sweet sounds of a choir practice as you stroll by any of Harlem's churches (which number in the hundreds). Attend dynamic cultural programs, author talks, and film screenings at the Schomburg Center for Research in Black Culture, or visit the Morris-Jumel Mansion for a trip back in time to Colonial New York.

QUICK BITES

- **Levain Bakery.** From coffee and cakes to breads and sticky buns, this bakery has something for every sweet tooth. But it's famous for giant cookies like chocolate-chip walnut, oatmeal raisin, and dark-chocolate chocolate chip. ✉ *2167 Frederick Douglass Blvd., between 116th and 117th Sts.* ⊕ *www.levainbakery.com* Ⓜ *Subway: B, C to 116th St.*

- **Make My Cake.** Matriarch Josephine Smith, affectionately called "Ma Smith," infuses her cakes with southern baking traditions and a dash of Harlem soul. Highlights include German chocolate cake, red velvet cake, and sweet potato cheesecake. ✉ *2380 Adam Clayton Powell Jr. Blvd., at 139th St.* ⊕ *www.makemycake.com* Ⓜ *Subway: 2, 3, C to 135th St.*

- **Manhattanville Coffee.** It may be on a quiet corner, but this light-filled, modern coffee shop is always buzzing, appealing to laptop-toting locals with a large communal table, tufted leather couches, and free Wi-Fi. ✉ *142 Edgecombe Ave., at 142nd St.* ⊕ *www.manhattanvillecoffee.com* Ⓜ *Subway: A, B, C, D to 145th St.; B, C to 135th St.*

Harlem is known throughout the world as a vibrant center of African American culture, music, and life. The neighborhood invites visitors to see historic jewels such as the Apollo Theater, architecturally splendid churches and brownstones, and cultural magnets like the Schomburg Center for Research in Black Culture, as well as an ongoing list of new and renovated sites and buildings.

A stroll along Harlem's 125th Street reveals the electric energy of the neighborhood, from impromptu drum circles to a bustling farmers market to sidewalk vendors hawking bootleg DVDs, incense, and African shea butter. This east–west stretch is the heart of the neighborhood, and home to some of the best people-watching in Manhattan. Bill Clinton's New York office is at 55 West 125th Street, and the legendary Apollo Theater stands at No. 253. A large number of chains (Starbucks, Red Lobster, H&M) make it hard to distinguish 125th Street from the city's other heavily commercialized areas, but there are still a few things that set it apart: the wide number of languages spoken, the aroma of West African spices for sale, and stylish locals who take pride in their fashions.

To get a feel for Harlem, spend time visiting its past and present. On 116th Street, particularly between St. Nicholas and Lenox Avenues (aka Malcolm X Boulevard), you'll find some of the area's most interesting religious buildings, from ornate churches to a green-domed mosque. Along Lenox Avenue and Frederick Douglass Boulevard between 110th and 130th Streets are chic restaurants, bars, and a few boutiques offering everything from bespoke cocktails and live music to Harlem-inspired gifts and high-end menswear.

◉ Sights

Hamilton Grange National Memorial
HOUSE | FAMILY | Founding father Alexander Hamilton and his wife raised eight kids in this Federal-style country home, which he called his "sweet project." Once located on Hamilton's 32 acres, the Grange, named after his father's childhood home in Scotland, has moved three times since it was built in 1802. It now stands in St. Nicholas Park and gives a lesson in Hamilton's life, from his illegitimate birth in the West Indies and his appointment as the nation's first Secretary of the Treasury to his authorship of *The Federalist Papers*

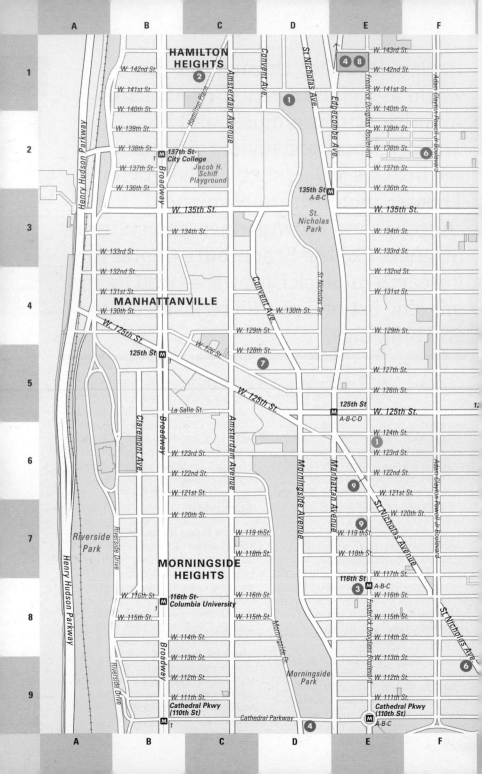

Harlem

KEY

1 Exploring Sights
1 Restaurants
1 Hotels

D.I.Y. Harlem Gospel Tours

Since 2000, the popularity of Sunday gospel tours has surged. While some in the community see it as an opportunity to broaden horizons and encourage diversity, others find tours disruptive and complain that tourists take seats away from regular parishioners (churches regularly fill to capacity). If you plan on attending a service, here are some tips:

Most churches have Sunday services at 11, but you may need to arrive as much as two hours early (depending on the church) to get in. Dress nicely (no shorts, sneakers, or jeans); be as quiet as possible; do not leave in the middle of the service; and do not take photos or videos or use your cell phone. Most important, remember that parishioners do not consider the service, or themselves, tourist attractions or entertainment.

A bus tour is generally an inauthentic (and more expensive) way to experience Harlem. Explore the neighborhood and churches on your own, or join a small tour like those led by **Harlem Heritage Tours**

(☎ 646/302 1575 ⊕ www.harlemheritage.com). Their tours (starting at $39) get high marks from past clients and are run by guides who were born and raised in Harlem. Groups are no larger than 25 people.

The following are some of the uptown churches with Sunday services:

Abyssinian Baptist Church (☎ 212/862–7474 ⊕ www.abyssinian. org) is one of the few churches that does not allow tour groups. Services for visitors are held at 11:30; arrive at least two hours ahead of time. **Canaan Baptist Church of Christ** (☎ 212/866–0301 ⊕ www.cbccnyc.org) has services at 10. **Convent Avenue Baptist Church** (☎ 212/234–6767 ⊕ www.conventchurch.org) has services at 7, 8, and 11. **First Corinthian Baptist Church** (☎ 212/864–5976 ⊕ www.fcbcnyc.org) has services at 7:30, 9:30, and 11:30. **Greater Refuge Temple** (☎ 212/866–1700 ⊕ www. greaterrefugetemple.org) has services at 11 and 4. **Memorial Baptist Church** (☎ 212/663–8830 ⊕ www.mbcvisionharlem.org) has services at 10.

and his death following a duel with Vice President Aaron Burr. The house's ground floor, formerly servants' quarters, hosts an interactive exhibit that includes a short film on Hamilton's life. Upstairs a parlor, study, dining room, and two guest rooms are open to view; note the beautiful piano, which belonged to his daughter Angelica. Self-guided tours of the furnished rooms can be made noon–1 and 3–4 only; 30-minute ranger-led tours are given at 10, 11, 2, and 4. ⊠ 414 W. 141st St., between St. Nicholas and Convent Aves., Harlem ☎ 646/548–2310 ⊕ www. nps.gov/hagr ⌨ Free ☉ Closed Mon.,

Tues. Ⓜ 1 to 137th St.–City College; A, B, C, D to 145th St.

Hamilton Heights

NEIGHBORHOOD | To envision this neighborhood's Harlem Renaissance days, walk down tree-lined Convent Avenue and cross over to **Hamilton Terrace** to see a time capsule of elegant stone row houses in mint condition. One of the neighborhood's most beautiful blocks, it's popular with film and TV crews. The **Hamilton Grange National Memorial,** founding father Alexander Hamilton's Federal-style mansion, is located at the southern end of the block, on 141st Street. Turn west

The Studio Museum features contemporary art by African American, Caribbean, and African artists.

and continue down Convent Avenue to see the looming Gothic spires (1905) of **City College.** Next, head east to visit **Strivers' Row.** ✉ *Convent Ave. between 135th and 150th Sts., Harlem* Ⓜ *A, B, C, D to 145th St.*

Masjid Malcolm Shabazz (*Mosque*)
RELIGIOUS SITE | Talk about religious conversions: in the mid-1960s, the Lenox Casino was transformed into this house of worship and cultural center, and given bright yellow arches and a huge, green onion dome that loudly proclaims its presence in a neighborhood of churches. Once functioning as Temple No. 7 under the Nation of Islam with a message of black nationalism, the mosque was bombed after the assassination of Malcolm X, who had preached here. It was then rebuilt and renamed in honor of the name Malcolm took at the end of his life, El-Hajj Malik Shabazz; its philosophy now is one of inclusion. To attend services, requests must be made in advance by writing to *msmosque@aol.com.*

These days the Sunni congregation has a large proportion of immigrants from Senegal, many of whom live in and around 116th Street. Next door is Graceline Court, a 16-story luxury condominium building that cantilevers somewhat awkwardly over the mosque. ✉ *102 W. 116th St., at Lenox Ave. (Malcolm X Blvd.), Harlem* ☎ *212/662–2200* 🏛 *themasjidmalcolmshabazz.com* Ⓜ *2, 3 to 116th St.*

Morris-Jumel Mansion
HOUSE | FAMILY | During the Revolutionary War, General Washington used this wooden, pillared 8,500-square-foot house (1765) as his headquarters, and when he visited as president in 1790, he brought along John Quincy Adams, Thomas Jefferson, and Alexander Hamilton. Inside rooms are furnished with period decorations; upstairs, keep an eye out for the hand-painted wallpaper (original to the house) and a "commode chair," stuck in a corner of the dressing room. Outside, behind the house, is a Colonial-era marker that says it's 11 miles to New York—a reminder of what a small

sliver of Manhattan the city was at that time. West of the house is the block-long Sylvan Terrace, a row of crisp two-story clapboard houses built in 1882. ⊠ *65 Jumel Terr., north of 160th St., between St. Nicholas and Edgecombe Aves., Harlem ☎ 212/923–8008 ⊕ www.morrisjumel.org 🖾 $10; guided tour $12 ☉ Closed Mon. Ⓜ C to 163rd St.*

Schomburg Center for Research in Black Culture

LIBRARY | Founded in 1925 and named a National Historic Landmark in 2017, the Schomburg Center for Research in Black Culture is one of the world's leading cultural institutions devoted to the research, preservation, and exhibition of materials focused on African American, African Diaspora, and African experiences. Established with the collections of Arturo Alfonso Schomburg, this research division of the New York Public Library features diverse programming and collections of over 11 million items that illuminate the richness of global black history, arts, and culture. Check the website for the latest exhibitions here. The Schomburg also serves the Harlem community as a space that encourages lifelong education and exploration. ⊠ *515 Lenox Ave. (Malcolm X Blvd.), between 135th and 136th Sts., Harlem ☎ 917/275–6975 ⊕ www.nypl.org/locations/schomburg ☉ Closed Sun. Ⓜ 2, 3 to 135th St.*

Strivers' Row

NEIGHBORHOOD | This block of gorgeous 1890s Georgian and Italian Renaissance Revival homes earned its nickname in the 1920s from less affluent Harlemites who felt its residents were "striving" to become well-to-do. Some of the few remaining private service alleys, used when deliveries arrived via horse and cart, lie behind these houses and are visible through iron gates. Note the gatepost between Nos. 251 and 253 on 138th Street that reads, "Private Road. Walk Your Horses." These houses were built by the contractor David H. King Jr.,

whose works also include the base for the Statue of Liberty and the oldest parts of the Cathedral Church of St. John the Divine. When the houses failed to sell to whites, the properties on these blocks were sold to African American doctors, lawyers, and other professionals; composers and musicians W. C. Handy and Eubie Blake were also among the residents. If you have the time, detour a block north to see the palazzo-style group of houses designed by Stanford White, on the north side of 139th Street. ⊠ *138th and 139th Sts., between Adam Clayton Powell Jr. and Frederick Douglass Blvds., Harlem Ⓜ B, C to 135th St.; A, B, C, D to 145th St.*

★ Studio Museum in Harlem

MUSEUM | Contemporary art by African American, Caribbean, and African artists is the focus of this small museum with a light-filled sculpture garden. Three artists in residence present their works each year, and lively Uptown Fridays! in summer feature DJs, cocktails, and a fashionable crowd. The gift shop is small but packs a punch; don't miss its fantastic collection of coffee-table books. ⊠ *144 W. 125th St., between Lenox Ave. (Malcolm X Blvd.) and Adam Clayton Powell Jr. Blvd., Harlem ☎ 212/864–4500 ⊕ www.studiomuseum.org 🖾 $7 suggested donation (free Sun.) ☉ Closed Mon.–Wed. Ⓜ 2, 3, A, B, C, D to 125th St.*

Sugar Hill

NEIGHBORHOOD | Standing on the bluff of Sugar Hill overlooking Jackie Robinson Park, outside the slightly run-down **409 Edgecombe Avenue,** you'd never guess that here resided such influential African Americans as NAACP founder W.E.B. DuBois and Supreme Court Justice Thurgood Marshall, or that farther north at **555 Edgecombe** (known as the "Triple Nickel") writers Langston Hughes and Zora Neale Hurston and jazz musicians Duke Ellington, Count Basie, and others lived, wrote, and played. It's also here that for more than 20 years musician Marjorie

Harlem's Jazz Age

It was in Harlem that Billie Holiday got her first singing job, Duke Ellington made his first recording, and Louis Armstrong was propelled to stardom. Jazz was king during the Harlem Renaissance in the 1920s and '30s, and though Chicago and New Orleans may duke it out for the "birthplace of jazz" title, New York was where jazz musicians came to be heard.

In the 1920s, socialites made the journey uptown to Harlem's Cotton Club and Connie's Inn (131st Street and 7th Avenue) to hear "black" music. Both clubs were white-owned and barred blacks from entering, except as performers. (The rules changed years later.) Connie's introduced New Yorkers to Louis Armstrong. The Cotton Club—Harlem's most popular nightspot by far—booked such big names as Fletcher Henderson, Coleman Hawkins, Duke Ellington, Cab Calloway, and Ethel Waters. After shows ended at the paying clubs, musicians would head to after-hours establishments with black patrons, such as Small's Paradise, Minton's Playhouse (which reopened in 2013), and Basement Brownies, where they'd hammer out new riffs into the wee hours.

Eliot has been hosting jazz concerts in her apartment (3F) at 3:30 pm every Sunday. Farther down, at No. 345, you can't miss the **Benzinger House** with its flared mansard roof. Amid all this history, the modern-looking **Sugar Hill Children's Museum of Art & Storytelling,** at 155th Street and St. Nicholas Avenue, gathers local families for programs that encourage the creative spirit of children. ✉ *From 145th to 155th St., between Edgecombe and St. Nicholas Aves., Harlem* [M] *A, B, C, D to 145th St.*

Swing Low: Harriet Tubman Memorial
PUBLIC ART | FAMILY | *Swing Low,* a bronze statue of abolitionist Harriet Tubman rising from a traffic triangle at the crossroads of St. Nicholas Avenue, West 122nd Street, and Frederick Douglass Boulevard, was created in 2007 by sculptor Alison Saar. Inspired by West African "passport" masks, the striking monument incorporates the faces of "anonymous passengers" of the Underground Railroad in Tubman's skirt. The granite base includes bronze tiles that depict pivotal events in Tubman's life and traditional quilting patterns. ✉ *Crossroads of St. Nicholas Ave., 122nd St., and Frederick Douglass Blvd., Harlem* 🌐 *www.nycgovparks.org* [M] *A, B, C, D to 125th St.; 2, 3 to 116th St.*

🍴 Restaurants

Harlem culinary renaissance? Yes, indeed. This historic northern neighborhood has seen an infusion of fantastic restaurants since 2010. There are still the standby southern and soul-food restaurants but also newer arrivals, making your journey here even more worthwhile.

BLVD Bistro
$$ | AMERICAN | Chef Carlos Swepson puts a contemporary spin on classic American soul food with down-home dishes like biscuits and sausage gravy, jumbo shrimp and grits, turkey meat loaf, seven-cheese macaroni, and fried chicken sliders. Owned and operated by Swepson and his wife, Markisha, the casual yet smart eatery is on the ground floor of a renovated brownstone. **Known for:** busy brunch scene; friendly and attentive waitstaff; homemade buttermilk biscuits. [$] *Average main: $22* ✉ *239 Lenox Ave.*

(Malcolm X Blvd.), at 122nd St., Harlem ☎ 212/678-6200 ⊕ boulevardbistrony. com ⊘ Closed Mon. Ⓜ 2, 3 to 125th St.

Harlem Shake

$ | AMERICAN | FAMILY | This festive, family-friendly burger joint on the bustling, brownstone-lined corner of 124th Street and Lenox Avenue has a retro malt-shop interior adorned with headshots of African American entertainers and vintage Jet magazine covers. The eatery's name is a clever take on the dance craze that went viral, and also gives a nod to its rich organic milk shakes—like the decadent Red Velvet, made with real cake and Blue Marble ice cream. Known for: tasty fries including jerk, sweet yam, and chili-cheese; open-mic nights on Friday; annual Miss and Mr. Harlem Shake contest. Ⓢ Average main: $8 ✉ 100 W. 124th St., at Lenox Ave. (Malcolm X Blvd.), Harlem ☎ 212/222-8300 ⊕ www.harlem-shakenyc.com Ⓜ 2, 3 to 125th St.

LoLo's Seafood Shack

$$ | CARIBBEAN | Helmed by husband-and-wife team executive chef Raymond Mohan and restaurateur Leticia Young, LoLo's offers a mash-up of island and New England beach grub from seafood boils and steam pots to fish-fry and crab-cake baskets with garlic fries. Old-school rap and soul album covers affixed to the wall in the front waiting area add urban flair to the otherwise minimalist decor of this "lolo"—the Caribbean name for a small traditional restaurant that serves local cuisine. Known for: daily happy hour with $5 food specials; warm-weather backyard patio with picnic tables; crowd-pleasing rum punch. Ⓢ Average main: $16 ✉ 303 W. 116th St., between Frederick Douglass Blvd. and Manhattan Ave., Harlem ☎ 646/649-3356 ⊕ www.lolosseafoodshack.com Ⓜ 2, 3, B, C to 116th St.

Miss Mamie's Spoonbread Too

$$ | AMERICAN | FAMILY | From uptown church ladies to former president Bill Clinton, Miss Mamie's Spoonbread Too attracts a diverse clientele with a common goal—to enjoy a hearty helping of comforting soul food. The uncluttered interior is mostly beige, with family portraits hanging on the walls, and former model and best-selling cookbook author Norma Jean Darden satisfies her patrons with mouthwatering passed-down recipies like fried or smothered chicken, fried or baked catfish, barbecue ribs, collard greens, and baked macaroni and cheese. Known for: longtime neighborhood favorite; tempting desserts from sweet potato pie to peach cobbler; Miss Mamie's sampler platter (for those who can't decide). Ⓢ Average main: $20 ✉ 366 W. 110th St., between Columbus and Manhattan Aves., Harlem ☎ 212/865-0700 ⊕ spoonbreadinc.com ⊘ No lunch weekdays Ⓜ B, C to Cathedral Pkwy.–110th St.

★ Red Rooster Harlem

$$$ | AMERICAN | Marcus Samuelsson, who earned his celebrity chefdom at Aquavit in Midtown for his take on Ethiopian-accented Scandinavian cuisine (fusing the food of his birthplace with that of where he grew up), moved to Harlem in 2010, creating a culinary hot spot in this casual, jazzy-looking space with wall murals, wooden tables, and bistro chairs. The comfort-food menu reflects the ethnic diversity of modern-day New York City, from jerk chicken to braised short ribs. Known for: lines for Sunday brunch with gospel music; veal meatballs with potato hash and lingonberry sauce; prix-fixe lunch option. Ⓢ Average main: $32 ✉ 310 Lenox Ave. (Malcolm X Blvd.), between 125th and 126th Sts., Harlem ☎ 212/792-9001 ⊕ www.redroosterharlem.com Ⓜ 2, 3 to 125th St.

Seasoned Vegan

$$ | VEGETARIAN | At this East Harlem vegan and raw eatery, you won't be tempted to ask "Where's the beef?" Mother-and-son team Brenda and Aaron Beener take tasty comfort food staples and "veganize" them: for example, the

raw lasagna consists of raw zucchini, spinach, cashew cheese, and marinara sauce; the barbecue riblets are a blend of lotus root and fermented soy; and the po'boy sandwich is made with fried yam or burdock root protein that mimics shrimp or crawfish, respectively. **Known for:** global vegan flavors; weekend late-night menu after 10 pm; colorful artwork-adorned walls. *$ Average main: $17* ⊠ *55 St. Nicholas Ave., at 113th St., Harlem* ☎ *212/222–0092* ⊕ *www. seasonedvegan.com* ⊙ *Closed Mon. No lunch weekdays* Ⓜ *2, 3 to Central Park North–110th St.; B, C to Cathedral Pkwy.–110th St.*

Sushi Inoue

$$$$ | SUSHI | At this eponymous eatery from chef Shinichi Inoue (who earned a Michelin star at Sushi Azabu in TriBeCa), little details lurk: he makes two types of rice (one for heavier fish and one for lighter), just as he makes lighter and heavier soy sauces. And the chef hand-grates real wasabi for the ultrafresh sushi and sashimi this place is devoted to exclusively, whether you choose the various *omakase* options or à la carte items. **Known for:** bluefin tuna tasting menu; expensive omakase options; exquisite attention to details. *$ Average main: $100* ⊠ *381 Lenox Ave (Malcolm X Blvd.), at 129th St., Harlem* ☎ *646/766–0555* ⊕ *www.sushiinoueharlem.com* ⊙ *Closed Mon. No lunch* Ⓜ *2, 3 to 125th St.*

Sylvia's

$$ | SOUTHERN | FAMILY | A Harlem mainstay, Sylvia's has been serving soul-food favorites like smothered chicken, barbecue ribs, collard greens, and mashed potatoes to a dedicated crowd of locals, tourists, and college students since 1962. Owner Sylvia Woods may have passed on in 2012, but her restaurant and signature sauces, jarred and sold online and in the restaurant, are more popular than ever. **Known for:** Sunday gospel brunch; famous smothered chicken;

cornmeal-dusted cafish. *$ Average main: $24* ⊠ *328 Lenox Ave. (Malcolm X Blvd.), near 127th St., Harlem* ☎ *212/996–0660* ⊕ *www.sylviasrestaurant.com* Ⓜ *2, 3 to 125th St.*

Vinatería

$$$ | ITALIAN | Proprietor Yvette Leeper Bueno and chef Mimi Weissenborn offer a thoughtful menu of Spanish- and Italian-influenced seasonal dishes, along with a welcoming atmosphere and sustainable design. The Mediterranean-focused wine list contains some unique finds and is accessibly priced but carefully curated, complementing menu highlights including spicy veal meatballs, black spaghetti with octopus and scallops, and pan-seared scallops with crispy pork belly. **Known for:** intentionally sourced by-the-glass and good value wine options; romantic, date-night ambience; seafood, pasta, and meat dishes that pair well with wine. *$ Average main: $26* ⊠ *2211 Frederick Douglass Blvd., between 119th and 120th Sts., Harlem* ☎ *212/662–8462* ⊕ *www.vinaterianyc. com* ⊙ *Closed Wed., Thurs. No lunch Mon., Tues., Fri.* Ⓜ *B, C to 116th St.*

🛏 Hotels

Aloft Harlem

$ | HOTEL | A reasonably priced option in an increasingly popular area of Harlem (Marcus Samuelsson's hot Red Rooster restaurant is nearby), this branch of the Aloft chain delivers with cheerful service and a fun atmosphere. **Pros:** good room size for the price; convenient to subways; ever-increasing local shopping and dining options. **Cons:** rooms have minimal space for hanging clothes; rooms get some street noise; far from city's main tourist attractions. *$ Rooms from: $169* ⊠ *2296 Frederick Douglass Blvd., between 123th and 124th Sts., Harlem* ☎ *212/749–4000* ⊕ *www.aloftharlem.com* ⇆ *124 rooms* ⊙ *No meals* Ⓜ *A, B, C, D to 125th St.*

▼ Nightlife

BARS

Corner Social

BARS/PUBS | With nearly 20 beers on tap, sports on big screens, and bar food that's anything but boring (everything from a raw bar to shrimp macaroni and cheese), it's no surprise that this neighborhood favorite is packed on weekends. In warm weather an outdoor patio gives you a front-row seat to the scene on Lenox Avenue. ✉ 321 Lenox Ave. (Malcolm X Blvd.), at 126th St., Harlem ☎ 212/510–8552 ⊕ www.cornersocialnyc.com Ⓜ 2, 3 to 125th St.

Cove Lounge

BARS/PUBS | This sophisticated, sleek bi-level dining and nightlife venue is known for its mix of Caribbean and southern-inspired cuisine. Well-heeled regulars flock here for Sunday brunch (shrimp and grits, or fried chicken and red velvet waffle), but it's also popular for late-night noshing, listening to live DJs, and sipping specialty cocktails. ✉ 325 Lenox Ave. (Malcolm X Blvd.), between 126th and 127th Sts., Harlem ☎ 212/222–5708 ⊕ www.covelounge.com Ⓜ 2, 3 to 125th St.

Ginny's Supperclub

BARS/PUBS | Head downstairs from Marcus Samuelsson's renowned Red Rooster restaurant and find yourself in a glamorous lounge that seems right out of the 1920s. The cocktails are classic with a modern flair, and there is live music and/or DJs throughout the week, as well as a Sunday gospel brunch. Walk-ins are welcome, but advance reservations are recommended. ✉ 310 Lenox Ave. (Malcolm X Blvd.), at 125th St., Harlem ☎ 212/421–3821 ⊕ www.ginnyssupperclub.com Ⓜ 2, 3 to 125th St.

Harlem Hops

BARS/PUBS | Launched by three graduates of historically black colleges, this cozy pub specializes in "beer, booze, bites, and beats." The menu is casual (bites include a Bavarian soft pretzel, craft beer bratwurst, and cheesy lobster pie) and pairs well with an accessible collection of innovative small-batch beers. ✉ 2268 Adam Clayton Powell Jr. Blvd., between 133rd and 134th Sts., Harlem ☎ 646/998–3444 ⊕ harlemhops.com Ⓜ 2, 3 to 135th St.

Harlem Public

BARS/PUBS | A juicy burger, live music, and more than a dozen craft beers on tap make this the type of neighborhood watering hole every New Yorker wants on their corner. Plenty of stools fill the sprawling space, along with a scattering of tables on the sidewalk during warm weather. It's an unfussy spot to raise a glass after a day of exploring vibrant Harlem. ✉ 3612 Broadway, at 149th St., Harlem ☎ 212/939–9404 ⊕ www.harlem-public.com Ⓜ 1, A, B, C, D to 145th St.

Shrine

BARS/PUBS | It doesn't look like much from the outside, but this bar and small performance venue with a global slant hosts multiple events each night, including live music, DJs, spoken word, and dance. These days there's usually a crush of out-of-towners during showtimes, but the music remains stellar and the establishment itself is the stuff of legend. ✉ 2271 Adam Clayton Powell Jr. Blvd., between 133rd and 134th Sts., Harlem ☎ 212/690–7807 ⊕ www.shrinenyc.com Ⓜ 2, 3 to 135th St.

Solomon & Kuff Rum Hall

BARS/PUBS | Well-heeled locals flock to this large, hip industrial-style bar and restaurant with Caribbean-leaning cuisine, an ample rum selection (more than 100 choices), DJ nights, and a festive weekday happy hour. ✉ 2331 12th Ave., at 133rd St., Harlem ☎ 212/283–1819 ⊕ www.solomonandkuff.com Ⓜ 1 to 137th St.–City College.

JAZZ VENUES

Minton's Playhouse

MUSIC CLUBS | The jazz institution that once featured big-name performers such as Dizzy Gillespie and Duke Ellington is now a sophisticated supper club with a roster of house-band jazz performers and featured musicians. The southern-revival food is garnering acclaim (the kitchen is shared with the Cecil Steakhouse next door). It's not a cheap night out (or weekend brunch), but worth the splurge. Patrons should dress to impress; reservations are recommended. ⊠ *206 W. 118th St., near Adam Clayton Powell Jr. Blvd., Harlem* ☎ *212/243–2222* ⊕ *www.mintonsharlem.com* Ⓜ *2, 3, B, C to 116th St.*

🎭 Performing Arts

FILM

Maysles Documentary Center

FILM | Founded by legendary filmmaker Albert Maysles, this snug theater showcases an array of independent documentary films as well as panel discussions. ⊠ *343 Lenox Ave. (Malcolm X Blvd.), between 127th and 128th Sts., Harlem* ☎ *212/537–6843* ⊕ *www.maysles.org* Ⓜ *2, 3 to 125th St.*

MUSIC

Apollo Theater

MUSIC | Michael Jackson, Ella Fitzgerald, and James Brown are just a few of the world-class performers who have appeared on this equally famed stage, which first opened back in 1934. If the Apollo's Amateur Night doesn't get you up to 125th Street on a Wednesday, consider the theater's Thursday comedy night and the intimate late-night music series, Apollo Music Café, on select Friday and Saturday nights, featuring a variety of jazz, pop, hip-hop, and rock performers. ⊠ *253 W. 125th St., between Frederick Douglass and Adam Clayton Powell Jr. Blvds., Harlem* ☎ *212/531–5300, 800/745–3000 for tickets* ⊕ *www.apollotheater.org* Ⓜ *2, 3, A, B, C, D to 125th St.*

PERFORMANCE CENTERS

Harlem Stage

ARTS CENTERS | Set in a perfectly restored landmark built in 1890 as part of the Croton Aqueduct system, Harlem Stage is a cozy 200-seat venue for jazz music, theater, and dance. ⊠ *The Gatehouse, 150 Convent Ave., at 135th St., Harlem* ☎ *212/281–9240* ⊕ *www.harlemstage.org* Ⓜ *B, C to 135th St.; 1 to 137th St.–City College.*

🛍 Shopping

Fashionable New Yorkers and visitors alike flock to Harlem for custom-made hats, eclectic mom-and-pop shops, imported crafts and jewelry, and creative gift items.

CLOTHING

Harlem Haberdashery

CLOTHING | Home goods, accessories, and ready-to-wear fashions from shoes to jackets for men and women are handsomely displayed in the former home of civil rights leader Malcolm X. The bespoke boutique is owned and operated by celebrity tailor Guy Wood Sr. (also known for 5001 Flavors, his custom clothing company) and his wife, Sharene. Harlem Haberdashery makes it a family affair by carrying limited collections designed by the couple's adult children and Sharene's brother. ⊠ *245 Lenox Ave. (Malcolm X Blvd.), at 122nd St., Harlem* ☎ *646/707–0070* ⊕ *www.harlemhaberdashery.com* Ⓜ *2, 3 to 125th St.*

GIFTS AND SOUVENIRS

NiLu

GIFTS/SOUVENIRS | Owned and operated by husband-and-wife team Mark and Katrina Parris, NiLu specializes in locally made home goods and furnishings, apparel, books, and crafts. The Harlem residents named the kitschy gift shop after their two sons, Nigel and Luke. The couple emphasizes fair trade products and is dedicated to showcasing the rich culture, artistry, and unique attributes of

Harlem and other special places around the world. ⊠ *191 Lenox Ave. (Malcolm X Blvd.), between 119th and 120th Sts., Harlem* ☎ *646/964–4926* ⊕ *shopnilu.com* Ⓜ *2, 3 to 116th St.*

JEWELRY AND ACCESSORIES
Calabar Imports Harlem
JEWELRY/ACCESSORIES | Sister store to the original Calabar Imports in Crown Heights, Brooklyn, the shop offers stylish, eclectic, and affordable clothing, accessories, jewelry, home decor, and gifts from West Africa, Southeast Asia, and South America. Owned and operated by mother-and-daughter entrepreneurs Heloise Oton and Atim Annette Oton, it also hosts art exhibits, dance and meditation workshops, trunk shows, pop-up shops, holiday markets, and other community events. ⊠ *2504 Frederick Douglass Blvd., at 129th St., Harlem* ☎ *646/964–5062* ⊕ *www.calabar-imports. com* Ⓜ *A, B, C, D to 125th St.*

Hats. By Bunn
JEWELRY/ACCESSORIES | Master milliner Mr. Bunn caters to a fashion-forward clientele who want "classic originals made for all seasons." The former shoemaker's coveted handcrafted caps, fedoras, derbies, bowlers, and sun hats for men and women are suited to any occasion—from Easter Sunday to supper club—and come in a variety of colors and materials. ⊠ *2283 Adam Clayton Powell Jr. Blvd., between 134th and 135th Sts., Harlem* ☎ *212/694–3590* ⊕ *hatsbybunn.com* Ⓜ *2, 3 to 135th St.*

MARKETS
Malcolm Shabazz Harlem Market
OUTDOOR/FLEA/GREEN MARKETS | FAMILY | This canopied marketplace offers an array of funky African and African-inspired jewelry, Afrocentric art and wood carvings, and festive clothing and fabrics peddled by vendors hailing from countries like Senegal, Nigeria, Kenya, and Ghana. On weekends with nice weather, more vendors open. It's a one-stop shopping experience: patrons can also groove to global tunes, sample traditional African cuisine, or get their hair braided. ⊠ *52 W. 116th St., between Lenox (Malcolm X Blvd.) and 5th Aves., Harlem* Ⓜ *2, 3 to 116th St.*

Chapter 14

BROOKLYN

Updated by
Giulia Pines

👁 **Sights**
★★★☆☆

🍴 **Restaurants**
★★★★★

🏨 **Hotels**
★★☆☆☆

🛍 **Shopping**
★★★☆☆

🍸 **Nightlife**
★★★★☆

NEIGHBORHOOD SNAPSHOT

TOP EXPERIENCES

- Eating and barhopping in Williamsburg
- Screaming at the top of the Cyclone roller coaster in Coney Island
- Smelling the roses, and everything else, at the Brooklyn Botanic Garden
- Catching a show at BAM or Barclays Center
- Walking across the Brooklyn Bridge
- Picnicking in Brooklyn Bridge Park
- Being awestruck by architecture in Brooklyn Heights or street art in Bushwick

GETTING HERE

Brooklyn is very accessible by subway from Manhattan; check the listings for subway info. Brooklyn Heights, Downtown Brooklyn, DUMBO, and Williamsburg are the closest neighborhoods to Manhattan. Coney Island and Brighton Beach are the farthest; budget about an hour each way if you're traveling from Midtown.

MAKING THE MOST OF YOUR TIME

You can't "see" Brooklyn in a day or even two, so don't even try. Focus on the neighborhoods and attractions that interest you most. The most picturesque way to get to Brooklyn is by its most majestic bridge. Walking along the wooden pedestrian path of the Brooklyn Bridge—a classic New York experience—takes about 30 or 40 minutes, worth it for the panoramic views of the skylines and the harbor. The path is almost always crowded, unless you go early in the morning. Exit the bridge onto Cadman Plaza on the Brooklyn side, then walk southwest to get to Brooklyn Heights, a charming neighborhood of 19th-century brownstone homes, or walk north into the hip neighborhood of DUMBO.

QUICK BITES

- **Almondine Bakery.** The best French bakery this side of Montmartre is on Water Street. You'll find excellent chocolate raspberry croissants, mille-feuille, macarons, and pear tarts, as well as baguettes, quiche, and sandwiches. ✉ *85 Water St., DUMBO* ⊕ *www.almondinebakery.com* Ⓜ *Subway: F to York St.*

- **Jacques Torres Chocolate.** Torres, from France, is New York's adopted Willy Wonka. He dishes out drool-worthy truffles and bonbons, and hot chocolate rich enough to make a Swiss miss blush. The shop has a café if you want to eat in. ✉ *66 Water St., DUMBO* ⊕ *www.mrchocolate.com* Ⓜ *Subway: A, C to High St.; F to York St.*

- **Juliana's.** Skip the lines at Grimaldi's and walk next door, where you'll find what many Brooklynites think of as the "real" Grimaldi's, offering deliciously charred New York–style coal-oven pizza, made by a master pizzaiolo in a brick oven that is generations old. ✉ *19 Old Fulton St., DUMBO* ⊕ *julianaspizza.com* Ⓜ *Subway: F to York St.*

Hardly Manhattan's sidekick, Brooklyn is a destination in its own right, with many diverse neighborhoods and a seemingly endless number of compelling sights and fabulous places to eat and drink and shop.

Across the East River from Manhattan, on Long Island's western edge, Brooklyn is one of New York City's five boroughs. At 71 square miles, it's more than three times the size of Manhattan, and with more than 2½ million people, if it were a city it would be the fourth largest in the United States, in terms of population. Brooklyn *was* a city until the end of the 19th century, with its own widely circulated newspaper (*The Brooklyn Eagle*), its own expansive park (Prospect Park), and its own baseball team that would eventually be called the Brooklyn Dodgers. In 1883 it also got its own bridge, the Brooklyn Bridge, which drew the attention of the entire country.

Brooklyn Heights and **DUMBO** are easily accessible from Manhattan by subway or via the Brooklyn Bridge; both neighborhoods have compelling but very different architecture (brownstones versus 19th-century warehouses) and fabulous views of Manhattan. **Carroll Gardens, Cobble Hill, Boerum Hill,** and **Fort Greene** all have plenty of lovely streets to stroll with thriving restaurant and bar scenes. The latter also has the Brooklyn Academy of Music. **Williamsburg** is the epicenter of trendsetting Brooklyn, which is overflowing into up-and-coming **Bushwick** and **East Williamsburg. Park Slope** and **Prospect Park** welcome with laid-back, family-friendly activities, while **Prospect Heights** and **Crown Heights** are home to heavy hitters like the Barclays Center,

the Brooklyn Botanic Garden, Weeksville Heritage Center, and the Brooklyn Children's Museum. **Coney Island** and **Brighton Beach** have Brooklyn's subway-accessible beaches, boardwalks, and amusement parks, including the legendary Cyclone roller coaster.

Brooklyn Heights

Brooklyn Heights is quintessential "brownstone Brooklyn." It's the oldest neighborhood in the borough, and the original village of Brooklyn; almost the entire neighborhood is part of the Brooklyn Heights Historic District. This is still very much the neighborhood of shady lanes, cobblestone streets, centuries-old row houses, and landmark buildings that Walt Whitman rhapsodized about, and the magnificent postcard views of the Manhattan skyline and the Brooklyn Bridge have inspired countless artists and photographers since. In the early to mid-20th century, Brooklyn Heights was a bohemian haven, home to such writers as Arthur Miller, Truman Capote, Henry Miller, Alfred Kazin, Carson McCullers, Paul Bowles, Marianne Moore, Norman Mailer, and W.E.B. DuBois.

The majestic **Brooklyn Bridge** has one foot in Brooklyn Heights, near DUMBO, and a walk across it either to or from Lower Manhattan is one of the classic New York experiences.

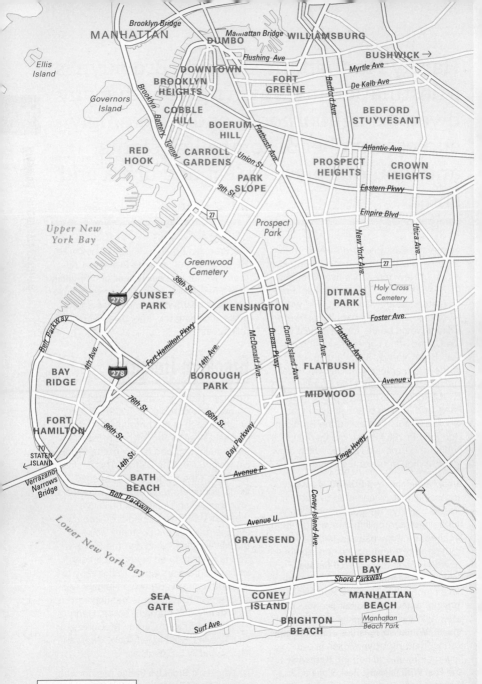

Brooklyn

Brooklyn Is Book Country ◉

Brooklyn has been a mecca for writers and literature since the days of *Uncle Tom's Cabin*, written by a preacher's daughter in Brooklyn Heights. Since then, writers have flocked here for the cheap rent and quiet streets. Henry Miller, Norman Mailer, Truman Capote, Arthur Miller (with Marilyn Monroe), Paul and Jane Bowles, Carson McCullers, James Purdy, and Walt Whitman created more than one masterpiece here.

Today, amid the gentrification, Brooklyn continues to lure famous and near-famous writers and musicians from all over the world.

Perhaps reflecting the plethora of writers in the neighborhood, the borough has a relatively high density of both used and new bookstores, and also several small presses, including Melville House, a publisher with a storefront.

And with all these writers so close by, it only makes sense that Brooklyn has a fabulous book festival, to boot. The Brooklyn Book Festival happens every year at Borough Hall, on the third weekend in September. Authors gather for readings and signings, and independent publishers display their wares.

◉ Sights

★ Brooklyn Bridge (Brooklyn Entrance)

BRIDGE/TUNNEL | While the majority of tourists usually walk across the Brooklyn Bridge from Manhattan, you'll get better views if you enter and walk from the Brooklyn side. It's a suprisingly long walk of more than a mile that normally takes about 40 minutes, but the exhilarating views are good payment for your exercise. Since many office workers (and bicyclists) commute this way, the walkway is particularly busy during the morning rush hour from 7 to 9 am and in the afternoon from 4 to 6. It's most magical and quietest in the early morning, but while you won't be able to avoid the crowds, it's worth the trip at sunset in the summer, when the lights of Manhattan come to life after 8. There are two pedestrian access points for the bridge on the Brooklyn side. One is at the intersection of Tillary Street and Boerum Place; the second is the Washington Street underpass, which leads to a staircase up to the walkway. ⊠ *Brooklyn Heights* Ⓜ *A, C to High St.; F to York St.; 2, 3 to Clark St.*

Brooklyn Borough Hall

BUILDING | Built in 1848 as Brooklyn's city hall, this Greek Revival landmark, adorned with Tuckahoe marble, is one of the borough's handsomest buildings. The statue of Justice atop its cast-iron cupola was part of the original plan but wasn't installed until 1988. Today the building serves as the office of Brooklyn's borough president and the home of the Brooklyn Tourism & Visitors Center ⊠ *209 Joralemon St., Brooklyn Heights* ☎ *718/802–3700* ⊕ *www.explorebk. com* ⊗ *Closed weekends* Ⓜ *2, 3, 4, 5 to Borough Hall; R to Court St.; A, C, F, R to Jay St.–MetroTech.*

★ Brooklyn Bridge Park

CAROUSEL | **FAMILY** | This sweeping feat of green urban renewal stretches from the Manhattan Bridge in DUMBO to the Brooklyn Bridge and south all the way to Pier 6, carpeting old industrial sites along the waterfront with scenic esplanades and lush meadows. The park has playgrounds, sports fields, food concessions, the wonderfully restored Jane's Carousel, and lots of grass for lounging. You can access the park at various points; just head down the hill toward the East River and you can't miss it. ⊠ *Brooklyn waterfront, Brooklyn Heights* ☎ *718/222–9939* ⊕ *www.brooklynbridgepark.org* Ⓜ *2, 3 to Clark St.; A, C to High St.; F to York St.*

★ Brooklyn Heights Promenade

PROMENADE | FAMILY | Strolling this mile-long path, famous for its magnificent Manhattan views, you might find it surprising to learn that its origins were purely functional: the promenade was built as a sound barrier to protect nearby brownstones from highway noise. Find a bench and take in the skyline, the Statue of Liberty, and the Brooklyn Bridge; in the evening, the lights of Manhattan sparkle across the East River. Below are the Brooklyn–Queens Expressway and Brooklyn Bridge Park. ⊠ *Between Remsen and Cranberry Sts., Brooklyn Heights* Ⓜ *2, 3 to Clark St.; A, C to High St.; R to Court St.*

★ Brooklyn Historical Society

HISTORIC SITE | Four centuries' worth of art and artifacts bring Brooklyn's story to life at this marvelous space. Housed in an 1881 Queen Anne–style National Historic Landmark building, the society surveys the borough's changing identity through interactive exhibitions, landscape paintings, photographs, portraits of Brooklynites, and fascinating memorabilia. The gift shop features an eclectic assortment of Brooklyn-themed books and tchotchkes. Stop by the society's second location in DUMBO's Empire Stores (55 Water Street) for special exhibits like the family-friendly "Waterfront." ⊠ *128 Pierrepont St., Brooklyn Heights* ☎ *718/222–4111* ⊕ *www.brooklynhistory. org* 🖾 *$10 suggested donation* ☉ *Closed Mon., Tues.* Ⓜ *2, 3, 4, 5 to Borough Hall; R to Court St.; A, C, F, R to Jay St.–MetroTech.*

"Fruit" Streets

HISTORIC SITE | The quiet blocks of Pineapple, Cranberry, and Orange Streets contain some of Brooklyn Heights's most picturesque brownstones and brick homes. A few homes made of wood still exist here, too, although new construction of this type has been banned in this area as a fire hazard since the mid-19th century. The wood-frame Federal-style house at 24 Middagh Street dates to the 1820s, its lane commemorating one Lady Middagh, whom we can thank for bestowing such memorable fruit-themed names on this enclave. ⊠ *Pineapple, Orange, and Cranberry Sts., Brooklyn Heights* Ⓜ *2, 3 to Clark St.; A, C to High St.*

New York Transit Museum

MUSEUM | FAMILY | Step down into an old 1930s subway station to experience this entertaining museum's displays of vintage trains and memorabilia. You can wander through trains and turnstiles and sit behind the wheel of a former city bus (it's not only the kids who do this). Original advertising, signage, and upholstery make this feel like a trip back in time. The gift shop carries subway-line socks, decorative tile reproductions, and other fun stuff. ⊠ *99 Schermerhorn St., Brooklyn Heights* ☎ *718/694–1600* ⊕ *www. nytransitmuseum.org* 🖾 *$10* ☉ *Closed Mon.* Ⓜ *2, 3, 4, 5 to Borough Hall; A, C, G to Hoyt–Schermerhorn Sts.; A, C, F, R to Jay St.–MetroTech.*

🍴 Restaurants

Brooklyn may be the place to eat these days, but Brooklyn Heights has always been more pleasing to the eye than to the taste buds.

★ Colonie

$$ |ꞌMODERN AMERICAN | The key to this perpetually popular restaurant's success lies in its use of ultrafresh ingredients, sourced from local purveyors and presented with style in an upscale-casual space that honors its neighborhood's historical roots. There's always an oyster special, along with a selection of small plates. **Known for:** locally sourced ingredients; daily oyster special; open kitchen.

Brooklyn Heights is well known for its multitude of picturesque brownstones.

$ *Average main: $20* ✉ *127 Atlantic Ave., Brooklyn Heights* ☎ *718/855–7500* ⊕ *www.colonienyc.com* ⊗ *No lunch weekdays* Ⓜ *2, 3, 4, 5 to Borough Hall; R to Court St.*

★ The River Café

$$$$ | **MODERN AMERICAN** | A deservedly popular special-occasion destination, this waterfront institution complements its exquisite Brooklyn Bridge views with memorable top-shelf cuisine served by an unfailingly attentive staff. Lobster, lamb, duck, and strip steak are among the staples of the prix-fixe menu ($138 for dinner, $47 for Saturday lunch, $60 for Sunday brunch). **Known for:** unforgettable location; top-shelf cuisine; refined atmosphere. $ *Average main: $138* ✉ *1 Water St., Brooklyn Heights* ☎ *718/522–5200* ⊕ *www.therivercafe.com* ⊗ *No breakfast weekends, no lunch Sun.–Fri., no brunch Mon.–Sat.* Ⓜ *2, 3 to Clark St.; A, C to High St.; F to York St.*

🛍 Shopping

FOOD AND TREATS

★ Sahadi's

FOOD/CANDY | Inhale the aromas of spices and dark-roast coffee beans as you enter this Middle Eastern trading post that's been selling bulk foods in Brooklyn since 1948. Bins, jars, and barrels hold everything from nuts, dried fruit, olives, and pickled vegetables to cheeses, chocolate, candy, those intoxicating coffees, and all manner of spices. There's a large selection of prepared food and groceries as well. ✉ *187 Atlantic Ave., between Clinton and Court Sts., Brooklyn Heights* ☎ *718/624–4550* ⊕ *www.sahadis.com* Ⓜ *2, 3, 4, 5 to Borough Hall; R to Court St.; A, C, F, R to Jay St.–MetroTech.*

Two for the Pot

FOOD/CANDY | The name of this narrow shop, in business since 1973, refers to the indulgent practice of adding two extra scoops of coffee grounds to every pot you brew, and if you're at all fond of indulging your coffee or tea tastes, you

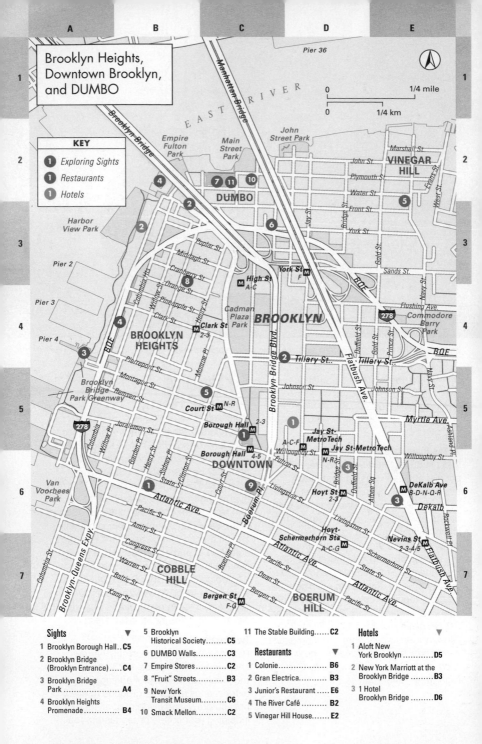

Brooklyn Heights, Downtown Brooklyn, and DUMBO

KEY

- ① Exploring Sights
- ① Restaurants
- ① Hotels

EAST RIVER

Pier 36

0   1/4 mile
0   1/4 km

Manhattan Bridge

Brooklyn Bridge

Empire Fulton Park

Main Street Park

John Street Park

VINEGAR HILL

Marshall St
Evans St
West St

John St
Plymouth St
Water St
Front St
York St

DUMBO

Harbor View Park

Pier 2

Poplar St.
Middagh St.
Cranberry St.
Orange St.
Pineapple St.
Clark St.

High St
A-C

Cadman Plaza Park

BROOKLYN

Sands St.

Flushing Ave.
Commodore Barry Park

278

BQE

Pier 3

Columbia Hts.

Pier 4

BROOKLYN HEIGHTS

Clark St
2-3

Pierrepont St.
Montague St.
Remsen St.
Joralemon St.

Monroe Pl.

Court St
N-R

Borough Hall
2-3

Borough Hall
4-5

DOWNTOWN

Brooklyn Bridge Park Greenway

278

Willow Pl.
Garden Pl.
Henry St.
Sidney Pl.
Clinton St.
State St.

Atlantic Ave.
Pacific St.
Amity St.
Congress St.
Warren St.
Baltic St.
Kane St.

Van Voorhees Park

Brooklyn-Queens Expy.

Columbia St.

COBBLE HILL

Court St.

Boerum Pl.

Livingston St.

Tillary St.
Tillary St.

Johnson St.
Johnson St.

Jay St-MetroTech
A-C-F
Jay St-MetroTech
N-R-C

Willoughby St.
Fulton St.

Hoyt St
2-3

Hoyt-Schermerhorn Sts
A-C-G

Bergen St
F-G

Bergen St.

Dean St.
Pacific St.

BOERUM HILL

Flatbush Ave.
Myrtle Ave.

Willoughby St.

Ashland Pl.

DeKalb Ave
B-D-N-Q-R
Dekalb

Nevins St
2-3-4-5

Schermerhorn St.
State St.

Atlantic Ave.
Pacific St.

Rockwell St.

Duffield St.
Gold St.
Prince St.
Navy St.

BQE

Flatbush Ave.

Brooklyn Bridge Blvd.

Sights ▼

1 Brooklyn Borough Hall .. **C5**
2 Brooklyn Bridge (Brooklyn Entrance) **C4**
3 Brooklyn Bridge Park **A4**
4 Brooklyn Heights Promenade **B4**
5 Brooklyn Historical Society **C5**
6 DUMBO Walls............ **C3**
7 Empire Stores **C2**
8 "Fruit" Streets........... **B3**
9 New York Transit Museum........... **C6**
10 Smack Mellon............ **C2**
11 The Stable Building...... **C2**

Restaurants ▼

1 Colonie.................. **B6**
2 Gran Electrica........... **B3**
3 Junior's Restaurant **E6**
4 The River Café **B2**
5 Vinegar Hill House....... **E2**

Hotels ▼

1 Aloft New York Brooklyn **D5**
2 New York Marriott at the Brooklyn Bridge **B3**
3 1 Hotel Brooklyn Bridge **D6**

must stop in here. The wide selection of top-quality coffees and teas is complemented by brewing paraphernalia, artisanal honey, and hard-to-find brands of U.K. sweets and other comestibles. ✉ *200 Clinton St., Brooklyn Heights* ☎ *718/855–8173* [M] *2, 3, 4, 5 to Borough Hall; R to Court St.; A, C, F, R to Jay St.–MetroTech.*

Downtown Brooklyn

Downtown Brooklyn is modern and bustling, and other than a few notable restaurants, there isn't much to attract visitors—but it's convenient to the Brooklyn Bridge and Brooklyn Heights, and walking distance to neighborhoods like Cobble Hill, Boerum Hill, and DUMBO.

🍴 Restaurants

Even though it's filled with neoclassical courthouses and glass skyscrapers, there isn't much reason to come to Downtown Brooklyn—unless, of course, you want to eat at the original location of the famous Junior's.

Junior's Restaurant
$$ | **DINER** | **FAMILY** | Famous for its thick slices of cheesecake, Junior's has been a quintessential Brooklyn eatery since 1950. Classic cheeseburgers looming over little cups of coleslaw and thick French fries are first-rate, as are the sweet-potato latkes and pretty much all the breakfast offerings. **Known for:** cheesecake; diner classics; quintessential Brooklyn. [$] *Average main: $15* ✉ *386 Flatbush Ave., Downtown Brooklyn* ☎ *718/852–5257* 🌐 *www.juniorscheesecake.com* [M] *2, 3, 4, 5 to Nevins St.; B, Q, R to DeKalb Ave.; A, C, G to Hoyt–Schermerhorn Sts.*

🛏 Hotels

Aloft New York Brooklyn
$ | **HOTEL** | **FAMILY** | A funky boutique chain operation in the heart of Downtown Brooklyn, Aloft is a lively yet comfortable space. **Pros:** easy subway access; reasonable prices; guests have access to the adjacent Sheraton's indoor swimming pool and room service. **Cons:** neighborhood can be noisy; no on-site restaurant; small closets. [$] *Rooms from: $180* ✉ *216 Duffield St., Downtown Brooklyn* ☎ *718/256–3833* 🌐 *www.marriott.com/hotels/travel/nycyl-aloft-new-york-brooklyn/* 🔑 *176 rooms* 🍽 *No meals* [M] *2, 3 to Hoyt St., A, C, F, R to Jay St.–MetroTech.*

New York Marriott at the Brooklyn Bridge
$ | **HOTEL** | **FAMILY** | The rooms at this well-situated hotel are classic Marriott—large and enhanced by high ceilings, massaging showerheads, and other nice touches. **Pros:** near some of Brooklyn's hipper neighborhoods; traditional full-service hotel; good subway access. **Cons:** on a busy downtown street; Wi-Fi isn't free; design feels a bit cookie-cutter. [$] *Rooms from: $299* ✉ *333 Adams St., Downtown Brooklyn* ☎ *718/246–7000* 🌐 *www.marriott.com* 🔑 *665 rooms* 🍽 *No meals* [M] *2, 3, 4, 5 to Borough Hall; A, C, F, R to Jay St.–MetroTech.*

DUMBO

For sheer jaw-dropping drama, few city walks are as cinematic as strolling the DUMBO waterfront. The photogenic area pairs 19th-century warehouses and refurbished industrial buildings on cobblestone streets with rumbling trains and soaring bridges overhead. (The latter gives the district its name, an acronym of Down Under the Manhattan Bridge Overpass.) Across the East River, the glittering Manhattan skyline provides epic views and popular backdrops for wedding proposals, fashion shoots, and innumerable selfies. Major galleries and performance hubs imbue the neighborhood with artistic élan, and the adjacent Navy Yard is a booming example of Brooklyn's revitalized industrial waterfront.

An integral part of DUMBO is the Brooklyn Bridge Park, and its renovated piers and rolling green spaces. Crowds of locals and tourists alike flock to its riverfront benches and tiny beaches to sunbathe or simply to ponder the magnificence of one of the city's finest views.

👁 Sights

DUMBO Walls
PUBLIC ART | Keep an eye out under and around the Manhattan Bridge and the Brooklyn-Queens Expressway, where walls display street art by the likes of CAM, Shepard Fairey, and MOMO. The project is sponsored by the DUMBO Improvement District and Two Trees Management Co., along with the New York City Department of Transportation Urban Art Program, the Jonathan LeVine Gallery, and the Wooster Gallery. ✉ DUMBO Ⓜ F to York St.

★ Empire Stores
BUILDING | Housed in a sparkling renovation of an enormous 19th-century warehouse, this collection of shops and restaurants features a 7,000-square-foot rooftop garden with East River and Manhattan views. It's also home to a 3,200-square-foot exhibition space from the Brooklyn Historical Society that has small displays and a gift shop in a modern, industrial-chic space. Other tenants include area businesses, a West Elm store with a Brooklyn Roasting Company café, and the first Brooklyn location of the Soho House, called DUMBO House. ✉ 53–83 Water St., DUMBO ⊕ empirestoresdumbo.com Ⓜ A, C to High St.; F to York St.

Smack Mellon
ARTS VENUE | The transformation of an industrial boiler house into an edgy arts compound is quintessential DUMBO. This 12,000-square-foot structure now hosts large-scale avant-garde exhibitions and runs a prestigious residency program. Don't be surprised if you pass a smartphone-clutching event planner on your way in: the 5,000-square-foot gallery here is also a popular wedding venue. ✉ 92 Plymouth St., DUMBO ☎ 718/834–8761 ⊕ www.smackmellon.org ⊘ Closed Mon., Tues. Ⓜ A, C to High St.; F to York St.

★ The Stable Building
MUSEUM | Although the Galapagos Art Space moved to Detroit, the site continues its arts legacy, housing four first-floor gallery spaces that were previously part of the 111 Front Street gallery collective. Minus Space shows artists specializing in "reductive abstract art" (simple materials, precise craftsmanship, monochromatic or limited color, repetition of shapes). United Photo Industries (UPI) shows work by emerging photographers and those working in new photography styles. The Klompching Gallery focuses on fine-art photography. Masters Projects represents artists working in all sorts of media, including paint, mixed media, street art, photography, and installations. Gallery hours vary, but weekday and Saturday afternoons are your best bet to visit; most are closed Monday. ✉ 16 Main St., DUMBO Ⓜ 2, 3 to Clark St.; A, C to High St.; F to York St.

🍴 Restaurants

Once upon a time, the primary reason for a hungry person to come to DUMBO was to eat pizza at Grimaldi's. The past few years have seen the growing gentrification of these loft-strewn cobblestone streets, which today are sprinkled with toothsome eateries and cute boutiques. Now that the Brooklyn waterfront has been fully developed you can walk off your meal on a romantic stroll.

Gran Eléctrica

$$ | MEXICAN | FAMILY | Few restaurants are equally suited to neighborhood families and trendy twentysomethings, but Gran Eléctrica's street-food-centric Mexican menu pleases all palates. In addition to multiregional tacos and small plates, the buzzy, stylish space has an impressive tequila list and pours balanced cocktails. **Known for:** multiregional Mexican dishes; balanced cocktails and diverse tequilas; buzzy space that's family-friendly. $ *Average main: $16* ⊠ *5 Front St., DUMBO* ☎ *718/852–2700* ⊕ *www.granelectrica. com* ☾ *No lunch weekdays* Ⓜ *A, C to High St.; F to York St.*

Vinegar Hill House

$$$ | MODERN AMERICAN | Outfitted with candlelit tables and a twinkling rear patio, this romantic destination is well worth the sloping walk up from the waterfront. Seasonal menus include inventive new American fare and crowd-pleasing brunch dishes; wait times can be considerable, but the cozy bar pours potent cocktails, local beer, and wine by the glass. **Known for:** romantic space with a twinkling backyard; seasonal, sustainably sourced new American dishes; weekend brunch. $ *Average main: $25* ⊠ *72 Hudson Ave., DUMBO* ☎ *718/522–1018* ⊕ *www. vinegarhillhouse.com* ☾ *No lunch* Ⓜ *F to York St.*

Hotels

★ 1 Hotel Brooklyn Bridge

$$$ | HOTEL | An eco-friendly ethos underscores this hip, beautifully designed outpost of the 1 Hotels fleet, including details such as headboards made from upcycled corrugated steel in many guest rooms; a living wall punctuates the tiered, buzzy lobby filled with low-slung leather sofas. **Pros:** beautifully designed and environmentally conscious; near Brooklyn Bridge Park; hotel guests have priority to rooftop bar on weekdays. **Cons:** east-facing rooms overlook busy thoroughfare; no nearby transit options;

uneven service. $ *Rooms from: $479* ⊠ *60 Furman St., DUMBO* ☎ *347/696–2500* ⊕ *1hotels.com/brooklyn-bridge* ⊷ *195 rooms* ⦿ *No meals.*

Shopping

BOOKS AND STATIONERY

powerHouse Arena

BOOKS/STATIONERY | FAMILY | Edgy art-book publisher powerHouse is a vision in concrete and steel at this bright showroom that sells illustrated titles, children's books, and works by authors from Joseph Mitchell to Gary Shteyngart. The space also hosts publishing parties, book launches, readings, and discussion groups. ⊠ *28 Adams St., between Front and Water Sts., DUMBO* ☎ *718/666–3049* ⊕ *www.powerhousearena.com* Ⓜ *A, C to High St.; F to York St.*

CLOTHING

Front General Store

CLOTHING | Outfitting DUMBO's cool kids since 2011, this shop sells his-and-hers vintage Ralph Lauren blazers, 1940s Royal Stetson hats, and other well-chosen odds 'n' ends, including antique Mexican glassware and Chesterfield-esque leather armchairs. ⊠ *143 Front St., between Pearl and Jay Sts., DUMBO* ☎ *646/573–0123* ⊕ *frontgeneralstore.com* Ⓜ *A, C to High St., F to York St.*

Nightlife

BARS

Cecconi's Dumbo

BARS/PUBS | Already known for its upscale eateries around the world, Cecconi's made a splash joining the polished DUMBO culinary and cultural scene in 2017. The Italian menu and stunning East River–facing outdoor terrace are enough to warrant a visit; but no matter the season or weather, the roomy bar, outstanding service, and inviting furnishings make this a hot spot well worth a trip to this historic district. ⊠ *55 Water St., DUMBO*

☎ *718/650–3900* ⊕ *cecconisdumbo.com* Ⓜ *A, C to High St.; F to York St.*

Superfine

BARS/PUBS | The narrow bi-level floor plan might seem a little odd, but friendly service and convivial, colorful crowds transform this renovated warehouse into a welcoming, quirky neighborhood spot. The kitchen's organic menu changes seasonally, but the real action is at the bar, where stiff concoctions are poured near the orange-felt pool table. There are also weekend DJs and monthly local artist shows. ⊠ *126 Front St., DUMBO* ☎ *718/243–9005* ⊕ *www.superfine.nyc* Ⓜ *F to York St.*

🎭 Performing Arts

THEATER

★ St. Ann's Warehouse

ART GALLERIES—ARTS | The latest iteration of this cutting-edge arts institution (originally launched in the East Village in 1980) occupies a stunningly refurbished tobacco warehouse from 1860 that sits beneath the Brooklyn Bridge in Brooklyn Bridge Park. The 24,000-square-foot space features original brick archways, an elegant outdoor courtyard, an exhibition space, and a theater hosting such performances as an all-female production of *Henry IV* and the American premiere of Irish playwright Edna Walsh's first opera. ⊠ *45 Water St., DUMBO* ☎ *718/254–8779* ⊕ *stannswarehouse.org* Ⓜ *A, C to High St.; F to York St.*

Carroll Gardens

Named for Charles Carroll, the only Catholic signatory of the Declaration of Independence, and the lush front gardens that line the neighborhood's brownstones, Carroll Gardens was a well-kept secret until the 1980s. Traditionally an Italian neighborhood, many old-school vestiges, including some that have served the area for well over a half century, still remain. Court and Smith Streets are the backbone of the community, and now feature a mix of top-notch restaurants and bistros, handsome cocktail lounges and craft-beer bars, and boutiques selling the most current styles, to go along with original mom-and-pop bakeries and butcher shops. A recent influx of French expats makes the neighborhood's annual Bastille Day festival and *pétanque* (like lawn bowling but played on sand using heavy metal balls) tournament a high point each July.

🍽 Restaurants

Carroll Gardens has standout restaurants, which lure even those Manhattanites who might be loath to cross the river.

Buttermilk Channel

$$$ | **AMERICAN** | This new-regional-American bistro draws epic brunch lines and a legion of neighborhood families (the Clown Sundae is legendary among Carroll Gardens kids). But when day turns to night, Buttermilk Channel transforms into a surprisingly serious restaurant with an excellent, mostly American wine list. **Known for:** fried pork chop or chicken with cheddar waffles; three-course Monday-night prix fixe; unusual ingredient combinations. Ⓢ *Average main: $25* ⊠ *524 Court St., Carroll Gardens* ☎ *718/852–8490* ⊕ *www.buttermilkchannelnyc.com* Ⓜ *F, G to Smith–9th Sts.*

Frankies Spuntino 457

$$ | **ITALIAN** | A longtime favorite culinary pioneer in Carroll Gardens, Frank Castronovo and Frank Falcinelli's Italian-American restaurant has atmosphere to spare between the backyard and former blacksmith stable. Choose from the well-conceived menu's shareable salads (many with vegetables roasted or marinated with the Frankies' own Sicilian olive oil); handmade pastas like the cavatelli with hot sausage, sage, and brown butter; meatballs; and crusty sandwiches that ask to be shared. **Known for:**

Carroll Gardens, Cobble Hill, Boerum Hill, and Fort Greene

KEY

1 Restaurants
1 Hotels

Restaurants ▸

1 Buttermilk Channel........**B3**
2 Frankies Spuntino 457....**B3**
3 Roman's........................**G1**
4 Walter's........................**G1**

Hotels ▸

1 NU Hotel Brooklyn........**D1**

outdoor dining; menu options for all kinds of eaters; less-than-warm staff. $ *Average main: $20* ✉ *457 Court St., Carroll Gardens* ☎ *718/403–0033* ⊕ *www.frankiesspuntino.com* Ⓜ *F, G to Carroll St. or Smith–9th Sts.*

🛍 Shopping

FOOD AND TREATS

★ **G. Esposito & Sons Jersey Pork Store**

FOOD/CANDY | The epitome of an old-school Italian butcher and specialty shop, Esposito's has been serving the area once known as South Brooklyn for almost 100 years. Brothers and co-owners John and George Esposito run the store their grandfather opened in 1922 and are still producing home-made sausages, dry-aged soppressata, and hero sandwiches made on Caputo's bread. Order up an Italian Combo with the works, or the habit-forming Santino's "Fluffy" Combo, stuffed with chicken cutlets, sweet peppers, Asiago cheese, pesto, and oil and vinegar, and grab a seat in neighboring Carroll Park to chow down. ✉ *357 Court St., between Union and President Sts., Carroll Gardens* ☎ *718/875–6863* Ⓜ *F, G to Carroll St.*

GIFTS AND SOUVENIRS

Swallow

GIFTS/SOUVENIRS | If you're looking for a gift or a special trinket for that hard-to-shop-for friend or family member who has exquisite taste and an appreciation for the fine designs of nature, head to Swallow. Anatomy- and nature-inspired jewelry, vases, painted gold-leaf mirrors, chimes made of obsidian shards and dried eucalyptus, and other objets d'art and curiosities are just some of the offerings. Browsing here is a bit like traveling down the rabbit hole into a grown-up's housewares wonderland. ✉ *361 Smith St., between Carroll and 2nd Sts., Carroll Gardens* ☎ *718/222–8201* ⊕ *www.dearswallow.com* Ⓜ *F, G to Carroll St.*

Cobble Hill

Cobble Hill stands out for its 19th-century architecture, leafy and compact park, and more recently, for escalating real estate prices. Dutch residents called the area Cobleshill in reference to a Revolutionary War–era land mound, which was flattened by British soldiers to prevent strategic use by George Washington's troops. These days, most of the 22-block neighborhood is landmarked as Brooklyn's second-oldest district, a mix of brick town houses, brownstones, and Victorian schoolhouses, where only the Gothic Revival churches exceed a 50-foot height limit. Historically working-class, the neighborhood has adopted all the trappings of haute Brooklyn, especially along busy Court Street.

🛍 Shopping

BOOKS AND STATIONERY

Books Are Magic

BOOKS/STATIONERY | **FAMILY** | Author Emma Straub opened this spacious and well-stocked bookstore after neighborhood landmark BookCourt closed, and even used her predecessor's tall wooden bookshelves in creating the new space. Books Are Magic hosts author events—many with celebrated writers who happen to live in Brooklyn—several days a week. Don't miss the excellent kids' area in the back. ✉ *225 Smith St., at Butler St., Cobble Hill* ☎ *718/246–2665* ⊕ *www.booksaremagic.net* Ⓜ *F, G to Bergen St.*

CLOTHING

Bird

CLOTHING | Looking for the chic-est women's wear in Brooklyn? You'll find it at this beloved boutique known for its high prices attached to enviable items from Rachel Comey, Dries Van Noten, Jesse Kamm, and Ulla Johnson, as well as its own collection of seasonal dresses. Everything from knit sweaterdresses and cardigans to statement shoes and delicate gold jewelry share the cozy space. There are a few items for men available at the Williamsburg location, one of four NYC stores (plus an outpost in Los Angeles). ✉ *220 Smith St., at Butler St., Cobble Hill* ☎ *718/797–3774* ⊕ *www.birdbrooklyn.com* Ⓜ *F, G to Bergen St.*

ⓨ Nightlife

BARS
Clover Club
BARS/PUBS | Long recognized for excellent drinks—both classic and inspired by the classics—and a cozy vibe, this is one of the best cocktail bars in Brooklyn. Passionate mixologists cook up seasonal cocktail menus and tasty bites to pair with them. Weekends get busy, especially with a brunch service, but head here on weeknights to sit at the bar and call bartender's choice. ✉ *210 Smith St., Cobble Hill* ☎ *718/855–7939* ⊕ *www. cloverclubny.com* Ⓜ *F, G to Bergen St.*

Boerum Hill

Understated elegance defines Boerum Hill, where redbrick town houses and brownstones line quiet tree-lined thoroughfares from 4th Avenue to Smith Street and Schermerhorn to Baltic. The neighborhood saw an influx of immigrants in the late 1800s, with completion of the Brooklyn Bridge and the emergence of trolley cars, but fell into disrepair after World War II. Now fully gentrified, the setting is laden with beautiful cafés and plays host to Atlantic Antic, NYC's largest street festival and unofficial fall kick-off, each September. Despite its air of sophistication, Boerum Hill presents moments of levity, namely artist Susan Gardner's sparkly mosaic-covered brownstone at 108 Wyckoff Street.

Hotels

NU Hotel Brooklyn
$ | HOTEL | The hip-yet-affordable NU, on one of Brooklyn's main nightlife and shopping streets, is perfect for visitors seeking a perch near the best of the borough. **Pros:** great Brooklyn launching pad; knowledgeable staff; 24-hour fitness center. **Cons:** subway or cab ride to anything in Manhattan; bar area can be a little too quiet; limited in-room amenities. Ⓢ *Rooms from: $200* ✉ *85 Smith St., Boerum Hill* ☎ *718/852–8585* ⊕ *www. nuhotelbrooklyn.com* ↪ *93 rooms* ⱺ *Free Breakfast* Ⓜ *F, G to Bergen St.; A, C, G to Hoyt–Schermerhorn Sts.*

ⓨ Nightlife

★ **Grand Army**
BARS/PUBS | Housed in a former corner market, this easygoing neighborhood bar may not appear to take its craft cocktails and quality beer list seriously. But the staff, led by master bartender and co-owner Damon Boelte, know precisely how to mix a classic libation or one from the sophisticated, themed menu that changes each fall and spring. ✉ *336 State St., at Hoyt St., Boerum Hill* ☎ *718/643–1503* ⊕ *www.grandarmybar.com* Ⓜ *A, C, G to Hoyt–Schermerhorn Sts.*

ⓞ Shopping

BEAUTY
★ **Twisted Lily**
PERFUME/COSMETICS | One of the most comprehensive collections of independent and natural fragrances hides behind this elegant storefront on busy Atlantic Avenue. The knowledgeable staff know their way around hundreds of scents and will happily help you find your favorite, but be prepared to want to take more than a few home. The boutique also carries candles and skin-care, grooming, and beauty products. ✉ *360 Atlantic Ave., between Hoyt and Bond Sts., Boerum*

Hill ☎ 347/529–4681 ⊕ twistedlily.com Ⓜ A, C, G to Hoyt–Schermerhorn Sts.

GIFTS AND SOUVENIRS
Regular Visitors
GIFTS/SOUVENIRS | Part housewares store (see: Kinto mugs and Fog Linen towels), part luxe apothecary (e.g., Marvis toothpaste and French Girl dry shampoo), part artisanal grocer (peruse local honeys and Mexican hot sauces), and then some— this bright, thoughtfully designed neighborhood shop has everything you didn't know you needed. There's also a wall of magazines (many independent and hard to find), and the store doubles as a coffee shop, with just a few counter seats in the window for laptop-toting creatives and friends catching up. ⊠ 149 Smith St., at Bergen St., Boerum Hill ☎ 646/766–0484 ⊕ www.regularvisitors.com Ⓜ F, G to Bergen St.

HOME DECOR
The Primary Essentials
CERAMICS/GLASSWARE | Stock up on handcrafted ceramics, textiles made by artisans in India, candles and perfumes from Mexico, desk accessories from Japan, and artwork fit for a renovated loft at this Brooklyn design store from former stylist Lauren Snyder. The boutique is pleasant and relaxed—nearly as elegant as the products it stocks—and carries designers found nowhere else in New York. A new location just opened in NoLIta, too. ⊠ 372 Atlantic Ave., between Hoyt and Bond Sts., Boerum Hill ☎ 718/522–1804 ⊕ theprimaryessentials.com Ⓜ A, C, G to Hoyt–Schermerhorn Sts.

Fort Greene

Art institutions, flatteringly lit eateries, and the sort of showstopping architecture that sends real estate agents into early retirement make Fort Greene irresistible. Bookended by the Pratt Institute and the former Williamsburg Savings Bank Tower (now 1 Hanson Place)—a four-sided clock tower that was once the borough's tallest building and remains a local landmark—the neighborhood has a central location and an illustrious past. Climb the 96 steps or the grassy slopes of Fort Greene Park and you'll be greeted by vistas of the Manhattan skyline, while standing in the silhouette of the 149-foot tall Prison Ship Martyrs' Monument—dedicated to the thousands of Americans who died on British prison ships during the Revolutionary War. Everyone from Walt Whitman to Spike Lee has called these iconic streets home.

🍴 Restaurants

Fort Greene has become one of the most desirable neighborhoods in Brooklyn, the lovely brownstone apartments attracting young professionals and many of the borough's established writers and artists. It's also a garden of culinary delights with restaurants leading the locavore farm-to-table movement. And who knows? Maybe even a famous director or author will be sitting at the table next to you.

Roman's
$$$ | ITALIAN | Part of an all-star Brooklyn restaurant group that includes Williamsburg favorites Diner and Marlow & Sons, this seasonally focused eatery has an Italian accent. Menus change daily and include farm-fresh fare like wintry fennel salads or pork meatballs in brodo, or delicacies like artichoke-studded housemade spaghetti in summer. Known for: seasonal menu; hip scene; great for special occasions. 💲 Average main: $26 ⊠ 243 DeKalb Ave., Fort Greene ☎ 718/622–5300 ⊕ www.romansnyc.com 🕐 No lunch Ⓜ C to Lafayette Ave.; G to Clinton–Washington Aves.

Walter's
$$ | AMERICAN | A sister restaurant to Williamsburg's Walter Foods, this buzzy bistro has a menu of upscale comfort food, a comely crowd, and rosy-hued lighting that gives the space a glamorous

vibe. Stop in for a cocktail after a day in Fort Greene Park, or come for a seasonal repast courtesy of Walter's raw bar, satisfying main dishes (fried chicken with garlic mashed potatoes is a winner), and market-fresh veggie sides. **Known for:** fun bar scene; upscale comfort food; great cocktails. $ *Average main: $20* ✉ *166 DeKalb Ave., Fort Greene* ☎ *718/488–7800* ⊕ *www.walterfoods.com/walters* Ⓜ *B, Q, R to DeKalb Ave.; C to Lafayette Ave.; G to Fulton St.*

🔴 Performing Arts

PERFORMANCE CENTERS
★ **Brooklyn Academy of Music** (*BAM*)
ARTS CENTERS | Founded in 1861 and operating at its current location since 1908, BAM is a multidisciplinary performing arts center that has grown to span three edifices, including the Beaux Arts seven-story Peter Jay Sharp building. It's known for innovative performances of many types, and the facilities include an unadorned "black box" theater, dance venues, a four-screen movie theater, an opera house, and an open-plan performance and restaurant space. ✉ *Peter Jay Sharp Bldg., 30 Lafayette Ave., Fort Greene* ☎ *718/636–4100* ⊕ *www.bam. org* Ⓜ *2, 3, 4, 5, B, D, N, Q, R to Atlantic Ave.–Barclays Ctr.; G to Fulton St.; C to Lafayette Ave.*

Williamsburg

These days, it's impossible to walk through North Brooklyn without encountering something new. Fabulous boutiques, vintage shops, and forward-thinking restaurants crop up constantly, lending an energy that verges on overwhelming. The neighborhood has certainly glossed itself up in recent years, evinced by pricey cocktail bars, highrise waterfront condos, and expensive boutiques. But Williamsburg's past is also endlessly intriguing: for much of the 20th century this industrial area on the East River was home to a mix of working-class Americans. Rising Manhattan rents in the 1990s sent an influx of East Village artists and musicians onto the L train, and since then the area has rapidly, albeit creatively, gentrified. And while some side streets may appear graffitied and creepy, rest assured that there's likely to be a DIY concert-gallery space in one of those seemingly abandoned factories.

Williamsburg's 70-plus galleries are distributed randomly, with no single main drag. Plan your trip ahead of time using the online **Brooklyn Art Guide** at ⊕ *www. wagmag.org.* (You can also pick up a copy at neighborhood galleries and some cafés.) Hours vary widely, but most are open weekends (call ahead). To be honest, serendipitous poking is the best way to sample the art, rather than seeking out a specific gallery.

New York City Urban Adventures Tours
WALKING TOURS | For a glimpse into Brooklyn's illustrious past as the nation's brewing capital (once home to 48 breweries), book a spot on the **Brewed in Brooklyn** walking tour ($82 per person). The tour includes a stroll through historic Brewers Row with stops that include a 19th century German brewery once operated by Otto Huber, lunch at Danny's Pizzeria, and, of course, a craft beer at each watering hole along the way. Another popular tour is **Neighborhood Eats: Brownstone Brooklyn,** which is without a doubt the best way to sample the eclectic bites of BoCoCa (Boerum Hill, Cobble Hill, Carroll Gardens) in one afternoon. ✉ *Williamsburg* ☎ *347/618–8687* ⊕ *www. newyorkcityurbanadventures.com.*

Sights

City Reliquary
MUSEUM | **FAMILY** | Subway tokens, Statue of Liberty figurines, antique seltzer bottles, and other artifacts you might find

in a time capsule crowd the cases of this museum that celebrates New York City's past and present. Recent temporary exhibits here have included one about the last doughnut shops in NYC and another about the Empire Rollerdrome skating rink (birthplace of roller disco). ⊠ *370 Metropolitan Ave., Williamsburg* ☎ *718/782–4842* ⊕ *www.cityreliquary. org* 🎫 *$7* 🕙 *Closed Mon.–Wed.* Ⓜ *L to Lorimer St.; G to Metropolitan Ave.*

Domino Park

CITY PARK | FAMILY | Brooklynites may still be mourning the demise of the Domino Sugar Factory, but the developers have made good on at least one of their promises: They've turned a large swath of the former complex into a sprawling riverside park, complete with a playground, a garden, dancing fountains, and refinery remnants along Artifact Walk. You'll see locals hanging out at the bocce court or playing with their pooches at the dog run, but most of all, you'll be able to marvel at a truly spectacular view of the Williamsburg Bridge, seemingly right above your head, and the Manhattan skyline beyond. ⊠ *15 River St., Williamsburg* ⊕ *www. dominopark.com* Ⓜ *J, M, Z to Marcy Ave.; L to Bedford Ave.*

🍴 Restaurants

Still probably the hippest, happening-est neighborhood in the five boroughs, Williamsburg is also one of the hottest destinations on the culinary landscape. You'll find plenty of decadent twists on farm-to-table cuisine, dressed-up comfort-food classics, and killer cocktails.

★ Diner

$$ | AMERICAN | The word "diner" might evoke a greasy spoon, but this trendsetting restaurant under the Williamsburg Bridge is nothing of the sort. Andrew Tarlow—the godfather of Brooklyn's farm-to-table culinary renaissance— opened it in 1999 and launched an entire movement. **Known for:** trailblazing restaurateur; farm-to-table fare; intimate space in a vintage dining car. 💲 *Average main: $21* ⊠ *85 Broadway, Williamsburg* ☎ *718/486–3077* ⊕ *www.dinernyc.com* Ⓜ *J, M, Z to Marcy Ave.*

Fette Sau

$$ | BARBECUE | It might seem odd to go to a former auto-body repair shop to feast on meat, but the funky building and courtyard are just the right setting for the serious barbecue served here. A huge wood-and-gas smoker delivers brisket, sausages, ribs, and even duck—all ordered by the pound. **Known for:** Southern-style barbecue; excellent whiskey list; no reservations. 💲 *Average main: $13* ⊠ *354 Metropolitan Ave., Williamsburg* ☎ *718/963–3404* ⊕ *www. fettesaubbq.com* 🕙 *No lunch Mon.* Ⓜ *L to Lorimer St.; G to Metropolitan Ave.*

Le Barricou

$$ | FRENCH | The team behind nearby Maison Premiere operates this Parisian-style brasserie serving escargots, coq au vin, and other French bistro classics. Diners sit at rustic wooden tables, and the walls are collaged with vintage French newspapers. **Known for:** French bistro classics; popular brunch spot; old-world atmosphere. 💲 *Average main: $18* ⊠ *533 Grand St., Williamsburg* ☎ *718/782–7372* ⊕ *www.lebarricouny.com* Ⓜ *L to Lorimer St.; G to Metropolitan Ave.*

★ Marlow & Sons

$$ | AMERICAN | With its green-and-white-striped awning, you might easily mistake this buzzy bistro for an old-timey grocery store, but this is a wood-paneled dining room packed nightly with foodies for remarkable locavore cuisine. Part of the Andrew Tarlow empire, Marlow & Sons serves food that sounds simple until you take that first bite. **Known for:** pioneering restaurateur; inspired locavore fare; vintage grocery store–inspired design. 💲 *Average main: $23* ⊠ *81 Broadway, Williamsburg* ☎ *718/384–1441* ⊕ *www. marlowandsons.com* Ⓜ *J, M, Z to Marcy Ave.*

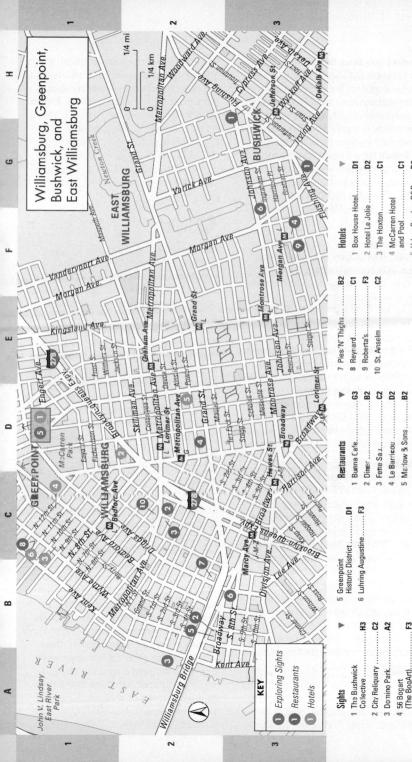

Williamsburg, Greenpoint, Bushwick, and East Williamsburg

KEY

🔵 Exploring Sights

🔴 Restaurants

🟢 Hotels

Sights ▶

1 The Bushwick Collective................H3
2 City Reliquary..............C2
3 Domino Park..............A2
4 56 Bogart (The BogArt)..............F3
5 Greenpoint Historic District............D1
6 Luhring Augustine.........F3

Restaurants ▶

1 Buona Cafe..............G3
2 Diner..............B2
3 Fette Sau..............C2
4 Le Barricou..............D2
5 Marlow & Sons..............B2
6 Peter Luger Steak House..............B3
7 Pies 'N' Thighs.............B2
8 Reynard..............C1
9 Roberta's..............F3
10 St. Anselm..............C2

Hotels ▶

1 Box House Hotel..............D1
2 Hotel Le Jolie..............D2
3 The Hoxton..............C1
4 McCarren Hotel and Pool..............C1
5 Urban Cowboy B&B.....D2
6 Wythe Hotel..............C1

★ Peter Luger Steak House

$$$$ | STEAKHOUSE | Steak lovers come to Peter Luger for the exquisite dry-aged meat and the casual atmosphere. You can order individual steaks, but the porterhouse is highly recommended and served only for two, three, or four people. **Known for:** excellent steak; historic Brooklyn ambience; no credit cards. $ *Average main: $80* ⊠ *178 Broadway, Williamsburg* ☎ *718/387–7400* ⊕ *www.peterluger.com* ▭ *No credit cards* Ⓜ *J, M, Z to Marcy Ave.*

Pies 'N' Thighs

$$ | SOUTHERN | Opened by two Diner alums, this little restaurant takes its moniker seriously, serving famously delicious fried chicken and pies made with organic and local ingredients. Perched on chairs from an elementary school, diners enjoy Southern-style meals that come with a protein (catfish and pulled pork for those who don't want chicken) and two sides (grits, mac 'n' cheese, and biscuits are favorites). **Known for:** fried chicken and pies; fun, casual vibe; good value. $ *Average main: $15* ⊠ *166 S. 4th St., Williamsburg* ☎ *347/529–6090* ⊕ *www.piesnthighs.com* Ⓜ *J, M, Z to Marcy Ave.*

★ Reynard

$$$ | MODERN AMERICAN | Reynard has all the hallmarks of a Williamsburg venture, with farm-to-table fare highlighting the season's freshest ingredients, and everything made in-house, even the granola. The grass-fed burger is always available, but the rest of the menu changes often enough that you'll want to come back to try it all. **Known for:** farm-to-table fare; urban-rustic digs in the Wythe Hotel; great sourdough bread. $ *Average main: $26* ⊠ *Wythe Hotel, 80 Wythe Ave., Williamsburg* ☎ *718/460–8004* ⊕ *www.reynardnyc.com* Ⓜ *L to Bedford Ave.*

St. Anselm

$$ | STEAKHOUSE | This modest spot grills high-quality meat and fish, all sustainably and ethically sourced, and at very reasonable prices. The sides, ordered à la carte, deserve special attention: the spinach gratin is dependably hearty, and the seasonal special of delicata squash with manchego cheese is divine. **Known for:** grilled meat and fish; casual vibe; no reservations. $ *Average main: $23* ⊠ *355 Metropolitan Ave., Williamsburg* ☎ *718/384–5054* ⊕ *www.stanselm.net* ☾ *No lunch weekdays* Ⓜ *L to Lorimer St.; G to Metropolitan Ave.; J, M, Z to Marcy Ave.*

🛏 Hotels

Hotel Le Jolie

$ | HOTEL | This no-frills favorite has excellent service and is convenient not only to Williamsburg's arts, culture, and dining scenes but also to the subway and the Brooklyn-Queens Expressway, the latter handy should you want to get into Manhattan via car. **Pros:** good value; free parking on a first-come, first-served basis; convenient part of Brooklyn. **Cons:** proximity to highway can mean noise; can feel remote even though near to subways; not hip or trendy. $ *Rooms from: $249* ⊠ *235 Meeker Ave., Williamsburg* ☎ *718/625–2100* ⊕ *www.hotellejolie.com* ⇥ *52 rooms* ❐ *Free Breakfast* Ⓜ *L to Lorimer St.; G to Metropolitan Ave.*

The Hoxton

$ | HOTEL | Built on the site of a water tower factory, this hipster hotel pays homage to the area's industrial past with exposed brick, raw concrete, and steel girders, while nodding to its trendy present with bright, high-ceilinged spaces, quirky fonts and patterns, and three dining spots—Klein's, Backyard, and Summerly—run by local luminaries, plus a rooftop bar. **Pros:** monthly events that attract locals; three restaurants and a rooftop bar; room views of the Manhattan skyline. **Cons:** rooms can be small for Brooklyn; area can get a bit dead during the day and noisy at night; connections to the rest of the city must go through the sometimes-unreliable L train. $ *Rooms from: $159* ⊠ *97 Wythe Ave., Williamsburg*

Williamsburg has become one of the most popular (and hip) neighborhoods in Brooklyn.

☎ 718/215–7100 ⊕ thehoxton.com/new-york/williamsburg/hotels ⇥ 175 rooms ⦿ Free Breakfast Ⓜ L to Bedford Ave.

McCarren Hotel and Pool
$ | HOTEL | With a plum location overlooking McCarren Park and a rooftop bar offering sundowner happy hour cocktails, this hotel sizzles with scenester savvy. **Pros:** high hip factor; quality rooftop restaurant-bar, close to main thoroughfare Bedford Avenue. **Cons:** potential for noise from concerts in McCarren Park; some room details like lighting controls could be more user-friendly; the pool gets crowded in summer. ⓢ Rooms from: $295 ⌂ 160 N. 12th St., Williamsburg ☎ 718/218–7500 ⊕ www.mccarrenhotel.com ⇥ 64 rooms ⦿ No meals Ⓜ L to Bedford Ave.

★ Urban Cowboy B&B
$ | B&B/INN | Williamsburg's only B&B, which occupies a renovated 100-year-old town house, combines the neighborhood's renegade spirit with an eye for design. **Pros:** beautiful design with personal touches; backyard Jacuzzi;

personable staff. **Cons:** most rooms share a bathroom; a bit far from Williamsburg's main attractions; it can get a bit noisy. ⓢ Rooms from: $250 ⌂ 111 Powers St., Williamsburg ☎ 347/840–0525 ⊕ www.urbancowboy.com ⇥ 5 rooms ⦿ Free Breakfast Ⓜ L to Lorimer St.; G to Metropolitan Ave.

★ Wythe Hotel
$$ | HOTEL | A former cooperage on the Brooklyn waterfront has found new life as the Wythe Hotel, a stunner for its Manhattan-skyline views, locally sourced design touches and amenities, and supercool restaurant (Reynard) and bar (Ides). **Pros:** Brooklyn-based design and environmentally friendly products; fabulous views from rooms or rooftop bar; destination-worthy restaurant. **Cons:** somewhat removed from the subway; no room service; the rooftop bar gets crowded. ⓢ Rooms from: $300 ⌂ 80 Wythe Ave., at N. 11th St., Williamsburg ☎ 718/460–8001 ⊕ www.wythehotel.com ⇥ 72 rooms ⦿ No meals Ⓜ L to Bedford Ave.

🛍 Shopping

CLOTHING

★ Brooklyn Tailors

CLOTHING | The husband-and-wife team behind this men's tailor has been crafting bespoke, made-to-measure, and off-the-rack suits, shirts, and overcoats for the well-dressed gents of New York since 2007. The store also carries a curated range of shoes, sweaters, grooming products, and other accessories from brands like Drake's and Joseph Cheaney, and full collections from Camoshita. ✉ *327 Grand St., between Havemeyer St. and Marcy Ave., Williamsburg* ☎ *347/799–1646* ⊕ *www.brooklyn-tailors.com* Ⓜ *L to Lorimer St.; G to Metropolitan Ave.*

In God We Trust

CLOTHING | This NYC-based brand is as popular for its simple, classic jewelry as it is for clean-lined clothes. The women's wear tends to be boxy and menswear-inspired, and the store also carries a curated selection of bags, accessories, and home decor from other designers. Jewelry pieces like signet rings and heart pendant necklaces can be engraved; some are sold already engraved with whimsical phrases. ✉ *129 Bedford Ave., between N. 9th and 10th Sts., Williamsburg* ☎ *718/384–0700* ⊕ *ingodwetrustnyc.com* Ⓜ *L to Bedford Ave.*

HOME DECOR

Leif

BOOKS/STATIONERY | A lifestyle store that embodies the, well, Brooklyn lifestyle, this bright little boutique has a curated collection of housewares, jewelry, beauty products, and prints by local artists. Find geometric rugs and pillows, linen tablecloths, hand-painted ceramic pitchers, tassel earrings, colorful knit accessories, fragrant candles, and more. ✉ *99 Grand St., between Wythe Ave. and Berry St., Williamsburg* ☎ *718/302–5343* ⊕ *www.leifshop.com* Ⓜ *L to Bedford Ave.*

🍸 Nightlife

BARS

Barcade

BARS/PUBS | Stop reminiscing about your arcade-loving youth and start playing the more than 30 vintage video games (most cost a mere quarter) lining the walls of this high-spirited bar-arcade. Challenge yourself with favorites like Ms. Pac-Man or rarities like Rampage. Barcade isn't just about the games, though: there's a good selection of microbrews, as well as snacks. ✉ *388 Union Ave., Williamsburg* ☎ *718/302–6464* ⊕ *www.barcadebrooklyn.com* Ⓜ *G to Metropolitan Ave.; L to Lorimer St.*

★ Ides Bar2

BARS/PUBS | One of the buzziest bars in Williamsburg, the Ides benefits from its privileged position on the Wythe Hotel's rooftop. Well-heeled patrons from all over the world line up for entry ($10 after 6 pm on Friday and Saturday) and the jaw-dropping views of the Manhattan skyline. It's a hot spot on weekends, and crowded—it's more than worth it to go early and have that memorable view all to yourself. This is one of NYC's rare gratuity-free bars, and the only slightly higher menu prices reflect it. ✉ *Wythe Hotel, 80 Wythe Ave., 6th fl., Williamsburg* ☎ *718/460–8006* ⊕ *www.wythehotel.com/the-ides* Ⓜ *L to Bedford Ave.*

★ Maison Premiere

BARS/PUBS | Step inside this buzzy bar and restaurant, marked only by a small "Bar, Oysters" sign, and you'll instantly feel whisked away to New Orleans. Sip expertly made cocktails at the horseshoe-shape bar, or dine on platters of oysters at one of the café tables (there are full dinner and brunch menus as well). The back garden (closed only in winter) is a lush oasis with cast-iron tables amid wisteria and palms. ✉ *298 Bedford Ave., Williamsburg* ☎ *347/335–0446* ⊕ *www.maisonpremiere.com* Ⓜ *L to Bedford Ave.*

Radegast Hall & Biergarten

BREWPUBS/BEER GARDENS | The vibe is boisterous at this sprawling beer garden, with plenty of communal tables that foster a convivial atmosphere. The Central European beers on tap and in bottles pair well with hearty foods like schnitzel, goulash, and delicious hot pretzels. There's free live music every night. ✉ *113 N. 3rd St., Williamsburg* ☎ *718/963–3937* ⊕ *www.radegasthall.com* Ⓜ *L to Bedford Ave.*

Spuyten Duyvil

BARS/PUBS | You might need to be a beer geek to recognize the obscure names of the more than 100 imported microbrews available here, but the connoisseurs behind the bar are more than happy to offer detailed descriptions and make recommendations. They'll also help you choose cheese and charcuterie platters to match your beverages. The space is narrow, with limited seating: all the more reason to take advantage of the huge backyard in summer. ✉ *359 Metropolitan Ave., Williamsburg* ☎ *718/963–4140* ⊕ *www.spuytenduyvilnyc.com* Ⓜ *L to Lorimer St.; G to Metropolitan Ave.*

The Water Tower

BARS/PUBS | Perched atop the Williamsburg Hotel, overlooking its rooftop pool, this new, ambitious bar may represent a new chapter in the annals of Brooklyn history. Not one of New York's actual iconic water towers, but rather a conical glass structure made in tribute to them, the bar is unabashedly upscale in a "Manhattan" sort of way, with cocktails starting at $22 and going up to $150, and a caviar tasting that costs $525. Still, the 360-degree views are some of the city's best, and if you're looking for a comprehensive night out, starting with drinks and ending with a DJ dance party, this is your ticket. ✉ *96 Wythe Ave., Williamsburg* ☎ *718/362–8100* ⊕ *www.thewilliamsburghotel.com/bars-restaurants* Ⓜ *L to Bedford Ave.*

BREWERIES

Brooklyn Brewery

BREWPUBS/BEER GARDENS | This brewery put the borough's once-active craft beer scene back on the map when it opened in this former matzo factory in Williamsburg in 1996. Free 15-minute guided tours are offered on weekend afternoons, and there are always at least 8 or 10 offerings in the convivial taproom: the signature lager is popular, as is the Belgian-inspired Local 1, or try one of the seasonal options. Note that no open-toed shoes are allowed on the tours. ✉ *79 N. 11th St., Williamsburg* ☎ *718/486–7422* ⊕ *www.brooklynbrewery.com* Ⓜ *L to Bedford Ave.; G to Nassau Ave.*

LIVE MUSIC VENUES

Bembe

DANCE CLUBS | This steamy bi-level lounge is Williamsburg's answer to Miami clubbing, though decorated with salvaged items including an old redwood front door from a New York State winery. The crowd is as eclectic as the DJ-spun beats that range from reggae to Brazilian— often accompanied by live drumming. The tropical bar menu adds to the place's Latin cred. ✉ *81 S. 6th St., Williamsburg* ☎ *718/387–5389* ⊕ *www.bembe.us* Ⓜ *J, M, Z to Marcy Ave.*

Music Hall of Williamsburg

MUSIC CLUBS | This intimate tri-level music venue in a former mayonnaise factory has excellent acoustics, so it's no surprise that it draws die-hard fans of rock and indie music. There's balcony seating and an additional bar upstairs. If you love Manhattan's Bowery Ballroom, you'll feel the same way about this venue; it's also run by the bookers at Bowery Presents, so you can expect the same quality lineups. ✉ *66 N. 6th St., Williamsburg* ☎ *718/486–5400* ⊕ *www.musichallofwilliamsburg.com* Ⓜ *L to Bedford Ave.*

Union Pool

BARS/PUBS | A former pool-supply store now serves as a funky multipurpose venue, complete with a corrugated tin–backed bar, a photo booth, a small stage for live music, and cheap PBR. It's a popular spot on the Friday-night circuit, especially for late-night dancing. The back patio has a taco truck and a fire pit. ✉ *484 Union Ave., Williamsburg* ☎ *718/609–0484* ⊕ *www.union-pool.com* Ⓜ *G to Metropolitan Ave.; L to Lorimer St.*

🎭 Performing Arts

FILM

★ Nitehawk Cinema

FILM | The only movie theater of its kind in the New York City area, Nitehawk shows first-run and repertory films in three theater spaces and serves a full menu in-theater, as well as popcorn and snacks. Themed dining specials are paired with each indie film. Movies often sell out on weekends, so buy tickets ($12) in advance. After the film, bring your ticket stub down to the ground-level bar for $4 beers and well drinks. ✉ *136 Metropolitan Ave., Williamsburg* ☎ *718/782–8370* ⊕ *www.nitehawkcinema.com* 🎟 *Tickets $12* Ⓜ *L to Bedford Ave.*

Greenpoint

Greenpoint, Brooklyn's northernmost neighborhood, above Williamsburg and below Queens, is often described as "up and coming," but Greenpointers know it's already arrived—again. A major 19th-century hub, first for shipbuilding and later for glassmaking, printing, and other manufacturing pursuits, Greenpoint prospered by welcoming successive waves of German, Irish, Italian, and Polish immigrants. Still predominantly Polish today, the area retains a village feel even as upscale businesses open and new residents move in. It has evolved more slowly than nearby Williamsburg, in part because the subway line that services Greenpoint is the borough's only one that doesn't travel to Manhattan. With more than 7,500 new housing units planned by around 2025—some in repurposed factories, others, among them the waterfront Greenpoint Landing development, new construction—the mood could shift. For now, though, Greenpoint plays amiable host to outstanding restaurants, creative bakeries, independent boutiques, and cozy bars. All of these, along with the now-ended HBO hit *Girls,* whose main character, Hannah, lived here, have raised Greenpoint's contemporary profile, but it's still easy to get a sense of the area's layered history. Town houses from the 1800s add architectural gravitas to the side streets off Manhattan Avenue, the neighborhood's main artery; a half mile west, the waterfront is a striking juxtaposition of spruced-up parks and the remnants of the area's industrial past.

👁 Sights

Greenpoint Historic District

BUILDING | Landmarked in 1982, this historic district is lined with beautiful town houses. The area extends roughly from Calyer Street north to Kent Street, between Manhattan Avenue and Franklin Street. The brick homes date to the 1850s, when Greenpoint was a major hub for shipbuilding and the manufacturing. Walking along Franklin Street, north of Greenpoint Avenue, it's easy to feel like you've stepped into an Edward Hopper painting. ✉ *Calyer St. to Kent St., Greenpoint* Ⓜ *G to Greenpoint Ave.*

🛏 Hotels

Box House Hotel

$$ | HOTEL | Adventurous travelers are drawn to this all-suites hotel, formerly a door factory, in industrial northern Greenpoint, where suites feel like stylish New York City apartments, with kitchens, living rooms, and homey touches like shelves lined with books (some also have terraces). **Pros:** exciting, developing neighborhood; huge suites with kitchens and living rooms; free neighborhood transportation. **Cons:** functional bathrooms not particularly luxurious; no blackout curtains; isolated location in industrial area isn't for everyone. $ *Rooms from: $349 ⊠ 77 Box St., Greenpoint* ☎ *646/396–0251* ⊕ *www.theboxhousehotel.com* ⊅ *127 rooms and suites* ❍I *No meals* Ⓜ *G to Greenpoint Ave.*

Nightlife

BARS
★ Diamond Lil
BARS/PUBS | Locals flock to this low-key neighborhood spot for great cocktails at affordable prices by a bartender who trained in the Milk & Honey school developed by the late, legendary bartender Sasha Petraske (the man responsible for New York's speakeasy craze). The sophisticated art nouveau–inspired design—complete with embossed wallpaper and a beaded lamp—gives the place a warm, Prohibition-era vibe. Settle into one of the forest green booths and sample tipples like the Frozen Painkiller or the Valparaiso Sour (made with pisco, Campari, lemon, and strawberry). ⊠ *179 Nassau Ave., Greenpoint* ⊕ *www.diamondlilbar.com* Ⓜ *G to Nassau Ave.*

⊕ Shopping

★ In God We Trust
CLOTHING | Stylish shoppers love this boutique for the homespun clothes and cheeky accessories, like gold penne pasta on a delicate chain or business-card cases emblazoned "Talented Mother Fucker." Of the two Brooklyn locations, the Bedford Avenue shop in Williamsburg gets the most foot traffic, but the clothes and jewelry are made in the studio behind this Greenpoint Avenue outpost. ⊠ *70 Greenpoint Ave., Greenpoint* ☎ *718/389–3545* ⊕ *www.ingodwetrustnyc.com* Ⓜ *G to Greenpoint Ave.*

Bushwick

Bushwick is young and cool, and also gritty and very industrial—working factories make everything from wontons to plastic bags—but it's definitely where to go if you're interested in street art: check out the Bushwick Collective and the streets surrounding it. The neighborhood also has pockets of cafés and restaurants, including Roberta's—making some of the best Neapolitan-style pizza this side of the Atlantic.

◉ Sights

★ The Bushwick Collective
PUBLIC ART | For evidence of art's ability to transform lives, visit this colorful outdoor street art gallery curated by Joseph Ficalora, a Bushwick native who came of age during the neighborhood's period of decline and channeled his grief over losing both of his parents into a space where street artists create temporary works of art. Pixel Pancho of Turin and Baltimore-based Gaia are among the established artists featured at this urban street-art destination. ⊠ *427 Troutman St., Bushwick* ⊕ *thebushwickcollective. com* Ⓜ *L to Jefferson St.*

56 Bogart (The BogArt)
ARTS VENUE | Many young Bushwick galleries showcase edgy and experimental work—visiting this converted warehouse is an easy way to see a lot of art in one shot. The BogArt contains large studios and more than a dozen galleries. Standouts include Robert Henry Contemporary, Theodore:Art, David & Schweitzer Contemporary, and Fuchs Project. ■**TIP→ Gallery hours vary, but the best time to visit is on Friday and weekends, when most of them are open.** ⊠ *56 Bogart St., Bushwick* ☎ *718/599–0800* ⊕ *www.56bogartstreet.com* Ⓜ *L to Morgan Ave.*

On a walk through Bushwick and East Williamsburg, you'll find plenty of dynamic local street art.

🍴 Restaurants

The big draw in Bushwick is Roberta's. The neighborhood is still pretty industrial, but there are new restaurants and bars out here creating a scene.

Bunna Cafe

$ | **ETHIOPIAN** | The best way to sample the diverse flavors, many quite spicy, of Ethiopian cuisine at this stellar restaurant are the combination platters—for one or to share—though you can also order individual dishes. If the delicious, seasonal *duba wot* (spiced pumpkin) is available, definitely include it in your platter. **Known for:** shareable plates; traditional Ethiopian coffee ceremony and teas; live music events featuring Ethiopian artists. ⓢ *Average main: $11* ✉ *1084 Flushing Ave., Bushwick* ☎ *347/295–2227* ⊕ *bunnaethiopia.net* Ⓜ *L to Morgan Ave.*

★ Roberta's

$$ | **PIZZA** | A neighborhood groundbreaker since it opened in 2008, this restaurant in a former garage is a must-visit, especially for pizza connoisseurs. The menu emphasizes hyperlocal ingredients—there's a rooftop garden—and the wood-fired pizzas have innovative combinations of toppings like fennel, pork sausage, and pistachio. **Known for:** award-winning, nationally recognized pizza; seasonal patio with outdoor tiki bar; impressive beverage menu includes curated coffee program. ⓢ *Average main: $17* ✉ *261 Moore St., Bushwick* ☎ *718/417–1118* ⊕ *www.robertaspizza.com* Ⓜ *L to Morgan Ave.*

East Williamsburg

Industrial East Williamsburg, between Williamsburg and Bushwick, has become an enclave of street art, up-and-coming art galleries, cafés, and restaurants.

👁 Sights

Luhring Augustine

MUSEUM | Probably the neighborhood's most established gallery, this annex of the Chelsea original is worth a stop to

see whatever show is up and to appreciate the soaring space and its cantilevered
ceiling. ⊠ *25 Knickerbocker Ave., East
Williamsburg* ☎ *718/386–2746* ⊕ *www.
luhringaugustine.com* ⊗ *Closed Mon.–
Wed. Sept.–June and Sun.–Tues. in July
and Aug.* Ⓜ *L to Morgan Ave.*

⛾ Nightlife

BARS
★ Featherweight

BARS/PUBS | The cocktail list at this small
spot is full of the hits you'd expect at a
bar run by the experts behind the two
Weather Up spaces in Manhattan and
Prospect Heights. Part of the allure,
though, is that bartenders will mix a
cocktail to your precise specifications.
Prime time here is late night. Finding the
entrance is part of the fun: look for the
painted feather and the three-story-tall
mural of a boxer. ⊠ *135 Graham Ave.,
East Williamsburg* ☎ *202/907–3372*
⊕ *www.featherweightbk.com* Ⓜ *J, M to
Lorimer St.; L to Montrose Ave.*

Park Slope

Full of young families, dog walkers, dou-
ble-wide strollers, and impeccably curated shops, the neighborhood that literally
slopes down from Prospect Park can feel
like a veritable Norman Rockwell painting. Add to all that a slew of laptop-friend-
ly coffeehouses and turn-of-the-20th-
century brownstones—remnants of the
days when Park Slope had the nation's
highest per-capita income—and it's no
surprise that academics and writers have
flocked here. Park Slope's busiest drags,
5th and 7th Avenues, present plenty
of shopping and noshing opportunities.
Head to the elegant, 585-acre Prospect
Park for long strolls or bicycle rides past
lazy meadows, shady forests, and lakes
designed by Olmsted and Vaux of Central
Park fame (look out for free summertime
concerts). Adjacent is Brooklyn Botanic

Garden, which features a variety of
public classes and the springtime Cherry
Blossom Festival. Also perched on the
park is the Brooklyn Museum, lauded for
collections of American, Egyptian, and
feminist art.

⊙ Sights

Lefferts Historic House

BUILDING | FAMILY | A visit to this Dutch
Colonial farmhouse, built in 1783 and
moved from nearby Flatbush Avenue
to Prospect Park in 1918, is a window
into how Brooklynites lived in the 19th
century, when the area was predominantly farmland. Rooms are furnished
with antiques and reproductions from
the 1820s, when the house was last
redecorated. ⊠ *452 Flatbush Ave.,
Prospect Park* ☎ *718/789–2822* ⊕ *www.
prospectpark.org/lefferts* ⊠ *$3 suggested
donation* ⊗ *Closed weekdays* Ⓜ *B, Q, S
to Prospect Park.*

LeFrak Center at Lakeside

CITY PARK | FAMILY | The highlight of this
26-acre space in Prospect Park is the
all-season ice- and roller-skating rink. The
walkways, the esplanade near the lake,
and the Music Island nature reserve—
all part of the original Olmsted and
Vaux plans—make for a pleasant stroll.
Themed roller-skating night takes place
on Friday, April through October; in winter, the rink hosts hockey and curling clin-
ics for all ages. The Bluestone Café offers
sunny outdoor seating year-round. ⊠ *171
East Dr., Prospect Park* ☎ *718/462–0010*
⊕ *www.lakesidebrooklyn.com* ⊠ *Skating
$6 weekdays, $9 weekends; rentals
$6–$7* ⊗ *Rink: closed days vary by
season* Ⓜ *B, Q, S to Prospect Park; Q to
Parkside Ave.*

Old Stone House & Washington Park

BUILDING | FAMILY | This reconstructed
Dutch farmhouse dating to 1699, played
a central role in the Battle of Brooklyn,
one of the largest battles of the Revolutionary War, and survived until the 1890s.

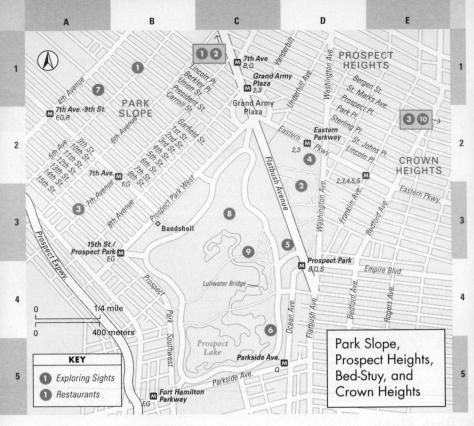

Park Slope,
Prospect Heights,
Bed-Stuy, and
Crown Heights

KEY
1 *Exploring Sights*
1 *Restaurants*

The small museum here focuses on the Revolutionary era in Brooklyn from 1776 until 1783. Art exhibits, concerts, plays, and other community events take place year-round, including a ball game to celebrate the Brooklyn Baseball Club, which started here and gave rise to the Brooklyn Dodgers. ⊠ *Washington Park/J. J. Byrne Playground, 336 3rd St., Park Slope* ☎ *718/768–3195* ⊕ *www. theoldstonehouse.org* ✉ *$3 suggested donation* ⊙ *Closed Mon.–Thurs.* Ⓜ *R to Union St.; F, G, R to 4th Ave.–9th St.*

★ Prospect Park

ARTS VENUE | FAMILY | Brooklyn residents are passionate about Prospect Park, and with good reason: lush green spaces, gently curved walkways, summer concerts, vivid foliage in autumn, and an all-season skating rink make it a year-round getaway. In 1859 the New York Legislature decided to develop plans for a park in the fast-growing city of Brooklyn. After landscape architects Frederick Law Olmsted and Calvert Vaux completed the park in the late 1880s, Olmsted remarked that he was prouder of Prospect Park than of any of his other works—Manhattan's Central Park included. Many critics agree that this is their most beautiful work. On weekends, those not jogging the 3.35-mile loop gravitate to the tree-fringed Long Meadow to picnic, or play cricket, flag football, or Frisbee. The park's north entrance is at Grand Army Plaza, where the Soldiers' and Sailors' Memorial Arch (patterned on the Arc de Triomphe in Paris) honors Civil War veterans. On Saturday, year-round, a green market at the plaza throngs with shoppers.

A good way to experience the park is to walk the Long Meadow and then head to the eastern side, where you'll find the lake and most attractions, including the Lefferts Historic House, Prospect Park Audubon Center, and the LeFrak Center. The Prospect Park Carousel, built in 1912, still thrills the kids. The annual Celebrate Brooklyn! festival takes place at the Prospect Park Bandshell from early June through mid-August. The many other events include free yoga classes on the Long Meadow in summer and the Sunday Smorgasburg outdoor food market at Breeze Hill, April through October. ⊠ *450 Flatbush Ave., Prospect Park* ☎ *718/965–8951* ⊕ *www.prospectpark. org* ✉ *Carousel $2.50* ⊙ *Carousel closed Mon.–Wed.* Ⓜ *2, 3 to Grand Army Plaza; F, G to 7th Ave. or 15th St.–Prospect Park; B, Q to 7th Ave.*

★ Smorgasburg

$ | |MARKET | More than a hundred of New York City's best and brightest cooks and culinary artisans unite in Prospect Park (replacing the Brooklyn Bridge Park Pier 5 location) every Sunday to form the city's hottest foodie market. An offshoot of the Brooklyn Flea, this food bazaar extravaganza has launched countless culinary crazes (ramen burger, anyone?), and most vendors are small-scale, home-grown operators. Lines can grow long and vendors can sell out as the afternoon goes on, so head over early in the day if possible. There is also an outpost on the Williamsburg waterfront (between Kent Avenue and North 7th Street) on Saturday, as well as smaller Smorgasburg pop-ups in Queens, at Coney Island, at the South Street Seaport, and at Central Park SummerStage events. A collaboration with the Winter Flea is held weekends at 625 Atlantic Avenue, across from Barclays Center. The larger Smorgasburgs are seasonal and generally take place from May through October, but check the website to confirm. ⊠ *Breeze Hill, Prospect Park* ⊕ *www.brooklynflea.com* Ⓜ *B, Q, S to Prospect Park; F, G to 15th St.–Prospect Park.*

🍴 Restaurants

Park Slope's reputation precedes it: this handsome, gay-friendly family neighborhood also happens to be a great place to fill the tummy. Restaurant-crammed 5th

The boathouse in Prospect Park, built in 1905, was one of the first buildings in New York City to be declared a historic landmark.

Avenue is not for the indecisive; there's everything from Mexican to Italian to Thai, and it's all quite good.

★ al di là Trattoria

$$$ | ITALIAN | Roughly translated as "beyond," al di là has been consistently packed since it opened in 1998, and it's easy to understand why: perfectly prepared dishes from northern Italy in a cozy atmosphere. The warm farro salad with seasonal ingredients and goat cheese is perfectly al dente; the hand-pinched ravioli are delicious; and meatier entrées like braised rabbit, pork loin scaloppine, and charcoal-grilled young chicken are highlights. **Known for:** knowledgeable servers; ragù; not taking reservations. [$] *Average main: $26* ✉ *248 5th Ave., Park Slope* ☎ *718/783–4565* 🌐 *www.aldilatrattoria.com* [M] *R to Union St.*

Fonda

$$ | MEXICAN | Authentic and flavorful contemporary Mexican food, perfectly mixed cocktails, and amiable staff define this cozy restaurant—the first of three in New York City overseen by award-winning chef and cookbook author Roberto Santibañez. It's tempting to order by sauce alone: enchiladas with mole, scallops and shrimp with avocado serrano sauce, and poblano peppers with roasted-tomato chipotle sauce. **Known for:** happy hour at the bar; duck zarape; tight seating when crowded. [$] *Average main: $24* ✉ *434 7th Ave., Park Slope* ☎ *718/369–3144* 🌐 *www.fondarestaurant.com* 🕒 *No lunch weekdays* [M] *F, G to 7th Ave. or 15th St.–Prospect Park.*

Shopping

GIFTS AND SOUVENIRS

Annie's Blue Ribbon General Store

GIFTS/SOUVENIRS | FAMILY | The perfectly giftable, Brooklyn-made products at this variety store include Apotheke candles and diffusers, Bellocq teas, Claudia Pearson's hand-drawn tea towels, Brooklyn Slate, and Bocce's Bakery birthday-cake treats for your favorite canine. Brooklyn-themed tchotchkes, ecofriendly cleaning supplies (including a Common Good Refill station), stationery, and toys round out the selection. ✉ *232 5th Ave., between President and Carroll Sts., Park Slope* ☎ *718/522–9848* ⊕ *www.bluerib-bongeneralstore.com* Ⓜ *R to Union St.*

TOYS
Brooklyn Superhero Supply Co.

TOYS | **FAMILY** | If you can't crack a smile in this store—where all proceeds from superhero costumes, gear, and secret identity kits benefit 826NYC's writing and tutoring programs for kids—step immediately into its Devillainizer cage. Once cleansed, browse superpowers like telekinesis, chutzpah, and gumption, sold in plastic jugs and fake paint cans. The clever labels listing "ingredients" and "warnings" are worth every ounce of the tongue-in-cheek products. If you want to visit, do call ahead because it's staffed by volunteers, though it's usually open Tuesday through Sunday from noon to 6. ✉ *372 5th Ave., between 5th and 6th Sts., Park Slope* ☎ *718/499–9884* ⊕ *www.superherosupplies.com* ☾ *Closed Mon.* Ⓜ *F, G, R to 4th Ave.–9th St.*

ⓨ Nightlife

BARS
★ Union Hall

BARS/PUBS | This neighborhood stand-by has something going on just about every night. On the main floor, two bocce courts and a library nook with couches and fireplace are popular hangouts; downstairs, there are smart comedy shows with both high-profile and up-and-coming performers, eclectic talks, or DJs spinning. The outdoor patio is open in good weather. The menu of perfectly tasty burgers, sandwiches, and bar snacks (beer cheese is a highlight) means the patrons tend to settle in for the evening. Events are either free or have a modest cover ($5–$20). ✉ *702 Union St., Park Slope* ☎ *718/638–4400* ⊕ *www.unionhallny.com* Ⓜ *R to Union St.*

LIVE MUSIC VENUES
★ Barbès

MUSIC CLUBS | Outstanding regulars like the Django Reinhardt mantle-bearer Stephane Wrembel, western-swingers Brain Cloud, and Slavic Soul Party spin threads of folk and "ethnic" into 21st-century music, while the Erik Satie Quartet keeps Satie, Britten, and other classical composers relevant. Performances take place in the back room, where a pitcher is passed to collect the $10 suggested cover. Up front, the somewhat musty, Parisian-like bar has a laid-back vibe and a full cocktail menu. ✉ *376 9th St., Park Slope* ☎ *347/422–0248* ⊕ *www.barbesbrooklyn.com* Ⓜ *F, G to 7th Ave.*

🎭 Performing Arts

THEATER
Puppetworks

PUPPET SHOWS | **FAMILY** | Marionette puppets have been enacting classic fairy tales like *Beauty and the Beast*, *Goldilocks and the Three Bears*, *Jack and the Beanstalk*, and *Pinocchio* for children at this storefront theater since 1990. A friendly puppeteer preps the young audience on theater etiquette before each performance. Afterward, theater education continues with a Q&A. Public performances are given on weekends only; call or email for reservations. ✉ *338 6th Ave., Park Slope* ☎ *718/965–3391* ⊕ *www.puppetworks.org* 🎟 *$11* Ⓜ *F, G to 7th Ave.*

Prospect Heights

An influx of creative young professionals and impressive eats has lifted Prospect Heights out from the shadow of nearby Park Slope. Swing by Grand Army Plaza on a Saturday to hit the borough's flagship farmers market, where cooking demos and fresh produce entice the food-loving hoards. Or gorge on everything from lobster rolls to Korean tacos at the plaza's Food Truck Rally held on select Sundays, May through October. Vanderbilt Avenue and Washington Avenue are the main drags for restaurants and bars.

👁 Sights

Barclays Center

ARTS VENUE | FAMILY | This rust-tinted spaceship of an arena houses two sports franchises—basketball's Brooklyn Nets and ice hockey's New York Islanders—and hosts events from rock concerts to circuses. With a capacity rivaling Madison Square Garden's, Barclays Center also has plenty of room to offer concessions courtesy of local restaurateurs, including Paisano's Burger, BK Ballers, and Calexico. ✉ *620 Atlantic Ave., Prospect Heights* ☎ *917/618–6100* 🌐 *www.barclayscenter.com* [M] *2, 3, 4, 5, B, D, N, Q, R to Atlantic Ave.–Barclays Ctr.; G to Fulton St.; C to Lafayette Ave.; LIRR to Atlantic Terminal.*

★ Brooklyn Botanic Garden

GARDEN | FAMILY | A verdant 52-acre oasis, the BBG charms with its array of "gardens within the garden," including an idyllic Japanese hill-and-pond garden, a stunning rose garden, and a Shakespeare garden. The Japanese cherry arbor turns into a breathtaking cloud of pink every spring. There are multiple entrances, and a variety of free garden tours are available with admission; check the website for seasonal details. ✉ *990 Washington Ave., Prospect Heights* ☎ *718/623–7200* 🌐 *www.bbg.org* 🎫 *$15* 🕒 *Closed Mon. except major holidays* [M] *2, 3 to Eastern Pkwy.–Brooklyn Museum; 2, 3, 4, 5 to Franklin Ave.; S to Botanic Garden; B, Q to Prospect Park.*

★ Brooklyn Museum

MUSEUM | FAMILY | First-time visitors may well gasp at the vastness of New York's second-largest museum (after Manhattan's Metropolitan Museum of Art) and one of the largest in America at 560,000 square feet of exhibition space. The colossal Beaux Arts structure houses one of the best collections of Egyptian art in the world and impressive collections of African, pre-Columbian, and Native American art. It's also worth seeking out the museum's works by Georgia O'Keeffe, Winslow Homer, John Singer Sargent, George Bellows, Thomas Eakins, and Milton Avery. The museum is also well known for very contemporary, cutting-edge special exhibits. The monthly (except for September) First Saturday free-entry night is a neighborhood party of art, music, and dancing, with food vendors and several cash bars. ✉ *200 Eastern Pkwy., Prospect Heights* ☎ *718/638–5000* 🌐 *www.brooklynmuseum.org* 🎫 *$16 suggested donation, $25 combo ticket with Brooklyn Botanic Garden* 🕒 *Closed Mon., Tues.* [M] *2, 3 to Eastern Pkwy.–Brooklyn Museum.*

🍴 Restaurants

Once referred to as the "new Park Slope," the neighborhood on the other side of Flatbush has come into its own. Leafy brownstone-laden streets are increasingly filled with great restaurants.

Chuko Ramen

$$ | JAPANESE | A small, reliably tasty menu of signature ramen headlines this Prospect Heights institution for noodle bowls, buns, gyoza, beer, and sake. Long waits for a table have (slightly) abated since the operation moved in 2016 to this (slightly) larger location offering 20 more seats, but expect crowds, especially during winter months. **Known for:** ramen; very popular; lines. [$] *Average main: $14* ✉ *565 Vanderbilt Ave., Prospect Heights* ☎ *347/425–9501* 🌐 *www.chukobk.com* [M] *2, 3 to Bergen St.; C to Clinton–Washington Aves.; B, Q to 7th Ave.*

Bed-Stuy and Crown Heights

Crown Heights and nearby Bedford-Stuyvesant (known as Bed-Stuy) are vast and historic neighborhoods with a tumultuous past. Long since the 1991 riots that escalated tensions between the area's Hasidic and black communities, these days Crown Heights is more likely to inspire thoughts of diverse stoops and row houses, rapid gentrification, and authentic Caribbean fare. Crown Heights is also home to the Brooklyn Children's Museum and Weeksville Heritage Center.

◉ Sights

Brooklyn Children's Museum
COLLEGE | FAMILY | What's red, yellow, and green, and shaped like a spaceship? The Brooklyn Children's Museum, an interactive space where kids can run, touch, and play with abandon. Exhibits range from a working greenhouse to art experiences. The cornerstone is World Brooklyn, a warren of rooms dedicated to various NYC cultures that includes an Italian pizza shop, Hispanic bakery, and a replica MTA bus. ✉ 145 Brooklyn Ave., Crown Heights ☎ 718/735-4400 ⊕ www.brooklynkids. org ☜ $11 ⊘ Closed Mon. Ⓜ C to Kingston–Throop Aves.; 3 to Kingston Ave.; A, C to Nostrand Ave.

Weeksville Heritage Center
BUILDING | FAMILY | Honoring the history of the 19th-century African American community of Weeksville, one of the first communities of free blacks in New York (founded by James Weeks), this Crown Heights museum comprises an industrial-modern building by Caples Jefferson Architects, botanical gardens, and three houses that date as far back as 1838. The restored homes, along the historic, gravel Hunterfly Road, are now period re-creations depicting life in the 1860s, 1900s, and 1930s. Walk-in tours ($8) are Tuesday to Friday at 2 and 4 pm. ✉ 158 Buffalo Ave., Crown Heights ☎ 718/756-5250 ⊕ www.weeksvillesociety.org ☜ $8 house tours; grounds free ⊘ Closed Sat.–Mon. Ⓜ A, C to Utica Ave.; 3, 4 to Crown Heights–Utica Ave.

Coney Island

Coney Island is practically synonymous with the sounds, smells, and sights of a New York City summer: hot dogs and ice cream, suntan lotion, roller coasters, excited crowds, and weathered old men fishing.

Named Konijn Eiland (Rabbit Island) by the Dutch for its wild rabbit population, the Coney Island peninsula has a boardwalk, a 2½-mile long beach, amusement parks, and the **New York Aquarium**, which was heavily damaged during Hurricane Sandy in 2012 and underwent extensive renovations, culminating with the opening of the long-awaited exhibition *Ocean Wonders: Sharks!* in 2018. Nathan's Famous on Surf Avenue is the quintessential hot dog spot.

Among the other entertainments out here are the freakish attractions at **Coney Island Circus Sideshow** and the heart-stopping plunge of the granddaddy of all roller coasters—the **Cyclone**. The Mets' minor-league baseball team, the Cyclones, plays at MCU Park, where music concerts are also held in summer. The area's banner day is during the raucous Mermaid Parade, held in June. A fireworks display lights up the sky Friday night from late June through Labor Day.

◉ Sights

Coney Island Circus Sideshow
ARTS VENUE | The cast of talented freaks and geeks who keep Coney Island's carnival tradition alive include sword swallowers, fire-eaters, knife throwers, contortionists, and Serpentina the snake

A stroll on the boardwalk at Coney Island is a New York summer tradition.

dancer. Every show is an extravaganza, with 10 different acts to fascinate and impress. ⊠ *Sideshows by the Seashore, 1208 Surf Ave., Coney Island* ☎ *718/372-5159* ⊕ *www.coneyisland.com/sideshow.shtml* 🎫 *$10* ⊙ *Closed Oct.–Mar.* Ⓜ *F, Q to W. 8th St.–NY Aquarium; D, F, N, Q to Coney Island–Stillwell Ave.*

The Cyclone

AMUSEMENT PARK/WATER PARK | **FAMILY** | This historic wooden roller coaster first thrilled riders in 1927, and it'll still make you scream. Anticipation builds as the cars slowly clack up to the first unforgettable 85-foot plunge—and the look on your face is captured in photos that you can purchase at the end of the ride. The Cyclone may not have the speed or the twists and turns of more modern rides, but that's all part of its rickety charm. It's one of two New York City landmarks in Coney Island; the other is Deno's Wonder Wheel. ⊠ *Luna Park, 834 Surf Ave., Coney Island* ☎ *718/373-5862* ⊕ *www.lunaparknyc.com* 🎫 *$10* ⊙ *Closed hrs vary, but are generally mid-Oct.–early*

May; check website for details Ⓜ *F, Q to W. 8th St.–NY Aquarium; D, F, N, Q to Coney Island–Stillwell Ave.*

Deno's Wonder Wheel Amusement Park

AMUSEMENT PARK/WATER PARK | **FAMILY** | The star attraction at Deno's is the towering 150-foot-tall Wonder Wheel. The Ferris wheel first opened in 1920, making it the oldest ride in Coney Island, and the spectacular views from the top take in a long stretch of the shoreline. Other rides for tots here include the Dizzy Dragons, the Pony Carts, and a brightly painted carousel, plus the new virtual reality arcade game Stop the Zombies. ⊠ *1025 Riegelmann Boardwalk, Coney Island* ☎ *718/372-2592* 🎫 *Free admission; pay-as-you-ride* ⊙ *Closed Nov.–early Mar.; hrs vary* Ⓜ *F, Q to W. 8th St.–NY Aquarium; D, F, N, Q to Coney Island–Stillwell Ave.*

★ New York Aquarium

ZOO | **FAMILY** | The oldest continually operating aquarium in the United States is run by the Wildlife Conservation Society; its mission is to save wildlife and wild places worldwide through science, conservation action, and education. The aquarium occupies 14 acres of beach-front property and is home to hundreds of aquatic species. At the Sea Cliffs, you can watch penguins, sea lions, sea otters, and seals frolic: the best action is at feeding time. The Conservation Hall and Glovers Reef building is home to marine life from Belize, Fiji, and all over the world, including angelfish, eels, rays, and piranhas. The new *Ocean Wonders: Sharks!* exhibit opened in summer 2018 and features 12 species of sharks including sand tiger sharks, nurse sharks, and sandbar sharks. The exhibit highlight is a 40-foot coral-reef tunnel that provides 360-degree views of an Indo Pacific reef, and a 350,000-plus-gallon representation of the Hudson Canyon's edge. ■ TIP➔ **Purchase tickets online for discounted rates.** ✉ *602 Surf Ave., Coney Island* ☎ *718/265–3474* ⊕ *www.nyaquarium.com* 🔌 *$12* Ⓜ *F, Q to W. 8th St.–NY Aquarium; D, F, N, Q to Coney Island–Stillwell Ave.*

★ **Riegelmann Boardwalk**
BEACH—SIGHT | FAMILY | Built in 1923, just one year before legendary Totonno's Pizzeria opened its doors on nearby Neptune Avenue, this famous wood planked walkway is better known as the Coney Island Boardwalk, and in summer it seems like all of Brooklyn is out strolling along the 2½-mile stretch. The quintessential walk starts at the end of the pier in Coney Island, opposite the Parachute Jump—you can see the shoreline stretched out before you, a beautiful confluence of nature and city. From here to Brighton Beach is a little over a mile and should take about a half hour at a leisurely amble. Those modernistic, rectangular structures perched over the beach are new bathrooms and lifeguard stations. ✉ *Between W. 37th and Brighton 15th Sts., Coney Island* Ⓜ *D, F, N, Q to Coney Island–Stillwell Ave.; F, Q to W. 8th St.–NY Aquarium; B, Q to Brighton Beach; Q to Ocean Pkwy.*

🍴 Restaurants

It's no longer an island, but this amusement park on the sea is salt-of-the-earth paradise. Think pizza and hot dogs and calorie-laden carnival fare. If you're in town during July 4, a Big Apple must-see is the annual Nathan's Famous hot-dog-eating contest where hundreds of people gather to watch "professional" eaters scarf down tubular meat.

★ **Nathan's Famous**
$ | HOT DOG | Nathan Handwerker, a Polish immigrant, founded this Coney Island hot dog stand in 1916, and what followed can only be described as a quintessential American success story. With a $300 loan and his wife Ida's secret spice recipe, Nathan set up shop and his success was almost instantaneous—Al Capone, Jimmy Durante, and Cary Grant became regulars early on, President FDR served Nathan's dogs to the king and queen of England, local girl Barbra Streisand had them delivered to London, and Walter Matthau asked that they be served at his funeral. **Known for:** world-famous hot dogs; quintessentially Brooklyn; annual hot-dog-eating contest. Ⓢ *Average main: $5* ✉ *1310 Surf Ave., Coney Island* ☎ *718/333–2202* ⊕ *www.nathansfamous.com* Ⓜ *D, F, N, Q to Coney Island–Stillwell Ave.*

Totonno's Pizzeria Napolitana
$$ | PIZZA | FAMILY | Thin-crust pies judiciously topped with fresh mozzarella and tangy, homemade tomato sauce, then baked in a coal oven—at Totonno's you're not just eating pizza, you're biting into a slice of New York history. Not much has changed since Anthony (Totonno) Pero first opened the pizzeria, in 1924, right after the subways started running to Coney Island—the restaurant is at the same location and run by the same family, who use ingredients and techniques that have been handed down through four generations. **Known for:** legendary New York pizza; family-run; historic

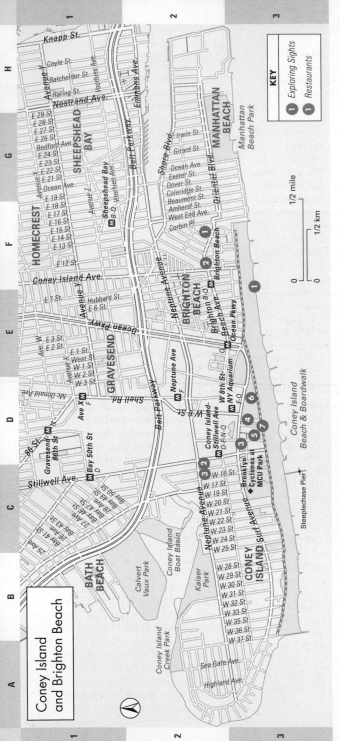

Coney Island and Brighton Beach

KEY

- ❶ Exploring Sights
- ❶ Restaurants

Sights ▶

1 Brighton Beach..............**F3**
2 Brighton
  Beach Avenue..............**F2**
3 Coney Island
  Circus Sideshow............**D3**
4 The Cyclone..................**D3**
5 Deno's Wonder Wheel
  Amusement Park........**D3**
6 New York Aquarium......**D3**
7 Riegelmann
  Boardwalk..................**D3**

Restaurants ▶

1 Kashkar Cafe...............**F2**
2 Nathan's Famous.........**C2**
3 Totonno's Pizzeria
  Napolitana.................**C2**

0   1/2 mile

0   1/2 km

location. $ *Average main: $17* ✉ *1524 Neptune Ave., Coney Island* ☎ *718/372–8606* ⊕ *www.totonnosconeyisland.com* ⊙ *Closed Mon.–Wed.* ═ *No credit cards* Ⓜ *D, F, N, Q to Coney Island–Stillwell Ave.*

🛍 Shopping

FOOD AND TREATS
Williams Candy

FOOD/CANDY | FAMILY | Selling homemade candy apples, marshmallow sticks, popcorn, nuts, and giant lollipops for more than 75 years, this old-school corner candy shop with the yellow awning is a Coney Island mainstay. Owner Peter Agrapides used to visit the store with his mother when he was a kid; he's been the proud owner for 30 years. ✉ *1318 Surf Ave., between W. 15th St. and Stillwell Ave., Coney Island* ☎ *718/372–0302* ⊕ *www.candytreats.com* Ⓜ *D, F, N, Q to Coney Island–Stillwell Ave.*

Brighton Beach

A pleasant stroll just down the boardwalk from Coney Island is Brighton Beach, named after Britain's beach resort. In the early 1900s Brighton Beach was a resort in its own right, with seaside hotels that catered to rich Manhattan families visiting for the summer. Since the 1970s and '80s Brighton Beach has been known for its 100,000 Soviet émigrés. To get to the heart of "Little Odessa" from Coney Island, walk about a mile east along the boardwalk to Brighton 1st Place, then head up to Brighton Beach Avenue. To get here from Manhattan directly, take the B or Q train to the Brighton Beach stop; the trip takes about an hour from Midtown Manhattan.

👁 Sights

★ Brighton Beach

BEACH—SIGHT | FAMILY | Just steps from the subway, this stretch of golden sand is the showpiece of Brooklyn's oceanside playground. Families set up beach blankets, umbrellas, and coolers, and pickup games of beach volleyball and football add to the excitement. Calm surf, a lively boardwalk, and a handful of restaurants for shade and refreshments complete the package. That spit of land in the distance is the Rockaway Peninsula, in Queens. ✉ *Brighton Beach Ave., Brighton Beach* Ⓜ *B, Q to Brighton Beach; Q to Ocean Pkwy.*

Brighton Beach Avenue

NEIGHBORHOOD | The main thoroughfare of "Little Odessa" can feel more like Kiev than Manhattan. Cyrillic shop signs advertise everything from salted tomatoes and pickled mushrooms to Russian-language DVDs and Armani handbags. When the weather's good, local bakeries sell sweet honey cake, cheese-stuffed *vatrushki* danishes, and chocolatey rugelach from sidewalk tables. ✉ *Brighton Beach Ave., Brighton Beach* Ⓜ *B, Q to Brighton Beach.*

🍴 Restaurants

The subway trains that shuttle people out to this beachside neighborhood could be nicknamed the "time machine," because strolling the wide boardwalk along the sea feels like you've dropped into another time and space. Odessa in the 1980s comes to mind. After all, it was around that time when a mass migration of Russian immigrants settled in Brighton Beach. Today you'll hear more Slavic than English, and you'll most certainly be tempted by the vodka and highly entertaining Russian restaurants that line the boardwalk.

Kashkar Cafe

$ | **ASIAN** | Uyghur cuisine, from the Chinese region of Xinjiang, is the focus of the menu at this postage-stamp-size café. Standouts include *naryn* (lamb dumplings), *samsa* (empanada-like lamb pies), pickles, vinegary salads, and clay-oven-baked bread. **Known for:** Uyghur and Uzbek cuisine; large portions; colorful restaurant. [$] *Average main: $6* ✉ *1141 Brighton Beach Ave., Brighton Beach* ☎ *347/991–1111* [M] *B, Q to Brighton Beach.*

QUEENS, THE BRONX, AND STATEN ISLAND

15

Updated by
Giulia Pines

⊙ Sights	🍽 Restaurants	🛏 Hotels	🛍 Shopping	🍸 Nightlife
★★★☆☆	★★★★☆	★★☆☆☆	★★★★☆	★★★☆☆

NEIGHBORHOOD SNAPSHOT

TOP EXPERIENCES

- Sampling ethnic eats and local brews in Queens
- Catching a game at Yankee Stadium or Citi Field
- Taking a free ride on the Staten Island Ferry
- Soaking up modern art at Long Island City museums

GETTING HERE

Queens is served by many subway lines. To get to Astoria, take the N or W train. For Long Island City, take the E, M, G, or 7 train. To get to Jackson Heights, take the 7 train to the 74th Street–Broadway stop. You can also take the E, F, M, or R train to Jackson Heights–Roosevelt Avenue. The 7 brings you out to the attractions of Flushing Meadows Corona Park, as well as Citi Field.

The Bronx is serviced by the 1, 2, 4, 5, 6, B, and D trains. The attractions in the Bronx are spread out across the borough, though, so you need to take different lines to get where you want to go, and it's not necessarily convenient to make connections across town. The B, D, and 4 trains all go to Yankee Stadium, and the B and D continue uptown to the vicinity of Arthur Avenue. The 2 and 5 trains take you close to the Bronx Zoo and Arthur Avenue. Some Metro-North Railroad trains from Grand Central Terminal stop at the New York Botanical Garden.

From the scenic (and free) Staten Island Ferry, you can catch a local bus or hop in a taxi to hit up attractions that are farther afield. Tell the driver where you're going, and ask about the return bus schedule or taxi pickup.

PLANNING YOUR TIME

You can see a few highlights of any of these three boroughs in a day, but if you want to explore deeper, you'll need more time. And don't forget that Flushing has some of the city's best Chinese food. Arthur Avenue in the Bronx is famous for its Italian restaurants.

QUICK BITES

- **Pugsley Pizza.** Get a quality slice or pie at this fun, family-run neighborhood favorite and hangout for nearby Fordham University students. ⊠ *590 E. 191st St., Belmont, Bronx* Ⓜ *Subway: 4, B, D to Fordham Rd.*

- **SingleCut Beersmiths.** Named for a body style of guitar, this craft brewery has a taproom that also serves food like empanadas, flatbread pizzas, and brats. It's closed Monday through Wednesday. ⊠ *19–33 37th St., Astoria, Queens* Ⓜ *Subway: N, W to Astoria–Ditmars Blvd.*

- **Taqueria Coatzingo.** Order a taco *al pastor* (stuffed with spit-grilled pork marinated in citrus and spices) and take a seat among the locals in this authentic, bare-bones Mexican taqueria. ⊠ *7605 Roosevelt Ave., at 76th St., Jackson Heights, Queens* Ⓜ *Subway: E, F, M, R to Jackson Heights–Roosevelt Ave.*

- **White Bear.** The wontons at this tiny hole-in-the-wall are worth the trek to Flushing. Order the No. 6: a dozen wontons with hot chili oil for $6.50. ⊠ *135-02 Roosevelt Ave., entrance on Prince St., Flushing, Queens* Ⓜ *Subway: 7 to Flushing–Main St.*

Many tourists miss out on Queens, the Bronx, and Staten Island—the three boroughs of New York City other than the biggies for tourism, Manhattan and Brooklyn—and that's a shame. There are some noteworthy restaurants, museums, and attractions, and the subway's handful of express trains means that they're closer than you might think.

Queens

Just for the museums and restaurants alone, it's truly worth it to take a short 15-minute trip from Midtown on the 7, E, or M train to **Long Island City** or a slightly longer ride on the N, W, M, or R train to **Astoria**. In Long Island City, major art must-sees are **MoMA PS1** and the **Noguchi Museum.** No trip to Astoria—once nicknamed "Little Athens"—is complete without sampling some of the city's finest Greek and Mediterranean fare and a stop at the **Museum of the Moving Image.**

Jackson Heights boasts a diverse cornucopia of culture and cuisine and is home to one of the city's busiest Indian shopping districts. It's a wonderful place to spend an afternoon browsing shops and dining in one of the many authentic ethnic restaurants.

Top reasons to trek out to **Flushing** and **Corona** include seeing a ball game at the New York Mets' stadium, **Citi Field,** spending time at the expansive **Flushing Meadows Corona Park,** especially if you're traveling with kids, and devouring Asian

dim sum in Flushing's Chinatown. You may want to venture out to the **Rocka-ways** for the beach scene.

Astoria

Head to Astoria for authentic Greek restaurants, shops, and grocery stores. Here you can buy kalamata olives and salty sheep's (or sheep-and-goat's) milk feta from store owners who can tell you where to go for the best gyro or spanako-pita. Taverna Kyclades is well-known for classic Greek seafood dishes, while just a few blocks up the road, SingleCut Beersmiths runs free brewery tours and pours some tasty ales and lagers. Astoria, named for John Jacob Astor—America's first multimillionaire—has been the center of Greek immigrant life in New York City for more than 60 years. Today substantial numbers of Arab, Asian, Eastern European, Irish, and Latino immigrants have also joined the dwindling Greek and Italian populations that call Astoria home. The presence of the Greek community is still evident on strips along both 23rd Avenue and Ditmars

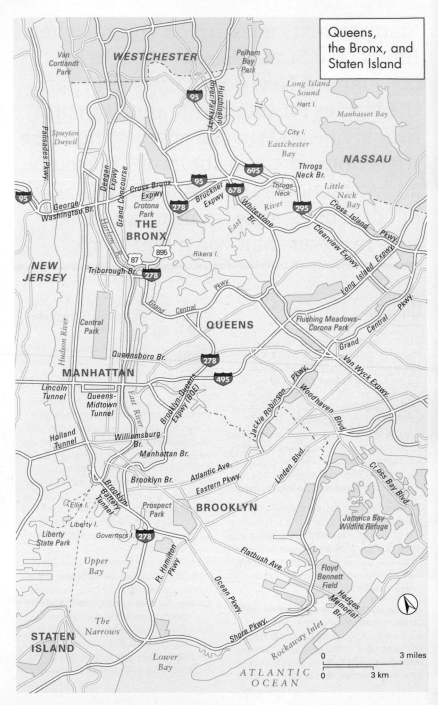

Queens,
the Bronx, and
Staten Island

WESTCHESTER

Van Cortlandt Park

Pelham Bay Park

Long Island Sound

Hart I.

Manhasset Bay

95

Hutchinson River Parkway

Spuyten Duyvil

City I.

Eastchester Bay

NASSAU

Palisades Pkwy.

695

Throgs Neck Br.

95

Deegan Expwy

Grand Concourse

Cross Bronx Expwy

678

Throgs Neck

Little Neck Bay

Crotona Park

278

Bruckner Expwy

Whitestone Br.

295

Cross Island Pkwy.

THE BRONX

East River

Clearview Expwy.

Long Island Expwy.

95

George Washington Br.

Harlem R.

87

895

Rikers I.

NEW JERSEY

Triborough Br.

278

Grand Central Pkwy.

QUEENS

Flushing Meadows-Corona Park

Grand Central Pkwy.

Van Wyck Expwy.

Central Park

Hudson River

Queensboro Br.

278

495

Jackie Robinson Pkwy.

Woodhaven Blvd.

MANHATTAN

Lincoln Tunnel

Queens-Midtown Tunnel

East River

Holland Tunnel

Williamsburg Br.

Brooklyn-Queens Expwy (BQE)

Manhattan Br.

Brooklyn Br.

Atlantic Ave.

Eastern Pkwy.

Linden Blvd.

Cross Bay Blvd.

Brooklyn Battery Tunnel

Ellis I.

Prospect Park

BROOKLYN

Jamaica Bay Wildlife Refuge

Liberty I.

Liberty State Park

Governors I.

278

Upper Bay

Ft. Hamilton Pkwy

Flatbush Ave.

Ocean Pkwy.

Floyd Bennett Field

Hodges Memorial Br.

STATEN ISLAND

The Narrows

Shore Pkwy.

Rockaway Inlet

Lower Bay

ATLANTIC OCEAN

0   3 miles

0   3 km

Boulevard. Another busy thoroughfare is 30th Avenue, with almost every kind of food store imaginable. Astoria is also home to the nation's only museum devoted to the art, technology, and history of film, TV, and digital media: the Museum of the Moving Image.

Sights

★ Museum of the Moving Image

MUSEUM | The Museum of the Moving Image is full of Hollywood and television memorabilia, but the core exhibition, *Behind the Screen,* demonstrates how movies and TV shows are produced and shown, including stations where visitors can create their own short animation, experiment with sound effects, or view the behind-the-scenes editing process of a live Mets baseball game. The *Jim Henson Exhibition* tells the stories behind many of Henson's film and TV works and has a build-a-muppet station. A wide range of films (more than 400), from classic Hollywood to avant-garde works to foreign-festival hits, is generally shown weekend evenings and afternoons. In addition, there are other special programs including film retrospectives, lectures, and workshops. ✉ *36 01 35th Ave., at 37th St., Astoria* ☎ *718/777–6888* 🌐 *www.movingimage.us* 🎟 *$15 (free Fri. after 4)* 🕒 *Closed Mon., Tues.* [M] *M, R to Steinway St.; N, W to 36th Ave.*

Restaurants

After you're finished with the sights, end your day with dinner at one of Astoria's legendary Greek restaurants (on or near Broadway), or venture to the Middle Eastern restaurants farther out on Steinway Street.

Taverna Kyclades

$$ | **GREEK** | The current powerhouse of Hellenic eats in the neighborhood, Taverna Kyclades serves Greek classics at a higher level than you might expect, given the simple decor and unassuming location. Fried calamari and grilled octopus make appearances at rock-bottom prices, despite their obvious quality, as do more out-of-the-ordinary dishes like "caviar dip" and swordfish kebabs. **Known for:** most authentic Greek fare this side of the Acropolis; lamb chops; no reservations. [$] *Average main: $18* ✉ *33-07 Ditmars Blvd., Astoria* ☎ *718/545–8666* 🌐 *www.tavernakyclades.com* [M] *N, W to Astoria–Ditmars Blvd.*

Hotels

Paper Factory Hotel

$ | **HOTEL** | **FAMILY** | Space, style, access to intriguing local neighborhoods, and seriously good value—this paper factory–turned–chic hotel provides many reasons to stay in Queens. **Pros:** excellent value; one-minute walk to subway; stylish, good-size rooms with kitchenettes. **Cons:** some street noise reaches rooms; neighborhood feels a bit remote; Wi-Fi can be unreliable. [$] *Rooms from: $199* ✉ *37-06 36th St., Astoria* ☎ *718/392–7200* 🌐 *www.paperfactoryhotel.com* 🛏 *125 rooms* 🍴 *No meals* [M] *M, R to 36th St.*

Nightlife

Bohemian Hall & Beer Garden

BARS/PUBS | Warm summer nights and cold, frothy beers have been savored by locals for over 100 years at the Bohemian Hall & Beer Garden. With pitchers of beer, picnic tables, live music, and Czech dishes from the kitchen, this sunny garden is an ideal spot for getting together with old friends—or making new ones over big mugs of Staropramen and Pilsner Urquell. While some of the outdoor seating is covered, in the event of rain, the well-worn indoor bar is just as inviting, though comparatively tiny. ✉ *29-19 24th Ave., Astoria* ☎ *718/274–4925* 🌐 *www.bohemianhall.com* [M] *N, W to Astoria–Ditmars Blvd.*

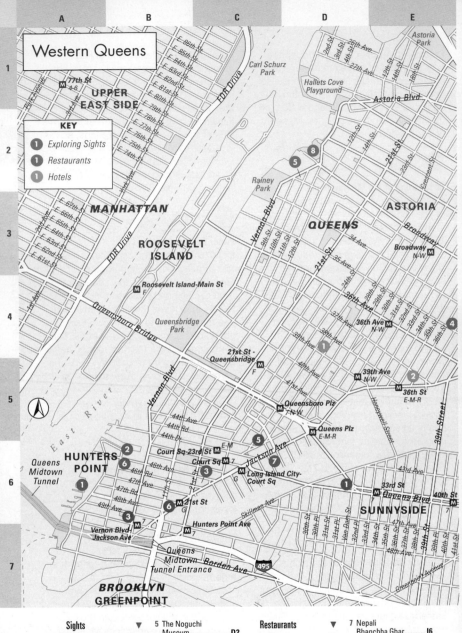

Western Queens

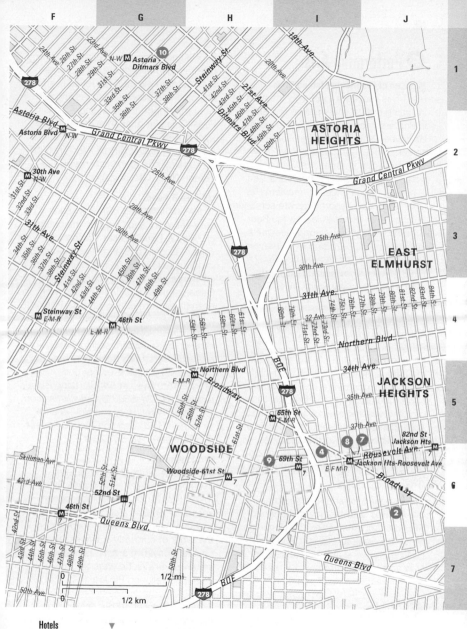

Hotels ▼

🎟 Performing Arts

Museum of the Moving Image films

FILM | This museum touts two theaters, including both a show palace and an intimate screening room, where classic Hollywood and foreign titles share the screen with experimental works, new films from the international festival circuit, live musical collaborations, and in-person appearances by moviemaker luminaries. Daily short films are screened in Tut's Fever Movie Palace, a fab Red Grooms and Lysiane Luong–designed installation. ✉ 36-01 35th Ave., between 36th and 37th Sts., Astoria ☎ 718/777–6888 ⊕ www.movingimage.us/films Ⓜ M, R to Steinway St.; N, W to 36th Ave.

Long Island City

Long Island City (LIC) is the art capital of Queens, with MoMA PS1, which presents experimental and innovative contemporary work; the Noguchi Museum, showcasing the work of Japanese American sculptor Isamu Noguchi in a large, peaceful garden and galleries; and the Socrates Sculpture Park, with large outdoor installations fronting the East River.

Worth noting for art buffs, the free LIC Art Bus shuttles guests between Socrates Sculpture Park, the Noguchi Museum, SculptureCenter, and MoMA PS1 on weekend afternoons between May and early September. It runs every 45 minutes between 1 and 6 pm.

👁 Sights

Gantry Plaza State Park

CITY PARK | Mosey down to this 12-acre waterfront park for sweeping views of Midtown Manhattan across the East River. The atmospheric stretch comes with piers, manicured lawns, Adirondack chairs and well-designed benches, and interesting relics that nod to Long Island City's industrial past, including towering, restored old gantries (once used as shipping lifts between barges and rail cars) that fringe the river and a massive Pepsi-Cola sign that once stood atop a factory here. ✉ 4-09 47th Rd., at Center Blvd., Long Island City ☎ 718/786–6385 ⊕ nysparks.com/parks 🎟 Free Ⓜ 7 to Vernon Blvd.–Jackson Ave.

LIC Flea & Food

$ | MARKET | |MARKET | On weekends between April and October, the outdoor LIC Flea & Food market welcomes visitors to peruse stands from some 85 vendors selling foodie fare and handcrafted wares. Sample snacks from many Queens-based food vendors hawking everything from ethnic eats like Filipino lumpias (spring rolls) to fresh-baked bundt cakes. Wash it all down at the alfresco beer garden, selling Queens-brewed beers from Rockaway Brewing Company, Finback Brewery, and more. ✉ 5-25 46th Ave., at 5th St., Long Island City ☎ 718/224–5863 ⊕ www.licflea.com ⊙ Closed weekdays, and Nov.–Mar. Ⓜ 7 to Vernon Blvd.–Jackson Ave.; G to 21st St.; E, M to Court Sq.–23rd St.

★ MoMA PS1

MUSEUM | A pioneer in the "alternative-space" movement, MoMA PS1 rose from the ruins of an abandoned school in 1976 as a sort of community arts center for the future, focusing on the work of currently active experimental and innovative artists. Long-term installations include work by Sol LeWitt, James Turrell, and Pipilotti Rist. Every available corner of the enormous building is used; discover art not only in former classrooms–turned–galleries, but also in the boiler room, and even in some bathrooms. On summer Saturdays, MoMA PS1 presents Warm Up, an outdoor dance party series that attracts a hip art-school crowd, held in the courtyard noon–9. Similarly, their Sunday Sessions are held fall through spring (hours and

The Noguchi Museum is dedicated to the work of visionary sculptor Isamu Noguchi.

dates vary) in the VW Dome and include various artistic installations, scholarly lectures, and special performances. ✉ 22-25 Jackson Ave., at 46th Ave., Long Island City 🕾 718/784–2084 ⊕ www.momaps1. org ✉ $10 suggested donation (free with MoMA entrance ticket, within 14 days of visit); Warm Up $18 in advance, $22 at the door; Sunday Sessions $15; free to NYC residents ⊙ Closed Tues., Wed. Ⓜ 7, G to Court Sq., E, M to Court Sq.–23rd St.; G to 21st St.

The Noguchi Museum
MUSEUM | In 1985 the Japanese American sculptor Isamu Noguchi (1904–88) transformed this former industrial plant into a place to display his modernist and earlier works. A peaceful central garden is surrounded by galleries, and there are some 200 pieces in stone, metal, clay, and other materials on display. Temporary exhibits have examined his collaborations with others, such as industrial designer Isamu Kenmochi, architect and inventor R. Buckminster Fuller, and choreographer Martha Graham. The museum is about a mile from subway stops; check the website for complete directions. ■TIP➔ There are extended hours on the first Friday of the month, May through September. ✉ 9-01 33rd Rd., at Vernon Blvd., Long Island City 🕾 718/204–7088 ⊕ www.noguchi.org ✉ $10 (free 1st Fri. of month) ⊙ Closed Mon., Tues. Ⓜ N, W to Broadway.

Rockaway Brewing Company
WINERY/DISTILLERY | At the epicenter of the Queens microbrew boom, this laidback brewery offers a taproom serving up tasty handcrafted brews (take-home growlers and cans are available), as well as free brewery tours on weekends. Evenings—though it closes at 9 or 10— and weekends are the best times to visit. ✉ 46-01 5th St., at 46th Ave., Long Island City 🕾 718/482–6528 ⊕ rockawaybrewco. com ⊙ Closed weekday afternoons Ⓜ 7 to Vernon Blvd.–Jackson Ave.; G to 21st St.; E, M to Court Sq.–23rd St.

SculptureCenter

MUSEUM | Founded by artists in 1928 to exhibit innovative contemporary work, SculptureCenter now occupies a former trolley repair shop that was renovated by artist Maya Lin in 2002 and expanded by Andrew Berman Architect in 2014; it's not far from MoMA PS1. Indoor and outdoor exhibition spaces sometimes close between shows; call ahead before visiting. ⊠ *44-19 Purves St., at Jackson Ave., Long Island City* ☎ *718/361–1750* ⊕ *www.sculpture-center.org* ⊠ *$5 suggested donation* ⊗ *Closed Mon., Tues.* Ⓜ *7, G to Court Sq.; E, M to Court Sq.–23rd St.; 7, N, W to Queensboro Plaza.*

Socrates Sculpture Park

PUBLIC ART | FAMILY | In 1986 local artist Mark di Suvero and other residents rallied to transform what had been an abandoned landfill and illegal dump site into this 4½-acre waterfront park devoted to public art. Today a superb view of the East River and Manhattan frames changing exhibitions of contemporary sculptures and multimedia installations. Free public programs include art workshops and an annual outdoor international film series (Wednesday evenings in July and August). ■TIP→ **Socrates is open 365 days a year, but the best time to visit is during warmer months.** Check online for a list of current and upcoming exhibitions. ⊠ *32-01 Vernon Blvd., at Broadway, Long Island City* ⊹ *From subway, walk about 8 blocks west on Broadway* ☎ *718/956–1819* ⊕ *www.socratessculpturepark.org* ⊠ *Free* Ⓜ *N, W to Broadway.*

🍴 Restaurants

Long Island City began attracting more visitors when MoMA PS1 opened back in the 1970s, and today it's getting more popular thanks to its hip but down-to-earth eateries and awesome views of the Manhattan skyline.

Adda

$$ | INDIAN | It can seem like hubris to open a contemporary Indian restaurant in the same borough as Jackson Heights, but this newcomer isn't aiming for quite the same crowd. With Indian dance music on the speakers and tabloid pages papering the walls, Adda broadcasts a hip, fun vibe, though the trendy decor almost belies what comes to the table: no fusion dishes, but rather authentic Indian favorites that draw inspiration from the greenmarket and grandma's cookbook. **Known for:** exquisitely spiced food; authentic dishes from saag paneer to goat-brain stew; BYOB for now. Ⓢ *Average main: $15* ⊠ *31-31 Thomson Ave., Long Island City* ☎ *718/433–3888* ⊕ *www.addanyc.com* ⊗ *Closed Sun.* Ⓜ *7 at 33 St.–Rawson.*

Casa Enrique

$$ | MEXICAN | Come for the tacos, stay for the margaritas: that's what a lot of local Long Island City folks do at this popular Mexican standout. The chef is from Chiapas but expect pan-Mexican fare, with tacos crammed with slow-cooked beef tongue or rich chorizo, among other meat options; also worthy are refreshing fish ceviche and the tender meatballs wading in a spicy chipotle-tomato sauce. **Known for:** different margaritas, including aguachile; interesting enchiladas; delicious mole. Ⓢ *Average main: $17* ⊠ *5-48 49th Ave., between Vernon Blvd. and 5th St., Long Island City* ☎ *347/448–6040* ⊕ *www.henrinyc.com/casa-enrique* ⊗ *No lunch weekdays* Ⓜ *7 to Vernon Blvd.–Jackson Ave.*

M. Wells Steakhouse

$$$$ | STEAKHOUSE | From the team that made Long Island City a dining destination with M. Wells Dinette inside MoMA PS1 comes this mecca devoted to meat. **Known for:** steak including grass-fed rib eye; venison T-bone; French onion soup. Ⓢ *Average main: $42* ⊠ *43-15 Crescent St., Long Island City* ☎ *718/786–9060* ⊕ *www.magasinwells.com* ⊗ *Closed*

Mon., Tues. No lunch Ⓜ 7, N, W to
Queensboro Plaza; E, M, R to Queens
Plaza.

Mu Ramen

$$ | **RAMEN** | Savory bowls of *tonkatsu*
(pork-bone broth) ramen are what this
cozy little shop is best known for: topped
with *ton toro* (pork jowl) and drizzled with
a black garlic oil, the ramen lacks only
nitamago (a seasoned soft-boiled egg),
which can be added to any ramen on the
menu. Popular with neighborhood locals,
this cash-only place attracts a crowd on
many nights (it opens at 5). **Known for:**
inventive fusion appetizers with world flavors; tonkatsu ramen; rib eye and ramen.
Ⓢ *Average main: $16* ✉ *12-09 Jackson
Ave., between 48th Ave. and 47th
Rd., Long Island City* ☎ *917/868–8903*
🌐 *www.muramennyc.com* ⊙ *Closed
Mon. No lunch* ▭ *No credit cards* Ⓜ *7 to
Vernon Blvd.–Jackson Ave.; G to 21st St.*

🛏 Hotels

Boro Hotel

$ | **HOTEL** | This industrial-chic proper-
ty in Queens (just two subway stops
from Manhattan) has spacious rooms,
balconies with skyline views, and
downright huge bathrooms. **Pros:** sleek
design; fantastic views of Manhattan
skyline; rooftop bar with lounge chairs.
Cons: isolated location; limited dining
and drinking venues nearby; rooftop
bar is closed in winter. Ⓢ *Rooms from:
$179* ✉ *38-28 27th St., Long Island City*
☎ *718/433–1375* 🌐 *www.borohotel.com*
🛏 *108 rooms* 🍴 *No meals* Ⓜ *7, N, W to
Queensboro Plaza; E, M, R to Queens
Plaza.*

🍸 Nightlife

Dutch Kills

BARS/PUBS | The dark bar with cozy
wooden booths at Dutch Kills—a cocktail
den with a nod to the neighborhood's
historic roots—serves up finely crafted
drinks at a couple of dollars cheaper

than similar Manhattan watering holes.
Expect precisely chiseled chunks of ice
and skilled bartenders who, with a few
queries into your preferences and curiosities, can create a concoction just to your
taste. (As the former industrial zone that
is Long Island City continues to gentrify
and turn residential, expect to see more
craft bars around the neighborhood.)
✉ *27-24 Jackson Ave., Long Island City*
☎ *718/383–2724* 🌐 *www.dutchkillsbar.
com* Ⓜ *E, M, R to Queens Plaza; 7, G to
Court Sq.; 7, N, W to Queensboro Plaza.*

Jackson Heights

Much more than just a hub for traditional Indian delicacies, Jackson Heights
resembles a giant international food
court. Even in the diverse borough of
Queens, it stands out for being a true
multicultural neighborhood. In just a few
blocks surrounding the three way intersection of Roosevelt Avenue, 74th Street,
and Broadway are shops and restaurants
catering to the area's strong Tibetan,
Nepalese, Bangladeshi, Colombian, Mexican, and Ecuadorian communities. Built
as a planned "garden community" in the
late 1910s, the area boasts many prewar
apartments with elaborate block-long
interior gardens as well as English-style
residences. Celebs who grew up in the
area include Lucy Liu and Gene Sim-
mons. It's also the birthplace of the board
game Scrabble, which has its own playful
commemorative sign at 35th Avenue and
81st Street.

🍴 Restaurants

Jackson Heights is home to a United
Nations of cuisine: from outstanding
Indian and Pakistani places to surprisingly
excellent taco carts. Look for small shops
selling juicy meat-filled *momos* (dumplings) and other Himalayan treats. The
nearby areas of Elmhurst and Woodside
offer some excellent global dining options
as well.

★ Ayada Thai

$$ | THAI | There are plenty of great Thai restaurants in Elmhurst, but Ayada tops them all (in fact, it announced plans to open a branch in Manhattan's Chelsea Market). Operating out of two storefronts directly next to each other (you go wherever there's a table, and it can get quite packed), Ayada serves up fiery, flavorful Thai favorites as well as some dishes you've never heard of before. **Known for:** spicy options for whole fish; raw shrimp salad; foodie and local favorite means longish wait times for a table. [$] *Average main: $20* ✉ *78-03 Woodside Ave., Elmhurst* ☎ *718/424–0844* 🌐 *ayadathaielm.com* [M] *7 to 74th St.–Broadway; E, F, M, R to Jackson Heights–Roosevelt Ave.*

Kababish

$ | PAKISTANI | For freshly baked *naan* (Indian-style flatbread) and grilled kebabs, pop in to this wee Jackson Heights takeout-only eatery churning out authentic Indian, Pakistani, and Bangladeshi fare. Everything is made to order, so consider calling ahead to avoid a wait; it's open late into the night. [$] *Average main: $10* ✉ *70-64 Broadway, at 72nd St., Jackson Heights* ☎ *718/565–5131* 🌐 *www.kababish.com* [M] *7 to 74th St.–Broadway; E, F, M, R to Jackson Heights–Roosevelt Ave.*

Nepali Bhanchha Ghar

$ | NEPALESE | The two-time winner of Jackson Heights's annual Momo Crawl, Nepali Bhanchha Ghar is an unassuming, cash-only storefront spot, known for its *jhol momo* (juicy dumplings in a rich, tomatoey, chutney-esque broth) and other Nepalese fare. Also on hand are a spicy, crispy noodle dish that will remind you of packaged ramen (though in a good way), *thali* platters vibrant with fiery, colorful curries, and a special savory doughnut served with a spicy tomato chutney. **Known for:** fried and steamed varieties of momos; sel roti doughnuts; some very spicy dishes. [$] *Average main: $8* ✉ *74-06 37th Rd., Jackson Heights* ☎ *929/522–0625* 🌐 *bhanchha-ghar-inc.business.site* ▭ *No credit cards* [M] *7 to 74th St.–Broadway; E, F, M, R to Jackson Heights–Roosevelt Ave.*

Phayul

$ | TIBETAN | Step through the doorway with the Himalayan eyebrow-threading sign above it, head up the twisting and turning stairway, then enter through a beaded curtain and you'll find yourself something of a delicious culinary anomaly: Tibetan Sichuan cuisine. The traditional *momos* (Tibetan dumplings stuffed with meat) are worth trying, but the most exciting fare here lies in the fusion of the two cultures, like spicy blood sausage or tofu in a fiery chili sauce. **Known for:** unique fusion cuisine (cash only); blood sausage; yak-cheese soup. [$] *Average main: $10* ✉ *37-65 74th St., 2nd fl., Jackson Heights* ☎ *718/424–1869* ▭ *No credit cards* [M] *7 to 74th St.–Broadway; E, F, M, R to Jackson Heights–Roosevelt Ave.*

★ SriPraPhai

$$ | THAI | A long-beloved, cash-only Thai option, SriPraPhai (pronounced "see-PRA-pie") has a huge menu, and it's hard to go wrong: just make sure you order the crispy watercress salad, *larb* (ground pork salad with mint and lime juice), sautéed chicken with cashews and pineapple, *kao-soy* (curried egg noodles), and/or roast-duck green curry. If you go with a few people, order the delicately flavored whole steamed fish. **Known for:** some of the top Thai in the Big Apple; charming seasonal backyard seating; notably spicy fare. [$] *Average main: $14* ✉ *64-13 39th Ave., Woodside* ☎ *718/899–9599* 🌐 *www.sripraphai.com* ▭ *No credit cards* 🕒 *Closed Wed.* [M] *7 to 69th St.*

Flushing and Corona

To New Yorkers, making the trip to Flushing usually means catching a baseball game at Citi Field or hunting down the best the Far East has to offer in its vibrant Chinatown. The historic town

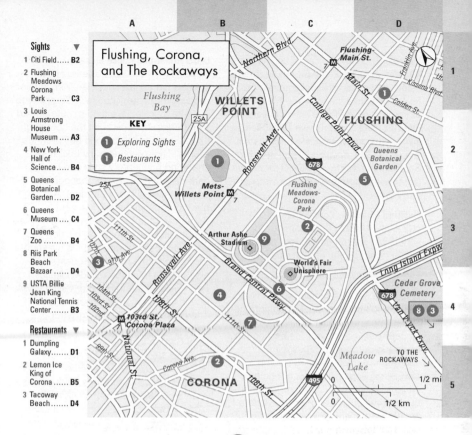

Flushing, Corona, and The Rockaways

KEY

① Exploring Sights

① Restaurants

of Flushing is a microcosm of a larger city, with a bustling downtown area, fantastic restaurants, and the bucolic Flushing Meadows Corona Park nearby. Flushing may seem like a strange name for a neighborhood, but it's an English adaption of the original (and hard-to-pronounce) Dutch name Vlissingen (the Dutch named it for a favorite port city in the Netherlands).

Next door, quiet Corona could easily be overlooked, but that would be a mistake, with attractions like the Queens Zoo, Queens Museum, and New York Hall of Science spilling over into the neighborhood from within Flushing Meadows Corona Park. Here you also find two huge legacies: the Louis Armstrong House Museum and the cooling Italian ices at neighborhood institution the Lemon Ice King of Corona.

◉ Sights

★ Citi Field

SPORTS VENUE | FAMILY | Opened in 2009, the Mets' stadium was designed to hark back to Ebbets Field (where the Dodgers played in Brooklyn until 1957), with a brick exterior and lots of fun features for fans of all ages, from a batting cage and Wiffle-ball field to the original giant apple taken from the team's old residence, Shea Stadium. Even those who aren't Mets fans but simply love baseball should come to see the Jackie Robinson Rotunda, a soaring multistory entrance and history exhibit dedicated to the Dodgers player who shattered baseball's color barrier. While here, don't miss the chance to taste your way through the fabulous food court, Taste of the City, set behind center field (on the Field Level), where you'll find Shake Shack burgers, Blue Smoke barbecue, close to 40 beer varieties at the Big Apple Brews stand, and more. Still feeling nostalgic for the old Shea? Stop by the Mets Hall of Fame & Museum. ■TIP➜ **Ballpark tours ($13) are available year-round; see mets.com/tours for schedule and ticketing info.** ⊠ *123-01 Roosevelt Ave., at 126th St., Flushing* ☎ *718/507–8499 for tickets* ⊕ *www.mlb.com/mets* Ⓜ *7 to Mets–Willets Point.*

Flushing Meadows Corona Park

CITY PARK | FAMILY | The gleaming Unisphere (an enormous 140-foot-high steel globe) might tip you off that this 898-acre park was the site of two World's Fairs. Take advantage of the park's barbecue pits, seasonal boat rentals, sports fields, and big cultural festivals, but don't forget the art museum, science hall, zoo, theater, carousel, indoor pool, ice-skating rink, pitch-and-putt golf and minigolf course, and model-airplane field. Aim to hit a few primary spots in a day, noting that while several are clustered together on the northwest side of the park, visitors should be prepared for long peaceful walks in between.

The **Queens Night Market** (⊕ *www.queensnightmarket.com*) is an outdoor market held Saturday evening, late April through October, in the park near the New York Hall of Science. It's reminiscent of Asia's popular food markets, and you can expect to find about 100 vendors serving flavorful, often adventurous global fare. ■TIP➜ **The flat grounds are ideal for family biking; bike rentals are available at two locations from March to October.** The park is open from 6 am to 9 pm, 365 days a year (as in most city parks, exercise caution when visiting outside of daytime hours). ⊠ *Between 111th St./Grand Central Pkwy. and Van Wyck Expressway/College Point Blvd., Flushing* ⊕ *www.nycgovparks.org/parks/fmcp* ☞ *Free parking available* Ⓜ *7 to 111th St. or Mets–Willets Point.*

Louis Armstrong House Museum

MUSEUM | For the last 28 years of his life, the famed jazz musician lived in this modest three-story house in Corona with his wife, Lucille. Take a 40-minute guided tour (required; departs on the hour until 4), and note the difference between the rooms vividly decorated by Lucille in charming midcentury style and Louis's dark den, cluttered with phonographs and reel-to-reel tape recorders. Although photographs and family mementos throughout the house impart knowledge about Satchmo's life, it's in his den that you really begin to understand his spirit. Exclusive to the museum, guests can also tune in to intimate audio clips of Louis playing the trumpet or telling jokes on his home-recorded private tapes. The museum also hosts Armstrong-related special events and a Hot Jazz / Cool Garden summer concert series. ⊠ *34-56 107th St., at 37th Ave., Corona* ☎ *718/478–8274* ⊕ *www.louisarmstronghouse.org* ⊠ *$12, includes guided house tour* ⊗ *Closed Mon.* Ⓜ *7 to 103rd St.–Corona Plaza.*

New York Hall of Science

MUSEUM | FAMILY | At the northwestern edge of Flushing Meadows Corona Park, the New York Hall of Science has more than 450 hands-on exhibits that make science a playground for inquisitive minds of all ages. Climb aboard a replica of John Glenn's space capsule, throw a fastball and investigate its speed, explore Charles and Ray Eames's classic Mathematica exhibition, or check out the exhibition in the iconic Great Hall, *Connected Worlds,* which demonstrates the interconnectedness of ecosystems via animation and motion-activated displays. Note that the 3-D Theater, Rocket Park Mini Golf, and Science Playground require extra fees. ⊠ *47-01 111th St., at 48th Ave., Corona* ☎ *718/699–0005* ⊕ *www.nysci.org* ⊠ *$16 (free Fri. 2–5 pm and Sun. 10–11 am); parking $10* Ⓜ *7 to 111th St.*

The big matches for the U.S. Open happen at Arthur Ashe Stadium, part of the USTA Billie Jean King National Tennis Center.

Queens Botanical Garden

GARDEN | FAMILY | Adjacent to Flushing Meadows Corona Park, these 39 acres include rose and herb gardens, an arboretum, and plantings especially designed to attract bees and birds. An environmentally friendly visitor center uses solar energy and recycles rainwater. ⊠ *43-50 Main St., Flushing* ☎ *718/886–3800* ⊕ *www. queensbotanical.org* ⌷ *$6 (free Nov.– Mar.); parking $6–$10* ⊙ *Closed Mon.* Ⓜ *7 to Flushing–Main St.*

Queens Museum

MUSEUM | Between the zoo and the Unisphere in Flushing Meadows Corona Park lies the Queens Museum. Don't miss the astonishing Panorama of the City of New York, a nearly 900,000-building model of NYC made for the 1964 World's Fair, and the world's largest scale model. There are also rotating exhibitions of contemporary art, a massive map of the NYC water supply system, and a permanent collection of Louis Comfort Tiffany stained glass. Parking is free but limited. ⊠ *Flushing Meadows Corona Park, New York City Building, Corona* ⏻ *From the subway, the museum is about a 15-min walk southwest through Flushing Meadows Corona Park* ☎ *718/592–9700* ⊕ *www.queensmuseum.org* ⌷ *$8 suggested donation* ⊙ *Closed Mon., Tues.* Ⓜ *7 to Mets–Willets Point.*

Queens Zoo

ZOO | FAMILY | Flushing Meadows Corona Park is home to the intimate Queens Zoo, dedicated to the animals of North and South America. The 11-acre facility features pumas, Andean bears, Canadian lynx, and pudus, the world's smallest deer species. The zoo also maintains a farm with domesticated animals like sheep, goats, horses, rabbits, and more. The last ticket is sold 30 minutes before closing. ⊠ *53-51 111th St., at 53rd Ave., Corona* ☎ *718/271–1500* ⊕ *www. queenszoo.com* ⌷ *$8* Ⓜ *7 to 111th St.*

USTA Billie Jean King National Tennis Center

SPORTS VENUE | Each year, from late August through early September, 700,000 fans come here for the U.S.

Open, which claims the title of highest-attended annual sporting event in the world. The rest of the year, the 34 courts (19 outdoor and 12 indoor, all DecoTurf, plus 3 stadium courts) are open to the public for $24–$68 hourly. Make reservations up to two days in advance. Parking is free but limited. ⊠ *Flushing Meadows Corona Park, Flushing* ⚐ *Walk 3 mins down the ramp from the subway* ☎ *718/760–6200* ⊕ *www.ntc.usta.com* ☉ *Closed 1 month around U.S. Open (roughly late Aug.–early Sept.)* Ⓜ *7 to Mets–Willets Point.*

🍴 Restaurants

Food lovers know there's one train to take to some of the best eats in the city. The 7 snakes its way through the middle of Queens, and conveniently through some of the best dining neighborhoods in New York. At the end of the line is Flushing, home to the second-largest Chinatown (after San Francisco's) in the United States. Wide streets have few tourists and many interesting stores and restaurants, making the trip worth it. A couple of tips: bring cash, because not many of these restaurants accept credit cards, and be prepared to encounter language difficulties, as English speakers are in the minority. In Manhattan, catch the 7 train at Times Square or Grand Central Terminal.

Dumpling Galaxy

$ | **CHINESE** | Originally a tiny stall in an underground mall, Helen You's restaurant has expanded to become a banquet-size space with a colorful accompanying cookbook. The gargantuan menu can seem overwhelming, but it's a thrilling testament to just how varied the definition of "dumpling" can be. **Known for:** fried and steamed dumplings, from vegetarian options to all kinds of meat and seafood; dessert dumplings such as strawberry seasame; banquet-style space. Ⓢ *Average main: $7* ⊠ *42-35 Main St., in the back of the Arcadia Mall,* *Flushing* ☎ *212/518–3265* ⊕ *www.dumplinggalaxy.com* Ⓜ *7 to Flushing–Main St.*

Lemon Ice King of Corona

$ | **FAST FOOD** | **FAMILY** | If you're looking for an authentic Queens experience, there are few as true as eating an Italian ice from the Lemon Ice King of Corona on a hot summer day. A neighborhood institution for more than 70 years, this place has dozens of flavors to dig into (just note there are no seats). Ⓢ *Average main: $5* ⊠ *52-02 108th St., at 52nd Ave., Corona* ☎ *718/699–5133* ⊕ *www.thelemonicekingofcorona.com* ⊟ *No credit cards* Ⓜ *7 to 103rd St.–Corona Plaza.*

The Rockaways

"Hitch a ride to Rockaway Beach" by taking the A train to its southernmost terminus, where the transformation of the once-neglected Rockaways (an area spanning several neighboring beach communities along the skinny Rockaway Peninsula) into a sort of Williamsburg-on-the-waterfont is fully under way. Its anti-Hamptons hipster beach scene is back on track following damage sustained during Hurricane Sandy in 2012. Throughout beach season (late May through mid-September), buzzy restaurants and beach bars (including the Riis Park Beach Bazaar at Jacob Riis Park) draw crowds, as do the sandy shores, with plenty of water activities beyond swimming, like surfing, Jet Skiing, and even whale- and dolphin-watching cruises.

👁 Sights

Riis Park Beach Bazaar

MARKET | This outdoor fair features over two dozen local food-and-drink vendors. Try the ribs and pulled pork from **Fletcher's Brooklyn Barbecue** or ice cream from Brooklyn-based **Ample Hills Creamery,** and check out cultural offerings (like free weekend concerts), beach activities (volleyball, kite flying, and more), and assorted handicrafts vendors on the waterfront at **Jacob Riis Park Beach.** Facilities and vendors are generally open from Memorial Day through Labor Day, with most activity unfolding on weekends. Each off-season highlights the latest restaurant-in-residence at the Art Deco pavilion, with a heated dining room and flat screens showing local sports teams. ✉ *Jacob Riis Park, Gateway National Recreation Area, 16702 Rockaway Beach Blvd., Rockaway Park, Queens* 🌐 *www.riisparkbeachbazaar.com* 🕒 *Bazaar closed Labor Day–Memorial Day. Restaurant closed Tues. Labor Day–Memorial Day (check website for latest hrs).*

🍴 Restaurants

Tacoway Beach

$ | MEXICAN | This small, cash-only, mostly outdoor eatery is an oasis; once you're inside, it becomes hard to remember that you're actually still in New York City rather than some more typical beach destination. For the perfect post-beach pit stop, order some Mexican-style street tacos (try the fried fish) and a cerveza, and bask in the chill surfer vibes as the sun goes down. **Known for:** superior fish tacos; surfboards on the wall; summer-only hangout for surfers, locals, cool kids. [$] *Average main: $5* ✉ *302 Beach 87th St., at Rockaway Fwy., Queens* 🌐 *www.tacowaybeach.com* 🕒 *Closed Labor Day–Memorial Day* 💳 *No credit cards* [M] *A-Shuttle to Beach 90th St.*

The Bronx

Whether you're relaxing at a Yankees game, indulging in fresh mozzarella and cannoli on Arthur Avenue, or scoping out exotic species at the zoo, there's plenty of fun to be had here. Named for the area's first documented European settler, Jonas Bronck, the Bronx may be the city's most misunderstood borough. Its reputation as a gritty, down-and-out place is a little outdated, and there's lots of beauty if you know where to look. There is more parkland in the Bronx than in any other borough, as well as one of the world's finest botanical collections, the largest metropolitan zoo in the country, and, of course, Yankee Stadium.

👁 Sights

★ Arthur Avenue (Belmont)

NEIGHBORHOOD | Manhattan's Little Italy is overrun with mediocre restaurants aimed at tourists, but Belmont (meaning "beautiful hill"), the Little Italy of the Bronx, is a real, thriving Italian American community. Unless you have family in the area, the main reason to come here is for the food: eating it, buying it, looking at it fondly through windows, and chatting with shopkeepers so you can get recipe advice.

Nearly a century after pushcarts on Arthur Avenue catered to Italian American workers constructing the zoo and botanical garden, the area teems with meat markets, bakeries, cheese makers, and shops selling kitchenware (espresso machines, pasta makers, etc.). There are debates about which store or restaurant is the "best," but thanks to generations of Italian grandmothers, most vendors here serve fresh, handmade foods.

Although the area is no longer solely Italian—many Latinos and Albanians share this neighborhood now—Italians dominate the food scene. The covered **Arthur Avenue Retail Market** (2344 Arthur Ave.) is a terrific starting point. It houses some dozen vendors, including the Bronx Beer Hall. Regulars mostly shop on Saturday afternoon; many stores are shuttered on Sunday and after 5 pm. ✉ *Arthur Ave. between Crescent Ave./184th St. and 188th St., and 187th St. between Lorillard Pl. and Cambreleng Ave., Belmont* 🌐 *www.bronxlittleitaly.com* [M] *4, B, D to Fordham Rd., then it's about a 15-min walk (or take Bx12 bus).*

Two bronze rhinoceros statues stand at the entrance to the Keith W. Johnson Zoo Center at the Bronx Zoo. They're modeled after a rhino named Bessie, who lived at the zoo from 1923 to 1962.

★ Bronx Zoo

ZOO | FAMILY | With 265 acres and more than 10,000 animals representing 700-plus species, this is the largest metropolitan zoo in the United States, opened in 1899. See exotic creatures in outdoor settings that re-create natural habitats; you're often separated from the animals by no more than a moat or wall of glass. Don't miss the **Congo Gorilla Forest,** a 6½-acre re-creation of a lush African rain forest with western lowland gorillas, as well as mandrills, okapis, and red river hogs. At **Tiger Mountain** an open viewing shelter lets you get incredibly close to Siberian tigers. As the big cats nap at midday, visit in the morning or afternoon. **Madagascar!** is a verdant re-creation of one of the world's most threatened natural habitats, with lemurs and hissing cockroaches.

Go on a mini-safari via the **Wild Asia Monorail,** May through October, weather permitting. Here you can view Asian elephants, Indo-Chinese tigers, Indian rhinoceroses, and other species. Try to visit popular exhibits, such as Congo Gorilla Forest, early to avoid lines later in the day. In winter the outdoor exhibitions have fewer animals on view, but there's plenty to savor indoors. Some exhibits have an extra charge; to see everything, consider purchasing the Total Experience ticket. ⊠ *2300 Southern Blvd., near 187th St., Belmont* ☎ *718/220–5100* ⊕ *www.bronxzoo.com* ✉ *General admission $22.95–$25.95 (extra charge for some exhibits); Total Experience ticket $28.95–$38.95; free entry Wed. (suggested donation; some attractions extra)* ☞ *Last entry to exhibits is 30 mins before closing; check website for seasonal discounts available when purchasing tickets online; parking $16* Ⓜ *2, 5 to Pelham Pkwy.; BxM11 express bus to Bronx River entrance.*

Edgar Allan Poe Cottage

HOUSE | The beloved American poet-writer's legacy is detailed at this historic house museum, tucked into a bustling section of the Bronx. The small farmhouse, dating to 1812, housed Poe; his

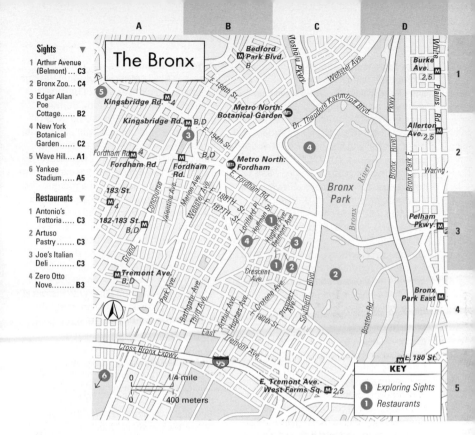

The Bronx

KEY

1 Exploring Sights

1 Restaurants

---

young, ailing wife, Virginia; and his mother-in-law during his final years, from 1846 to 1849. Rooms are filled with reproduction period pieces, as well as a handful of personal effects that may have inspired the enduring poems Poe wrote here, like "Annabel Lee" and "The Bells." The surrounding green space in Poe Park lends well to the transporting back-in-time feeling of a visit here. Audio and guided tours are included with admission. ✉ *2640 Grand Concourse, at Kingsbridge Rd., Fordham, Bronx* ☎ *718/881–8900* ⊕ *bronxhistoricalsociety.org/poe-cottage* 🖼 *$5* ⊘ *Closed Mon.–Wed.* Ⓜ *4, B, D to Kingsbridge Rd.*

★ New York Botanical Garden

GARDEN | FAMILY | Considered one of the leading botany centers in the world, this beautiful 250-acre garden is one of the best reasons to make a trip to the Bronx. Built around the dramatic gorge of the Bronx River, the garden is home to lush indoor and outdoor gardens and acres of natural forest, and offers classes, concerts, and special exhibits. In June and September, be astounded by the captivating fragrance of the Peggy Rockefeller Rose Garden's 4,000 roses of more than 650 varieties; see intricate orchids that look like the stuff of science fiction; or relax outside in the leafy Thain Family Forest or indoors in the calm of the conservatory. You can also explore the Everett Children's Adventure Garden, a 12-acre, indoor-outdoor museum with a boulder maze, giant animal topiaries, and a plant discovery center.

There's plenty to see year-round. The Victorian-style **Enid A. Haupt Conservatory** houses re-creations of misty tropical rain forests and arid African and North

American deserts, as well as exhibitions such as the annual Holiday Train Show and Orchid Show. The **All-Garden Pass** gives you access to the conservatory, Rock Garden (April–October), tram tour, Everett Children's Adventure Garden, and other special exhibitions. ⊠ *2900 Southern Blvd., Belmont* ☎ *718/817–8700* ⊕ *www.nybg.org* ⊠ *All-Garden Pass $28 weekends, $25 weekdays. Grounds-only admission is free Sat. 9–10 and all day Wed. (available otherwise only to NYC residents for $15)* ⊘ *Closed Mon.* ⟳ *Parking $17 weekdays, $20 weekends and special events* Ⓜ *4, B, D to Bedford Park Blvd.; then walk about 8 blocks downhill to the garden (or take the Bx26 bus). Metro-North (Harlem local line) to Botanical Garden.*

Wave Hill

GARDEN | Drawn by views of the Hudson River and New Jersey's dramatic Palisades cliffs, 19th-century Manhattan millionaires built summer homes in the Bronx neighborhood of Riverdale. One of the most magnificent, Wave Hill, is today a renowned 28-acre public garden and cultural center that attracts visitors from all over the world. Its themed gardens, from an aquatic garden to a shade border, are exquisite. Grand beech and oak trees tower above wide lawns, an elegant pergola overlooks the majestic river view, and benches on curving pathways provide quiet respite. Open year-round, Wave Hill House (1843) and Glyndor House (1927) host art exhibitions, Sunday concerts, wellness-minded activities, and art and gardening workshops. It's worth the schlep if you are a garden fan. ⊠ *649 W. 249th St., at Independence Ave., Riverdale* ☎ *718/549–3200* ⊕ *www. wavehill.org* ⊠ *$8 (free Tues. and Sat. 9–noon); parking $8* ⊘ *Closed Mon.* Ⓜ *1 to Van Cortlandt Park–242nd St. (free shuttle service seasonally; see website); A to Inwood–207th St., then Bx7 or Bx20 bus to 252nd St.; Metro-North Hudson Line to Riverdale (free shuttle service seasonally; see website).*

★ Yankee Stadium

SPORTS VENUE | FAMILY | From April through October, you can see one of baseball's great franchises, the "Bronx Bombers," in action at their 2009-debuted, $1.5 billion Yankee Stadium (set right across the street from the site of the original stadium, aka "the House that Ruth Built"). Tickets can be pricey, but the experience is like watching baseball in a modern-day coliseum. It's quite opulent: a traditional white frieze adorns the stadium's top; inside, limestone-and-marble hallways are lined with photos of past Yankee greats. History buffs and hard-core fans should visit the Yankees Museum (set on the main level and open till the end of the eighth inning), filled with historical team memorabilia, and Monument Park (closes 45 minutes prior to first pitch), with plaques of past Yankee legends, by center field. ■TIP➜ **Pregame and off-season one-hour stadium tours are held on a near-daily basis year-round; visit the Yankees website for more info on times and ticketing.** ⊠ *1 E. 161st St., at River Ave., South Bronx, Bronx* ☎ *718/293–4300* ⊕ *newyork.yankees.mlb.com* Ⓜ *4, B, D to 161st St.–Yankee Stadium.*

🍴 Restaurants

People don't really wander into this borough—as they do into Brooklyn and Queens, hoping to stumble on some gem of an ethnic eatery—but the Bronx has a lot going for it, if you know where to look. Dotted throughout the borough are some great Mexican taquerias, African eateries, and old-school Italian joints. Skip Manhattan's Little Italy and head to the Bronx's Arthur Avenue for a red-sauce treat; it's a much more authentic Italian American neighborhood.

Antonio's Trattoria

$$ | ITALIAN | Antonio's bills itself as "an Italian restaurant serving simple food," but this casual spot is underselling itself. This is fantastic salt-of-the-earth Italian American fare: start with the

mini-meatballs wading in a marinara sauce and move on to baked clams, house-made ravioli, fettuccine carbonara, or excellent pizza, baked in a brick oven in the Neapolitan manner. **Known for:** classic red-sauce joint; brick-oven pizza; a bit off the main "Little Italy" strip. $ *Average main: $22* ⊠ *2370 Belmont Ave., Belmont* ☎ *718/733–6630* ⊕ *www.antoniostrattoria.com* Ⓜ *B, D to 182nd–183rd Sts.*

Artuso Pastry

$ | **BAKERY** | Step inside this neighborhood mainstay near Arthur Avenue for a delectable selection of cakes, cookies, and pastries, perfect for an on-the-go snack while you're exploring the Arthur Avenue area. Artuso's has been run by the same Italian American family since 1946, and the impassioned proprietors and community vibe only add flavor to the shop's outstanding selection of sweets. **Known for:** signature cannoli; multiple favors of biscotti; seasonal specialties including Italian ices. $ *Average main: $4* ⊠ *670 E. 187th St., at Cambreleng Ave., Belmont* ☎ *718/367–2515* ⊕ *artusopastry.com* Ⓜ *4, B, D to Fordham Rd., walk 15 mins east.*

Joe's Italian Deli

$ | **ITALIAN** | Seven shops within four blocks of Arthur Avenue make fresh mozzarella daily, but Joe's is the one you don't want to miss (the trick is, they add the perfect amount of salt). For lunch, dive into one of the gigantic hero sandwiches, a generous portion of chicken parmigiana, or one of the other daily specials from the hot bar. **Known for:** delicious, good-value sandwiches; limited seating, so eat your treat elsewhere; old-school Italian deli vibe, including meats hanging from ceiling. $ *Average main: $10* ⊠ *685 E. 187th St., at Crescent Ave., Belmont* ☎ ⊕ *www.joesitaliandeli.com* Ⓜ *4, B, D to Fordham Rd., walk 15 mins east.*

Zero Otto Nove

$$ | **ITALIAN** | Tucked among the family-owned food shops of Arthur Avenue, Zero Otto Nove is one of the city's better Italian restaurants, with a good-size bar, seating on two levels, and murals painted on the walls. The draw is a menu that nicely balances authentic Italian fare with good Italian American classics; you might try a wood-oven-fired pizza, perfectly chewy and loaded with buffalo mozzarella. **Known for:** good list of Italian wines; pastas including mafalde e ceci; gets pretty loud when it's busy, as it often is. $ *Average main: $20* ⊠ *2357 Arthur Ave., Belmont* ☎ *718/220–1027* ⊕ *www.zeroottonove.com* ⊘ *Closed Mon.* Ⓜ *B, D to 182nd–183rd Sts.*

Staten Island

A free 25-minute ferry voyage from the southern tip of Manhattan to Staten Island provides one of the city's best views of the Statue of Liberty and the downtown Manhattan skyline. When you arrive in the St. George neighborhood, it's hard to miss the **waterfront promenade,** with its Manhattan skyline views and "Postcards" 9/11 memorial, or the Richmond County Bank Ballpark, the home of the **Staten Island Yankees** (⊕ *www.siyanks.com*), where minor leaguers in pinstripes affectionately known as "Baby Bombers" dream of one day playing in the major league in the Bronx. At this writing, **Empire Outlets** (⊕ *www.empireoutletsnyc.com*) in St. George, the city's first outlet mall, is scheduled to open by mid-2019.

When you venture beyond the borough's northernmost tip, Staten Island is full of surprises. Along with suburban-type sprawl, there are wonderful small museums, including a premier collection of Tibetan art; walkable woodlands; and a historic village replicating New York's rural past. From the ferry terminal, grab an S40 bus to the **Snug Harbor Cultural Center** (less than 10 minutes) or take the S74 and combine visits to the **Jacques Marchais Museum of Tibetan Art** and **Historic Richmond Town.**

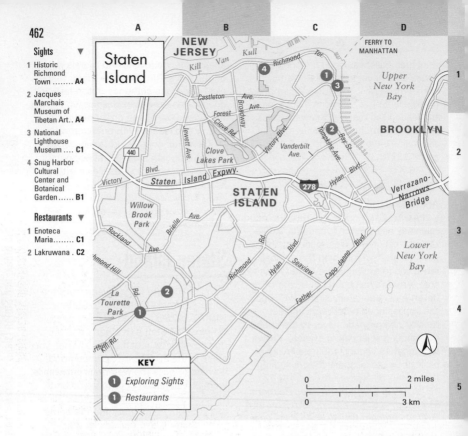

Staten Island

KEY

1 *Exploring Sights*

1 *Restaurants*

0 ——— 2 miles

0 ——— 3 km

Legally part of New York City since 1898, Staten Island is in many ways a world apart. The city's most suburban borough (sometimes called the "Forgotten Borough" by locals) is geographically more separate, less populous, politically more conservative, and ethnically more homogeneous than the rest of the city.

◉ Sights

Historic Richmond Town

MUSEUM VILLAGE | FAMILY | Think of a small-scale version of Virginia's Colonial Williamsburg, and you'll understand the appeal of Historic Richmond Town, NYC's only living-history museum. This 100-acre village, constructed from the 1670s to the early 20th century, was the site of Staten Island's original county seat. Fifteen of the site's 30 historic buildings (28 landmarked) are open to the public.

Highlights include the Gothic Revival **Courthouse,** the one-room **General Store,** and the **Voorlezer's House,** the oldest schoolhouse in America (it served as a residence and place of worship, in addition to an elementary school). Also on-site is the **Staten Island Historical Society Museum,** built in 1848 as the second county clerk's and surrogate's office, which now houses Staten Island artifacts plus changing exhibits about the island. There are guided tours Wednesday through Friday at 1:30 and weekends at 1:30 and 3.

You may see staff in period dress demonstrate Early American crafts and trades such as tinsmithing or basket making, though the general era meant to be re-created is 1820–1860. Check the website for special events and educational programs held throughout the year. ✉ *441 Clarke Ave., at St. Patrick's Pl., Richmondtown* ✦ *Take the S74 bus (30–45 mins) or a car service (about $20) from the ferry terminal* ☎ *718/351–1611* ⊕ *www.historicrichmondtown.org* ✉ *$8 (free Fri.); free parking* ⊘ *Closed Mon., Tues.* Ⓜ *S74 bus to Richmond Rd./St. Patrick's Pl.*

Jacques Marchais Museum of Tibetan Art

MUSEUM | At the top of a hill sits this replica of a Tibetan monastery containing one of the largest collections of Tibetan and Himalayan sculpture, paintings, and artifacts outside Tibet. Meditate with visiting Buddhist monks, or just enjoy the peaceful views from the terraced garden. ✉ *338 Lighthouse Ave., Lighthouse Hill* ☎ *718/987–3500* ⊕ *www.tibetanmuseum.org* ✉ *$6* ⊘ *Closed Mon., Tues.* Ⓜ *S74 bus to Lighthouse Ave. (35–45 mins from ferry terminal) and walk uphill 15 mins; cab fare from ferry terminal is about $20.*

National Lighthouse Museum

MUSEUM | Just a short stroll from the ferry terminal, this museum sheds "light" on lighthouse history throughout America. It's housed in a 1912 foundry that was once part of an 18-building complex for the U.S. Lighthouse Service General Depot, which was the center of all lighthouse operations in the country from 1864 to 1939. Only six structures remain, including underground vaults, an administration building where architects designed the country's lighthouses, and buildings where Fresnel lenses were assembled. Self-guided visits through the small museum take in exhibits and artifacts surrounding the history, technology, and keepers behind lighthouses, illustrating the role they collectively played in American maritime history. The museum is a five-minute walk south of the Staten Island Ferry terminal. ✉ *200 The Promenade at Lighthouse Point, St. George* ☎ *718/390–0040* ⊕ *lighthousemuseum.org* ✉ *$5* ⊘ *Closed Mon.*

★ Snug Harbor Cultural Center and Botanical Garden

MUSEUM | **FAMILY** | Once part of a retirement center for sailors, this 83-acre cultural center is now a popular spot to engage with contemporary art and historical collections. Enjoy the **Staten Island Children's Museum** ($8 ⊕ *www.sichildrensmuseum.org*), or take a stroll through lush gardens. All on-site attractions here can be visited—and, if applicable, ticketed—independently of each other.

Made up of 26 landmarked buildings, nine botanic gardens, 10 acres of wetlands, and a 2-acre farm, Snug Harbor is also home to an outpost of the **Staten Island Museum** ($8 suggested donation ⊕ *www.statenislandmuseum.org*), with exhibits spanning art, history, and science; the **New York Chinese Scholar's Garden** ($5); and dance and music studios, art galleries, and residency programs. Main Hall—the oldest building on the property, dating to 1833—is home to the **Eleanor Proske Visitors Center** (free) and the **Newhouse Center for Contemporary Art** ($5), which exhibits artworks connected to Snug Harbor's history. Next door, the **Noble Maritime Collection** (suggested donation ⊕ *www.noblemaritime.org*) maintains historic collections specific to Staten Island and Snug Harbor's maritime past. **Harbor Eats,** Snug Harbor's on-site outdoor café, is open May through October. Packing a picnic is also recommended. ✉ *1000 Richmond Terr., between Snug Harbor Rd. and Tysen St., Livingston* ✦ *From the Staten Island Ferry terminal, take the S40 bus 2 miles (about 7 mins) to Snug Harbor Rd. Otherwise, grab a car service at the ferry terminal (about $8)* ☎ *718/448–2500* ⊕ *www.snug-harbor.org* ✉ *Grounds and Botanical Gardens free; Chinese Scholar's Garden and Newhouse Center combo ticket $8; free parking* ⊘ *Children's Museum closed Mon. Staten Island Museum closed Mon., Tues. New York Chinese Scholar's Garden closed Mon. (summer–fall);*

Did You Know?

Many New Yorkers consider the Staten Island Ferry the ultimate inexpensive date. Its decks provide romantic waterfront views of the Statue of Liberty and Lower Manhattan without costing a cent (and beer is a bargain).

Mon., Thurs. (winter–spring). Newhouse Center closed Jan.–Mar.; Mon., Tues. (Apr.–Nov.); Mon.–Wed. (Dec.). Noble Maritime Collection closed Mon.–Wed. Ⓜ *S40 bus to Snug Harbor Rd. (from ferry terminal).*

🍴 Restaurants

If you made your way here on the free ferry from Whitehall Terminal and want to explore, you'll find plenty of homespun, no-frills eateries.

Enoteca Maria

$$ | ITALIAN | Just a short walk from the Staten Island ferry, Enoteca Maria may look, smell, and seem like an ordinary Italian eatery, but scratch beneath the ragù and you'll find something interesting. The restaurant does not employ one chef but a dozen or so, all Italian *nonne,* or grandmas, each one cooking regional dishes on different nights; there are international nonne from other countries cooking as well. **Known for:** rotating Italian grandmas cooking regional fare; permanent menu of Italian fare; Italian wines. Ⓢ *Average main: $15* ✉ *27 Hyatt St., at Central Ave., St. George* ☎ *718/447–2777* ⊕ *www.enotecamaria.com* 🕒 *Closed Mon.–Wed.* Ⓜ *Ferry to Staten Island.*

Lakruwana

$$ | SRI LANKAN | FAMILY | Few outsiders know this, but Staten Island has a sizable Sri Lankan community, which means it's the perfect place to get a taste of this cuisine. Among a cluster of restaurants and grocery stores, this brightly decorated restaurant stands out as a local favorite, with fiery curries that make the most of ingredients from the island, including tamarind, cashews, pineapple, and lots of coconut. **Known for:** coconut curries; "string hopper" rice noodles; popular cash-only lunchtime weekend buffet. Ⓢ *Average main: $15* ✉ *668 Bay St., St. George* ☎ *347/857–6619* ⊕ *www.lakruwana.com* 🕒 *Closed Mon.* Ⓜ *S76 or S86 bus from the Staten Island Ferry Terminal (10 mins).*

🛍 Shopping

New York City's first outlet mall, which is adjacent to the St. George Ferry Terminal, has been under construction since 2015. It finally opened in May 2019 and will have over 100 stores when fully complete.

Index

472

Photo Credits

Notes

Notes

Fodor's NEW YORK CITY 2020

Publisher: Stephen Horowitz, *General Manager*

Editorial: Douglas Stallings, *Editorial Director*; Margaret Kelly, Jacinta O'Halloran, Amanda Sadlowski, *Senior Editors*; Kayla Becker, Alexis Kelly, Teddy Minford, Rachael Roth, *Editors*

Design: Tina Malaney, *Design and Production Director*; Jessica Gonzalez, *Graphic Designer*; Mariana Tabares, *Design & Production Intern*

Production: Jennifer DePrima, *Editorial Production Manager*; Carrie Parker, *Senior Production Editor*; Elyse Rozelle, *Production Editor*; Jackson Pranica, *Editorial Production Assistant*

Maps: Rebecca Baer, *Senior Map Editor*; Mark Stroud (Moon Street Cartography), *Cartographer*

Photography: Jill Krueger, *Director of Photo*; Namrata Aggarwal, Ashok Kumar, Carl Yu, *Photo Editors*; Rebecca Rimmer, *Photo Intern*

Business & Operations: Chuck Hoover, *Chief Marketing Officer*; Robert Ames, *Group General Manager*; Tara McCrillis, *Director of Publishing Operations*; Victor Bernal, *Business Analyst*

Public Relations and Marketing: Joe Ewaskiw, *Senior Director Communications & Public Relations*; Esther Su, *Senior Marketing Manager*; Ryan Garcia, Thomas Talarico, Miranda Villalobos, *Marketing Specialists*

Fodors.com Jeremy Tarr, *Editorial Director*; Rachael Levitt, *Managing Editor*

Technology: Jon Atkinson, *Director of Technology*; Rudresh Teotia, *Lead Developer*; Jacob Ashpis, *Content Operations Manager*

Writers: Annie Bruce, Kelsy Chauvin, David Farley, Laura Itzkowitz, Giulia Pines, Josh Rogol, Cameron Todd, Caroline Trefler

Editors: Doug Stallings, Teddy Minford, Linda Cabasin

Production Editor: Carrie Parker

ISBN 978-1-64097-162-2

ISSN 0736–9395

Library of Congress Control Number 2019903719

SPECIAL SALES
This book is available at special discounts for bulk purchases for sales promotions or premiums. For more information, e-mail SpecialMarkets@fodors.com.

PRINTED IN THE UNITED STATES OF AMERICA

10 9 8 7 6 5 4 3 2 1